Human Development

Human Development

A Life-Span Approach

Fourth Edition

Karen L. Freiberg, Ph.D.
Department of Psychology
The University of Maryland
Baltimore County

JONES AND BARTLETT PUBLISHERS

Boston   London

Editorial, Sales, and Customer Service Offices
Jones and Bartlett Publishers
One Exeter Plaza
Boston, MA 02116
1-617-859-3900
1-800-832-0034

Jones and Bartlett Publishers International
P O Box 1498
London W6 7RS
England

Library of Congress Cataloging-in-Publication Data

Freiberg, Karen L., 1944–
    Human development : a life-span approach / Karen L. Freiberg.—4th ed.
        p.   cm.
    Includes bibliographical references and index.
    ISBN 0-86720-323-4
    1. Developmental psychology.   2. Human growth.   I. Title.
BF713.F74 1992
155—dc20   92-5015
                                                            CIP

Cover: *Alexander Cassatt and His Son Robert,* by Mary Cassatt Reprinted with permission from the Philadelphia Museum of Art: W. P. Wilstach Collection and gift of Mrs. William Cox Wright.

Printed in the United States of America
96 95 94 93   10 9 8 7 6 5 4 3 2

Photo Credits

Photo credits continue on page 514, which constitutes an extension of the copyright page.

Contents

9 The Thirties and Forties *322*

10 The Fifties and Sixties *364*

11 The Later Years *394*

12 Death and Bereavement *430*

Preface

This text is intended to give you, the reader, a view of human development as multidimensional. While most life-span textbooks cover cognitive and psychosocial aspects of development well, few present such a vast array of intervening influences—factors such as health and illness, diet and nutrition, stress and coping skills, individual differences, race and ethnicity, religion and culture. This text focuses holistically on the ecology of living. You will learn to appreciate the importance of diverse and sundry influences on behaviors. You are not simply a product of your genes and the socialization skills of your parents and teachers. You are unique and complicated.

Human development is not a scientific field of facts; rather, careful researchers have given us a body of knowledge of best guesses. The probability that a specific behavior is caused by factors A, B, and C may be only 95%. What about the person who experiences factors A, B, and C but does not behave in the predicted fashion? This textbook presents the developmental questions and the research "partial answers." It then allows you to make up your own mind about the solution or solutions to problems. Do you like to think for yourself? This book asks you to do so.

The organization of *Human Development* is chronological by age. First, two introductory chapters examine determinants of development, research methodologies, and theoretical viewpoints. Then, nine chapters cover the time span from conception to late adulthood and carefully emphasize the significance of biology as well as psychological growth and change. The last chapter looks at death and bereavement throughout the life span, introducing the reader to a fairly new and rapidly expanding area of research.

Changes in this text include the addition of many new references and sources of information. The publisher and author concluded that a full color atlas of human anatomy would be especially useful for the students. It is located in the center of the textbook. References are made to the atlas frequently to help readers understand how both psychological and physiological concepts relate to anatomical human development. Twelve intriguing profiles of famous persons introduce the chapters. These ask you to think about your own assumptions about stages of life. The new graphics include functional photographs, line drawings, charts, tables, and boxed topics. Key concepts are listed at the end of each chapter, and are set in bold type when they first occur in the text. Definitions of these terms are handily provided in a glossary. Questions for review at the end of each chapter assist you in examining your feelings about important topics. Suggested further readings and extensive references enable you to explore topics that interest you.

A variety of ancillary materials are available to accompany the text. For the student, there is a study guide which follows the text chapter by chapter with outlines, summaries, guided learning questions, and practice exams. For the instructor—and free to all adopters of the text—there is an instructor's resource manual with chapter outlines and summaries, an audiovisual resource list, and suggested classroom activities and research projects; a computerized test bank consisting of over one thousand questions; a set of forty colored transparencies covering key topics and concepts; and a specially selected set of videos on related topics.

The author has experienced first-hand many of the quirks of life about which she writes. She has seen her parents grow old and die, and has guided her children into young adulthood. She has lived and worked cross-culturally, in poverty and otherwise, as a public health nurse, a school-nurse teacher, a child development clinician, a writer, and a developmental researcher. Currently she is professor of psychology at the University of Maryland, Baltimore County.

Thanks to the many academicians who provided suggestions for this revised edition of *Human Development:*

Eugene Audette, University of St. Thomas
William Bailey, Eastern Illinois University
Linda Bakken, Wichita State University
Patricia Bence, Tompkins Cortland Community College
Doris Bergen, Miami University
Catherine Burns, Oregon State University
Padraic Burns, Boston University School of Medicine
Veronica Casey, J. M. Wright Technical School
Debra Chasanoff, Union County College
Harold Chipman, Pepperdine University
Stephanie Clancy, Southern Illinois University at Carbondale
Madonna Combs, Marshall University
Ann Daniel, Providence Hospital School of Nursing
Sara DeHart, University of Minnesota
Mary DeLucci, University of Missouri
Barbara Drysdale, Halfway House of Northern Illinois
Joseph Fitzgerald, Wayne State University
Mary Kay Jordan Fleming, College of Mount Saint Joseph
Alice Galper, Mount Vernon College
Aline Garrett, University of Southwestern Louisiana
Margaret Goldern, State University of New York at Morrisville
Alice Grady, Fort Sanders School of Nursing
Vernon Haynes, Youngstown State University
Thomas Hess, North Carolina State University
John C. Johnson, Weatherford College
Laura Kamptner, California State University
Steven Krantz, University of Missouri, Kansas City
Sister Paschaline Kutac, Victoria College
Shelley MacDermid, Purdue University
Frances Murphy, Eastern Illinois University
Carol Raupp, California State University, Bakersfield
Paul Roodin, State University of New York at Oswego
Nancy Ryan-Wenger, Ohio State University, College of Nursing
Robert Rycek, University of Nebraska at Kearney
David Saarnio, Northern Illinois University
Susan Schaffer, Old Dominion University

John Schulenberg, University of Michigan, Ann Arbor
Lawrence Shelton, University of Vermont
Carol Sigelman, University of Arizona
Stephen Small, University of Wisconsin
Tim Snyder, Lander College
James Speer, S. F. Austin State University
Laura Thompson, New Mexico State University
Fred Vondracek, Pennsylvania State University
Barbara Wagner, Parma School of Nursing
Eleanor Walker, Bowie State University.

A special word of appreciation to my husband, Bill, and my daughter, Signe, who made it possible for me to spend considerable time at home writing this edition. Thanks to Joseph E. Burns, Vice President of Jones and Bartlett Publishers, and to the editorial and production people who turned my manuscript into a book: Paula Carroll, Judy Songdahl, Heather Stratton, Carolyn Artin, and Herbert Nolan. Lastly, a big thank you to Madelon Kellough for her faithful typing assistance.

Human Development

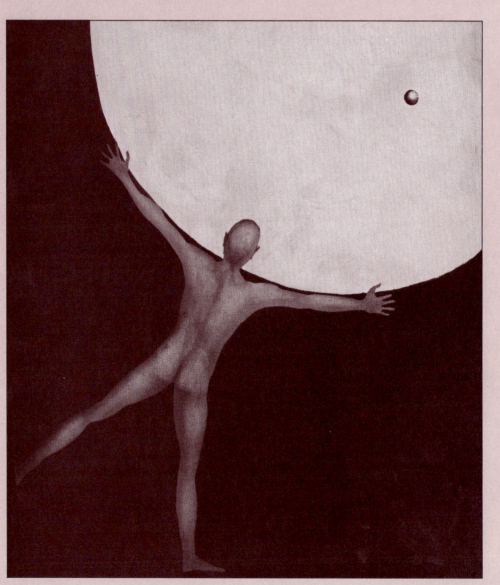

The Study of Human Development

1

Development

How can one proceed through one's life span in a meaningful, perhaps artful, way? Most people spend long moments searching for meaning in life. Poets and scribes have suggested some answers to the question of life's meaning, philosophers and psychologists have provided others. In fact, there are no simple answers. Life is complicated. Its meaning differs for every unique individual participating in its drama, and for every individual, the meaning of life changes as time marches on.

This textbook is dedicated to every reader searching for answers to life's mysteries. Right here, up front, you should realize that a study of life-span human development will provoke new questions as well as provide only partial answers to old questions. Life cannot be completely comprehended because it consists of so many surprises coming from so many unpredictable sources.

Youth is wholly experimental.
—*Robert Louis Stevenson*

At thirty, man suspects himself a fool;
Knows it at forty, and reforms his plan.
—*Edward Young*

And man not old, but mellow, like good wine.
—*Stephen Phillips*

Life is short and the art long.
—*Hippocrates*

Specific Determinants of Development

Ecology

Ecology is the study of the relations between people and the resources and sociocultural patterns in their environment. Urie Bronfenbrenner (1979) presented an ecological model of human development that helps to explain the complications of living. There are a multitude of influences accosting every human every day, creating pressures for reacting in different ways. In addition, every human very actively helps shape the systems of influence in which he or she lives. Bronfenbrenner describes three major psychological systems: the macrosystem, the exosystem, and the microsystem (see Figure 1-1).

The **macrosystem** is a large, enduring system. It contains the ideologies of the culture and subcultures and the beliefs of the people living in the system. It is influenced by ideologies of past systems and by hopes for future systems. While effects of the greater macrosystem may not be readily visible in the life of any one unique person, it has profound repercussions on all of our lives.

The **exosystem** is a collection of influences in which each unique human has indirect participation: as a second party, or distant associate. Local politics, the mass

Larry grew up in a walk-up apartment in a rugged Brooklyn neighborhood. His immigrant parents ran a bar-and-grill under the tracks of the el—the elevated train. When Larry was ten years old, a police officer picked him up and explained that Larry's dad had died of a heart attack. The policeman told Larry that he should be the man of the house now. His father had left little money, so Larry, his mother, and his brother had to move into an attic apartment and live on welfare. Larry was mischievous, but his mother always called him her little angel. She would never believe bad things about him nor apply discipline. Larry was raised as much by his neighborhood buddies as by his mother. He spent most of his time at sports fields, the movies, the candy store, the front stoop, or the street corner lamppost. As a teenager, he belonged to the Warriors, a gang of sorts. He was a school troublemaker who earned terrible grades. After high school, he bounced through a series of odd jobs. He eventually saved enough money to take a bus south. In Miami, he serendipitously found work as a disc jockey on a radio station. His fortunes soared. He soon had his own talk show, with celebrity guests. He married a beautiful Playboy bunny. Eventually, however, he began to gamble and play around. He lost his job and his wife and was arrested for grand larceny. Larry had gone from celebrity to notoriety. He did not, however, remain down. The larceny charges were resolved, he filed for bankruptcy, and he began picking up the pieces of his life. Larry is Larry King, the host of the Ace Award winning CNN talk show and the Peabody Award winning Mutual Radio talk show, perhaps the best talk show in the history of radio.

As King's life illustrates, human development is never static, it is always in a state of flux. Larry went from rags to riches to rags to riches. Do people form patterns of responses? Could anyone have predicted the course of Larry's life from his childhood experiences?

*King L. (1982). *Larry King by Larry King*. New York: Simon & Schuster.

media, financial resources, environmental quality, and the like (see Figure 1-1) have repercussions on the lives of every human in these exosystems.

The **microsystem** is the sum of all the spheres in which each unique human has direct, one-on-one participation. Examples include interactions with family, peers, school, work, associates, neighbors, religious leaders, and health service providers.

Bronfenbrenner called an interrelationship between two or more microsystems a **mesosystem** (*meso* is a combining form meaning "in the middle"). The unique person may be pressured to react quite differently to the combination of family and religion,

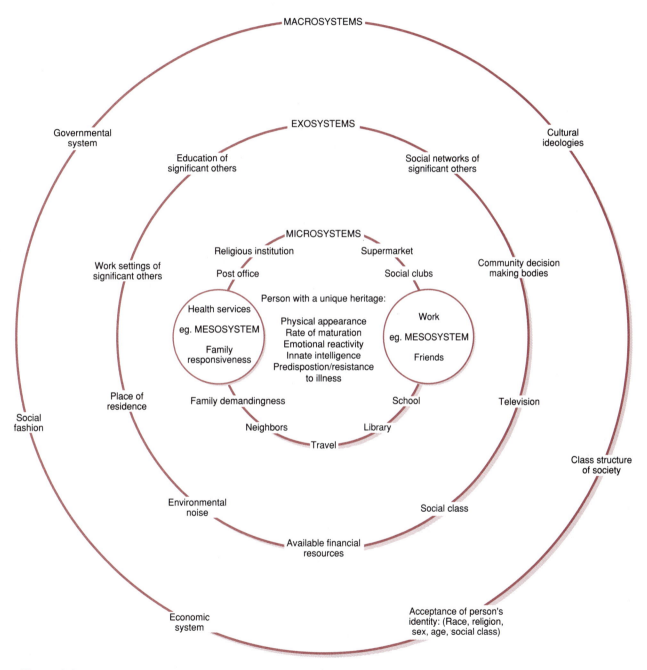

Figure 1-1

An overview of some of the macrosystems, exosystems, microsystems, and mesosystems that influence human development.

(Adapted from Bronfenbrenner, U. (1979) *The Ecology of Human Development.* Cambridge, MA: Harvard University Press, with the permission of Urie Bronfenbrenner.)

Figure 1-2
A mesosystem linkage between microsystems such as a religious institution and the family may produce a different effect on the person than either microsystem could by itself.

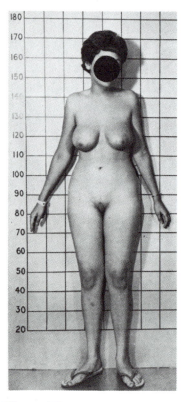

Figure 1-3
External appearance of an adult chromosomal male (XY) with androgen-insensitivity syndrome.

for example, than he or she would be to just the family or to just the religion. Mesosystems are common between microsystems and can be very influential on human development. Nevertheless, it makes it more difficult to analyze the influences on a unique human being's development when one must consider the ever-changing combined systems (mesosystems), as well as macro-, exo-, and microsystems (see Figure 1-2).

In the center of the ecology of human development is the unique individual. Every infant arrives in the world quite different from every other person who has ever lived. Even identical twins, who share genetic heritage, experience slightly different environments in the uterus and increasingly different environments after birth and, thus, are unique. Each person, with his or her physical features, health, emotional reactivity, intelligence, and spirituality, shapes all the surrounding systems. As the person grows, changes, and matures, his or her effects on the surrounding systems change as well. No wonder it is so difficult to proceed through one's life span in a meaningful, comprehensible way. Life is short, and the art of life is long!

Heredity

Heredity refers to the transmission of physical characteristics of parents to their offspring by means of genes passed to the offspring through the ovum (egg) and sperm at the moment of conception. Hereditary factors assure that there is a great deal of sameness in the rates and principles underlying both **ontogeny**, the unfolding life history of the individual person, and **phylogeny**, the unfolding life history of the human species. Some forces have primarily a hereditary base, such as sex, biological maturation, race, and predisposition or resistance to certain illnesses, but we cannot say that any one aspect of human development is determined exclusively by either heredity or environment. There are always ways in which the two interact.

Can we say "Boy is a boy is a boy" the way Gertrude Stein said "Rose is a rose is a rose"? The answer is a resounding *no* for several reasons. Inheritance of one X chromosome and one Y chromosome confers the **genotype**, or genetic make-up, of a male. But if a genetic male has a rare disease called androgen-insensitivity syndrome, he will have a **phenotype**, or the external appearance, of a female. In this case, because his body cells are insensitive to androgens (masculinizing hormones), he will have undescended testes and a penis small enough to be mistaken for a clitoris, and at puberty his breasts will enlarge under the influence of the estrogens (feminizing hormones) that are present in all humans, whether male or female. In spite of the female phenotype, the individual with androgen-insensitivity syndrome is a chromosomal male (see Figure 1-3).

Although gender (or sex) has a strong hereditary basis, it is affected by the environment in many ways. The mother's prenatal status, for example, may induce changes in her developing embryo/fetus. During pregnancy, diabetic mothers may be given supplemental estrogen, which has the potential of feminizing male offspring. Similarly, some pregnant women are given artificial progestins (another sex hormone that sometimes has androgenic properties) in order to prevent spontaneous abortions. Progestin-affected female fetuses are often masculinized. These prenatal environmental events pale, however, in comparison to all of the postnatal environmental influences on sexual identity. Boys reared to be extremely masculine according to their own culture's norms for masculinity may be considered feminine according to another culture's norms. Boys can also be reared to be very feminine or to be androgynous (having positive aspects of both male and female behaviors). Boys may wish they were girls and consciously adopt feminine behaviors despite their rearing; similarly, girls may consciously adopt masculine behaviors. Sex hormone secretions may also be affected by many environmental events, including stress, diet, drugs, steroids, accidents, and illnesses. If as simple a "hereditary" dimension as being male or female can be so obfuscated by environmental events, imagine how much more complicated are dimensions that are not as clearly determined by genes!

Environment

Environment refers to all the external conditions and influences affecting the life and development of an organism. Many forces have primarily an environmental base, such as air quality, climate, food supplies, the resources of the community, and education. An individual's traits and characteristics, however, are influenced by both environment and inborn traits. The interaction between nature and nurture is complex.

Lung cancer is a leading cause of human death. Scientists have determined that cigarette smoking causes lung cancer. Why, then, can some individuals chain smoke for many years without getting lung cancer? Is heredity involved? *Yes.* Scientists have also determined that oncogenes are involved with the onset of cancer. If a person inherits the oncogene for lung cancer, the tars and nicotine inhaled with cigarette smoking can trigger the oncogene to begin the formation of a malignant tumor. (For further information about oncogenes, see Chapter 10, page 373.) A person who does not inherit an oncogene for lung cancer may escape tumor formation.

Sports are a leading recreational choice of many humans. Can a characteristic with a strong underlying environmental base, such as sports choice, be free of heredity influence? The answer is *no.* Sports choice can be affected by a number of genetic and biological factors: physical size and strength, health, sex, intelligence, state of biological maturation, or possibly by the effects of hormones (high prenatal estrogen exposure has been associated with lower assertiveness, while high postpubertal testosterone levels have been associated with more physically aggressive behaviors: Tieger, 1980). (See Figure 1-4.)

Figure 1-4
Why do so few females choose to wrestle? Are environmental factors exclusively responsible for females' decisions to compete in other sports?

The Family

The family has been, at various times, both held sacred and considered a scourge. For many people it is regarded more often as one than the other. It is difficult to cast the contemporary North American family into one mold, for, although the functions that families perform may be similar, their composition and their social and emotional climates can be vastly dissimilar. (See Figure 1-5.)

A primary function of families in relation to their children is physical care. Human children require years of feeding, clothing, sheltering, and protecting before they can take care of themselves without adult help. A second important function of families is socialization of children. Social values and appropriate social behaviors need to be taught. The family more than any other institution has the responsibility for instilling religious

Figure 1-5
The form a family takes may vary considerably from the mainstream norm of father, mother, and children.

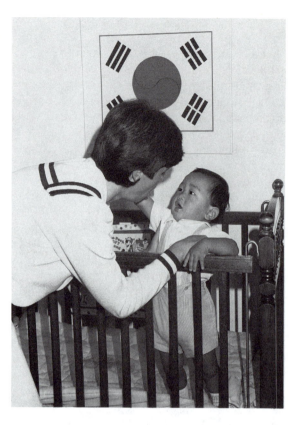

and moral training and for providing discipline. A third important function of the family is to provide a sense of belonging for all its members. A family connotes ancestors, traditions, intimacy, family rituals, even private passwords or jokes. The tie to one's family is felt and enduring, even if family members feud or change frequently or if the home is crisis prone. A fourth important function of families is the provision of an affection bond. Parents should be a source of love to each other, to their offspring, and to all those who reside in the family household. Provision of a tender, loving, caring, supportive feeling is one of the most important ways in which a family can optimize the development of its members (see Table 1-1).

Table 1-1 Some Basic Functions of the Family and Community

Family	Community
Physical care; food, clothing, shelter	Social feedback for mores
Socialization; discipline, moral education	Social networking; support systems
Attachment bonds; sense of belonging	Social control; law enforcement
Affection bonds; love	Employment; economic welfare
	Public education

The Community

Sociology and anthropology have shown us that community customs are important determinants of development. Although one culture may be appreciably influenced by a given set of variables (for example, sex roles and social status), it does not follow that all cultures will be affected by the same standards. Nor does it follow that every individual within a culture will be moved to behave like every other person due to the prevailing **mores** (folkways that are considered conducive to the welfare of society and so develop the force of law).

Open country

City apartment

Suburbia

City slum

Figure 1-6
Family and community settings vary considerably even within a small radius of land space.

Although the family may start the work of instilling society's values in its children, the community is the testing ground on which all of these values and beliefs are tried. Various community settings tend to shape and perpetuate certain behaviors (see Figure 1-6). All aspects of the socialization process are affected by community interactions. Consider two aspects of psychosocial development described by Erik Erikson (discussed in Chapter 2, page 33). He believed that the first social lesson learned by human infants is trust in caregivers. Community members, in the form of babysitters, daycare center staff, neighbors, friends, relatives, religious group members, and interested others, either enhance an infant's trust or instill feelings of mistrust. The second social lesson, which is learned in toddlerhood, is autonomy. The child begins to view the self as a separate person, able to stand alone. Community members can either enhance the child's sense of autonomy or foster in the child a sense of shame and doubt. Community members who are critical or abusive can make a child feel mistrustful and dependent again.

Having a **social network** is essential to the well-being of humans. Children and adults alike, when deprived of social contact, suffer breakdowns in their psychosocial health. Law enforcers, for example, have long been aware that solitary confinement is the most severe form of punishment. Community members supplement or sometimes replace family members as sources of social support; they provide companionship, reassurance, and emotional security. They also give one another mutual support when tasks or problems arise that are too great to bear alone, for example, emergency disaster relief (see Figure 1-7).

Community members share in the tasks of social control by making and altering rules, adhering to them, and providing law enforcement institutions in their community.

Figure 1-7
The community becomes a strong social support network in times of crisis when the needs of many are great.

They share the task of assuring economic welfare by providing jobs for one another. The community also is responsible for providing free and appropriate public education to its citizenry.

Throughout the following chapters you will find references to family influences and community influences. Remember, human existence is complex: No research methodology, no theory, and no textbook can ever fully describe all its complexities. Consider yourself. Can anyone else ever fully understand you? Do you completely understand yourself?

Historical Overview

The earliest cave dwellers probably pondered the meaning of human existence as we do today. Evidence suggests that as early as 500 B.C. a group of Greeks known as Sophists (wise persons) had already concluded that it is pointless to look for absolute truths about humans because the truth is different for each individual (Greer, 1982). Socrates attacked this theory of relative truth. He felt the unexamined life was not worth living. He was condemned to death for supposedly corrupting the youth of Athens by challenging them to "know thyself" (see Figure 1-8).

Figure 1-8
The ancient Greek teacher, Socrates, was condemned to drink poison hemlock because he refused to stop searching for the truth about human existence.

Older Perspectives about Humans

The Renaissance philosophers, in keeping with the scientific revolution and the age of enlightenment, again tried to understand the meaning of life. They used the scientific method of **inductive reasoning**. They searched for psychological functions in the mind (brain) and reasoned from the particulars they found in unique individuals toward generalities (universals) of human development. They also continued to practice **deductive reasoning**, pondering life's meaning from generalities to particulars, or from the universal to the individual.

The thinking of the Renaissance philosophers was mired in controversy. René Descartes (1596–1650) (see Figure 1-9) believed infants are born with souls, separate from their physiological bodies. Souls, he believed, have innate powers for thinking and reasoning. Religious rituals that sanctify or purify the soul at birth embrace this view. John Locke (1632–1704), on the other hand, believed infants arrive in the world as *tabula rasa* (clean slates): They learn their thoughts and behaviors from social interactions. Thomas Jefferson, in the Declaration of Independence of the United States, embraced the idea that all men are created equal. Which side of this controversy do you favor? Are infants born with innate reason, or are they born as blank slates?

Charles Darwin (1802–1882) added new fuel to the fires of debate about the nature and origin of human behavior with his theories of evolution and "survival of the fittest." His baby biography, "A Biographical Sketch of an Infant" (1877), emphasized the potency of heredity over environment. It not only argued for genetic determination of many

Figure 1-9
The Renaissance philosopher, Descartes, believed humans have innate souls with consciousness, volition, and reason.

Figure 1-10
Galton linked eminence in humans to heredity. He failed to consider that all his eminent men shared upper-class status, good nutrition, educational tutors, patronage, and other privileges. (Photo courtesy of *The National Library of Medicine, Bethesda, Maryland.*)

human behaviors but also made baby biographies a subject of scientific inquiry and initiated the study of child development.

Darwin's cousin, Francis Galton (see Figure 1-10), supported Darwin's thesis with a book called *Hereditary Genius* (1892). Galton compared 977 eminent men and contrasted them to some women (whom he believed to be not only physically weaker but also intellectually inferior) and some mentally retarded persons. He pointed out that ability seemed to depend on descent. On the basis of chance, 1 out of the 977 men should have had an eminent relation. Instead, 322 of them had relatives as famous as themselves.

Galton's attempts to prove the preponderance of heredity over environment failed to consider external factors such as social class, education, nutrition, social support networks, patronage, and luck, common to all the eminent men he considered. Galton, in an unsuccessful attempt to separate heredity from environment, also made the first known scientific study of twins. He applied statistical measures to his work, developing one of the most important measurements, the correlation coefficient (see p. 20).

Newer Perspectives about Humans

Psychology emerged as an independent study separate from philosophy scarcely more than 100 years ago. It built upon the foundation provided by earlier great thinkers. From the laboratories of Wilhelm Wundt in Germany came an insistence that human behavior be studied through rigorous experimentation using the scientific method rather than through reasoning processes. The **scientific method** is to state a problem, form a hypothesis, experiment, observe, and draw conclusions. All statements are considered mere supposition by the true scientist until they can be proved true or false by experimental testing. Furthermore, tests must be explicit enough so that other scientists can replicate (repeat) them. Wundt insisted that a dependable knowledge of psychology could be established only in this fashion. No opinions or long-held beliefs could be substituted for facts. Wundt wanted nothing to be taken for granted.

Experimental psychology, especially Wundt's method of structuralism (isolating the elements of mental content) with subjective introspection (self-analysis), was soon augmented by behaviorism, created by John Watson in the United States (after the work of the Russian physiologist Ivan Pavlov). This approach is described in more detail in Chapter 2.

Descriptive psychology, which attempts to describe the unique complexity of individuals rather than discover general laws about psychological processes, developed alongside experimental psychology but often in opposition to it. Descriptive psychologists criticized rigorous experimentation for losing sight of the idiosyncrasies of human behavior. Branches of psychology that used descriptive research techniques rather than the pure scientific method of experimentation included psychoanalysis and clinical psychology, following work done by Sigmund Freud in Austria; cognitive psychology, following work done by Jean Piaget in Switzerland; and humanist psychology, following work done by Abraham Maslow and Carl Rogers in the United States. (These approaches will also be described in more detail in Chapter 2.)

Developmental psychology combines experimentation and description. It is the study of humans focusing on developmental changes from conception through old age (see Figure 1-11). Developmental psychology still struggles with questions such as the degree to which behaviors are innate or learned. However, the focus today is more on the changes that occur. Scientists now recognize that both heredity and environment affect development. Older theories about humans ignored most changes. One hundred years ago, children were looked on as miniature adults. Many were employed in mines and factories for long hours each day (Aries, 1962). In portraits of children by the old masters, affluent children are dressed in adult clothing (see Figure 1-12).

Infancy and childhood emerged as important, separate fields of study in the 1920s, especially through the work of Piaget and two Americans. Arnold Gesell at Yale and

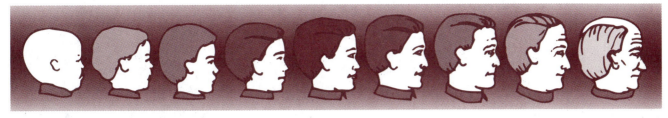

Figure 1-11
Developmental psychology studies changes in humans from conception through old age.
It embraces various theories about the hows, whens, and whys of change.

John Watson at Johns Hopkins had contradictory views: Piaget and Gesell stressed heredity and maturation, whereas Watson emphasized learning and conditioning as foundations for new child behaviors.

Adolescence as a subject of scientific study began in the 1920s, as G. Stanley Hall's *Adolescence* (1904) became widely read. He described adolescence as a period of *Sturm und Drang* (storm and stress). Later, anthropologists, especially Margaret Mead in *Coming of Age in Samoa* (1928) and *Growing Up in New Guinea* (1953), suggested that storm and stress are not a universal phenomenon. Rather, there are cultural variations in the period called adolescence.

G. Stanley Hall pioneered work in the psychology of old age as well as adolescence. At the age of 78, he added *Senescence: The Last Half of Life* (1922) to his list of publications. Gerontology (the study of old age) became an independent discipline in the 1940s with the creation of a Gerontology Research Center in Baltimore, headed by Nathan Shock, under the auspices of the National Institutes of Health (see Figure 1-13). Now called the National Institute of Aging, this facility has been studying the aging process for 50 years. As the elderly population has increased, research on aging is being correspondingly augmented.

Figure 1-12
Prior to the 20th century, children were viewed as miniature adults after they could walk and talk.

Figure 1-13
New theories about humans focus on lifelong changes. Dr. Nathan Shock began aging research in Baltimore in the 1940s.

Research Methodology

Research is a controlled, objective, systematic, and patient study carried out to learn more about a subject. If the research is undertaken for the primary satisfaction of knowing and understanding the subject, it is called **basic research**. If it is entered into for the purpose of knowing a subject well enough to make changes, it is called **applied research**. The findings of basic research often have applications, however, and applied research may make important contributions to the basic knowledge of a field.

In the field of human development, questions asked by basic or applied researchers reflect many concerns. Some common inquiries might be stated in the following ways. Try substituting a question that interests you (such as jealousy, competition, or altruism) in the blank spaces:

How does _____ get its start?

How often does _____ occur?

Why does _____ occur?

What is the result of _____ occurring?

What is a normal pattern for _____?

What constitutes "abnormal" for _____?

Can "abnormal" _____ be prevented?

Can "abnormal" _____ be reversed to normal?

What is the most efficient way to achieve normal _____?

Could occurrence of _____ with A, B, and C persons predict the occurrence of _____ with X, Y, and Z persons? Under what conditions?

It is important that you understand some of the basic methods of research. In textbooks, journals, newspapers, television reports, or even word-of-mouth communications, people will report research findings to you. Some of the reports will be quite reliable and worthy of your trust. Others will be contrived or based on faulty logic. You, as a consumer of research, should be able to question how conclusions were reached. You should also be able to make an intelligent estimate of how reliable the results are, based on the research methodologies used. Very often the same question can be researched in different ways and the resulting answers will be in conflict. Which study should you believe? The following brief introduction to research methodology cannot make you an expert judge of research quality. However, it can make you aware of problems inherent to all research methodgies used to study human development. If you emerge from a careful reading of the following descriptions feeling skeptical about the 100% accuracy of any human relations research result, this chapter will have accomplished its first goal. If you begin to question how research results are obtained in the future, a second important goal will have been met.

Cross-Sectional versus Longitudinal Studies

Cross-sectional studies, which measure different subjects at the same time, are used more frequently than **longitudinal studies**, which measure the same subjects over a period of time, because they can be completed more quickly (see Figure 1-14). However, cross-sectional studies tend to ignore the individual and his or her unique growth and development. This drawback can be especially hazardous if the subjects under study are going through an especially rapid period of growth and change, such as infancy or adolescence. For example, when infants ranging in age from birth through three months are grouped together for study, their individual differences, which are vast, are ignored.

Another hazard of cross-sectional research involves the dangers of comparing groups of individuals of different ages. Findings may be determined by social and generational differences between the age groups as much as by the variable under study. Consider, for example, the impact on people of World War II in the 1940s, the Vietnam War in the 1960s, and the Persian Gulf War in 1991. These situations influenced the social and emotional development of the people who experienced them. Would a research finding such as "A belief in war increases with age" make you skeptical if you knew the persons studied were all either fifty or seventy years old? Wouldn't you

Year of birth			Longitudinal															
'83	Jim at 2	Kay at 2	Ann at 2	Al at 2	Eve at 2	Bob at 2	Joe at 2	Ina at 2	Ed at 2	Sue at 2	Lee at 2	Ted at 2	Mae at 2	Ken at 2	Liz at 2	Deb at 2	Don at 2	Pat at 2
'84	Jim at 3	Kay at 3	Ann at 3	Al at 3	Eve at 3	Bob at 3	Joe at 3	Ina at 3	Ed at 3	Sue at 3	Lee at 3	Ted at 3	Mae at 3	Ken at 3	Liz at 3	Deb at 3	Don at 3	Pat at 3
'85	Jim at 4	Kay at 4	Ann at 4	Al at 4	Eve at 4	Bob at 4	Joe at 4	Ina at 4	Ed at 4	Sue at 4	Lee at 4	Ted at 4	Mae at 4	Ken at 4	Liz at 4	Deb at 4	Don at 4	Pat at 4
'86	Jim at 5	Kay at 5	Ann at 5	Al at 5	Eve at 5	Bob at 5	Joe at 5	Ina at 5	Ed at 5	Sue at 5	Lee at 5	Ted at 5	Mae at 5	Ken at 5	Liz at 5	Deb at 5	Don at 5	Pat at 5
Cross-sectional '87	Jim at 6	Kay at 6	Ann at 6	Al at 6	Eve at 6	Bob at 6	Joe at 6	Ina at 6	Ed at 6	Sue at 6	Lee at 6	Ted at 6	Mae at 6	Ken at 6	Liz at 6	Deb at 6	Don at 6	Pat at 6
'88	Jim at 7	Kay at 7	Ann at 7	Al at 7	Eve at 7	Bob at 7	Joe at 7	Ina at 7	Ed at 7	Sue at 7	Lee at 7	Ted at 7	Mae at 7	Ken at 7	Liz at 7	Deb at 7	Don at 7	Pat at 7
'89	Jim at 8	Kay at 8	Ann at 8	Al at 8	Eve at 8	Bob at 8	Joe at 8	Ina at 8	Ed at 8	Sue at 8	Lee at 8	Ted at 8	Mae at 8	Ken at 8	Liz at 8	Deb at 8	Don at 8	Pat at 8

Figure 1-14
A schematic representation of cross-sectional and longitudinal samples of research subjects.

question whether the positive evaluation of war was really a result of what each subject had experienced in his or her youth? Would twenty-year-olds express a belief in the efficacy of war today?

When cross-sectional research is used to study groups of individuals who are similar in age and background, the criticism of differential experiences is less meaningful. Comparisons of associates that are carefully designed to eliminate problems of intragroup or social and cultural differences can be fruitful as well as convenient ways of learning a great deal about human behavior.

Longitudinal research is desirable for ascertaining the stability or instability of individual characteristics over time. Many concerns of human development research (such as physical functions or intelligence) are better studied longitudinally than by means of a one-time investigation. The Baltimore Longitudinal Study of Aging, for example, has been studying volunteers since 1958. Each volunteer has his or her own biological profile, so that individual changes can be measured as each one ages.

Longitudinal research, like cross-sectional research, has many problems. One obvious difficulty is that longitudinal research takes so much time. Subjects in longitudinal research get "lost" (quit, move away, die), and the expenses incurred by the researchers over time are enormous. It is also possible that subjects in a longitudinal study will become "investigation wise" (anticipate what the researchers want to see), will lose their motivation to give their best efforts to the research, or will remember how they responded in the last session.

Several methods of combining cross-sectional and longitudinal research are possible. Appelbaum and McCall (1983) have presented three general approaches: cohort-sequential, time-sequential, and cross-sequential. A **cohort** is a person born about the same time and into the same society as the individual under study. A person born ten or more years earlier or later than you might experience a kind of "generation gap" from you and therefore would not be your cohort. **Cohort-sequential** research looks at cohorts longitudinally with sequential times of measurement and is replicated using cohorts born in different years, usually until the oldest subjects in the last study reach the age of the oldest subjects in the first study (see Figure 1-15). A **time-sequential**

Year of birth	Year of measurement																	
	'84	'85	'86	'87	'88	'89	'90	'91	'92	'93	'94	'95	'96	'97	'98	'99	'00	'01
'83	Cal at 1	Cal at 2	Cal at 3	Cal at 4	Cal at 5	Cal at 6	Cal at 7	Cal at 8	Cal at 9	Cal at 10	Cal at 11	Cal at 12	Cal at 13	Cal at 14	Cal at 15	Cal at 16	Cal at 17	Cal at 18
'84		Nan at 1	Nan at 2	Nan at 3	Nan at 4	Nan at 5	Nan at 6	Nan at 7	Nan at 8	Nan at 9	Nan at 10	Nan at 11	Nan at 12	Nan at 13	Nan at 14	Nan at 15	Nan at 16	Nan at 17
'85			Ray at 1	Ray at 2	Ray at 3	Ray at 4	Ray at 5	Ray at 6	Ray at 7	Ray at 8	Ray at 9	Ray at 10	Ray at 11	Ray at 12	Ray at 13	Ray at 14	Ray at 15	Ray at 16
'86				Zoe at 1	Zoe at 2	Zoe at 3	Zoe at 4	Zoe at 5	Zoe at 6	Zoe at 7	Zoe at 8	Zoe at 9	Zoe at 10	Zoe at 11	Zoe at 12	Zoe at 13	Zoe at 14	Zoe at 15
'87					Hal at 1	Hal at 2	Hal at 3	Hal at 4	Hal at 5	Hal at 6	Hal at 7	Hal at 8	Hal at 9	Hal at 10	Hal at 11	Hal at 12	Hal at 13	Hal at 14
'88						Flo at 1	Flo at 2	Flo at 3	Flo at 4	Flo at 5	Flo at 6	Flo at 7	Flo at 8	Flo at 9	Flo at 10	Flo at 11	Flo at 12	Flo at 13
'89							Vi at 1	Vi at 2	Vi at 3	Vi at 4	Vi at 5	Vi at 6	Vi at 7	Vi at 8	Vi at 9	Vi at 10	Vi at 11	Vi at 12

A. Cohort-sequential   B. Time-sequential   C. Cross-sequential

Figure 1-15

A schematic representation of (a) cohort-sequential, (b) time-sequential, and (c) cross-sequential samples of research subjects.

study is done cross-sectionally and is replicated at different times of measurement, usually until the oldest subjects in the last study reach the age of the oldest subjects in the first study (see Figure 1-15). Finally, in a **cross-sequential** study several cross-sections of cohorts are studied longitudinally with the same times of measurement without regard to age (see Figure 1-15). These methods combine the desirability of analyzing the unique individual differences of subjects with the relative ease of looking at a greater number of subjects in a shorter time. Again, however, there is a risk that subjects may become investigation wise or lose their motivation over time.

Experimental Studies

An **experiment** is a technique that can determine causal relationships between a manipulated variable and one or more **dependent variables**. When one conducts an experiment, one controls a host of factors to prevent them from confusing the action of the manipulated variable, called the **independent variable**. Consider the following study:

> Courage (1989) used forty-eight cooperative four-year-old children of normal intelligence to demonstrate the efficacy of training procedures on performance in the game of Twenty Questions. All of the children made many errors on the pretest (first playing of the game). Experimental subject children were given training in how to play: They were taught to ask categorical questions to identify the target. In a posttest immediately following the training, the experimental group of subject children asked categorical questions and played the game of Twenty Questions efficiently. In a posttest one week later, the subject children still asked categorical questions and played the game efficiently. A group of control children who had no training in how to ask categorical questions made many errors in both posttests (second and third playings of the game).

In the ideal experiment, in order to demonstrate that there is a relationship between the variables, a **control group** is used. The control group is not subjected to the manipulation of the independent variable under study as the experimental group is. Both groups are observed carefully. If the dependent variables occur only in the experimental group, then it can be assumed that the manipulation of the independent variable was effective in bringing about a consequence that ordinarily would not occur. In the above experiment, the researcher strove for equality of age, sex (there were an equal number of boys and girls in both the subject and control groups), intelligence (all children had normal intelligence), and cooperation (uncooperative children were replaced). This provided her with a degree of confidence that the one independent variable manipulated (training in how to ask categorical questions) caused the changes observed in the experimental subjects but not in the controls.

When a scientist can demonstrate that a research method accomplished what it set out to accomplish, was well-grounded, effective, and honest, then the scientist can claim that the research was valid (see Figure 1-16). **Validity** means truthfulness and trustworthiness. Because an experiment can demonstrate that a manipulation of the independent variable causes changes in dependent variables while other factors are held constant, it is usually considered internally valid. However, it is often difficult to generalize the results observed in an experimental situation to other settings. In the real world, one can seldom prevent a host of extraneous factors from having effects on behaviors. Thus, experiments may not always be externally valid: They may not always be trustworthy to describe how a manipulation of one independent variable will change behavior when extraneous factors are not controlled.

A correctly done experiment is a reliable way to conduct science because it is so carefully designed and controlled. The capable researcher describes every step of the study from start to finish so that another researcher can repeat the study by following the same steps. A repetition of a study is called a **replication**. When a research study produces the same results each time it is replicated, it is said to have a high degree of reliability. **Reliability** in research means that the same observations or procedures

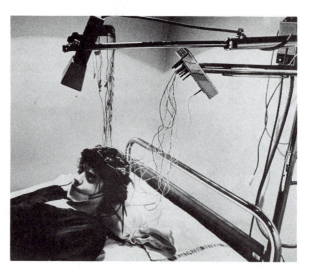

Figure 1-16
Modern electronic equipment allows researchers to validly measure brain activity in response to the manipulation of an independent variable.

will produce the same or similar results each time they are repeated. Experiments that have been reliably replicated give us confidence that a known independent variable will produce certain changes in certain dependent variables when all the other factors in the environment are controlled.

In order to make experiments applicable to the real world, a **random sample** of subjects is selected for study. A random sample gives every person of the group under study an equal chance of participating in the research. For example, suppose we wanted to study receptive language in two-year-olds. We might find all the two-year-olds in a city by going to the Bureau of Vital Statistics and looking at birth registrations. Suppose there were 2000 two-year-olds and we only wanted to test a sample of 100. First, we would number the toddlers from 1 to 2000. Then we would use a table of randomized numbers from a statistics book, or from a computer program, and select 100 of these random numbers. If some of the first 100 toddlers randomly chosen could not participate in the study (e.g., they were non-verbal, health disabled, not willing), we would continue selecting toddlers at random until our sample size reached 100. This way, we should have a group of toddlers representative of the population of the city (e.g., all ethnicities, all economic levels). If the city has a population that has approximately the same percentage of ethnic and economic groups as the country, then the results of the study might be generalized country-wide. It is honest to generalize only to the type of population from which the random sample was selected.

One criticism frequently voiced about experimental research is that, because it is so highly manipulated and controlled, it does not give a very good picture of what actually occurs in the real world. It is true that there is a degree of artificiality about experimental research, but this does not always negate its value. The kinds of stimuli that can be used as independent variables and the kinds of responses that can be used as dependent variables in experimental situations are confined within narrow bounds. An experiment will rarely employ more than one or two independent variables, and these are usually of a fairly simple nature. This kind of research cannot contribute much to our knowledge of such things as thought processes, emotional feeling tones, or unconscious inhibitors of behavior. It is a rigorous, precise, replicable way of doing research on a limited number of topics in human development.

Observational Studies

An **observation** in science is the gathering of research data from the real world by recognizing and noting facts or behaviors as they occur. Following the scientific method, observational studies attempt to be as valid as possible. They are not able to achieve the same degree of internal validity as experiments because extraneous factors are not controlled. It is difficult to prove that one variable observed to influence another variable will do so again and again under different circumstances or settings. However, observational studies may have a higher degree of external validity than experiments. Observational findings can be more trustworthy to generalize to the larger population because they note facts or behaviors as they occur in the real world rather than in an experimental, manipulated, setting.

> *Friend Of Who Has Children came to our house one day while my father was away. He was a Red Clay. My mother and I were just starting to eat, and she told him to eat with us. There was only one spoon, and we all used it. Once, as the man was using the spoon, my mother asked for it. He handed it to her, and she reached over and took it. After we'd eaten my mother went out with the herd, and he went away.*
>
> *When my father came home he asked me, "Was anyone here today?" I said, "Yes." "How many people came today?" I said, "Only one." He asked me who it was. I knew the man very well, and I said, "Friend Of Who Has Children. He came, and we ate with him." "Where'd he sit while you were eating?" my father asked. I said, "On the north side." "Where'd your mother sit?" "On the west side, close to this man." "Where'd you sit?" "I was sitting on the south side." And I added, "We ate with the spoon. The man had the spoon, and my mother took it away from him." My father got up, picked up the spoon and handed it to me. "Now you hand it to me just as the man handed it to your mother." I handed it to him. "Just like this," I said. He took the spoon, "Now," he said, "I'm the man, and you're your mother. How'd she take hold of the spoon?" "This way," I said, and I did just as my mother had done. After I told him all this he got on his horse and rode away.**

In this vignette, the young Navajo boy was an astute observer of behaviors. He did not understand the sexual significance of what he saw. Nevertheless, he replicated the behaviors to someone who understood. Thus, he created problems for his mother. Should the father have trusted his son as a reliable witness?

Any observation of humans is impossible to see again in exactly the same way, in the same setting. Does this mean we cannot ascribe reliability (repeatability) to observations? Scientists using experiments usually rely on test–retest measures of reliability. Scientists using observations usually rely on interrater measures of reliability. If two or more observers agree that they saw the same thing at the same time, the finding may be considered reliable. Modern audio–video equipment allows for the recording of naturalistic observations. Behaviors can thus be repeated through replays, allowing a very high degree of confidence in the accuracy of the observations (see Figure 1-17).

Observations can be done on random samples of the population under study, can be done on subject groups and control groups, and can be analyzed statistically. They can also be conducted in laboratories. Consider the procedures of the following observational study (Jasnow, et al., 1988):

> The observation took place in the Interpersonal Communications Laboratory when each infant was four months post-partum. So as to ensure as much uniformity as possible in the infants' state level, mothers were asked to arrive at the laboratory just prior to the infant's next feeding. Mothers were asked to feed their infant in the room where the recording was to take place. This period allowed both mother and infant to acclimate to the laboratory setting. During the recording session, the infant was placed in an infant seat which was itself placed on a table at an elevation such that mother and infant could comfortably achieve eye contact. In order to record the vocal exchanges, a specially constructed bib into which a wireless microphone had been sewn was tied on the infant. The mother used a clip-on wireless microphone. Video recordings were made in addition to audio recordings. A special effects generator was used to allow split-screen recordings of infant and mother on the same video tape. The mother was told, "I would like you to talk to your baby and try to get your baby to talk to you."

Figure 1-17
Researchers today can capture naturalistic observations on film. Several people can then analyze the same sequence of behavior. A high degree of interrater reliability makes an observation more scientifically precise.

**SOURCE:* Walter Dyk, *Son of Old Man Hat: A Navajo Autobiography* reprinted with permission of University of Nebraska Press, 1966.

Figure 1-18
A specialized computer system can transform vocalizations of an infant and adult into a diagrammatic representation. The numbered line at the bottom represents 250-millisecond units of time. V stands for vocalization, P for pause, SP for switching pause, ISS for interruptive simultaneous speech, and NSS for noninterruptive simultaneous speech. The arrows that point down denote the end of the infant's turns; the arrows that point up denote the end of the adult's turns.

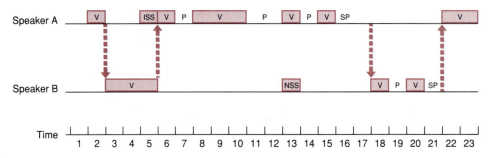

In this study, the researchers were interested in how infants coordinated the time of their vocal behavior with that of their mothers and vice versa. A specialized computer system allowed the researchers to analyze speaking turns, vocalizations, pauses, switching pauses, and simultaneous speech (see Figure 1-18).

Observational studies are sometimes considered to be less scientifically rigorous than experiments. The above study was an observational study conducted in a laboratory. Do you think it fell short in scientific rigor?

Electronic recording devices (audiovisual equipment, special effects generators, videotapes, sound spectrograms) make it possible to record behavior as it occurs and then to analyze segments of the behavior carefully and repeatedly at a later date. Newer techniques are continually being developed that make the analysis of naturally occurring behaviors even easier. Observational studies still have many methodological problems, however. The behaviors to be isolated for analysis must be carefully identified and defined. All persons trained to extract these elements must understand the definitions fully. They must reach a high level of agreement (called interrater reliability) among themselves about what they are seeing. Further, they should not have any preconceived notions about what they ought to be seeing, as preconceptions can distort their perception of what they see. This state or quality of observing phenomena without bias, in a detached, impersonal way, is called **objectivity**. The opposite is **subjectivity**: a state or quality of imposing personal prejudices, thoughts, and feelings into one's work. It is hard to overcome subjectivity in an observational study of human behavior. Experimental studies that deal with counting responses or gathering measures of quantity avoid subjectivity better than observational studies that rely more heavily on measures of the quality of responses.

In **field studies**, there are limits on the activities and events that are catalogued in any instances of observing naturally occurring behaviors. The researcher must first have a good idea of the variables she or he is looking for. This requirement may prevent looking at a random sample of a population if one or more variables under study are person specific (for example, male breast cancer). Comparing certain behaviors observed in different groups (such as men with breast cancer and men without) may result in invalid conclusions. How can the researcher be sure that any group differences observed are due to the cancer and not some extraneous variable? Although results of field studies are inconclusive, they contribute a great deal of information to our knowledge of human development.

Participant observation is a special form of field study in which the researcher attempts to become immersed in the way of life to be studied to the point that she or he becomes a part of the social context. Anthropologists and sociologists are most apt to use this technique to study human behavior. Most people tend to change what they do and say when they know they are being observed. The participant observer, by becoming a part of the environment, assures that her or his own behaviors do not significantly affect the actions and reactions of others. The disadvantage of the participant observer approach is that it involves a considerable investment of time to become a part of a "real life" situation and to become accepted by people on their own terms.

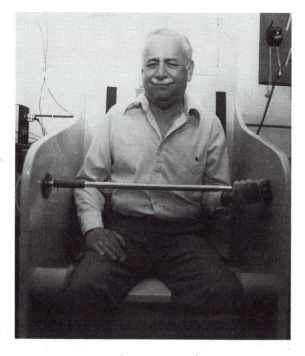

Figure 1-19
Clinical investigations involve
many observations as well as
tests and measurements.

   Clinical investigations are usually studies done in facilities where people come
to receive advice or treatment for problems. Consequently, they often deal with mal-
adjustments of some kind. They may, however, also be used to study healthy people.
Clinical investigations may involve in-depth laboratory tests, physical examinations,
radiological scans, interviews, or surveys, as well as observations by professional
specialists, depending on the nature of the study. Sharing of information by an interdisciplinary team allows each participant to have a better picture of the individual under
study (see Figure 1-19).

   The result of intensive investigation of the past history and/or current influences
on the subject is most apt to be a **case study**. The focus is on the individual and his
or her uniqueness. Research using case studies may try to find commonalities among
people with particular problems or experiences. There are dangers inherent in this kind
of research. The investigator may try to force different experiences into the same
classification for the sake of doing statistical analyses, or the researcher may affect the
results of the analyses by interpreting the data according to some preconceived notions.
Nevertheless, case studies can provide us with a wealth of new information. Some
case studies are done by lay persons in the form of autobiographies, biographies,
diaries, collections of letters, record books, baby books, and the like. Many insights
have been discovered, or rediscovered, in such sources.

Correlational Studies

   In **correlational research** two or more variables are examined in order to
determine if they are related to each other. This co-relationship, if it exists, may be
positive or negative (see Table 1-2). If two variables go together in the same direction
(e.g., kinship and intelligence), they are positively related. They are positively related
regardless of whether they go up together, as kinship and intelligence do, or down
together, as mother's education and involvement in her son's school activities do. If
two variables covary in such a way that one goes up when the other goes down (e.g.,
reading ability and time spent naming pseudo-words), they are negatively related.

   Relationships between variables never demonstrate cause and effect. Which came
first, the chicken or the egg? Every correlation has the same dilemma. Whether two

Table 1-2 Selected correlation coefficients for child development variables

Child development variables	Correlation	Source of Data
Positively Related Variables		
Identical twins reared together and intelligence scores	$r = +.86$ (strong)	Bouchard and McGue (1981)
Mother's education and her involvement in her son's school activities	$r = +.53$	Stevenson and Baker (1987)
Parental encouragement and time viewing "Sesame Street"	$r = +.36$	Pinon, Huston, and Wright (1989)
Family income loss and father's indifferent behavior to his children	$r = +.17$ (weak)	Elder, Van Nguyen, and Caspi (1985)
Negatively Related Variables		
3rd grade superior reading ability and measures of time and errors on pseudo-word naming task	$r = -.72$ (strong)	Stanovich, Nathan, and Zolman (1988)
Marijuana smoking during pregnancy and duration of newborn's cry	$r = -.58$	Lester and Dreher (1989)
14-year-old boys value of intellectual matters and hard drug use	$r = -.35$	Block, Block, and Keyes (1988)
Maternal attention to younger sibling and cooperation between siblings	$r = -.17$ (weak)	Stocker, Dunn, and Plomin (1989)

variables go up together, down together, or in opposite directions from each other, we can only say with confidence that they covary. The question of which came first, or which caused the other, or whether both were caused by another factor must be further explored with some other research methodology.

Interviews or questionnaires are frequently used to obtain data about things that a scientist suspects may be correlated. The strength of any correlations, positive or negative, can be determined with a statistic called a correlation coefficient. Correlations range from -1.0 (a perfect negative covariance) to $+1.0$ (a perfect positive covariance). If two variables are totally unrelated, their correlation coefficient will be 0. Correlation coefficients are symbolized with an r equal to a number between -1.0 and $+1.0$ (see Table 1-2). Numbers close to 1 (whether negative or positive) mean variables have a strong magnitude of relationship to each other. Numbers close to 0 (whether negative or positive) mean variables have a weak magnitude of co-relationship. Strong statistical relationships are of most interest to scientists. However, further studies (e.g., experiments, observations, tests) must be developed to try to determine why the variables go together, if one causes the other, or if both are caused by some other factors (e.g., similar intelligence test scores of identical twins may be the result of similar environmental stimulations).

Standardized Tests

Standardized tests are tests that have been administered to a great many people representing the population for whom they were designed in order to determine statistical norms (standards) for that population. Subjects used in the process of standardization should reflect all the characteristics (e.g., age, sex, culture, occupational background) of the population on which the test will be used. We say a test is valid if it can be trusted to show how close or distant a subject, from the population it was designed to assess, falls from the norms. Herein lies a problem with standardized tests. They are often used to assess people quite different from the population used for the standardization of norms. Most intelligence tests, for example, have been standardized standardization of norms. Most intelligence tests, for example, have been standardized with predominantly Caucasian middle-class subjects. Are they then valid for testing the intelligence of black or Hispanic subjects, or for testing the intelligence of the very rich, or the very poor? Often a test is standardized in only one area of a country. The test makers carefully match their standardization sample to the demographic characteristics of that area (see Box 1-1). Can this test then be valid for use with persons in other areas of a country with different demographic characteristics, or in other countries?

Some examples of standardized tests are intelligence tests, achievement tests, personality tests, normal development screening tests, and tests of neurological damage. In order to be valid, a test should measure what it is supposed to measure. Herein lies another problem. What constitutes intelligence, or achievement, or neurological damage? Can all aspects of intelligence, or achievement, et cetera, be measured? Because of problems with definitions, and additional problems of finding ways to test all aspects of any defined concept, standardized tests may not be completely valid.

If a standardized test yields the same or similar results each time it is taken, we say it has good test–retest reliability. Can you think of a reason why a subject might score close to the same when repeating a test? Many standardized tests have two or more forms making repeated tests slightly different. This assures that subjects are not remembering their answers from the first test. The question that remains is, "How equivalent are the two forms of the same test?" You may have wondered about this if you took the same standardized test twice, in different forms; for example, the Scholastic Aptitude Test (see Figure 1-20).

There is considerable controversy in the social and behavioral sciences about testing, not only about how concepts should be measured and the precision of those measurements, but also over the meaning of the constructs themselves (Green, 1981). A benefit of standardized tests is that they allow rapid and cost-efficient assessment of the abilities of many persons. A limitation is that despite scientific rigor in the

---

**BOX
1-1**

How 5000 subjects might be selected from "Our Area" as the standardization population for our fictitious test of reading skills.

Demographic characteristics of "Our Area" and standardization sample

	"Our Area"	Sample		"Our Area"	Sample
Age Groups			*Cultural backgrounds*		
1–10	8%	6%	African–American	17%	16%
11–20	9%	10%	Anglo–American	47%	48%
21–30	17%	18%	Asian–American	11%	12%
31–40	24%	24%	Hispanic–American	22%	22%
41–50	22%	22%	Native–American	3%	2%
51–60	11%	12%			
61–70	3%	4%			
71–80	3%	3%	*Occupational backgrounds*		
81–90	2%	1%	Professional	17%	19%
91–100	1%	—	Skilled laborers	20%	19%
			Semi-skilled Laborers	26%	25%
Sex					
Male	47%	50%	Unskilled Laborers	15%	16%
Female	53%	50%	Unemployed	8%	7%
			Students	14%	14%

Figure 1-20
Many standardized tests, such as achievement tests, are given more than once. A slightly different form is used each time. Are alternate forms equivalent?

standardization of norms, they may discriminate against some normal persons, who, for various reasons, score distant from these norms. The reader of this text is encouraged to reach his or her own opinions about the use of standardized tests in research.

Interviews and Surveys

Interviews are used to collect data about people's behaviors in the past (called **retrospective studies**) or about their current attitudes or behaviors. Although a great deal of information can be obtained in this way, there are a number of factors that can make responses suspect. First, there is the obvious fact that most people like to cast themselves in a favorable light. Second, many persons, in an attempt to please the interviewer, will give the answer they feel is desired. Third, the way that a question is worded or asked can often influence what response will be given. Fourth, people are forgetful. Even if memories are excellent, no one perceives every aspect of every experience. Many times people remember only what they want to remember. Finally, everyone experiences changes of mind. Truthful answers that are given one day may no longer reflect how one feels after a day, a week, or a month (see Figure 1-21).

Surveys and questionnaires are susceptible to many of the weaknesses of interviews. Answers may reflect lack of frankness, forgetfulness, selective memory, confusion about wording, or vacillating attitudes. Subjects may be nervous, which affects their ability to remember or reason, or bored, which can lead to carelessness and decreased efforts to concentrate on the questions, or they may lack motivation to participate. Nevertheless, when respondents strive to be honest and are motivated to add to a body of research data, these methods can amass a great deal of information that cannot be gathered in other ways.

Figure 1-21
Interview data can be deceptive. Interviewees may misunderstand questions, hedge, forget, or change their minds, as well as speak the unvarnished truth.

Ethical Considerations

Regardless of the research methodology adopted, any study using human participants must observe caution to protect the welfare of the subjects. The researcher must strive to preserve and protect their dignity, worth, and fundamental human rights. The American Psychological Association (1981) proposed the following ethical considerations for research with human participants:

- Prior to participation, the investigator clarifies the obligations and responsibilities of each subject and explains all aspects of the research about which the participants inquire.
- If concealment or deception is necessary, the investigator ensures that the participants are provided with sufficient explanation as soon as possible.
- The investigator respects the individual's freedom to decline to participate in or to withdraw from the research at any time.
- The investigator protects the participant from physical and mental discomfort, harm, and danger unless the research has great potential benefit and fully informed and voluntary consent is obtained from each participant. Procedures for contacting the investigator within a reasonable time following participation if stress, harm, or related concerns arise must be given.
- The investigator is responsible for the ethical treatment of subjects by collaborators, assistants, students, and employees.
- After the data are collected, the investigator provides the participant with information about the nature of the study and attempts to remove any misconceptions that may have arisen.
- If research results in undesirable consequences, the investigator has the responsibility to remove or correct these consequences.
- Confidential information obtained about a research participant during an investigation is protected.

The Society for Research in Child Development (1990) listed fourteen ethical principles for research with children (see Table 1-3).

Table 1-3 Ethical Standards for Research with Children

Principle	Description
Non-harmful procedures	No operation may harm the child either physically or psychologically.
Informed consent	Inform the child and answer the child's questions. Let the child choose to participate or not.
Parental consent	Parents' consent should be obtained in writing after learning the features of the research.
Additional consent	Other persons (e.g., teachers) interacting with the child during the study should be informed and consent.
Incentives	Incentives must be fair and not exceed the range of the child's normal incentives.
Deception	If deception is necessary, it must have no negative effects on the child or child's family.
Anonymity	Anonymity of information should be preserved and only used for that purpose for which permission was obtained.
Mutual responsibilities	Responsibilities of subject and investigator are defined. Investigator honors all promises.
Jeopardy	Investigator bears responsibility to discuss with parents any information that may jeopardize child.
Unforeseen consequences	Investigator corrects unforeseen undesirable consquences immediately.
Confidentiality	Subjects' identity should be concealed in written and verbal reports of the results of the study.
Informing participants	Investigator reports general findings to subjects in terms appropriate to their understanding.
Reporting results	Caution should be exercised in reporting results, making evaluations, or giving advice.
Implications of findings	Findings are presented with care for social, political, and humane implications.

Statistical Treatment of Data

Methods of statistical analysis have been developed to evaluate data obtained in research. Methods of statistical analysis help to shape the format of research and, in so doing, are part and parcel of research methods. Although statistics is a branch of applied mathematics in its own right, with roots in probability theory, its value is stressed here as a tool of human development research. The following brief overview will help you understand some of the statistical terms in research reports.

Descriptive statistics describe and summarize to help a reader understand the characteristics of data. *Means, medians,* and *modes* are descriptive statistics used frequently to represent a set of measures as a single number. The mean is the arithmetic average. The median is the middle number in any ordered series. The mode is the numerical term that occurs most frequently in the data. For instance, if you have scores of 62, 62, 63, 84, and 94, the mean value will be 73, the median 63, and the mode 62.

Descriptive statistics that assess the spread of a set of data are the range and the standard deviation. The highest and lowest values of the data indicate the **range.** The degree of spread from the center of the data is described by the **standard deviation**. For normal distributions approximately 68% of all scores will be expected to fall within one standard deviation above and below the mean. Approximately 95% will fall within two standard deviations and 99% within three standard deviations above and below the mean (see Figure 1-22).

A frequently used term in statistics is the **correlation coefficient**. It is a numerical value that indicates the degree and direction of the relationship of two variables to one

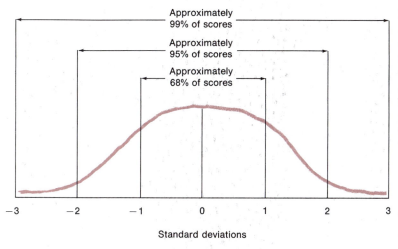

another. When two variables change in the same direction (such as height and weight), they are said to be positively correlated. When two variables change in the opposite direction (such as high blood pressure and life expectancy), they are said to be negatively correlated. Most correlation coefficients range between $+1.0$ and -1.0 and are therefore fractions (for example, $+.25$, $-.55$, $+.90$) that indicate some low, moderate, or high degree of positive or negative association between two variables.

Inferential statistics go beyond description. The characteristics of a population are inferred from the characteristics of a *sample* of that population. For example, from a knowledge of the birth weights of a sample of infants, one can infer the birth weights of the larger population of infants. Based on sample values, statistical methods can be employed to estimate population values with varying degrees of confidence.

There are many kinds of statistical tests used on different sets of data to answer different types of questions. For example, t-tests are often used in evaluating differences in mean outcomes of two treatments. Analyses of variance are used to evaluate differences in mean outcomes among three or more treatments. Chi-square tests are used to evaluate how variables are distributed in a population. Regression analysis is used in testing for significance of relationships among two or more variables.

Confidence intervals are mathematical expressions that define a range into which a certain proportion of the values of a variable will fall. They are derived from a knowledge of the characteristics of a sample. For instance, we could mathematically define a 95% confidence interval that would include the birth weights of 95% of infants in a population, based on our knowledge of the mean and standard deviation of the birth weights of a random sample of infants drawn from that population. Weights falling outside of this 95% confidence interval would be considered distinctly unusual. They could be expected to occur by chance with a **probability** (expressed as p) of no more than 5% (expressed as $p \leq .05$). The highest and lowest values of the confidence interval are called the confidence limits. Influenced by experience, researchers may say that a value of a variable is unusual and has **statistical significance** if its chance of occurring is less than 5% ($p < .05$) or less than 1% ($p < .01$).

Summary

The ecology of every human's development consists of changing sociocultural systems and resources. Textbooks such as this can never fully explain the art of living or the meaning of life but can aid in one's understanding of both.

Heredity and environment interact in a multitude of ways to determine human development. It is not possible to assign any human characteristic an exclusive heredity label, or an exclusive environmental label.

The family has long been held responsible for a child's development. While family members certainly influence development, each child helps shape his or her family as well. The functions families perform are similar but the ways in which they carry them out can be very diverse. The community helps determine how each unique person develops by shaping and reinforcing some behaviors and ignoring others. Community members are important sources of social, economic, and emotional support for each other.

Historical debates about human development focused on questions such as the innate soul and the acquired effects of education and discipline. The theory of evolution triggered a multitude of questions about the genetic predetermination of human characteristics. Contemporary studies of human development focus more on the description of behaviors, the ways in which behaviors change, and the causes of behavior change. The study of development is the concern of the biological sciences as well as the social sciences. Specialized studies frequently concentrate on only one aspect of human life in order to learn as much as possible about a specific area. Interdisciplinary sharing helps round out our picture of how development proceeds.

Research can be cross-sectional (studying many different persons at the same time) or longitudinal (studying the same persons over a period of time). These methods can be combined in cohort-sequential, time-sequential, and cross-sequential studies. Three major kinds of research—experimental, observational, and correlational—have been applied to the study of human development. Experimental research is contrived. It can provide control of variables, is objective, and is replicable; however, it has a limited application to the study of areas such as thought processes and feelings. Observational research is a look at "real life." It can contribute a great deal of information about many different subjects; however, it must rely on some subjective judgments and may not be easily replicated. Correlational studies show positive or negative correspondence between two or more variables but do not necessarily imply causation. They can usually be conducted with a minimum of interference in people's lives.

Standardized tests may not be valid for persons outside the group on whom the norms were standardized. They allow rapid and cost-efficient assessment of many traits and behaviors. They are often used in conjunction with other research methods. Interviews obtain information about conscious intentions or about personal or opinionated data. Surveys collect similar information indirectly, in writing. Both interviews and surveys can be biased and can suggest answers or restrict answers. People being interviewed or filling out surveys can lie, hide information, or answer carelessly. These research methods are ways to obtain information about personal opinions or conscious intentions and are used in conjunction with other research methods. Regardless of the research method(s) chosen, ethical considerations must always be observed to protect the participants in studies of human development.

The data obtained from any type of research are usually analyzed with statistics. Results are expressed numerically in terms of their mean, median, mode, and standard deviation. Relations between variables can be expressed in terms of correlation coefficients or chi-square tests. Inferential statistics extend analysis beyond simple description to predict characteristics of the population from those of a sample.

Key Concepts

ecology	inductive reasoning	independent variables	case study
macrosystem	deductive reasoning	control group	correlational research
exosystem	scientific method	validity	standardized tests
microsystem	experimental psychology	replication	interview
mesosystem	descriptive psychology	reliability	retrospective study
heredity	developmental psychology	random sample	descriptive statistics
ontogeny	basic research	observation	standard deviation
phylogeny	applied research	objectivity	correlation coefficient
genotype	cross-sectional studies	subjectivity	inferential statistics
phenotype	longitudinal studies	field study	confidence intervals
environment	cohort	participant observation	probability
mores	experiment	clinical investigations	statistical significance
social network	dependent variables		

Questions for Review

1. Which of the following are microsystem influences? exosystem influences? macrosystem influences?
   - depletion of ozone layer
   - economic recession
   - school board decision
   - grandparents' divorce
   - Sunday school attendance
   - pen pal's letter
2. Why is it so difficult for humans to accept that both heredity and environment influence behaviors? What factors make us want to believe, for example, that our intelligence was inherited from our parents?
3. Sir Francis Galton felt women were intellectually inferior to men. What environmental factors may have led him to this conclusion?
4. Describe an experimental, observational, or correlational study you would be interested in doing. Discuss some of the problems you might have in conducting this piece of research
5. List the pros and cons of using the experimental method in doing research on human development.
6. Why are experiments often considered more scientific than observational or correlational forms of research?
7. Some feminists say that very little of the research already done in human development is useful for statements about women since most of it was done by men using male subjects, who have had different experiences than women. Do you agree or disagree with this criticism? Why?

Further Readings

Aries, P. (1962). *Centuries of childhood: A social history of family life.* New York: Vintage/Random House.
 Historically precise account of the evolution of the concept of childhood and the image of children with rich detail and vivid descriptions of the familial and educational worlds of children of the past.

Bronfenbrenner, U. (1979). *The ecology of human development: Experiments by nature and design.* Cambridge, MA: Harvard University Press.
 A challenge to scientists and lay readers to consider all the layers of the environment that have a formative influence on children. The interactions of real children with the real world become very important in this ecological perspective.

Lewontin, R. (1982). *Human diversity.* New York: W. H. Freeman.
 Discussion of the heredity–environment controversy with an overview of genetic mechanisms. Presentation of human diversity and its basis in evolution, heredity, and environment.

Miller, S. A. (1987). *Developmental research methods.* Englewood Cliffs, NJ: Prentice Hall.
 A review of the scientific method and multiple research techniques. Gives advantages and disadvantages of each method along with many concrete examples.

Molyneaux, D., and Lane, V. W. (1982). *Effective interviewing.* Boston: Allyn and Bacon.
 A valuable resource for every person who wants to collect data on human behavior. It describes all the keys to success in interviewing, such as active listening, use of silence, and guiding the interview.

Theories of Human Development

2

Theories are not fact; they are merely speculations of hypotheses that individuals make for the purpose of explaining and predicting behavior. You have theories of your own. You may not have formalized them or put them in writing, but you have them. Some of your theories are quite firmly entrenched in your thought processes; others may change each time you discuss a topic, meet someone new, or read a book. Some of your theories are exclusively yours; others you may have borrowed or adopted from friends, from professors, or from reading. Because of the status of theories as "not well understood" or "not proved," many are frequently altered or exchanged for others.

Human development is a complicated and difficult area in which to construct research. The theories presented here are respected because of the *empirical* (founded on experiment or observation) evidence that supports their propositions. This is not to say that they are correct or incorrect; rather, they have received the attention and support of some experts and some of the public at large. Every time a person sets his or her theories down in print for others to read, that person leaves himself or herself open to agreement, praise, approval, and criticism. Carefully researched, well-organized, systematic theories with definitions of special terminology are more apt to gain support than poorly constructed or undocumented theories. Feel free to agree or disagree with part or all of any of the theories that follow.

> Everything has been thought of before, but the problem is to think of it again.
>
> —*Goethe*

> A great many people think they are thinking when they are merely rearranging their prejudices.
>
> —*William James*

Psychodynamic Theories

Psychodynamic psychology refers to the study of the conscious, the subconscious, and especially the unconscious elements in human behavior. There are many theories that fall under the umbrella term psychodynamic, each with its own slant but all sharing certain similarities. Psychodynamic theorists study what happened in childhood to learn about the adult. They look for instinctual drives to explain human actions and reactions, and they study how these basic drives have been gratified (successfully or unsuccessfully). All believe that people use defense mechanisms to avoid pain or anxiety and to modify the pressures of various drives. The underlying assumption of all the psychodynamic theorists is that conscious, subconscious, and unconscious mental processes regulate how energy is distributed or deployed and how drives are satisfied or modified.

Helen Keller was born in June of 1880 in a small Alabama town. She was a precocious baby who spoke her first words at six months and ran at twelve months. When she was nineteen months old, she contracted encephalitis. Although she lived, she never saw, nor heard, again. She spent her early childhood playing with the daughter of a family servant. She developed her own system of signs with which she tyrannized her playmate. The two of them were always getting into mischief. When Helen was almost seven, her parents consulted the best to find a teacher for her: Alexander Graham Bell and the head of the Perkins Institute for the Blind recommended Anne Sullivan.

Helen tried to dominate Miss Sullivan the way she had her family and friend, but to no avail. Anne Sullivan was patient. She tried to break through Helen's dense fog by continually showing Helen objects and finger-spelling them into her hand. One day Helen understood the connection between water on her hand and the finger-spelled word "water." She later wrote, "That living word awakened my soul, gave it light, hope, set it free!"* After that, she clamored to learn everything Anne Sullivan could teach her. She learned to read Braille and to write on a special typewriter. She "heard" people by reading their lips with her finger and spoke with her own voice, even if she could not hear. She eventually graduated from college with honors and became a celebrated author and lecturer.

How did Anne Sullivan achieve this miracle? Freud might have suggested that Helen's libido provided her with a sense of pleasure at the water on her hand, which increased her desire to learn a name for it from Miss Sullivan. A behaviorist would explain her learning on the basis of Miss Sullivan's stimulus-response-reinforcement techniques. A social-learning theorist might add that Helen also practiced self-reinforcement. A cognitive theorist would emphasize Helen's concrete operational thinking, which linked the water and the finger-spelling word. A humanistic psychologist would probably focus on Helen's self-concept and the way her needs for love, belonging, and self-esteem influenced her actions and reactions. Other theorists could give alternative explanations for the life of Helen Keller and the miracle worker, Anne Sullivan. Theories are guesses, not facts. How would you account for the successes of Helen and Anne?*

*Keller, H. (1902). *The Story of My Life*. New York: Doubleday.

Freud's Psychosexual Stages

The father of all psychodynamic theories was Sigmund Freud (see Figure 2-1). Many of his assumptions have become so firmly established in the language of our times (for instance, libido, id, unconscious) that we regard them as facts rather than suppositions.

Freud believed that sexual desire is the primary motivator of behavior. He described **libido** as a life force, a source of energy, especially dominated by "demands of sexual desire . . . for pleasure" (Freud, 1966, p. 142). Sexual desire, he felt, is present in some form in most physical pleasures. Many of the sexual conflicts he believed to be developmental were probably once true of children raised during his lifetime (1856–1939) in Europe. However, they may not be true of all children today.

Freud devised the technique of **free association** of ideas in a "relaxed" setting to counteract his patients' tendencies to organize and censor their thoughts before speaking them aloud. The image of a psychiatrist sitting back in a chair while the patient reclines on a couch originated in his Vienna office. Early in his career, Freud also hypnotized patients to help them review their earlier life experiences. He often used dream analysis to help them gain more insight into their needs, desires, fears, and anxieties.

Freud postulated that personality has three components: the id, the ego, and the superego. The **id**, according to Freud, is the hedonistic (pleasure-seeking) part of the personality. Instincts, sexual impulses, the hunger drive, and aggressive urges are all housed there. Freud felt that the psychic energy, or libido, of the id is composed of two types of drives (or instincts). One, **Eros**, is a life force, aimed at survival and self-propagation. It motivates one to seek food, shelter, creature comforts, and sexual satisfaction. The other, **Thanatos**, is a death force, aimed against the world and the self. The energy of Thanatos builds up until it must be discharged either against others (aggressive drive) or against the self in some self-destructive manner. While a death force may seem the antithesis of hedonism, it is not. Many people will attest to the

Figure 2-1
Sigmund Freud (1856–1939) emphasized sexual libido, three aspects of personality, childhood events, and unconscious memories as determinants of behavior.

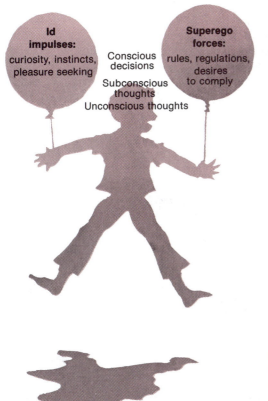

Id impulses:
curiosity, instincts, pleasure seeking

Conscious decisions

Subconscious thoughts

Unconscious thoughts

Superego forces:
rules, regulations, desires to comply

Figure 2-2
Freud postulated three aspects of the personality: the id, the ego, and the superego.

pleasure they derive from putting their lives in danger (drag racing, sky diving, and so on). Freud believed that id impulses, with their untamed, animal-like drives, are in constant need of control. The **superego**, he believed, is the controlling, moral arm of the personality. According to Freud, it serves as a watchdog, ensuring that our dominant id impulses do not motivate us to engage in socially unacceptable behaviors (see Figure 2-2 on page 31). It is learned in accordance with the religious teachings, moral standards, and ethics and mores of our parents and culture. It is composed of the conscience, which is a prohibitive influence on our behavior, and the ego-ideal, which motivates us to do good deeds. The superego supposedly develops slowly over the course of one's childhood and adolescence. The id, in contrast, is the aspect of the personality that houses and directs psychic energy from birth.

Between the id and the superego is the **ego**. Freud saw the **ego** as the realistic aspect of the personality. Ego is the self: the problem-solving, perceiving, remembering, judging, speaking mediator of all conscious, subconscious, and unconscious drives. At times a person is more id controlled and at other times he or she is more influenced by the superego. However, Freud felt that these personality components, and the relative way they balance and counterbalance each other, become established by the end of adolescence. By this point, one has a typical response pattern to frustrations, conflicts, and threats. Freud felt that major changes in adult personality could be accomplished only with analysis of childhood events and understanding of the forces that shaped the id, ego, and superego.

Freud believed that all human behavior is rooted in mental processes at one of the levels of consciousness: conscious, unconscious, and subconscious, (see Figure 2-3). He felt that ideas buried in the **unconscious** mind influence us in ways that are beyond our ability to control. The ego has repressed memories and prevents them from gaining access to the conscious (knowing) mind. Unconscious ideas, however, have the power to affect behaviors. At the **subconscious** level people may be only vaguely aware of the roots of their ideas. For example, you may have feelings about a person or a place without being able to get a firm grasp on what those feelings are or where they came from. In therapy some of the unconscious or subconscious thoughts may be revealed to the therapist through free association, dream analysis, slips of the tongue ("Freudian slips"), flashes of insight (the "aha" experience), or hypnosis.

As Freud sought to understand how childhood conflicts create problems in adulthood, he proposed a sequence of developmental stages (see Table 2-1). Each stage, he believed, is based on instincts related to body zones that bring sexual pleasure. If a child passes through each stage without trauma (and few can, in Freud's opinion), he

Figure 2-3

In Freudian theory, the unconscious, containing all memories not able to be retrieved, is the largest level of the mind. The subconscious, with only partially retrievable memories, is also larger than the level of conscious awareness.

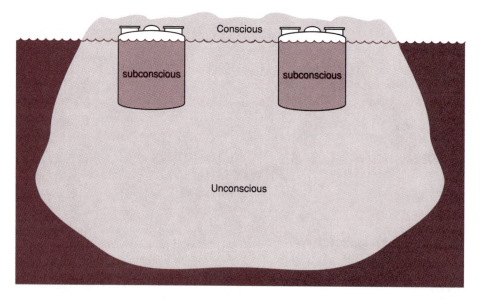

Table 2-1   Freudian Stages of Psychosexual Development

Stage	Sex Drives Related to:	Possible Results of Trauma
Oral	Feeding and weaning	Features of oral fixations: nail biting, cigarette smoking, gum chewing
Anal	Toilet training	Features of anal fixations: parsimony, orderliness, punctiliousness, obstinacy, pedantry, possessiveness
Phallic	Genital manipulation	Oedipal complex: boy overly attached to mother fears father may castrate him (castration complex); or Electra complex: girl overly attached to father, wishes to be a man, has "penis envy"
Latent	(Sex drives repressed)	Prolonged or exaggerated Oedipal or Electra complex
Genital	Puberty	Failure to develop mature, socially acceptable modes of attaining sexual gratification

or she will become a "well-adjusted" adult. Trauma during any given stage will result in some **fixation** (arrest of psychosexual development) or complex of the personality based on that stage. The origin of abnormal behavior in adults can often be traced back to too much or too little gratification during one or more of these developmental stages of childhood.

Some of the **defense mechanisms** that Freud proposed as guards against sexual anxieties have received wide acceptance. Many of these hypothesized behaviors are

BOX 2-1

Defense Mechanisms.

Compensation: Effort to win respect or prestige in one activity as a substitute for inability to achieve in some other realm or endeavor.

Denial: A refusal to believe or accept something as it is bur rather to perceive it as one wishes it would be.

Displacement: Transfer of emotion away from the person or situation that incurred the strong feeling and toward an inappropriate person or object.

Fantasy: Imagination of what one could have said or will say, could have done or will do; daydreaming.

Intellectualization: The separation of events and/or ideas or concepts from the emotions that impinge on them.

Introjection: Taking into one's own personality the characteristics of another.

Projection: Attributing one's own motives, emotions, or characteristics to someone else.

Rationalization: Concealment of motive for behavior by assigning some socially acceptable reasons for the action.

Reaction formation: Distortion of a drive to its opposite—for example, acting kindly toward a person whom one dislikes.

Regression: Reactivation of behaviors more appropriate to an earlier stage of development.

Repression: Burying something in the subconscious or unconscious levels of thought.

Sublimation: Discharge of libido in socially acceptable activity rather than using it to obtain sexual gratification.

now accepted as learned reactions to anxiety that an individual habitually adopts when frustrated. Some of the most common defense mechanisms are described in Box 2-1. All of these defense mechanisms are characteristic ways in which the ego avoids pain, modifies expression of strong emotions, and relieves excessive anxiety. Overuse of any of the defense mechanisms, however, can be self-defeating. They can interfere with one's coping and adapting and restrain one in abnormal behaviors.

Freud based his theory primarily on what he saw and heard from patients who sought his psychiatric treatment. He did not use personality tests, experiment, or collect data for quantitative analysis. However, he did check his theory continually against the evidence as he saw it. This resulted in may revisions of his concepts and eventually in a theory that has endured.

Erikson's Psychosocial Conflicts

Erik Erikson (b. 1902) believed that social and cultural factors influence the manner in which an individual resolves the various conflicts brought about by biological maturation. Thus, his theory is called *psychosocial* rather than psychosexual. Erikson met Freud and studied psychoanalysis under Freud's daughter, Anna. He agreed with Freud's postulation that maturation brings conflicts revolving around oral, anal, phallic, latent and genital stages of psychosexual development. However, he believed that psychosocial development continued after the resolution of the sexual conflicts. He proposed eight conflicts of life: The first five parallel Freud's psychosexual stages, the last three occur during adulthood (see Figure 2-4).

The eight conflicts proposed by Erikson are referred to as **nuclear conflicts**. By nuclear, he meant central: the issues about which behaviors are focused, those of crucial importance to the personality at that stage of life. In infancy, for example, the conflict revolves around the biological need for food and the maturation of the sucking reflex associated with feeding. Erikson, like Freud, believed that oral gratification brings sexual (libidinous) gratification as well. Erikson called his first nuclear conflict *trust versus mistrust,* however, reflecting his belief that social forces are more powerful mediating forces than sexual forces in bringing about the gratification of needs. If an infant is fed lovingly and is supported in other biological needs, that infant will develop a sense of trust in his or her world. Experiences of being left hungry will result in a sense of mistrust. Each of Erikson's eight nuclear conflicts will be discussed in detail in Chapters 4 through 10.

It is possible—in fact, probable, in Erikson's view—that at any stage of life, the solving of a conflict will be somewhere between a perfect positive and a total negative. Obviously, it is desirable to have a more positive than negative resolution of each conflict. The way in which each conflict is resolved will affect adjustments to all subsequent conflicts. Also, during subsequent conflicts the individual will still spend some time re-resolving earlier conflicts. Erikson (1968) wrote that every adult carries residues of childhood conflicts in the recesses of his or her personality. These conflicts are constantly being re-resolved. It is never too late in life to change a negative resolution of an old conflict into a more positive resolution.

Freud felt that only the id component of personality is present at birth. Erikson disagreed. He suggested that newborn babies also have an immature ego. This ego is reshaped by the self and the social world during each progressive nuclear conflict. The ego, as it matures, is a unifying force between the perceived identity and all societal forces.

Erikson's theory is considered an epigenetic theory. *Epigenesis* refers to that which is built upon (*epi*) the original (*genesis*). Past experiences affect present behavior. Each new nuclear conflict is resolved by examining (consciously or unconsciously) the results of behaviors or experiences of the past. One's behavior thus becomes much more differentiated the more one has experienced socially and culturally in the process of

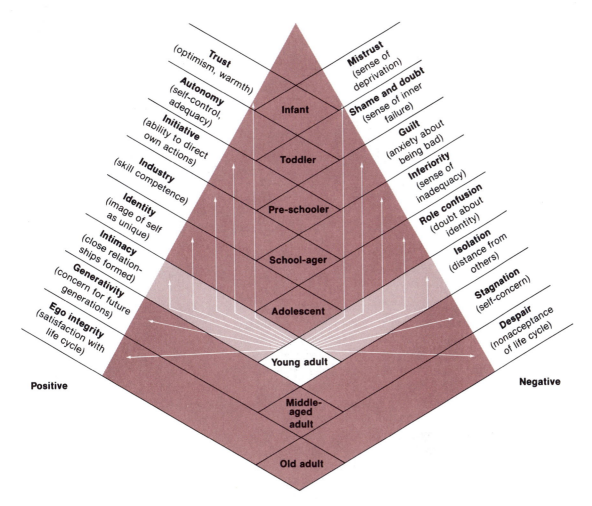

Figure 2-4
Erikson's psychosocial theory emphasized eight nuclear conflicts. At each stage of life, one conflict is at the forefront. The major conflict facing the young adult, for example, is intimacy vs. isolation. Attempts to resolve other conflicts exist (see arrows) but to a lesser degree. (Reprinted and adapted from Erikson, E. H. (1963). *Childhood and Society, 2nd Edition.* New York: W. W. Norton & Company, Inc., with the permission of W. W. Norton & Company, Inc.)

maturing biologically. More positive resolutions of each past conflict contribute to an easier evolution of a new, well-adjusted ego. More negative resolutions contribute to more confusion in the quest for identity. However, even negative experiences contribute to the learning, changing, maturing process. Erikson hoped that, by working at all conflicts to some degree throughout life, all humans could achieve a healthy personality.

Contributions of Other Psychodynamic Theorists

Carl Jung (b. 1875), a student of Freud, introduced the concept of inherited **archetypes** to psychodynamic theory. Archetypes are unconscious figures typically seen in fantasies, dreams, or other situations when the imagination is active. These archetypes (Great Mother, Wise Old Man, Hero, Divine Child) predispose a person to act in the way one's ancestors acted. Jung (1931) theorized that a deeper level of consciousness exists than Freud's unconscious. He called it the **collective unconscious.** He proposed that human beings have inherited the wisdom and experience of previous centuries through this collective unconscious. Religious or mystic experiences, deep trances, dreams, or

Figure 2-5
Jung proposed that personalities may be more extraverted, more introverted, or a synthesis of the complementary polarities.

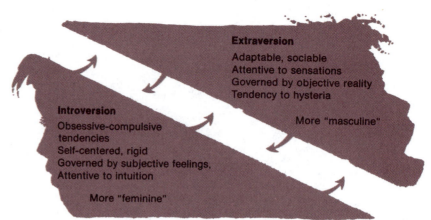

Extraversion
Adaptable, sociable
Attentive to sensations
Governed by objective reality
Tendency to hysteria

More "masculine"

Introversion
Obsessive-compulsive tendencies
Self-centered, rigid
Governed by subjective feelings,
Attentive to intuition

More "feminine"

hallucinations, Jung felt, might occasionally shed some light on these collective memories.

Jung's most famous concepts are those of extraversion and introversion (see Figure 2-5). The **extravert** directs his or her interest to phenomena outside the self rather than to his or her own experiences and feelings. An **introvert** directs his or her interest toward the self rather than to outside phenomena. "Normal" personalities are better able to bring together the complementary polarities that divide them than are the more "obsessive-compulsive" introverts or "hysterical" extraverts.

Alfred Alder, another associate and contemporary of Sigmund Freud, believed that people are motivated to move from a position of **inferiority** (feeling of inadequacy) toward security, power, and **superiority** (feeling of high value and worth). He saw the drive for superiority and power to be a more potent motivator of behavior than sexual libido. He wrote extensively about inferiority complexes and the defense mechanisms of compensation and overcompensation that some people use to hide their feelings of inferiority. The well-adjusted individual overcomes his or her self-absorption and places the interests of others side by side with personal strivings.

Karen Horney (1937) saw basic anxiety rather than sexual desire as the primary motivator of behavior. She felt that this anxiety begins with the infant's birth into a frightening world. Unless adequate defenses are developed against this anxiety, one of three abnormal behaviors may develop: moving toward people, moving away from people, or moving against people. Horney believed that normal people have some of all three personality characteristics affecting their behavior, depending on the situations in which they find themselves. Functioning in only one of the stereotypic modes constitutes abnormal behavior (see Figure 2-6).

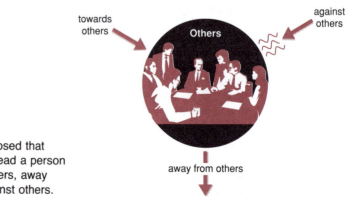

towards others

Others

against others

away from others

Figure 2-6
Karen Horney proposed that basic anxiety may lead a person to move toward others, away from others, or against others.

Behaviorist Theories

Psychodynamic theories are based on the premise that the roots of a person's behavior lie in that individual's earlier experiences. Behaviorist theories believe that new behaviors can be substituted for old behaviors after a relatively short period of time. New behaviors can be taught to, or conditioned in, the individual.

Watson's Classical Conditioning

At the turn of the century, a Russian physiologist, Ivan Pavlov, introduced the idea of changing behavior through a process known as **classical conditioning**. He trained a dog to salivate at the sound of a bell by coupling the bell with every presentation of food over an interval of time. After a while the dog associated the sound of the bell with the arrival of food and, whenever he heard the bell, began salivating (a natural reflex) in anticipation. The food was called the *unconditioned stimulus* (US), the salivation that it initiated the *unconditioned response* (UR). The sound of the bell (or any other arbitrary stimulus) was labeled the *conditioned stimulus* (CS). After the CS was paired with the US a number of times, learning took place such that the CS brought about salivation all by itself. Salivation to the bell was called the *conditioned response* (CR) (see Figure 2-7).

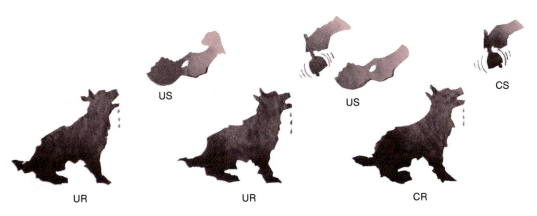

Figure 2-7
Ivan Pavlov's classical conditioning paradigm: A US produces a response; pair a CS with a US when eliciting a response; soon the CS alone will elicit the response.

An American psychologist, John Watson, introduced **behaviorism** (the objective, experimental study of human behavior) to the field of psychology in the 1920s. He wanted more of a separation between psychology and the realms of philosophy and religion. Behaviorists, using classical conditioning techniques, could observe, measure, and unambiguously state what was learned in technical, scientific language. Behaviorists did not try to speculate about the hidden causes of behavior for which no proof could be supplied. Instead, behavioral psychologists produced evidence that anxieties and phobias could be both created and cured by behavioral means. Watson and Raynor (1920) classically conditioned fear in an 11-month-old infant (Albert) by pairing the presentation of a white furry rat (the CS) with the noise of a sharp blow on a steel bar (the US). The noise of the steel bar being struck frightened Albert (UR). Since the noise was always paired with the presentation of the rat, Albert soon learned to fear the presentation of the rat (CR). He generalized this learned fear to other white, furry things as well (a rabbit, cotton, wool, and so on).*

---

*The ethics of this experiment has been a matter of much controversy. Such research would probably not be approved today.

Mary Cover Jones (1924), a student of Watson's, later published a paper in which she detailed her success in helping a small boy overcome his fear of furry things. She conditioned him to tolerate a rabbit by coupling his lunches with the presentation of the animal. After a while the boy was able to eat calmly with the rabbit on his lap.

John Watson believed that many human behaviors are learned by association (pairing of CS with US to bring about a CR). In his book *Behaviorism* (1930), Watson stated:

> Give me a dozen healthy infants, well-formed, and my own specified world to bring them up in, and I'll guarantee to take any one at random and train him to become any type of specialist I might select—doctor, lawyer, artist, merchant-chief, and, yes, even beggarman and thief, regardless of his talents, penchants, tendencies, abilities, vocations, and race of his ancestors (p. 82).

Watson's advice had some impact on American parenting. It was modified to a great extent, however, by competing advice from Freud and his followers in the psychodynamic movement who stressed the developing child's need for a sense of security and a reduction of frustrations, pains, and anxieties.

Skinner's Operant Conditioning

B. F. Skinner (see Figure 2-8) popularized the concept of **stimulus–response learning** (S–R learning) and introduced the concept of operant conditioning procedures to behaviorism. His carefully controlled experiments and numerous publications of orderly data, his theoretical explanations of behaviorism, and his arguments for the uses of operant conditioning to modify and/or control human behavior made him a recognized leader of behaviorists from the 1940s through the 1980s. He published several influential and controversial books, including two best-sellers in which he argued that operant conditioning should be made an integral part of the social order: *Walden Two* (1948) and *Beyond Freedom and Dignity* (1971).

In Pavlov's classical conditioning paradigm, a stimulus that brings about an involuntary response (for example, salivation when food appears) is paired with a second stimulus, which is finally substituted for the original stimulus. This form of conditioning is not always feasible, however, because many of the responses desired for modifying behaviors are voluntary rather than involuntary. Skinner's operant conditioning approach provides a feasible method of altering voluntary responses.

In **operant conditioning** a voluntary response is associated with a stimulus by being rewarded (*reinforced*) when it occurs. Operant conditioning works because animals and humans tend to repeat actions that bring them pleasurable consequences. Skinner advocated the use of positive reinforcement to bring overt responses under the control of stimuli. Some other behaviorists introduced the use of some form of punishment to help terminate undesirable voluntary responses.

Skinner designed and built special electronic cages now referred to as "Skinner boxes" for use in many of his orderly experiments of conditioned responses in animals (see Figure 2-9). Into this apparatus he would place an animal such as a rat or a pigeon. When the animal pressed a level (pigeons needed to peck a disk), the specially constructed box would deliver a small quantity of food to the animal and record the response. At first responses were shaped by rewarding every response. Eventually, reinforcers were given on either a continuous (fixed) or an intermittent (variable) schedule of reinforcement. Intermittent reinforcement makes a conditioned response stronger and more resistant to fading away than giving a reward for every response.

Behavioral psychologists who apply Skinnerian principles to bring about operant conditioning may have to spend considerable time shaping desirable responses. At first, a response that approximates the behavior that the psychologist wants to develop is reinforced. In successive steps the rewards are made contingent on a response that more closely resembles, and finally becomes, the desired behavior. Box 2-2 presents

Figure 2-8
B. F. Skinner (1904–1990) demonstrated how behaviors are produced through operant conditioning with reinforcement contingencies.

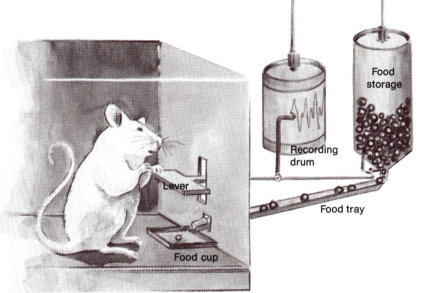

a problem and its solution as an example of operant conditioning in action. Procedures of operant conditioning are also known as **behavior modification**.

In laboratory experiments using operant conditioning, behavioral scientists have been able to demonstrate that their conditioning procedures, not any extraneous factors, are responsible for modifying responses. They can **extinguish** responses (cause them to die out) by deconditioning and bring them back by reconditioning. Although intermittent reinforcements strengthen responses in the conditioning process, they do not guarantee that the conditioning will be permanent. In order for behaviors to last in the course of everyday living, they must continue to evoke positive rewards for the person performing them.

Programs of behavior modification have been very useful in studying development in experimental situations. Behavior modification has been used successfully to alter overeating, smoking, alcoholism, poor study habits, and aggression. Some procedures can be put to destructive uses, as has happened with brainwashing. Behavior modifi-

---

BOX

2-2

Shaping Behavior.

The problem: Johnny won't approach his peers in nursery school but follows the teacher or her assistants around, demanding their attention.

Step 1: Obtain an operant level. Observe and count the number of approaches Johnny makes to any peer in a certain time interval. Also count the number of advances he makes to the teacher and her assistants.

Step 2: Shape the behavior desired. To begin, each time Johnny plays alone without following a teacher or demanding adult attention, reinforce him with attention. Ignore him when he makes advances toward the teach-

ers. As soon as he can spend short periods of time alone, make reinforcement contingent on a higher level of behavior (such as watching his peers play). When this is achieved, make the reward of attention contingent on a still higher level of behavior (such as interacting with peers) until Johnny reaches the desired level of behavior.

Step 3: Now make the reinforcement schedule variable rather than continuous. Never reward undesirable behavior, but use an intermittent reinforcement schedule for the conditioned behavior (in this case interacting with peers).

cation has been cast in a negative light in futuristic novels such as George Orwell's *1984* and Aldous Huxley's *Brave New World.* Humans are portrayed as becoming so conditioned that they lose their free will and individuality. Although conditioning can be put to evil uses, it is also a technique with potential for producing many desirable behaviors. Skinner, in *Beyond Freedom and Dignity* (1971), advocated its use to eliminate problems such as aggression, wastefulness, and injustice in our society.

Social-Learning Theories

Social-learning theories evolved out of behaviorism. They differ from behaviorist theories in that they do not hold that direct reinforcement is always necessary for learning. In operant conditioning procedures, reinforcements must be carefully controlled. No rewards must be given for undesirable acts, and the desired behaviors must be attended to continuously at first. Some semblance of a response must also occur naturally before it can be shaped into a more desirable response with reinforcement. **Social-learning theory** accounts for learning that takes place when responses, or some approximation of them, do not occur naturally. Neal Miller and John Dollard (1941) suggested imitation as an explanation of how novel behaviors are acquired. This idea was demonstrated and expanded by many psychologists in the following two decades.

Bandura's Modeling Theory

The writings of Bandura and Walters (1963), Bandura and Rosenthal (1966), and Bandura (1969) exemplify the belief in learning by imitation, or **modeling**. Many of the experiments of Albert Bandura (b. 1925) and his colleagues involved observing the behaviors of children after they had watched models demonstrating various actions or feelings. Models were varied, from real life, to filmed, to cartoon or animal models. Children were found to imitate the behavior of models more frequently if the models were perceived to be powerful or if some form of positive reinforcement was given to the models for the behaviors or emotions they demonstrated. Some modeled behaviors elicited *similar* behaviors rather than exact imitations. Much important learning was observed to take place vicariously (experienced by one person through his or her imagined participation in another person's experience). Further, some behaviors could be inhibited or extinguished if children observed that they brought about undesirable consequences for another person (see Figure 2-10).

There are many things that children and adults may perceive as positive reinforcers for given behaviors: material rewards (money, food, gifts), praise, nurturance, inclusion in a group, attention, even criticism if it is seen as a form of attention. Bandura identified two other kinds of reinforcement that may influence social learning: *vicarious reinforcement* and *self-reinforcement.*

In vicarious reinforcement the person imitating some modeled behavior obtains pleasure from the act not because he or she is rewarded but because the model or some other person was rewarded. The reinforcement of the model takes the place of one's own reward.

In self-reinforcement the learner actually rewards himself or herself for behaviors or emotions deemed meritorious. Self-administered reinforcers are considered very important in the learning of complex social behaviors.

Bandura's theory moves beyond the suggestion that imitation accounts for the acquisition of novel behaviors to an explanation based on observational learning, or "no-trial" learning, in which behaviors are not necessarily imitated to be learned. Children (and adults) are exposed to a vast number of social behaviors that they learn without overt modeling. They watch behaviors on television, in movies, and in real life, of parents, peers, teachers, neighbors, and the like. They listen to interactions. They

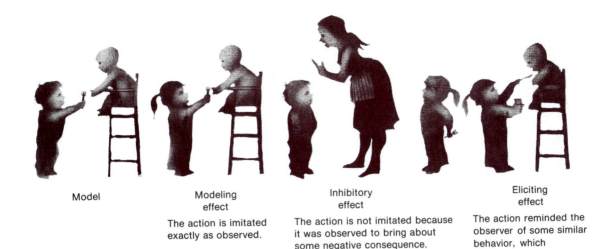

Model | Modeling effect | Inhibitory effect | Eliciting effect

The action is imitated exactly as observed.

The action is not imitated because it was observed to bring about some negative consequence.

The action reminded the observer of some similar behavior, which was then imitated.

Figure 2-10
Behaviors may be exact replications of a model or they may be similar actions. Models can inhibit behaviors if their actions are observed to be punished.

read about interactions. These exposures result in observational learning whenever conditions are right.

Bandura (1977) suggested four intervening conditions between a modeled (observed) event and its acquisition (or learning):

1. attention,
2. retention,
3. motor reproduction, and
4. motivation.

Bandura identified many subcomponents of these four component processes underlying observational learning. Adequate attending, for example, requires the observer to be aroused, to be able to take in information through the senses, to be able to perceive it, and to have some past experiences of reinforcement for similar attention. Adequate retention requires some cognitive processes. The observer must be able to organize what he or she is observing, retain it in some symbolic way (visual image, verbal), and rehearse it in some way (verbal, visual, or motor). To have adequate motor reproduction of the modeled behavior, the observer must have the physical abilities to perform the action, some self-monitoring of the quality of the reproduction, and some feedback as to its accuracy. Finally, to be sufficiently motivated to learn through observation, the person must have some anticipation of a desirable reinforcement for an overt performance of the behavior. The expected reinforcement can be a vicarious reinforcement, a self-reinforcement, or an external reinforcement.

Bandura did not view the person as a mere point between some environmental stimulus and some conditioned response. He suggested a process of reciprocal determinism in learning: The person, the behavior, and the environment all interact with each other. Each affects the others in any actions or reactions.

Sears's Identification Theory

Robert Sears applied social-learning principles to the socialization of children. Sears felt that parents are the earliest and most frequent models for children's imitations. Children do what they see and hear their parents do, not just what their parents tell them to do.

Figure 2-11
Identification grows out of imitation of a powerful and rewarding model.

Sears and his colleagues (1965) proposed three phases of social learning from infancy through childhood:

1. rudimentary behaviors,
2. secondary behavioral systems, and
3. secondary motivational systems.

In rudimentary behaviors the infant is motivated to interact with others to avoid pain and reduce the displeasures brought about by physiological processes (hunger, elimination, temperature regulation). When these needs are met, the infant learns which behaviors (crying, kicking, grasping, smiling) produce the most rapid reduction of pain and which ones are least effective. Each infant behavior becomes associated with a parental response that affects the quality of the infant's next behavior and with the quality of the parents' next response. In other words, Sears suggested that behavior is both the cause and the effect of later behavior. Individual differences emerge in each parent–infant pair in both their interactive responses and in the reinforcers they use with each other.

Sears stressed the importance of looking at *dyads* (units of two) in order to understand developmental learning. In his second phase of social learning, called secondary behavioral systems, dyadic interactions lead to expectations of behaviors on the part of both participants (usually mother and child). Discrete behaviors become linked together into a behavioral system in which one behavior acquires the power to elicit the other behaviors that are linked in the same chain. For example, a hunger call not only brings mother and food but also a whole chain of interactive behaviors while eating. Gradually a mother will give more positive reinforcement (affection, praise) for the child's efforts to imitate the family's behavioral patterns. The child relies on the family for these reinforcements and imitates increasingly more complex social behaviors (self-feeding, dressing, toileting).

Sears (1957) used social learning by imitation to explain how identification occurs. The child, dependent on the mother, father, or primary caregiver, comes to enjoy her or his affectionate nurture. The child imitates this powerful and rewarding model. The act of imitation itself then acquires a secondary rewarding (reinforcing) value. Imitating the gestures and actions of the loved one will bring pleasure to the child in the loved one's absence. This imitation then becomes habitual and is known as **identification**.

Sears stressed that the expectancies of the primary caregivers should be in keeping with the maturational level of the child. The learning process is enhanced when the child strongly identifies with the primary caregivers and is rewarded for compliance with requested behaviors (see Figure 2-11). The strength of identification varies with

1. the amount of affectionate nurture given the child,
2. the demands placed on the child,
3. the extent to which the primary caregiver uses withdrawal of love, and
4. the amount of absence of the persons with whom the child identifies.

Sears's third phase of developmental learning, that of acquiring secondary motivational systems, begins when the child moves beyond reliance on the family for reinforcements of behavior. Persons in schools, peer groups, and networks such as religious, sports, music, or service groups become potential reinforcers of behavior. The child is motivated to learn and imitate many of the behaviors of group members to obtain gratifications. By this time the child can also use self-reinforcement as much as desired and becomes quite self-reliant.

Social-learning theorists continually modify their theories to account for more behavioral phenomena. Because they limit their research to carefully controlled experiments, observe ethical considerations, and report their findings completely, they are highly respected. Because past experiences, especially the highly charged emotional experiences that are the concern of the psychodynamic theorists, cannot be investigated in experimental situations, and because recounting of them is so subjective, they are intentionally left unstudied.

Cognitive Theories

Cognitive-developmental theories deal with perception and thinking. They concentrate on the process of *how* an individual comes to perceive, think about, and understand his or her environment. They emphasize biological changes and maturation and only peripherally touch on emotional aspects of behavior. The most systematic explorations of **cognition** (the process of knowing and perceiving) were carried out by Jean Piaget between 1920 and 1980.

Piaget's Cognitive Stages

Piaget began his career as a biologist, earning a Ph.D. for a study of mollusks. He found employment in Paris, standardizing intelligence tests for humans. He became fascinated with the confusing way children reason to arrive at answers to questions (see Figure 2-12). His biological background led him to question how it is that humans come to adapt to their world and to reason with abstract logic. Thus began his investigations of cognitive development and **genetic epistemology** (the study of the origin, nature, method, and limits of knowledge). How does the infant who "knows" the world through reflex actions eventually come to understand mature hypothetical concepts? Piaget's theory explains the qualitative differences in methods of thinking used by children and adolescents rather than enumerating the quantity of right answers that children can provide at different ages.

Piaget used his own three children as subjects for many of his early descriptive studies. He was an astute observer of changes in their behavior that indicated a more advanced stage of intellectual development. In addition to observing, he invented many little problems or games to test their reasoning abilities. For example, when his daughter Jacqueline was five months and five days old, Piaget (1962) reported:

> I then tried the experiment of alternately separating and bringing together my hands as I stood in front of her. She watched me attentively and reproduced the movement

Figure 2-12
"Why did you put sand in Phyllis's car?" "The shovel made me do it." Piaget was fascinated with the reasons behind children's answers to questions.

three times. She stopped when I stopped and began again when I did, never looking at her hands, but keeping her eyes fixed on mine.

At 0;5(6) (five months, six days) and 0;5(7) (five months, seven days) she failed to react, perhaps because I was at the side and not in front of her. At 0;5(8), however, when I resumed my movement in front of her, she imitated me fourteen times in just under two minutes. I myself only did it about forty times. After I stopped, she only did it three times in five minutes. It was thus a clear case of imitation. (pp. 15-16)

Piaget, like the social-learning theorists, found that imitation is one of the important skills that children have to help them learn about and adapt to the adult world. He saw organization and adaptation as two basic functions of all organisms. In their adaptation to the world, humans practice the interrelated processes of assimilation and accommodation. **Assimilation** refers to an individual's taking in (perceiving) some new pieces of information from the environment and using the current cognitive framework to deal with the information. **Accommodation** refers to modifications of the current cognitive framework that the individual must make due to the impact of some newly assimilated pieces of information. Previous concepts may be radically altered in the process of accommodation. Children are continually revising and refining their thought processes through assimilation and accommodation, thus becoming cognitively more mature.

Piaget introduced the concepts of **equilibrium** and **disequilibrium** to help explain cognitive development. Equilibrium refers to a state of relative balance between assimilation and accommodation of environmental stimuli. In equilibrium one does not have to disturb one's thought processes too much to assimilate the information at hand. When the mind must work to form new concepts into which the information can fit, a state of disequilibrium is present. The mind continually fluctuates between relative equilibrium and disequilibrium as learning takes place. This portion of Piaget's theory parallels the concept of **stimulus–response (S–R) learning** of behavioral theory. The information that upsets a state of equilibrium is comparable to a stimulus, for which a response (new learning accommodation) is necessary to restore the balance.

Piaget postulated that intellectual development occurs by stages (see Table 2-2). At the end of each hypothetical stage, children attain a feeling of near equilibrium in

Table 2-2 Piaget's Four Stages of Cognitive Development.

Stage	Substages	Characteristics
Sensorimotor period	Reflexes Primary circular reactions Secondary circular reactions Coordination of secondary schemas Tertiary circular reactions Invention of new means through mental combinations	The apparatus of the senses and of the musculature become increasingly operative.
Preoperational period	Preconceptual phase Intuitive phase	The child has the emerging ability to think mentally.
Concrete operations period		The child learns to reason about what he or she sees and does in the here-and-now world.
Formal operations period		The individual has the ability to see logical relationships among diverse properties and to reason in the abstract.

their assimilation and accommodation of environmental events. The remaining inconsistencies then serve to usher in a new phase of higher learning. (Each of these stages is explained in more detail in the cognitive development sections of Chapters 4, 5, 6, and 7.) Piaget found that progression through these stages is gradual and orderly. In his opinion, the development of intelligence is biologically determined. Every child goes through all of the stages at his or her own pace.

Piaget's goal was to study epistemology—how we come to know things—not education. However, he preferred educational programs that allow children free exploration of materials rather than providing them with too many structured learning experiences. Through the manipulation of materials and the experience of experimenting with them, children assimilate and accommodate the aspects of the stimuli that are novel to them yet familiar enough to be fitted into preexisting schemas. A **schema**, in Piaget's theory, is a basic cognitive unit (such as an activity or a thought process) that the child or adult is capable of performing. Many concepts that adults try to teach children in formal lessons either may lack novelty and thus be repetitious and boring or may be too novel to fit into any pre-existing schemas (see Figure 2-13).

Piaget arrived at many of his conclusions about cognitive development by asking different questions of each child, rather than by uniformly testing a large number of children on the same concepts. Questions can be used to explore a child's reasoning abilities in depth without suggesting that any answers are right or wrong. Questions can be kept at a level that each child understands, and any spontaneous, interesting answers can be pursued. In short, this clinical method allows the examiner to explore each child's unique reasoning processes with very few constraints.

Piaget is recognized as "the great child psychologist of the twentieth century" (Cohen, 1983). His descriptions of the development of reasoning abilities during infancy, childhood, and adolescence are rich and voluminous (he authored over 30 books and more than 400 papers). However, many of his beliefs have been empirically questioned.

Figure 2-13
If a concept has already been acquired, the task bores the child. If a concept is too complicated, the task is "over the child's head." Pleasure and excitement are generated by learning while doing.

Infants, for example, seem to be more intelligent than he allowed, and adolescents seem to be less logical. Piaget also neglected to consider social influences on development. He disregarded Freudian concepts such as the unconscious and psychosexual conflicts. He looked only at children's rational utterances, not at their irrational behaviors. He collected data predominantly on white subjects from the area around Geneva. He did not indicate whether he found sex differences, cultural differences, or differences related to factors such as the adequacy of nutrition. Some children also have their own individual styles of problem solving that do not conform to the Piagetian stage model. In spite of drawbacks, replications of his studies have supported much of his theory of cognitive development.

Contributions of Other Cognitive Theorists

Jerome Bruner (1966) suggested that cognitive development can be viewed as an acquisition of increasingly more complex modes of representation of external objects, events, and experiences. He proposed three representational systems: the enactive, the iconic, and the symbolic. These modes are acquired in the fixed order given but do not necessarily supersede each other. All modes remain active and involved in information processing throughout life. At birth, the infant has an innate ability to exercise certain reflexes (grasping, head turning, looking, listening, sucking) that enable him or her to process some information from the environment. These behaviors and other sensory and motor activities that mature in the first two years (smelling, tasting, touching, crawling, walking, pushing, pulling, manipulating objects) allow for an *enactive mode* (through activity) of representing information. Soon the toddler acquires the ability to form mental images (icons) of objects, events, and experiences to store in his or her memory. Bruner calls this the *iconic mode* of representation. Finally, language is learned and a symbol (word) can be used for processing and storing information—the *symbolic mode*. As the child acquires each of these modes of representation, his or her internal structures for processing information become more sophisticated, with a greater use of rules and strategies (see Figure 2-14).

Bruner's theory stresses the external environmental incentives for change. Parents and teachers need to challenge children to exercise their representational strategies. They need to encourage children to use language to classify objects and events into related mental categories and to be ever more efficient in symbol use. Children's

Figure 2-14
One can experience an apple by smell and taste (enactive mode), by visualizing it mentally (iconic mode), or by using the word "apple" for it (symbolic mode).

cognitive development is enhanced by increased language and symbol usage (as with computer programming languages, for example). However, children must adjust their behavior to fit cultural conventions (not all adults are conversant in computer languages). Cultures that encourage sophisticated symbol use by children also encourage greater cognitive development.

Two Russian psychologists, A. R. Luria and L. S. Vygotsky, working on cognitive studies concurrently with Piaget in the 1920s and 1930s, stressed the role of language in cognition.

Vygotsky (1962) felt that, without language, thinking would be impossible. At first an infant's behaviors are controlled by the directions and speech of the adult caregivers. As the child acquires language, self-directions are given overtly (publicly). Later the child controls behavior with covert (private) language. Thinking and reasoning then develop, based on internalized language, or **inner speech**.

Luria (1976) tested areas of cognition such as perception, generalization, deduction, reasoning, imagination, and ability to analyze one's own inner life. He found that people in more primitive social structures had thought processes that were concrete, based on practical activities, and centered on situational experiences. More technological systems produced people whose cognitions were more abstract and more theoretical and who had more self-awareness and social awareness. Luria theorized that cognitive development must be viewed in terms of the dynamic environment to which each individual is exposed. Specifically, the use of a language that allows one to abstract, codify, and generalize is linked with more complex cognitive processes (Luria, 1982).

Lawrence Kohlberg extended Piaget's theory of how children learn the moral standards of their social order. Piaget wrote of only two basic moral orientations: that of moral realism, in which rules are seen as sacred and unalterable, and that of moral relativism, in which rules are seen as modifiable. Kohlberg (1984) described stages of moral development (see Table 2-3). In a twenty-year longitudinal study, Colby, Kohlberg, and others (1983) documented the basic assumptions of Kohlberg's theory. Acquisition of the highest levels depends on previous cognition, experience, and acquisition of each of the lower levels. Kohlberg also found that moral judgments are correlated with age, socioeconomic status, IQ, and education. Each of Kohlberg's stages will be discussed in more detail in Chapters 6 and 7.

Table 2-3 Brief Summation of Kohlberg's Stages of Moral Development.

Level	Stage	Characteristics
Premoral	Stage 1	Punishment and obedience orientation
	Stage 2	Acts that are satisfying to self and occasionally satisfying to others defined as right
Conventional morality	Stage 3	Morality of maintaining good relations and approval of others
	Stage 4	Orientation to showing respect for authority and maintaining social order for social order's sake
Postconventional morality	Stage 5	Morality of accepting democratically contracted laws

Humanistic Theories

There is no one master builder of **humanistic psychology**, as Freud was of psychodynamic theory and Piaget of the study of cognition. It grew in part out of existential philosophies. Humanistic theories are also often called *phenomenological* theories, referring to the fact that subjective reality—what a person perceives his or her world to be—is more important than external reality.

The humanistic viewpoint is that people are born basically good. They strive throughout their lives to become all they are capable of being. The ways in which people define their experiences within their family and their society may either hinder or enhance their potential for growth. All humans are different because of their varying experiences and the unique meanings that these experiences have for them.

A central tenet of humanistic psychology is that people cannot love others unless they first love themselves. Child-rearing, according to the humanists, should involve freedom to grow and become what one can be. Guilt feelings, hostilities, punishments, and the like are counterproductive to the development of self-esteem. When family members feel loved and accepted for what they are, they feel freer to pursue joy, love, rational behavior, and self-actualization.

Maslow's Needs Hierarchy

Abraham Maslow exemplified the positive approach of the humanists. In Maslow's view, basic needs are organized into a hierarchy of relative potency. At the top of the hierarchy is the need for **self-actualization**, a state of being open, autonomous, spontaneous, accepting, loving, creative, and democratic—in short, being a happy, fulfilled human being. Unfortunately, self-actualized people are rarely found, because this state is not manifest in people who have lower-order needs unfilled. The most potent (most basic) needs are the physiological requirements for food, water, and shelter (see Figure 2-15). Maslow (1954) saw the need for safety as secondary to physiological necessities. Many persons do not feel safe. The high crime rate contributes to this insecurity, as does fierce competition in schools and places of employment.

When safety needs are satisfied, a person seeks out kinship and belonging and a sense that he or she is loved. Maslow saw many adults struggling to fill the requirement for love and belonging. Maslow also saw many people struggling with the next need for self-esteem. One does not have to accomplish great deeds, or wield power, to have self-esteem. One simply needs to feel satisfied with one's own role and skills. Given this sense of competence, a person can finally be motivated to achieve the higher-order need of self-actualization.

Self-actualized people are focused on problems outside themselves. They are characterized by passions for justice, honesty, equality, and personal freedoms. Their

Figure 2-15
Maslow's needs hierarchy goes from the lowest-order need for food and water to the highest-order need for self-actualization.

friendships tend to cut across racial, ethnic, age, sex, educational, political, and social class barriers. Maslow saw self-actualized people as normal people with nothing taken away. Maslow saw two other higher-order needs that motivate behavior in some people: the need to know and understand, and the need for art and beauty (aesthetics).

Maslow (1965) included in his theory the concept of **peak experiences**, which he defined as moments of intense happiness or ecstasy. During a peak experience one has a momentary sense of unity with the whole world. The grass seems greener, the sky bluer; the secrets of living seem within reach, and one feels more noble, free, and at peace. Maslow felt this phenomenon of peaking is within the reach of everyone, although some people may not recognize the brief peak experience when it occurs.

Maslow encouraged people to help one another move toward the highest level of growth through mutual acceptance:

> If we would be helpers, counselors, teachers, guiders, or psychotherapists, what we must do is to accept the person and help him learn what kind of person he is already. What is his style, what are his aptitudes, what is he good at, not good for, what can we build upon, what are his good raw materials, his good potentialities? (Maslow, 1968, p. 693)

The holistic health movement today is an application of Maslow's theory. Rather than focusing on the treatment of ill health, holistic medicine anticipates people's physiological and psychosocial needs. It concentrates on preventing illness (both physical and mental) by helping people assume responsibilities for meeting all of their needs: physiological, safety, love and belonging, esteem, and self-actualization.

Rogers's Phenomenological Approach

Carl Rogers believed that we all help shape our own personalities. In order to change we must acknowledge to ourselves what we are. Self-acceptance marks the beginning of change. He developed the method of client-centered therapy in which the therapist refrains from making value judgments or giving advice. Instead the client is helped to discover what behaviors to change and how to change them.

Central to Rogers's personality theory is the **phenomenological approach**, the belief that only the person involved can know his or her own phenomenological world. (*Phenomenological* refers to what is perceived or experienced as real, rather than the external reality itself.) What is important for understanding a person's behavior is knowledge of how he or she perceives and experiences the phenomenological world that constitutes his or her "reality." Rogers (1951) believed that as experiences occur in one's life they are handled in one of three ways:

1. They are perceived and organized into a congruent (corresponding, agreeing) relationship with the self.
2. They are ignored because they are perceived to have no relationship with the self.
3. They are denied perception and organization (symbolization) or distorted in their symbolization because they are inconsistent with the self.

When one's phenomenologic field of experiences is predominantly congruent with one's self-concept, there is a relative freedom from strain and anxiety and one is said to be well-adjusted (see Figure 2-16). However, when many experiences are distorted in their symbolization or are denied awareness, there is psychological tension and one is said to be maladjusted.

Rogers (1961) tried to see the world of the other person as that person saw it. He never offered a negative evaluation of others but maintained *unconditional positive regard* for them. His theory proposed that each person can, through organization of personal experiences, learn to become healthy.

Figure 2-16
The difference between a well-adjusted person and a maladjusted one, according to Rogers, is how the person perceives and experiences the world in relation to the self.

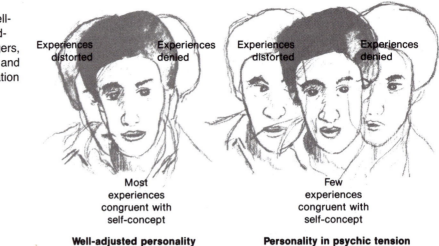

Experiences distorted   Experiences denied   Experiences distorted   Experiences denied

Most experiences congruent with self-concept

Few experiences congruent with self-concept

Well-adjusted personality   **Personality in psychic tension**

Ellis's Rational-Emotive Theory

Albert Ellis (b. 1913) developed an approach called **rational-emotive theory**. Ellis believed that abnormal behaviors are often the result of irrational thought processes (Ellis and Harper, 1961). Many people talk nonsense to themselves: They convince themselves that they are afraid, unattractive, or in some way inferior. Ellis suggested that it is not the event (A) that causes an emotional reaction (C) but rather the world (B) known only to the person experiencing it (what one thinks, how one interprets a happening, what one feels.) This A-B-C theory is schematically represented in Figure 2-17.

Ellis (1974) listed four human life goals:

1. to survive,
2. to be happy,
3. to get along with members of society, and
4. to relate intimately with a few select persons.

These four goals regulate an enormous part of one's life. Humans tend to make assumptions about how to achieve these goals. Some of these assumptions are rational (based on sound judgment); others may be irrational (based on faulty logic). When a person's belief systems are based on many irrational assumptions, their emotional reactions to events are disturbed. Abnormal behaviors can be eliminated by changing belief systems.

Figure 2-17
Ellis proposed that the event (A) does not cause the reaction (C). Rather, one's beliefs (B) about the event cause the reaction.

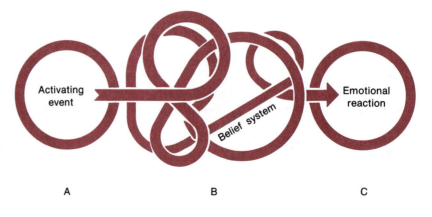

Activating event

Belief system

Emotional reaction

A   B   C

Comparisons of Theories

There are many other theorists who have made important contributions to the study of human development. Portions of some of these theories are presented elsewhere in this textbook. Most theories do not so much contradict each other as speak to separate aspects of the developmental process.

Psychodynamic theories are oriented toward explaining the reasons for development of abnormal behaviors in psychosexual and psychosocial aspects of living. They look to the past to explain present behaviors. They have been influential not only in the development of therapies to ameliorate abnormal behaviors of children and adults but also in the development of advice for parents on aspects of child-rearing.

Behaviorist theories are oriented toward understanding the development of responsive behaviors to various stimuli. They look at the pattern of reinforcers in a person's environment to explain specific behaviors. They have been influential in helping us understand not only how specific behaviors are acquired but also how specific behaviors can be extinguished and how new behaviors can be gradually shaped and learned through reinforcers. Behavior theory can be applied to the learning of thousands of specific behaviors, which can be either classically or operantly conditioned. The theory intentionally ignores concepts such as the unconscious, the ego, libido, and defense mechanisms.

Social-learning theories are oriented toward understanding the development of behaviors for which reinforcers may not obviously be present. They focus on observational learning experiences within the social world and identification processes. They have been influential in helping us understand the role of modeling in behavior acquisition. They bridge the gap between psychodynamic personality theories and cognitive theories, incorporating concepts of both psychic tensions and cognitive processing. They have given us a great deal of information on more positive ways to rear children using concepts of modeling and identification strength.

Cognitive theories are oriented toward explaining how humans acquire and process information and become knowledgeable about the world around them. They look for changes in cognitive processes from infancy, through childhood and adolescence, and into adulthood. They have been influential not only in helping us learn what to expect cognitively from children, adolescents, and adults, but also in helping us to understand how to challenge and stimulate learning.

Humanistic theories are oriented toward explaining the maintenance of healthy personalities. They focus on the here-and-now aspects of behavioral functioning, on personal experiencing, and on the meanings that the individual assigns to feelings, events, and subjective phenomena. By studying healthy personalities, humanistic psychologists have been influential in showing us the potential that all people have for enhancing their lives.

Summary

Theories are not facts. They are "best guesses" put forth to explain a phenomenon or set of phenomena. There are many theories of human development. This chapter has not covered all theories of human development but has tried to present a flavor of some of the popular theories, including the psychodynamic, behaviorist, social-learning, cognitive, and humanistic.

Psychodynamic theories usually focus on the impact and influences of past experiences. Freud described motivators of behavior; the personality components of id, ego, and superego; defense mechanisms; and stages of psychosexual development. Erikson proposed eight nuclear conflicts of life, the first three paralleling Freud's first three stages of psychosexual development, the latter five stressing interactions within society. Jung emphasized lifelong personality development, a collective unconscious, and the concepts of introversion and extraversion. Adler emphasized felt inferiority and the mechanism of compensation. Karen Horney stressed basic anxiety.

Behaviorists effect behavior changes after relatively short periods of behavior therapy using conditioning. Watson popularized the use of classical conditioning to effect behavioral changes in human subjects. Skinner popularized operant conditioning and stimulus–response (S–R) learning. He used positive reinforcement (rewards) to change behavior. Some behaviorists also use punishment.

Social-learning theorists explain how social behaviors are acquired in childhood in the absence of direct reinforcement. Bandura proposed modeling as a fundamental means for acquiring new behaviors. Sears added identification to explain new actions.

Cognitive theories are concerned with how we understand our world. Piaget stressed the need for maturation and experience for cognitive growth. He described the learning processes of assimilation and accommodation and postulated four stages of cognitive development. Bruner suggested three representational systems to explain increased cognitive awareness: the enactive, iconic, and symbolic modes. Luria and Vygotsky emphasized the role of language in cognitive development. Kohlberg explained how children acquire moral behaviors.

Humanistic psychologists study healthy personalities. Their theories stress people's goodness and need for freedom in order to become open, spontaneous, and independent. The ideal, as described by Maslow, is to meet needs in order to be *self-actualized*. Rogers stressed the phenomenological sense of self and each person's abilities to change. Ellis wrote that people should learn to be more rational in their belief systems in order to live more fully.

Key Concepts

psychodynamic	fixation	behaviorism	assimilation
libido	defense mechanisms	stimulus–response learning	accommodation
free association	nuclear conflict	operant conditioning	disequilibrium/equilibrium
id	archetypes	behavior modification	schema
Eros	collective unconscious	extinction	inner speech
Thanatos	extravert	social-learning theory	humanistic psychology
superego	introvert	modeling	self-actualization
ego	inferiority	identification	peak experience
unconscious	superiority	cognition	phenomenological approach
subconscious	classical conditioning	genetic epistemology	rational-emotive theory

Questions for Review

1. Imagine you would like to see a counselor for some problem you are having. Would you choose someone with a psychodynamic, a cognitive, a behaviorist, or a humanist viewpoint? Explain.
2. Compare Freud's psychodynamic theory with behaviorism. Are there any shared beliefs? In what areas are the viewpoints diametrically opposed?
3. Do you agree or disagree with the humanistic view that child-rearing should allow for the self-actualization of each person involved? Discuss.
4. Contrast cognitive theory with humanistic theory. What beliefs are shared? Did cognitive psychology fuel the humanistic movement? Why or why not?
5. Develop an eclectic (composed of material from various sources) theory of your own. Choose five ideas from this chapter that best characterize your beliefs about human development. Upon which theoretical orientation have you leaned most heavily?

Further Readings

Salkind, N. J. (1985). *Theories of human development,* 2nd ed. New York: Wiley.
    A help to link theory with human development in practice. Boxes summarizing empirical studies accompany the discussion of each of the popular theorists of human development.
Lerner, R. M. (1986). *Concepts and theories of human development,* 2nd ed. New York: Random House.
    Discussion of the philosophical and historical bases of the key ideas found in the study of human development and how these ideas influence different theories.
Miller, P. H. (1989). *Theories of developmental psychology,* 2nd ed. New York: W. H. Freeman.
    A review of the major theories that have influenced developmental psychology with a critical analysis of their impacts.
Erikson, E. H. (1982). *The life cycle completed.* New York: Norton.

A final book by Erikson. He discusses the eight stages of the life cycle with an integrated view of ego integrity throughout the lifespan.

Ginsburg, H., and Opper, S. (1988). *Piaget's theory of intellectual development,* 3rd ed. Englewood Cliffs, NJ: Prentice-Hall.

A warm account of Piaget's life and work by his former students. Portions of his research reports are translated to illustrate how he arrived at his theoretical formulations.

Buckley, K. W. (1989). *Mechanical man: John Broadus Watson and the beginnings of behaviorism.* New York: Guilford Press.

A biography of Watson showing his human side as well as his passion for demonstrating the powers of conditioning.

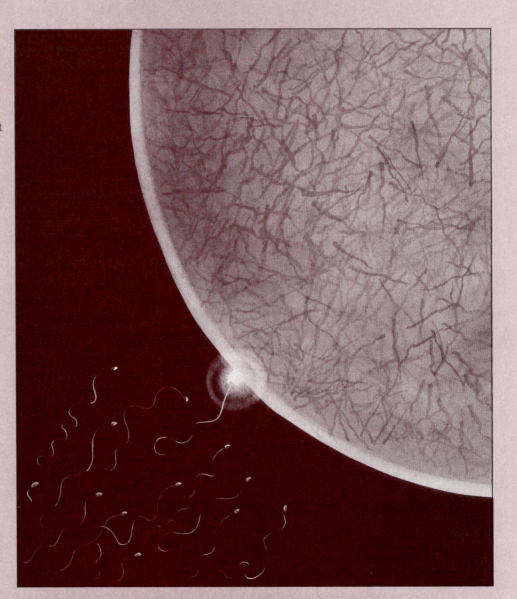

Prenatal Development 3

Conception is any beginning. In human physiology, conception is the impregnation of an ovum by a sperm. The infusion of a live sperm cell into a live ovum (see Figure 3-1) begins a series of cell divisions which, given adequate genes and environment, may result in a new human being.

> God could not be everywhere, so he made mothers.
>
> —*Yiddish saying*

Caroline and her classmates had been given a pretest on the first day of their nursing class in Obstetrics. A multiple-choice question had asked, "Where does impregnation of a human ovum occur?" Possible answers included the stomach, the mouth, the vagina, the Fallopian tube, and the ovary. As the professor went over the answers, she laughed at this question. "Can you believe somebody in this class actually still believes you can get pregnant from kissing?" she joked. When the laughter subsided, she continued, "Someone here must also still believe the myth about swallowing watermelon seeds. Or perhaps this person believes that swallowed sperm can reach an ovum through the stomach?" There were a few embarrassed giggles. Caroline hoped that her grin would hide the fact that she didn't know the correct answer. She peeked at her roommate. Rikke's blush told Caroline that Rikke had probably selected either mouth or stomach. Caroline had guessed vagina. This, too, was wrong. The correct answer was Fallopian tube. Caroline had never heard of such a structure, despite having had a sex education class in high school. She felt angry at the professor for ridiculing their ignorance and ashamed that she knew so little about human conception herself.

Many persons, including those who have had offspring, know very little about the anatomy and physiology of reproduction. Conception of a new human being occurs when sperm and ovum meet in the Fallopian tube within a woman's abdomen, close to one of her ovaries. Let us trace the course of sperm and ova that can lead to this miracle of life.

Prenatal Physiological Processes

Can you recall any of your own early naive concepts about "where babies come from"? Did you ever wonder if pregnancy resulted from kissing? From overeating? From swallowing a watermelon seed? History suggests that many early people believed that some spirit entered a woman at the moment when she first felt her baby move (Hartland, 1909). They believed that impregnating spirits came from the wind, the trees, the sun, the moon, food, and water. During the Renaissance, people believed that new babies

Cilla was an Air Force child who moved from base to base every two or three years. She was always afraid of not being accepted by new people. When she was 14, she found herself not only accepted, but also pursued, by the rock and roll superstar Elvis Presley. For the next several years, she accommodated herself to his wishes. As she wrote in her autobiography, "He taught me everything: how to dress, how to walk, how to apply make-up and wear my hair, how to behave, how to return love. . . . Over the years, he became my father, husband, and very nearly God. . . ."*

Cilla discovered she was pregnant shortly after her marriage in 1967. She was angry with Elvis, who had forbidden her to take birth-control pills. She wanted a honeymoon year, with exotic travel and adventures. She was determined not to get fat. She gained only four pounds from her non-pregnant weight during the nine months. She never wore maternity clothes. She danced ballet, rode her motorcycle, rode horses, went on hayrides, had snowball fights, and kept up with Elvis in every way. She wanted to remain at his side and make him happy. She ignored the admonitions of her superstitious family members who told her that standing would make her legs swell so that she couldn't walk, or that brushing her hair over her head would make the umbilical cord wrap around the baby.

Exactly nine months after her marriage, Cilla gave birth to Lisa Marie, a tiny but otherwise perfectly normal, healthy baby girl. She had lots of silky black hair just like her father. Was Priscilla Beaulieu Presley just lucky? Most obstetricians recommend at least a twenty-five pound weight gain during pregnancy. Could Cilla's excellent health help protect Lisa Marie prenatally? Was her diet, though meager, balanced and nutritious? Was her exercise, despite the concern of her family, reasonable and safe?

*Presley, P.B. (1985). *Elvis and Me.* New York: G. P. Putnam.

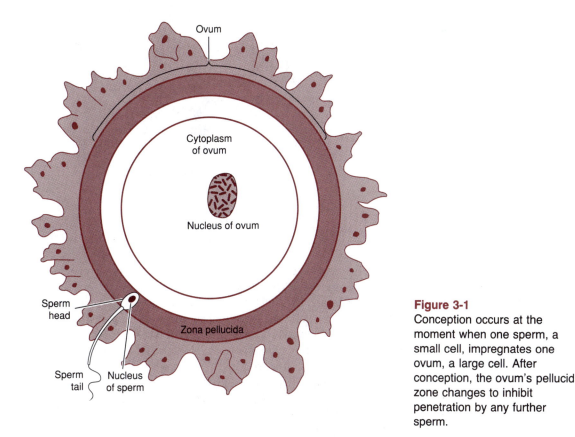

Figure 3-1
Conception occurs at the moment when one sperm, a small cell, impregnates one ovum, a large cell. After conception, the ovum's pellucid zone changes to inhibit penetration by any further sperm.

were contained in male sperm (Needham, 1959). They needed only to be planted in a woman to grow. Anton van Leeuwenhoek, experimenting with the first microscope, believed he saw miniature human beings in sperm cells. Indeed, our knowledge of the principles of genetic inheritance after the ovum–sperm union is relatively new.

Precursors of a New Human Being

Human development begins with the impregnation of an ovum by a sperm. The ovum and sperm have to mature separately before they merge.

The Ovum.   The *ovum* (egg) originates from one of the two female *ovaries* located on either side of the **uterus** (muscular organ in which the embryo/fetus is developed and protected) (see Figure 3-2 and Plate 15 in the center of this textbook). About every thirty days during a woman's fertile years (from puberty to menopause or approximately ages 12 to 50), a mature ovum is set free. This event is called **ovulation.** The ovum can then be fertilized if sperm are present. Usually only one ovum is ovulated, but sometimes two or more are released, presenting the possibility for multiple, fraternal births. The two ovaries alternate months in which they release ova (plural of ovum).

The process of ovulation is controlled by an intricate feedback loop in the endocrine system (see Figure 3-3). The hypothalamus is the regulator of the system, a thermostat of sorts. When all the conditions are right, the hypothalamus sends out a hormone to stimulate the pituitary gland: luteinizing hormone releasing hormone (LHRH). The pituitary gland, in turn, sends out hormones to stimulate the ovaries: follicle-stimulating hormone (FSH) and luteinizing hormone (LH). FSH and LH trigger ovulation. During the process of ovulation, the ovaries produce their own hormones: **estrogen** and **progesterone.** The hypothalamus responds to elevated levels of estrogen and progesterone by inhibiting FSH and LH for a while. When estrogen and progesterone levels drop, a burst

Figure 3-2
The female reproductive tract includes two ovaries, two Fallopian tubes, and one uterus. The uterus is connected to the vagina by a narrow muscular neck called the cervix.

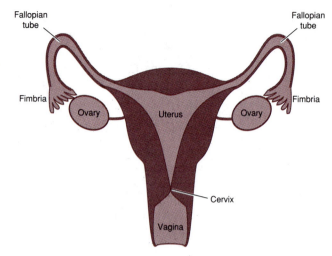

of hypothalamic LHRH triggers more pituitary FSH and LH, and a new cycle starts.

If estrogen and progesterone levels remain high, the hypothalamus will inhibit the pituitary's production of FSH and LH, and the ovaries will not produce ova. This happens when a woman is pregnant or taking birth-control pills and sometimes during lactation. Other hormones, especially the stress hormones released when a woman is seriously ill, severely stressed, or on a starvation diet, also influence the hypothalamus. It can sense when conditions are wrong for a pregnancy. It continuously regulates when and if the pituitary produces FSH and LH to trigger ovulation (Ganong, 1987).

Each female has approximately 700,000 rudimentary ova in her ovaries at the time of birth (Sadler, 1985). Each immature ovum is contained in a primordial (primitive) follicle. Every month from puberty through menopause from 5 to 12 of the primordial follicles begin to grow under the influence of FSH, but usually only one reaches full maturity. Durig the average woman's life, a maximum of about 500 follicles will fully

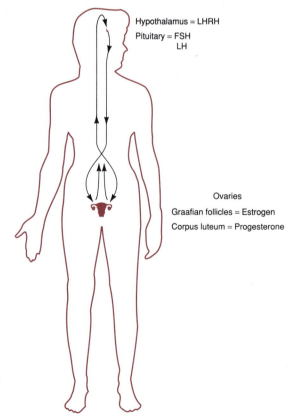

Figure 3-3
The hormone feedback loop that regulates the production of ova and ovulation.

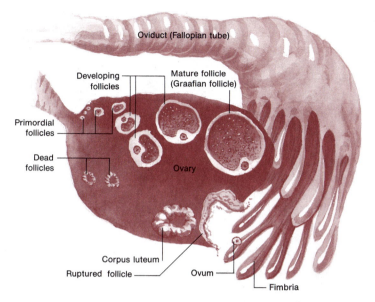

Figure 3-4
Schematic summary of the maturation and discharge of an ovum from the ovary (ovulation).

ripen and release their ova (one per month for about 35 fertile years, subtracting months of pregnancy, birth-control pill use, and/or illnesses affecting ovarian functions). All the follicles that begin to develop each month produce estrogen. Luteinizing hormone triggers the release of one ovum from a fully ripened follicle (called a **Graafian follicle**) and from the surface of the ovary (ovulation) (see Figure 3-4).

BOX 3-1

Natural Family Planning.

Knowledge of how to recognize one's most fertile period (around the time of ovulation) has led to several methods of natural contraception or natural family planning. A woman can measure her basal body temperature (BBT method), calculate her expected ovulation by the calendar, check her cervical mucous secretions (cervical mucous method), or combine these observations (symptothermic method).

In order to use the BBT method, a woman must take a daily early-morning reading of her body temperature. While follicles are ripening, prior to ovulation, BBT is slightly low, below 98.6°F. At ovulation, BBT rises about one degree and then remains elevated until shortly before the next menstrual period. A woman's BBT may also be elevated in the morning due to infection, inadequate sleep, or consumption of alcoholic beverages the night before. Thus, she must take these factors, as well as ovulation, into account when noting a rise in BBT.

The calendar method is based on the individual woman's normal menstrual cycle, which can vary from twenty-four to thirty-four days. Ovulation occurs approximately fourteen days before each menstrual period. By charting the beginning of each menses and then counting back two weeks, a woman can estimate when she ovulated retrospectively.

The number of days required between the beginning of menstrual bleeding and a new ovulation counting forward is highly variable from woman to woman depending on the length of time her follicles need to mature. Ovulation can be delayed if a woman is dieting or malnourished, has an infection, has an endocrine disturbance, or has undergone unusual physical or emotional stress.

Ovulation can also be estimated as occurring when cervical mucous secretions become slippery and clear, like raw egg white. While a woman's fertile period lasts only for the life of the ovum (twelve to twenty-four hours), a man's sperm may survive in the oviduct awaiting ovulation for seventy-two hours. Consequently, a pregnancy may result if intercourse occurs two to three days prior to ovulation. Women trained to watch for changes in their cervical mucous secretions are better able to predict when they are two or three days prior to ovulation than are women who rely only on basal body temperature changes and the calendar.

The three methods combined (symptothermic) are more reliable than any one method alone. The natural family planning method is free and does not alter a woman's natural biologic rhythms. It has been demonstrated to be 80–90% effective (Tatum, 1987).

After ovulation the several partially developed follicles degenerate. Under the influence of LH, the Graafian follicle develops into a structure called the **corpus luteum.** The corpus luteum secretes estrogen and progesterone, which help the uterus prepare to accept a fertilized ovum. If the ovum is fertilized, the corpus luteum increases its production of estrogen and progesterone during pregnancy. If the ovum remains unfertilized, the corpus luteum begins to degenerate. Then, in about fourteen days, the uterus sheds, through menstruation, the lining it had prepared for the possibility of pregnancy.

As the ovum escapes from the Graafian follicle and from the surface of the ovary, it passes briefly through the abdominal cavity before it is picked up by the fimbriated (fringelike) ends of the Fallopian tube. The ovum moves slowly down the four-inch tube and reaches the uterus after four to seven days. Unless it is fertilized by a sperm within twelve to twenty-four hours after escaping from the ovary, it dies (Sadler, 1985). Knowledge of a woman's fertile period can be used to practice contraception and/or plan for pregnancy (see Box 3-1 on page 59).

The Sperm.   Whereas women are born with all the ova they will ever have, men continually produce *sperm* (male sex cells) at the rate of several hundred million every few days. (Most men continually produce sperm from puberty until death.) The sperm are formed in the two *testes* (male sex glands) that lie in the scrotum suspended below the abdomen (see Figure 3-5 and Color Plate 15 at the center of the textbook). This location outside the abdomen is necessary for fertility because **spermatogenesis** (formation of sperm) requires a temperature lower than that of the body. The scrotum hangs loosely when warm and pulls closer to the body when cool to maintain a relatively stable temperature.

From birth, males have in their testes dormant spermatogonia or primordial germ cells that are the early precursors of sperm. Beginning at puberty these primordial germ cells multiply. A sperm diminishes in size during this maturation transformation. The cell nucleus condenses and is concentrated into a "head" region, and most of the cell cytoplasm (the gluelike, semifluid matter outside the nucleus) is cast off. A long, whiplike tail, called a flagellum (plural = flagella), forms. This structure permits the sperm great mobility.

Fully developed sperm move from the seminiferous tubules in the testes to the *epididymis* (excretory duct at the rear, upper surface of each testis) (see Figure 3-5), where they may remain for several weeks. They are lubricated and acquire greater mobility while in the epididymis. When ejaculation occurs, a few hundred million sperm travel from the epididymis through the long *vas deferens* (duct that carries sperm) to

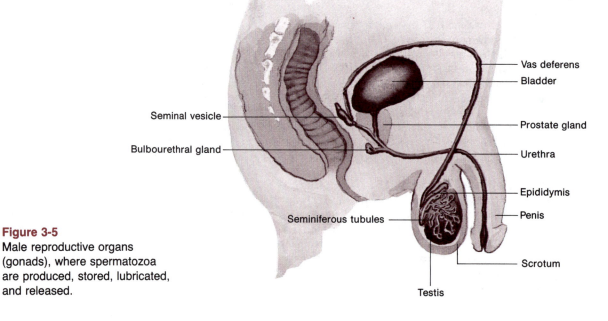

Figure 3-5
Male reproductive organs (gonads), where spermatozoa are produced, stored, lubricated, and released.

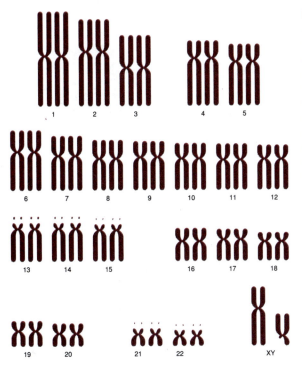

Figure 3-6
All human cells (except ova and sperm) have 23 pairs of chromosomes. One member of each pair is contributed by each biological parent. The pairs can be numbered according to size and shape. The last pair, the sex chromosomes, are alike (XX) if the human is female, but are different (XY) if the human is male.

the penis. En route they are further lubricated by fluids from the *seminal vesicles,* the *prostate gland,* and the *bulbourethral* glands. These fluids both nourish the sperm and provide them with further means of transport. Finally, the sperm are expelled from the penis. During sexual intercourse the sperm are deposited in the vagina near the small opening to the uterus known as the cervix (refer back to Figure 3-2).

A woman's body does not make it easy for sperm to reach an ovum. The cervix is protected by mucous secretions through which the sperm must pass. Then they must cross the uterus, enter the oviducts, and travel to the ends nearest the ovaries in order to fertilize an ovum. While over a million sperm may be deposited near the cervix, only a few hundred may reach the portion of the oviducts near the ovaries. Sperm travel fastest right after ejaculation and slow down considerably after two hours. Some sperm can be expected to reach the ovarian ends of the oviducts after about one hour, and others arrive later. The whiplike movements of the flagella help the sperm "swim." Sperm can remain alive for about seventy-two hours waiting to fertilize an ovum (Katchadourian, 1989).

Sperm undergo still another transformation within the female genital tract. They lose a coating on their heads, which allows special enzymes to escape. These enzymes help break down the protective coating on the ovum so that a sperm can penetrate it. Only one sperm fertilizes an ovum. Once the head of a sperm enters the pellucid zone of the ovum a change occurs on the surface of the ovum that renders it impermeable to all other sperm (refer back to Figure 3-1).

Chromosomes. *Chromo* (Greek for "color") combined with *soma* (Greek for "body") makes **chromosome,** or "colored body." This is what early scientists doing microscopic studies of cells at the turn of the 20th century saw in the stained nuclei of cells. The cells of some creatures had many rod-shaped colored bodies, others very few. For example, in a crustacean cell, over 100 chromosomes were counted, while in a fruit fly only four could be seen. Erroneously, early scientists believed each human cell contained 48 chromosomes (Trattner, 1942). We now know that all human cells except mature ova and sperm contain 46 chromosomes. Ripe ova and sperm contain only 23 chromosomes. Each chromosome contains thousands of discrete portions of deoxyribonucleic acid (DNA) molecules that code the hereditary information that de-

Figure 3-7
Sex of the offspring is determined by the sex chromosome contributed by the father's mature sperm (X or Y). All the mother's mature ova contain X chromosomes.

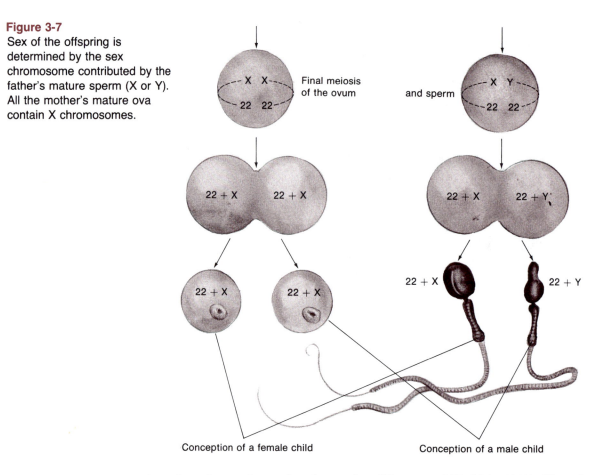

Conception of a female child   Conception of a male child

termines the unique makeup of each organism (Weaver and Hedrick, 1989). We call these basic units of heredity **genes.**

The 46 chromosomes in the nucleus of every human body cell can be divided into 23 pairs (see Figure 3-6). Blueprints for half of the chromosomes (one of each pair) were supplied by the biological father at the moment of conception and blueprints for the other half of the chromosomes (the other of each pair) were supplied by the biological

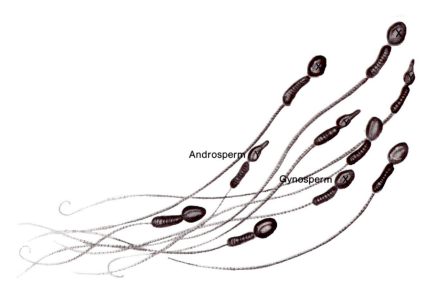

Figure 3-8
Schematic representation of mature spermatozoa. Those that will produce female offspring (carrying an X chromosome) have the larger, oval heads and shorter flagella.

Would You Preselect the Sex of Your Child?

The ancient Greeks believed that tying a string around a man's right testicle would produce male sperm, while a string around his left testicle would create female sperm. By 1970 in the United States, with a knowledge of the differences between androsperm and gynosperm to guide him, Dr. Landrum Shettles proposed a more effective method of preselecting a child's sex. In order to produce a son, he advised alkaline (baking soda and water) douches for females prior to intercourse and deep penetration by the male during intercourse, which should occur at the time of ovulation. If a daughter is preferred, he advised acid douching (vinegar and water), intercourse with shallow penetration two to three days before ovulation, and sexual abstinence at ovulation.

By the 1980s, two California scientists had developed Gametrics, a laboratory method of preselecting offspring's sex for which they claim a success rate of about 75% (Ericsson and Glass, 1982). Gametrics separates X- and Y-bearing sperm in glass columns. If a son is desired, a solution of albumin is used. The androsperm, with their long tails and small heads, can swim through the sticky substance to the bottom of the column faster than gynosperm. If a daughter is preferred, a gelatinous powder is placed in the column instead. Gynosperm fall through the powder to the bottom of the tube more rapidly because they are heavier. Once the separation of X- and Y-bearing sperm is accomplished, the prospective mother is artificially inseminated with the sperm of her choice extracted from her mate's semen.

mother at conception. Heredity is always a fifty–fifty proposition with equal numbers of chromosomes and genes being contributed by each parent.

The sex of offspring is determined by the sex chromosomes. Every mature ovum contains one large X sex chromosome. Every mature sperm contains either a large X or a small Y sex chromosome. If a sperm containing an X chromosome fertilizes the ovum, the offspring of this impregnation will be female. Likewise, if a sperm containing a Y chromosome fertilizes the ovum, the offspring will be a male (see Figure 3-7).

It has become possible to identify and differentiate sperm that will produce male and female offspring. Sperm that will produce male children (called **androsperm**) have longer tails and smaller heads and can be expected to reach the far ends of the oviducts most rapidly. However, the sperm that will produce female children (called **gynosperm**) can survive longer in the oviducts waiting for an ovum, due to the extra cytoplasm carried in their head region (see Figure 3-8). Knowledge of the differences in androsperm and gynosperm have allowed some parents to preselect the sex of their children (see Box 3-2).

Mitosis.   After impregnation of an ovum by a sperm, the new cell, the **zygote,** begins to divide by a replication cell division called *mitosis.* Each chromosome is composed of molecules of DNA in a double helix (see Figure 3-9). It can make a carbon

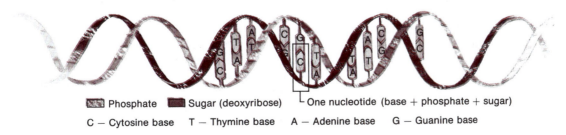

Phosphate   Sugar (deoxyribose)   └ One nucleotide (base + phosphate + sugar)

C — Cytosine base   T — Thymine base   A — Adenine base   G — Guanine base

Figure 3-9
Schematic representation of the deoxyribonucleic acid (DNA) molecule, showing its double helix arrangement.

Figure 3-10
During cell division the helical strands of DNA uncoil and find new complementary bases, phosphates, and sugars in the cell material, forming new identical strands into new identical chromosomes.

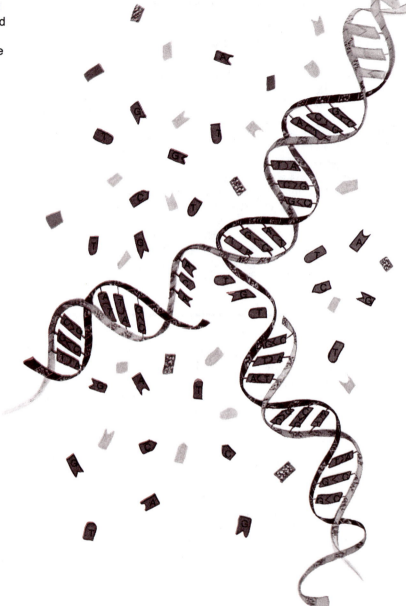

copy of itself by uncoiling its helical strands. It finds new materials (phosphates, sugars, and organic bases) in the cell to create new strands (see Figure 3-10). Each original strand then recoils with its new strand to form two absolutely identical chromosomes. Both the chromosome contributed by the father and the chromosome contributed by the mother do this for each pair of chromosomes. This process results in a replication, nucleotide by nucleotide, of the two strands of complementary DNA. Each DNA strand thus serves as a pattern for its complementary strand. By this process, the new set of chromosomes carries exactly the same nucleotides in a double-helix arrangement as the original. After the process of DNA replication, the number of chromosomes per cell has doubled. The cell must then undergo a division process to return the number of chromosomes back to the original level.

Mitosis occurs in a series of stages (see Figure 3-11). Every chromosome separates from its replica so that a newly formed cell can have genetic material that is perfectly equivalent to that of the original cell.

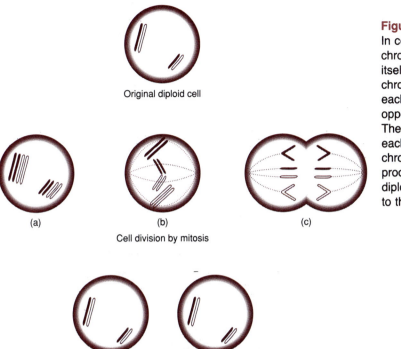

Original diploid cell

(a)   (b)   (c)

Cell division by mitosis

New diploid cells

Figure 3-11
In cell division by mitosis, each chromosome makes a copy of itself (a). The identical chromosomes separate from each other and move to opposite sides of the cell (b). The original cell cleaves in half, each side containing identical chromosomes (c). The final products of mitosis are two diploid cells absolutely identical to the original diploid cell.

Meiosis.   Mature ova and sperm contain 23 chromosomes. Immature ova and sperm have a full complement of 46 chromosomes. When the ova and sperm divide, the number of chromosomes is reduced by one half. This reduction division is called *meiosis*. It begins like mitosis. Each chromosome uncoils its helical strands of DNA and creates new strands of DNA from cell materials. Each original strand recoils with its new complementary DNA strand forming two identical chromosomes. However, unlike mitosis where the identical chromosomes separate from each other and move to opposite ends of the cell (refer back to Figure 3-11), in meiosis the identical chromosomes remain bound together by a tiny central structure called a **centromere** (see Figure 3-12a). Sometimes small sections of chromosomal material from the duplicated maternal chromosomes exchange places with complementary sections of the duplicated paternal chromosomes (see Figure 3-12b). This phenomenon is called **crossing-over.** It does not always occur, or may occur on some chromosome pairs but not on others. The cell will eventually cleave in half, forming two new cells (see Figure 3-12c). However, since the duplicated identical chromosomes remain bound together by the centromere, each new cell will contain 23 double chromosomes (see Figure 3-12d). The centromeres eventually break apart (see Figure 3-12e). Then, the duplicated chromosomes separate from each other and move to opposite ends of the cell (see Figure 3-12f). Finally, each cell cleaves in half again, forming four haploid cells, with 23 single chromosomes. Thus, the final product of meiosis is not two identical diploid cells as in mitosis, but four non-identical haploid cells each with only one-half the original number of chromosomes.

In meiosis of an ovum, one of these four final haploid cells retains more cytoplasm than the others and becomes the mature ovum. The other three cells, called polar bodies, degenerate. In meiosis of an immature sperm into four mature sperm, all four cells survive as haploid cells.

We cannot conclude this discussion of meiosis without a reminder of why it occurs. Were ova and sperm to divide by mitosis, retaining all 46 identical chromosomes, the zygote would have 92 chromosomes after impregnation. Meiosis of ova and sperm assure that generation after generation of humans have 46 chromosomes per cell, 23 inherited from a haploid ova and 23 inherited from a haploid sperm. The variation of chromosomes in each haploid cell plus the crossing-over phenomenon assure that siblings produced by the same biological parents will have their own unique combinations

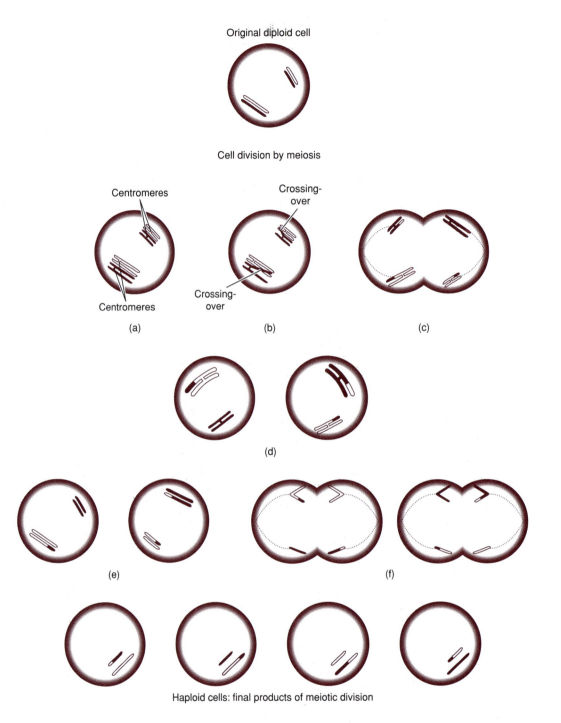

Figure 3-12

In cell division by meiosis, each chromosome makes a copy of itself. The identical chromosomes stay bound to each other by a central structure, the centromere (a). Small sections of chromosomal materials may be exchanged between chromosome pairs, a phenomenon known as crossing-over (b). The identical chromosomes, bound together by centromeres and possibly containing some crossed-over materials, move to opposite sides of the cell (c). The original cell cleaves in half, each side containing different, double chromosome pairs (d). The centromeres break apart (e). The duplicated chromosomes separate from each other and move to opposite sides of the cells (f). Each cell cleaves in half, each side containing non-identical chromosomes. The final products of meiosis are four haploid cells, each different from, and containing only one half the chromosomes of, the original diploid cell.

of chromosomes. Only identical twins, the result of the division of the original zygote into two persons, can have completely identical chromosomes and genes.

Genetic Inheritance

In 1970, this author was teaching a class about genes at a major U.S. university. I described them as hypothetical structures: structures assumed to exist but without final proof of existence. I went into detail about how Watson, Crick, and Wilkens won a Nobel Prize in 1962 for constructing a model of DNA (genetic material), and how contemporary researchers were attempting to synthesize a gene. I was about to move on to describe Mendel's laws of inheritance when a stately Indian woman in a sari arose from the back of the classroom. "Yes?" I asked her. "Do you read the newspapers?" she asked. "Excuse me?" She repeated and expanded the question, very articulately, "Do you read news, or listen to news?" I asked her what she meant. She explained that one of her countrymen, Har Gobind Khorana, had just successfully synthesized a gene, and that his feat was covered by all the news media. It was true. The gene was no longer hypothetical. I was mortified. To this day, I will not face a class until I have read or listened to the daily news. I have never forgotten Khorana's name, nor his contribution.

Genes on Chromosomes.   Each chromosome pair of the 23 human pairs is slightly different in size and shape (refer back to Figure 3-6). The amount of DNA on each chromosome pair, concurrently, is different. The amount of DNA that constitutes one gene is hard to determine. One gene is the sequence of DNA on a specific site of a chromosome that carries the information for a particular trait. Current estimates are that about 100,000 genes exist on the helical strands of DNA on the 46 chromosomes (Ayala and Kiger, 1984), about 3000 to 5000 genes per pair.

Each particular trait is determined by a gene on one chromosome contributed by the mother and by a gene on the other homologous (alike) chromosome of the pair contributed by the father. The different genes that occupy the same position on homologous chromosomes and determine a trait are called **alleles** (see Figure 3-13).

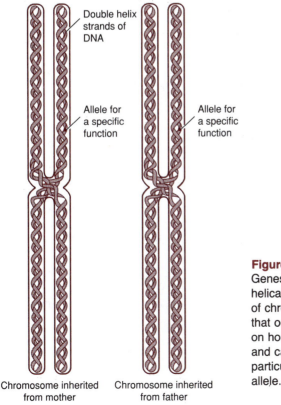

Double helix strands of DNA

Allele for a specific function

Allele for a specific function

Chromosome inherited from mother

Chromosome inherited from father

Figure 3-13
Genes are sequenced on the helical strands of DNA on a pair of chromosomes. The genes that occupy the same position on homologous chromosomes and carry a message for a particular trait constitute an allele.

Dominant, Recessive, and Interactive Genes. Gregor Mendel (1822–1884), an Austrian monk, growing sweetpeas in his monastery in the mid 1800s, noted and published his observations about inheritance. Traits such as size, shape, and color, he believed, were inherited as separate units. He postulated that different forms of genes, one inherited from each parent, worked together in dominant (controlling) or recessive (yielding) relationships. His speculations became accepted by plant breeders and scientists and were called Mendel's Laws.

Mendel's Laws apply to many human traits that we know are influenced by dominant or recessive allelic genes. Consider, for example, the disease cystic fibrosis. It is carried by a recessive gene. It is customary to designate a recessive genetic characteristic by a lower case letter. Thus, a person with cystic fibrosis will be designated as cc (one recessive gene on each allele). Dominant genetic characteristics are designated with capital letters. Thus, a person without cystic fibrosis, who does not carry a hidden recessive gene, will be designated as NN (one dominant normal gene on each allele). Suppose these two persons marry and produce children. Examine the possibilities for combinations of alleles for the trait cystic fibrosis from these parents:

Parent with CF

		c	c
	N	Nc	Nc
Parent without CF	N	Nc	Nc

Every child will inherit a dominant gene for no disease and a recessive gene for disease. The dominant gene will protect every child from ever having the disease. However, these children are called *carriers* because they carry the recessive gene for the disease. Now, suppose one of the children with the allele Nc marries and produces children with a person who is also Nc for cystic fibrosis (one dominant normal gene, one recessive disease gene). Examine the possibilities for combinations of alleles for the trait cystic fibrosis from these parents:

Parent carrier of CF

		N	c
	N	NN	Nc
Parent carrier of CF	c	Nc	cc

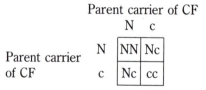

Theoretically, one out of four children will inherit two dominant normal genes and be free of the disease. When the allelic genes are the same, the person is said to be homozygous (alike) for those paired genes. Theoretically, two out of four children will inherit one dominant gene and one recessive gene. When allelic genes are different (i.e., when each parent has contributed a different form of the same gene), the person is said to be heterozygous (different) for those paired genes. Theoretically, one out of four children will inherit two recessive genes and will have the disease cystic fibrosis. This person will be homozygous (alike) for recessive genes. While in theory the offspring of two Nc parents will be 25% NN, 50% Nc, and 25% cc, the reality does not always follow theory. Two parents, both heterozygous for the trait cystic fibrosis, may produce all children homozygous for the dominant normal genes (NN), or all children homozygous for the recessive genes (cc), or a variety of heterozygous and homozygous children. Each new child they produce has a 1 in 4 chance of inheriting the disease, a 1 in 2 chance of being a carrier, and a 1 in 4 chance of being totally free of the recessive gene.

For many years, Mendel's laws of dominance and recessiveness of genes were believed to apply to all traits. We now know that one gene is not always dominant and the other recessive. Two genes often give separate controlling messages. If so, they are called interactive genes: both messages may be followed to some extent. Consider, for example, hazel eyes. These can be the result of a message for blue eyes from one gene and a message for brown eyes from the other gene. Skin color can also show intermediate effects of the colors requested by the two genes. Reality does not always follow interactive effect theory. Sometimes dominant genes do exert control as when two hazel-eyed parents produce a brown-eyed child, or as when two light-skinned parents produce a dark-skinned child. In co-dominant genes, both genes express their dominant message without recessiveness or interaction. Blood type AB, for example, is a co-dominance of type A from one gene and type B from the other gene.

Sex-Linked Genes.   On Figure 3-6, page 61, you will notice that the X chromosome on the last chromosome pair is approximately three times larger than the Y chromosome. The X chromosome carries a great many more segments of DNA (genes) than the Y. In the first 22 chromosome pairs, the members of each pair are alike. These chromosomes are called **autosomes.** Each gene has a complementary gene on its paired chromosome. The last pair of chromosomes are called **sex chromosomes** because, among other things, they determine the sex of the individual (see Figure 3-12). A female with two Xs has complementary alleles on each X. A male with one X and one Y has many genes on the X without any complements on the Y. These are called X-linked, or sex-linked genes. Because they lack counterparts on the Y, the sex-linked genes supply their message for traits to males without modification. Many conditions (e.g., color blindness, hemophilia) are carried as recessive genes by the female on the X but manifest predominantly in males who lack a complementary gene on the Y. Females will only inherit these conditions if the recessive genes causing them are found on both X chromosomes.

Genotype and Phenotype.   As discussed in Chapter 1, genotype refers to the genes on the chromosomes contributed by the mother and the father that determine the specific traits of a unique human being. Phenotype refers to the outward appearance of a unique human being. Dominance or recessiveness of allelic genes, interactive allelic gene effects, and environmental effects determine the phenotype.

> Jytte was a blonde woman of Danish ancestry. Joshua, her husband, had dark brown hair and Slovakian ancestry. When their first child was born with red hair, they were amazed. No living relatives on either side of their families had red hair. They thought the color would change as the child grew, but it only became more red. Their second child was also born with, and retained, very red hair. Wherever Jytte and Josh went with their children, they were asked to explain why the children were redheads. Not having any logical explanation, they used the repartee, "It came with the head."

There are many stories told, similar to the above vignette, about the phenotypic appearance of a person not matching an assumed genetic inheritance. Often the genotype for a given trait is not discovered until two persons with recessive genes for the same trait produce offspring who inherit the recessive genes from both parents. Thus, it finally becomes manifest in a phenotype, even though it may have been hidden (by a dominant gene) for many generations. The lay term, "throw-back," is often used to explain the appearance of a genotypic trait long hidden in the phenotypes of family members.

Table 3-1   The More Common Varieties of Spina Bifida.

Spina Bifida Occulta	Failure of one or two vertebrae to fuse.
Meningocele	A cleft forms where two or more vertebrae fail to fuse. A sac containing the meninges of the spinal cord bulges through the cleft.
Myelocele (Rachischisis)	The neural groove fails to close and neural tissue is exposed.
Meningo-myelocele	A more serious form of meningocele. The sac bulging through the cleft contains meninges and also portions of the spinal cord and neural tissue.
Arnold-Chiari malformation	Portions of either the medulla or the cerebellum project into a meningocele or meningomyelocele.

Polygenic Orchestration of Development.   Many traits require the action of more than one set of genes working together simultaneously. In some situations, the action of one set of allelic genes is dependent on the presence but not necessarily on the action of other genes. Traits that require several genes are called multifactorial traits or polygenic traits (Stenchever and Jones, 1987). An example of a polygenic inherited disease is spina bifida. It has several forms (e.g., occult, meningocele, meningo-myelocele, myelocele) dependent on the different genes involved (see Table 3-1).

Gene mapping, identifying the position and function of specific genes on specific chromosomes, is an active pursuit of geneticists today. It is also a challenging and difficult one. Organisms that reproduce rapidly and have large numbers of offspring (e.g., fruit flies, molds) are usually used to observe gene changes over generations. Chromosome banding and the use of hybrid cells are also helping scientists map the locations and activities of genes on chromosomes.

If, thus far, you have not come to a full appreciation of how genes (segments of DNA) on chromosomes orchestrate development, you are not alone. We are all still a long way away from being able to count the genes on each chromosome and describe their specific actions and interactive effects.

Stages of Prenatal Development

The growth and development of a single impregnated ovum into a full-term infant in approximately 266 days is a truly remarkable phenomenon. From fertilization until birth, every day is marked by notable changes in the baby-to-be. Three stages of prenatal development will be highlighted first: (1) the germinal period, (2) the embryonic period, and (3) the fetal period. A discussion of a multitude of environmental influences (both internal and external to the uterus) that can influence the developing organism will follow.

Germinal Period.   As soon as fertilization and the pairing of the twenty-three chromosomes of the ovum and sperm occur, the new cell becomes a *zygote*. This zygote is the prototype (model) for all body cells. It undergoes mitotic cell division within a day and becomes a two-cell structure, each cell a copy of the other. Within another day it will reach a four-cell stage. By three days the four cells will have divided twice again to make a sixteen-cell structure called a **morula.** The nucleus of each cell will contain the full complement of 23 pairs of chromosomes. These chromosome pairs are always identical to those formed at fertilization.

This early cell division occurs in the Fallopian tube as the zygote-changed-to-morula is slowly transported by peristaltic movements toward the uterus. The ball of cells floats freely in the uterus, growing progressively larger through mitotic cell division un-

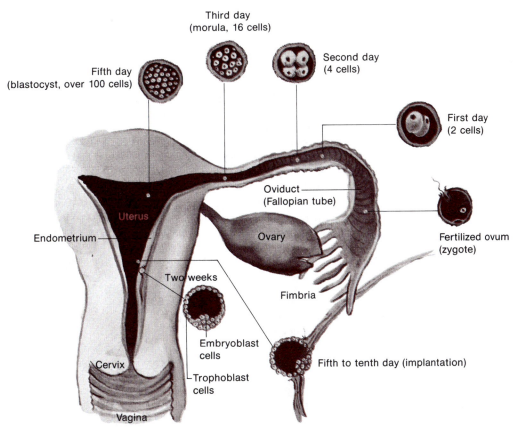

Figure 3-14
Schematic representation of the changes from zygote to implanted blastocyst in the germinal period.

til about the sixth to tenth day after fertilization. At this time it reaches a stage called the **blastocyst** and contains over one hundred cells. It will now burrow into the well-prepared mucosal lining, called the **endometrium,** on the wall of the uterus (see Figure 3-14). This period of time from fertilization to implantation is called the **germinal period.**

The endometrium was stimulated to grow by the hormones estrogen and progesterone produced by the corpus luteum after the ovum escaped from its Graafian follicle. The process by which the blastocyst burrows into the endometrium is called **implantation.** Some women will shed a little blood at this time. The bleeding may be mistaken for a menstrual period since it occurs about five to ten days after ovulation. It usually differs from a normal menstrual flow, however, in both amount and duration of bleeding.

If infertile couples opt for in vitro fertilization (a test-tube baby), the union of ovum and sperm and the growth from zygote to morula is accomplished in a petri dish rather than in the oviduct (see Box 3-3).

Several methods of noncoital reproduction have been developed (Thorneycroft, 1987). These procedures are controversial. While many governments have formed ethics committees to consider regulation of such reproductive practices, few laws have been passed to limit these new techniques. After reading the pros and cons in Box 3-4, you may form your own opinions about the ethics of this social issue.

The cells of the blastocyst differentiate into embryonic cells and trophoblastic cells as it implants into the uterus. The embryonic cells become the future baby. The *trophoblastic* cells will form the **placenta** (vascular organ in which the embryo/fetus develops), the *amniotic sac* (innermost membrane enveloping the embryo/fetus), and the *amniotic fluid* to surround, support, and protect the developing baby. Cells containing

BOX
3-3

Noncoital Reproductive Techniques.

In the technique called in vitro fertilization (IVF), the biological mother is given medicine to stimulate her ovaries to produce several ripe ova rather than just one at her monthly ovulation. The ova are surgically removed and placed on a culture medium. The biological father masturbates to produce sperm, which are combined with the ova on the culture medium. Impregnation of the ova occurs. After a few days, healthy looking products of IVF conception are transferred to the mother's uterus, in hopes that they will survive, become implanted, and result in a pregnancy (Edwards, 1981). Sometimes no transplanted fertilized ova survive. Other times more than one survives, resulting in multiple births. This technique, IVF, may involve the biological mother (the one who contributed the ova) or a surrogate mother. The biological father (the one who contributed the sperm) may be the biological mother's husband, or another sperm donor. It is also possible, in a marriage where infertility is the result of a woman's inability to produce ova, that donor ova are used but the gestational mother is the wife of the biological father.

Artificial insemination involves deposition of sperm in the vagina by mechanical means rather than through sexual intercourse. A biological father with a low sperm count may collect and store several ejaculates to assure a higher sperm count for insemination. The father's sperm mixed with donor sperm, or donor sperm only, may also be inseminated.

A surrogate mother is one who is artificially insemi-nated by the sperm of another woman's husband, with her consent, to conceive a child for them. If the surrogate mother is also to be the gestational mother, she sustains the pregnancy, bears the child, and gives it up to the couple, supposedly negating her rights to the child as its biological mother. Many surrogate mothers, like Mary Beth Whitehead of the "Baby M" case which became headline news in the United States in 1986, cannot do so (Whitehead, 1989).

Surrogacy embryo transfer (SET) involves the artificial insemination of a woman who serves as surrogate mother for only a short time (Robison, 1988). Donor sperm must reach her Fallopian tubes, impregnate her ovum, and the resulting conceptus (that which is produced as a result of conception, the embryo) must survive and begin growing as it travels down the tube and into the uterus. The embryo can then be removed and transferred to the uterus of the gestational mother (the woman who will sustain the pregnancy and bear the child).

In gamete intra-Fallopian transfer (GIFT), ova and sperm are transferred separately into a woman's Fallopian tube, allowing impregnation to occur in a natural environment (Robison, 1988). Ova may come from the wife or a donor, sperm may come from the husband or a donor. The resulting child may be genetically related to both, just one, or neither of the parents who will bear and rear the child.

BOX
3-4

The Pros and Cons of Noncoital Reproductive Techniques.

Pros

A man with a low sperm count may become a biological father through sperm collection and artificial insemination.

A woman who cannot produce ova may become a gestational mother with donor ova.

Infertile couples can have partially biological children using donor ova and/or donor sperm and/or surrogate gestational mothers.

Infertile couples can have 100% biological children using in vitro fertilization or gamete intra-Fallopian transfer.

Surrogate mothers may take over some or all of the gestational responsibilities for a biological mother.

Cons

Family members with partial or absent biological ties may feel alienated from each other.

Rearing responsibilities for non-biological children may be difficult to determine.

Men may be exploited to sell sperm for impregnating purposes.

Women may be exploited to rent out their uteruses for gestational purposes.

Payments for donor sperm, donor ova, embryos, or gestational services may commercialize human reproduction.

Defective children produced by high technology conception or surrogacy may be rejected.

Prospective parents may soon demand higher technology to produce a child to specifications (e.g., sex, appearance, personality, intelligence).

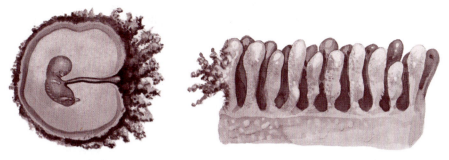

Figure 3-15
Early placental villi are short, stout projections into the uterine mucosa. Later they develop treelike side branches.

identical chromosomal and genetic materials in their nuclei can assume different roles because only limited numbers of genes are allowed to function in each cell.

Some of the trophoblastic cells form minute projections called **villi** (see Figure 3-15) which burrow into the endometrial lining of the uterus. Nutrients, oxygen, and other products obtained from the mother by diffusion to the placental villi are then transported to the baby through the umbilical cord.

Other trophoblastic cells, especially the *chorion* (the outermost membrane enveloping the embryo/fetus), begin excreting chorionic hormones within a few days after implantation, or about two weeks after fertilization. These hormones, *human chorionic gonadotropin* (HCG), *human chorionic somatomammotropin* (HCS), *thyrotropin, estrogen,* and *progesterone* cause the "morning sickness" that about 50% of women experience in their pregnancies. Other signs and symptoms of pregnancy are listed in Table 3-2.

Table 3-2 Early Physical Signs and Symptoms Used to Diagnose Pregnancy.

Presumptive	Probable	Positive
Missed menstrual period	Abdominal enlargement	Hearing fetal heartbeats
Nausea and vomiting	Uterine contractions (painless or with a sensation of tightening and pressure)	Feeling the outline of the fetus through the abdomen
Tingling sensation or pain in the breasts		X-ray film showing fetus
Fluttering sensation in the lower abdomen (caused by movement of the fetus)	Ballottement: when the physician taps the uterus from within the vagina the fetus bounces back, giving the sense of a floating object within the uterus	Ultrasound picture of fetus (safer than x-ray)
Urinary frequency and/or bladder irritability		Electrocardiogram of fetal heart
Constipation	Uterine souffle: a rushing sound heard through the abdomen caused by movement of maternal blood filling placental vessels and sinuses	Radioimmunoassay for HCG (very precise and accurate test)
Weight gain		
Fatigue		
Thinning and softening of the fingernails		
Elevation of basal body temperature		
Darkening of skin over the forehead, nose, and cheekbones		
Darkening of nipples and areolas		
Increased facial or body hair		
Enlargement of the breasts		
Protuberance of the lower abdomen		
Increased vaginal discharge		
Softening of the cervix		

SOURCE: Adapted from R. W. Hale (1984). Diagnosis of pregnancy and associated conditions. In R. C. Benson (ed.), *Current Obstetric and Gynecologic Diagnosis and Treatment,* 5th ed. Los Altos, Calif.: Lange. Reprinted by permission.

Embryonic Period.   The second to eighth weeks after impregnation make up the **embryonic period.** The placenta expands to form a balloonlike sac, the amniotic sac, inside which the embryo grows. The sac fills with amniotic fluid, which serves as a shock absorber for the floating embryo and keeps the walls of the uterus from restricting continued development.

As the embryo grows, its cells differentiate into *ectodermal, mesodermal,* and *endodermal* layers. These layers eventually become, respectively, the outer structures (skin, hair, teeth, nails, nerves), the middle structures (muscles, bones, heart, blood vessels), and the inner structures (intestines, endocrine glands, liver, pancreas, lungs, and respiratory tract). In the fourth week the embryo appears C-shaped. The brain and heart experience the most rapid growth. Thickened areas that will become eyes and ears are visible (see Figure 3-16). In the fifth week the buds that will become arms and legs appear. Growth of the brain is faster than that of all the other body parts. By the sixth week the head is bent over the abdominal bulge. The heart and circulatory system, lungs and respiratory system, liver, pancreas, kidneys, genitals, nervous system, mouth, stomach, and intestines are all undergoing very rapid development. A hand with webbed fingers appears. By the seventh week the fingers are all clearly visible and toes appear. The head becomes more rounded and is supported by a neck area. The abdominal bulge and the umbilical cord become smaller. By the eighth week the embryo has a distinctly human appearance. At this point it is called a fetus rather than an embryo.

The period of most rapid growth or development of any structure or function is called its critical period. The developing human is especially vulnerable to disruptive influences during the embryonic period. Spontaneous abortions (miscarriages) are most apt to occur either at implantation or during the embryonic period. They usually occur because there is faulty development in one of the critical organ systems. This can be viewed as nature's way of protecting the species from aberrations. The spontaneous abortion rate may be as high as 40% of all pregnancies (Durfee, 1987). Most women

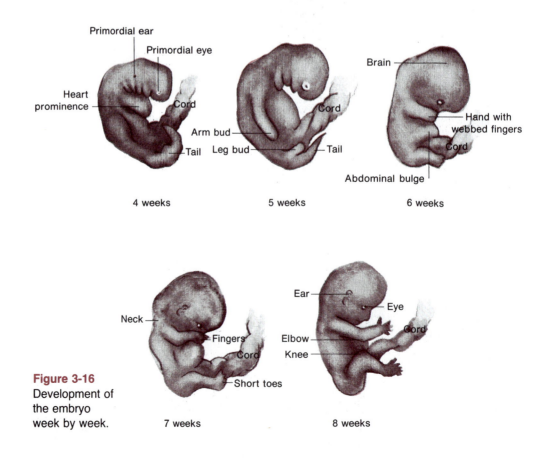

Figure 3-16
Development of the embryo week by week.

will not be aware that they are aborting an unhealthy product of conception. They will only experience a delayed menstrual period and more cramping and bleeding than is usual with menstruation.

Fetal Period. The fetal period lasts from eight weeks until birth. The fetus is less susceptible than the embryo to internal and external injuries to its organs, since the vital organs are usually past their critical period. The **fetal period** is characterized by growth and maturation of all of the structures that were formed in the embryonic stage (see Box 3-5). Weight gain is extraordinary. By the third month the sex of the fetus is distinguishable externally. By the fourth month the head is erect on the neck, the external ears are formed and stand out from the head, and the legs are well developed. By the fifth month the mother has usually felt movements of the legs or arms (called quickening). At first the movements can be compared to a bubble rising to the surface, or a butterfly fluttering, but later they are very noticeably kicks or punches that may cause the mother to wince. By six months the fetus has hair, eyebrows, and fingernails. Occasionally a fetus born around the twenty-sixth to twenty-ninth week (approximately seven months) can survive (see Figure 3-17). However, the mortality rate is high because the respiratory system is not yet adequately developed to support life outside the uterus.

The fetus's blood flows from the fetus through arteries in the umbilical cord into capillaries in the villi. Waste products are exchanged by diffusion, a process by which small substances (e.g., carbon dioxide and other wastes, oxygen and other nutrients) pass through a membrane but larger substances (e.g., blood cells) do not. The fetus's blood never meets or mixes with the mother's blood during pregnancy. The membranes of the placenta provide what is known as the **placental barrier.** Only substances small enough to diffuse through the placental membrane can be transmitted from mother to fetus and from fetus to mother. A fetal vein carries nutrients acquired from each villus back to the fetus through the umbilical cord (see Figure 3-18). The umbilical

---

BOX
3-5

Progression of Fetal Development.

9 Weeks: Head about half the length of fetus, about ¾ inches long. Fetus about 1½ inches long. Fingers, toes, eyelids, nose, and upper jaw evident. Central nervous system and muscle fibers forming.

12 Weeks: Head growth slows while body growth accelerates. Arms almost reach final relative length; legs remain short. External genitalia mature. Sucking and eyelid reflexive responses can be elicited.

16 Weeks: Legs lengthen. Some ossification of skeleton. Skin red and thin. Fingers and toes separated. Fetus about 9 inches long, weighs about 9 ounces.

20 Weeks: Mother feels fetal movements. Eyebrows and head hair visible. Eyes sensitive to light. Wake and sleep cycles evident. Some fat forming on body.

24 Weeks: Blood flow visible in vessels. Skin translucent and wrinkled. Weight gain accelerates. Brain grows rapidly. Kidney tubules branch out. Ovaries and testes developed.

28 Weeks: Eyes open and close. Good head of hair. Subcutaneous fat smooths out many wrinkles. Rhythmic breathing movements. Can usually survive premature birth. Fetus about 14 inches long, weighs about 2½ pounds.

32 Weeks: Fingernails and toenails present. Skin pink and smooth. Arms and legs develop fat and may appear chubby. Respiratory system and temperature regulating mechanism mature.

36 Weeks: Fetal heart heard through stethoscope. Slowing of growth as time of birth approaches. Mammary glands protrude in both sexes. Skin is white in fetuses of all races due to lack of melanin.

40 Weeks: Fully developed and optimally ready for birth.

Figure 3-17
Fetus in utero at about seven months, with vital organ systems formed but immature. Visibly lacking are the protective layers of fat that are added during the last few weeks of the third trimester of pregnancy.

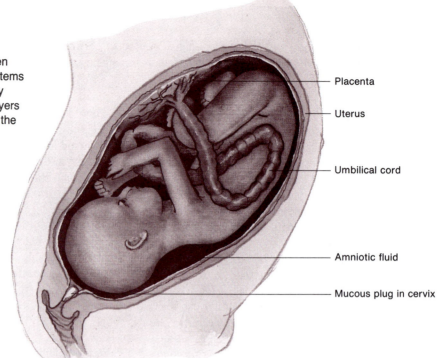

Placenta

Uterus

Umbilical cord

Amniotic fluid

Mucous plug in cervix

cord, with a continual circulation of blood through its arteries and veins, remains distended and firm. Despite rumors to the contrary, it is not slack enough to become knotted.

In the last two months of gestation the fetus rapidly accumulates fat deposits to

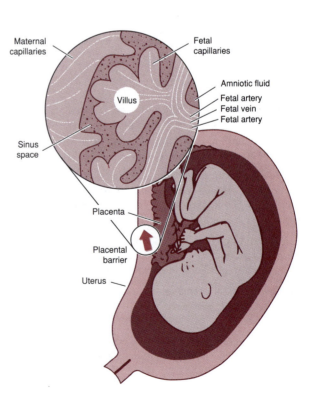

Maternal capillaries

Fetal capillaries

Amniotic fluid
Fetal artery
Fetal vein
Fetal artery

Villus

Sinus space

Placenta

Placental barrier

Uterus

Figure 3-18
The blood vessels of the mother and the fetus are not joined prenatally. Blood from maternal capillaries fills sinus spaces in the endometrium. Nutrients and waste products diffuse through the placental villi, called the placental barrier. A fetal vein in the umbilical cord brings wastes to the capillaries in the villi. Two fetal arteries in the umbilical cord carry nutrients obtained from the villi back to the fetus.

use in the neonatal period. The fatty tissues give the fetus a plump, smooth look. The fetus is usually expelled from the uterus about thirty-eight weeks (nine months, or 266 days) after conception. In spite of intensive research, the exact mechanisms that trigger hormone changes in the mother's blood, the fetus, and in the uterus and cause the uterus to contract and push out the fetus are not yet well understood (Ganong, 1983).

Possible Prenatal Problems

Considering the enormously complicated mechanism of the development of an individual from germ cells to birth, and considering the multitude of factors that can affect the organism in intrauterine life, it is amazing that abnormalities are not more frequent. In this section of the chapter we will describe various reasons for some of the imperfections that do occur. Remember, however, that these are not all risks in every pregnancy. The norm is for full-term, healthy infants, not defective ones, to emerge from the nine months of prenatal existence.

Chromosomal Abnormalities

Most chromosomal problems are due to chromosomal nondisjunction during meiosis of either ova or sperm. The centromere should split apart allowing the paired chromosomes to go to separate cells (refer back to Figure 3-12e). If this disjunction fails to occur, one cell will receive a double chromosome and the other cell will receive no chromosome of that pair (see Figure 3-19a). The sex chromosomes, X and Y, seem to be especially prone to nondisjunction. Those that survive gestation and contain extra or absent sex chromosomes are characterized as the following chromosomal abnormalities:

XXX—Metafemale—lowered intelligence

XXY—Klinefelter syndrome male—infertile, lowered intelligence

X0—Turner syndrome female—infertile, lowered intelligence

XYY—Double Y male—impulsive, lowered intelligence

Some persons with XXXX, XXXY, XXYY or even five sex chromosomes (e.g., XXXYY) have survived gestation. The greater the number of X chromosomes present, the greater the severity of mental retardation (Moore, 1988).

Nondisjunction of autosomal chromosomes usually results in products of conception that are spontaneously aborted. The exception to this principle is Down syndrome, caused by extra chromosomal material on the 21st autosomal chromosome pair. The condition is also called Trisomy 21, because three number 21 chromosomes are present. Down syndrome individuals have a variable degree of mental retardation and numerous physical malformations (Turkington, 1987). They have recognizable appearances characterized by flat, broad faces, predominant epicantal folds above their eyes, and poor nasal bridge development (see Figure 3-20).

Some Down syndrome individuals have only a portion of an extra 21st chromosome. This may be due to partial chromosomal nondisjunction (see Figure 3-19b). It also may be because a portion of another chromosome has broken off its base and attached itself to the 21st chromosome pair. This uncommon error is known as translocation. Rarely, a Down syndrome individual will have mosaic Down syndrome, in which some, but not all, cells will contain an extra 21st chromosome. This is due to the failure of some of the paired 21st chromosomes to divide in cells of the developing morula shortly after conception.

Trisomies of a few other autosomal chromosomal pairs (e.g., 13, 18) have survived

Figure 3-19
Autosomes or sex chromosomes that contain extra chromosomes or chromosomal materials contribute to abnormal human conditions. The usual reason for extra chromosomal materials is that the centromere fails to break apart during meiotic division. In nondisjunction, this results in one haploid cell having two chromosomes of one pair (a). In partial nondisjunction, one haploid cell has a portion of a second chromosome attached to one of its chromosomes (b).

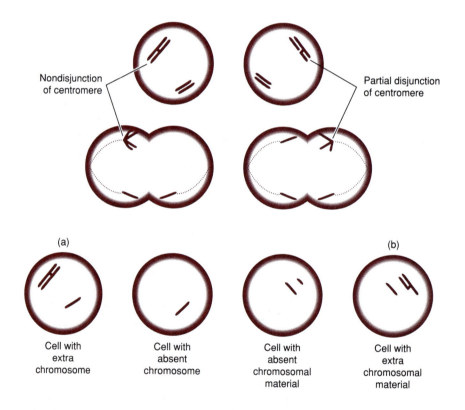

Original diploid cell

Products of 1st meiotic division

Nondisjunction of centromere

Partial disjunction of centromere

(a)

(b)

| Cell with extra chromosome | Cell with absent chromosome | Cell with absent chromosomal material | Cell with extra chromosomal material |

gestation. Individuals with these trisomies are born with severe multiple malformations and usually die in early infancy (Moore, 1988).

There is a positive correlation between chromosomal problems and age of parents (see Table 3-3). Teenage mothers and older mothers (those past age 35) more frequently have babies with chromosomal disorders (Stenchever and Jones, 1987). Older fathers

Table 3-3 Approximate Number of Children Born with Down Syndrome Relative to the Mother's Age.

18–30	1 per 1000
Age 40	1 per 100
Age 50	1 per 10

may also be implicated in faulty meiotic division of sperm resulting in inheritance of extra chromosomes or chromosomal materials (Tjossem, De La Cruz, and Muller, 1984).

Genetic Abnormalities

Most inherited diseases are caused by genes rather than chromosomal problems. Some genes that code messages for disease conditions are dominant in allelic gene relationships. Many of them create the diseased condition at different ages, in varying degrees, and under different environmental conditions, suggesting multifactorial or polygenic orchestration of development.

> Woody Guthrie was a famous U.S. folk singer and guitarist of the 1940s and 1950s. He wrote such famous songs as "This Land Is Your Land," and "So Long, It's Been Good to Know You." By the mid-1950s, he was diagnosed as having a debilitating neurological condition, called Huntington's disease, which is carried by a dominant gene. His son, Arlo, achieved fame of his own as a folk singer of the 1960s, even as his father lay dying. He played at numerous concerts, including the Woodstock festival of 1969. He worried that he, too, would develop Huntington's disease. His probability of acquiring it was 50%. In a quasi-fictional movie, *Alice's Restaurant*, he related how he failed to get deferred from military service in Vietnam due to his genetic potential for the disease. Instead, he got deferred by obtaining a criminal record: He dumped garbage illegally.

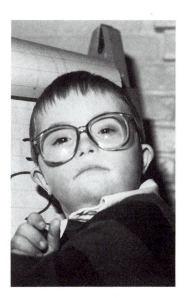

Figure 3-20
An individual with Down syndrome has characteristic facial anomalies: an epicantal fold above each eye, a short or absent nasal bridge, a flattened, broad face, and a protruding tongue.

The threat of acquiring a disease carried on a dominant gene is 50% if one parent carries the gene. To illustrate this in Huntington's disease, let the dominant genetic disease characteristic be designated with a capital H. No Huntington's disease is designated with a lower case n (normal).

Parent carrying
Huntington's disease
	H	n
Parent free of n	Hn	nn
Huntington's disease n	Hn	nn

The threat of acquiring a disease carried on a dominant gene is 75% if both parents carry the gene. (Both parents will also eventually acquire the disease.)

Parent carrying
Huntington's disease
	H	n
Parent carrying H	HH	Hn
Huntington's disease n	Hn	nn

Because of the high probability of passing a disease to offspring when even one parent is heterozygous for the disease, many couples with dominant gene diseases opt to remain childless, to adopt children, or to use noncoital reproductive techniques (see p. 72) to produce children carrying only the genes of the disease-free parent. Examples of other dominant gene diseases are cortical cataracts, some forms of deafness, Marfan's syndrome, muscular dystrophy, night blindness, and polycystic kidney disease (Stenchever and Jones, 1987).

In order for biological parents to pass a disease carried on a recessive gene to any offspring, both parents must carry the recessive gene. Even when they are both heterozygous for the disease, the probability of passing the disease to an offspring is only 25%. The probability that offspring will carry the recessive gene without having the disease is 50% (refer back to the discussion of cystic fibrosis on page 68). Some examples of recessive gene diseases are albinism, cystic fibrosis, dysautonomia, galactosemia, Gaucher's disease, glaucoma, phenylketonuria, sickle cell anemia, Tay-Sachs disease, and Wilson's disease (Stenchever and Jones, 1987). Many of these diseases are found predominantly in one ethnic group because of the high rate of intermarriage of persons within ethnic groups (see Table 3-4) Geneticists often talk of hybrid vigor in relation to human populations as well as in relation to plants. The mixing of the gene pool, as occurs when persons of different ethnic backgrounds marry and procreate, provides new genes (disease-free) to prevent the recessive genes from pairing up and producing a disease. Parents and children, siblings, and sometimes first cousins are legally prohibited from producing offspring with each other because of the high probability of pairing recessive (disease-producing) genes.

A small percent of the population, about 15%, inherit red blood cells that lack major **antigens** called **Rh factor** (Durfee, 1987). Antigens are materials that stimulate the body to produce a rejection response. People lacking the factor (Rh negative) will develop antibodies against the factor if red blood cells with the factor get into their blood. This risk is slight as blood is always typed and cross-matched before transfusions. Sharing of needles, as for intravenous injection of illegal drugs, however, may sensitize some Rh-negative mothers to develop antibodies against Rh-positive blood. If an Rh-negative mother who has antibodies against the Rh factor becomes pregnant with a child who inherits the Rh factor, problems ensue. The antibodies will cross the placental barrier and destroy the red blood cells of the fetus, resulting in a severe anemia (called erythroblastosis fetalis), and/or fetal death. If an Rh-negative woman inadvertently comes in blood-to-blood contact with Rh-positive blood, a drug called Rhogam can be given to prevent the development of antibodies. This drug is routinely given to Rh-negative mothers when they deliver babies, because of the danger of Rh-positive fetal blood getting into the mother's blood during the birth process (see Figure 3-21). Rh incompatibility problems occur in only a small percent of Rh-negative mothers gestating Rh-positive children because of the widespread use of Rhogam and the care taken with blood transfusions.

Another potential for antibody production exists between persons with type A, type B, and type O blood. If, for example, a mother with type O blood has type A blood introduced into her blood stream, she may develop antibodies against type A. These antibodies may cross the placental barrier and attack type A blood cells of the fetus. ABO incompatibility disease (hemolytic anemia) is much milder than Rh incompatibility disease (erythroblastosis fetalis). It usually does not develop until after birth and can usually be treated successfully with phototherapy. Full spectrum lights help destroy the attacking antibodies. Occasionally, an exchange transfusion may be necessary.

Table 3-4 Some Genetic Recessive Disorders and the Population Group They Most Frequently Affect.

Disorder	Extraction of Most Affected Persons
Cystic fibrosis	Northwestern European
Phenylketonuria	Northwestern European
Tay-Sachs disease	Ashkenazic Jewish, French-Canadian
Dysautonomia	Ashkenazic Jewish
Glucose dehydrogenase deficiency	African and Chinese
Mediterranean fever	Armenian, Italian, Greek
Adult lactose deficiency	Chinese
Adrenogenital syndrome	Eskimo
Sickle-cell anemia	African

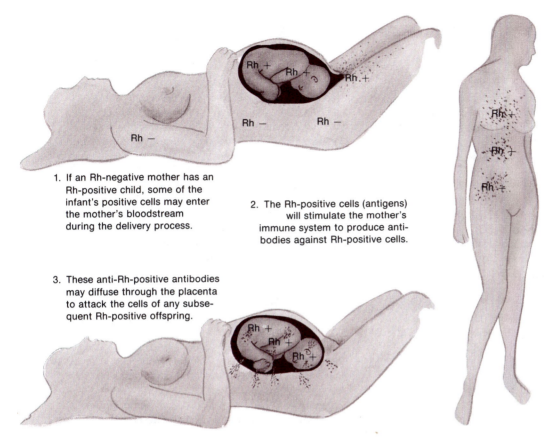

1. If an Rh-negative mother has an Rh-positive child, some of the infant's positive cells may enter the mother's bloodstream during the delivery process.

2. The Rh-positive cells (antigens) will stimulate the mother's immune system to produce antibodies against Rh-positive cells.

3. These anti-Rh-positive antibodies may diffuse through the placenta to attack the cells of any subsequent Rh-positive offspring.

Figure 3-21
Antigen–antibody response to Rh factor in an Rh-negative mother.

Parents who, through genetic counseling or past experience, know that they are at high risk for producing offspring with one of the chromosomal or genetically transmitted disorders may elect to have chorionic villus sampling or amniocentesis done early in pregnancy (see Figure 3-22). Several procedures used in prenatal testing are described in Box 3-6.

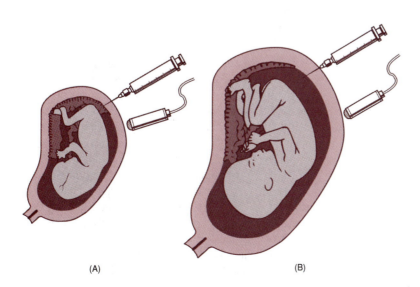

(A)   (B)

Figure 3-22
Chorionic villus sampling (CVS) and amniocentesis are procedures that extract fetal materials for culture and analysis in order to detect possible fetal disorders. In CVS, a needle is used to withdraw a portion of a fetal villus. The placement of the needle is guided by an ultrasound scanner (A). It can be performed at 8–10 weeks of gestation. In amniocentesis, the needle, guided by an ultrasound scanner, is used to extract amniotic fluid (B). It can be performed at 15–25 weeks of gestation.

Prenatal Testing.

There are several relatively safe procedures available today for pregnant women who have some reason to suspect that their gestating child may have a disorder (e.g., a family history of the disorder, the age of the mother or father, a previous child born with the disorder).

A blood test for alpha-fetoprotein (AFP) may suggest that either spina bifida or microcephaly (underdevelopment of the brain) is present if AFP levels are high. High AFP levels are not diagnostic, however: They are sometimes high with normal pregnancies. A low AFP may sometimes indicate a Down syndrome fetus. Further testing must be done after an abnormal AFP test.

An ultrasound image (sonogram) is formed when sound waves are bounced off the gestating embryo/fetus. If spina bifida or microcephaly is present, it can usually be detected by looking at a sonogram image.

Chorionic villus sampling (CVS) involves a removal of a small amount of villi (see page 81) after the eighth week of pregnancy. The villi are removed with a sterile needle. A sonogram helps the technician guide the needle to the villi. The villi, which are genetically identical to the developing embryo/fetus, can be cultured, incubated, and analyzed for possible chromosomal or recessive gene disorders. This procedure carries a slight risk of triggering a spontaneous abortion.

Amniocentesis involves a removal of a small amount of amniotic fluid (see page 81) after the fourteenth week of pregnancy. The fluid is removed with a sterile needle guided by a sonogram. The amniotic fluid is cultured, incubated, and analyzed for possible chromosomal or recessive gene disorders. This procedure can detect more abnormalities than CVS, and carries less risk of triggering an abortion, but must be postponed until the second trimester of pregnancy. An induced abortion is more dangerous at this time.

Fetoscopy involves inserting a lighted needle into the placental sac after the eighteenth week of pregnancy. The fetus can thus be inspected directly. This procedure carries a slight risk of introducing an infection to the fetus or of triggering a spontaneous abortion.

Fetal cord sampling uses fetoscopy and takes the further step of removing a small amount of the umbilical cord for analysis. It is done after the twentieth week of pregnancy. It carries a slight risk of traumatizing the fetus. Both fetoscopy and fetal cord sampling are done late in pregnancy after an induced abortion becomes a higher risk procedure.

Environmental Concerns

The influences of heredity and environment cannot be separated. From impregnation the environment provided by the mother begins to exert an influence. The genetic make-up of the organism provides a potential for functioning for any given trait in that individual. This potential may or may not then be utilized, depending on the prenatal environmental influences. One tends to think of environment as something experienced after birth, but there are many areas in which environment before birth can effect changes in the growing, developing embryo/fetus.

Uterine Condition.   The uterus of the human female is prepared for the gestation of babies monthly between the approximate ages of twelve (menarche) and fifty (menopause). During these years, hormones cause the ovaries to release one ovum per month. Hormones also cause the endometrial lining to thicken each month for the eventuality of a pregnancy. If a blastocyst fails to implant, the lining is shed as menstrual flow. While gestation is possible from menarche to menopause, the endometrium of younger fertile women (approximately 12 through 17) and that of older fertile women (approximately 35 through 50) often does not provide as optimal an exchange of wastes and nutrients. Younger and older mothers have the highest rates of stillborn infants and infants born with serious disorders. Women aged 20–29 have the lowest rates of infant death or abnormality (Bhatia, Sokol, and Pernoll, 1987). Age, as discussed on page 78, often contributes to faulty meiosis of ova and sperm. Younger and older mothers have the highest rates of infants born with chromosomal errors.

The status of a woman's uterus and Fallopian tubes for gestation may be jeopardized by sexually transmitted diseases and by pelvic infections. Chlamydia and gonorrhea most frequently cause problems with infertility or ectopic (tubal) pregnancies. These sexually transmitted diseases frequently create no symptoms in females until the infection has spread from the vagina and uterus up into the Fallopian tubes. Then, the woman may experience pelvic pain, fever, and vaginal discharge. Antibiotic therapy should be given immediately. Infected tubes can adhere together, causing infertility, or may be occluded to the extent that a fertilized ovum cannot get through, causing the blastocyst to implant in the Fallopian tube (known as an ectopic pregnancy). A single episode of pelvic inflammatory disease has been shown to cause infertility or ectopic pregnancies in 12–18% of women (Hemsell, et al., 1987).

Nutrition.   In order for the embryo/fetus to develop optimally within the uterus, the gestating mother must provide an ample supply of nutrients. It is current practice to recommend weight gains of 22–27 pounds during pregnancy (Taylor and Pernoll, 1987). Underweight mothers may be asked to gain more, while overweight mothers may be requested to gain less.

A classic study followed the children of women in Holland who were subjected to a World War II famine during their pregnancies (Stein, et al., 1975). The research suggested that poorly nourished women typically lost their babies due to the wartime famine. However, normally well-nourished healthy women gave birth to healthy babies who developed into healthy adults, despite the famine. These data led many people to assume that nutrition in pregnancy was not very important as long as a woman was healthy prior to her pregnancy. Recent research contradicts this assumption. Women who are poorly nourished during their pregnancies, especially if they are protein deficient, have a higher incidence of premature and low-birthweight babies (Taylor and Pernoll, 1987). Nearly 50% of premature and low-birthweight infants experience some learning disabilities later in life (Drillien, Thomson, and Bargoyne, 1980).

Excessive weight gain during pregnancy will not produce overly large babies. Very large babies are usually the result of maternal hormonal disorders (e.g., diabetes) or genetic factors. Babies typically account for only about one third of the weight gain in pregnancy (Taylor and Pernoll, 1987). The remainder of the weight gain can be accounted for by placenta, amniotic fluid, and extra maternal tissues and fluids (see Table 3-5).

The most important nutritional supplements for optimizing prenatal development are protein, calcium, iron, and vitamins (especially folic acid). Prenatal vitamin and mineral supplements, which contain all the recommended daily allowances, can be obtained by prescription. Megadoses of vitamins (more than recommended) may be unsafe during pregnancy (Dwyer, 1984). Vitamins should not be substituted for inadequate food intake. Pregnant women should strive to eat two or more servings each day from the four basic food groups: (1) proteins, (2) vegetables and fruits, (3) milk, and (4) breads and cereals. They do not need empty calorie foods (e.g., sugars, sodas, heavily salted snacks).

Teratogenic Drugs.   The Food and Drug Administration of the United States requires that all drugs be labeled as to their potential for causing birth defects. This potential is called *teratogenicity*. A **teratogenic drug** is any drug that can cross the placental barrier and disturb the growth and development of the embryo/fetus. *Terat* is Greek for monster and *genesis* is Greek for origin, therefore, teratogenicity refers literally to the potential for creating monsters. Most drugs have some teratogenic properties. Physicians prefer that pregnant women check with them before taking any medications.

If a drug is totally free of any human fetal risk, it is designated Category A. If it has a known fetal risk but may be given in life-threatening situations, it is designated Category D. Categories B and C are used for drugs with animal risks and possible human risks. A fifth classification, X, is used if the drug is absolutely contraindicated during pregnancy.

Pregnant women should read labels of all medicines carefully for available infor-

Table 3-5   Where Does a Mother Gain Weight During Pregnancy?

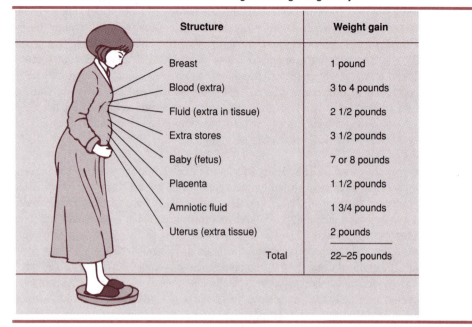

Structure	Weight gain
Breast	1 pound
Blood (extra)	3 to 4 pounds
Fluid (extra in tissue)	2 1/2 pounds
Extra stores	3 1/2 pounds
Baby (fetus)	7 or 8 pounds
Placenta	1 1/2 pounds
Amniotic fluid	1 3/4 pounds
Uterus (extra tissue)	2 pounds
Total	22–25 pounds

Reproduced, with permission, from Snowman, M. (1986). *Food and Fitness.* Syracuse: New Readers Press.

maiton on teratogenicity. They should never hesitate to call a physician if they are unsure of a medicine's safety. Many over-the-counter drugs, usually quite safe, can be very dangerous during pregnancy. Some examples are acne medications, cough syrups, laxatives, diet pills, and psoriasis preparations (see Table 3-6).

Because women can and do ask about legal drugs, they usually do not take them during pregnancies. Illegal drugs, therefore, present a much more serious teratogenic threat today. A national estimate in 1988 suggested that 11% of pregnant women in the United States use illegal drugs and that 375,000 newborns each year are damaged by such illegal drug exposure (Miller, 1989).

Leila lived in an affluent suburban area of California with Jack and Kristy. They laughed when people made the comparison between them and the characters on the TV sitcom "Three's Company." Leila and Jack were independently wealthy. Only Kristy worked, occasionally, as an actress. They used uppers (cocaine, amphetamines) and downers (barbiturates, tranquilizers) and followed the party scene. All three roommates mainstreamed (intravenously injected) their cocaine and amphetamines for quick lifts. They shared needles indiscriminately. When Leila and Jack conceived a child, they had blood tests to determine if they were HIV positive (had AIDS antibodies). Jack was positive, but Leila was negative. She decided to move away from her roommates during her pregnancy to protect the child. She continued to use uppers and downers, however. She needed them to function and to help her forget how much she missed her friends. Her baby girl was born prematurely weighing less than three pounds. She had several physical anomalies. Leila put her up for adoption, but nobody chose to adopt her defective baby. Leila's daughter remained hospitalized for two months, then was moved from foster home to foster home. At two years of age, she died of an uncorrected congenital heart defect.

Drug exposed babies are often born prematurely, with low birth weights and multiple physical anomalies, as was Leila's daughter. Illegal substance abuse during pregnancy occurs in all social and economic classes. When pregnant women seek help for their drug dependencies, they often cannot get it. A 1989 survey conducted by a U.S. Congress Select Committee reported that two out of three hospitals said that they had no place to refer substance-abusing pregnant women for treatment (Miller, 1989).

Table 3-6 lists some possible sequelae to the abuse of specific legal and illegal drugs during pregnancy. The problems are usually most pronounced if the gestating mother takes the drug during the first trimester of pregnancy, the critical period for development of all the organ systems.

Physicians do not like to prescribe sleeping pills, sedatives, or tranquilizers for pregnant women because of their teratogenic risks. However, stress also places a gestating mother and her fetus at risk. For many years, alcohol (in moderation) was considered a safe alternative to reduce anxieties during pregnancy. Now scientists have ample evidence that daily heavy use of alcohol during pregnancy can lead to fetal alcohol syndrome (FAS) (Mulvihill, 1986). Infants born with FAS are mentally retarded. They have characteristically small heads, widely spaced eyes, and flattened noses (see Box 3-7).

Total abstinence from smoking during pregnancy is now strongly advised (Sexton

Table 3-6   The Possible Teratogenic Effects of Select Drugs if Taken by Women Early in Their Pregnancies.

Drug	Effect	Source
Accutane (acne medication)	Small brain; ear defects; heart defects	*Physicians Desk Reference,* 1988
Alcohol	Learning disabilities; Fetal Alcohol Syndrome	Mulvihill, 1986
Amphetamines; many diet pills	Transposition of great vessels; cleft palate	Taylor and Pernoll, 1987
Androgenic steroids	Ambiguous genitals; females masculinized	Moore, 1988
Cocaine	Low birthweight; attention deficits	Chasnoff, et al., 1989
Cough syrup with iodine	Thyroid disorders; growth retardation	Moore, 1988
Heroin; opium products	Withdrawal symptoms in neonate	Taylor and Pernoll, 1987
LSD	Chromosomal abnormalities	Taylor and Pernoll, 1987
Marijuana	Premature delivery; low birth weight	Zuckerman et al., 1989
Methotrexate (psoriasis medication)	Multiple congenital abnormalities	Taylor and Pernoll, 1987
Nicotine	Premature delivery; low birth weight; perinatal respiratory problems	Bodde, 1984
PCP	Neonatal behavioral abnormalities	Goden, Sokol, and Rubin, 1980
Phenobarbital; many sleeping pills	Multiple congenital abnormalities	Taylor and Pernoll, 1987
Podophyllin (in many laxatives)	Multiple congenital abnormalities	Taylor and Pernoll, 1987
Streptomycin (antibiotic)	Hearing disabilities; 8th nerve damage	Warkany, 1986
Tetracycline (antibiotic)	Stained, underdeveloped dental enamel	Moore, 1988
Tranquilizers	Cardiac defects	Taylor and Pernoll, 1987

BOX
3-7

Fetal Alcohol Syndrome.

The third most common type of birth defect (after Down syndrome and spina bifida), and one that is completely preventable, is fetal alcohol syndrome (FAS). It is characterized by a thin upper lip, flat upturned nose, short, fissured eyelids, small head, growth deficiency during childhood, joint abnormalities, and, in many cases, a heart or other major organ defect. While physical appearance is unique, it is relatively minor compared to the major outcome of FAS: mental retardation (Darby, Streissguth, and Smith, 1981).

How much alcohol can a mother-to-be consume during her pregnancy without the risk of FAS and mental retardation? The answer is unknown. Chronic consumption of six or more alcoholic drinks per day places any woman at high risk. However, even regular intake of one or two ounces of absolute alcohol per day may result in FAS, especially if a woman is malnourished, smokes heavily, or uses other drugs. The danger of regular alcohol consumption is greatest during the first trimester, when fetal development of brain tissue and other vital organs is most rapid (Holzman, 1982). No "safe" lower limit for alcohol consumption at any time during pregnancy has been set (Furey, 1982). Alcohol use later in pregnancy, below that needed to produce FAS, has been associated with low arousal and poor habituation in newborn infants (Streissguth, Barr, and Martin, 1983).

and Hebel, 1984). The nicotine and carbon monoxide introduced into the blood stream through the lungs easily cross the placental barrier (see Figure 3-23). They contribute to growth retardation, postnatal respiratory problems, and learning difficulties (Bodde, 1984). They put the fetus in jeopardy of premature birth (Shiono, Klebanoff, and Rhoads, 1986). They may also put the infant in jeopardy of pre- or post-natal death.

Stress. Many women use alcohol, cigarettes, and/or tranquilizers to cope with stress. These drugs are all contraindicated during pregnancy, but stress itself can be teratogenic. Maternal stress causes activation of her central and autonomic nervous systems. The brain sends messages to the endocrine system for the release of stress hormones (e.g., epinephrine, cortisol). These in turn effect maternal bodily changes such as more rapid heart beat and breathing, more tense muscles, perspiration, and a narrowing of the blood vessels carrying blood to both the digestive organs and the uterus. The fetus, thus, has less access to the nutrients that should typically cross the placental barrier. A mother who experiences a great deal of stress throughout her pregnancy may contribute to growth retardation, prematurity, and low birthweight of her fetus. In addition, stress hormones cross the placental barrier and cause the fetus to experience more rapid heartbeat and breathing and more muscle tension. Infants born to mothers who have been stressed throughout their pregnancies may be more hyperactive in childhood and have more problems with eating and sleeping (Campbell and Werry, 1986).

Stress management can be accomplished without drugs. Exercise, good nutrition, adequate sleep, daily relaxation, decreased anger and hostility, and increased social support are several keys to coping with stress. It may, however, be difficult for some women to achieve these goals. Some pregnant women are advised to seek the help of counselors, therapists, or support groups to learn stress management, relaxation techniques, anger reduction, and/or social networking. A variety of pamphlets, books and videotapes are available that recommend specific exercise routines during pregnancy to increase cardiovascular fitness without jeopardizing the fetus. Often a daily exercise routine will also reduce insomnia and ensure a better night's sleep (see Figure 3-24).

Diseases. Women with chronic, irreversible disease conditions often have high-risk pregnancies. High-risk pregnancies are those in which mother, fetus, or newborn is, or will be, at increased risk for morbidity or mortality before or after delivery (Bhatia, Sokol, and Pernoll, 1987). Women with severe heart disease, chronic hyptertension,

1. Inhaled smoke, containing tar, nicotine, carbon monoxide, and other toxins, enters a mother's lungs via mouth and windpipe. The lungs serve as a way station where blood excretes carbon dioxide and takes in fresh oxygen.

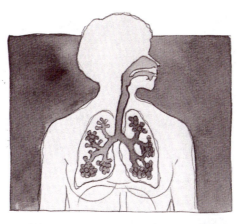

Figure 3-23
Nicotine and carbon monoxide enter a mother's lungs via mouth and windpipe (a). Inside the lungs, tobacco smoke releases nicotine and carbon monoxide into the maternal blood stream and prevents the blood from taking up enough fresh oxygen (b). Arteries and capillaries carry the mother's blood to her uterus, which holds the fetus (c). In the placenta, the mother's blood delivers nicotine and carbon monoxide to the fetus via the umbilical cord (d). Research evidence suggests that a smoking mother may deprive her fetus of the oxygen it needs for full growth.

2. Inside the lungs tobacco smoke releases small particles of toxic substances into the maternal bloodstream and prevents the blood from taking up enough fresh oxygen.

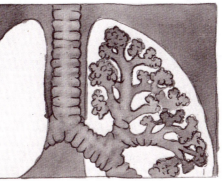

3. Arteries, arterioles, and capillaries carry the mother's blood to different organs, including her uterus, which holds the fetus (unborn baby) and placenta.

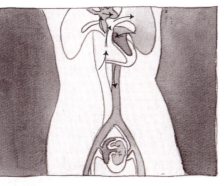

4. In the placenta the mother's blood delivers wholesome nutrients to the fetus as well as any harmful substances she eats, drinks, or inhales. The umbilical cord carries the blood to the fetus where it is distributed to its developing tissues and organs. Research evidence suggests that the higher levels of carbon monoxide in the blood of a smoking mother may deprive her fetus of the oxygen it needs for full growth.

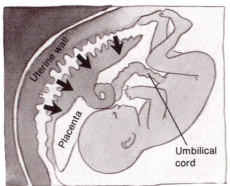

Uterine wall

Placenta

Umbilical cord

Figure 3-24
Regular mild exercise during pregnancy improves blood circulation, reduces fatigue, improves sleep, aids digestion, and plays an important role in stress management.

diabetes, sickle cell disease, cancer, or severe renal (kidney) disease are often advised to adopt children or to use a surrogate gestational mother (see page 72). If they choose to become pregnant themselves, they should be supervised closely throughout the pregnancy. The professional who provides the prenatal care may advise hospitalization during the last trimester and/or early delivery of the fetus.

Some normally healthy women develop acute diseases during their pregnancies. In general, illnesses caused by larger bacterial organisms such as streptococci (strep throats, impetigo), staphylococci (boils, conjunctivitis), or pneumococci (pneumonia) will not cross the placental barrier. The embryo/fetus is more at risk from the mother's fever than from the bacterial agents. Care must be taken to prescribe drugs for the mother that have no teratogenic properties (see page 83).

Maternal illnesses caused by viruses, or other small organisms, can and do cross the placental barrier. In some cases, viral infections that reach the embryo or fetus are fatal. They cause spontaneous abortions or stillborn infants. In other cases, they cause congenital abnormalities. Women can be immunized against several dangerous viruses before pregnancy (e.g., measles, mumps, rubella, diphtheria, tetanus, polio). An immunization against chicken pox may have been made available by the time you read this chapter. A woman who is already pregnant should not be given immunizations, since the injections contain viral materials. Many disease-producing organisms are potentially dangerous during pregnancy, especially in the first trimester (see Table 3-7). Pregnant women should avoid close contact with anyone with any acute infectious disease.

Table 3-7   Some Select Infections That Will Affect the Developing Embryo/Fetus Prenatally.

Maternal Infection	Effect on Development
Herpes simplex I (cold sores); Herpes simplex II (genital sores)	Neonatal systemic herpes; possible death
Herpes zoster (shingles); Varicella (chickenpox)	Mental retardation; visual defects; limb and digit defects; muscle atrophy
Cytomegalovirus	Deafness; mental retardation
Hepatitis	Neonatal hepatitis; possible death
Syphilis	Mental retardation; paresis
Tuberculosis	Neonatal tuberculosis; cerebral palsy
Toxoplasmosis	Spasticity of muscles; visual impairment; seizures; small brain; mental retardation

Some normally healthy women develop what is commonly called "toxemia" during their pregnancies. The medical term for toxemia is pre-eclampsia. This disease is characterized by edema (accumulation of fluid in body tissues and swelling), by high blood pressure, and by the loss of protein in the urine. It usually does not appear until the last trimester of pregnancy, and its cause is unknown (Mabie and Sibai, 1987). While physicians may restrict the salt intake of women with pre-eclampsia, it is not caused by eating too much salt. It is more common in teenage mothers, older mothers, mothers bearing their first child, and black mothers. If untreated, it may progress to eclampsia, an extreme toxic condition in which the mother has seizures. Women with pre-eclampsia are usually hospitalized to monitor their blood pressure, diet, and rest to prevent eclampsia. Drugs to lower blood pressure must be used sparingly because of possible teratogenic effects on the fetus. If the blood pressure is very difficult to control, and the fetus is old enough to survive premature birth (28 weeks or older), the usual therapy is to induce labor and delivery. Uncontrolled high blood pressure and eclampsia are life threatening to both mother and fetus.

Radiation.   High-frequency electromagnetic waves such as x-rays and ultraviolet rays are teratogenic. Rads from radiation exposure accumulate in the body where they have the potential to cause mutations of chromosomes and genes. Men and nonpregnant women should always have their gonads (testes and ovaries) covered by a lead shield during x-radiation. Pregnant women should not be x-rayed unless absolutely necessary in life-threatening situations. Radiation that reaches an embryo/fetus may cause mental retardation, growth retardation, and chromosomal injury (Brent, 1986). The severity of the damage is related to the absorbed dose, the dose rate, and the stage of embryonic or fetal development at the time of exposure. Exposure to ultraviolet radiation, as from sun lamps or natural sunlight, should also be avoided during pregnancy.

Expectant Parenthood

The news that conception has occurred and that a new human being is developing brings about heightened emotionality in both mother and father: awe, fear, hope, happiness, perhaps sadness (see Figure 3-25). Depending on special circumstances such as age, marital status, school or employment situations, or other children, expectant parenthood may require a mutlitude of changes in lifestyle. Even in situations where a baby has been desired and awaited, pregnancy creates the need for some transitions and adjustments.

The psychological factors to which expectant parents must adapt vary with the trimester of the pregnancy. In the first trimester, it is common for both mother and father to have mixed feelings about the pregnancy. The woman has to alter her self-concept to include the concept of herself as a gestational mother. She may go through a period of ambivalence about whether or not she wants to sustain a pregnancy with all its inherent risks. When she first accepts the pregnancy as a part of her self, she focuses not so much on the baby-to-be as on "my pregnancy" (Benson, 1987). She concentrates on the symptoms she may be experiencing (see Table 3-8). About 50% of women are troubled by nausea and vomiting between two and twelve weeks' gestation (Taylor and Pernoll, 1987). Drugs are contraindicated, so the mother-to-be must try to allay such symptoms with rest and frequent smaller meals of light, dry foods. Most women have some fears associated with both their mental and physical health during early pregnancy.

Fathers-to-be usually become introspective in the early months of pregnancy. They ask themselves questions such as "Can I parent?" and "What will this do to our relationship?" Many men, even experienced fathers, lack knowledge or have misinformation about pregnancy. They do not expect, or know how to cope with, the mother's symptoms of pregnancy. They may be confused as well by the mother's emotional

Figure 3-25
Many husbands take a very active role in their wives' pregnancies, participating in nutrition, stress management, exercise, and birth preparation programs. It is not unusual for them to use figures of speech such as "our" pregnancy and to mimic being pregnant too. This pride and concern can enhance both the couple's relationship and future parenting practices.

Table 3-8   Common Physical and Psychological Changes in Women Early in a Pregnancy.

Physical	Psychological
Nausea and vomiting	Mood swings
Breast enlargement and tenderness	Emotional detachment
Urinary frequency	Ambivalence about pregnancy
Constipation	Less interest in usual pursuits
Fatigue	More dependency on others

liability. These deficits in knowledge may lead them to become better informed and more nuturant towards the mother, or, conversely, they may look for ways to escape from her. Some men with unresolved dependency needs may become more demanding. They ask the pregnant woman to give them more time, more attention, and more nurturance (Osofsky, 1983).

In the second trimester, both mother and father begin to focus more on the baby than on the symptoms of pregnancy (Benson, 1987). The first perception of fetal movement occurs between fourteen and twenty weeks (Taylor and Pernoll, 1987). Feeling the baby move helps both parents focus on the fact that a new life is developing. If a sonogram is done, the parents can see the image of the child. Many parents use a stethoscope to listen to the sounds of the fetal heartbeat (see Figure 3-26). As the fetus seems more real, mothers and fathers may experience doubts and fears about their ability to care for this separate individual. They may pull together and form a tighter union in response to future parenthood, or they may experience less security about their relationship.

Women usually experience more interest in sexual intercourse in the middle of a pregnancy (Benson, 1987). Men may fear that sex will jeopardize the pregnancy. Alternately, they may believe that a pregnant woman is not a proper object of sexual desire. In fact, sexual intercourse is safe and can help sustain a more nurturant relationship between prospective parents. Abstinence can increase friction and lead to resentment of the future baby.

In the third trimester, the mother usually feels less attractive and more uncomfortable with her abdominal enlargement. She may experience problems with balance and coordination. She may notice stretch marks on her breasts and abdomen and/or varicose veins on her legs. The expanded uterus squeezes other abdominal organs so she may have heartburn, shortness of breath, and a frequent need to urinate. Both parents begin to hope the baby will be early, not late.

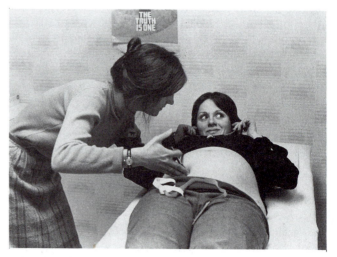

Figure 3-26
Hearing a fetal heartbeat helps expectant parents accept the reality that a separate individual is growing and developing within the gestating mother.

Birth

Approximately 266 days after conception, the new human being is ready to emerge into the outside world. Most obstetricians give mothers-to-be an expected due date, or EDC (expected day of confinement), figured from the last menstrual period by means of Nägele's rule. Seven days are added to the first day of the last menstrual period. Then three months are subtracted from this date. For example, if Mrs. K.'s last period began October 13, adding seven days would bring one to October 20, and subtracting three months would bring one to July 20. Mrs. K.'s due date would then be given as July 20. Only a very small fraction of women actually deliver on their due dates. Most deliver within ten to fifteen days before or after the estimated date.

The uterine contractions that expel the fetus and the placenta are known as labor. Labor differs for every woman and with every succeeding child, so statements about what it is like are at best generalizations. Jacklin and Maccoby (1982) reported that the length of labor for mothers giving birth to boys is longer than that for mothers giving birth to girls. The average length of labor for a first child is thirteen hours; for subsequent children, it is eight hours. Labors lasting twenty-four to thirty-six hours and precipitous deliveries that occur on the way to the hospital are not uncommon.

Mild contractions called **Braxton–Hicks contractions** occur throughout pregnancy, preparing the uterus for its eventual task of expelling the fetus and placenta. They are painless early in pregnancy but may be felt as "false labor" toward term. These contractions may begin thinning out and enlarging the uterine floor prior to actual labor. False labor may also accompany the dropping of the baby's head into the brim of the pelvis. This is variously known as "lightening," "settling," or "dropping" (see Figure 3-27). With first babies it may occur as much as two weeks before labor. Lightening usually makes a pregnant woman feel more comfortable and allows a greater range of motion. Since the pressure on her diaphragm is relieved, she can breathe more easily.

As the baby's head presses down on the uterine floor, **dilation** and **effacement**

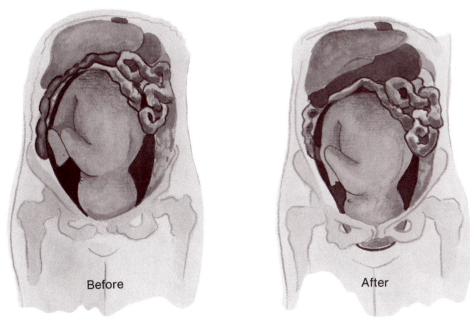

Before   After

Engagement of the head late in pregnancy
(known as lightening, settling, or dropping)

Figure 3-27
When the baby's head descends into the pelvis, the mother feels some relief from the pressure on her abdominal organs.

Figure 3-28
Effacement and dilation of the
cervix in the first stages of labor.

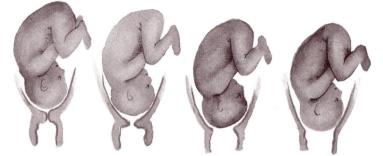

occur. The pressure against the opening to the uterus (the cervix) causes it to *dilate* (enlarge) and *efface* (thin out). As this happens, a mucous plug, which has been keeping the cervix closed during pregnancy, is expelled. It is frequently streaked with blood and is referred to as the "bloody show." Real labor usually begins after the mucous plug is discharged and when the cervix begins dilating and effacing more rapidly (see Figure 3-28).

Stages of Labor

There are four stages of labor. In the first stage the cervix effaces and dilates until it is wide enough (usually around four inches, or ten centimeters, or five fingers) to allow the baby's head to pass into the vagina. In the second stage the baby emerges from the vagina. In the third stage the placenta (or afterbirth) is expelled. The fourth stage is the immediate postpartum period.

Presentations

Presentations refer to how the fetus is positioned during delivery. In about 96% of pelvic deliveries the top of the skull (vertex) comes out first. If the spine of the fetus is adjacent to the abdomen of the mother, the head descends in an *anterior lie*. If the spine of the fetus is to the left or right side, the head descends in a *transverse*

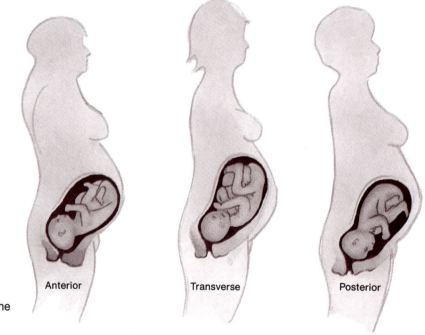

Anterior   Transverse   Posterior

Figure 3-29
Commonly seen positions of the
fetus in the uterus.

lie. With anterior or transverse lies the back part of the skull emerges first, which is the easiest way for it to pass the pubic arch bones. If the spine of the fetus is lined up against the spine of the mother, the head descends in a *posterior lie.* The posterior position often causes the mother to experience more back pain during labor. (See Figure 3-29.)

The bones of the fetal skull are not yet completely formed. The membrane-covered spaces between the bones allow the bones to overlap each other slightly. This overlap process is known as **molding.**

Fetuses who do not emerge with the top of their skulls first may present with their brow, their face, their shoulder, or in a breech (buttocks or feet first) position (see Figure 3-30).

Brow, face, shoulder, and breech presentations are difficult because the diameter of each of these presenting parts is too large to slip through the pelvic arch. Usually the baby is delivered surgically through an incision made through the abdomen and uterus of the mother (**Caesarean section**).

Aids to Delivery

Analgesics help the laboring mother relax and lose her sensitivity to the pain of the uterine contractions. Anesthesia takes away all the sensations either by putting the mother to sleep (general inhalation anesthesia) or by deadening the sensations in a portion of her body (regional or local anesthesia).

Some anesthesia must be used for Caesarean section deliveries. Once uncommon (4% of deliveries in the 1950s), "C-section" births are now rising precipitously. Brody (1981) reports that in some hospitals they constitute about 40% of deliveries, whereas the overall percentage of deliveries by Caesarean in 1980 was 18%. This increase reflects many physicians' desire to deliver the baby as quickly as possible if any signs of fetal distress occur.

All anesthetic agents share a common hazard. They can be transmitted across the placental membrane to the fetus. This transmission can contribute to a drowsy infant at birth who may have difficulty initiating his or her own respiration. Failure to initiate respirations can lead to **anoxia** (severe deficiency of oxygen in the tissues). Without oxygen, brain tissue can be damaged or destroyed. Other negative outcomes associated with anesthetics include alternations in heart rate and abnormal patterns of sleep and wakefulness (Broman, 1983). The baby may also have trouble feeding in the first two to three days after delivery. Some evidence exists that the effects of anoxia at birth may be long lasting. Hollenbeck and colleagues (1984) found that both smiling and infant–parent touching were diminished at one month when labor medication doses produced a depressed neonate. Inhalation anesthetics especially are associated with

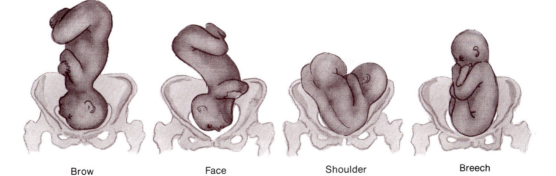

Brow   Face   Shoulder   Breech

Figure 3-30
Atypical presentations of the fetus.

poor neuromotor and psychomotor functioning throughout the first year (Broman, 1983). The American Academy of Pediatrics (1978) recommended that obstetricians administer the lowest effective doses of safe obstetric medications during labor.

The use of anesthesia during labor may necessitate the use of obstetrical **forceps,** tongs that fit over the head of a fetus and grasp it without compressing it. They are used if a mother loses her ability to push the fetus out due to the effects of medication or exhaustion. Forceps frequently leave marks showing where they were placed on the infant's head, but such marks disappear in a few days.

Many women have an **episiotomy** during delivery. In this procedure a straight cut is made from the vagina back toward the anus but slightly to one side to enlarge the vaginal opening just before the head delivers. A straight cut is easier to sew up and heals better than a ragged-edged tear. An episiotomy also gives the baby more room to get out.

Allowing the mother to assume a squatting position during her labor reduces the pain of contractions and allows the best relaxation and optimum stretch of the perineal muscles. It is also a good posture to help the rotation of the fetus's head inside the pelvis. Many hospitals now have birthing chairs, which allow the mother to be supported in a vertical, semi-squat posture during contractions. Other maternity units allow laboring women to find for themselves a posture in which they are most comfortable during contractions, whether a squat, a kneeling position, or simply bending forward.

Natural childbirth is the delivery of an infant without the use of anesthetics or instrumentation. Prepared childbirth refers to the fact that the mother (and usually a partner, such as the father) has been educated beforehand about the physiology of pregnancy, knows what to expect during labor and delivery, and has been taught perineal muscle-building exercises, relaxation techniques, breathing mechanisms, and comfort aids to assist in the birth (see Figure 3-31). In the United States such preparation usually comes from a series of six to eight evening meetings conducted in the **Lamaze method of delivery** or the Grantly Dick-Read method. Prepared childbirth encourages parents to experience birth together. It discourages the mother from relying on drugs, although it does not necessarily mean drugless labor. Use of drugs may be initiated at the discretion of the doctor or midwife (a nurse specially trained to help women in childbirth).

The **LeBoyer method of delivery** was developed to reduce fetal birth trauma. The delivery room is kept dark and quiet. Sometimes soft music is played. The newborn is immediately immersed in warm water to simulate amniotic fluid. Then the infant is gently stroked and massaged as it adjusts to the external world. Finally, the neonate is put to the mother's breast while she is still in the delivery room, to facilitate an immediate bonding between mother and child. The father is also encouraged to be present and to participate in holding, bathing, cuddling, and stroking his newborn.

Evidence exists that the presence of the father, or some other companion, to support a mother during labor and delivery has many beneficial effects. Kennell (1982), in a comparative study of twenty mothers with and without a supportive companion during labor, found that labor was shortened a mean time of ten hours for mothers with support. In addition, the supported mothers remained awake longer after delivery and stroked, talked to, and smiled at their infants more.

Possible Birth Difficulties

Precipitous (sudden or abrupt) deliveries can be dangerous to the fetus, as can prolonged labors and premature or low-birth-weight deliveries.

A **precipitous delivery** is dangerous to the fetus because the skull bones are compressed rapidly rather than molding gradually. This can cause tears in the membranous coverings of the brain. Another danger of precipitous labor is that the fetus may be born unattended. Such labors last less than three hours.

With **prolonged labor** (over twenty-four hours) the fetus runs the risk of acquiring an infection, suffocating, or sustaining brain damage from insufficient oxygenation.

Figure 3-31
Lamaze classes, or similar childbirth preparation classes, increase parental support and perception of control as well as provide information about the last weeks of pregnancy and the labor and delivery process.

Obstetricians may provide rest for the mother with weak contractions in order to improve them, may stimulate contractions with drugs, or may perform a Caesarean section to deliver the infant.

Preterm infants (born before thirty-seven weeks) are now differentiated from low-birth-weight (less than five and a half pounds or 2500 grams) infants. Small-for-gestational-age (SGA) infants have weight inappropriate for gestational age, whether born before thirty-seven weeks or at term. These variables, while given separate definitions, may occur in the same baby. These infants have respiratory problems, poor temperature control, limited nutrient deposits, difficulties with sucking and swallowing, poor resistance to infection, fragile blood vessels that may hemorrhage, poor kidney function, and poor liver functioning. Factors associated with low birth weight, preterm delivery, and SGA include youthfulness or agedness of the mother, maternal prenatal infections, maternal prenatal drug abuse, malnutrition, or emotional traumas during pregnancy. Saco-Pollitt (1981) found that high-altitude living (14,000 feet above sea level) also contributes to low birth weight. Infants born with low birth weights may also have a genetic inheritance for small size. Whatever the reason for their size, these babies need extra warmth, nutrition, protection, and possible assistance with cardiac and respiratory functioning.

Summary

The uterus of the mother is the primary prenatal environment. The progress of prenatal development depends on the interactions of the genetic materials inherited from each parent. The ovum and sperm divide by meiosis as they mature and become haploid cells, with only half the normal complement of chromosomes. Conception of a new human being occurs with the union of one ovum with one sperm. This union produces one new cell with chromosomes inherited from each parent. This new cell proceeds to divide again and again, by mitosis, reproducing other cells, each carrying the same genetic materials inherited from the parents. The period of growth and development in the uterus lasts for nine months. In the germinal period implantation occurs, and the cells differentiate. In the embryonic period all the vital organs form and the embryo acquires a distinctly human appearance. For the remainder of the prenatal period, the baby-to-be is called a fetus, and all the structures grow and mature.

While the norm is for fetuses to survive the nine prenatal months and emerge as healthy full-term infants, some imperfections do occur. Down, Klinefelter, and

Turner syndromes are examples of problems caused by chromosomal defects. Huntington's disease, Tay-Sachs disease, and sickle-cell anemia are examples of problems caused by genetic defects. Rh and ABO incompatibility diseases also have a genetic link.

The embryo/fetus also can be harmed by teratogenic factors in the mother's environment, such as poor nutrition, many drugs, alcohol abuse, stress, infections, and radiation.

Expectant parenthood requires transitions and adjustments for both parents. These transitions vary across stages of pregnancy and according to unique individuals anticipating parenthood.

At the end of nine months the fetus is ready to emerge into the external world as a unique individual. The contractions that push the baby out are called labor. Most babies are expelled head first. The average length of labor for a first child is thirteen hours, and for subsequent children it is eight hours. If either the fetus or mother has problems that might interfere with a normal vaginal delivery, the baby may be delivered by surgery through the abdomen of the mother (Caesarean section).

Considering the enormously complicated process from formation of mature haploid ova and sperm to fertilization to implantation to delivery of a full-term baby, it is amazing that normal infants are the rule, not the exception. Never again in the life span will growth and change be quite as rapid or quite as comprehensive.

Key Concepts

uterus	zygote	placenta	molding
ovulation	centromere	villi	Caesarean section
estrogens	crossing over	embryonic period	anoxia
progesterone	alleles	fetal period	forceps
Graafian follicle	autosomes	placental barrier	episiotomy
corpus luteum	sex chromosomes	antigens	Lamaze delivery
spermatogenesis	morula	Rh factor	LeBoyer delivery
chromosomes	blastocyst	teratogenic drugs	precipitous delivery
genes	endometrium	Braxton-Hicks contractions	prolonged labor
androsperm	germinal period	dilation	
gynosperm	implantation	effacement	

Questions for Review

1. Outline the fertilization process by stating what, where, when, and how it occurs.
2. Cystic fibrosis is inherited as a recessive condition. If a couple, neither of whom has cystic fibrosis, give birth to a child with cystic fibrosis, what ratio of children also affected would be expected among their subsequent offspring?
3. Many women have diets that consist of high amounts of carbohydrates and low amounts of protein. Discuss what effects this kind of diet may have on a developing fetus.
4. Write a short letter persuading a friend to give up smoking during her pregnancy. Give her reasons for doing so.
5. How do teratogens reach the embryo/fetus?
6. What are typical concerns of expectant parents over the course of the three trimesters of pregnancy?

Further Readings

Brown, J. E. (1983). *Nutrition for your pregnancy: The University of Minnesota Guide.* Minneapolis: University of Minnesota Press.
  Scientifically up-to-date information about nutrition and its effects on maternal and fetal health based on years of research at the University of Minnesota and elsewhere.

Ewy, D., and Ewy, R. (1982). *Preparation for childbirth: A Lamaze guide.* Boulder, CO: Pruett.
  A guide to prepared childbirth written for the lay reader in simple terms without sacrificed detail or accuracy. Illustrated with multiple photographs and line drawings.

Nilsson, L. (1990). *A child is born: The completely new edition.* New York: Delacorte Press.
Sensational photographs of prenatal development by the Swedish photographer, Lennart Nilsson, with accompanying text by Lars Hamberger.

Tilton, N., Tilton, T., and Moore, G. (1985). *Making miracles: In vitro fertilization.* New York: Doubleday.
A comprehensive coverage of the in vitro process told through the eyes of a couple who experienced it.

Todd, W. D., and Tapley, D. F. (eds.) (1988). *The Columbia University College of Physicians and Surgeons complete guide to pregnancy.* New York: Crown.
Several physicians collaborated to produce an articulate, easy-to-read account of conception, prenatal development, pregnancy lifestyle considerations, diets, exercise, and health maintenance recommendations. Includes a complete glossary of medical terms.

Infancy

4

The miracle of birth . . . the wonder of postnatal development—the awe of infancy. Growth and development in infancy is only exceeded by the rapidity of prenatal change. The much-touted adolescent growth spurt pales in comparison with growth in the first year of life: Weight triples, length doubles, the brain doubles its birth weight (Sinclair, 1978). The helpless neonate becomes a walking baby. Language changes from cries to understandable speech.

The word infant derives from the Latin "infans," which literally translates to "without language." Infants can, however, communicate feelings and thoughts through cries and coos (a language of sorts). A disproportionate amount of the research on human development has focused on infancy, because there are so many wondrous changes occurring. We will try to capture some of the excitement of infancy in this chapter.

A favorable ratio of basic trust over basic distrust is the first step in psychosocial adaptation.
—*Erik Erikson*

If you approach people with trust and affection, you will have a ten-fold trust and affection returned to you.
—*Gandhi*

Physical Development

The brain, heart, and lungs of a neonate are mature enough to make extrauterine life possible at birth, although many other organ systems are still quite immature. They undergo rapid changes during infancy, resulting in a metamorphosis from a totally dependent, reflex-bound neonate to a toddling, talking, thinking child. Let us examine the physiological status of the neonate first. This will provide a base from which to compare the physical growth and development that take place in the months of infancy.

Physical Status of the Neonate

The term **neonate** refers to an infant from birth through the first month of life. The term **neonatorium** refers to the first month of life. At birth the infant must literally conform to a whole new world. The era of floating in a warm amniotic sac filled with fluid, and of having all the necessities of life supplied through the umbilical cord, ends. The transition from intrauterine to extrauterine existence requires many adaptations (see Figure 4-1).

Transitional Changes. Survival of newborns requires that circulation be transferred from the umbilical cord to the heart. First the cord is "stripped." This means that the doctor or midwife pushes all the extra blood and nutrients from the cord toward

Steveland was born in 1950 with about the same visual acuity as most infants, although he was born prematurely. In order to help him maintain normal body temperature, protect him from infections, and prevent the respiratory distress that is common in premature infants, he was placed in an incubator. Oxygen was then added to the total space within the incubator to enrich the air the baby breathed. The extra oxygen affected all body tissues, not just the lungs, including the retinal tissue of the eyes. It caused destruction to the retina known as *retrolental fibroplasia*. This happened to many premature babies in the 1950s. It happened to Steveland. The damage to his eyes was extensive and permanent. His blindness could not be reversed.

Steveland's mother was a religious woman. She at first sought out faith healers and prayer groups to help restore her infant son's sight. Eventually she came to accept the handicap as a gift from God rather than as something that needed correcting. She concentrated on helping Steveland accept his blindness. He reported, "My mother taught me never to feel sorry for myself, because handicaps are really things to be used, another way to benefit yourself and others in the long run."*

Blind infants learn to see the world through their other senses: hearing, touch, taste, and smell. Steveland's family members were instrumental in helping him develop his sense of hearing. They expected him to do the things other people do by using sound instead of vision. He not only learned to recognize people by their voices but to discern their moods by their tones of voice. He sang everywhere, including on neighbors' porches. One lucky day, a professional singer heard Steveland and asked his parents' permission to take him to a recording studio for an audition. The president of the record company hired Steveland on the spot. Steveland became "Little Stevie Wonder" at age ten. The rest of Steveland's history is well known. Despite his busy schedule as a recording star, Stevie Wonder has given countless hours to working with children, especially those with handicaps.

Would Stevie's musical talents have developed to the same extent so early in his life if he had been sighted? Did Stevie Wonder's parents help him or hinder him by asking him to do so much for himself despite his blindness?

*Haskins, J. (1976). *The Story of Stevie Wonder*. New York: William Morrow.

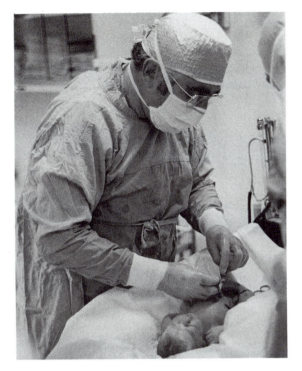

Figure 4-1
The transition from intrauterine to extrauterine life is a giant step for a neonate. Breathing and blood circulation are transferred from mother to baby as the umbilical cord is severed.

the baby's body. Then the cord is clamped shut close to the infant's abdomen. Finally, the cord is cut between the clamp and the placenta (afterbirth). The cord stump remaining on the baby dries up and falls off in one or two weeks. The umbilical site heals to form the navel. Two heart openings, present prenatally, now close. The *ductus arteriosus*, which is a shunt between the aorta and the pulmonary artery, obliterates by about age three months. The *foramen ovale*, which is the connection between the right and left atria of the heart, functionally closes with a flap by the first week of life, although it may not obliterate completely until much later (Wolfe and Wiggins, 1984).

Survival of newborns also requires that the exchange of oxygen and carbon dioxide be transferred from the placenta to the lungs. Respiratory reflexes become activated within seconds after birth. Infants usually breathe spontaneously and cry, thereby allowing full expansion of their lungs with air. However, if the respiratory passages are blocked with amniotic fluid, breathing will be impaired. For this reason babies are held upside down after delivery, allowing fluid to drain out. Some hospitals also routinely suction the respiratory tracts of newborns to hasten free breathing. The belief that the doctor or nurse must slap the baby to start it crying is false. Spanking, back slapping, or immersing the baby in cold water can be dangerous. Instead, the newborn's heels are flicked or tapped lightly. If infants do not begin to breathe within sixty seconds of birth, resuscitation measures may be instituted to prevent cell damage or death from lack of oxygen (called *anoxia*). The demands of the neonate's brain for oxygen are huge. The blood vessels that supply the brain with oxygen are still quite fragile. In addition, the muscular support system for the head is weak. Consequently, the baby's head must be supported carefully.

Survival of the neonate requires that warmth be provided in the period immediately following birth. The temperature-regulating mechanism of the nervous system is not yet sufficiently mature to allow the baby to shiver or sweat to raise or lower temperature. Also, the intrauterine environment is much warmer than room temperature. The fetus was accustomed to an environment of 98.6° F. The baby finds it easier to breathe when warm. Therefore, in hospitals, infants are dried and placed in warm bassinets or carriers as soon as respirations are established and the cord is clamped. Many times stockinette caps are put on the infants' heads to help retain body heat.

The neonate is seldom very hungry immediately following delivery. First feedings are either sweetened water or colostrum. **Colostrum** is a sweet, thin fluid that is produced by the breast for two to three days before milk comes in. Milk is generally not tolerated well for a day or two, although it then becomes the only necessary source of nutrients for the first few months of infancy.

Sleep is the infant's major activity throughout the first few weeks of life. Some babies stay awake for an hour and a half before their first sleep; others fall asleep after delivery and do not wake up fully until the second or third day.

Appearance.   Right after birth, the neonate is seldom as cute as new parents expect. Neonates like to stay curled up in fetal posture. In the first hours of life, the skin may appear wrinkled. Imagine how your skin looks shortly after you have been swimming, or soaking in a tub. The neonate, remember, was floating in amniotic fluid for nine months. The head appears huge. It is approximately one fourth of the total body length (Sinclair, 1978). However, with the arms and legs curled up, the head often seems to be nearly half the total body length. The head may also be misshapen from molding or have forceps marks from a forceps-assisted delivery. While most babies have very little head hair, some babies may have abundant hair, extending beyond the head onto the back and shoulders. Neonates also have fine body hair called **lanugo**. During the prenatal period, the fetus was covered with a waxy substance, called **vernix caseosa**, to protect the skin. Splotches of this waxy vernix may remain on the neonate, sometimes causing the baby to look as if he or she has been dusted with flour (see Figure 4-2.)

The birth attendant adds to the neonate's less-than-adorable appearance by adding an umbilical clamp (or tie, or band) to the navel and by instilling silver nitrate or antibiotic drops into the eyes to protect against infection. The eye drops often cause the neonate's eyelids to become swollen and red for a day or two. Maternal hormones that crossed the placental barrier prenatally cause swollen breasts and genitals in both male and female neonates. When the neonate cries hard, one can see pulsations of the blood vessels on the **soft spots** on the head (Gill, 1987). The soft spots are the spaces where the skull bones remained open prenatally to allow the head to mold during delivery (see p. 103). The lateral spaces (see Figure 4-3) close right after birth. The posterior fontanelle closes at about two months and the anterior fontanelle (commonly called "the soft spot") closes between ten and fourteen months after birth (Silver, 1984).

The neonate usually flushes very red when crying. Dark-skinned parents may be

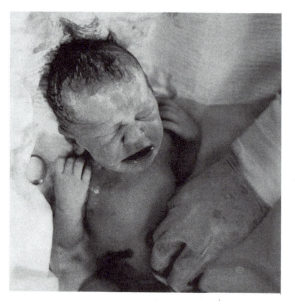

Figure 4-2
A healthy newborn may appear to have been dusted with flour. White splotches of vernix caseosa contrast with the deep flush that develops when a baby cries.

Figure 4-3
Schematic representation of sutures and fontanelles (soft spots) of a neonate's skull.

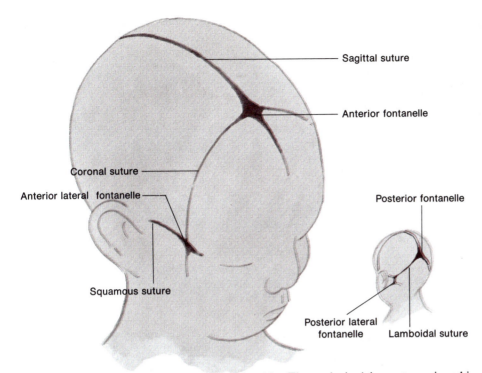

surprised to see that their neonate has light skin. The melanin (pigment causing skin color) develops to a greater extent after birth. Most neonates have smoky grey-blue colored irises in their eyes for a short period after birth. The iris pigments also lack melanin but will eventually develop into a final eye color during infancy.

Many new parents are afraid to hold their neonates for fear they will break. In fact, most of the bones of a neonate have not yet undergone **ossification** (change from cartilage to bone). The bones that ossify prenatally are those that protect the neonates' vital organs: skull, vertebrae, sternum, ribs (see Figure 4-4). The shafts of the bones of the arms, legs, fingers, and toes have started to ossify, but they are not yet joined to each other except by cartilage.

Physiologic jaundice, a yellow coloration of the skin and of the sclera (white area) of the eyes, appears in about one-third of full-term neonates in the first three days of life (Koops and Battaglia, 1984). It is caused by the presence of high levels of bilirubin (a bile pigment that is a breakdown product of fetal hemoglobin) in the bloodstream. It usually disappears by one week of age, at which time the infant's liver has developed the ability to metabolize the bilirubin, allowing its excretion. If the bilirubin level climbs too high, the neonate may be placed under full-spectrum lights (phototherapy), which enhances the breakdown of bilirubin. The baby's eyes must be covered for their protection if phototherapy is used.

Visual acuity is poor in the newborn: A neonate can see at 20 feet what an adult with normal visual acuity can see approximately at 300 feet (Banks and Salapatek, 1983).

Eye muscles are weak and the eyes may occasionally drift to a crossed or wall-eyed position. Visual focus is fairly rigid, and the neonate will see objects best if they are from 9 to 20 inches from the eyes, the distance the mother's face is from the baby when she is breast-feeding.

Hearing develops in the uterus, where the fetus is exposed to the sounds of the mother's heartbeat, intestinal rumblings, and blood flow. The neonate will turn to sounds immediately after birth and often sleeps more peacefully when background noises are present. For this reason many newborn nurseries play a tape or record of the "Lullaby of the Womb."

Taste and smell are both present at birth. Neonates seem to prefer the smell of

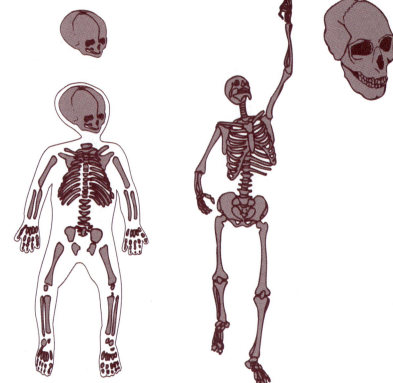

Figure 4-4
Ossification of the skeleton of a neonate. The vital organs are protected by ossified bone. The limbs are still predominantly cartilage. Compare this with the ossified skeleton of an adult here and on Plate 1 in the center of the text.

their own mothers (Russell, 1976) and by six days of age, if breast-fed, prefer the taste of their own mother's milk (Cernoch and Porter, 1985). They prefer sweet tastes (Crook, 1978) and will purse their lips, turn their heads, and grimace to sour or bitter tastes (Steiner, 1979).

The lips of neonates are their most sensitive areas of touch. This is why they root with their lips to find food (see Figure 4-5) and probably why Freud called the first psychosexual stage of life the oral stage (see Chapter 2, p. 33).

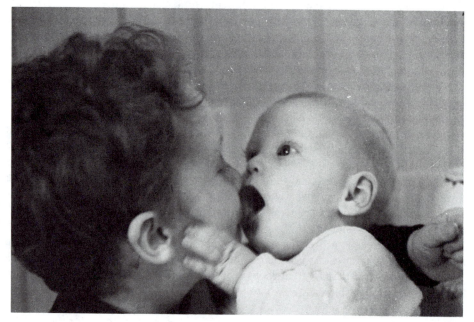

Figure 4-5
To root means to poke around in order to find something. The rooting reflex of human infants leads to a turning of nose and mouth in the direction of any facial touch. This may lead to food or to other novel encounters.

Assessment.   Within one minute of the neonate's extrauterine existence, he or she must pass a first test. Failure of this examination, called the Apgar, means going to a special neonatal intensive care unit rather than to a shared room with "Mom" or to the regular newborn nursery. If you were born after 1958, you probably also had this first examination of your life.

The **Apgar evaluation** is a scale for assessing the state of the neonate at one minute post-partum and again after five minutes. It evaluates five conditions: heartbeat, respiratory effort, muscle tone, reflex irritability, and color; with a score of 0, 1, or 2 each (see Table 4-1). Infants with total scores from 0–4 need emergency measures to keep them alive. Infants with scores from 5–7 need some help to improve their vital signs. Infants with scores of 8–10 are considered healthy. Infants who score less than 6 after five minutes are usually taken to intensive care nurseries.

After hospital delivery, the neonate is cared for by members of the pediatric staff while the birth attendant continues to care for the mother. The neonate gets a full physical examination within the first day of life. Hospitalization following delivery of a normal infant is seldom more than 6–36 hours unless the mother had a C-section. In this case, both mother and neonate may remain hospitalized 4–5 days. Before discharge, the neonate is given a discharge examination. Often today this includes the **Brazelton Neonatal Behavioral Assessment Scale (NBAS).** Brazelton (1973) developed this relatively simple procedure to assess the baby's behavioral repertoire with 20 reflex items and 27 items that relate to response to stress, ability to control state, motor capabilities, and information processing. The NBAS is useful for identifying babies who are in need of special care or attention and for discussing infant responses with parents.

A modification of the NBAS was developed by Als, Brazelton, and other colleagues (1982) to assess preterm infants. Called the Assessment of Preterm Infant Behavior (APIB), it examines a series of interactions between the observer and the preterm infant to determine the preterm's abilities to organize and integrate behaviors.

Another new form of neonatal assessment is brain electrical activity mapping (BEAM). It utilizes neurological techniques that have been available for years, the electroencephalogram and sensory evoked potentials, and makes the data more visible with computerized tomographic mapping. An extension of BEAM, called significance probability mapping (SPM), can be used to delineate regions of difference between two BEAM images. This neurophysiological technique may make it possible to distinguish between neurologically normal and abnormal neonates in the first three days of life (Duffy, Burchfiel, and Lombroso, 1979).

Reflexes are involuntary actions. Several reflex behaviors are innate in healthy human infants. If they cannot be elicited, or are weak, the infant must be evaluated

Table 4-1   The Apgar Scoring Method.

Sign	0	1	2
Heart rate	Absent	Below 100	Over 100
Respiratory effort	Absent	Minimal; weak cry	Good: strong cry
Muscle tone	Limp	Some flexion of extremities	Active motion; extremities well flexed
Reflex irritability (response to stimulation on sole of foot)	No response	Grimace	Cry
Color	Blue or pale	Body pink; extremities blue	Pink

SOURCE: From Virginia Apgar, *Anesthesia and Analgesia*, 32:260, 1953. Reprinted by permission.

Table 4-2 Some Reflex Activities of Neonates.

Reflex	Description
Rooting	Directing mouth toward source of any facial stimulation and beginning sucking movements.
Sucking	Plying the tongue and lips to take in food or liquid to the back of the mouth.
Swallowing	Muscle movements of the throat allowing food or liquid to pass from the mouth to the esophagus.
Coughing	Expelling air from the lungs suddenly with an explosive sound.
Sneezing	A sudden, violent, spasmodic, and audible expiration of breath.
Blinking	Quickly closing, then opening, the eyelids.
Smiling	Turning lips upward in happy expression.
Grasping	Very tight contraction of hand muscles around an object, allowing neonate to support own weight.
Moro	Swinging arms and legs out, then rapidly back in, to hug oneself into a curled ball.
Babinski	Toe fanning up and out in response to foot stroking.
Head turning	Moving face to left or right to free airway when placed face down on surface.
Crying	Making a loud and plaintive calling sound.
Tonic neck	Extending arm and leg to side in fencing posture when head is turned to side.

further to discover why. Table 4-2 presents several reflex behaviors normally seen in infants. Most of them have some life-preserving function. Rooting, for example, helps an infant find food (see Figure 4-5). The sucking and swallowing reflexes help the baby ingest the food thus found. The grasping reflex helps to assure that the baby will not fall if dropped. The smile reflex and the cry reflex both serve to gain and maintain the presence of caregivers.

Perhaps the simplest way to assess a neonate's status is to listen to his or her cry. Zeskind and Lester (1978) demonstrated that biological differences between normal and abnormal neonates can be detected with spectrographic analyses of cry features, even in babies who show no other abnormal physical, behavioral, or neurological signs (see Box 4-1).

Behaviors.   The neonate is a unique individual at birth. While infants, in general, can be described in terms of behavioral states present after birth, each infant develops his or her own rhythms and response patterns.

The neonate spends the majority of the day either eating or sleeping. Both breast- and bottle-fed infants tend to suck more slowly in the first few days than they will later, as sucking becomes more proficient (Pollitt, Consolazio, and Goodkin, 1981). They also take many pause intervals between bursts of sucking behavior. Their digestive tracts are not fully developed, and digestion requires a tremendous expenditure of energy. Some neonates seem to need to rest several times during each feeding cycle. Newborns who are affected by obstetrical medications given the mother during labor may have weak sucking responses and be especially slow feeders (Brackbill, 1979). The pauses between feeding intervals are often a time for rapt staring at the parent by the neonate and some form of parental response (e.g., smiling, talking, singing). These behaviors are important to early bonding of parent and infant (see Figure 4-6).

The sleep states of neonates range from regular sleep, in which the infant is at full rest, to periodic sleep, in which the infant has bursts of rapid, shallow breathing interspersed with deep slow respirations, to irregular sleep, in which the infant has irregular breathing, facial grimaces, limb movements, and rapid eye movements. These

Figure 4-6
A rapt stare between parent and infant during feeding or play is a form of entrapment, causing each to fall more in love with the other.

BOX
4-1

What's in a Neonate's Cry?

Zeskind (1980) asked parents to report what response they would make to neonates that they heard crying on tape. Some of the cries were of normal infants, others were of high-risk infants. Parents consistently responded with tender and caring behaviors for "sick" sounding cries and with behaviors that would effectively terminate crying for "distressing" and "urgent" sounding cries. No parent chose a "'wait and see" or "give a pacifier" response for the cry of a high-risk neonate. The urgent, distressing, sick sounds are functional in eliciting appropriate caregiving behaviors.

When the cries of normal and high-risk neonates are subjected to sound analysis using a spectrograph, a machine that can plot the threshold, latency, activity, and frequency of cries, the differences heard by students, parents, and everyone else can clearly be seen. Neonates who appear "normal" on routine physical and neurological examinations may be spotted by spectrum analysis to really be "at risk."

The cries of malnourished infants are harder to elicit, are shorter in duration, and contain more high-pitched sounds than the cries of normal infants (Zeskind, 1983). Different types of cries can signal different risks. Down syndrome babies, for example, tend to have

unusually low-pitched cries. There are indications that infants at risk for sudden infant death syndrome may also produce low-pitched cries. Preterm babies produce "urgent" high-pitched cries. Babies exposed to narcotics prenatally give characteristically short first cry expirations (Huntington, Hans, and Zeskind, 1990).

Adult listeners are aroused by high-pitched cries. While the initial effect is fuctional and produces caregiving, over time the effect may be paradoxical. An aroused adult may feel inadequate, frustrated, and hostile toward the crying baby, especially if all attempts to soothe the infant fail. There is some evidence that high-pitched crying may be associated with later parental abuse.

Could a parent intervention program for preterm neonates with high-pitched cry sounds reduce the risk of eventual abuse? Zeskind and Iacino (1984) began a program to help mothers of hospitalized high-risk neonates increase their contact and familiarity with their babies and develop more realistic expectations for their behaviors. Unexpectedly, this intervention had another positive effect. It faciliatated the recovery and reduced the hospitalization time of the preterm high-pitched-crying neonates in the study.

rapid eye movements (REM) signal a special kind of sleep state (REM sleep) in which dreams occur. Infants spend approximately 50% of their time in REM sleep, compared to adults, who spend about 20% of their sleep time in the REM state (Roffwarg, Muzio, and Dement, 1966).

The awake behaviors of neonates range from drowsiness, to alert inactivity, to alert activity (moving the body, head, or limbs), to crying. The cry sounds of each human neonate are usually very successful elicitors of adult behaviors. Untrained adults who are inexperienced with infants and who have had no lessons on the meanings of cry sounds seem to have an intuitive sense of what to do for a crying baby (Zeskind and Lester, 1978).

Duane signed up for a Child Development course at his college to please his girlfriend. His professor asked him to participate in a research project that involved listening to a baby's crying and making a decision about his response to the cry. Duane protested, "I don't know anything about babies." His girlfriend encouraged him, so he tried the project. To his utter amazement, he was able to decide such things as when the cry sounds indicated urgent or not urgent responses and when they indicated that the baby was sick or healthy, distressed or not distressed. Duane asked the professor, "How did I know such things? Is it instinctive? unconsciously learned? both? Can other naive students also do this?" The professor answered, "We're not sure how, but yes, many inexperienced people can perceive both meaning and needs from the simple sounds of the baby's cry."

Can you tell males from females by cry sounds? No, you cannot. Are there other sex differences between male and female infants in the neonatorum? If both males and females are dressed in the same color unisex pajamas, can you tell them apart? No, you cannot. (See Figure 4-7.) Some researchers have suggested that males are more

Figure 4-7
Can you tell newborn male babies from female babies by their facial expressions, their cries, their activities?

active motorically than females: They wriggle, squirm, thrash, turn their heads, and generally move their large muscles more than females (Fairweather, 1976; Maccoby and Jacklin, 1974). These research findings recognize unique individual differences: While in general infant males show more large muscle motor activity, some female babies are very active. A high activity level in the neonatorum may reflect greater birth trauma. Research studies for many years have documented the relatively greater physiological maturity of females at term and their easier births, and the corollary, the relative physiological immaturity of males at term and throughout the first year of life (Sinclair, 1978). "High-risk" newborns are more likely to be male than female (Harvey et al., 1982). Some reasons for being considered "high-risk" will be discussed in the next section.

Another factor that probably contributes to increased motor activity in male neonates is the practice of circumcision. In this procedure, the prepuce (foreskin) of the penis is removed. When performed as a religious rite, it is usually done several days after hospital discharge. When performed for hygienic reasons, it is usually done in the hospital a day or two after birth. The discomfort caused by circumcision can increase wriggling and squirming movements for several days. The American Academy of Pediatrics has stated that there is no medical reason for neonatal circumcision (Koops and Battaglia, 1984). Parents are encouraged to learn the pros and cons of the procedure and make informed decisions for each individual child.

High-Risk Neonates

Infants at high risk of disability or death are low-birth-weight infants who weigh less than 5½ pounds (2500 grams). They may be preterm (born before thirty-seven weeks) or small for gestational age (SGA), with weight inappropriate for gestation, whether born before thirty-seven weeks or at term.

Infant deaths and disabilities are high in Canada and the United States relative to other industrialized nations (Wegman, 1987). Why should this be when we have good sanitation, clean water, relatively inexpensive foods, and available medical care? The infant mortality rate in the United States is 11.2 infants per thousand, or about 39,000 deaths to babies per year (Nazario, 1988). The number of high-risk babies left with permanant disabilities is much higher. A large percentage of these deaths and disabilities could have been prevented if the pregnant mother had sought and practiced quality prenatal care.

While high-risk neonates differ, depending on their weight, gestation, and possibility of other major problems (such as chromosomal or genetic anomalies), most of them face problems with respiration, temperature maintenance, susceptibility to infection, feeding, nutrition, and liver functioning.

A common sequela to low birth weight is **respiratory distress syndrome** (also known as hyaline membrane disease of the lung). The immature lungs lack **surfactant**, a substance that lubricates the air sacs and helps them inflate. The airways must be kept open mechanically. This is now accomplished with continuous positive airway pressure (CPAP) delivered into an incubator, a hood, or tubes in the infant's nose or mouth. The pressure is continued until the neonate produces the surfactant. When CPAP is in use, measurements of the oxygen and carbon dioxide of the neonate's blood can be taken continuously across the skin. When CPAP is discontinued, another monitoring device is attached to the incubator or bassinet to emit a warning signal should respirations cease.

Another common sequela to low birth weight is a large ductus arteriosis, which allows too much blood to be pumped into the lungs with each heartbeat. In the majority of cases, this problem can be alleviated by injecting an intravenous drug that triggers closure of the duct. If drug therapy doesn't work, surgery may be required to prevent heart failure.

Low-birth-weight infants have both limited fat deposits to protect them from heat loss and poor temperature-regulating abilities. Consequently, they must be kept warm in incubators or bassinets set to maintain skin temperature between 96.8° and 98.6°F. Provision of adequate heat allows the neonate to use the calories taken in for growth rather than heat expenditure. Incubation also helps prevent infection. Parents may still visit their tiny baby and even provide care through incubator windows (see Figure 4-8).

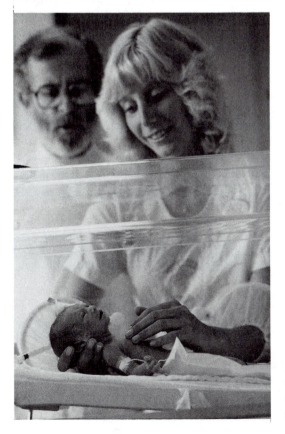

Figure 4-8
High risk infants need tender loving care (TLC) and human touching, despite their fragile status.

Nutritional status is often poor in low-birth-weight, preterm, and SGA infants. Many have limited stores of iron, which can lead to later anemia. Many are also hypoglycemic (low blood sugar) and deficient in folic acid. Correcting nutritional imbalances and maintaining adequate postnatal nutrition are extremely critical, yet difficult. Low-birth-weight infants have weak sucking, swallowing, gag, and cough reflexes, leading to difficulty in feeding and danger of aspiration (Koops and Battaglia, 1984). They often require intravenous feeding. Frequent blood samples are taken to assure that the neonate has sufficient glucose, which can be added to the special low-birth-weight-infant formula. The formula has extra protein as well as vitamins, carbohydrates, and fats balanced to support rapid postnatal growth.

Since liver functioning is not well developed, many low-birth-weight neonates develop jaundice caused by an excess of bilirubin. This can be corrected with phototherapy.

Low-birth-weight and preterm babies often have poor muscle control, poor orienting responses, and abnormal reflex activity. Researchers have discovered that equipping incubators with oscillating waterbeds and rhythmic sounds (Burns et al., 1983), or providing manual rocking and sound stimulation to incubator babies (Barnard and Bee, 1983) will improve their motor responsiveness. Frequent gentle massage can actually stimulate the growth of preterm infants (Scafidi et al., 1990).

Transfer from an incubator to a bassinet is usually accomplished when the neonate reaches 4 to 4½ pounds (1800 to 2000 grams). Weaning from intravenous to oral feedings is accomplished gradually when the neonate is strong enough to suck and swallow without aspirating the formula. Discharge from the hospital is accomplished when the neonate eats well, has all existing medical problems under control, and weighs from 4½ to 5½ pounds (2000 to 2500 grams).

The long-term prognosis for surviving low-birth-weight, preterm, or SGA infants is much better than it used to be. Still, most will show some delays in sensorimotor, personal-social, and gross motor abilities for one to two years (Ungerer and Sigman, 1983). Some will have permanent neurological difficulties, learning and perceptual problems, or mental retardation. Permanent handicaps are greatest in the neonates who are the tiniest or the most neurologically abnormal at birth (Pape and Fitzhardinge, 1981).

The physical status of a low-birth-weight neonate is improved when parents become actively involved in care during the time while the neonate is still hospitalized (Holmes, Reich, and Pasternak, 1984). Most intensive-care nurseries not only allow this but also teach mothers and fathers how to relate to their babies. Some parents report many negative reactions to having an infant in intensive care. They are uncertain about the prognosis, inconvenienced by the distance and expense of traveling to the hospital and the need to find babysitters for the children at home, alienated from the tiny baby who seems to belong more to the hospital staff than to them, resentful that they cannot take their baby home, and worried about the special care their infant will need after discharge (Jenkins and Pederson, 1985). Home intervention programs following discharge can help improve performance of high-risk babies (Ross, 1984). When mothers have social support networks to help them care for their premature infants, they interact more positively with their babies, and their babies, in turn, are more socially competent (Crnic et al., 1983).

Physical Changes in the First Two Years

The physical changes of infancy progress in an orderly, sequential way for all normal babies, although the exact age at which each change occurs varies widely from baby to baby. In the 1930s and 1940s, Arnold Gesell, Frances Ilg, and other colleagues at the Yale University Clinic for Infant and Child Development filmed and studied sequences of infant development. Out of this "cinemanalysis" came the conclusion that growth proceeds in certain developmental directions: from head to foot (called the **cephalo-caudal** direction), from the center outward (called the **proximal-distal** direction), and from **general to specific** movements. Cephalocaudal direction is well illustrated by the fact that the head accounts for about one-fourth of the infant's length at birth. By about one year of age the circumference of the chest finally becomes equal to that of the head. Proximal-distal development can be illustrated by the fact that the first bones to ossify are those close to the central, vital organs (skull, clavicle, spine) that are formed before birth. The bones of the fingers and toes do not begin to ossify until the end of the first year of life. General to specific development can be illustrated by grasping. Infants can crudely hold larger objects with both hands by about four months. They can hold smaller objects in one hand between thumb and forefinger (**pincer grasp**) by about one year of age. Figure 4-9 illustrates these developmental directions.

Gesell's studies also indicated that development does not progress in a straight line but rather oscillates back and forth between periods of rapid and slower maturing.

Visual acuity develops rapidly during infancy. While a neonate's vision is about 20/300, a six-month-old's acuity is closer to 20/100 (Banks and Salapatek, 1983). Color perception is similar to that of adults by three months, and infants can discriminate among forms. The ability to accommodate the curvature of the lens to shift from focusing on near objects to far objects (or vice versa) also becomes rapid and quite accurate by age three months. Very young babies seem to perceive depth, as measured by changes in their heartbeats, even though infants generally do not avoid falling from heights until they are old enough to crawl (Campos, Langer, & Krowitz, 1970).

Hearing is well developed at birth. Recent research suggests that infants are relatively more sensitive than adults to high-frequency sounds (Aslin, Pisoni, and Jusczyk, 1983). Many infants seem to prefer the higher pitched, slower rhythm voices of women (*motherese*) to the lower pitched voices of men (Fernald, 1985). Infants will attend to changes in rhythm or pitch of voice. If you want a baby to listen, change your voice; the melody is the message (Fernald, 1989).

Infants tend to gain an average of about 20 grams (two-thirds of an ounce) per day during their first five months and 15 grams (half an ounce) per day for the remainder of their first year of life. They can be expected to double their birth weight by about five months, triple it by one year, and quadruple it by two years of age. Length during

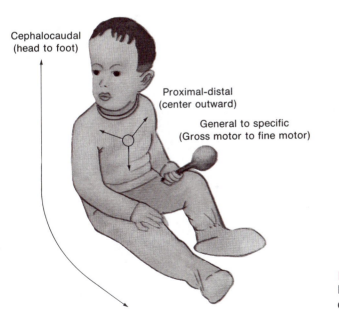

Cephalocaudal
(head to foot)

Proximal-distal
(center outward)

General to specific
(Gross motor to fine motor)

Figure 4-9
Principles of developmental direction.

infancy can be expected to increase by about 25 to 30 centimeters (10 to 12 inches) during the first year and by about 12 more centimeters (5 inches) at the end of the second year. The weight of the brain multiplies most rapidly during infancy as cells enlarge, acquire longer, branched processes, and gain myelin sheathing. At the end of the first eighteen months, the brain is 75% of its adult weight. By the fourth year, 90% of its final weight has been attained (Holt, 1977).

Nutrition is vitally important to an infant's physical development. Milk is sufficient to meet all of a baby's needs for the first six months of life. It may be mother's milk, formula, or a combination of both. Breast-feeding is encouraged because the mother's milk, in addition to being less expensive, always ready, sterile, and at the right temperature, has many nutritional advantages. It contains higher levels of lactose (milk sugar), vitamin C, and cholesterol than cow's milk and less protein. It also has a more efficient nutritional balance between iron, zinc, vitamin E, and unsaturated fatty acids (O'Brien and Hambridge, 1984). Human milk seems particularly suitable for rapid brain cell development. The additional cholesterol in early infancy may induce the production of enzymes required for cholesterol breakdown in adulthood. Another advantage of breast milk is that it also contains anti-infectious agents, which protect the baby from gastrointestinal and upper respiratory disease. Still another benefit of breast-feeding is that the process of **lactation** (secretion of milk by the mammary glands) stimulates the uterus to shrink more rapidly to its normal nonpregnant size (see Figure 4-10).

Some mothers are discouraged from breast-feeding because it takes so long. Neonates require long feeding times, whether breast- or bottle-fed. By one month of age, all babies speed up their feeding time as they become more proficient at sucking, even though the amount they consume remains the same (Pollitt, Consolazio, and Goodkin, 1981).

Breast-feeding may be discouraged if the mother is in poor health, malnourished, or taking medicines that may diffuse into the breast milk. On occasion a nursing mother may also develop an abscess (swollen, inflamed area) on one of her nipples that prevents her from feeding her infant. Breast-feeding may also be discouraged if the infant is low-birth-weight, SGA, or premature or suffers from a cleft (split) lip or palate. Sometimes the mothers' milk may be pumped and fed to these infants until they are able to suckle.

Many commercial formulas are available, fortified with vitamins and modified in protein content. Formulas may also be prepared at home from milk, water, and sugar

Figure 4-10
Both breast- and bottle-feeding parents can satisfy an infant's need for tender loving care (TLC). Face-to-face attention and cuddling should accompany feedings.

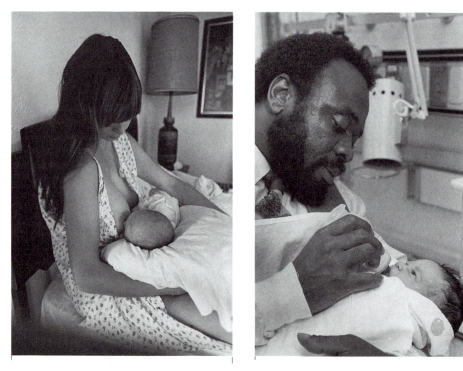

in a ratio determined by the health care provider. Many infants have adverse reactions to cow's milk (rashes, wheezing, diarrhea). For this reason many of the commercial formulas substitute vegetable proteins for cow's milk.

Care must be taken when bottle-feeding to assure cleanliness and psychological stimulation (touching, fondling, and so on). Either breast- or bottle-feeding can be satisfying if accompanied by tender loving care. Infants should not, however, be fed by propping bottles in their cribs. In addition to emotional deprivation, this may cause obstruction of the eustachian tube and ear infections, or dental cavities in the baby teeth.

Solid foods are generally started after six months, depending on the advising health care provider. Only a few teaspoons of all new foods are introduced at a time. They are continued for a day or two to ensure that no allergic manifestation (such as rash) or other evidence of intolerance (for example, diarrhea) will occur before starting another new food (see Figure 4-11).

Infants generally show a decrease in appetite between about twelve and eighteen months of age. They are no longer growing as rapidly and therefore do not need as many calories. "Empty calories," such as those found in candy and soda pop, should especially be avoided.

Sleep needs and patterns oscillate greatly during the first two years, both in the life of a single child and between infants. Immediately after birth, infants spend most of their nonfeeding time in sleep. The sleep–wake cycles are short, however, and the neonate can be expected to wake up every two to three hours (even during the night). The age at which the baby sleeps through the night (considered about a six- to eight-hour stretch) varies greatly from infant to infant. Some babies surprise their parents by doing this shortly after birth, whereas others cannot do so until they are from four to seven months old. Between ages one and two most infants adapt their schedules to a morning and an afternoon nap and a full night (about twelve hours) of sleep.

The ages at which infants reach the **motor milestones** of development (see Table 4-3) vary considerably. The "average" baby, determined by mean values of hundreds of infants, does not exist. Normative data can often be misleading. Each idosyncratic human being develops at his or her own rate on each of the motor tasks. In general, girls are ahead of boys in skeletal maturity and motor development (Silver, 1984).

Motor milestones depend on genetic factors, biologically rooted tempos of growth, maturation of the central nervous system, skeletal ossification, nutrition, physical health, environmental space, freedom, stimulation, and even psychological well-being. On the "average," one-month-old infants can lift their chins up above a surface when lying on their stomachs. By two months they can probably lift their chests up slightly and gaze around. At about three months their locomotor maturation is sufficient to hold their heads steady as they are pulled up. They also begin to roll over and reach for objects

Figure 4-11
Solid foods are usually introduced about the sixth month, depending on the infant's size and the health care provider's preferences. Feedings should be relaxed, pleasant times for both baby and caregiver.

Table 4-3 Motor Milestones of Infant Development.

Achievement	Approximate Age
Chin up off mattress	1 month
Chest up off mattress	2 months
Rolls over	3 months
Sits with support	4 months
Sits without support	6 months
Stands holding on	6 months
Crawls	7 months
Gets to sitting position alone	8 months
Pulls self to stand	8 months
Walks	12 months
Walks backward	15 months
Climbs stairs	18 months

SOURCE: Adapted from *Denver Developmental Screening Test* (DDST), by W. K. Frankenburg and J. B. Dodds. Copyright 1967 by the University of Colorado Medical Center, Reprinted by permission.

that attract their attention. At about four months they may grasp and hold objects for which they reach. By age five months infants can generally bear weight on their legs. They can also hold their heads steady when in an upright position. At six months many infants sit alone. Their grasp is also now practiced enough to allow them to transfer objects from hand to hand. Between seven and nine months, babies may assume a sitting posture on their own, learn to creep or crawl, or stand with support. Between nine and twelve months they begin to take walking steps when their hands are held or to walk along by holding the furniture or some other support (see Figure 4-12). They also have practiced their grasp enough to have moved from a whole-hand carry to a pincer grasp. Most babies can walk alone by twelve to fifteen months. By eighteen months they may be able to run stiffly and even climb stairs.

The ages for eruption of teeth in infancy are far more varied than the ages for accomplishing motor tasks. An occasional infant is born with a tooth. Other infants show no signs of teething until well past their first birthday. Early and late teething patterns appear to have genetic bases and are not related to other aspects of physical and motor development. Infants are often irritable and have increased salivation while teething, but teething does not cause diarrhea, fever, or other systemic disturbances (Beedle, 1984). Teething rings may hasten tooth eruption as well as provide pain relief when infants chew on them.

Health Maintenance

One of the most important ways in which caregivers provide for infant health is by supplying appropriate nutrients in a loving manner. Caregivers have the responsibility to ensure that the nutrients provided are appropriate, germ-free, available in sufficient supply when requested, and offered concurrently with tender loving care. As infants mature, it is necessary to add to the diet to ensure that they have sufficient protein, iron, calcium, and vitamins for the most active growth period of their life.

A second important aspect of infant health maintenance is protection from infection. The infant is highly susceptible to disease. Persons with known active infections (such as colds, influenza, "strep" or "staph" infections) should not kiss, cuddle, or be in close contact with infants. If the primary caregiver becomes ill, another person should help meet the baby's needs until the caregiver can recover.

Because infant skin is sensitive, it must be protected, especially from diaper rash. Diaper rashes are common, even in the cleanest homes, because of the ammonia that forms from urine in wet diapers. Ammonia burns and irritates the skin, causing redness

Figure 4-12

There is considerable variation in the age at which each infant begins to walk independently. Most babies require some support in their early attempts to step out into the world.

Table 4-4 Recommended Infant Immunizations.

DPT (diphtheria, pertussis, tetanus)	Ages 2, 4, 6, and 18 months
OPV (oral polio vaccine)	Ages 2, 4, 6, and 18 months
MMR (measles, mumps, rubella)	Age 15 months
HIB (hemophilus influenza type B)	Age 24 months

or blisters. Protective powders or creams may be necessary to supplement prompt changing of wet diapers.

Many infections that contributed in the past to high infant mortality and morbidity in later life can now be prevented through a series of immunizations: diphtheria, whooping cough (pertussis), tetanus, poliomyelitis, measles, mumps, and rubella. All babies should be taken to a physician or well-baby clinic for immunizations. The usual schedule is presented in Table 4-4. Injections are not given at the scheduled time if an infant has an active upper respiratory infection or other illness. The exact timing of immunizations is not nearly as important as the fact that the infant receive all of the injections. Records of immunizations should be carefully kept with other important documents. Some school systems will need to see these records before enrolling the child in kindergarten or first grade.

Some parents fear the whooping cough (pertussis) vaccination because it has been associated with adverse side effects. It is somewhat more risky than the other immunizations (Harding, 1985). Tenderness at the inoculation site and fever are common sequelae. Many physicians routinely advise aspirin for two to twelve hours following immunization. A more serious risk is central nervous system (CNS) reactivity. This has been estimated to occur in 1 out of 310,000 vaccinations (Fulginiti, 1984). The occurrence of any CNS symptoms is an absolute contraindication to giving further doses. Parents must be sure to report convulsions or collapse after injections to the physician. Even when CNS symptoms have developed after the whooping cough vaccine, few infants have suffered permanent sequelae. In contrast, the disease itself is most severe in infancy. Of all the deaths from pertussis in the United States in a recent seven-year period, 72% were infants (McIntosh and Lauer, 1984). Several hospitals have reported outbreaks of the disease in the last decade. Unfortunately, antibiotics are ineffective during the paroxysmal "whooping cough" stage of the disease, when deaths may occur from lung collapse.

Regularly scheduled visits to a doctor's office or clinic during infancy are important for health maintenance above and beyond immunizations (see Figure 4-13). Trained health care providers determine the presence of any possible disorders or developmental

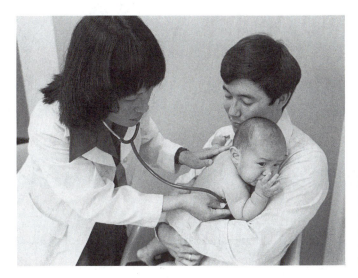

Figure 4-13
Regular well-baby examinations by a health care practitioner can prevent problems and identify and treat minor problems before they become severe.

delays that may require attention. They can provide nutritional guidance and counseling for psychological problems.

An additional important aspect of health maintenance is accident prevention. Motor vehicle accidents are the leading cause of accidental death in infancy. Even in nonaccidents infants may be killed because of sudden stops and turns (Agran, 1981). Safety seats for infants are now mandated in the United States and must be used. They should comply with the Federal Motor Vehicle Safety Standard and contain the words "dynamically tested," which means they have passed a crash situation test. Infants must be protected from falls: out of cribs with bars down or full-sized beds, down open stairwells, off furniture. They must be kept away from open heaters and fireplaces, matches, hot stoves, and hot radiators and out of the paths of motor vehicles. Poisons, pins and nails, and any small objects that could be swallowed must be kept out of reach. Any large containers of water (bathtubs, swimming pools) are especially hazardous. Infants must be watched carefully and taught to respect and obey the command "no" for their own safety's sake.

Should a serious accident occur, the baby should be rushed to the nearest doctor's office or hospital with someone telephoning ahead. If the problem is aspiration and the infant chokes and turns blue, a caregiver should first try to dislodge the object blocking the airway with blows to the back. The infant should be straddled over the adult's arm with the chest and head supported in one hand and the head held lower than the body (see Figure 4-14). Then four rapid blows are carefully administered between the baby's shoulder blades. If the object is not dislodged, place the free hand over the infant's back and, supporting the head, turn the baby over and administer four chest compressions in rapid succession. Again, be certain the head is lower than the body and supported well.

Common Health Problems in Infancy

Infections of the digestive system and the respiratory tract are the leading health problems of infants. Colic is not a disease. It affects about 20% of all infants for reasons as yet unknown (see Box 4-2).

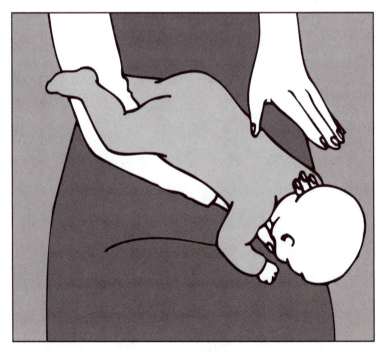

Figure 4-14
Do not use the Heimlich maneuver on a choking infant. Use rapid back blows to dislodge the object instead.

Diarrhea and vomiting are usually related to irritation of the digestive system by new foods, contaminated foods, or nonfood substances. Infants become dehydrated very quickly when they lose fluids. Consequently, diarrhea and vomiting must be treated promptly.

Projectile vomiting (hurled forward) and constipation may signal *pyloric stenosis*, a narrowing of the end of the stomach. This occurs in 1 out of 500 infants, four times more commonly in males, for unknown reasons. Treatment is surgically to enlarge the pyloric opening.

Malnutrition problems arise if infants are weaned too early from milk and are not given other foods equally rich in proteins. The effects of malnutrition on brain cell development are profound. Infancy is a critical period for growth of brain tissue. This can be illustrated by outcomes of kwashiorkor (disease caused by severe protein deficiency) in humans. Babies acquiring the disease in early infancy suffer irreparable brain damage. Those who are affected by kwashiorkor in later infancy (from fifteen to twenty-nine months) have a milder residual mental retardation. Children who do not get the disease until they are beyond age three can recover normal intelligence once they are cured of their disease. Infant malnutrition can cause developmental lags (Grantham-McGregor et al., 1982) and learning disabilities during the elementary school years (Galler, Ramsey, and Solimano, 1984).

Another danger of inadequate infant nutrition is **iron deficiency**. As many as 35%

BOX
4-2

What's in a One- to Three-Month-Old's Cry?

While neonatal cries may indicate developmental risk (see Box 4-1), periods of explosive, inconsolable crying between the ages of approximately two weeks and three months of age may betoken nothing more serious than **colic**. Nothing more serious? To parents of the 20% of babies who have colic, such a phrase will seem a gross understatement. Yet colicky babies are healthy, not diseased. They gain weight and are physically robust. They also have screaming attacks, often accompanied by twisting, turning, or stiffening, which last more than three hours a day, occur at least three days a week, and continue for at least three weeks (usually into the third month of life), for which no physical cause can be found.

Almost all infants have some periods of unexplained fussiness in this age period. You will hear descriptions such as "a touch of colic," or "very colicky" offered to explain cries. There are gradations of colic. What sets colicky crying apart from plain crying is the severity and inconsolable nature of the colic attacks, their persistence and repetition, the abrupt and dramatic mood shifts seen in the colicky baby, and the failure to explain the attacks with any medical or environmental causes.

Many myths exist about colic. Weissbluth (1985) assures that colic is *not* due to birth order, sex, intelligence of the baby, educational status of the mother, the nursing mother's diet, the failure to breast-feed, any food allergy, any gastrointestinal problem, fresh air, or maternal anxieties. While its fundamental cause is still unknown, research suggests that colic is set off by one or more physiological factors, including disordered regulation of breathing, temperament, sleep cycles that are not synchronized with other body rhythms, or abnormal levels of naturally occurring substances such as prostaglandins or progesterone (Weissbluth, 1985). The problem usually corrects itself by about three to four months.

Can anything be done to "cure" colic and stop the screaming attacks before three or four months? No. Some physicians advise changing formulas, burping the baby more frequently, applying warm water bottles, giving herbal tea, or tranquilizing the baby (or tranquilizing the mother!). The colic continues to wax and wane until it has run its natural course. Some physicians will prescribe dicyclomine (Bentyl), a smooth muscle relaxant that eases spasms of the intestines. (It may also calm the baby's nervous system.) It does not cure colic, but it makes crying spells shorter and less frequent and makes the baby more consolable. Most experts advise soothing the colicky infant with rhythmic motions until each attack abates: rocking, jiggling, bouncing, patting, massage, a ride in the car—whatever works to console him or her.

The baby should never be left alone to cry it out for hours at a time in the first few months of life. A classic study by Bell and Ainsworth (1972) demonstrated that ignoring early cries leads to more crying later, while responding to early cries leads to less crying later. Parents must be patient and loving during the many trying hours of colic attacks in the first few months. The baby is normal and the colic will disappear.

of infants in the one to three age range are iron deficient, according to the National Health Nutrition Examination Survey (Honig and Oski, 1984). Infants have iron stores from prenatal development sufficient to last them for about four months. After that, they must obtain additional iron from breast milk, iron-fortified infant formulas, or iron-containing solid foods. Signs of iron deficiency in infants include irritability, weakness, poor appetite, and susceptibility to infections (Githens and Hathaway, 1984). Iron-deficient infants also perform poorly on mental development scales. Their performance dramatically improves within two weeks of treatment with intramuscular iron injections (Honig and Oski, 1984). Honig and Oski noted that iron-deficient infants also manifest very solemn faces. All efforts to establish positive rapport and obtain smiles fail. This is an important behavioral index that can be used to alert health caregivers to which babies need medical screening for potential iron deficiency.

Fat babies are at increased risk of infection (O'Brien and Hambridge, 1984). Over-fed babies develop additional fat cells to store the unused energy sources (Fomon, 1974). The hypothesis that these fat cells that proliferate in infancy continue to replace themselves as children grow has not been supported with research evidence. However, adults who were fat as infants are frequently obese or have difficulty holding their weight down to the normal range for their size. Some researchers believe there is a genetic predisposition for obesity (Stunkard et al., 1986). An alternate theory about the effect of infant overfeeding on adult obesity is that eating patterns become habits that are difficult to change. Whatever the explanation, fat babies tend to become overweight adults.

Eczema is a manifestation of allergic reaction to one or more foods or other substances. It is characterized by inflammation of the skin and intense itching. It may be a wet form with running sores or a dry form with bright red patches of scales. The tendency to become allergic is inherited, but an infant's eczema may be a reaction to a food or substance quite different from the food or substance to which the parents are allergic. Doctors frequently have difficulty determining the source(s) of the infant's problem. Until they do, medication is usually prescribed to help relieve the itching.

Respiratory illnesses common in infancy include croup, influenza, colds, bronchitis, pneumonia, and ear infections. **Croup** is a mild form of tracheobronchitis common in infancy. It produces a loud spasmodic cough that can be very frightening (it may sound like the infant is strangling). Croup is rarely serious unless the airway becomes obstructed.

Crib death, called **sudden infant death syndrome (SIDS)** occurs when apparently normal, well-developed infants suddenly stop breathing. The fundamental cause of SIDS is unknown, although Steinschneider (1972) and Guilleminault and colleagues (1979) found increased episodes of apnea in infants who later died from SIDS.

SIDS is most common between two and four months. It can occur in any infant but is more common in urban, low-income, male, twin, low-birth-weight, and premature babies, and in infants born to teenage parents.

In most major hospitals today infants who have frequent apnea episodes are watched closely. At discharge from the hospital their caregivers may be instructed to monitor breathing with the help of a machine that signals apnea occurrences. Usually just moving the baby is enough to restore breathing. As the infant matures, the apnea episodes become less frequent and are eventually outgrown.

Failure-to-thrive syndrome (FTTS), in which apparently normal infants fail to maintain established patterns of weight gain and fall below the third weight percentile, (see Figure 4-15), is another condition whose fundamental cause is unknown. FTTS infants have characteristically bizarre eye behaviors. They gaze wide-eyed, scan the environment continuously, and avoid eye contact. Neurologically, they are either spastic and rigid or floppy with a near absence of muscle tone (Barbero, 1982). FTTS may involve a deprivation of loving, sensitive caregiving. Drotar and Malone (1982) reported that mothers of FTTS infants have diminished responsiveness to their infants and

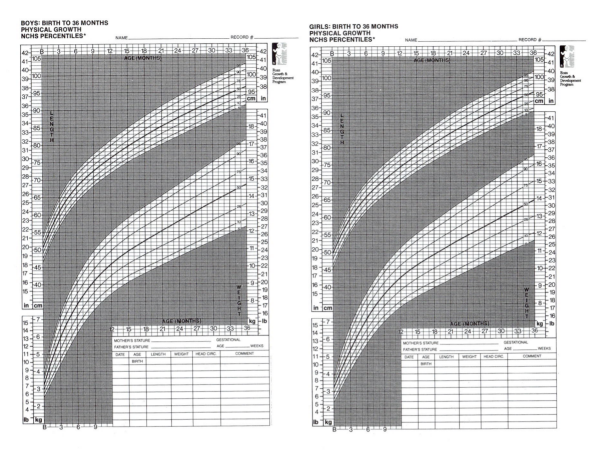

Figure 4-15
Standard percentiles for length and weight of infants from birth to three years in three-month increments. Each healthy infant tends to stay near the same line of trajectory over time.

tension-laden interactions when they do respond. Gagan, Cupoli, and Watkins (1984) found that mothers of FTTS infants have poor social support networks. Barbero (1982) reported that mothers of FTTS infants have histories of some emotional trauma: deprivations in their own childhoods, problems during their pregnancies, disruptions in the neonatal period, or current life stresses (marital strains, financial crises). FTTS babies do gain weight when hospitalized and appropriately nurtured. This, however, is only the beginning of treatment. Therapy must be continued in the home to encourage a more adaptive attachment between mother and infant and to assure future nurturing and sensitive caregiving.

Cognitive and Language Development

Some people believe that infant behaviors are taught by sensitive caregivers. Other people feel that infant behaviors will gradually evolve, regardless of caregivers, as the baby matures. Before reading on, consider these two explanations of new behaviors by infants. Which one seems more correct to you? There is an inseparable element of interplay between maturation and teaching in infant learning. In recent years educators have accepted the idea that many aspects of cognitive behavior are controlled by maturation. Until the central nervous system reaches the necessary degree of maturity for any given skill, no amount of teaching will enable the infant to accomplish the task.

Brain Maturation

The central nervous system (brain and spinal cord) is one of the more immature organ systems in the neonate. The three major regions of the brain are the cerebrum, the cerebellum, and the brain stem (see Figure 4-16). The brain stem consists of the pons, medulla, midbrain, and diencephalon. At birth these structures are developed more fully than the rest of the brain. They help regulate respiration, heartbeat, blood pressure, coughing, sneezing, swallowing, postural reflexes, and some motor coordination. Less well developed in the neonate is the cerebellum, through which balance and joint position sense are coordinated. It develops very rapidly in the early months of life. The cerebrum consists of two large lobes called cerebral hemispheres, which control learning, thought, and memory. The growth of the cerebrum is slow, spanning infancy, childhood, and adolescence.

All portions of the brain are composed of nervous tissue that consists of three elements: nerve cells, nerve fibers, and the supporting structure of cells known as the neuroglia, or simply glia. The glial cells (named from the Greek word for glue) account for approximately 90% of all brain tissue. Nerve cells, called neurons, in spite of their relatively small number (10% of the brain cells, or approximately 10 billion cells) sustain life, control thought, consciousness, and memory, direct all our involuntary and voluntary muscle movements, and are in charge of all the senses. When we speak of brain cells, we usually mean neurons, the workers, rather than glia, the supporters.

At birth all of the neurons that the brain will ever have are present. Glial cells may continue to be added during infancy. The rapid growth and development of the brains of infants consist mainly of additions of glial cells and increases in size of existing neurons. The increase in the size of neurons is due to increases in materials in the cells, increases in the length and branchings of the cell processes (the axon and dendrites), and the growth of a layer of fatty, insulating material called **myelin** around the axon and dendrites (see Figure 4-17). Myelin sheathing allows messages to be transmitted with greater speed and ease across the cell processes. Glial cells (supporting cells) can be curtailed by insufficient dietary protein (Winick, 1976). In addition, lack

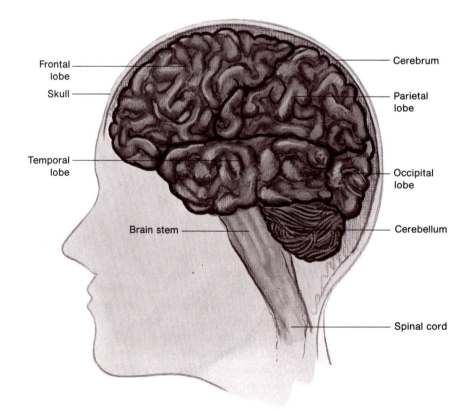

Figure 4-16
The major structures of the human brain are the brain stem, the cerebellum, and the cerebrum.

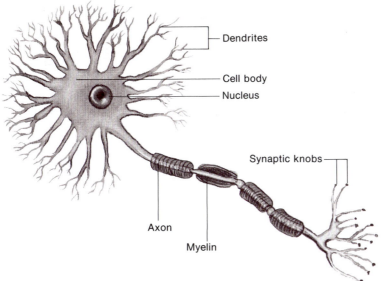

Figure 4-17
Schematic view of a neuron,
showing myelin sheathing
around the axon.

Dendrites

Cell body

Nucleus

Synaptic knobs

Axon

Myelin

of protein reduces branchings of the nerve fibers, enlargement of cell bodies, and myelinization of the cell processes.

Brain growth during infancy involves an increase in the number of **synapses** (junctions between cell processes of neurons) and the development of **neurotransmitters** (chemical substances that facilitate the transmission of impulses across the synapses between nerve endings). Eventually each neuron will be able to receive input from about 1000 other neurons and send messages to hundreds more. There are indications that the more activity a region of neurons gets, the greater the chance of creating extra dendritic branches and synaptic connections (Lenard, 1983). There is also evidence that environmental stimulation in infancy will produce the neuronal activity that, in turn, will increase dendritic growth (Greenough and Juraska, 1979). The same is probably true of environmental stimulation in childhood, adolescence, and even adulthood, although the dendritic branching occurs at increasingly slower rates as we age.

While neurons can generate new fibers, the cell body of a central nervous system neuron cannot be replaced once it is destroyed. For this reason, the infant brain must be carefully protected.

Piaget's Sensorimotor Stage

Jean Piaget's theory of cognitive development stresses four major periods through which humans pass in the course of intellectual maturation: (1) sensorimotor intelligence in infancy, (2) preoperational thinking in early childhood, (3) concrete operational thought in later childhood, and (4) formal or logical intelligence in adolescence and adulthood. In Piaget's first stage of **sensorimotor intelligence** an infant's knowledge of the world comes about primarily through sensory impressions and motor activities. Piaget saw the sensorimotor period of intellectual development as having six distinctive substages (see Table 4-5). Some infants pass through the succession of stages earlier than others. The rate of intellectual development depends not only on maturation but also on genetic factors, physical and emotional health, nutrition, and the kinds of stimulation that the infant receives from the environment. Piaget and his colleagues were hesitant to attach an expected age of emergence on any of the substages of sensorimotor development.

As infants experience various phenomena through their motions and senses, the complementary processes of assimilation and accommodation are put into play. *Assimilation* refers to the process of absorbing new information from the environment and using current structures to deal with the information (see Chapter 2). Any objects or

Table 4-5   Some of the Achievements in the Six Substages of Piaget's Sensorimotor Stage.

(1) Reflexes	(2) Primary Circular Reactions	(3) Secondary Circular Reactions	(4) Coordination of Secondary Schemas	(5) Tertiary Circular Reactions	(6) Mental Combinations
Exercises innate behavioral patterns	Causality: Repeats simple, pleasurable activities	Causality: Shows abbreviations of intentional actions; combines actions	Causality: Shows expectations of events or behaviors	Causality: Recognizes causes other than self and differentiates cause and effect	Causality: Perceives causality mentally and is able to detour simple forms of action
	Imitation: Imitates actions that have previously been performed	Imitation: Successfully imitates modeled activity if it is familiar	Imitation: Begins to imitate novel behaviors	Imitation: Adept at novel imitations including sounds	Imitation: Can imitate model no longer present
	Object concept: Coordinates looking and hearing	Object concept: Conducts visual or tactile search if behavior was ongoing	Object concept: Employs a variety of searching behaviors	Object concept: Correctly follows visual sequence of object's movements	Object concept: Can infer object's location even when tricks of perception are introduced
			Means to ends: Uses purposive behavior to attain goal	Means to ends: Experiments with new means to attain ends	Means to ends: Uses short cuts by thinking rather than groping
			Object in space: Discovers perspective in depth	Object in space: Sees spatial relationships enough to fit different shapes into corresponding openings	Object in space: has symbolic representation of space; can solve detour problems

events that elicit exploring behaviors from the infant are being assimilated. *Accommodation* refers to the process whereby the infant (or child, or adult) alters his or her behaviors and adjusts existing schemas to the requirements of the object or event just assimilated. Assimilation and accommodation allow infants to integrate new learning with old and thus adapt to their ever-expanding environments. As a result of infants' encounters with new stimuli, they acquire increased numbers of *schemas*. These, according to Piaget (1952), are mentally organized patterns of behaviors. When any structures are assimilated and accommodated into sharply defined schemas, a state of relative equilibrium is said to exist. This equilibrium, however, sows seeds for its own destruction. Inconsistencies and gaps previously ignored become salient. They usher in a new disequilibrium requiring more exploration of newly perceived phenomena that, in turn, become new schemas.

The first stage of sensorimotor intelligence is the *reflex stage*. Piaget felt that for the first month of life the primary learning that takes place is bound to naturally occurring reflexes: rooting, sucking, swallowing, head turning, crying. He proposed that assimilation of these reflexes occurs because the infant has a basic tendency to exercise any available behaviors and make them function. In exercising reflexes such as sucking, the infant learns more about the environment. The infant will suck not only a nipple but also a finger, a blanket, someone else's cheek, a piece of clothing, or anything that happens to come in contact with the mouth. During the first stage the infant learns to differentiate among various stimuli and accommodate to them. Thus, before long, when hunger is strong, only a nipple will elicit strong sucking movements. A blanket may elicit a loud howl of protest instead.

The second stage of sensorimotor intelligence is the stage of *primary circular reactions*. Examples of some primary circular reactions (behaviors that become habits) are sucking on a specific object (thumb, finger, pacifier, toy), turning to look in the direction of a sound, reaching for and grasping an object, smiling at a friendly face, and showing anticipatory behaviors before routine procedures (feeding, diapering, being put to bed) (see Box 4-3).

During the phase of primary circular reactions, infants seem content to focus on objects or events that occur naturally. Soon, however, maturational processes make it possible for them to begin experimenting with novel actions of their own. At first such experimental actions occur by accident. Serendipity! Infants arrive at the fortunate discovery that they can alter stimuli themselves and thus make them slightly novel and more interesting.

Piaget called the third substage in infancy the period of *secondary circular reactions*. "Secondary" refers to the idea that habits developed in the preceding substage can now be embellished with new, more advanced actions. "Circular" refers to the fact that these behaviors are continually repeated by the baby in play. This stage is believed to characterize infants ranging in age from about four months through about eight to ten months. During this phase of development an intentionality in the babies' behaviors becomes apparent. Infants show evidence of finding ways to make interesting events last or be repeated. During the phase of secondary circular reactions infants will imitate models if the patterns of behavior being demonstrated are familiar. They cannot yet copy novel actions.

Piaget called the fourth stage the *coordination of secondary schemas*. It commences

---

BOX 4-3

Observations of P. through the Sensorimotor Substages.

1. *Reflexes* At 0;0(21)* P. is lying quietly in her crib when K. begins to cry. P. also begins to cry. K.'s cry seems to be the stimulus which set P.'s reflex in motion.

2. *Primary circular reactions* At 0;3(1) P. has been amused by a mobile above her with a string from it loosely attached to her foot so that the mobile moves when her foot moves. The string slips off her foot. She continues moving her foot and watching the mobile. When nothing happens, she moves her foot more vigorously, causing the mobile to move slightly as the crib jiggles.

3. *Secondary circular reactions* At 0;4(16) P. is lying on her back in her crib watching a mobile move as she shakes her right hand. A string is attached from the mobile to her right wrist. Her babysitter removes the string from her right wrist and slips it over her left wrist. She shakes her right wrist vigorously. She then shakes both hands as she becomes agitated. When the mobile moves, she continues shaking both hands more calmly. Soon she shakes only her left hand. (On following days, she becomes accustomed to shaking only the hand to which the loop is attached after one or two trials when the mobile–string game is presented.)

On 0;4(20) when the mobile is presented without a string, she shakes both hands until she fortuitously hits

the side of her crib, making the mobile move. In time she discovers that kicking the side of the crib to which the mobile is attached causes greater movement. Thereafter she experiments with the rate and rhythm of her kicks to make this interesting sight last.

4. *Coordination of secondary schemas* At 0;8(13) P. spends a great deal of time walking in a walker. Her mother has tied a string to the walker to "haul it in" when P. gets too close to forbidden objects. On this day, P. is sitting on the floor and she spies the walker. She does not know how to crawl but after looking around a while she notices the string. She picks it up and "reels in" the walker.

5. *Tertiary circular reactions* At 1;2(5) P. accidentally drops a toy on the floor of the car. She cannot retrieve it herself because she is buckled into a carseat. After only a moment's hesitation, she reaches for her mother's hand and pushes it down toward the object, indicating her desire to have the toy returned.

6. *Mental combinations* At 1;6(18) P. has tired of K., as he has been at her house for 5 hours. When K.'s mother comes in the door, P. immediately goes and gets K.'s coat and happily waves "bye-bye," without a word being said about K.'s need to leave.

---

*Numbers indicate years, months, and days in age at time of observation. The observations were made of a friend's child by the author.

when indications arise that babies have a defined goal in mind for what they are doing and so is often referred to as the "'means–ends stage." The approximate age range is from eight to twelve months. By this time infants are more mobile. They can sit alone, reach and grasp, creep, crawl, or perhaps even pull to stand or take a few unassisted steps. "Coordination of schemas" refers to the idea that infants now need and use more than one pattern of behavior to attain the goal they have in mind. They may use one schema as a means for attaining the goal and a second for dealing with the goal. Active experimentation is also evident as infants combine schemas in different ways.

Infants expect people to act in certain ways, indicating their appreciation of the laws of causality. They also acquire the ability to imitate novel behaviors of models. They now show a variety of searching behaviors for vanished objects (see Figure 4-18).

In substage five, *tertiary circular reactions,* babies can both incorporate the actions of combining schemas and remember results. Piaget located the beginnings of rational judgment and intellectual reasoning in this cyclic behavior. When confronted with obstacles, infants can now invent new means for handling them. They do not have to rely solely on schemas that were successful before. They recognize causes and effects quite clearly. Object concept is so well established that, even if something is hidden in a succession of places, the infant will search for it in the last place seen.

The last of the sensorimotor phases is the *invention of new means through mental combinations.* By this time infants can understand and use language to form mental symbols for behaviors. Infants try to think about problems and develop solutions on a mental rather than a physical level. Simple new forms of behavior are initiated and carried through without the past trial-and-error steps. Imitations of behaviors that occurred some time earlier can be seen.

Some people feel that infants may be able to generate mental hypotheses about their experiences sooner than Piaget surmised. J. J. Gibson (1966) and E. Gibson (1969) have argued that infants can pick up perceptual information from birth. Bruner (1973) argued that even from the outset the infant's motor activities show intention. Kagan (1979) reported that infants develop a concept of an object's permanence (as evidenced by searching behaviors) much sooner than Piaget predicted. Baillargeon and colleagues (1987, 1988, 1989, 1990) devised a series of ingenious experiments to demonstrate that infants do indeed have object permanence by four months, and location memory between six and eight months of age. Piaget's work, however, still stands as an accurate description of the sequence of infant cognitive advances and sensorimotor intelligence.

Language Beginnings

The ability to understand the spoken word is called passive or receptive language. It is, in fact, the primary or fundamental aspect of language. The ability to produce meaningful utterances is called expressive language.

Understanding of language becomes increasingly proficient as babies get older. Whether they are responding to intonation, to actual words, or both, it is possible either to soothe or to upset a baby of three to four months with comforting or frightening statements. By nine to eleven months receptive language is organized to the point that infants will obey spoken commands (give me the ball, play pat-a-cake, finish your juice).

It is interesting that the expressive speech center in the brain, which is located in the frontal lobe on the left side of the cerebrum (the right side in some left-handed persons), borders on the areas of the motor cortex that control both mouth–tongue movements and hand movements. This proximity of the speech center to the hand-control area of the motor cortex is important. We all express ourselves with our hands as well as with our mouths. Infants especially use many gestures in association with simple words as they acquire language.

The earliest sounds made in infancy are cries (Table 4-6). By about two weeks of age infants add new sounds to their repertoire such as coos and goo sounds, which are

Figure 4-18
Babies like to cause things to happen during the fourth state of sensorimotor development. The "drop the toy" game is usually a favorite as they coordinate secondary schemas.

Table 4-6 Progression of Expressive Language with Approximate Ages of Emerging Ability.

Language Characteristic	Age of Emergence
Crying	Birth
Wide variety of meaningless speech sounds	1– 6 months
Babbling syllables (such as "mamamama")	3–12 months
Phonetic drift (frequent practice of phonemes of "mother tongue")	6–18 months
Echolalia (imitation of simple sounds such as "dog, hat, pop")	6–18 months
Holophrasing (one-word sentences)	12–24 months
Telegraphic speech (subject–verb–object communiques)	18–36 months
Complete sentences	24–48 months

easily formed in the back of the mouth with undifferentiated tongue movements. These sounds have a nasal quality because the epiglottis is very close to the soft palate. The larynx and nasopharynx are short and high in the neck, the mouth is flat because of the absence of teeth, and the tongue more nearly fills the mouth (see Figure 4-19). The tongue moves mostly back and forth as for sucking and swallowing. In fact, the earliest sounds seem to be passive reflex activity, by-products of feeding and sucking (Oller, 1980).

When infants first babble, they string together consonants such as b, c, d, g, h, m, n, p, t, and w with vowels. These sounds are easily made by interrupting the flow of air from the lungs to the mouth with the lips (e.g., baba, mama, papa), the tongue (e.g., dada, nana, tata) or the back of the tongue and the soft palate (e.g., coo, goo). The vocal cords (voice box), of the larynx (see Figure 4-19), vibrate as air passes from the lungs to the mouth. This can create variations in sounds. When infants babble, they typically explore all the possible sounds they can make by changing the force of the airstream as it passes their vocal cords and by varying the positions of their tongue and mouth.

Many cultures use labels for primary caregivers that are combinations of these consonants plus vowels, perhaps because they are the sounds infants make (such as papa, mama, dada, nana). Infants in all cultures produce all the possible sounds of every known language. They try out whistles, snorts, chuckles, squeals, guttural sounds, trills, glides, even "Bronx cheers." These "babbles" reflect anatomical changes. Rasp-

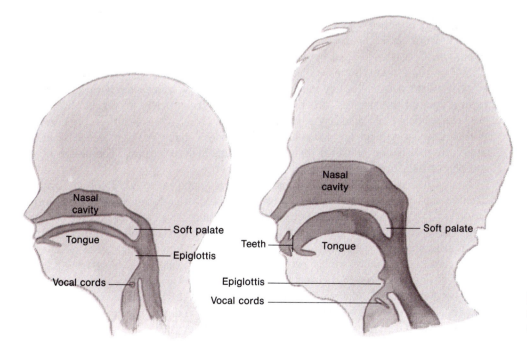

Figure 4-19

Comparison of vocal tracts of an infant and an adult.

berry sounds are evidence of increased air pressure in the mouth as the larynx and nasopharynx disengage, squeals and growls become possible as the larynx descends into the neck, and noncry yelling becomes possible as motor coordination between the respiratory system and the larynx improves (Kent, 1980).

Between approximately six and twelve months of age infants begin imitating the sounds they hear repeated by their primary caregivers more often than they reproduce their own unique sounds. This is known as **phonetic drift**. The phonemes produced more nearly approximate the phonemes of their "mother tongue." In the English language, there are 45 phonemes. Some languages have fewer phonemes (Hawaiian has 13), and some languages use far more sounds (Abkhazian has 71).

It is during the stage of phonetic drift that the speech of deaf infants begins to differ from that of normal hearing infants. Deaf infants will imitate the head movements, facial expressions, and lip movements of their caregivers, but they cannot hear the sounds they make, nor the sounds of others. Their own speech production continues to be undifferentiated babble. Gradually, they produce fewer and fewer sounds. It is at this point that a profound hearing impairment is usually diagnosed. Most professionals recommend that infants be taught an alternate form of communication as soon as deafness or severe hearing impairment is diagnosed. In addition to learning sign language with caregivers at home, hearing-disabled infants and children are usually also enrolled in special education programs as early as possible.

As early as age three months infants show a tendency to babble more when they are alone. When a caregiver approaches, they quiet to attend to the caregiver's utterances. They may try to repeat sounds that adults make if the sounds are ones they have already produced and practiced. By about ten months they may succeed at imitating novel sounds, ones that they have not practiced previously. The imitation of words spoken by others, whether perfect or imperfect, is called *echolalia*. Many babies make their first meaningful words through echolalia.

In all cultures the first meaningful words of babies are usually nouns. Next to emerge are verbs, the action words. The early utterances usually refer to subjects or objects on which the baby acts, not familiar things to which caregivers attend (such as diapers). Between ages one and two infants generally acquire the ability to produce **holophrases**, one-word sentences that convey a complete message ("Up"). Next, infants learn to expand their holophrases by attaching them back-to-back to other nouns or verbs. They thus form two-word sentences ("Mommy milk, Daddy come"). The one- and two-word sentences used by babies are generally accompanied by many gestures that, together with the context, make them comprehensible. For example, the single word *chair* might mean "I want to get up in the chair," "I want the chair moved," or "I want you to get out of the chair," or it may simply be a label ("This is a chair") or a question ("Is this a chair?"). The words produced by infants are usually the most salient portions of any message. Early speech is often referred to as **telegraphic speech** because, as in telegram messages, the articles, pronouns, prepositions, conjunctions, and auxiliary verbs are omitted (see Figure 4-20). In organizing and coding receptive language, infants acquire an understanding of the most meaningful units of speech. No one teaches them to use nouns and verbs first. They learn this sequence on their own.

Noam Chomsky (1968) proposed that humans (as opposed to other species) have an innate capacity to learn language, which he labeled the **language acquisition device (LAD)**. During infancy, as neurological maturation proceeds, the unique ability of the brain to sort out basic sounds and to extract from sentences the most meaningful elements becomes apparent. During early childhood the brain's language acquisition ability becomes even more sophisticated. Children will implicitly use underlying rules for constructing sentences in their native tongue. They will invent new sentences that they have never heard adults utter. They will also make rule-based mistakes (for example, adding -er and -s incorrectly to irregular verbs and nouns). These aspects of language development will be discussed further in Chapter 5.

Figure 4-20
Examples of infants' telegraphic messages.

Caregiver Communication	*Telegraphic Speech*
Where is our paper?	Paper desk.
What is this?	Daddy desk.
Where is Daddy?	Daddy go car?
No, Daddy's car is here, but where is Daddy?	Daddy sleep.
Did Daddy tell you that he wanted to stay in bed?	Daddy stay bed.
Would you like to go and take a nap like Daddy?	No, no nap!

Fostering Learning

Parents and other caregivers can have an enormous influence on their infants' intellectual and language development. The more infants are talked to directly, the better. From birth on, caregivers should talk to their babies when they are awake and alert, as during bathing and diaper changes. This early practice helps form habits of talking to infants that are invaluable later. This early talking also helps soothe babies and allows them to become familiar with and form attachments to their caregivers. Many parents are not sure what they should say to their babies. It is not important what is said, only that speaking occurs. Infants can be told the plans for the day. They can be sung to or told nursery rhymes. There is an old Norwegian saying that a much nicknamed baby is a much loved baby. Infants can be called all kinds of affectionate things and can be complimented over and other without any damage (see Figure 4-21).

At about three or four weeks, when infants begin cooing, caregivers can increase the rate at which babies play with sounds by imitating some of them. These vocal games should continue right up to and beyond the time when infants produce their first words. Caregivers should show enthusiasm and encourage infants to label things as well, even if the baby's word for an object is incomprehensible. Questions may be asked and, after a few moments, answered. All of these verbal activities will stimulate language development in infants.

Reading to babies can begin at birth (Trelease, 1982). Read poetry at first, because infants love to hear the rhythms, the pitch, and the melody of language. By about two

Figure 4-21
Language development is enhanced by face-to-face vocal interactions between infant and adult. The infant enjoys both hearing the adult's words and hearing her own sounds imitated back to her.

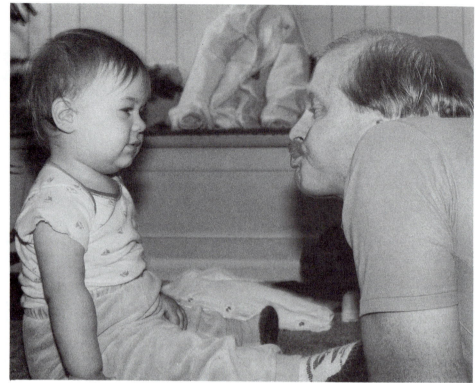

to three months, caregivers can introduce picture books, especially those with large figures and bright colors. Babies can usually help hold a book or turn pages by about six months. Their attention span and reading time can increase. If reading is a time for TLC, the infant will learn to love books.

Singing to babies should also begin at birth. Most infants prefer the voices of their caregivers, however good or bad the vocal quality. They will listen to any songs: rap, rock, golden oldies, arias, lullabies. Music stimulates both language and creativity.

Once babies begin making holophrases, every attempt should be made to understand these messages. If caregivers cannot comprehend, they can ask the baby "Show me." Sometimes, if another child is present, the child will understand what the baby is saying. When caregivers grasp what infant vocalizations mean, they should expand the holophrases or gestures into longer sentences, both encouraging the baby's word and modeling additional language (for example, "Up."—"Up? Very good! Billy wants to go up. Up Billy goes. Up into the chair.").

The same kinds of verbal stimulation that are useful in fostering language also

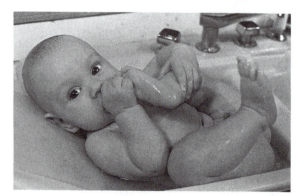

Figure 4-22
Babies explore everything they can reach with their mouths. Be sure that the objects baby can reach are safe.

encourage cognitive growth. Caregivers should be responsive to infants' calls for information, for encouragement, for a change of play materials, or for a change of scenery.

By about three months infants begin to reach for things and should be given opportunities to do so. Mobiles or toys can be strung on strong elastic and placed over the crib or across infant recliner seats. When infants can grasp toys, it is important to keep safety in mind. Babies should be given large, handled toys, not objects small enough to swallow, wooden toys with slivers, or paint-chipped toys. Babies explore everything with their mouths as well as with their hands (see Figure 4-22).

The right learning toy for a baby at any age is one that produces pleasure and excitement and is safe. Hunt (1964) called finding such toys "the problem of the match." If the toy is too familiar, the baby will be bored. If it is too novel, the baby will ignore it. The best learning toys are ones with both familiarity and challenge (something new to be assimilated and accommodated). Toys with various colors or sounds or textures or shapes should be provided. Several safe, manipulatory objects can be kept in one place to present to babies at playtimes. This allows them to select their own "match."

Babies learn a great deal from walks, from visits to stores or other people's houses, and from being with adults and other children in their own homes. Although playpens have their uses, it is good to give babies freedom to explore more than just a small square space from day to day. Back, front, or shoulder carriers are available that allow caregivers to take infants wherever they go with minimal difficulty.

When babies begin walking, they will explore anything they can touch, which necessitates putting unsafe things away. This is a time of active learning. Caregivers should respond to babies' bids for help, movement, encouragement, and the like. Play objects that no longer attract attention should be removed and new ones provided (see Box 4-4). It is also good to organize days so that changes of play objects or scenery occur frequently enough to prevent boredom.

**BOX
4-4**

Choosing Infant Toys.

Burton White (1975) divided the first thirty-seven months of life into seven progressive developmental phases and provided detailed lists of instructions for toys, strategies, and parental practices aimed at enhancing cognitive (also physical and psychosocial) development during these phases. He wrote that most families do quite well for the first six to eight months, but few provide adequate mental stimulation during the especially crucial phases between eight to fourteen months and fourteen to twenty-four months. He suggested taking the child out of restrictive devices such as playpens, jump seats, and gated areas by these ages and accident-proofing the living area instead so the infant can roam freely and explore. He suggested toys such as graduated-size containers to fit into each other, hinged objects, stiff-paged books, surprise boxes (such as a Jack-in-the-box), busy boxes, collections of safe small objects, balls, dolls, and water-play objects for eight- to fourteen-month-olds. Ridenour (1982) warned that the common practice of putting infants in this age range in walkers is inherently dangerous. The infant walker does not accelerate the onset of walking and the infant must be constantly supervised to prevent accidents.

Fourteen- to twenty-four-month-old infants can benefit from four-wheel devices on which they can sit and move, smaller toy cars and trucks with movable (but not removable) wheels to spin, doll carriages, swings and small slides, safe stairs to climb, pull toys, Ping-Pong balls and footballs, small plastic human and animal figures, pots and pans, pails, boxes, plastic jars and containers, small chairs and tables, full-length door mirrors, paper, crayons, simple puzzles, stacking toys, toy telephones, plastic pop beads, and stuffed animals. DeStefano and Mueller (1982) suggested that when two infants in this age group are playing together, smaller toys foster conflict while larger toys encourage more positive interactions. White (1975) discouraged such common activities as placing the infant in front of the television (even the educational programs) at these ages or doing any forced teaching (ABC's, numbers). He also warned against giving the child expensive but unstable tricycles, wind-up toys that require an adult to wind them, and popular but dangerous metal soldiers or small cars with parts that can be pulled off.

One additional important way in which families can foster intellectual development in infants is to provide diets with enough protein (including milk and milk products, meat, poultry, fish, beans) for maximum neurological development. Diets also need to be balanced out with other essential foods (fruits, vegetables, cereals, and grains). They should not be so calorie laden, however, that infants become too fat to move about freely.

Psychosocial Development

Many of the things families do to foster learning also foster psychosocial development. The most important person in any infant's life is the primary caregiver, usually the mother. Fathers, other family members, and community members are also very important persons to infants' psychosocial development.

Social Milestones

As babies grow, their waking social periods lengthen. Table 4-7 shows how "'social" human beings develop during infancy. By about two months babies will smile spontaneously at any human face. If the recipient responds, babies will usually make happy noises. Between two and five months babies begin reaching for and grasping objects, including human noses, glasses, hair, and clothing. At about the half-year mark babies begin trying to help feed themselves. By seven to nine months social games such as peek-a-boo and drop and fetch are fun. At about this time babies also become shy or anxious around strangers (called **stranger anxiety**). They may cling and vigorously protest any separation from the primary caregiver(s).

By about one year of age babies begin indicating what they want with holophrases. If babies do not receive gratification when they seek it, or if they are thwarted or frustrated, they may have angry outbursts (temper tantrums). Mealtimes may be chosen as prime times to test the word *no*. Food likes and dislikes may be exaggerated in the process.

By age eighteen months most babies are walking and finding additional ways to satisfy their curiosity. They imitate many of the behaviors of their caregivers. They will attempt to undress and dress themselves—the first rather well, the second with many frustrations. Jealousies become evident—of other adults, other children, even of pets or time-consuming activities such as housework or phone conversations. As you can see, by the end of infancy babies have already experienced a fairly wide range of social-emotional reactions (among them, distress, delight, attachment to caregivers, anxiety with strangers, curiosity, pleasure, frustration, anger, and jealousy.

Bonding

You will recall from the description of the Leboyer method of delivery (p. 94) that contemporary childbirth attendants frequently ask the mother and/or the father to hold and caress their neonate as soon as possible after birth. Frequently, the newborn is placed on the mother's abdomen for stroking, or even to her breast for breast-feeding, while the episiotomy is being stitched. Fathers who participate in delivery are often asked to give the newborn its first gentle bath. These requests encourage the new parents to participate in a synchronous behavior known as **bonding**. It is synchronous because as the mother and father are getting to know their baby, the baby looks at their faces, hears their voices, smells them, and responds to their touches. Newborns are generally quietly alert for the first hour after birth with wide open eyes. They can focus on objects from 8 to 12 inches away from their faces and can make brief eye-to-eye contact. Their hearing is well developed (see p. 103), and they seem to like to listen to the changes in pitch and rhythm that accompany human speech. The

Table 4-7 Selected Social Milestones of Infancy with Approximate Average Age of Emergence.

Milestone	Age of Emergence
Regards face	1 month
Social smile evoked by face	2 months
Selective smiles to familiar faces	5 months
Plays social games (for example, peek-a-boo)	7 months
Shy with strangers	8 months
Resists separation from caregiver	10 months
Holds own cup for drinking	12 months
Uses spoon to feed self	18 months
Removes own clothing	18 months
Plays interactive games (such as hide and seek)	24 months

neonate generally responds to the touch of another human by relaxing and snuggling. Their lips are especially sensitive to touch, and a gentle touch on a newborn's lips usually elicits a smacking response, not unlike a kiss.

When a baby makes eye contact, listens to a voice, turns toward a familiar smell, snuggles, or makes a kissing noise, the parent eliciting such behaviors has a hard time not falling in love (bonding) with the baby! The synchronous baby, in turn, seems to be falling in love with the parent(s).

Biologists have long known that early contact between some mammalian mothers and their offspring is necessary for caregiving behaviors to begin. If an ewe, for example, does not have contact with her lamb until two to three hours after birth, she will not let the lamb nurse, but instead butts it and shoves it away (Campos et al., 1983). Likewise, rats, monkeys, and goats need to have early contact with their offspring in order to initiate maternal behaviors.

During the early 1970s, many pediatricians began to suspect that a similar phenomenon might be operating between human mothers and infants. Research by Leifer and colleagues (1972), for example, demonstrated that mothers of full-term babies, who could hold their neonates, were very different in behaviors from mothers of premature babies who were kept in incubators. The mothers of full-term babies smiled at their infants more often and held them closer to their bodies. Leifer also compared two groups of mothers of premature infants. One group of premie mothers could have contact with their infants through the incubator windows, handling them and participating in normal caregiving procedures. The other group of premie mothers were separated from their infants except for visual contact. The mothers who had contact with their premature infants engaged in more affectionate touching and more close holding of their infants in the post-discharge observations. The mothers who were separated from their premature infants experienced more divorce, more emotional disturbance, and more often put their babies up for adoption. Child developmentalists wondered if they should try to augment early mother–infant contact. Klaus and his colleagues (1972) used research data to demonstrate that early contact made a dramatic difference in later caregiving. Bonded mothers were shown to be more attentive and more loving (see Figure 4-23).

Kennell, Voos, and Klaus (1970) reported that mothers who had extensive contact with their neonates in the first three days after birth had more secure attachments with their infants at one year than did mothers who held their neonates only at feeding. Reva Rubin (1963) described the bonding contact. The new mother, at first tentatively, very gently explores her neonate with a fingertip, stroking a small area (hair, profile). She behaves very much like a person in the first throes of courtship. Gradually, she braves a whole-hand stroke. Using palm as well as fingers she makes contact with larger areas of her baby (back, head, buttocks). Finally she uses her arms as an extension of her whole body. Rodholm and Larsson (1982) reported similar behavior patterns when fathers first approach their neonates. They begin by touching the infant's ex-

Figure 4-23
Early contact between parent(s) and infant with tender stroking and talking enhances a bonding phenomenon.

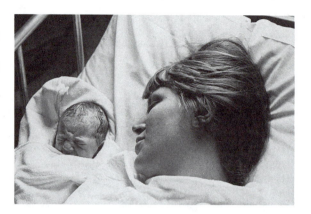

tremities, then the trunk, and finally the face, using their fingertips first, then proceeding to their palms.

Klaus and Kennell (1982) eventually wrote a controversial book in which they hypothesized that there is a sensitive period, lasting two to three days after birth, in which mothers and infants must bond. Without such early contact, they feared, attachment would not reach an optimal level later in life.

While studies suggest benefits from early parent–infant bonding, they do not prove that bonding must occur in the neonatorium. Many infants who have experienced early separation have later become securely attached to parents or parent substitutes. Chess and Thomas (1982), in a review of the literature on bonding, suggested that the attachment of parent and infant in the early neonatal period is not crucial to the child's later psychosocial development. Goldberg (1983) argued that we do not yet know how important (or unimportant) bonding is due to a lack of appropriate research. She warns that while early contact should be supported, parents must not be made to feel that they are already failures if, for some reason, they cannot establish an early bond (see Figure 4-24).

Attachment

In the 1940s and 1950s a few studies were made of infants raised in overcrowded orphanages. In general, the foundlings received only physical care. They were kept in cribs with covered sides, possibly to prevent the spread of infections, and were picked up only on alternate days for baths. Bottles were propped in the cribs. Visual contact with the caregivers and other babies was minimal due to the covered crib sides. Verbal stimulation was limited, and no toys were provided. Rene Spitz (1946) found that after two years of such care 37% of the infants had died, and the survivors seemed emotionally starved. In another study, Wayne Dennis found that over 60% of such deprived infants could not sit up alone at age two, and 80% could not walk by age four (Dennis and Najarian, 1957). Today many of these orphans would be diagnosed as having failure-to-thrive syndrome and the suggested cause would probably be a failure of attachment.

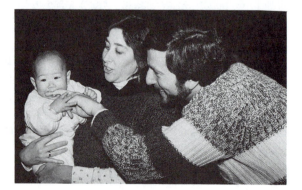

Figure 4-24
Most adopted infants become securely attached to their adoptive parents despite a failure to bond in the first few days after birth.

John Bowlby (1951), a psychoanalyst working in England with parents and children separated by long-term illnesses or the havoc worked by World War II, described the serious sequelae in children separated from adults to whom they had already become attached. In his writings, Bowlby emphasized the importance of an infant's developing a primary attachment to a caring, responsible adult.

Harry and Margaret Harlow (1965) demonstrated the importance of cuddling (**contact comfort**) for attachment and emotional well-being when they raised newborn rhesus monkeys with either chicken wire-covered or terry cloth-covered "surrogate" (substitute) mothers. Infant monkeys spend much more time with the warm, cloth-covered mothers even when they were fed from bottles placed in the wire mothers. When a frightening object like a moving toy was placed in their cages, they ran to the cloth-covered mother for comfort. If the warm, cloth-covered mothers were absent, the baby monkeys became extremely agitated. They did not seem to be comforted by the presence of the wire mothers. The Harlows suggested that human infants also have a psychological need for close contact with a warm, soft person to whom they can become attached.

Infants are aware of strangers and use their mother for a security base as early as two to four months after birth (Mizukami et al., 1990). An attachment has nearly always developed by the second half of the first year.

Ainsworth and her colleagues (1978) studied patterns of attachment. In their studies, which have become prototypes for many other studies of the mother–infant attachment, the infants were briefly separated from their mothers twice. In the first instance, the mother left the baby in a laboratory room with a stranger. In the second separation, the mother left the baby in the room alone. Of special interest to Ainsworth was the baby's behavior in the two reunion episodes following separation. About two-thirds of the babies sought to be close to their mothers on reunion, and if picked up they tended to resist being put down again (Ainsworth, 1982). They were labeled as having *secure attachment.* About one-quarter of the babies reacted by avoiding their mothers on reunion. They had not seemed to be very disturbed by the separation. They were called *insecurely attached, anxious/avoidant type.* Less than 10% of the babies reacted by seeking proximity to their mothers on reunion but behaving in an ambivalent or even angry fashion. These babies had been acutely distressed in the separation episodes. They were labeled *insecurely attached, anxious/ambivalent type.*

Ainsworth and her colleagues were able to correlate mothering behaviors with infant attachment types. Mothers of securely attached infants were most sensitive to their babies' needs and communications. Mothers of insecurely attached infants were less emotionally expressive and felt more aversion to close bodily contact with their babies. Durrett, Otaki, and Richards (1984) reported that mothers of securely attached infants perceived fathers as being more supportive than did mothers of insecurely attached infants. In a similar study, Egeland and Farber (1984) found that mothers of anxious/avoidant babies tended to have negative feelings about motherhood and to treat their babies with more careless indifference.

Many researchers have studied patterns of attachment on a longitudinal basis. By age two, securely attached infants are more independent and have better spatial abilities (Hazen and Durrett, 1982). They also are more playful, have longer attention spans, and have larger vocabularies (Main, 1983). By ages four to five, securely attached infants become more independent and positive in nursery school settings, while insecurely attached infants show signs of high dependency as well as resistant and avoidant behaviors (Sroufe, Fox, and Pancake, 1983).

Securely attached infants may have attachments to multiple caregivers. Kotelchuck (1976) demonstrated that infants can be securely attached to both parents, father as well as mother. Teti and Ablard (1989) showed that in a parent's absence, a securely attached infant may seek contact comfort from an equally secure older sibling. Infants can also become attached to other primary caregivers (e.g., grandmothers, day care attendants, babysitters) (see Figure 4-25).

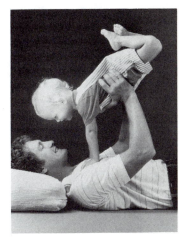

Figure 4-25
Most infants form attachments to their fathers as well as to their mothers.

Kagan (1978) advised caution in concluding that insecure attachment in infancy produces irreversible consequences. He studied infants in an isolated subsistence farming village in Guatemala who typically spent their first year of life confined in a small dark hut. They were hardly spoken to, not played with, and poorly nourished. When they emerged from the hut in their second year of life, attachment was minimal, and they were socially and intellectually retarded. However, by adolescence most of these slow starters performed nearly as well as other children on standardized tests. He suggested that the mind and the personality are elastic in early childhood: easily deformed by shearing forces but able to rebound when and if the deforming forces are removed. Sroufe (1979) wrote that the lasting consequences of early inadequate care may be subtle and complex. Insecurely attached infants may have increased vulnerability to repeated stress in later life.

Erikson's Trust versus Mistrust

Erik Erikson postulated that humans go through eight stages of psychosocial development in the life span (see Chapter Two). At each stage there exists a nuclear conflict. Although nuclear conflicts are never completely resolved during the stage in which they emerge, a satisfactory resolution of most of the conflict leaves a person with the judgment and ability to handle repeated upsurgings of the basic conflict throughout life. A person who has not passed through a stage successfully experiences a feeling of insecurity related to that "sense" throughout life.

Erikson proposed that, in infancy, the most crucial sense to be formed is a sense of **trust**, a feeling of confidence and reliance that caregivers will provide adequate care. Erikson's sense of trust does not explicitly deal with attachment: it is implicit, however, in the theory that an attachment does form between the infant and the caregiver as trust develops. Erikson (1963) suggested that when a mother meets the infant's needs consistently, with sameness and continuity, the infant learns to rely not only on the external provider but also on himself or herself. Trust is learned very early through situations such as feedings and diaperings. If infants are fed when hunger first appears rather than being allowed to develop strong hunger pangs, they are more comfortable in their surroundings. Likewise, if they are diapered when they first wet rather than being left cold and dirty, a feeling that the world is a good place is more apt to develop. **Mistrust**, the alternative, develops when infants are allowed to experience frequent bouts of overwhelming hunger or are left dirty, uncomfortable, irritated, and irritable. Table 4-8 presents some of Erikson's descriptions of the sense of trust versus the sense of mistrust and some adult behaviors that foster each attitude.

Effective caregiving for the development of a sense of trust involves far more than just taking care of an infant's bodily needs. It prospers with warm, tender touching, verbal soothing, verbal stimulation. Fathers do not spend as much time feeding and changing diapers as mothers (Parke, 1982). They are more likely to play with their infants, and their play is more physical and rousing, especially with sons (Power and Parke, 1982). The vigorous physical play between fathers and male infants may have a beneficial effect. The boys may learn to regulate their physical aggression as a result of experiencing competent rough and tumble play in which nobody gets hurt (Parke, 1982).

Fathers engage in more feeding and diapering if a mother undergoes Caesarean section delivery (Entwisle and Doering, 1980). Fathers are also more apt to feed and diaper if their infant is premature, low-birth-weight, or small for gestational age. There is some evidence that an infant's development is enhanced by more paternal participation (Pederson, Rubenstein, and Yarrow, 1980). Other evidence suggests that a mother's competence in caregiving is enhanced by paternal support of her efforts (Pederson, 1981). While the research does not suggest that a father's participation is essential to the development of trust, it does suggest that it is very beneficial.

Table 4-8 Erikson's First Nuclear Conflict: Trust versus Mistrust.

Sense	Eriksonian Descriptions	Fostering Adult Behaviors
Trust	Ease of feeding, depth of sleep, relaxation of bowels	Caregiving techniques with consistency, continuity, and sameness
	Feeling of inner goodness	Sensitive attention to the baby's individual needs
	Reliance on outer providers	Firm sense of personal trustworthiness; conviction that there is meaning to what one is doing
	Trust in the capacity of one's own organs to cope with urges	
versus Mistrust	Sense of having been deprived, divided, abandoned	Inconsistent, neglectful caregiving
	Anxiety, rage, lack of control of urges	Withdrawal from situations where baby tests the relationship and demands attention to his or her needs

SOURCE: Based on material from "Eight Ages of Man" from *Childhood and Society* (2nd ed., revised) by Erik H. Erikson, with the permission of W. W. Norton & Company, Inc. Copyright 1950, © 1963 by W. W. Norton & Company, Inc.

Infant Daycare

While nearly one-half of mothers of infants work, most of them provide for infant care in the homes of relatives or friends, or in their own homes with babysitters, husbands, or other relatives (see Figure 4-26). In **infant daycare** situations, a few adults provide care for several infants. This poses certain limitations on the establishment of close, one-to-one relationships between infants and caregivers. Administrators of most infant daycare centers are aware of the importance of attachment in an infant's life and will make efforts to have one or two adults care for the same babies every day. There are problems, however. Infants are brought to daycare centers early in the morning before the hour that the parent must be at his or her own job. They are picked up to be taken home late in the afternoon or early in the evening, after the parent has finished work and perhaps run a few errands. An infant's time at the daycare center averages eight and a half to ten hours a day. Employees of daycare centers usually work eight-hour days and, in addition, may leave for holidays, vacations, lunch or coffee breaks, and sick days. Thus, in spite of efforts to have just one or two adults

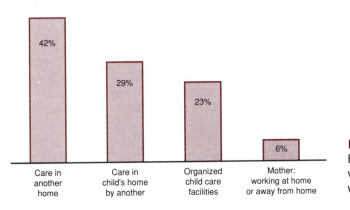

Figure 4-26
Employed mothers choose a variety of options for infant care while they are at work.

provide most of the care for any given infant, that infant will in fact experience an array of caregivers over time.

Infants will also experience the need to share their favorite caregiver (the one to whom they become most attached) with other infants. They will have experiences of waiting and watching while other infants are being held, cuddled, fed, changed, and entertained by their adult. If they become sick, their caregiving is either taken over by a relatively unfamiliar nurse in the daycare center or they must remain at home, often with an equally unfamiliar babysitter. In spite of some of these roadblocks, however, many daycare centers do a good job of providing sensitive attention to each infant's individual needs (see Figure 4-27).

The best centers are those with fewer children and more staff who work shorter hours and do not have housekeeping as well as childcare responsibilities (Howes, 1983). A special program in Syracuse, New York, tied routine caregiving activities such as feeding and diapering into joyful emotional encounters aimed at providing the maximum in a living, loving environment for its babies (Lally and Honig, 1977). This center, with an enriched cognitive stimulation program as well, is a model for many of the excellent infant daycare centers being run at present. It trains caregivers in workshops and through its manual, *Infant Caregiving: A Design for Training* (Honig and Lally, 1972).

In extensive reviews of research studies of infants in daycare, Clarke-Stewart and Fein (1983) and Scarr (1985) reported that infants do form close relationships with daycare staff. These attachments do not replace nor weaken the parent–infant primary attachment bond. A host of research reports have documented the idea that securely attached infants, despite long hours in daycare, still prefer their mother, go to her for help, stay closer to her, approach her more often, go to her when distressed or bored, and interact with her more. Infants who have experienced high quality daycare have more social competence with peers and adults and do better on measures of intellectual development. On the other hand, poor quality (overcrowded, understaffed) daycare or unresponsive babysitters have been associated with poor cognitive, language, and social outcomes (Scarr, 1985).

Honig (1983), in an attempt to evaluate various infant programs, pointed out that it is difficult to compare programs and rate their effectiveness because each has different staff, methods, goals, durations, and populations served. Although research demonstrates that good infant daycare is not detrimental, it does not suggest that it is better than care by parents. Many experts on infant and early child development feel that working mothers should be allowed extended leaves of absence from their jobs during the early months of their infants' lives. Many experts also support government subsidies to infant daycare facilities, as well as development of more centers at the mothers' working places. The United States lags behind the countries of Western Europe as well as China, Japan, and the Soviet Union in the support it provides for families with young children.

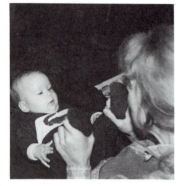

Figure 4-27
High quality infant daycare can meet a baby's needs for TLC as well as for feedings and diaperings.

Temperament

Each infant comes into the world with his or her own unique characteristics. Normal babies differ remarkably. Some infants, when held, cling. Others behave more like rag dolls. Some infants sleep a great deal more than others. **Individual differences** in babies have been noted in their activity, rhythmicity, adaptability, approach, threshold, intensity, moods, distractibility, and persistence (Thomas and Chess, 1977). Babies also differ in the amount of their crying, soothability, and capability for self-comforting behavior.

In a longitudinal study of more than 200 infants in New York City, Thomas and Chess (1977) identified three different types of temperaments in infants. They defined **temperament** as behavioral style, the "how" of behavior in contrast to the "what" (abilities) and the "why" (motivation). Others prefer to define temperament as individual differences in the expression of emotionality and arousal (Campos et al., 1983). The three types of temperament classified by Thomas and Chess are difficult, easy, and slow-to-warm-up. *Difficult* babies do not have predictable rhythms; they react intensely, approach slowly, adapt slowly, and are more frequently negative in mood. *Easy* babies do have predictable rhythms, react mildly, approach and adapt quickly, and are more frequently positive in mood. *Slow-to-warm-up* babies approach and adapt slowly and are more negative in mood. However, they are not as intense as difficult infants. They react mildly and have a relatively low activity level. Infants with difficult temperaments are much more fearful of strangers (Berberian and Snyder, 1982). They are in Erikson's polar conflict scheme, least trusting (see Figure 4-28).

Parenting styles and infant temperamental patterns work in synchrony with each other. Mothers of infants with more difficult temperaments have less interpersonal coordination of their speech with their babies and longer pauses between speaking (Feldstein et al., 1990a). Feldstein and his colleagues (1990b) have suggested that interpersonal timing of speech patterns may have a hereditary basis. Infants' patterns of speech are very similar, whether they are talking to their mothers or to strangers.

Twin studies demonstrate that temperamental styles are not simply a result of parenting practices. Identical twins are much more alike on temperament ratings than same-sexed fraternal twins, both at nine months (Torgersen and Kringlen, 1978) and at four and seven years (Goldsmith and Gottesman, 1981). Weissbluth and Green (1984) also found that difficult temperaments may be associated with low plasma progesterone levels in infancy, reflecting individual differences in neurophysiology.

Many studies have shown sex differences in infant temperaments. Boy babies have been shown to be more active, both awake and in sleep, to fuss and cry more, and to soothe less easily, which may eventually lead to fewer attempts to soothe them by caregivers. Girl babies have been shown to babble to faces and voices more and in turn to receive more face-to-face vocal exchanges. Carey and McDevitt (1978), who developed a reliable and widely used infant temperament questionnaire, reported that girls are less approaching toward strangers at four to eight months than boys are. As infants move into their second year of life, boys have been observed to show more aggression and independence, whereas girls have been observed spending more time close to familiar adults, vocalizing. Arguments as to whether observed sex differences are genetically or environmentally induced, or both, are unresolved. Most research suggests socialization factors heavily affect the outcome. The differences in uniquely individual infants can be detected in the first three days of life and tend to be stable over time. For example, Korner and associates (1985) compared activity monitored in infancy with activity levels in the same children at four to eight years of age. They found that the least vigorous infants became the least active children.

Ethnic differences in temperament have been seen as early as a few days after the birth. Kagan, Kearsley, and Zelazo (1978) reported that Chinese American infants

Figure 4-28
Temperamentally easy babies are usually positive and adapt readily to new situations. Babies with difficult temperaments react intensely and negatively to changes in routine.

are less vocal, less active, more socially inhibited, and more negative in mood than non-Chinese infants. When Hsu, Soong, and their associates (1981) used the Carey Infant Temperament Questionnaire in Taiwan to assess Chinese babies, they found them to be more withdrawing, less adaptable, less distractible, and more negative in mood than Chinese American babies. Weissbluth (1982) found Chinese American babies to have, on the average, a shorter total sleep duration than non-Chinese infants. Weissbluth associated decreased duration of night sleep with more negative mood. Ethnic differences in temperament may exist, but they may be associated with environmental as well as genetic differences.

Is it useful to label infants by temperament type, especially when research cannot prove that all temperaments remain stable or clearly explain why differences exist? Carey (1981) gave many reasons why assessing temperament and discussing results with parents are useful. One need not use the labels "difficult" or "slow-to-warm-up." However, parents will not feel as inadequate, guilty, apprehensive, or angry if they realize that their infant's slow approach to foods or people, intensity, or negative moods, for example, are temperamental characteristics that are inborn. Temperament assessments can help parents anticipate their infant's probable behaviors and emotional expressions. With this insight, they can shift their interaction patterns to mesh with their baby's reactions and prevent potentially serious family problems.

Discipline

Discipline refers to limit setting, to training that develops self-control. It is a very important part of helping babies feel safe and secure. It is best brought about through consistent, predictable caregiving routines (see Figure 4-29).

At birth infants' wake–sleep–hunger cycles are irregular. Initially, it is a good idea to offer food each time babies awaken from sleep, although before long babies will develop their own feeding schedules. In general, periods of hunger vary from two and a half to four hours apart. Soon caregivers will recognize hunger cycles and will discover the approximate rhythm of their own infants. Knowing the approximate length of time between hunger cycles will help establish another rhythm, the day–night sleep pattern. Most neonates will automatically have one longer nap (ranging from four to eight hours) per day and several shorter ones (ranging from one to three hours). The longer nap does not necessarily occur at night, but a knowledge of the approximate time between hunger pangs during the short nap periods will enable caregivers to "move" the longer nap to night. They simply can wake the baby for feedings every two and a half (or three, or four) hours during the day and provide a warm, dark, quiet atmosphere conducive to sleep at night. The "longer" night nap may only be four hours initially, but it gradually lengthens until babies "sleep through the night." Other ways that caregivers can demonstrate consistency and continuity and help establish disciplined,

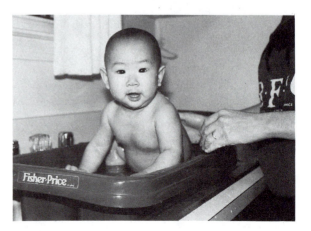

Figure 4-29
Baths, naps, meals, and other routines help discipline infants and make them feel safe and secure.

patterned days for their infants are by bathing the baby at approximately the same time each day and by making feedings routine.

Food likes and dislikes are common in infancy. To avoid confrontations over foods, caregivers should try a new food when the baby is neither tired nor painfully hungry. If babies resist, caregivers should stay calm. They can try the food again later.

Biting usually follows teething. Infants learn what not to bite (caregivers, siblings, furniture) and what is acceptable (teething toys, dry toast, biscuits) through the caregiver's prompt substitution of appropriate teething materials for inappropriate ones.

Mobility requires a certain amount of household and outdoor engineering. Household engineering consists of such things as moving dangerous items out of reach or locking them away, using gates as necessary on stairwells or off-limits areas, putting safety plugs in electrical outlets, and keeping pins, scissors, nails, or other sharp or poisonous items off the floors. Outdoor engineering consists of providing a fenced-in play yard, teaching the baby never to cross a street without holding an adult hand, checking toys and playground equipment for sharp edges or toxic paint flakes, and never leaving the baby alone around open water (see Figure 4-30).

Infants also learn to respect and obey the word *no*. If it is used only when needed and reinforced by removing the infant from the temptation (or vice versa), it will be heeded. If it is voiced often and indiscriminately with no follow-up, however, it will eventually be ignored.

Temper tantrums are much more likely to occur when babies are hungry and tired than when they are fed and rested (see Box 4-5). Likewise, they occur more frequently

Figure 4-30
Babies love to play in water. Never leave an infant unattended around water. Even a shallow puddle can be hazardous.

BOX 4-5

What's in a Four- to Twelve-Month-Old's Cry?

By four to six months of age, the cry sounds of an infant are not indicative of a high-risk neonate (see Box 4-1) or of colic (see Box 4-2). Do all older babies' cry sounds become similar? Not at all. Each unique baby has a repertoire of cries by this age to communicate such things as hunger, pain, sleepiness, or boredom, and the primary caregiver(s) can tell which cry is which. Nevertheless, some babies' cries are generally more irritating and "spoiled" sounding than the repertoire of cries of other babies. Lounsbury and Bates (1982) asked mothers of four- to six-month-old infants to rate the taped cries of twelve unrelated same-aged infants in terms of their emotional responses to the cries. Would the crying induce sadness, a desire to mother the baby, irritation, or a perception that the infant on the tape was "spoiled"?

Each infant whose crying had been taped had previously been classified by temperament type, difficult to easy. Unrelated mothers, not knowing the temperament ratings, were expert at picking out the "difficult" babies. They were the babies who sounded "spoiled" and whose cries were most irritating. Spectrum analysis of the cries of difficult babies reveal that they have longer pauses within and between cry sounds.

Are babies with "'difficult' temperaments spoiled? Weissbluth (1985) advised that, while the temperament is inborn, the caregivers' reactions to the irritating crying can either reduce its frequency or exacerbate the screaming ("spoil" the baby) after four to six months. His recommendation: "During the first few months, always respond promptly to your baby's crying. After four, five, certainly six months, it is time to change your tactics" (p. 135). Weissbluth focused on night crying or crankiness between midnight and 5 A.M., which he called "trained night crying." A baby who fusses all night will not be pleasant the next day (just like an adult!). The caregiver should shift the baby's sleep schedule. Weissbluth recommends waking the baby early, allowing no naps after 11 A.M., and imposing bedtime at 9 P.M. The bedroom should be kept dark (no night light) and quiet, and the baby should be left alone, even if he or she cries. Within a few days, the crying will occur less frequently, for shorter and shorter durations, and soon the baby will "learn" to sleep through the night. Parents need to be consistent with this imposition of discipline. Weissbluth adds a word of caution. If the baby habitually snores and appears to have difficulty breathing at night, parents should consult a pediatrician. If the baby awakens agitated and frightened from nightmares or night terrors, parents should check to see if he or she has a fever. If night terrors are common, parents should consult a pediatrician or perhaps a child psychologist.

when toys, scenery, or social contacts thwart or frustrate some goal than when babies are able to observe or explore phenomena that interest them. If an infant desires something forbidden and must be thwarted with a *no*, it is a wise caregiver who can quickly find an acceptable substitute goal for the baby or in some way distract attention to another interesting stimulus.

Summary

The neonate must make many transitions from prenatal to extrauterine existence. The first month is a high-risk period. The appearance of a newborn differs significantly from that of cute babies in media advertising. Several assessments are made of the neonate to assure normal development and behaviors. High-risk neonates (preterm, low birth weight, small for gestational age) need specialized care to survive. Their parents also need supportive services.

Growth and change are rapid in the first two years of life. Development proceeds from head to foot, from near to far, and from general to specific. Good nutrition is vital to growth, as is sufficient sleep. Health maintenance requires that infections be treated promptly; many can be prevented through a series of immunizations. Safety precautions to prevent accidents are essential. Common health problems include digestive and nutritional disorders and respiratory infections. Sudden infant death syndrome and failure-to-thrive syndrome affect a smaller number of infants each year.

Piaget described a sensorimotor stage to explain the cognitive changes that occur during infancy. In six progressively more complex phases, babies move from predominant exercise of preexisting reflexes to actions that require remembering and planning. Contemporary researchers are demonstrating that infants may be smarter earlier than Piaget thought.

Learning to talk has its roots in receptive language.

The baby listens to communications of others and begins to sort out meaning. Babbling shows a drift towards the phonemes of the mother tongue. Expressive language (talking) usually begins with nouns and verbs. Eventually the baby begins to string nouns and verbs together ("Daddy come"). Early speech is described as telegraphic because only the most salient words are reproduced. Human infants probably have an innate ability to acquire language.

Tender loving care is a crucial ingredient in the make-up of emotionally healthy infants. Babies may bond to parents in the first few days of life. They need contact comfort as well as feeding and diapering. They become attached to their primary caregivers and show joy at reunion and anxiety at separation. Quality infant day care has not been shown to be detrimental to psychosocial development.

Erikson described the most crucial social learning in infancy as trust, a sense of confidence and reliance in the caregivers. Trust develops when caregivers are consistent with schedules and discipline as well as sensitive to the baby's needs.

Babies show individual differences in temperament early. Babies shape their caregivers' behaviors as well as respond to them. Discipline requires that all caregivers involved with an infant should be sensitive to the baby's needs and temperament and consistent with schedules.

Key Concepts

neonate	cephalocaudal development	croup	telegraphic speech
colostrum	proximal-distal development	SIDS (sudden infant death syndrome)	language acquisition device (LAD)
lanugo			
vernix caseosa	general to specific development	FTTS (failure-to-thrive syndrome)	stranger anxiety
soft spots			bonding
ossification	pincer grasp	myelin	attachment
Apgar scale	lactation	synapse	contact comfort
Brazelton scale	motor milestones	neurotransmitters	trust versus mistrust
reflexes	colic	sensorimotor intelligence	infant daycare
respiratory distress syndrome	iron deficiency anemia	phonetic drift	individual differences
	eczema	holophrases	temperament
			discipline

Questions for Review

1. Describe the process that occurs immediately after birth, when the baby adapts from intrauterine to extrauterine life.
2. Describe a normal and an abnormal cry of a neonate, a two-month-old, and a ten-month-old, discussing probable reason(s) for the abnormal cry you have described at each of the ages.
3. Your friend has written to ask you whether you think she should breast-feed or bottle-feed her infant.
   Write a letter in response giving pros and cons of each.
4. Your neighbor's infant has been diagnosed as having non-organic failure-to-thrive syndrome. What does this tell you? Can you help your neighbor?
5. Discuss how families can foster cognitive development in infancy.
6. Infants may reside in foster homes for a number of months, often being moved from one home to another. Consider the future implications of this lifestyle on such children. Speculate as to the resolution of Erikson's trust–mistrust conflict in these situations. Also, discuss the consequences in terms of formation of the attachment bond.
7. Infants require a great deal of attention to both their physical and psychological needs. Describe some of their psychological needs.

Further Readings

Field, T. M. (1990). *Infancy*. Cambridge, MA: Harvard University Press.
   An enjoyable exposition on infant development covering motor, perceptual, cognitive, social, and emotional processes.

Kaye, K. (1982). *The mental and social life of babies*. Chicago: University of Chicago Press.
   Subtitled "How parents create persons," this book also emphasizes "How babies create parents." It details the many ways in which reciprocal relationships affect behaviors.

Lewis, M., and Worobey, J. (eds.) (1989). *Infant stress and coping*. San Francisco: Jossey-Bass.
   Separate chapters cover hormonal responses to stress, stress and illness, frustration and anger, mother–infant separation, prenatal and postnatal stresses.

Oates, J., and Sheldon, S. (eds.) (1987). *Cognitive development in infancy*. East Sussex, U.K.: Lawrence Erlbaum/Open University.
   A collection of 18 papers on cognition divided into sections on the cultural and biological content, learning, perception, object concept, social behavior, and continuity.

O'Shea, J. S. (1988). *Under three*. New York: Van Nostrand Reinhold.
   A comprehensive guide to caring for a baby written in nontechnical language by a pediatrician and a team of child-care experts. Beautifully illustrated.

Scarr, S. (1985). *Mother care, other care*. New York: Basic Books.
   A review of research of the risks and advantages of placing children in out-of-home day care.

Early Childhood 5

Somewhere between eighteen and thirty months of age infants develop motor coordination and speech skills to such an extent that their parents and other adults view them as toddlers rather than as babies. They walk, they have increased success with talking, and they strive for a measure of self-reliance and independence. This chapter will describe the various aspects of development separately. These boundaries serve only to help the reader visualize the changes in each area more clearly. Try, if you can, to visualize children you know (or have known) who are approximately ages two, three, four, and five. Keep each whole child in mind as you read about development in the separate areas. The two-year-old is quite different from the five-year-old. In each section the contrasts between younger and older children will be stated.

Early childhood encompasses the ages from two through five, after infancy but before kindergarten. You may have heard the terms Terrible Twos, Conforming Threes, and Out-of-Bounds Fours. Preschoolers are often described as "brats": They exaggerate, brag, tattle, threaten, alibi, and call names. Are these behaviors the result of too much luxury? too little discipline? Are they rooted in biology? Let us take a close look at what is known as early childhood.

> From the day your baby is born, you must teach him to do without things. Children today love luxury too much. They have detestable manners, flout authority, have no respect for their elders. They no longer rise when their parents or teachers enter the room. What kind of awful creatures will they be when they grow up?
>
> —*Socrates*

Physical Development

Physical development can be defined as that which primarily affects the body as contrasted with the mind. The two are truly inseparable because of constant interactive effects. Nevertheless, before examining the development of cognition, language, and psychosocial changes, we will look at the body changes of early childhood. Nutrition, health status, physical disabilities, accidents, and social factors play an important part in determining how each unique child grows physically.

Growth Progression

The rate of growth in the early childhood years is slower than in infancy but follows the same general principles. It is orderly and sequential. It proceeds from head to foot (cephalocaudal direction), from the center outward (proximal-distal direction), and from general to specific movements (see Chapter 4). To illustrate cephalocaudal development, let us look at head and leg circumferences of five-year-olds. Mean head circumference is approximately 50 centimeters, or about 90% of its adult size. In contrast,

143

George was a frail, tow-headed, introverted little boy. He had several big brothers who enjoyed working and playing with their father at the Jorgensen Construction Company. They encouraged George to be like them, but George remembers that he always preferred to stay home and play with his sister, Dolly. Dolly had long blonde hair and wore dresses. George wanted long hair and dresses too. He was very upset to be told that a little boy needed to wear trousers and have his hair cut short. It puzzled him so much that he challenged his mother with whys. She tried to explain that God made both men and women because there are different things men and women need to do to make the world work, and God made George to be a man to do a man's work. George didn't like this answer. He replied "I don't like the kind of surprise God made me."*

Five-year-old George wanted a doll for Christmas. He prayed to God to send him one with long, golden hair. Instead he found a bright red railway train under the tree. He was disappointed, his feelings were hurt, and he desperately wanted to cry, but he had been taught that little boys must not cry.

George spent as much time with his Grandmother as he could. She understood that he loved beautiful things like her fine porcelain, her needlepoint, her crocheted doilies, her flowers, and especially her lavender perfume. He confided to her that he did not like to participate in rough-and-tumble games or fist fights with his brothers. He recalled fearfully running away from his brothers to his Grandmother's house after some childish altercation. She reassured him that it was all right for him to refuse to fight. She told him, "Fighting is the ugliest part of life. To live without fighting is much more important, and much more satisfying."*

George took a piece of his Grandmother's needlepoint with him when he began school, as a security blanket of sorts. A teacher found it and shamed him in front of his class. She told him it was an inappropriate thing for a red-blooded boy to have. His classmates tittered. George was too young to realize that a love for beauty was not the sole property of females. The ridicule made him doubt himself. George told his Grandmother what had happened. She championed his cause as she always did when others laughed at his "sissified" ways. She gently told him he mustn't mind, and gave him another piece of needlework.

George continued to be taunted for his feminine mannerisms throughout late childhood and adolescence. When he was twenty-five, he went to Denmark, the country from which his beloved Grandmother had emigrated. There he had the world's first successful transsexual operation. He returned to New York as Christine Jorgensen. Christine went on to become a spokeswoman for the advancement of medical science and for the sympathetic understanding of persons with transsexuality.

In her autobiography, Christine presented her opinion that the basic feelings about sexual identity are an integral part of a person from birth. She did not believe that her feminine ways were due to the fact that she played with her sister or spent so much time with her Grandmother in early childhood.

How much of sexual identity is influenced by external environmental factors? Would George have developed a masculine gender role if his beloved Grandmother had pushed him in that direction in his formative preschool years? How does ridicule affect self-concept in early childhood? How important are early childhood feelings?

*Jorgensen, C. (1967). *Christine Jorgensen: A personal autobiography.* Middlebury, VT: Paul S. Eriksson, Inc.

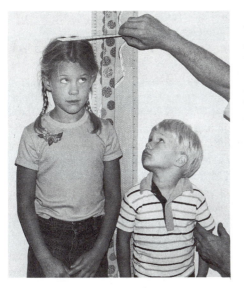

Figure 5-1
The cephalic (head) development of these 7- and 4-year-olds is nearly identical as measured by head circumference. It is the length of the arms, legs, and trunk that give the 7-year-old her larger appearance.

leg circumference is only about 22½ centimeters, less than 45% of its adult size (see Figure 5-1). As an example of proximal-distal development, the young child will develop the ability to use the muscles of the upper arms (pushing) and upper legs (jumping) long before the ability to use the finger muscles (molding clay) or toe muscles (picking up marbles). To illustrate the principle of development from general to specific, consider finger muscles again. First, the young child will have the gross motor ability to push a lump of clay from round to flat then to round again. Later, the fine muscles will acquire the necessary coordination to push the clay into a shape roughly resembling what the child desires (such as a dog or a car).

To help you appreciate some of the physical changes that occur in early childhood, **motor norms** (the average motor achievements by age for a large number of children) are presented in Table 5-1. Gross motor accomplishments are those that involve the

Table 5-1   Gross and Fine Motor Accomplishments of Early Childhood.

Gross Motor Accomplishments	Age Range in Years	Fine Motor Accomplishments	Age Range in Years
Throws ball overhand	2–2½	Imitates vertical line	2–3
Balances on one foot 1 second	2–3¼	Dumps raisin from bottle	2–3
Jumps in place	2–3	Builds tower of eight cubes	2–3¼
Pedals tricycle	2–3	Copies circle	2¼–3¼
Broad jumps	2–3¼	Imitates bridge with three cubes	2¼–3½
Balances on one foot 5 seconds	2½–4¼	Picks longer line, three of three	2½–4¼
Balances on one foot 10 seconds	3–6	Copies plus sign	2¾–4½
Hops on one foot	3–5	Draws man, three parts	3¼–5
Heel-to-toe walk	3¼–5	Imitates square (demonstrated)	3½–5½
Catches bounced ball	3½–5½	Copies square	4½–6
Backward heel-to-toe walk	3¾–6	Draws man, six parts	4½–6

SOURCE: Adapted from Frankenburg & Dodds, Denver Developmental Screening Test (DDST), University of Colorado Medical Center, 1967. Reprinted by permission.

use of the large muscles (arms and legs). Fine motor tasks are those that require use and coordination of smaller muscles (especially fingers).

The average North American two-year-old stands about 81 to 84 centimeters high (32 to 33 inches) and weighs about 11 to 13 kilograms (26 to 28 pounds). By age five the average child stands about 109 to 111 centimeters high (40 to 44 inches) and weighs about 18 to 19 kilograms (39 to 41 pounds). Remember that "average" refers to the sum of many quantities divided by the number of quantities that were added together. No one child should be expected to be average in every respect. Weight gain in early childhood averages about 2 kilograms (4 pounds) per year, and height increases range from 6 to 8 centimeters (2½ to 3½ inches) per year.

Studies of well-nourished European and American children over the past one hundred years have revealed a trend toward increased height each decade up through the 1960s. In countries such as England and Norway and in the upper socioeconomic strata of the United States, this growth seems to have leveled off (Roche, 1979). In many countries where food supplies are scarce, this growth trend (called the **secular growth trend**) has not been seen. When you next visit a museum with artifacts from the early days of American colonization, notice how much smaller the people must have been to wear or use the items on display.

Although the average two-year-old may be about 82 centimeters tall and weigh 12 kilograms, there is a wide range of normal heights and weights for children of every age. These can be found by referring to a table of standard measurement percentiles for age (see Figure 5-2). Individual variations in height and weight are influenced by

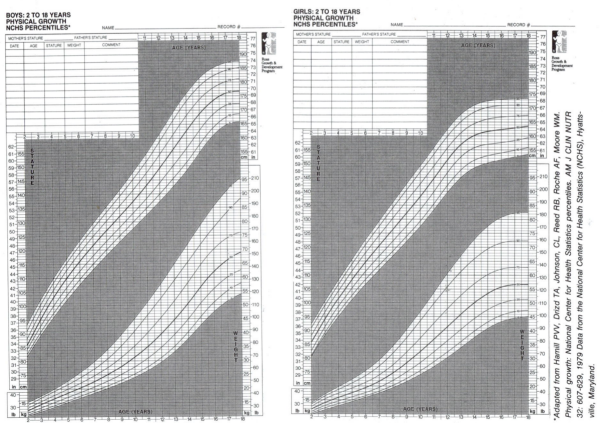

Figure 5-2

Standard measurement percentiles for height and weight of children.

such factors as inheritance, ethnicity, sex, hormones, nutrition, health, and living conditions. Each child's growth in height and weight tends to follow a **growth trajectory** (curved path) that maintains its place in relation to other children's height and weight trajectories over time. Thus, a two-year-old child whose height is in the 90th percentile can be expected to continue to be tall for his or her age, following the 90th percentile trajectory throughout childhood into adulthood. (Weight is more susceptible to dietary factors and cannot be predicted as successfully.) Improvements in nutrition and living conditions can increase height only within certain limits imposed by genetic inheritance and secretions of growth-promoting hormones.

Physical changes occur at a relatively slow, even, and continuous pace. Only occasionally will starts and stops be noticeable. Sometimes a child will concentrate so intently on one aspect of development (for example, tricycle riding) that other emerging abilities will seem to falter or even regress (for instance, bladder sphincter muscle control). Most children will also show some seasonal variations in the speed of their growth. Increases in height occur more rapidly in the spring, whereas increases in weight occur more rapidly in the fall. Illnesses and periods of malnutrition can temporarily slow children's rates of growth, but when diseases are cured or missing nutrients supplied, a catch-up phenomenon usually occurs (see Figure 5-3).

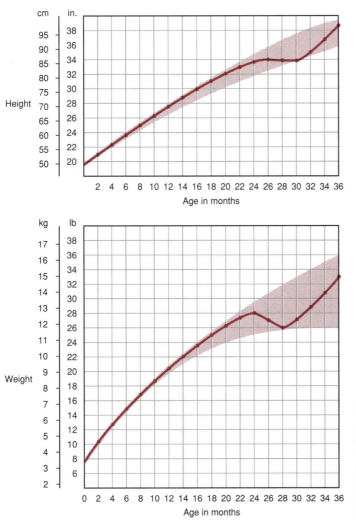

Figure 5-3

An illness can temporarily slow a child's physical development. When it is cured, however, a catch-up growth phenomenon will assure that the child once more achieves her place on her growth trajectory.

Figure 5-4
The arms of two-year-olds are so short that only their hands extend above their heads when they raise their arms. Adult arms are so long that the elbow usually extends above the head.

The **catch-up growth** may be as much as 400 percent above normal and will continue until appropriate norms are achieved, at which point growth slows to normal (Ganong, 1980). Exceptions depend on the length and severity of the disease or malnourished state, on the organs affected, and on the emotional state of the child. The brain is more susceptible to permanent injury because its cells are not replaced once they are destroyed. (To some extent, other brain cells may take over the functions of the missing cells.)

Arms and legs grow fastest during early childhood, trailed by trunk growth. Head growth follows at a much slower pace, mainly because brain weight has already reached approximately 75% of its adult size by age two. The top-heavy, short-legged appearance of babyhood changes to proportions more nearly resembling those of adults between ages two and five. When two-year-olds bend over, they can usually touch their heads to the floor without bending their knees. By age five they can simply place their hands flat on the floor without bending their knees. When two-year-olds wave goodbye, their arms go straight up without any elbow bending, yet their hands reach only slightly above their heads (see Figure 5-4). Five-year-olds' hands reach considerably higher up into the air. Potbellies are typical of toddlers, due to the forward placement of the bladder in their relatively short trunks and to the lordosis (curvature) of their as yet unelongated spines. By age five to six potbellies and the lordosis disappear.

Visual acuity improves dramatically during early childhood. Remember from Chapter 4 that vision at birth is about 20/300. By age one, it may improve to about 20/100, by age two to about 20/40, by age three to about 20/30, and finally by age four to "normal" acuity of 20/20 (Silver, 1984). Accommodation of the lens to shift from near to far focus on different objects is rapid, and convergence—bringing the image seen by each eye to a central point where it appears the same—is smooth.

Consider the following comparisons of neuromuscular skills of toddlers and preschoolers. At age two children walk upstairs holding onto a hand, rail, or wall. They place both feet on each step before proceeding to the next. By age three they begin to alternate their feet, one to a step. By age four they have usually ceased to hold on to anything and alternate steps going both down and up. By age five they may well run up the stairs. For many two-year-olds, holding a glass of liquid and drinking without spilling is a feat. By age three children can drink well and feed themselves complete meals with very little assistance. At age three children undress (quite successfully) and attempt to dress (less successfully). By age five, children dress without assistance, including washing face and hands and brushing teeth. Five-year-olds may even be able to tie the laces of their shoes in neat bows. Three-year-olds learn to jump over or off objects and maintain their balance. Five-year-olds learn to jump rope in rhythm. Two-year-olds may or may not be toilet trained for daytime (there will be more on toilet training later in this chapter). If they are, there are still generally some accidents. Three-year-olds may or may not be night trained. Five-year-olds generally take care of their own toilet needs, unannounced and unassisted.

The Denver Developmental Screening Test (DDST) is a reliable and widely accepted normative schedule that allows an examiner to ascertain how much a child has matured in various areas (see Figure 5-5). It has bars that represent the age span between which 25% and 90% of children perform each item. It alerts professionals to the possibility of developmental delays so that appropriate diagnostic studies may be pursued. Screens are not meant to diagnose. The DDST does not give an intelligence quotient (IQ) or developmental quotient (DQ). An even shorter form of the DDST has been developed (Frankenburg, 1981). It is a prescreen, to use before the full DDST. If parents have a high school education, the prescreen consists of a ten-item questionnaire. If the parents are not educated, the prescreen consists of twelve performance items for the child to accomplish. If one or more of the prescreen items indicate delay, the full DDST is given. Together, the two forms of the new prescreens are known as the Prescreening Developmental Questionnaire (PDQ).

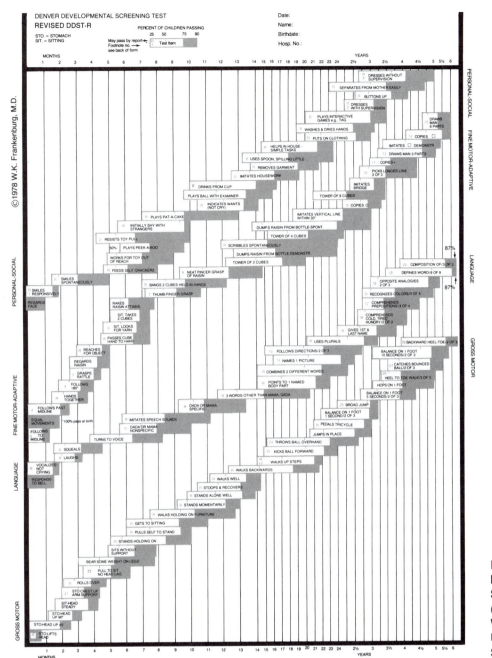

Figure 5-5
Denver Developmental
Screening Test (DDST).
(Reprinted by permission of Dr.
William K. Frankenburg,
University of Colorado Health
Sciences Center.)

Frankenburg and Caldwell also constructed a screening test for potential school problems, to be given to children between birth and age six in their own homes. Known as the Home Screening Questionnaire (HSQ), it may be useful in determining which preschoolers need a longer, more comprehensive evaluation for potential school problems. With early diagnosis and early intervention, difficulties may be alleviated.

Nutrition

Adequate nutrition consists of a diet balanced with proteins, carbohydrates, and fats plus sufficient vitamins and minerals. It can be achieved by giving children two or more servings every day from each of the four basic food groups: (1) milk, (2) vegetables

Table 5-2 Examples of Foods in the Four Basic Food Groups.

Milk	Fruit/Vegetables	Protein	Grains
milk	tomatoes	dry beans	cereals
buttermilk	citrus fruits	nuts	bread
yogurt	berries	eggs	pasta
custard	melons	poultry	rice
ice cream	pitted fruits	fish	crackers
soft cheese	dried fruits	beef	muffins
hard cheese	leafy vegetables	pork	pancakes
cream cheese	root-type vegetables	mutton	noodles
sour cream	stem-type vegetables	tofu	tapioca
sour milk	pod-type vegetables	seeds	tortillas
condensed milk	potatoes	shellfish	barley

and fruits, (3) meat (or protein), and (4) breads and cereals (see Table 5-2). However, a well-balanced diet may be more difficult to attain during early childhood than it was during infancy. Appetites decrease and fluctuate from day to day. Children use mealtimes to test their independence with food refusals, food jags, or dawdling. They discover "junk" foods and demand them. Between-meal snacks are common. They are also sometimes necessary because active young children burn up their intake of mealtime calories rapidly. Nevertheless, snacks may interfere with intake of more nutritious foods at mealtimes. Caregivers can help assure adequate nutrition in early childhood by providing snacks with substantive nutritive value (milk, cheese, nuts, whole grain cereals or bread, fruit, vegetables). If young children have not been allowed to spoil their appetites with junk foods and if their food refusals do not receive a great deal of attention, they will eat most of the foods served at meals in imitation of their caregivers. Food dislikes are generally related to highly seasoned or strong flavors or the foods that the caregivers also dislike. Vitamin supplements are rarely necessary if young children have balanced diets. Some health care professionals recommend vitamins with iron if the child shows signs of iron deficiency anemia. Others may recommend fluoride pills to help prevent tooth decay.

Some children develop an abnormal craving for certain unnatural "foods" (dirt, laundry starch, play-dough, chalk, chips of paint, or plaster). This craving is called **pica.** The ingestion of flakes of paint or plaster with lead in them or other leaded substances (e.g., solder, brass alloys, home-glazed pottery) or inhalation of lead (as from fruit tree sprays and fumes from burning batteries) can lead to moderate to severe anemia with weakness, irritability, and weight loss. If more than 0.5 mg of lead per day is ingested, the child can have a toxic reaction (lead poisoning) or lead encephalopathy (inflammation of the brain) (Rumack, 1984). Even relatively low levels of body lead in children are associated with poorer cognitive functioning than expected (Bergomi et al., 1989), often before any signs of gross motor impairment are seen. About 4% of American children have elevated lead levels in their blood and should receive medical treatment. Pica may also be related to psychosocial problems that need investigation and treatment.

Health Maintenance

Some active, impetuous preschoolers go from ages two to five without an accident, a sniffle, or a sneeze. Most little children, however, become very well acquainted with their health care providers. Parents can promote good health in early childhood in a number of ways:

- have child immunized,
- provide nutritious meals,
- teach child cleanliness,
- have child brush teeth,
- schedule dental check-ups,
- establish good sleep habits,
- teach safety precautions,
- respond to child's needs,
- schedule medical check-ups,
- report symptoms of illnesses promptly.

About 5–10% of preschool children have some kind of visual impairment (Schmitt, 1984). Parents may begin to suspect that vision is faulty if they see their child hold an object very far from or very close to the face while examining it. Friends or neighbors may point out problems such as squinting or crossed eyes that parents ignore.

Most young children are normally hyperopic (farsighted). When the globe of the eye expands to rounder, fuller, more adultlike proportions at about ages four to six, this farsighted condition will correct itself. However, some children with a higher grade of **hyperopia** in early childhood may experience headaches from this refractive error. If so, they should be fitted for glasses. Glasses will not interfere with the progressive development of the eye and the accompanying decrease of hyperopia. Two other refractive errors of the eyes that young children may experience are **myopia** (near-sightedness) and **astigmatism.** In astigmatism one or more of the refractive surfaces of the eye have unequal curvature, which interferes with clear focusing. Glasses will correct the errors of both myopia and astigmatism and should be prescribed for and worn by young children as soon as the defects are discovered (see Figure 5-6).

Strabismus (crossed eyes, walleyes) may lessen with the passage of time. The more usual course of events, however, is for the child habitually to use only one eye. This may eventually cause the wandering eye to lose its visual function. Uncorrected strabismus is one of the leading causes of monocular (one-eyed) blindness. It is preventable: In general, vision can be saved if the deviating eye is brought back into binocular (two-eyed) functioning as early as possible.

Mild or moderate hearing defects occur in approximately 1% of young children (Schmitt, 1984). Caregivers may suspect a hearing defect if children do not attempt to speak by age two, if they fail to respond to out-of-sight noises, or if they tilt their heads while listening. The majority of hearing defects are acquired in early life as a result of inadequately treated ear infections or accidental ear injuries. If a hearing defect cannot be corrected with a hearing device, a child may be started in lip reading and sign language instructions as early as two to three years of age. Caregivers should also learn to communicate in sign for the benefit of the child.

Accidents are the leading cause of death in early childhood. Young children are especially vulnerable to hazardous conditions in their environments because of their cognitive immaturity and their strivings for autonomy and initiative. They cannot be trusted to remember and obey safety rules. Young children also often act impulsively to gratify their immediate egocentric needs or desires, rather than thinking about rules.

Motor vehicles account for nearly one-half of the fatal accidents of early childhood. Caregivers have a dual teaching responsibility in relation to automotive safety: precautions for riding in a motor vehicle and precautions while playing near areas where motor vehicles travel.

Seatbelts for children are the law! In addition, children must be taught to keep their hands and feet away from the driver. The back seat is, in general, a safer place for children than the front, and the center seat is safer than the window seats. A child riding on an adult's lap is not safe.

Young children should not be allowed to play in streets or busy driveways at any

Figure 5-6
Young children should wear glasses if they have any visual impairments. Glasses will not interfere with the development of the eye and physiological corrective processes.

Figure 5-7
Small children can be expert at climbing to reach almost everything they want.

time and should be supervised while playing in areas accessible to roadways. In addition, toddlers and preschoolers should cross streets only with adult supervision. Young children should be taught "stop, look, and listen" procedures whenever they are near traffic.

Young children frequently ingest poisonous substances (Rumack, 1984) (see Figure 5-7). The four household areas from which toddlers and preschoolers most often take and taste poisonous materials are the cabinet under the kitchen sink, the medicine cabinet, the bedroom dresser, and the garage (or storage area for shop, automotive, and garden supplies). Mothers frequently fail to realize that detergents can seriously injure or kill children in relatively small quantities. All household cleaning products should be stored on a high shelf out of children's sight and reach. Likewise, beauty products, paints, petroleum products, fertilizers, insecticides, and the like should be high and hidden from view. Medicine cabinets should be kept locked, and medicines should never be stored with foods. If cough syrups or liquid antibiotics must be refrigerated, they should be kept separate from foods in covered containers. Safety caps should be replaced securely. When medicines are necessary, caregivers should caution the child that the substance is a medicine, not a candy, and should only be taken when given by a known adult. The chart in Figure 5-8 may be copied and given to parents of young children to remind them of safety precautions and first aid measures. Caregivers should fill in all the phone numbers at the bottom of the chart. If they do not know their nearest poison control center, they can call the toll free information number 1-800-555-1212 and ask for the number of the poison center in their city or state. Table 5-3 lists some common poisonous substances that children ingest.

Other accidents that are seen frequently in early childhood include burns and scalds, animal bites, drowning, electrocution, head injuries, and sprains from falls. If a preschooler experiences a brief loss of consciousness, a seizure, irritability, drowsiness, vomiting, or an unsteady gait following a head injury, he or she may have a concussion. Medical attention should be sought immediately.

Table 5-3   Some Common Household "Poisons" That Young Children May Ingest.

Alcohol-based hair tonic	Drain cleaners	Nitroglycerin
Alcoholic beverages	Eyedrops	Permanent wave lotion
Ammonia	Fabric softener	Permanent wave neutralizer
Antihistamines	Fingernail polish	
Antiperistaltics (especially Lomotil)	Fingernail polish remover	Phisohex
	Floor wax	Photographic solutions
Aspirin	Fumigants	Rodenticides
Bath oil	Fungicides	Rubbing alcohol
Bleach	Gasoline	Sedatives
Boric acid	Hair spray	Shampoo
Cement and glue	Heart medicine	Shaving lotion
Charcoal lighter fluid	Insecticides	Shoe polish
Clinitest tablets	Iodine	Silver polish
Cologne, toilet water	Iron pills	Sleeping pills
Contraceptive pills	Kerosene	Solder
Deodorizers	Laxatives	Toilet bowl cleaners
Depilatories	Leaded paints	Toxic houseplants
Detergents	Leakage from batteries	Turpentine/paint thinner
Diet pills	Lighter fluid	Vitamins
Disinfectants	Metallic hair dye	Washing soda
Diuretics	Moth balls	Weed killers

PREVENTING CHILDHOOD POISONINGS

Each year, thousands of children are accidentally poisoned by medicines, polishes, insecticides, drain cleaners, bleaches, household chemicals, and garage products. It is the responsibility of adults to make sure that children are not exposed to potentially toxic substances.

Here are some suggestions:
(1) Insist on safety closures and learn how to use them properly.
(2) Keep household cleaning supplies, medicines, garage products, and insecticides out of the reach and sight of your child. Lock them up whenever possible.
(3) Never store food and cleaning products together. Store medicine and chemicals in original containers and never in food or beverage containers.
(4) Avoid taking medicine in your child's presence. Children love to imitate. Always call medicine by its proper name. Never suggest that medicine is "candy"—especially aspirin and children's vitamins.
(5) Read the label on all products and heed warnings and cautions. Never use medicine from an unlabeled or unreadable container. Never pour medicine in a darkened area where the label cannot be clearly seen.
(6) If you are interrupted while using a product, take it with you. It only takes a few seconds for your child to get into it.
(7) Know what your child can do. For example, if you have a crawling infant, keep household products stored above floor level, not beneath the kitchen sink.
(8) Keep the phone number of your doctor, Poison Center, hospital, police department, and fire department or paramedic emergency rescue squad near the phone.

FIRST AID FOR POISONING

Always keep syrup of ipecac and Epsom salt (magnesium sulfate) in your home. The former is used to induce vomiting and the latter may be used as a laxative. These drugs are used sometimes when poisons are swallowed. Only use them as instructed by your Poison Center or doctor, and *follow their directions for use.*

Inhaled Poisons If gas, fumes, or smoke have been inhaled, immediately drag or carry the patient to fresh air. Then call the Poison Center or your doctor.

Poisons on the Skin If the poison has been spilled on the skin or clothing, remove the clothing and flood the involved parts with water. Then wash with soapy water and rinse thoroughly. Then call the Poison Center or your doctor.

Swallowed Poisons If the poison has been swallowed and the patient is awake and can swallow, give the patient only water or milk to drink. Then call the Poison Center or your doctor. *CAUTION:* Antidote labels on products may be incorrect. Do not give salt, vinegar, or lemon juice. Call before doing anything else.

Poisons in the Eye Flush the eye with lukewarm water poured from a pitcher held 3–4 inches from the eye for 15 minutes. Call the Poison Center or your doctor.

DOCTOR_____   POISON CENTER_____   AMBULANCE_____

POLICE_____   FIRE DEPARTMENT_____   HOSPITAL_____

(This page may be reproduced for purposes of education in poison prevention. Courtesy of Rocky Mountain Poison Center, Denver, Colorado.)

Figure 5-8
This chart should be reproduced and placed in a prominent spot in homes with young children. Be sure to fill in the local phone numbers for emergency services.

Common Health Problems

Young children are more susceptible to the common cold than their elders are because they have had less opportunity to build up antibodies against the numerous viral organisms that cause it. Their shorter eustachian tube and shorter respiratory tract also contribute to more cold sequelae: otitis media (ear infection), pharyngitis (sore throat), strep throat, tonsillitis, bronchitis, and pneumonia. The sooner colds are treated, the less chance of more severe outcomes. Colds should not be treated with aspirin (see Box 5-1).

Earaches can develop quickly in young children as organisms travel up the eustachian tube (see Figure 5-9). Schmitt and Berman (1984) estimate that one-third of the pediatrician's time is spent in the management of ear infections (**otitis media**). Symptoms include fever, irritability, sleep difficulty, or tugging at the ear. In some cases, the eardrum will have ruptured and caregivers will see watery fluid or pus draining from the ear. Treatment is a full ten- to fourteen-day course of antibiotics. Caregivers must give the medicine for the complete time prescribed even if the child appears completely well in two or three days.

Strep throat, caused by streptococcal bacteria, is another illness for which caregivers must provide the full ten-day course of antibiotics, even if the child's sore throat clears up in one or two days. Inadequately treated strep may lead to more serious illness, such as scarlet fever, pneumonia, or meningitis. A strep infection may travel far from the respiratory tract to the skin (causing impetigo), to the heart (causing rheumatic heart disease) or to the kidneys (causing nephritis).

A boil (furuncle) originates in a hair follicle. It becomes red, swollen, hot, and painful and fills with pus. Treatment may include incising and draining the area and a course of antibiotics.

Conjunctivitis is the most common of all pediatric eye disorders (Ellis, 1984). Symptoms include redness of the conjunctiva ("pink eye"), a purulent discharge, and sticking together of the eyelids in the morning. It is usually treated with antibiotic ointment instilled into the eye several times a day.

Chickenpox is caused by a viral organism of the herpes family: herpes zoster. (Other herpes lesions will be discussed in Chapter 7.) Chickenpox is characterized by crops of itchy skin vesicles. It is usually a mild disease in young children. Some parents have "chickenpox parties," intentionally exposing their children to a child with chickenpox in hopes that they will contact the disease while young. (It has more serious sequelae in adolescents and adults.) Treatment consists of cool baths or calamine lotion to relieve the itching. Aspirin should not be given to a child with chickenpox (see Box 5-1).

Symptoms of gastrointestinal infections such as vomiting, cramps, or diarrhea should always be reported to a medical practitioner. It is not safe to assume that the child has the "flu." The problem may be one of a magnitude requiring surgery, such as appendicitis or intussusception. Even if the gastrointestinal upset is due to the flu,

BOX
5-1

Aspirin and Reye's Syndrome.

The common cold, gastrointestinal flu, and chickenpox are the result of infection with one or more viral agents. There is some suggestion that acetylsalicylic acid (aspirin) and other salicylate drugs may interact with viruses causing illnesses in children to produce the rare condition known as Reye's syndrome. Other causes have also been suggested (insecticides, herbicides, metabolic defects), but none has been conclusively linked (together with a virus) as the cause of the disease. Until more is known about Reye's syndrome, however, aspirin bottles now carry a warning not to give the product to children nineteen years and under with chickenpox or flu without first consulting a physician. Vulnerability seems to be limited to childhood.

Symptoms suggestive of Reye's syndrome are vomiting, irrational behavior, restlessness, convulsions, progressive stupor, and coma (Silverman and Roy, 1984). The diagnosis of Reye's syndrome can be confirmed or denied with laboratory tests. Treatment is supportive and life-saving in about 70% of affected children. However, some residual neurologic damage is common, especially in children whose Reye's syndrome was preceded by chickenpox.

There is no indication that giving aspirin to children for the pain or fever accompanying bacterial infections, toothaches, or headaches or the pain accompanying minor accidental injuries carries any risk when given as directed.

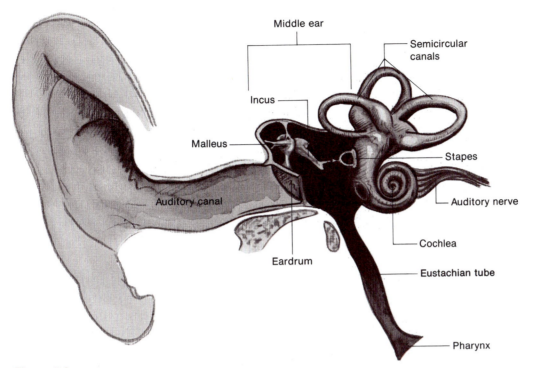

Figure 5-9
Middle ear infections (otitis media) are common sequelae to colds. Middle ear infections can cause the eardrum to bulge painfully and sometimes to rupture (see also Plate 16 in center of textbook).

young children can become seriously dehydrated quite quickly. They may go into shock from loss of fluids after vomiting and diarrhea.

Urinary tract infections are uncommon in boys but quite frequent in preschool girls. They usually result from fecal contamination of the short female urethra situated so close to the anus and from infrequent voiding. They are usually treated with antibiotics. Inadequate treatment may result in a more serious kidney infection. Little girls should be taught to wipe themselves carefully from front to back after every bowel movement to prevent infection.

Cancers unfortunately claim the lives of many preschoolers each year. The predominant forms of cancer of early childhood are leukemia and Wilms' tumor. **Leukemia** of early childhood involves a proliferation of abnormal white blood cells. It nearly always has an acute onset with anemia, bruises, limb pain, and fever. The cause remains unknown. Treatment involves antileukemic chemotherapy and blood transfusions. Some leukemia can be treated with bone marrow transplants if a suitable donor is available. With aggressive chemotherapy many leukemic children can survive free of disease for five years or longer (Tubergen, 1984). The word "cure" as applied to leukemia is difficult to define, but there are increasing numbers of long-term survivors.

Wilms' tumor is a cancerous mass that develops in the kidneys of some young children. There are usually no symptoms before the mass is felt by a caregiver while washing or dressing the child. Treatment involves surgical removal of the tumor and chemotherapy. The cure rate is excellent, from 80 to 90%.

Cognitive and Language Development

Psychobiology has altered the way contemporary human developmentalists look at learning and speech. The processes by which the human brain takes in new information, sorts it, and sends some into short-term memory and some further into a long-term memory store are fascinating. How much information reaches the long-term store? At present, we can only guess based on the amount of information that can be retrieved from memory (remembered). However, neurophysiologists believe we store more than we can retrieve (Rosenfield, 1988). Children learning language, for example, know rules of syntax that they do not know they know (cannot retrieve). We will start our discussion of cognition and language with a simple explanation of memory processes.

Memory Processes

Memory probably has three stages: **sensory memory, short-term memory** (often called "telephone-number" or "scratch-pad" memory) and distant, **long-term memory** (see Figure 5-10).

Very brief, momentary visual memories (icons) and auditory memories (echoes) are considered part of the sensory store. Have you had the experience of knowing that someone just asked you a question, but not knowing what they asked? You say something like "Could you repeat that?" Then, before they can repeat the question, you remember what they asked. Your memory gives you an echo of the question from your sensory store. Smells, tastes, and feelings can also remain briefly in a sensory store, usually for less than a second (Atkinson and Shiffrin, 1968).

The short-term memory store holds information about half a minute. Most people can hold from five to nine pieces of information for this long. Short-term memory is often called telephone number memory because we only need to remember phone numbers for a few seconds while we dial, and because phone numbers are usually seven digits. You can remember seven digits, or seven letters, or seven words, or a combination of seven items (digits, letters, and words) in short-term memory.

The long-term memory store is probably unlimited and probably holds information forever (Tulving, 1974). It is not unusual to find old people who can retrieve vast amounts of information about their childhood. Often they will say "It's funny, I hadn't thought about that for years" after relating some story. The problem with long-term memory is not being able to retrieve the information you know, rather than not knowing it. Have you had the experience of watching a TV quiz show, or playing a game of questions and answers, and knowing the answer as soon as someone else says it? Retrieval is sometimes enhanced in strange ways: by smells, sights, sounds, tastes. Often one memory will let loose a flood of other memories (see Figure 5-11).

There is a great deal we do not yet understand about memory processes. Our brains may truly be the last frontier, the least understood topic of scientific study. Some information (bad memories) automatically goes into a long-term store, even against our will, although the long-term store seems to resist other information (textbook material), try as we will to keep it.

Sensory and short-term memories are believed to consist only of electrical impulses. The electrical activity that is generated by the millions of bits of incoming material perceived by the brain every minute may be so brief and shallow as to be dissipated rather quickly, before there is a chance to send anything into a long-term memory

Figure 5-10
Memory is held for less than a second in the sensory store and less than a minute in the short-term store, but it can be retained for a lifetime in the long-term store.

Figure 5-11
Often a simple stimulus (e.g., the buzz of a bee) will trigger a flood of memories from the long-term store.

storage system. On the other hand, some bits of incoming information may excite a great deal of electrical activity, enough to overflow the boundaries of the sensory and short-term registration systems and to generate some longer-term retention of knowledge with potential for retrieval.

Research suggests that the limbic system plays a vital role in pushing some information into a retention process rather than allowing it to dissipate and be forgotten (see Figure 5-12). The **limbic system** is part of the brain stem. Its major function appears to be the regulation of emotions. Bits of information registered in the brain that excite some emotional reactions are more apt to be converted into long-term memories than are such things as telephone numbers.

The role of the limbic system in discriminating between trivial information and relevant material to commit to memory is very important to intellectual functioning. The Russian cognitive psychologist A. R. Luria (1968) (see Chapter 2) reported a case study of a man who sent too many things into his long-term memory bank. Although he could reproduce lengthy series of numbers or words or describe minute details of any given scene, he appeared to be dull-witted. He remembered whole situations rather than singling out key points. Consequently, his understanding of the meaning of any given subject matter was poor. He also could not forget images he no longer needed. New impressions collided with old in a chaotic manner. He appeared demented rather than gifted.

About 5% of children also have the ability to remember minute details of a situation

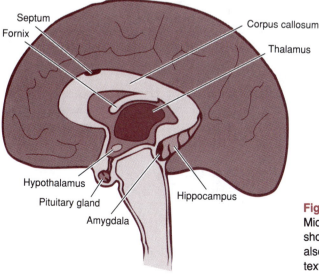

Figure 5-12
Midsagittal view of the brain showing the limbic system (see also Plate 11 in center of textbook).

(Haber, 1969). We call this **eidetic memory.** It is sometimes also referred to as photographic memory since the whole picture rather than important material seems to be retained. Eidetic imagery is usually lost in the maturation process, since intelligence requires the ability to blot out irrelevant stimuli and send only the most salient elements of a situation into memory.

Research studies have given us reason to believe that chemical changes and the synthesis of new protein materials by the brain cells are involved in the transfer of bits of incoming information from short- to long-term memory. Will and colleagues (1977) found increases in glial cells (supportive cells), in cholinesterase (an enzyme present in glial cells), and in acetylcholinesterase (an enzyme involved in synaptic transmission of neural impulses) in rats after they had been raised in separate, well-equipped cages and taught new tasks. Furthermore, rats raised in stimulating environments or trained in various skills have heavier brains than unstimulated rats raised in common barren cages. Likewise, rats fed high-protein diets learn more efficiently than malnourished rats.

A variety of drugs have been found that improve the brain's ability to fix memories. However, these drugs have side effects: some are poisonous; some cause convulsions; some are addictive. It may be possible that in the future safer drugs will be manufactured that will help synthesize the necessary chemicals to store the memories we wish, when we wish them stored. In the meantime, we are left with the knowledge that too much remembering is chaotic, and our ability to focus on some things and forget others is essential to intelligent behavior.

Piaget's Preoperational Stage

Preoperational thought, which characterizes young children, is advanced over sensorimotor intelligence because children have the emerging ability to remember and use their memories. The acquisition of expressive language marks the beginning of the preoperational stage. A word is one limited kind of mental sign. It refers to an object or situation, the meaning of which the child shares with all others in the environment (up, milk, Daddy). Other mental images are very personal (the feeling of cold and fright that accompanies being put on an adult toilet seat rather than on a child's seat or potty chair). Although mental symbols may have words associated with them, they are also partly nonverbal. You can appreciate this if you consider your own thoughts. When you think in words, your mental progress is considerably slower than when you allow whole images to flash by at a time.

Piaget gave specific names to both the mental images that a child forms to represent an object or situation and the objects or situations themselves. The mental images (words, nonverbal symbols) are called signifiers. The objects or events to which they refer are called the significates. In the dual processes of assimilation (taking in and consolidating information) and accommodation (changing concepts to fit with the newly assimilated information), young children apply signifiers to more and more diverse phenomena (significates). (See Figure 5-13.)

The ability to use mental images, though a major achievement in cognitive development, does not become refined for a number of years. Young children have difficulties differentiating between the real and the unreal, or between actual events and their fantasies. They seem glued to their perceptions of things and resist reasonable explanations of phenomena. Perceptions supersede reason. They also have a limited appreciation of the point of view of anyone but themselves. They try to find explanations for things based on their own personal needs and experiences. Their receptive and expressive language abilities, though expanding daily, leave them puzzled about many things they see, hear, or experience. They are unable to phrase adequate questions to clarify all of their confused thoughts. In many cases, they do not feel confused but simply "understand" events in illogical ways based on their perceptions. Piaget referred to this early phase of mental reasoning as *preoperational.* Young children's reason does

Figure 5-13
A signifier can be both a word (for example, "Rex"), and all the nonverbal, sensory, perceptual feelings that accompany a child's mental image of his dog.

not function according to "operations." Piaget defined operations as systematic, orderly ways of mentally turning an action over to its starting point again and again and integrating it with other reversible actions (Piaget and Inhelder, 1956). This reversible, thoughtful operating does not begin to emerge until about age seven.

Piaget subdivided the preoperational period into two phases: preconceptual and intuitive. In the first phase the child groups together facts as they are acquired, not separating the real from the fantasized and not classifying events in a systematic manner. In the second phase the child separates objects and events into some rudimentary classifications. However, the classifications are still faulty by standards of adult logic. Piaget described several characteristics of preoperational thought (see Table 5-4).

One reason young children are so perception-bound is their susceptibility to centration. **Centration** refers to a young child's tendency to focus attention on one object or event at a time. This "singlemindedness" is not obstinacy, as many adults label it, but a desire to finish assimilating and accommodating the self to the properties of a novel object or event. Thus, a child asked to sort a mixture of circles, squares, and triangles into three piles may ignore the circles and squares and just play with the more novel triangles. A birthday child may, likewise, refuse to participate in games and eating after opening a new gift that captures her attention.

Closely related to centration is **egocentrism.** This refers to the preoperational child's exclusive interest in objects or events that have some bearing on his or her own activities to the exclusion of all other objects or events. Consider your own dream life to understand this. When you dream, everything in your dream relates to you. In real (awake) life, you are an observer of many other objects and events that may have no direct bearing on your life. A preoperational child centers only on those things that relate to the self (ego). This "tunnel vision" creates perceptual distortions of the real world. A further characteristic of egocentric reasoning is that young children believe other people are also focusing on the objects or events to which they are attending. They may ask questions which appear to be vague simply because they believe the person being questioned sees (or hears, or perceives) the same things they are sensing.

Preoperational children deal with things exactly as they appear to them in their here-and-now egocentric perception. Piaget called this perception **realism.** Psychological events such as thoughts, dreams, and names are things of substance to the

Table 5-4 Some Characteristics of Preoperational Cognition Described by Piaget.

Characteristic	Definition
Centration	Focus on one and only one aspect of an object or event; blindness to others' points of view
Egocentrism	Self-centeredness; consideration of oneself and one's own interests to the exclusion of others
Realism	Belief that names, thoughts, and so on have objective reality; thinking something so makes it so
Animism	Belief that inanimate objects (such as wind, fire, and water) have life, feelings, and purpose
Artificialism	Belief that all objects and events exist to serve needs of humans, especially the self
Syncretism	Belief that co-occurring events belong together; for example, good china on table means that Grandma will come
Transductive reasoning	Reasoning from particular to particular; assignment of co-occurring events as cause and effect

child. For example, names are believed to be inherent in a thing. When Piaget (1933) asked a young child how people knew that the sun was called the sun, he got this answer: They saw it was called the sun because they could see it was round and hot. For another example of realism, Piaget discussed preschoolers' views of dreams. They are believed to come from outside, sometimes from God; they can be made of wind and sometimes can punish their viewer for misdeeds of the day.

Facts acquired by young children can be described as animistic, artificialistic, and syncretistic (see Table 5-4). **Animism** refers to the child's endowment of life, consciousness, and will to physical objects and events (pincushions feel the prick of a pin, clouds feel rain, and grass feels hurt when it is pulled). However, animistic notions may be fleeting (the pincushion may not be sentient until stabbed; grass may not feel the child playing on it but only another person's pulling on it). Dolgin and Behrend (1984) found animism strongest in five-year-olds. Physical similarity to animates (stuffed animals, dolls) and apparent self-movement of inanimates (vehicles) contributed to their animistic beliefs. **Artificialism** refers to the child's tendency to believe that all objects and events in the world were made by humans for humans (clouds exist to give us shade, rain comes to make splashy mud puddles, and lakes were put on earth for swimming or boating. Night comes so we can sleep). **Syncretism** refers to the child's tendency to fuse a multitude of diverse phenomena together. If you ask a young child the question "Why does the water flow downstream?" the answer is apt to be based on some co-occurring phenomenon: "The rocks push it down."

Reasoning in the preoperational period is most apt to be from particular to particular. Piaget called this **transductive reasoning.** It is midway between the two forms of reasoning that adults use—inductive and deductive. When we induce something, we use a few particulars to arrive at generalizations. For example, after meeting several persons from Denmark, all of whom have blond hair, we might generalize that all Danes are blond. When we deduce something, we reason from general to particular. For example, after observing many college students wearing jeans, we might word an invitation to a student "Wear your jeans," assuming that he or she must own a pair. The results of young children's transductive reasoning may or may not be logical by adult standards (they are always logical to the child). They are usually fascinating. Piaget (1962) provided these examples:

J. at 2 years, 9 months: "She hasn't got a name" (a little girl a year old).—Why?—
"Because she can't talk."
J. at 2 years, 10 months (showing a postcard): "It's a dog."—I think it's a cat.—"No,
it's a dog."—Is it? Why?—Why do you say it's a dog?—Why do you think it's a dog?—
"It's grey." (p. 232)

Time and number concepts are hazy in early childhood since a genuine understanding of them requires the operation of classification. Toddlers can learn to "wait a minute" and to recognize times for bodily activities like eating and sleeping. The concepts of yesterday and tomorrow gradually become meaningful, but even though preschoolers may voice the words *next month* or *next year,* they have little appreciation for the length of time involved. Thus they may wait impatiently for Christmas in September, regardless of their knowledge of the three-month wait. They may count numbers fluently yet be unable to select correctly which array has the most candies if one is piled and the other is spread out. Even after counting the candies, they are apt to choose the array that perceptually looks bigger to them, although it actually has fewer candies.

Piaget's descriptions of preoperational thinking appear to be valid cross-culturally. Most of the disagreements with his theory focus on age of onset and age of attainment of abilities rather than their sequence and characteristics (Dasen and Heron, 1981). Piaget felt that progression through cognitive stages has biological roots: Each child goes through all of the stages at his or her own pace (see Chapter 2, p. 45).

Language Acquisition

In Chapter 3, we previewed the rudimentary speech sounds that eventually lead to language (e.g., cries, coos, babbles, phonetic drift, holophrases, telegraphic speech). Holophrases are single words used by infants and toddlers which express an entire message and are understood by caregivers as a part of the mother tongue. This author's son, at age two, used the holophrase, "sockaz" to ask "Where is the sockaz?", or to request "May I have some sockaz?", or to label all the sockaz he saw. I understood. My husband, however, asked "Why does he talk about socks so often?" "Not socks," I answered, "chocolate!" The pronunciation of toddlers' words often leaves a lot to be desired. When do toddlers move from holophrastic speech to longer utterances? Why do they make so many mistakes in early speech? Who speaks sooner? What difference does it make if a toddler acquires language early or late? There are vast individual differences between toddlers in their speech and articulation patterns. We will begin by looking at commonalities in language development and then explore some of the differences and the possible reasons for them.

Some toddlers will use one-word language for several months before they begin to combine two or three words to make rudimentary sentences. Other young children move very rapidly from holophrasing to telegraphic speech (two- or three-word utterances). When toddlers begin to combine words into sentences, they seem very frugal. They only produce the most meaningful words. My son, for example, did not move from "sockaz" to "Mommy, may I please have another piece of chocolate?" but rather tried "More sockaz?", and then, when that didn't produce results, tried "More sockaz, Mama!" We call this telegraphic speech because telegrams, for which the number of words determines the cost, are typically also composed of only the most relevant parts of speech. Early sentences of toddlers are usually composed of nouns (e.g., chocolate, Mama) and verbs. (In my son's case, he used the adverb *more* to express the verb *have*.)

Some toddlers make their sentences longer by adding a vowel (usually *a*) to the end of the last word they speak. These additions (e.g., I go potty-a; more milk-a; stay downstairs-a) are usually dropped when the toddler learns to expand the sentence correctly with auxiliary parts of speech (e.g., adjectives, prepositions, articles, pronouns) placed before, between, or after nouns and verbs.

Many toddlers shorten the messages they want to convey into two or three telegraphic sentences rather than embed ideas next to one another, using noun clauses or prepositional phrases the way adults do. For example, you might say, "Could you bring me a tissue from the blue box on the table in the kitchen?" The toddler, affirming that he or she understood, might repeat, "Bring tissue. On table. Blue box in kitchen?"

Subtractions are much more typical of toddler speech than additions. Not only do young children shorten sentences, they also shorten many words into just one or two syllables (e.g., chocolate becomes sockaz, the name Elizabeth becomes E'Beth).

When expressive language first develops, most toddlers use one word to mean many things, a process known as overextension. Thus, the word "car" may mean not only every automobile but also every vehicle on four wheels including trucks, buses, and vans; every toy with four wheels such as tinker toys, transformers, and wagons; and even things usually seen in a car such as a steering wheel, a gear shift stick, or a toddler's car seat. Nouns are most frequently overextended to refer to multiple objects. The referential pronoun, *me,* is also often overextended to be both subject (e.g., me go car) and object (e.g., Mamma carry me).

Not all nouns are overextended. Familiar nouns are frequently underextended; the label is reserved for use for one and only one thing. Consider the following vignette:

> Three-year-old Jerome and his older brother, Doug, were playing at the neighborhood playground on a seesaw. Doug saw a friend from his school enter the playground and sit by the basketball court to watch a game in progress. Doug announced, "There's Lad! Come on, let's go over and see Lad." Jerome cried, "No, not Lad!" Doug frowned and asked, "Why? Are you afraid of Lad?" "No, no, not Lad!", Jerome replied. Doug tried another idea: "You don't want to stop seesawing? It's all right. After we say Hi to Lad, we'll come back and seesaw some more, OK?" "No, no, no! Not Lad," insisted Jerome. Doug tried to pull his brother off the seesaw. Jerome stubbornly resisted, saying "Not Lad!" Finally, Doug understood. "Yes, his name is Lad, too. Our dog isn't the only Lad in the world, you know." Jerome finally followed his brother to meet the new boy, still insisting "Not Lad! Lad home. Lad my puppy."

Many labels (e.g., Kitty, Grandma, Slinky) become underextended for short periods of time. This is due to the cognitive limitations of centration and egocentrism.

When children first begin telegraphic speech, they usually use the correct forms of irregular nouns and verbs (e.g., sheep went bye-bye, mice saw Cinderella). Later, they begin to add an *s* to pluralize every noun, and an *ed* to make the past tense of every verb (e.g., sheeps goed bye-bye, mouses seed Cinderella). Since many of the more commonly used verbs in the English language are irregular (this is also true of other languages), children begin to make many grammatical errors (see Table 5-5). The use of such rule-based mistakes is called overgeneralization. Toddlers make many

Table 5-5   Examples of Language Errors Made by Children Applying "Rules" to Irregular Words.

Plurals		Past Tenses			Contractions
sheeps	seed	*or*		sawed	amn't
foots	goed			wented	donen't
gooses	braked			broked	willn't
tooths	singed			sanged	she've
mices	gived			gaved	he've
oxs	doed			dided	they's
serieses	knowed			knewed	we's
deers	beginned			beganned	
loafs	bited			bitted	
childs	swimmed			swammed	
mans	bringed			broughted	
halfs	choosed			chosed	
mooses	camed			comed	
leafs	doed			dided	
trouts	writed			wroted	
knifes	ringed			ranged	
lifes	rided			roded	
thiefs	shaked			shooked	

contractions of words incorrectly as well, through overgeneralization (e.g., didn't becomes doen't, won't becomes willn't). They also follow the rule for adding self to all possessive pronouns, as in myself, yourself, herself, and "hisself" rather than himself. All of these overgeneralizations of rules are relatively long-lived. They must be corrected by adults many times before they are replaced by the correct "exceptions" to the rules. Children probably make these rule-based overgeneralizations rather than repeat words as they hear because they are born with an innate language acquisition device (LAD) which allows them to discern the syntax (rules) of the language they hear spoken (Chomsky, 1957). A LAD obliterates the need for caregivers to teach syntactic structures. Rather, they need only correct the speech of the child that is rule-based rather than following an exception to a rule (e.g., teeth, not "tooths"; went, not "goed"; himself, not "hisself"). Children around the world make rule-based mistakes in the grammar of their mother tongue when they first acquire language, presumably because of this innate LAD.

Parents and other adults do not coach toddlers in grammar. Most caregivers correct mispronunciations (e.g., choc-o-late, not "sockaz"), prohibit the repetition of dirty words or curse words, and request that the child use polite words (e.g., please and thank you). Many adults also expand children's telegraphic speech into complete sentences some of the time. Many children hear a cacophony of sounds from television, loud music, dissonant caregivers, other children at play, animals, and various people in neighborhood environments (e.g., stores, health clinics, religious meetings, playgrounds). How do they discriminate syntax from all this spoken language? Children who hear language directed at them, face to face, and who have their telegraphic sentences expanded frequently, tend to speak earlier and have larger vocabularies at younger ages than less stimulated children, but they do not have a permanent advantage. Children who seldom hear complete sentences, who seldom have language directed at them, and who never have their speech corrected or praised still learn to talk. They also learn the rules of the language(s) they acquire.

Toddlers, in the throes of learning language, are seldom silent. They seem to grab every opportunities to exercise their newly acquired skills. They practice "show and tell" with almost anyone who will listen. They ask questions, often with little interest in the answers they hear. It is as if they just want to hear any language spoken.

> Sean, a three-year-old, watched a new neighbor unload his furniture into a duplex apartment. When the new tenant found an outside water spigot and paused to have a drink, Sean approached. "Hi, who are you?" "I'm Mr. Gavin." "What are you doing?" "I'm having a drink of water." "Why?" "Because I'm thirsty." "Why?" "Because I've been sweating a lot." "Why?" "Because I've been carrying heavy furniture." "Why?" "Because I'm moving into this house." "Why?" "Because I need a bigger place to live." "Why?" "Because my wife and I had a baby." "Why?" "Because we wanted a child?" "Why?" "Hmm, that's a good question."

When toddlers cannot find anyone to converse with them, they talk to inanimate objects (stuffed animals, dolls, toys) or to themselves. Vygotsky (1934, 1962) called this egocentric speech *inner speech*. He believed that language is a very important determinant of both cognitive development and autonomy. Children learn to control their own behaviors by talking to themselves as they think, reason, and make judgments. If an adult did all the talking, all the directing, all the reasoning, and made all the judgments, the toddler would remain cognitively limited and dependent. However, normal children do a great deal of self-directing. While acquiring language, toddlers talk to themselves publicly and aloud. Later, inner speech becomes more covert, private, and silent. Toddlers use private speech to self-praise, to start or stop their behaviors, to label, to describe events, to focus their attention, to make transitions, and to answer their own questions.

Many of the incorrect words used by toddlers are not simply overextensions or underextensions of known labels or overgeneralizations of rules. Toddlers use their knowledge of language to invent words as well. For example, Damon asked his mother to let him wear his "up-sleeved" shirt (short-sleeved). Christine, after being shown the morning star, saw the moon in the sky and described it as the "daymoon."

The rapidity of children's language acquisition, once they get "off and running," is really quite astounding. While some children may not start holophrasing until very late, and some children may holophrase for many months before they begin to create telegraphic sentences, the speed of acquiring nouns and verbs to use in functional telegraphic sentences (subject–verb–object) is phenomenal. It is not unusual for a toddler to move from under 20 holophrastic words to over 600 nouns and verbs in less than six months.

Birth-order studies have suggested that second-born and subsequent children talk later, and less, than first-born children, presumably because the first-born receives more one-on-one language stimulation from parents (Dunn, 1983). While parents may talk less to younger siblings directly while older siblings are present, they still talk. When they converse with the older children, the younger child listens. Dunn and Shatz (1989) found that by age three toddlers become quite proficient at intruding themselves into conversations between their parents and older siblings. Not only do they intrude, they frequently turn the topic of conversation toward themselves. This ability to obtain attention through language is a social language skill more typical of later born than first born children.

Do girls speak sooner than boys? For a majority of people, the area of the cerebrum specialized for speech production (called Broca's area) is located in the left frontal lobe. In a small percentage of left-handed persons, and in persons with childhood injuries to the left frontal lobe, it may be located in the right hemisphere (Lennenberg, 1967). This location of Broca's area in the left hemisphere has led many people to speculate that this may provide a biological reason for girls speaking sooner than boys. The female human brain, at age 4, may have greater left hemispheric myelination (Petersen, 1979). It may maintain this advancement over males until close to puberty (Buffery and Grey, 1972).

An alternate explanation for the commonly held belief that girls speak earlier than boys is that girls may get more attention for the talking they do. In an extensive review of the literature on differential socialization practices with boys and girls, Block (1979) found that parents provided more physical closeness for daughters. Parents, conversely, encourage more independence, achievement, personal responsibility, and control of emotions in their sons. Block (1983) reported additional findings that girls play closer to their mothers and are given more homebound chores, while boys are given more freedom to explore and more chores taking them out of the house. Due to this closeness, parents may perceive that their daughters are talking more than their sons.

Weitzman and colleagues (1985) reported that mothers, regardless of their attitudes towards women's rights and gender roles, verbally stimulate their 2½- to 3½-year-old sons more than they do their same-aged daughters on a number of language variables. They ask more "what" questions, more "other" questions, provide more numbers and more action verbs, do more verbal teaching, and are more explicit when speaking. From the toddler's side, Cook and colleagues (1985) reported that boys both talk more and are more verbally assertive in their social interactions from early ages (see Figure 5-14).

The questions of gender differences in language are not yet adequately answered. We do not know for sure whether neurological differences or socialization practices account for earlier acquisition of language or more verbosity in one sex or the other.

The research on twin language is fascinating. Face-to-face babbling between twins stimulates more production of sounds. Twins help structure and support each other's speech, although neither twin can shape the other's sound productions toward words of the mother tongue. ("Mamama" would be shaped by an adult or older child to "Mommy.") As a consequence, twins often invent words to be part of their own language. A babble may be directed at a toy: "patata" may be vocalized while playing with a puppet. The other twin will reach for the toy and imitate the babble. Soon both twins accept the sound "patata" as the name of the puppet. Single children also invent

words when they do not know how to refer to something (e.g., up-sleeved shirt, day moon) but soon replace their inventions with the correct designation supplied by someone else. Twins are more apt to continue to use the invented words because they reinforce each other's use of neologisms (new words).

Many caregivers and older siblings find the neologisms of twins cute and begin to use the terms themselves. This can make such terms last a lifetime. While occasional neologisms that only the twins or their immediate fmaily understand are not harmful, allowing twins to develop an elaborate system of private speech can be. There have been pairs of twins whose extensive private languages have impaired their abilities to interact normally with all other people in their world. In rare cases where twin language caused abnormal social development, the adult caregivers were both distant from, and relatively noncommunicative with, the twins. When caregivers provide a normal environment of language stimulation, tender loving care, and reinforcement of words of the mother tongue, twins' language development proceeds normally.

Mark's parents brought him to the United States from Egypt at age three so they could pursue advanced academic work. They wanted him to learn to speak both Egyptian and English without confusing the languages. They decided to speak only Egyptian inside their apartment and only English everywhere else. Mark continued to learn Egyptian rapidly at home and slowly began to use English holophrases and telegraphic speech at his babysitter's house, in stores, and other out-of-home places. When an English-speaking cleaning lady began to speak to him in English, in his apartment, however, he began to answer her with interlanguage, a mixture of Egyptian and English. His use of interlanguage became more pronounced when his parents bought a television. In an effort to help Mark keep the two languages separate, his parents placed the TV in a small room designated as an "English speaking" room. They had the cleaning lady work only when Mark was not at home. The interlanguage ceased. At age 4½ Mark developed a strong friendship with a Spanish-speaking boy who lived in his apartment complex. He soon also learned to speak some Spanish with this friend and the friend's parents while playing in the friend's house.

Many children are exposed to more than one language in early childhood. Children who learn two or more languages simultaneously generally learn both languages more slowly than they would learn one language. However, they do seem to be able to learn both adequately, to acquire the syntax of both, and to keep words of both separate. At first, they seem to discern the syntactical rules which are common to all languages. Later, they learn the rules specific to each of the languages they are learning and keep them separate (Vihman, 1985). While interlanguage is more common in children whose parents model interlanguage, toddlers seem to have some cognitive and linguistic processes at work that help them avoid many mixed-language utterances. When caregivers find some method of using two or more languages in different situations (e.g., inside versus outside the home; one language with each adult; one language in the morning, another in the afternoon), the bilingual or multilingual child learns each language more rapidly and produces fewer mixed utterances (see Box 5-2).

Many psycholinguists have suggested that the exercise of learning more than one language system with syntax, phonology, and grammar in early childhood may be advantageous. Children who learn more than one language do not develop accents—they make the phonetic sounds of each language correctly. An English-speaking adult, in contrast, whose phonetic production has been limited to the 45 phonemes of English for several years, will give the phonemes of any foreign languages a decided "English" pronunciation.

Diaz (1985) and Hakuta (1987) have demonstrated that children with balanced bilingualism (equal facility in both languages) may have advantages in several other cognitive abilities. This is presumably because early practice in separating two grammars and two syntactical structures can lead to greater cognitive flexibility and a superior use of verbal mediators to guide cognitive activity.

Studies of early school bilingual education programs have demonstrated that young children can acquire a second language quite rapidly and have very few problems with interlanguage. Children learning a second language progress just as well in the first language as do children learning subjects only in the first language (Holobow et al., 1987). When they learn to read in one language, they can transfer their reading skills to a second language and differentiate between reading in both languages (Kendall et al., 1987).

Early Schooling

Today caregivers may be able to choose (depending on their locale) from a vast array of specialized preschool programs. How and if these programs will enhance a

---

BOX 5-2

When Should a Child Learn a Second Language?

If the sensitive period for speech center development is from birth to puberty, shouldn't children learn second (or third, or fourth) languages while young? Yes. Research and experience have shown that adults learn foreign languages slowly and speak with accents, whereas children are able to learn languages rapidly and speak without accents.

Should you wait until a child has learned the syntax and a large number of words in one language before you teach another? Not necessarily. If parents are bilingual (or multilingual), they can teach their children two or more languages from infancy. In fact, this is what many experts recommend.

Won't children mix up the words and syntax of two languages if they learn them simultaneously? In many countries where the population is bilingual or multilingual (Czechoslovakia, Switzerland) children learn two or more languages with ease. Garcia (1980) cautioned that there may be a temporary use of interlanguage (incor-

poration of two languages in speech). However, between the ages of three and seven, children sort out the separate grammars, and by age seven they can usually keep the languages totally separate.

Is there a way to help children avoid interlanguage? Yes. Parents can make learning two or more separate grammars easier by using the languages in different situations. Some examples: Spanish in the home, English outside the home; Spanish at meals, English except at meals; Spanish before 3 P.M., English after 3 P.M.; Spanish when Mom is present, English when Mom is absent. There are many other possibilities. Parents must also be careful not to model interlanguage usage.

Children learning two languages simultaneously may not acquire fluency in either one as rapidly as monolingual children do. However, they may have less difficulty learning subsequent foreign languages because they develop larger, more flexible cerebral speech centers (Albert and Obler, 1978).

child's intellectual and social-emotional development depends on many factors. The child's unique personality must be considered. Some programs serve the needs of shy children better than others. Likewise, some programs and teachers are more effective with active children. Some stress only the acquisition of cognitive or language skills. Others stress social adjustment. Many are eclectic (composed of material gathered from various sources). Some children enjoy a program more if it is not too long or too frequent (perhaps half-days two or three times a week). Others enjoy full-day programs five days per week. The reasons why caregivers send children to early childhood education programs can also influence the children's enjoyment and progress in the centers. If parents believe in the programs and cooperate with the teachers, their children are more apt to find the atmosphere pleasant than are children whose parents resent the intrusions of the daycare center or the school or feel guilty for leaving their children a part of the day (see Figure 5-15).

Some experts worry that early schooling can make children prematurely anxious about failure and deprive them of the wonderful world of play (Ames and Chase, 1974; Suransky, 1982) or will create "hurried children." Hurried children (those who grow up too fast, too soon) make up a large portion of the older troubled children experiencing school failure, drug dependence, trouble with the law, or chronic psychophysiological illnesses (Elkind, 1981).

Some experts worry that public schools do not continue to support children who are given good starts in enriched preschool programs. In many cases, the transition from a high-quality preschool to a public school with a low adult-to-child ratio has produced student problems in personal-social adjustment (Honig, Lally, and Mathieson, 1982). Clarke-Stewart (1982), in a review of contemporary daycare programs, pointed out that they appear to accelerate children's peer relationships while not hindering parent–child relationships. Some programs may also accelerate children's development of independence, knowledge, curiosity, inventiveness, and problem-solving abilities. (See also the discussion of daycare in Chapter 4.)

Fostering Learning

Experiences—opportunities to see, hear, taste, smell, or touch a multitude of objects—are the *sine qua non* for fostering intellectual growth. Without experiencing phenomena children cannot assimilate and accommodate them into their mental structures. In addition, the emotional climate in which a child learns about the world should

Figure 5-15
Preschool programs can provide an opportunity for children to interact with other children and to participate in many activities not readily available in their own homes.

be relaxed. An insecure, frightened, unhappy child seldom evinces much curiosity or interest in the events taking place around him or her other than those things that relate directly to his or her emotional problems. Nutrition is also important to learning. A hungry child is often lethargic and seldom very curious. Severe malnutrition can limit a child's ability to form new memories as well as interfere with interest and attention. Chronic health problems also interfere with energy and interest levels.

The right learning environment is one that produces pleasure and excitement in children. In such a setting parents and others involved in the child's care will not have to push. The child's interests will propel him or her to explore and discover more and more. The stimuli in the environment must satisfy what Hunt (1964) called "the problem of the match." Stimuli must not be too familiar, or they will bore children. But if stimuli are too novel, they will be ignored. Outings, trips, toys, games, and household articles that have elements of both familiarity and novelty will best capture and hold children's interests (see Figure 5-16).

Verbal stimulation is also important to children's intellectual development. Parents should spend time every day talking and listening to their children in face-to-face communication. It is not the amount of speech heard by children that fosters language but the way in which communications occur. A child may be bombarded with human vocalizations throughout the day (from television, other children, adults), but, unless words are spoken to a child directly, they will have little meaning. The most meaningful communications come from the adults to whom the child is attached. Significant adults can foster language by encouraging children's efforts to communicate. Holophrases and short sentences can be repeated approvingly and then expanded into longer sentences. Adults can explain objects or events to a child as they interact. It is important that adults attend to children's questions. Although a steady stream of "whys" can be exasperating, children who ask them want either information, attention, or both. The best time to provide both is when children are open and receptive. Caregivers who repeatedly say "Not now" or "Wait" and then fail to find a few minutes to spend with the child will discourage communication.

Reading aloud to children will entertain and stimulate them. Children can ask for and get instant replays of scenes. In addition to being able to turn pages back, ask questions, and discuss interesting aspects of the pictures in books, reading provides a warm emotional climate between children and caregivers (see Figure 5-17).

Figure 5-16
Outings, books, games, and plenty of one-on-one interaction will stimulate a child's cognitive development.

Some adults have a profound impact on cognitive achievements. Effective caregivers give specific, well-organized instructions, encourage children to ask questions or talk about activities, engage children in interactions, and praise their progress. White (1971) found that caregivers of competent children provided safe environments with a variety of toys and interesting household objects where children had a great deal of freedom for exploration. He also found that these caregivers set definite limits on dangerous behaviors and were available as consultants to answer questions, give directions, or provide encouragement when children needed it.

Psychosocial Development

The process of socialization is no longer viewed as a one-way street with family and community members acting on the child to bring about socialization. Children's unique characteristics and ways of interacting with the world influence the ways in which others react to them. Socialization is thus seen as a reciprocal process in which children influence adult behaviors as certainly as adults influence children's behaviors. Children's patterns of behavior range from shy to bold, passive to active, cuddly to distant, lethargic to alert, serious to carefree. The same adult behaviors aimed at socialization of each child can have different effects.

Havighurst (1972) suggested that there are nine developmental tasks to be accomplished during infancy and early childhood:

1. achieving physiological stability,
2. learning to take solid foods,
3. learning to talk,
4. learning to walk,
5. forming simple concepts of social and physical reality,
6. learning to relate emotionally to parents, siblings, and other people,
7. learning to control the elimination of body wastes,
8. learning to distinguish right and wrong and develop a conscience,
9. learning sex differences and sexual modesty.

The first five tasks were discussed in Chapter 4. In this section we will discuss the last four tasks, and Erikson's nuclear conflicts.

Erikson's Conflicts of Early Childhood

Given a sense of trust in the caregivers to whom they are attached, children move into what Erik Erikson described as the second nuclear conflict of life, that of achieving **autonomy versus shame and doubt** (see Table 5-6). Erikson, as a psychodynamic theorist, followed Freud's lead in viewing toilet training and anal functioning as a foremost concern of the child at about age two. As young children develop the sphincter control necessary for holding on and letting go, caregivers begin to ask them not to wet or mess their pants. Children have the power to obey or disobey, which, for them, can be a heady feeling. If accidents are cleaned up without much fuss, if children are encouraged to hold on long enough to get to a toilet, and if praise is given for toileting successes, children will gain a sense of self-control, of inner goodness, and of pride. These feelings are basic to autonomy as Erikson described it. However, if children are punished and made to feel foolish for their accidents, a sense of shame will develop. If they are kept in diapers and given no opportunities to control their urges, a sense of doubt will be fostered. Feelings of shame and doubt are not healthy personality attributes. As Erikson (1963) stated: "Too much shaming does not lead to genuine propriety but to a secret determination to try to get away with things, unseen—if, indeed, it does not result in defiant shamelessness" (p. 253). Doubt is the brother of shame. It is a sense of inner badness and secondary mistrust with a need to look back or behind. Erikson believed that many adult persecution complexes may have their origins in the compulsive doubting that begins in early childhood.

Although toilet training methods (to be discussed later in this chapter) play a role in the nuclear conflict of learning autonomy versus learning shame and doubt, they are by no means the only caregiving techniques involved. During the second and third years of life, toddlers are actively trying to stand on their own two feet. Increased neuro-muscular development gives them the capabilities for walking, running, climbing, pushing, pulling, holding on tight, and exploring their worlds in ways heretofore impossible. Likewise, cognitive and language development make it possible for them to think about their actions and make their wills known to their caregivers. "No!" and "Me!" (meaning "Let me do it myself") are oft-repeated holophrases of two- and three-year-olds. Caregivers do not have an easy time time helping children develop a sense of autonomy in all the activities of daily living. Toddlers need many experiences of being able to choose among alternatives (to play inside or outside, to wear the blue pants or the brown pants, to have a peanut butter or a cheese sandwich). However, caregivers

Table 5-6   Erikson's Second Nuclear Conflict: Autonomy Versus Shame and Doubt.

Sense	Eriksonian Descriptions	Fostering Adult Behaviors
Autonomy	Sense of inner goodness	Encouragement to stand on own feet
	Sense of self-control	Firm control of child's anarchy due to lack of sense of discrimination
	Sense of good will and pride	Gradual and well-guided experiences of free choice
versus		
Shame	Sense of premature or foolish exposure	Shaming as punishment technique
	Sense of being too visible	Suppression of self-expression
	Desire to sink out of sight	Overcontrol of actions Little free choice
Doubt	Sense of inner badness	Critical of self-help efforts.
	Secondary mistrust with a need to look back or behind	Overprotective

should phrase questions for children to allow situations in which either choice will be acceptable. When a particular behavior is necessary (such as going to bed, holding hands to cross a street, letting go of another child's hair), caregivers should not give a choice (see Figure 5-18). Erikson stressed that young children do not have the wisdom to know what behaviors are acceptable or unacceptable, healthy or unhealthy. If caregivers give in too often to children's stubborn demands, children may develop long-lasting conflicts. They may become fearful of their own powers. If their willfulness leads them into too many unfortunate accidents, they may develop what Erikson describes as a sense of self-doubt. Autonomous behaviors are best nourished in a climate where both experiences of free choice and firm control of anarchy are continuously available.

In the preschool period (about ages four to five) children begin the work of resolving Erikson's third nuclear conflict, that of acquiring a sense of **initiative versus guilt** (see Table 5-7). Having discovered that they can do for themselves, they become curious about how much they can do, and when, and where. They also wonder about who else they can be. They explore answers to these questions by pretending to be other people and by scrutinizing more and diverse phenomena. Acquiring a sense of initiative involves thrusting out into a wider world of childhood and assuming new interests and activities. Energy levels are high, curiosity is profound, and explorations are vigorous.

Erikson, following Freud, saw elements of genital interest and sexual conflicts accompanying the nuclear conflict of acquiring initiative versus assuming guilt. Curiosity and cognitive maturity lead young children to take note of the differences between males and females. Their role-playing imitations of other people include pretending to be husband and pretending to be wife. Children most frequently assume the roles of the adults in their lives whom they recognize as sharing sexual sameness. According to psychoanalytic theory, Oedipal and Electra complexes are common at this time. Oedipus was a legendary Greek king who killed his father and married his mother. A boy with an Oedipal complex presumably wants to replace his father as his mother's husband. Many boys become very attached to the females in their lives during the preschool period. Electra was a legendary Greek woman who harbored an intense love for her murdered father and bitterly hated her mother, whom she blamed for her father's death. A girl with an Electra complex supposedly wishes to replace her mother as her father's wife. While a dislike of mothers may not occur, many preschool girls do become very attached to the men in their lives during early childhood (see Figure 5-19).

Erikson (1963) wrote that rivalry is part of the conflict of initiative versus guilt. As he stated it, "Initiative brings with it anticipatory rivalry with those who have been there first and may, therefore, occupy with their superior equipment the field towards which one's initiative is directed" (p. 256). Rivalry can also be directed at other children (siblings, friends) and at other adults.

The development of a sense of initiative involves creativity and assertiveness. Children need to be given opportunities to plan for and carry out their own activities

Figure 5-18
Toddlers need experiences in which they can choose activities, but adults need to control choices where the young child lacks the ability to discriminate right from wrong, safe from unsafe.

Table 5-7 Erikson's Third Nuclear Conflict: Initiative Versus Guilt.

Sense	Eriksonian Descriptions	Fostering Adult Behaviors
Initiative	Quality of undertaking, planning, and "attacking" a task	Provide opportunities for child to plan and carry out own activities
versus		
Guilt	Anxiety about own behavior being bad	Inhibit child from starting own activities
	Fear of wrongdoing leading to over-control and overconstriction of own activities	Deride child's efforts at doing for self

during the preschool years. They need to begin to develop a feeling that they are, to some extent, masters of their own fates.

During this period the *superego* becomes apparent. Preschoolers begin to show signs of anxiety about their misbehaviors, even while they find it difficult to control their impulsive actions. Erikson (1963) calls this feeling of concern about misdeeds a sense of guilt. Preschoolers are harsher critics of their own behaviors than are their caregivers. Children who are frequently criticized may learn to overcontrol themselves to the point of extreme shyness. No child emerges from early childhood without some feelings of guilt for initiating forbidden behaviors. Learning the rules, regulations, and limits of behavior involves occasional overstepping of bounds. Adults need to help children establish a sense of right and wrong without laying on their shoulders an unduly heavy burden of guilt for the mistakes that naturally occur.

Parent–Child Relationships

Much has been written about the "new" style of parenting. Mothers take brief maternity leaves and return to work. Children spend their days with babysitters, relatives, or in organized child-care facilities. Some parents register their children for what they consider the best child-care facility in town before the child is born. Children come home to tired parents. Is this maternal deprivation? Is this paternal deprivation? As Socrates asked of the children of the ancient Greeks, "What kind of awful creatures will they be when they grow up?"

Working Mothers.   Many people are concerned that the increased percentage of mothers of preschoolers working outside the home will weaken identification bonds and jeopardize children's feelings of autonomy and initiative. Chapter 2 introduced identification as a major element in Robert Sears's social-learning theory of child development. Sears believed that identification with caregivers follows attachment bonding (Sears, Rau, and Alpert, 1965). Children learn to enjoy and look forward to contact with the caregivers who are their primary sources of nurture and affection. This attachment bond motivates children to imitate the behavior of the loved adult(s). Imitations are performed not only in the caregivers' presence but also in their absence. Sears pointed out that imitating absent caregivers has a secondary reinforcing value. It makes the caregivers seem closer. Children's incorporations of adult behaviors into their own acts can give them a sense of autonomy and initiative and can aid them in controlling their own emotions and behaviors.

Albert Bandura (1977) found that adults who are recognized as wielding power and controlling status are more salient as identification models than are those adults or children who are simply rewarding. Knowledge of this perception-of-power component in strong identification bonds may bring comfort to some parents who fear the effects of babysitters, daycare staff, peer models, television models, or super-rewarding (spoiling) adult models on their children. Although children practice many different roles in their play, they are most apt to take on the characteristics of the most loved, nurturing, and powerful people in their lives, usually their parents.

Pederson and colleagues (1982) found that employed mothers spend more time interacting with their children in the evening hours than do nonworking mothers. Easterbrooks and Goldberg (1985) found that maternal employment outside the home had little effect on the security of the toddlers they studied. They warned, however, that there may be "sleeper effects" of early maternal employment. If they exist, they can only be discerned with longitudinal research. Bronfenbrenner, Alvarez, and Henderson (1984) found that employed mothers perceive their three-year-old daughters in more favorable ways than they do their sons. Fathers exhibit the same pattern. Further research is needed to discern what differential effect, if any, full-time maternal employment has on the socialization of young sons and daughters.

Many researchers today feel convinced that children are resilient and malleable. There are a multitude of ways to help them realize their potentials. Care by loving, nurturing, stimulating adults is important, but these adults can be babysitters, relatives, or professional child-care providers as well as parents. Maternal employment need not have ill effects (Rutter, 1987).

Discipline. It would be much easier to be a parent if experts in child development could produce an easy formula for it. They cannot. There is an abundance of advice available on how to discipline children, but it is not simple or straightforward. It is full of ifs, ands, and buts. This is because children are not all alike, and their behaviors change from day to day, even from minute to minute. In addition, parents are not all alike, and parental behaviors are subject to mood swings just as children's are. The long-range goal of discipline is to help children develop consciences that will guide their behavior toward the positive and away from the negative. This conscience (or superego) formation involves gaining an understanding of moral codes (learning right from wrong). It also involves gaining mastery over one's own behavior (learning self-control). The short-term goal of discipline is to stop behaviors that are dangerous, destructive, pain producing, or annoying. Some forms of discipline are more effective in bringing about the long-range goal of helping children guide their own behaviors according to society's moral standards. Other forms of discipline better serve the short-term goal of stopping an ongoing set of bad behaviors.

Power-assertive discipline (physical punishment, threats of punishment, commands backed by force, shouting), and **love-withdrawal discipline** (scolding, refusing to look, listen to, or speak to a child, isolating the child, giving dirty looks, or explicitly stating dislike or disapproval) are more effective for bringing about immediate compliance with parental directives. However, **inductive discipline** (explaining reasons why behavior should change and explaining the consequences of the behavior) is more effective for bringing about the long-term goals of internalization of moral standards and self-regulation of behaviors (see Figure 5-20).

Identification with the powerful and nurturant parents or other caregivers helps the child model his or her behaviors, and adopt attitudes about right and wrong, as long as this brings the child security and/or external reinforcements. Beyond identifi-

Figure 5-20

Consequences of the predominant use of various forms of discipline.

Permissiveness	→	Lack of respect. Ill will toward person ignoring misbehavior.	→ Poor control of behavior. Less evidence of conscience.
Power assertion	→	Low guilt after punishment (score-is-even attitude). Hostility toward rule enforcer.	→ Behavior is controlled only when threat of detection and punishment exists. Less evidence of conscience.
Deprivation of approval or love	→	Variable guilt. High anxiety about loss of approval and love. Some resentment of person withholding affection.	→ Behavior is controlled to maintain good relations with others. Less evidence of conscience.
Inductive discipline (being made to feel responsible for consequences of behavior of others)	→	High guilt. Understanding of ramifications of selfish actions. High degree of empathy with others.	→ Behavior is controlled to avoid doing harm to others. More evidence of conscience.

cation comes *internalization,* a process whereby beliefs about right and wrong (and other attitudes) become so deeply inculcated that they continue to exist regardless of any external reinforcements. This internalization process can be equated with conscience development, the long-range goal of discipline.

Over the past twenty years, experts have been advising parents to avoid power-assertion and love-withdrawal discipline and use reason (inductive discipline) to foster internalization of moral values and development of a conscience to regulate behavior. Love withdrawal and power assertion are ineffective as techniques to enhance the development of a conscience and self-regulation of behavior in children. Furthermore, frequent use of love withdrawal is correlated with high anxiety levels in children and avoidance of the parent who withdraws the love. Inductive discipline, or "reason" can be applied in many ways, and the ways in which it is used are of utmost importance to its outcome.

Bearison and Cassel (1975) compared person-oriented reasoning (directed toward the feelings, thoughts, needs, or intentions of a person) with position-oriented reasoning (directed toward rules or status). Person-oriented reasoning is preferable. Children whose parents used person-oriented reasoning fostered more conscience development as it related to seeing the perspectives of others. Hoffman (1975) found that parents who use person-oriented reasoning do have more altruistic children, but only if they are concurrently loathe to use much power assertion.

Parents are not alike. They differ in the ways they assert power, withdraw love, or use inductive techniques of discipline. They differ in the relative amounts of each type of discipline they use. They also differ along two other important dimensions:

1. demandingness (high to low), and
2. responsiveness (high to low).

High demandingness can be defined as a large amount of regulation and control of a child's behavior by a caregiver, while low demandingness suggests few attempts to regulate or control a child's activities. High responsiveness can be defined as child-centered parenting with a great deal of time and attention spent engaging the child in activity or responding to the child's ongoing activities. Low responsiveness suggests parent-centeredness with little time and attention spent engaging or answering the child (see Figure 5-21).

Maccoby and Martin (1983) presented a fourfold scheme that characterizes caregivers who differ on these dimensions. Caregivers high on both demandingness and responsiveness fit the **authoritative parenting** pattern. Caregivers high on demandingness but low on responsiveness fit the **authoritarian parenting** pattern. Caregivers low on demandingness but high on responsiveness fit the **indulgent parenting** pattern, and caregivers low on both characteristics fit the **indifferent parenting** pattern.

The most positive parenting pattern in terms of conscience development (internalizing society's moral standards and gaining mastery over one's own behavior) is the authoritative pattern. Authoritative parents are most apt to raise children who are high in both self-esteem and self-control. They are also more independent and more socially responsible. Authoritarian parents are more apt to raise children who are low in self-esteem and self-control. The children are, however, highly controlled and obedient when in the presence of their autocratic parents or other adults. They tend to be shy and socially withdrawn with their peers as well as with adults.

The less positive parenting patterns in terms of conscience development are those that involve low demandingness from parents. Indulgent parents are apt to raise children who are immature. The children feel a need to rely on others for advice or help, and they tend to be socially irresponsible, impulsive, and often aggressive. The least positive pattern of parenting is the indifferent pattern. Children raised by neglecting parents are apt to become aggressive, impulsive, and delinquent. They show little evidence of internalization of moral standards or the ability to regulate their own behaviors. The consequences of the four patterns of parenting are less clear-cut when parents use a mixture of all four patterns of behavior as their children mature.

Many conflicts between adults and children are avoidable. Adults should be cog-

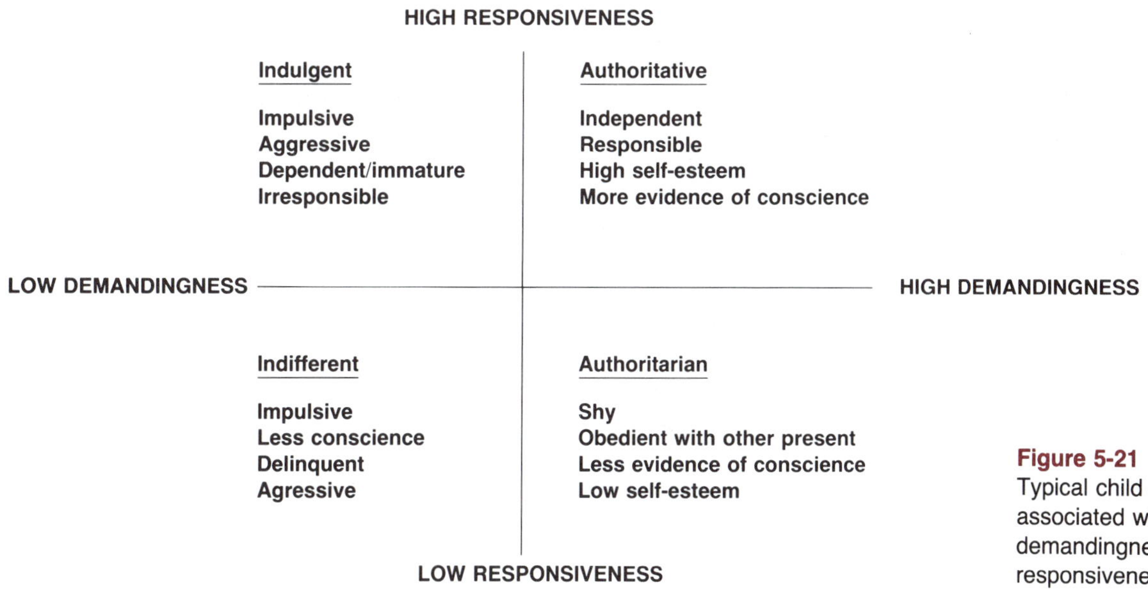

HIGH RESPONSIVENESS

Indulgent

Impulsive
Aggressive
Dependent/immature
Irresponsible

Authoritative

Independent
Responsible
High self-esteem
More evidence of conscience

LOW DEMANDINGNESS ————————————————— **HIGH DEMANDINGNESS**

Indifferent

Impulsive
Less conscience
Delinquent
Agressive

Authoritarian

Shy
Obedient with other present
Less evidence of conscience
Low self-esteem

LOW RESPONSIVENESS

Figure 5-21
Typical child outcomes associated with high or low demandingness and responsiveness.

nizant of normal behaviors of growing children at different ages. They should not become so responsive and so demanding as to intrude constantly in the lives of even their youngest children. Such overcontrol will interfere with the acquisition of autonomy and initiative. Nor should parents insist on rules and regulations that are beyond the child's ability to understand or obey.

Rudolf Dreikurs stressed giving children chores and responsibilities in order to help them feel wanted and needed (see Figure 5-22). Dreikurs wrote that unless children feel worthwhile they may go through one or more of four progressive stages aimed at capturing attention (Dreikurs and Soltz, 1964). **Dreikurs's stages** involve behaviors that are usually unpleasant for the adult(s) involved in parenting: (1) seeking attention directly through loud talking, interrupting, annoying, being cute; (2) seeking power through stubbornness, assertiveness, rebelliousness; (3) seeking revenge through aggressive acts aimed to injure or inflict pain; and, finally, (4) giving up altogether and retreating into a silent, passive stance.

Most children have times when they need to overcome feelings of inferiority by seeking attention, power, or revenge. Parents who reassure their children that they are loved and wanted can reduce these attention-seeking behaviors. Dreikurs feared that if children cannot achieve a feeling that they are worthwhile they may give up efforts to interact in a social way with others.

Discipline is not easy, but it is necessary. Children want and need help in controlling their impulsive actions in early childhood. Parents who are prepared to give this help in an inductive manner, with a relatively high level of responsiveness and demandingness, can be successful disciplinarians.

Child Abuse and Neglect.   Child abuse is defined as the intentional, nonaccidental physical or sexual abuse of a child by a parent or other caregiver entrusted with his or her care. It is not a new phenomenon, although research studies and media reporting have only recently brought it out from behind closed doors and into national awareness. In the early 1970s many states passed laws making it easier for doctors, nurses, social workers, and law enforcement officers to report cases of child neglect or abuse. In 1989, over 2.4 million cases of child abuse were reported in the United States (Lipsitt, 1990).

Serious physical abuse—resulting in permanent injury (or death)—is given the clinical name *battered child syndrome*. Physicians have a duty to evaluate battered children fully and to guarantee that no repetition of trauma will be permitted to occur (Kempe et al., 1985). Unfortunately, repetitions are common. Fatalities from abuse totaled 1237 in 1989 (Lipsitt, 1990). Fatal battering is most common in infants and toddlers.

Research indicates that abusive adults can be found in all socio-economic levels in our society and in all ethnic groups. Many factors, singly or in combination, contribute to high-risk situations in which child abuse is more likely to occur. Parents under stress, as from factors such as unemployment, poor marital relations, social isolation, depression, or health problems, may be at high risk for abusive behavior (Wolfe, 1985). So, also, are drug abusers (Lipsitt, 1990).

Certain child attributes or behaviors may also be very aversive to some parents and contribute to the incidence of abuse. Frequent crying, clinging, vomiting, sleep difficulties, bedwetting, aggressive outbursts, hyperactivity, or a difficult temperament may frustrate parents and lead to aggressive outbursts. There is also evidence that some abusive parents have misconceptions about children, little knowledge of normal child development, and an orientation toward physical punishment as a remedy for problems (Steele, 1975).

Many of the other factors contributing to child abuse are poorly understood because the data are sparse. Starr (1978, 1988) saw the need for research that considers the total ecology of the family: the abused child, the psychological characteristics of the

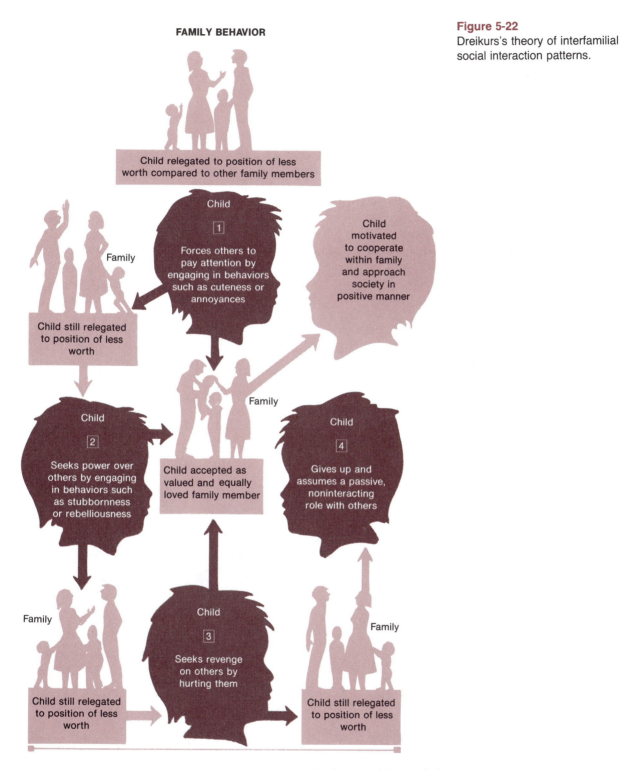

FAMILY BEHAVIOR

Figure 5-22
Dreikurs's theory of interfamilial social interaction patterns.

parent(s), the social forces impinging on the family, institutions, and the total character of the society.

Our relatively recent awareness of the prevalence of battered children in our society has led to new programs to help abusive parents and to intervene on behalf of injured children. Programs for adults should be multidisciplinary to provide aid in the many areas in which they suffer their seemingly insurmountable stresses and to educate them in areas of self-control and child-rearing techniques. Such programs should not be incriminating. Self-help groups and "parents anonymous" programs can be especially effective. Programs for children, such as specialized daycare centers, or summer camps, should emphasize the affectionate, trustworthy side of adults. They should also help abused children overcome their feelings of unworthiness and develop more positive self-concepts (see Figure 5-23). With increased understanding of the factors involved in child abuse, with increased efforts to provide intervention and treatment facilities in our communities, and with concern for psychological as well as physical health maintenance practices in our homes, it is hoped that child abuse (as well as other forms of violence in our society) will soon begin a downward spiral.

Sexual abuse, which was rarely reported just ten years ago, now accounts for about 20% of reported child abuse cases in some areas of the country. The incidence has probably not risen dramatically; rather, public awareness and willingness to report it has. Freud and his colleague, Breuer (1895), wrote about the effects of incest on adult women they saw as patients as early as the 19th century. A recent retrospective (looking backward) study of 200 prostitutes revealed that 60% of them had been unreported victims of sexual abuse as children (Silbert and Pines, 1981). About two-thirds of the prostitutes reported that the abusive figure was a father or father substitute. Goodwin, Cormier, and Owen (1983) reported that grandfather-granddaughter incest accounts for about 10% of intrafamilial sexual abuse. Other perpetrators reported quite frequently are uncles, cousins, brothers, stepbrothers, or close friends of the family. The victims can be either male (25%) or female (75%). Experts feel that children almost never make up stories about being sexually abused (Faller, 1984). They more commonly keep their victimization a secret. The trauma has extremely negative emotional, physical, and attitudinal impacts, especially on very young children.

Prevention of sexual abuse begins with early sex education, including information about the possibility of molestation, given by a loved and trusted source. Finkelhor (1984) suggested discussing touching with children, differentiating good, bad, and confusing touches. Confusing touches are those that make a child feel "funny" or "mixed

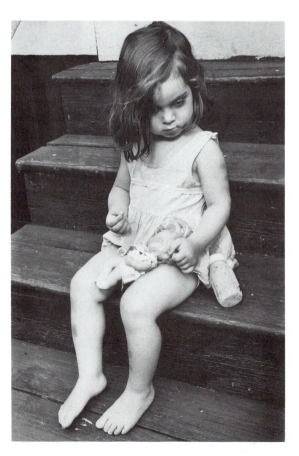

Figure 5-23
Special daycare programs and summer camps for abused children emphasize how lovable children are and how much they deserve hugs and affection.

Table 5-8 Prevention of Child Abuse and Neglect.

Primary Level of Prevention	Secondary Level of Prevention	Tertiary Level of Prevention
(Alter conditions that create abuse and neglect)	(Early detection and treatment of abuse)	(Reduce long-term consequences of abuse)
Child development classes Employment opportunities	Mandatory reporting	Counseling for abused
Good Samaritanism	Counseling for abusers	Social support for abused
Parenting seminars	Parents Anonymous groups	Rehabilitation programs for abusers
Media information on child care	Parenting hotlines	
Drug abuse prevention	Stress management help	
Social support networking	Social services help	
Affordable housing		
Available child care		

up," those that go under the pants, in private places, or all over. Children should be encouraged to tell someone right away about both bad touches (hitting, bullying, trapping) and confusing touches. They should understand that they have the right to refuse inappropriate touching and the right to keep their bodies private.

Child neglect is far more prevalent than child abuse (Wolock and Horowitiz, 1984). The consequences can be just as long lasting—physically, mentally, and emotionally. Child neglect is defined as being remiss in attending to any aspect of child care (nutrition, health care, accident prevention, cognitive stimulation, toilet training, discipline, or provision of a sense of being loved and wanted). Failure-to-thrive infants are frequently victims of neglect (see Chapter 4). Egeland and Sroufe (1981) documented the high incidence of neglect among parents who fit the indifferent pattern of parenting. These parents are detached, emotionally uninvolved, often depressed, and uninterested in the child they neglect.

Lally (1984) presented a view of child neglect that goes beyond the characteristics of the neglecting parent(s). Many such parents feel psychologically isolated from other adults. They may be caught up in nonnurturant social systems. Primary prevention aimed at teaching them how to care for the children they neglect is not enough. They need to be helped to find family and social support networks to decrease their feelings of isolation and helplessness. Links with community service agencies should be established, maintained, and strengthened so the parents will be able to find services (psychological, economic) when they need them. (See Table 5-8.) Beyond parent–child relationships and parent–social support system networks, Lally saw an association between child neglect and cultural beliefs. If a society espouses the concepts of survival of the fittest and achievement through aggressive competition, the weaker, less "fit" will be more apt to feel powerless. On the other hand, if a society embraces the concepts of cooperative efforts, good Samaritanism (willingness to help fellow beings in distress), and the fellowship of humankind, parents will be more apt to give nurturing to their children.

Toilet Training

Dorinne read a book on toilet training that suggested that the longer the training was delayed, the easier it would be. Therefore, when her best friend, Simone, bought a potty chair and began trying to toilet train her fifteen-month-old daughter, Suzy, Dorinne scoffingly told her she was wasting her time. Dorinne's son, Davy, took an interest in Suzy's potty chair. (The children played together daily.) Suzy was completely toilet trained when she was two years old. Davy asked for a potty chair for his second birthday. Dorinne bought it for him, but continued to diaper him and ignore the potty chair. One day when Davy was two and a half years old, he announced to Dorinne that he did not want to wear diapers anymore but would use the potty chair instead. She told him he needed to wear the diapers because he didn't have any underpants. Davy went to his father and asked for underpants. His father bought him some. Davy proudly put them on and kept them dry all day by using the potty. When his mother tried to diaper him at night, he fought the process, insisting that he was now a "big boy." She diapered him anyway, but was amazed to find him dry, and in his underpants, in the morning. She never diapered him again, and he never had an accident. Dorinne returned to work when her second child, Dawn, was six months old. She planned to toilet train Dawn in the same manner as Davy. However, Dawn's babysitter had other ideas. The babysitter bought and put underpants on Dawn at ten months and gave her small gifts whenever she used the potty chair. By Dawn's first birthday, she was consistently keeping her pants dry, between potty trips, although she continued to need diapers at night through the age of thirty months. Dorinne was incredulous. Could Davy have been trained earlier? Would Dawn be psychologically traumatized by such early training?

Most child development experts agree that **toilet training** should not begin too early. The child needs to have the ability voluntarily to control the muscles that allow the passage of urine from the bladder into the urethra and also an interest in this process. The age at which this motor skill is achieved varies greatly from child to child. Very rarely will this happen by one year of age. Dawn's early toileting successes may have been explained by regular urination habits and an astute babysitter who scheduled regular trips to the potty. In many cases unpleasant toilet training is associated with negative attitudes toward the whole pubic area and ultimately toward the genitals and sexuality. Physical readiness is seldom achieved before thirteen to eighteen months for the bowels (anal sphincter) and even later for the bladder. Starting earlier than this may result in disappointment for the parents and a sense of shame and doubt for the toddler. Mental readiness suggests that the child is old enough to find a mess in the diaper a nuisance. Toddlers are seldom as interested in cleanliness as their caregivers. In fact, they are often curious about their feces. Around thirteen to eighteen months children can understand that dry diapers (or training pants) are, in fact, more comfortable than wet or dirty ones. They also have a desire to imitate loved caregivers, and they appreciate the pleasure they give caregivers when they deposit their feces (and later urine) in a potty or toilet (see Figure 5-24). Mental readiness, then, suggests understanding of the benefits of dry over wet and motivation to please caregivers by using the toilet. Caregivers should be patient and casual about the training process. Sitting on a toilet should be kept to under ten minutes and should be a pleasant time. A child should never be strapped to a potty seat or forced to sit on the potty for a long time. Successes should be rewarded with a hug, applause, or other positive feedback. No negative feedback should be given for failures. It is emotionally easier for a toddler to be trained later than earlier. Ultimately all normal children do become toilet trained, and the process should not be allowed to damage the loving relationship between caregiver and child.

Figure 5-24
Toilet training should begin with a relaxed child who is interested in the process and who has voluntary control of defecation and urination.

Gender Identification. **Sex typing** (also called gender identification) does not occur all at once but continues gradually throughout the course of development. It is not an all-or-none phenomenon at any time. Many factors are related to the way in which young children perceive themselves as gender typed. Huston (1983) defined sex typing as multidimensional. It involves many constructs across many content areas. Masculine gender typing and feminine gender typing are not polar opposites. One can be more masculine in some constructs or content areas and more feminine in others and still be appropriately gender typed as male or female.

Freud (1933/1965) felt that cross-sex identifications (boys with their mothers and girls with their fathers) occur during early childhood. He believed that it is not until about age six that emotionally healthy boys and girls identify with the same-sex parent. Contemporary theories of the acquisition of gender typing have moved away from Freud's position because of the rather late age at which he felt appropriate gender identification takes place.

Social-learning theorists proposed that gender typing may occur soon after attachment bonds are formed (Mischel, 1966). Gender identity grows stronger with the passing of time. Boys are rewarded and praised for modeling masculine behaviors, whereas girls are rewarded and praised for modeling feminine actions. Both may be punished or ignored for inappropriate sex behaviors. According to social-learning theory, boys and girls learn appropriate sex behaviors because they imitate the behaviors of all the adults whom they find nurturant and powerful and because these appropriate behaviors bring rewards and attention (see Figure 5-25).

Kohlberg (1966) emphasized cognitive aspects of gender typing. Children model like-sexed persons because, first, they perceive their resemblance to those persons, and, second, they want to be like the persons whom they most closely resemble.

Martin and Halverson (1981) proposed an information-processing model. As children process information, they simplify it by trying to fit it into categories: "things for me" and "things not for me." Eventually their schemas will include the categories of gender, as gender differences are easily discriminated even by young children. "Things for me" will be broadened to include "things for (my sex)." They will change, modify, and refine their stereotypes over time.

Toddlers and preschoolers now usually all sport pants and shirts, regardless of sex. Many caregivers make a conscious effort to teach their sons to avoid fights, to express emotions, to nurture dolls, animals, or other children, and to help with cooking and housework. Daughters are rewarded for doing the same things but are also taught to assert themselves, to run, climb, and roughhouse, and to help with garbage collection and mechanical fix-it tasks. However, efforts to raise non-gender-typed children do not succeed. Even if parents studiously avoid labeling any activities, interests, personality attributes, or social behaviors as more appropriate for one gender than another, children will learn their culture's expectations from television, books, peers, other family members, and persons in the surrounding community (see Figure 5-26).

Marsha Weinraub and her colleagues (1984) found that a significant number of two-year-olds know their own gender identity. By three years of age, the majority of children know that men wear suits and shave, while women wear dresses and makeup. McLoyd and Ratner (1983) offered preschool children their choice of play with household

Figure 5-25
Gender identity is enhanced when children are praised for modeling the behaviors of same-sexed adults.

Figure 5-26
An example of the type of stereotyped message children may learn from books, peers, or television.

appliances or car appliances: girls preferred the house, boys the car. Ashton (1983) found that preschool children's toy preferences were directly related to the stereotypes found in picture books that they had just seen. O'Keefe and Hyde (1983) found that preschool boys chose gender-stereotyped jobs for themselves more frequently than did girls. This may reflect current efforts to encourage little girls to pursue traditionally male job options.

While acquiring sex-typed schemas about their worlds, children also became curious about the reasons for gender differences. In the process of being toilet trained, they learn that society deems modesty to be appropriate—they should not run around without pants outside their homes. Many preschoolers must prepare for a new sibling. Questions arise about pregnancy, birth, and sex of the baby. Sex education should begin in situations such as these and continue whenever children ask questions about gender differences, sex, or sexually related topics (see Box 5-3).

BOX 5-3

When and Where Should Sex Education Begin?

Sex education should begin in the home as soon as each child asks his or her first question about sex: "Does Mommy have a penis?" "Why doesn't Daddy have breasts?" "Where do babies come from?" "Why can't I touch my [genitals] in public?"

The child's major source of sex education should be the parents or primary caregivers. Most children acquire the bulk of their knowledge about sex in the preschool years. Sex education courses taught in schools, even if they are offered at the elementary school level, are usually too little, too late. Even extreme efforts to shelter children from a knowledge of sex differences usually end in failure. Sex differences are too obvious to remain unnoticed. If children learn that it is taboo to ask their caregivers questions about sex, they ask their siblings or friends or invent their own answers. Often they acquire a great deal of emotionally upsetting misinformation in this manner.

If parents and other caregivers are open and honest about sexual matters and answer all questions in a simple manner when and where they occur, children usually go back about their play. Most experts believe that sex education is best accomplished by such simple direct information given inside the home. However, it is not easy for all families to give on-the-spot, simple answers to questions, especially if they have had a lifetime's practice in keeping sexual matters hidden. Their embarrassment may be acute. Children can sense their parents' timidity and may quit asking questions.

Because about 25% of child sexual abuse occurs in early childhood (and 75% of victims are girls), parents need to teach youngsters that they have the right to keep their body private and that they must tell someone right away if anyone tries to touch them in private areas. This aspect of sex education should not be delayed until children are older. Many books for preschoolers are available to help families explain sex and gender roles. In order to help caregivers provide sex information, writers of such books present answers to the questions that they know preschoolers ask. These books are especially useful for parents who are too embarrassed to answer children's questions directly. Often the interaction required to read the book to the child will break the ice and allow the parents to continue giving factual information about sex, when the child desires it, in the future.

Sibling Relationships

The presence of one or more brothers or sisters in a family adds new dimensions to social development beyond the caregiver–child behaviors discussed so far. Children may form affectionate bonds to each other in spite of the fact that the outward demonstrations of their relationship seem to consist mainly of fights. They play, help, and nurture each other. They exchange language, ask questions, give directions, argue, correct, and in general provide a rich and varied environment for each other. The younger child takes great pleasure in imitating the older, more powerful child in every way possible. An older sibling will ask for a more complicated communication from a toddler than will an adult (often not appreciating the toddler's language limitations) and will also wait longer for, and even coach, the reply. When the age spacing between the older sibling and the toddler is wide, language stimulation is especially positive (Teti, Bond, and Gibbs, 1986).

Sibling rivalry varies from family to family. One factor that plays an important role in the formation of jealousies is the quality and quantity of time and attention that caregivers bestow on each individual child. The greater the differential treatment and favoritism shown, the more intense are the rivalries that develop (Stocker, Dunn, and Plomin, 1989). Although it is not always possible for caregivers to treat children equally, explanations should be given to children about the reasons for any preferential treatment that is protested as unfair. As much as possible, caregivers should try to be fair with the time, attention, and favors they give each child.

Three factors that have an interactive effect on sibling rivalry are sex, age spacing, and security of attachments. The stresses of sibling rivalry are greater between opposite-sex than between same-sex children (Minnett, Vandell, and Santrock, 1983). Children who are spaced closer together have more rivalry than children who are born further apart (Furman and Buhrmester, 1985). The most stressful spacing is under two years apart. The one- to two-year range is the period of time when toddlers are beginning to establish a sense of self. They struggle for a sense of autonomy and yet are vulnerable to feelings of shame and doubt. Their cognitive immaturity may prevent their understanding why the caregiver must spend time with the baby. Teti and Ablard (1989) found that if both the older sibling and the younger sibling are securely attached to the mother, they are apt to be friendlier. Insecurely attached siblings are more apt to develop antagonistic relationships.

Lynch (1982) found that mothers of children spaced less than two years apart experience the most stress. The toddler's competition for her attention is difficult for her to handle. She has less time for herself and is constantly fatigued. Mothers with new babies frequently expect their toddlers to regress in toilet training or eating habits, but they are unprepared for the behavior changes—the "different" way their children act (Lynch, 1982). Field and Reite (1984) found decreased activity, decreased sleep, and increased negative emotions in preschoolers whose mothers had just returned from the hospital with another child. Children should be helped to understand such feelings cannot be expressed in acts of physical aggression toward baby, mother, or self. Parents should spend as much time as possible with the toddler when the baby is asleep and reassure him or her of their love. Sibling rivalry can be further reduced by allowing the older child to help the adult nurture and protect the baby (holding, feeding, diapering, entertaining, and so on). (See Figure 5-27.)

Studies of large groups of firstborn, middle-born, and youngest children have revealed certain personality traits that are apt to characterize people of different **birth orders**. Although a significant number of persons of a particular birth order may share similarities, any one person can be quite different from the group and still be normal. Firstborn children have been shown to begin talking sooner. They model and identify more with their parents. By age thirty-three months, firstborns are more sociable with unfamiliar peers (Snow, Jacklin, and Maccoby, 1981). In school, they are superior to later-born children in both reading ability and achievement motivation (Glass, Neulinger,

Figure 5-27
Sibling rivalry is generally more intense when babies are born close together than when they are spaced a few years apart. The nurture of one sibling by another should be encouraged and praised.

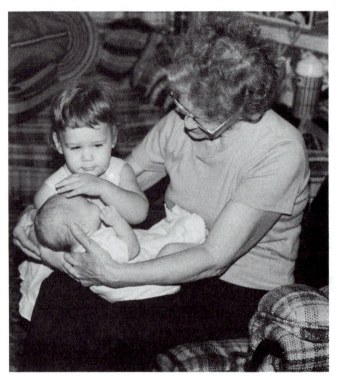

and Brim, 1974). They score higher on National Merit Scholarship exams (Breland, 1974), and more than a fair share of them achieve high-status employment for their adult years (doctors, lawyers, professors, engineers, architects, business executives).

Parents tend to spend more time with firstborn children. They pressure firstborns to perform more. They have higher expectations for them and give them more positive ratings (Baskett, 1985). If a firstborn female is followed by a second-born male, however, and a family places a great deal of emphasis on male achievement, the firstborn daughter may not experience as much parental involvement or support (Thomas, 1983). Sutton-Smith and Rosenberg (1970) described second- and middle-born children as more easygoing and cheerful or, occasionally, as neglected. The neglect of middle-born children has occasionally been documented (Kidwell, 1982) but is probably not as pervasive as folk wisdom suggests. Many middle-born children experience a strong sense of being loved, wanted, and attended. Kalliopuska (1984) found middle-born children more prone to empathize with the feelings of others than firstborns.

Youngest children have been variously described as more immature and self-conscious or as more popular and outgoing. When families are very large, children usually have fewer pressures on them in the cognitive and social realms. Zajonc (1976) suggested this as a reason for the lower intelligence of later-born children in large families. However, not all later-born children in large families have lower IQs than their older siblings. Families with six or more children usually insist on a handful of very firm rules but thereafter give the children a lot of freedom. In some families this freedom may have a positive effect on intelligence.

Peer Relationships

Parents, siblings, and others living under the same roof are usually the most significant forces in the ecology of early childhood. However, peers with whom the preschooler interacts regularly are also important microsystem influences (see Figure 5-28).

Play is the major means by which young children come to know and understand the world around them. It is also very important to their emotional development and mental health (Mueller, 1989). The play between parent and child is developmentally more sophisticated than the play between peers. The adult usually leads the play, motivates the child to continue, and uses more language to describe what is happening. In contrast, play between peers has more equality. It is relatively superficial and is based more on activity.

Will preschoolers learn more playing with an adult than playing with a peer? They will not necessarily learn more or less, but they will learn different things. Peer play is very important for learning exploration and mastery of physical objects with an "equal" (Mueller, 1989). In peer play, children learn to cooperate, take turns, and manage their tension without an adult authority giving directions.

Peer relations grow and change across early development (Hay, 1985). Two-year-olds usually engage in solitary play or onlooker play with their peers (see Table 5-9). They only join into parallel play with a peer when it suits what is momentarily of interest to them in terms of their own activity or object use (Shugar and Bokus, 1986). Confrontations over desired toys are common.

With increasing age, the child moves to more associative play in which some shared activity and communication occurs. Finally, around school age, children move to more cooperative play in which there are more rules and goals to their activities. Chance (1979) identified four kinds of play of young children: symbolic play, manipulative play, physical play, and games.

Symbolic play is one of the chief synthesizers of ego, emotions, cognition, and socialization in early childhood. Imitations are tried, not verbatim, but with the stress where the child desires. Children use symbolic play to adjust to reality and to get reality

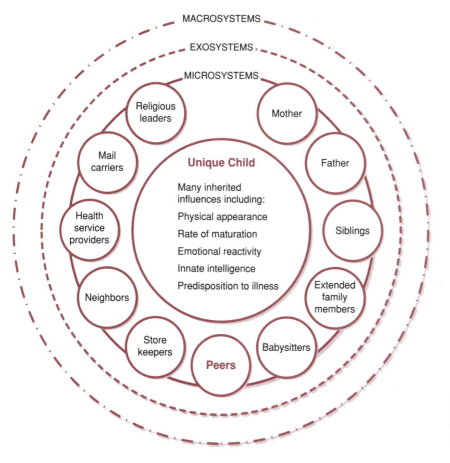

Figure 5-28
Peer play is a significant force in the psychosocial development of a young child.

Table 5-9 Changes in the Social Quality of Play with Age.

Type of Play	Characteristics
Onlooking	Observation of play of others with no actual participation beyond some communication (such as question/answer).
Solitary	Play of a self-contained nature; examining and manipulating toys, other objects, or people without reference to the other(s) in the vicinity.
Parallel	Play with one or more other companions but without any real exchange of interests or materials beyond a possible tug-of-war for some coveted object.
Associative	Play with one or more other companions loosely, doing the same thing with the same or similar materials, but separately, without a great deal of social interchange.
Cooperative	Play of relatively long duration and complexity with various roles and goals and sometimes leader(s) and follower(s).

to conform to their own personal needs and desires. They can act out conflicts. They can acquire power. They can project their shortcomings or limitations onto others. They can make their wishes come true. Play serves a multitude of functions. When you observe children in play, you will learn a great deal about what they are trying to comprehend. Consider for example, the following vignette:

> Sharon was left with a babysitter when her parents went to a concert. The next day she and a friend announced that they were going to a concert. They dressed up in her parents' clothes, then sat by Sharon's bed and began coloring. Her father, observing this, asked "Do you know what a concert is?" He then explained that it is a musical performance. Sharon led her friend into "Ring Around the Rosey" play, both singing and laughing gleefully, still in her bedroom.

Sharon was not only trying to understand about a concert, she was enacting a situation that had frustrated her. She had been quite unhappy about her parents' departure the previous evening. In her play she remained at home and gave herself a concert.

Manipulative play relies on sensory and motor exploration as well as on the cognitive task of trying to understand (such as how a broken toy came apart, how to assemble Lego blocks or puzzles). It may also be called skill-mastery play. Physical play emphasizes motor actions, such as running, jumping, hopping, swinging, and riding on vehicles. It enhances a child's perception of his or her body in space. It is more apt to be done with other children, but it can also be a form of solitary play. Game playing is social play. The child needs to interact with another child according to some rules or conventions. While games are more common in older children, any interaction between a young child and a peer that has a routine, turns-taking, sharing quality can be described as a game.

Many young children, especially those with few peers, develop imaginary playmates. In a review of the literature on these companions, Schilling (1985) reported that they typically make their appearance by age two-and-a-half to three years. While common in both sexes, they are slightly more frequent in girls. The evidence suggests that children who have imaginary companions may be more creative, more intelligent, and more verbal than other children. The imaginary friend can suggest activities to the child, be blamed when mistakes and accidents occur, compliment the child in the absence of adult approval, and participate (silently) in a great deal of symbolic play. Imaginary friends are part of the normal development of imaginative play behavior in some young children and should be treated with tolerant sensitivity and respect by adults. Increasing peer interactions will not necessarily make the imaginary playmate disappear. It is unusual for imaginary friends to persist beyond age five to six.

Television

Television is considered an important extrafamilial agent of socialization in North American culture today. Its role is similar to that of comic books, radio, and movies in past generations. It is not uncommon to see preschoolers incorporate characters from television into their fantasy play.

Professionals are concerned about the amount of television young children watch and also about the content of TV programming. The amount of time preschoolers spend watching television varies from child to child and from day to day but averages about three or four hours a day and more on cartoon day (Saturday). Children of working mothers who are cared for out of their own homes watch the educational *Sesame Street* less than children raised in their own homes (Pinon, Huston, and Wright, 1989).

The content of TV programming often teaches gender-role stereotypes and ethnic stereotypes. Males outnumber females in television roles. They are usually powerful, aggressive, assertive, and intelligent. In contrast, women more often play romantic or domestic roles. Commercials for boys' toys tend to be fast paced and full of action. Those for girls' toys are slow paced and accompanied by pastel colors and soft music. Ethnic minorities are under-represented on television.

The content of commercials directed at young children is of special concern to child development professionals. Evidence suggests that children younger than six do not understand that the purpose of advertising is to sell a product (Murray, 1989). They do not have the necessary cognitive abilities to defend themselves against skillful persuasion. In many cases, they cannot tell when programming ceases and advertising begins (see Figure 5-29). This is especially true when program characters promote products. Many of the newer "children's programs" are in fact little more than program-length commercials. They are released concurrently with a line of toys associated with the program's theme or characters to promote the toys. In some cases arrangements are made with broadcasters to share in the profits generated from the sales of toys

Figure 5-29
Television advertising makes children want products they do not need and that their families may not be able to afford.

when these program-length commercials are purchased by TV stations (Kunkel and Watkins, 1985).

Many of the cartoons made for children are violent, with an unrealistic view of death and resurrection. Gerbner (1972) took the time to count violent episodes in children's cartoons and got an average rate of 25.1 per hour. In a classic study in 1963, Bandura and his associates demonstrated that preschool children remember and subsequently perform violent acts that they see on television. It is difficult to predict how any given child will react to any given episode of TV violence. It has a large effect on a small percentage of youngsters and a small but significant effect on a large percentage of youngsters (Liebert, Sprafkin, and Davidson, 1982).

Television can have a positive influence on young children. Programs such as *Sesame Street* and *Mister Rogers' Neighborhood* increase skills in selective attention and task perseverance (Anderson, 1989). They teach tolerance, problem solving, health, and safety precautions. Children are cognitively active during television viewing. The type of learning that takes place is similar to that which occurs when children are read books. Optimal viewing time for good learning, however, is probably up to one hour, three times per day. Educational achievement declines with more than three viewing hours per day (Anderson, 1989).

Most early childhood educators and child psychologists feel that preschool television viewing should be guided by parents during the formative, preschool years (Huston et al., 1990). It should be limited to those programs designed to capture and hold the attention of the very young. It should not be used as a baby-sitter. Nor should children be placed in front of programs such as *Sesame Street* with the command "learn," especially if they are actively involved in some other creative activity. Viewing time should reflect their genuine interest time, no more.

Summary

Physically, children stretch out in early childhood. Arms, legs, and trunks grow, helping to alter the top-heavy, short-legged appearance of babyhood. Motor skills emerge and improve (running, stair climbing, tricycle riding, ball throwing).

Health maintenance requires adequate nutrition, sleep, exercise, affection, and protection from accidents. Regular check-ups, immunizations, and prompt diagnosis and treatment of infections can control many serious diseases and childhood disabilities.

Memory processes are not well understood. Some information disappears after sensory processing or short-term processing. Other information appears to go into a long-term memory store but is difficult to retrieve. Memories of little children are often based more on perceptions of reality rather than on reality itself.

Piaget described the cognitive developmental stage of early childhood as *preoperational*. Children explore, manipulate, and remember. The use of mental images makes possible rapid acquisition of language. Children do not yet classify and systematically define their thoughts. They view their worlds from an egocentric perspective. Quite often they are very persistent and self-centered about felt needs or desires.

Language development reflects the egocentricity of early childhood. *I, me,* and *mine* are often heard. *Why?* is also common. Word usage multiplies rapidly, going from the few holophrases of beginning speech to more than a thousand words in a year. The age of beginning speech varies greatly from child to child, some starting shortly after their first birthday, others waiting until after their third. One-to-one verbal stimulation fosters language usage.

Erikson described the nuclear conflicts of early childhood as first achieving a sense of autonomy versus shame and doubt and then thrusting out into the wider world with initiative rather than guilt. Learning self-help skills (feeding, dressing, toileting) and having freedom to explore and communicate are basic to autonomy and initiative.

Discipline is essential in early childhood. Three kinds may be used alone or in combination: power assertion, love withdrawal, and induction. Induction has the greatest potential for directing conscience formation. Both high demandingness and high responsiveness in parents are associated with more evidence of conscience and higher self-esteem in children.

Toilet training should begin in a relaxed fashion when the child is physically and psychologically ready. Toileting often leads to questions about sex differences. Gender identification is well established by the end of early childhood.

Siblings, peers, and television all have a profound impact on a young child's psychosocial development. Each provides a learning medium as well as helps synthesize ego, emotions, and socialization practices.

Key Concepts

motor norms	leukemia	animism	authoritarian parents
secular growth trend	sensory memory	artificialism	indulgent parents
growth trajectory	short-term memory	syncretism	indifferent parents
catch-up growth	long-term memory	transductive reasoning	Dreikurs's stages
pica	limbic system	autonomy versus shame	child abuse
hyperopia	eidetic memory	and doubt	child neglect
myopia	preoperational thought	initiative versus guilt	toilet training
astigmatism	centration	power-assertive discipline	sex typing
strabismus	egocentrism	love-withdrawal discipline	sibling rivalry
otitis media	realism	inductive discipline	birth order effects
strep infection		authoritative parents	

Questions for Review

1. Why do you think the age of two is commonly called the "terrible twos"?
2. How does the preoperational stage described by Piaget differ from the sensorimotor stage that occurs in infancy?
3. Do you support or oppose the practice of leaving a young child in an alternate care setting 40 hours a week while the mother works outside the home? Why?
4. What gifts (toys, games, and so on) do you think would be good for a child in early childhood? In your answer consider the developmental needs of a child at this time in the life span.
5. Do you agree or disagree that the violence seen on television and in other parts of society is producing more violence in children? Discuss.

Further Readings

Damon, W. (ed.) (1989). *Child development today and tomorrow.* San Francisco: Jossey-Bass.

The editor asked forward-looking researchers to write chapters examining the changing field of child development. The 20 articles point out future directions as well as explore current hot topics.

Douglas, J. (1989). *Behavior problems in young children.* New York: Routledge.

A psychologist gives good advice on eating problems, toilet training, bedtime and sleep problems, and emotional problems in young children.

Lande, J. S., Scarr, S., and Gunzenhauser (eds.) (1989). *Caring for children: Challenge to America.* Hillsdale, NJ: Lawrence Erlbaum.

A valuable resource for working parents and child care providers. Several child developmental experts voice their opinions on how to look after children well.

Rosenfield, I. (1988). *The invention of memory: A new view of the brain.* New York: Basic Books.

This book is written for the layperson. It requires a minimum of specialized knowledge to understand its concepts about neuroanatomy and neurophysiology.

Shengold, L. (1989). *Soul murder: The effects of childhood abuse and deprivation.* New Haven: Yale University Press.

The author draws on clinical case materials to document the effects of neglect and abuse on children.

Late Childhood

6

The years from six to twelve are called *middle childhood* as well as *late childhood*. The latter rubric will be used here as an inclusive term, as "middle childhood" suggests that the early-adolescent age range comprises late childhood, which most adolescents would consider a misnomer.

The most vivid memories of childhood are usually those from the late childhood period covered in this chapter: best friends (the "at home" ones such as neighbors and siblings and the "at school" ones who probably changed frequently); school; lunch hours at school; teachers and classes; after-school activities; homework; chores; sports; clubs; summer vacations; secrets; places to hide.

During late childhood, peers become extremely important. For this reason some writers call it the "gang age." It is also called the "dirty age" for reasons of both language and laundry. Piaget called it "the age of reason." It is a time of considerable development physically, socially, emotionally, cognitively, and linguistically. The old adage that a child's personality is set by age seven has not been supported by research. Personality is a dynamic phenomenon, influenced throughout life by all kinds of environmental pressures. One should not become locked into the notion that the late childhood years are simply a latent passage of time in which a child grows bigger but otherwise emerges unchanged.

Sweet childish days, that were as long
As twenty days are now.
—*William Wordsworth*

My salad days,
When I was green in judgement.
—*William Shakespeare*

One could do worse than be
a swinger of birches.
—*Robert Frost*

Physical Development

The physical appearances of elementary school children vary considerably within each age group. Consider the differences of your own peers when you were in first through sixth grade, not only by sex and race but also by such factors as height, weight, and physical build.

Growth Progression

Between the ages of six and twelve, children's proportions become more adultlike. Arms and legs get longer, giving more gangliness, the abdomen flattens, and the shoulders, chest, and trunk broaden. The lordosis (spinal curvature) of early childhood disappears, and the back appears straighter. Although the size of the head changes very little, facial proportions are altered considerably. The forehead broadens, the nose grows larger, the lips get fuller, and the jaw juts out from the chin. All of this takes place at a gradual but steady pace (see Figure 6-1). Height increases by about 5 to 7

Just before Malcolm was born, the Ku Klux Klan came to his home to get his father. His father wasn't home, and his mother was very pregnant, so the KKK just broke all the windows and rode away. After Malcolm was delivered, the family moved from Omaha to Milwaukee to be safe.

When Malcolm was four, the Ku Klux Klan again came to his home to get his father. The KKK fired their guns into the house and set it on fire. Malcolm recounted his first vivid life's memory: "We were outside in the night in our underwear, crying and yelling our heads off. The white police and firemen came and stood around watching us as the house burned down to the ground."* The family moved from Milwaukee to East Lansing to be safe.

When Malcolm was six, the Ku Klux Klan bashed in his father's skull and laid him across streetcar tracks to be run over. After the funeral, the insurance company refused to pay off the life insurance policy. They claimed that Malcolm's father had committed suicide. Malcolm's father was a minister. He taught his parishioners that they could rise up and accomplish whatever they wanted. He was an "uppity nigger"* who preached a better life until 1931, when he was murdered for his beliefs.

Malcolm's late childhood years were fraught with difficulties. From age 6 through age 12, his mother struggled to keep him and his seven brothers and sisters alive through the Great Depression. His mother was a light-skinned black who could initially pass as white. She would get household servant positions for a few days, but she would be fired as soon as her employers realized she was black. The social services gave her some welfare assistance, but they constantly conducted inquisitions and threatened to stop payments for minor grievances. She became deeply depressed. When Malcolm was 12, she was taken to a mental hospital where she languished for the next 26 years.

Malcolm coped with abject poverty by stealing food. He was considered a young juvenile delinquent: impulsive, aggressive, unmanageable. He was taken to a foster home at age 12. He was moved to a detention center at age 13. By the end of adolescence, he had earned the labels hoodlum, thief, dope peddler, and pimp. He was sent to jail at age 20 for burglary.

A popular theory about juvenile delinquents is that they are neglected in childhood, with low demands and low responsiveness from adults. Did Malcolm fit this mold? He admitted that he made so much noise whenever his mother asked him to do something that she negated her demands. She was so devastated and depressed by her situation that it was hard for her to be responsive to Malcolm.

This story could end with prison, but it does not. Malcolm X used his jail term to become well-read and self-educated. When he was released from prison, he joined a Black Muslim temple. He became the group's best-known spokesman. Malcolm X taught people that they didn't need to accept their situations, that they could change them. He questioned the legitimacy of the people in power. For the next 13 years, he helped lead the American Black Revolution. He was felled by an assassin's bullet at age 40.

How did the tumultuous late childhood of Malcolm X shape his life? Could he have survived from his father's death at age 6 through his mother's incarceration at age 12 without stealing? What life events might have motivated his decision to struggle for his whole race?

*Malcolm X (1964). *The Autobiography of Malcolm X.* New York: Random House.

Figure 6-1
During the grade school years, facial features lose their babyish look and become more adult-like.

centimeters (2 to 3 inches) a year, and weight gains vary from 1½ to 2½ kilograms (3 to 6 pounds) a year.

Normal, healthy children engage in plenty of activities that enhance large-muscle (gross motor) development—walking, running, jumping, climbing, throwing, catching, skating, swimming, dancing, and riding bicycles, skate boards, or horses. They also may be required by their families to engage in physical activities like daily chores. Small-muscle (fine motor) movement—eye–hand coordination—and manual dexterity become more precise with each advancing year, especially when opportunities exist for the exercise of the small muscles: printing and cursive writing, model building, sewing, weaving, painting, coloring, clay modeling, stamp collecting, dressing dolls, playing musical instruments, taking photographs.

Body types (short–fat, tall–thin) tend to remain stable even as height and weight are added. Sheldon (1940) identified three basic physiques: *endomorphy, mesomorphy,* and *ectomorphy* (see Figure 6-2). Endomorphs are short and round, mesomorphs are

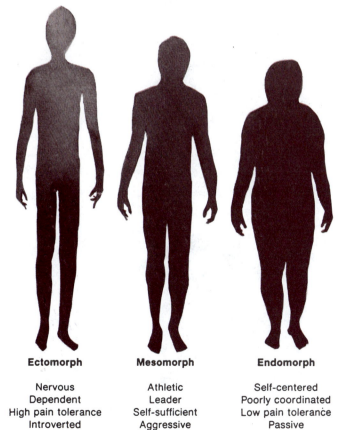

Ectomorph	Mesomorph	Endomorph
Nervous	Athletic	Self-centered
Dependent	Leader	Poorly coordinated
High pain tolerance	Self-sufficient	Low pain tolerance
Introverted	Aggressive	Passive
Restrained	Extraverted	Undisciplined

Figure 6-2
Studies correlating body build and temperament have had a profound influence on social stereotyping but remain controversial.

muscular with broad shoulders and narrow hips, and ectomorphs are long and lean. Sheldon assigned basic personality types to each body type. Research on body typology as it relates to behavior has waxed and waned over the last 40 years, with interest rekindled in the mid-1980s when a book by Wilson and Herrnstein (1985) suggested that a mesomorphic body build is associated with aggression and criminal activity. The assumption that body build determines personality remains highly criticized, however. There are too many exceptions to prove the rule (see Figure 6-2 and try to think of exceptions you know). A strong belief in a stereotyped personality to go with physical build may lead to a self-fulfilling prophecy effect. Current research leads us to suspect that genetic factors and hormone balances do make body build (especially bone structure,

BOX
6-1

Dental Caries.

A. Bacteria adhere to the teeth in the sticky coating called plaque. They convert the sugars in plaque to acids, which erode enamel.

B. The enamel is eroded unitl the acids reach the dentin. Dentin is destroyed more rapidly than enamel.

C. Eventually decay reaches the pulp and nerve; the tooth aches.

Teach children these tooth saving tips:
1. Don't eat sweets between meals
2. Avoid sticky or slow-dissolving sweets.
3. Brush after every meal.
4. Rinse your mouth with water if you can't brush.
5. Visit your dentist every six months.

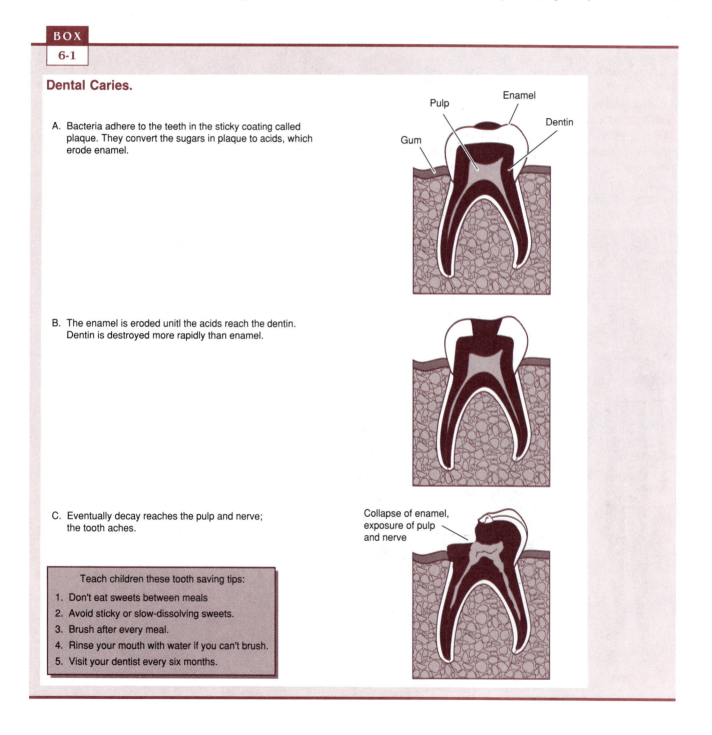

less so weight) relatively stable from childhood to adulthood. The pace of maturation may affect one's self-concept. Concentrations of hormones in the blood may also affect behavior, but there is not an invariant relationship between physique and personality.

Around the age of six or seven every child experiences the seemingly toothless grin caused by the shedding of deciduous teeth in preparation for the permanent ones. Throughout late childhood deciduous teeth are lost and permanent teeth are gained, until by age twelve most youngsters have twenty-eight out of the eventual thirty-two permanent teeth. (Lacking are the wisdom teeth that may or may not manage to arrive during adolescence.)

Numbers of children learn to cope (and sometimes even feel part of the gang) with their orthodontist visits and braces. Straightening of teeth not only gives a more pleasing appearance but also allows for a better bite and a more satisfactory development of the lower part of the face.

The leading noninfectious health problem in the Western world is **dental caries.** In spite of fluoridated water (which retards tooth decay), approximately 98% of North American children have some cavities and fillings in their teeth. They know the dentist as someone who drills and fills, rather than someone who examines and rewards. Biannual dental check-ups, fluoridated water, healthy diets, and frequent brushing can prevent caries (see Box 6-1).

Nutrition

Good nutrition during childhood does not necessarily mean eating the same foods as adults. For example, adult breakfasts are often toast and coffee or just coffee. What should a growing chilid have for breakfast? Television advertisements hawk packaged cereal, most of which are over 50% sugar. Many of these are eaten dry in the rush to get off to school. Other "fast" breakfasts taken in similar fashion are toast and jam or breakfast pastries. These meals of highly refined carbohydrates and sugar are digested rapidly and leave the child hungry again. Some children skip breakfast altogether. This is especially hard on the mind and the body because of the absence of any nutrients for an eight- to sixteen-hour period. Pollitt, Leibel, and Greenfield (1981) found that skipping breakfast significantly decreased the accuracy of responding to a number of problem-solving tasks in nine- to eleven-year-old children.

In a normal day a growing child should have three servings of milk or milk products, three servings of protein foods, three or four slices of bread or its equivalent (rice, pasta, cereal), one fruit or fruit juice, and at least two vegetables.

Vegetarian diets can provide adequate nutrition if they are supplemented with milk and cheese, or also with eggs. Pure vegetarian (vegan) diets are not recommended for children because they do not supply the complete proteins necessary for growth. Some protein food should be part of every meal (see Figure 6-3). Fat is usually found in protein foods in sufficient quantity to make it unnecessary to add separately. Sugar is not necessary to good nutrition.

Children do not usually need vitamin supplements. Some health care providers recommend iron supplementation if foods preferred are iron poor. Some school-aged children become vitamin conscious and buy "fad" nutrients in health food stores. They should be warned that the fat-soluble vitamins (A, D, E, and K) can build up to toxic levels when ingested in excess amounts.

Obesity affects from 5 to 10 percent of school aged children (O'Brien and Hambidge, 1984). Many obese children are poorly nourished because they eat predominantly high-carbohydrate foods. Obesity may also have a genetic basis or may result from learned family behaviors (as when all family members overeat) or from some body malfunction (such as underactive thyroid). Obesity can handicap a child physically and socially. Peers are often extremely cruel in their ridicule of an overweight child.

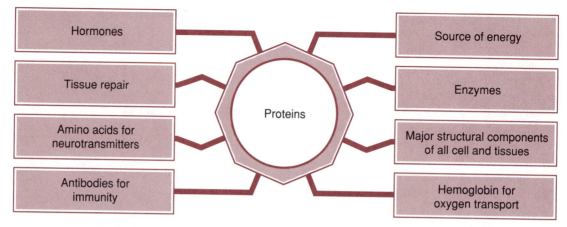

Hormones

Tissue repair

Amino acids for neurotransmitters

Antibodies for immunity

Proteins

Source of energy

Enzymes

Major structural components of all cell and tissues

Hemoglobin for oxygen transport

Figure 6-3
Proteins should be included in the meals of school children. They serve many vital functions.

A malnourished child may have growth retardation, fatigue, poor posture, and a lowered resistance to infection. In some cases, food deprivation may be a form of child neglect. More commonly, the malnourished child is fed, but for reasons of economics, ignorance, or convenience foods, the child is given insufficient protein, vitamins, and iron. High "empty-calorie" diets increase the need for thiamine, necessary for the metabolism of sugars. Lack of appetite may be due to filling up on empty-calorie snacks (soda, candy, cookies), emotional tensions, or a desire to be thin.

Medical professionals may examine children carefully if they do not grow taller in a year's time, but they do not get as concerned about failure to gain weight. This is because weight is influenced by exercise and environment as well as by diet. A well-fed, well-nourished child may get taller but not add kilograms (pounds) over a one-year time span and still be well within a normal range.

Health Maintenance

A school-age child's health should be safeguarded with an annual routine physical examination. There are conditions that may go unrecognized by parents (for example, heart murmurs, high blood pressure, anemia, hearing losses, developmental delays). Adequate sleep for school-age children decreases with age. A six-year-old should probably get from ten to twelve hours of sleep A twelve-year-old should probably get from eight to ten hours of sleep. Adequate sleep varies from child to child. If children go to sleep easily, sleep soundly, and wake refreshed, they are getting enough rest. Sleep disturbances such as restlessness, periods of wakefulness, and nightmares may be symptoms of emotional upset rather than excess sleep.

Roughly 25% of children need to wear glasses by late childhood. Most children are normally hyperopic (farsighted) until after about age six when their eyes begin to reach more adultlike proportions. Some children, however, are myopic (nearsighted), a problem that is not outgrown. Others have problems with astigmatism (faulty curvature of the cornea or lens) or strabismus (crossed eyes, walleyes; refer back to Chapter 5). Glasses can correct hyperopia, myopia, astigmatism, and strabismus and should be worn to prevent eyestrain or progressive loss of visual function (see Figure 6-4).

The more common illnesses of late childhood include the common cold, otitis media, tonsillitis, gastroenteritis, conjunctivitis, strep throat, impetigo, chickenpox, urinary tract infections, and boils (Schmitt, 1984). These diseases were discussed in more detail in Chapter 5. Infections account for approximately 70% of school absences.

Figure 6-4
Children should wear their prescribed glasses in school. Failure to do so can result in distorted images that interfere with learning.

Infections are less threatening than they were a generation ago because of the availability of antibiotics and immunizations, but untreated infections still may lead to serious complications (such as strep infection leading to rheumatic heart disease and glomerulonephritis). Accidents are the main cause of death and physical handicaps during childhood. School-age children most commonly get hurt in motor vehicle accidents. They also swallow or come in contact with poisons, burn themselves, have serious falls, have water-related accidents, get frostbite, or choke.

Child victims of major accidents should be considered seriously injured until their condition is proved stable. The first adult to arrive at the accident scene must be sure that the child can breathe. This may involve clearing debris (chewing gum, food) from the airway and positioning the head to the side. If there is any question of head or spinal injuries, the child should not be moved until trained medical personnel arrive. If the child is unconscious and pulses are not palpable, cardiopulmonary resuscitation (CPR) may be required. While it would be ideal for all adults to be trained in CPR, no adult who lacks sufficient knowledge of the procedure should attempt it.

If a child is bleeding, direct pressure should be applied over the hemorrhage site. If the child has been burned, a clean cool cloth should be placed on the burned area until help arrives. First aid for poisoning is presented in Chapter 5. Frostbite requires a prolonged (20-minute) rewarming of the affected area(s) with warm (38–40°C/100°F) water. If a child is choking, any older child or adult in the vicinity should immediately apply the **Heimlich manuever:**

1. The rescuer stands behind the victim and wraps his or her arms around the victim's waist.
2. The rescuer makes a fist with one hand and places the thumb side of the fist against the victim's abdomen, slightly above the navel and below the rib cage.
3. The rescuer grasps the fist with his or her other hand and presses it into the victim's abdomen with a quick upward thrust.
4. This thrust is repeated several times if necessary.

Figure 6-5
Children should obey safety precautions. Most of the 19 million annual accidental injuries to school-age children are preventable.

Although adults cannot always watch school-age children, they can repeatedly warn them against accident hazards, help them find safe play areas (see Figure 6-5), and teach safety consciousness.

Common Health Problems

Chronic illnesses such as hay fever, asthma and diabetes affect between 5 and 10% of the late-childhood population (Haggerty, 1984). Children with chronic illnesses may have to miss school or have special school arrangements made for them. When possible, it is preferable to keep the child within a normal school setting for the benefits to social and emotional development.

Some form of allergic reaction is normal in everyone who comes in contact with certain antigens (such as viruses or bee stings) for which they have no antibodies (see Chapter 3, p. 80). Some forms of antigens (also called *allergens*) cause reactivity only in certain members of the population (See Figure 6-6). **Hay fever** (inflammation of the nasal mucous membrane) occurs as a result of exposure to specific wind-borne pollens (Pearlman, 1984). Symptoms include itching, sneezing, eye tearing, swollen nasal passages, nasal speech, difficulty eating, and difficulty sleeping. In addition, children may develop headaches, sore throats, laryngitis, and otitis media as an extension of the allergic reaction. The acute symptoms can be treated with antihistamines, decongestants, and short-term use of steroid drugs.

Figure 6-6
Allergies are normal. Some forms of allergic reactions occur only in certain children and are triggered only by certain allergens.

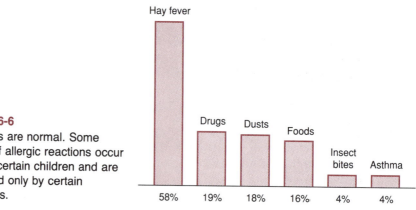

If the allergens can be identified, children may be given a series of injections of extremely small amounts of the substances to make them hyposensitive to those allergens in the future. Some physicians and parents may try environmental control instead, protecting the child from exposure to whatever substances incite the allergic reaction. In many cases, this may involve a move to another area of the country where the offending seasonal pollen does not exist. Children prone to hay fever may, however, develop new allergies to substances that exist in that area of the country after a few years.

Asthma is a reaction of the bronchial tubes to allergens (see Figure 6-7). Dust,

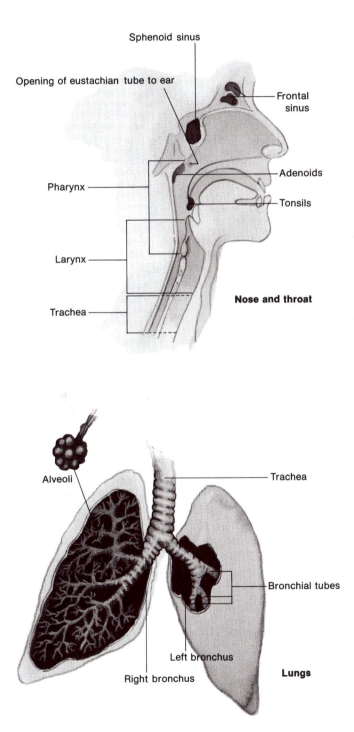

Sphenoid sinus

Opening of eustachian tube to ear

Frontal sinus

Adenoids

Pharynx

Tonsils

Larynx

Trachea

Nose and throat

Alveoli

Trachea

Bronchial tubes

Left bronchus

Right bronchus

Lungs

Figure 6-7

Hay fever usually causes an inflammation of the nasal passages and upper respiratory tract. Asthma typically involves the bronchial tubes and the lungs (see also Plate 13 in center of textbook).

plants, molds, insects, feathers, furs, pollens, foods, cooking odors, medicines, chemicals, smoke, paint fumes, changes in temperature or barometric pressure, overexercise, colds, or psychologic factors may trigger asthma (Pearlman, 1984). A child does not have to be allergic to have asthma, and even when the child does have a hypersensitivity to certain allergens, exposure to the allergens is seldom the only precipitating factor in an asthma attack.

An asthma attack involves bronchial wheezing that may become so serious that one wonders whether the child will be able to catch his or her next breath. Persons witnessing such attacks are often frightened. The asthmatic child becomes flushed and his or her skin becomes moist. Emergency care may involve aerosolized drug administration and transportation to a hospital for further supportive care. The child's fear, together with onlookers' fears, only makes the attack worse. It is more helpful if persons attending an asthmatic child remain calm and keep onlookers away. Parents can help their children most by understanding the underlying causes of attacks, reassuring the child of his or her continued worth and loved position in the family, setting definite limits on the child's behavior, and remaining calm and reassuring during and after the attacks. Meijer (1981) found that asthmatic children typically become very dependent on their mothers. The children need to be helped to assume more and more responsibility for their own care. Parents need to be helped to allow the child and others outside the family (such as school personnel) to assume some of the disease management as well. Many children outgrow or have a lessening in severity of their asthma after adolescence.

Diabetes mellitus, sometimes referred to as sugar diabetes, may begin in childhood. In the juvenile form of **diabetes,** with rare exceptions, insulin-producing cells in the pancreas are destroyed. For this reason, it is also called insulin-dependent diabetes, since insulin must be given by injection once or twice a day (Silver, Gotlin, and Klingensmith, 1984).

Symptoms of insulin deficiency include increased thirst, abdominal or leg cramps, loss of weight, frequent urination and emotional disturbances. Treatment consists of giving the child insulin (by injection) and regulating the child's diet and activity. A child may go into a hypoglycemic state (state of low blood sugar, also referred to as insulin shock) when he or she fails to consume enough carbohydrates, exercises too much, or takes too much insulin. A hypoglycemic state may first be noted by behavior changes such as inattention, confusion, sleepiness, or irritability. If the child does not ingest some form of sugar, loss of consciousness or convulsion may occur. For this reason diabetic children usually carry candy with them or ask for sweet food or drink whenever they experience any of the symptoms of hypoglycemia (see Figure 6-8).

Having diabetes may make children frustrated. They must always remember their medicine, watch their diet and their exercise, and be concerned about infections. They must also learn how to give themselves insulin injections safely. Their disease is not curable, only controllable with constant care.

Hagen, Anderson, and Barclay (1985) found that diabetic children have more problems than other children in a variety of areas beyond those of disease complications. While diabetic children have normal intelligence, they often underachieve and have social adjustment problems in school. They are at an increased risk for special education class placement and for repeating a grade in their early school years. Parents have a responsibility to monitor their entrance to school and their adaptation to the classroom environment. Each year, the parents must educate the child's teachers and other school staff (secretaries, administrators, food service personnel, coaches) about their diabetic child's special concerns and needs. Diabetic children should be treated as normally as possible and should be encouraged to perform up to their capabilities, without jeopardizing their medical disease management.

Seizures (loss of consciousness accompanied by convulsive muscle movements) may be due to low blood sugar, electric shock, high temperatures, brain infections, or

Figure 6-8
Diabetic children need to have a sweet drink or candy when they experience symptoms of hypoglycemia.

Table 6-1   Factors That May Be Associated with Bedwetting in Late Childhood.

Genetic: tends to run in families

Delayed physical maturation

Stresses of early childhood may have interfered with acquisition of control

Functional disorder of bladder (associated with frequent urination during the day as well)

Inadequate toilet training (neglected or excessively punitive)

Emotional or behavioral difficulties

Current environmental stress

Physical abnormality of urinary tract (rare)

SOURCE: Adapted from M. Rutter, *Helping Troubled Children* (New York: Plenum, 1975).

tumors. Such seizures are called symptomatic seizures. In **epilepsy** the underlying disorder in the brain causing seizures is not known.

In grand mal epilepsy the attack most often begins with a warning called an aura. The aura may take a variety of forms: the hallucination of a smell, taste, vision, or sound, an abnormal feeling in some part of the body. Immediately after that, consciousness is lost. The child falls to the ground and may suffer injuries in so doing. There then appears rigidity of the muscles, followed by sharp, short, interrupted jerking movements. When the convulsions stop, the child may remain unconscious for a few seconds or for a long period of time. He or she is generally sleepy and may have headaches for a few hours following each seizure.

In petit mal seizures children suddenly lapse into blank stares. They are unaware of their surroundings and may blink or smack their lips. The spell may only last ten to fifteen seconds. Children do not fall, have convulsive movements, or feel sleepy during or after petit mal seizures.

Much of the fear of epilepsy is rooted in misguided social attitudes (O'Shea, 1988). Once epilepsy has been diagnosed, the child can usually be kept symptom-free with daily medication. As with diabetic children, parents of epileptic children must educate the child's teachers and other relevant school personnel each year about the medical management and special concerns of their epileptic child. While seizures probably will not occur in a child controlled with medications, school staff should know how to recognize them and what to do in the event that one should take place in school.

By late childhood normal children should have day and night bladder and bowel control. Lack of bladder control, which most commonly occurs at night, is called **enuresis.** One in five children wets the bed occasionally at age seven, and one in fourteen still does so at age ten. Some of the possible reasons for this delayed control are given in Table 6-1. The treatment of enuresis depends on the cause of the problem. Medicines, behavior modification procedures, and family counseling have all been beneficial to some children.

Lack of bowel control, called **encopresis,** is a rarer problem in late childhood. Children who still soil their pants in the school years are usually suspected of having some emotional disturbance. Smearing the feces frequently accompanies the "accident." Some form of psychotherapy is usually necessary before encopresis is stopped.

Many boys (less commonly girls) develop some minor **motor tics** between the ages of six and twelve. These tics are involuntary, repetitive, nonpurposeful movements of a part of the body, such as eye blinks, facial twitches, tongue clicks, or jerking movements of the shoulders, arms, or legs. They occur at irregular intervals, increasing when the child is tense, decreasing during nonanxious concentration, and disappearing during sleep. These stereotyped motor tics may last from two weeks to usually not more than one year (Shapiro and Shapiro, 1980). No treatment is necessary unless the motor movement becomes severe and does not fluctuate and wane. Adults are advised not to criticize the child, call attention to the tic, or punish him or her for not stopping the behavior. Tics disappear most readily when the child's anxieties decrease and his or her self-confidence improves.

Cognitive and Language Development

Cognitive and language development move from the realm of parental concerns to the sphere of school interests during the years from six to twelve. An assortment of teachers help children learn increasingly complex cognitive skills and try to stimulate their drives for mastery and achievement. School becomes the center of children's extrafamilial lives, occupying about one-half of their waking hours Monday through Friday nine months of each year. Family members, leaders of groups (church, sports, music, art, dance, hobbies, scouts) and neighbors also become active teachers of children in late childhood.

The Learning Process

Children use many means of information processing. Some facts are stored only briefly (sensory memory, short-term memory), whereas others are retained over a longer period of time (long-term memory). (See Chapter 5, p. 156.) The hippocampi, structures that are part of the limbic system of the brain, seem to play a vital role in pushing some information into a retention process rather than allowing it to dissipate. The major function of the limbic system is the regulation of emotions. It does not seem merely coincidental that new information that arouses a personal emotional reaction is more apt to be remembered than information that is emotionally neutral.

School-age children learn new information best from personal experience, especially when they are aroused to attention and have some definite verbal or physical examples with which to encode and mediate their perceptions.

An awareness of memory processes by themselves is called **metamemory** (Flavell, 1970). With increasing age children develop strategies for remembering subject matter that they deem important. They learn to categorize incoming information in various ways. **Encoding** may be done with a word, with pictorial images, or with concepts. Encoding refers to the use of symbols or a code to represent something else. The

Figure 6-9
Reading contributes to competency in all cognitive skills: attending, encoding, mediating, remembering.

more experience children have in finding ways to remember subjects, the more adept they become at fixing memories.

When children can think about, talk about, and decide when to use different memory processes, we say they have **metacognition.** This is the knowledge of how to apply memory strategies in order to retain information or master new skills. Both meta-memory and metacognitive processes develop slowly over the course of late childhood.

Rehearsal involves repeating information in order to get it from a short-term to a long-term store. In general, trying to organize information using some encoding device is more expeditious than simple rehearsal. An elaborative rehearsal involves thinking about the new information and trying to relate it to existing knowledge.

The ability to store various objects and events in the memory is greatly enhanced by the comprehension and use of a large vocabulary. If children were asked to draw $\phi \, \psi \, \Omega$ from memory, they would have difficulty unless they had previously learned the Greek alphabet. If children know the Greek alphabet, they can use the names *phi, psi, omega* to mediate the image of the Greek symbols they see.

Mediation refers to a middle step between perceiving and remembering that aids memory. Verbal mediators, in the case of the Greek letters, would help children remember and respond with a correct drawing. This is much simpler than trying to remember the descriptions "circle with a vertical line through it, vertical line with a half circle open on top attached at midpoint," and so on. Mediation involves using skills already acquired to help develop new skills or acquire greater dexterity at old skills. Mediators are frequently verbal (that is, words we tell ourselves between taking in new information and responding to it). Reading increases school-age children's use of words as mediators (see Figure 6-9). Sometimes nonverbal mediators like pictures are used. The ability of deaf children to respond to new information quickly and accurately illustrates the use of some nonverbal mediators.

Piaget's Concrete Operations Stage

Piaget postulated that the period of **concrete operations** begins somewhere between ages six and eight, depending on each particular child and his or her maturation, physical experiences, and social interactions. Piaget did not equate early acquisition of concrete operations with greater intelligence.

As discussed in Chapter 5, the preoperational child (approximately age two to seven) gradually acquires the ability to see a few relationships between things and to handle some simple classifications. Piaget felt such successes were more intuitive than reasoned. The period of concrete operations is differentiated from preoperations by the fact that children now learn to reason about what they see and do (the age of reason). They develop the ability to apply rules to the new things they see and hear. Such rules help them understand and classify new phenomena. Rules may constantly undergo revisions and expansions (see Figure 6-10).

Another demarcation separating preoperational from concrete-operational children is the ability to comprehend **numbering.** Piaget explained that children become more adept at handling number correspondence and ordering problems during the concrete operations period because they use rules. When preschoolers are shown a bouquet of flowers bunched together and an equal-sized bouquet spread out, they will choose the separated bouquet as larger because it looks larger. Even when they count the flowers and determine that the two bouquets have an equal number of blossoms, they will again be deceived about size when one bouquet is spread out. Concrete-operational children handle problems of judging more, less, and the same by using a numerical count whenever possible (see Figure 6-11).

Piaget (1965) viewed numbering as a synthesis of two other operations: ordering and classifying. Preoperational children order objects haphazardly. Concrete-operational children develop the ability to order objects from largest to smallest or vice versa. If new gradients are introduced, the concrete-operational children will insert them cor-

Figure 6-10
Concrete operators find games like chess challenging. They apply rules, comprehend ordering and classifications, reverse mental calculations, and conserve equivalency.

rectly into their series. Concrete operators ascertain what objects belong to the same class, what objects differ, and how. They do this concurrently with ordering and ultimately with numbering. When presented with a box containing ten chocolates, five jelly beans, and five marbles and asked "Which is most—chocolates, candies, or toys?" a preoperational child will probably say that there are more chocolates than candies. They will not see that the chocolates are also in the class of candies. Concrete-operational children would not have this difficulty.

One of the hallmarks of children's ability to order and classify is their appreciation of where they are in relation to the rest of the universe (for example, Ten Hills section, City of Baltimore, State of Maryland, eastern seaboard, mid-Atlantic states, United States of America, northern hemisphere, continent of North America, planet Earth, solar system, Milky Way galaxy, cosmos). Their fascination with collections of various kinds (such as cards, rocks, shells, bottle caps, or stamps) reflects this interest in classification. Classification tasks are a good measure of a child's cognitive development (Gelman and Markman, 1987). By categorizing articles (e.g., cards, stamps), events, people, and places, children extend their knowledge and increase their desire for new information to classify.

Figure 6-11
Which box has more flowers? Concrete operators will count the flowers before giving an answer.

Trisha wandered away from the flea market in the church basement. She went upstairs to play in her Sunday School room. As she opened the door, she saw a baby in a stroller. She reasoned that a mother must be near because babies cannot take care of themselves. When a group of adults walked down the hall, Trisha looked them over to pick out the mother. To her surprise, a man came over and wheeled the baby in the stroller out of the room. Trisha had to revise her thoughts to include the fact that adults other than mothers can take care of babies.

Children who perform concrete operations can reverse their thoughts (called **reversibility**) and mentally imagine things as they were before any actions were taken. The child who had expected to see a mother can think back to the moment the baby was discovered alone and realize that, although a mother was expected, what he or she actually knew was that some adult must be near.

The ability to consider reciprocal relations also develops during the concrete operations stage. **Reciprocity** refers to the corresponding or interchangeable action or relation that one person or thing has on another. Using the example of the baby in the room, the child knew that some adult must take care of the infant. Caregiving includes many reciprocal associations—baby fusses, adult produces bottle; baby continues to fuss, adult rocks baby; baby quiets, adult talks to baby; baby coos and smiles, adult smiles and talks more to baby.

Reciprocity also involves understanding that the distance from A to B is the same as the distance from B to A. Children in the preoperations stage cannot do this.

Sanjay, age 4, attended a lecture on cognition with his mother and volunteered to answer some questions for the professor. "Which is greater, the distance from the floor to the ceiling, or the distance from the ceiling to the floor?" Sanjay thought for about a minute before he said, "It is further from the floor to the ceiling." "Why?" His answer, though demonstrating the faulty thinking of preschoolers, was interesting. "To get to the ceiling, you need to climb a ladder. That takes a long time. To get to the floor, you can jump. That is fast. So it is shorter from the ceiling to the floor."

The ability to use and reverse mental operations makes possible an important concrete skill described by Piaget, that of **conservation.** Conservation involves the ability to understand that a quantity does not change simply because the form it takes varies. For example, an amount of water does not change when it is poured from a tall thin glass into a short fat glass. Likewise, an amount of clay does not change when it is rolled from a ball shape into a snake shape (see Figure 6-12). In order to conserve, children must be able to analyze a problem. They must pay attention to more than one characteristic. They must be able to perceive changes in width as well as changes in height. They must reverse the operation mentally and visualize what the properties were like before the change occurred.

Conservation of mass or quantity develops first. Conservation of weight, where

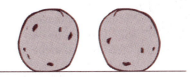
Two equal balls of clay

One is flattened to a snake shape
Which one has more clay now?

Figure 6-12
Which has more clay, the ball or the snake? Concrete operators will conserve equivalency from the original configuration.

children need to have a relative knowledge of the weights of different materials, develops more slowly. For example, if a child were given a scale and asked to measure two equal amounts of playdough and two much smaller but equivalent-weighted amounts of lead, the surprise would be that the lead is the same weight. By ages nine to twelve (depending on cognitive ability and experience), children will learn to attend to weight as well as size and know that two lumps of lead will weigh more than one lump of play dough. Conservation of volume seldom is achieved before age twelve. For this the child will have to realize that two equivalent amounts of material will both displace the same amount of water even though one is ball shaped and the other some other shape (such as flat as a pancake).

Time conceptions (days, months, years) become increasingly well differentiated during this stage, but ideas of historical time and far future may remain vague until ages ten to twelve. This author took her eight-year-old son to a Civil War battlefield and gave him a history lesson. When she was finished, he innocently asked her, "Mom, how old were you when that happened?"

Perception of self in space develops early. However, an understanding of geographical distances, such as those between states and countries, or of celestial distances, such as those between the earth, sun, moon, and stars, develops considerably more slowly.

Another notable achievement during the concrete operations period is an understanding of the differences between physical and psychological casuality. Young children with their animistic and artificialistic ideas (see p. 160) listen for or invent psychological causes for events. For example, many preschoolers who ask about the flame in a cigarette lighter would not be satisfied with an explanation of flints and lighter fluid. They would feel better answered if it were explained that the flame shot up so you could light your cigarette. As children grow older, they want to understand physical causes. Older children (even adults) may understand and be able to explain the physical

Table 6-2   Abilities Found in the Concrete Operations Stage.

Ability	Explanation
Classifying	Sorting a group of objects into related divisions (such as same size, same shape, same color)
Ordering	Placing a group of objects in succession (for examples, tallest to shortest, smallest to largest, by rank)
Numbering	Designating the place of objects in a series, taking into account classes and orders within classes
Conservation	The ability to understand that a material system remains unchanged while internal changes of any kind occur
of quantity	The amount of a material is neither increased nor diminished by changing its form
of weight	The heaviness of a material is neither increased nor diminished by changing its form
of volume	The space occupied by a material is neither increased nor diminished by changing the form of parts of the material
Reversibility	The ability to effect a change and then go back to the original condition by a physical or mental reversal of the change
Reciprocity	The ability to understand corresponding complementary, inverse relationships (for example, A to B is the equivalent of B to A)
Seeking physical causality	Looking for physical causes for events rather than believing in fantasy-based psychological causes
Applying rules	Use of established guides and regulations for actions and conduct rather than meeting egocentric desires
Spatial awareness	Knowing where one is in geographical distances
Time consciousness	Knowing where one is in relation to past, present, and future

cause for an occurrence (for example, a higher flame on a cigarette lighter resulting from more oxygen intake) yet speak of a psychological cause for the same occurrence as well ("Aha, the flame is shooting up to get you!").

The concrete-operational abilities do not all appear at once. They develop gradually as children have more and more experience manipulating objects and discovering rules about sizes, shapes, weights, classes, volume, time, space, and causality. All the operations become more refined and sophisticated with age and experience until children finally bridge the gap between concrete operations and the formal operations that characterize the reasoning of most literate adolescents and adults (see Table 6-2).

Language

Growth in vocabulary and use of language continue throughout adulthood. Children not only gain larger vocabularies during their late childhood years, they also correct grammatical and pronunciation errors and learn subtle meanings of old words. Puns and figures of speech finally become meaningful. Inflections allow children to alter the meaning of what they say. Language becomes fun! School-age children usually enjoy the play of words and invent or adopt word games that allow them to show off and improve their speech proficiency. Jokes based on double word meanings, slang, colloquialisms, curse words, feigned accents, secret languages, and ciphered messages abound between ages six and twelve. Children also try to use words that they do not fully understand (such as radar, communist, light year) and they often misinterpret expressions according to what they believe the words should mean.

> Duane and Craig, seven- and eight-year-old cousins, saw each other three times a
> year at family functions. Their first interaction was "Let me tell you the parrot joke."
> Each tried to be the first to tell it. Craig usually asserted his right to go first because
> he was older. When he was finished, Duane would tell the joke. Each telling was
> essentially the same with some slight variation added for ambiguity. Then both boys
> would laugh uproariously at the great good fun of the old joke.

McGhee (1979) links children's humor with cognitive development. When children begin to use concrete operations (e.g., reversibility, reciprocity, numbering), they appreciate ambiguity. They use their cognitive and language skills to tell jokes and listen for the punch lines. They especially appreciate riddles.

School-age children acquire new sophistication in their sentence constructions. Vocabulary has typically grown to about 14,000 words by age six (Carey, 1978). It may be five to ten times larger by adolescence. Sentences become longer and more complex as the child goes through school. The simple sentences (subject, verb, object) of early childhood are replaced by sentences containing prepositional phrases, relative clauses, and modification words (Menyuk, 1977). Children's understanding of certain syntactical forms (arrangements of words) in sentences also improves. Noam Chomsky (1972), who postulated the language acquisition device (LAD) in humans (see Chapter 4), believed there are two levels of language: surface and deep structures. For example, the sentences "Helen is easy to please" and "Helen is eager to please" have the same surface structure, but their deep structures, their underlying meanings, are very different. School-age children come to understand that Helen is the object of the first sentence (others try to please her), whereas she is the subject of the second and will try to please others. Younger children may have difficulty with the first sentence. They may be confused about what Helen is to do.

Some school-age children have problems with articulation, vocal quality, or the rhythm of their language. Common articulation problems are omissions of sounds (such as "at" for "hat"), substitutions ("dreth" for "dress"), distortions (such as /s/ in "sink" articulated like /z/), and additions ("go-a to the store-a"). Parents, teachers, and speech therapists can usually help the child correct the incorrect utterances as long as the cause of the disorder is not due to brain or nerve damage or oral-facial abnormalities (for example, cleft lip). Problems with vocal quality can be characterized as hypernasality (too much nasal emission during speech), hyponasality (too little nasal emission), or disorders of pitch (too high or too low), intensity (too loud or too soft), or flexibility (monotone). Children with such problems can usually be helped to find an acceptable voice in their repertoire and reinforce it until it is consistently used.

Some school children have problems with **stuttering** (the interruption of speech fluency through blocked, prolonged, or repeated words, syllables, or sounds) or cluttering (rapid, garbled, disorganized speech). Cluttering is often considered a form of stuttering. Stuttering is about four times more common in boys and usually begins before age eleven (Silver, 1984). Both organic and psychogenic factors are suspected causative factors. Gemelli (1982) stressed psychogenic factors such as ego functioning and parental patterns of behavior in cases of persistent stuttering. Many therapists feel that psychotherapy for both parents and child is a necessary adjunct to speech therapy for persistent stutterers.

The Concept of Intelligence

Pause for a moment from your steady reading to answer each of these questions in your own words: What is intelligence? What is common sense? What is street sense? What is rote memorization ability? What is speed reading? What is creativity? What is logic? Are these terms related? Which concepts are most applicable to you?

Many scholars have struggled to define the concept of intelligence in a manner that would appeal to others. The dilemma continues. Spearman (1927) proposed that intelligence consists of a "g" factor, for general abilities related to deduction and logical analysis, and an "s" factor, for specific abilities such as spatial reasoning and arithmetic skills. Thurstone (1938) proposed that intelligence could be defined by seven primary abilities: verbal comprehension, word fluency, number, space, memory, perceptual speed, and reasoning. Guilford (1967) proposed 120 factors of intelligence related to the dimensions of mental operations, contents, and products. Cattell (1971) proposed that intelligence consists of fluid intelligence (for innate capacities) and crystallized intelligence (for what one has learned).

Gardner (1983) posited the existence of seven separate "intelligences" that are exercised to carry out meaningful human fucntions (see Table 6-3). We do not perceive ourselves as having these different systems, however. We function as a unified self with a single consciousness or intelligence.

Sternberg (1988) described intelligence as mental self-management, a quality used every day at work, at play, and at rest, not just at school. He presented a triarchic theory of intelligence, looking at three manifestations:

1. intelligence and the individual's internal world (componential),
2. intelligence and the individual's external world (contextual), and
3. intelligence and the individual's experiences (experiential).

Sternberg proposed that we apply our intelligence to our internal world, external context, and personal experiences with three kinds of processes: meta-components, performance components, and knowledge-acquisition components (see Figure 6-13).

Table 6-3 Gardner's Seven "Intelligences"

1. Linguistic information
2. Logical-mathematical information
3. Spatial information
4. Bodily kinesthetic information
5. Musical information
6. Information about other individuals
7. Information about oneself

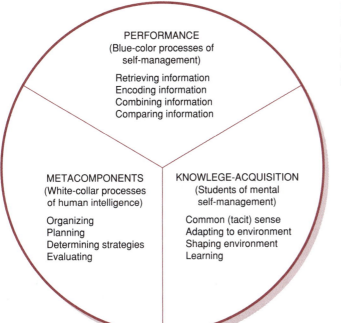

Figure 6-13
Sternberg's triarchic theory states that intelligence has meta-components, performance components, and knowledge-acquisition components.

Regardless of which definition (if any) appeals to you, can you propose a way to test for the concepts defined? Many scholars today feel that the intelligence tests we now have are, at best, achievement tests.

Alfred Binet and Theophile Simon standardized the first widely accepted intelligence test in France in 1905 for the purpose of determining which children were normal and could attend public schools and which ones were retarded and could not. Binet shunned the notion of formulating levels of intelligence beyond normal and subnormal. The concept of an intelligence quotient (IQ), giving degrees of mental difference, was proposed by a German, William Stern, in 1911 (Wolf, 1973). Lewis Terman at Stanford University revised the Binet–Simon test for use in the United States in 1916, changed its name to the Stanford-Binet test, and used Stern's concept of **intelligence quotients.**

An IQ is obtained by dividing tested mental age by chronological age and multiplying by 100. Thus if a six-year-old child answered questions on an intelligence test to the expected mental level of an eight-year-old, his or her IQ would be 133 (MA/CA × 100 = 8/6 × 100). If another six-year-old answered questions only at the expected mental level of a four-year-old, his or her IQ would be 66 (4/6 × 100). The average IQ is 100. Most IQs fall in a normal distribution range from 70 to 130 (see Figure 6-14). With a knowledge of where a child's tested IQ falls relative to a normal distribution of scores, one can determine whether a child belongs in a gifted class (IQ above 130), a special education class (IQ below 70), or a regular class (IQ between 70 and 130).

Wechsler (1949) developed an IQ test that scored verbal and performance abilities separately to get an idea of each individual's strengths and weaknesses. This approach allowed for special educational attention to be directed to areas of weakness. Both the Stanford-Binet and the Wechsler tests have to be administered to one person at a time by a trained tester and are therefore considered more trustworthy than IQ tests administered to a whole group by an untrained tester (such as a classroom teacher). However, group IQ tests are easier and far less expensive to administer and are, consequently, more prevalent. Today there are hundreds of IQ tests: individual tests, group tests, long forms, short forms, so-called culture-fair tests, even tests based on Piaget's studies in genetic epistemology. They have been developed to enable educators and others to classify students (or adults) by intelligence level and to place them in appropriate classes or jobs.

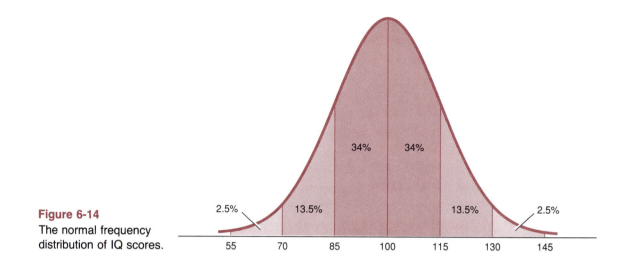

Figure 6-14
The normal frequency
distribution of IQ scores.

As the number, complexity, and uses of IQ tests have grown, so have the criticisms of them. Some advocates of IQ testing hail them as one of psychology's greatest achievements. IQ examinations can gauge how well or poorly a person has learned academic materials in comparison with others of the same age. IQ tests can also predict, to some degree, how well or poorly a person will continue to learn academic subjects in the future. Critics of IQ tests see them as one of psychology's most shameful bequests and often call for an abolition of their use (Scarr, 1978). In Washington, D.C., California, New York City, Philadelphia, and Minneapolis, IQ testing has been terminated.

One of the problems of IQ tests is that they can measure only a rather small set of the abilities known to be a part of intelligence. Different tests also give pictures of different factors of intelligence and, in effect, look at different "intelligences." No IQ test is known to measure the best (in theory) construct of intelligence (Carroll and Horn, 1981).

The testing of linguistic minorities as if they had exposure not only to the test materials but also to the language of the tester is an especially sensitive issue. In 1981 there were an estimated 3.5 million U.S. school-age children with limited English proficiency (Olmedo, 1981). These included Hispanics, Asians and Pacific Islanders, Native Americans, Eskimos, and recent immigrants from many other parts of the world. Many of these children, after IQ testing, were incorrectly labeled "learning disabled" or "mentally retarded."

Translated tests are most often translated into the formal form of the language rather than into the dialects used by the populations to which they are given (Samuda, 1975). Translated items also frequently lose the equivalent meaning of the original items. To be fair, children with limited English proficiency should be tested by examiners of their own ethnic and linguistic background or have a bilingual interpreter present. Even here problems arise. In which language should the directions be given first? Culture fair/culture free IQ tests are available that are also used to test children who have not had an equal exposure to the kinds of information found on the standard IQ tests. Research evidence indicates, however, that these tests are neither culture fair nor culture free, and they are not considered viable alternatives to the standard tests. See Figure 6-15 for an example of cultural biases on standardized tests.

Children may have tremendous fluctuations in their IQ scores from test to test, as much as from 20 to 30 points, depending on the circumstances surrounding the test administration. One child's tested IQ dropped 50 points after the death of his mother, and another's IQ score increased 30 points after psychotherapy relieved anxieties. When such variations due to environmental conditions are possible, the accuracy of any one measurement is open to question.

The one thing on which test advocates and critics agree is that a child's success

1. Which of these two objects go together?

"Correct" answer = Cup and saucer

Culture-bound possibilities that would be judged "incorrect" =

- spoon (for example, for soup) from saucer/cup
- mix (as for chocolate) in cup
- place cup on table
- place spoon on table

2. Pick the object that does not belong.

"Correct" answer = Oven (other objects are living)

Culture-bound possibilities that would be judged "incorrect" =

- rose (other objects relate to foods)
- clam (other objects exist on land; clam resides in water)
- tree (other items can be found inside a house)

in learning school subjects can sometimes be predicted by IQ tests. However, the reasons for this are unclear. Rosenthal and Jacobson (1968) demonstrated how influential expectation can be on actual performance in their widely known study *Pygmalion in the Classroom.* After intelligence tests were given to all the children in a class, teachers were told that certain children with just average test scores were going to bloom and show unusual academic growth during the school year. At the end of the year the children were retested. Those who were singled out as bloomers actually had improved and showed higher retest scores. The teachers' belief that they were going to bloom was held responsible for their higher scores. The treatment of a student according to some preconceived notion of how he or she will learn, which has the effect of eliciting the expected academic performance, has come to be known as the **Rosenthal effect.**

Arguments wax and wane about whether children inherit their intelligence or whether environmental factors motivate them to learn well. Most people believe that both heredity and environment influence intellectual ability. The argument became heated in the early 1970s after Berkeley psychologist Arthur Jensen (1969) published a review of several studies of intelligence. He concluded that about 80% of intelligence is inherited. He suggested further that "Caucasians inherit more intelligence than other races." This belief became known as **Jensenism.** He testified before a U.S. Senate Committee on Education that with only about 20% of intellect influenced by environment, the vast sums of money spent on compensatory education, in his opinion, were wasteful. Tempers flared, especially among educators trying to provide better educational opportunities for poor children of color. Jensen was accused of being a racist. Richard Herrnstein (1971) wrote in support of Jensen and added fuel to the fire of controversy. He suggested that since different people inherit different intellectual abilities, we should educate people for jobs according to their merit, or practice a system of **meritocracy.**

Figure 6-16
An impoverished environment with inadequate food, water, shelter, health care, and safety can supress a child's mental processes.

A Nobel Prize-winning physicist, William Shockley (1972), further suggested that persons with inherited low IQs might be monetarily rewarded for being sterilized to halt the production of more low-IQ children.

Counterarguments were abundant. Supporters of Head Start and other compensatory education programs emphasized that children given enriched environmental stimulation through early schooling could enhance the extent to which their genetic potential was realized. Others questioned whether the impoverished and suppressive environments of these children were not more responsible for failing to evoke and nurture their IQs (see Figure 6-16). In France in 1982, Schiff and his colleagues showed that infants of unskilled workers adopted by families from the top of the socioprofessional scale showed an increase in their IQ scores over time when compared to their siblings who remained in their natural homes.

In 1980 Jensen published a book defending his thesis. He put less emphasis on the data of the British psychologist Sir Cyril Burt, which he had cited in his 1969 article, because Burt's research has been revealed to be fraudulent (Hearnshaw, 1979). In his 1980 writing, Jensen supported the validity of IQ tests that have shown intellectual differences.

No valid answer can really be provided to the question of how much heredity and environment affect intelligence. No way has yet been found both validly and reliably to measure the components of intelligence.

Creativity

Creativity has been variously defined as the ability to think flexibly, divergently, imaginatively, inventively, or productively. Feldman (1989) defines it as a significant transformation of a body of knowledge (e.g., art, music, literature, science) such that the body of knowledge is irrevocably changed. Einstein's theory of relativity, Mozart's music, and Darwin's theory of evolution were clearly creative (Gruber, 1981). Creativity requires consciousness of a system of order, a perception that such a system is changeable, and the tendency to go outside the bounds of the system to change it (Feldman, 1989).

Is it good to be creative? A paradox exists in contemporary schools about creativity. Although its merits are extolled, its development is frequently inhibited. Novel, un-

Figure 6-17
Creative children are able to express their thoughts in original, unique ways. Adults can foster creativity by refraining from giving specific "how-to-do-it" directions.

conventional ideas, even though practical and correct in their own way, may be penalized. Children may be encouraged to make school products look like the models in workbooks or those that their teachers have made. Creative children can be criticized for work that differs from the norm. A child's attendance at school five days a week also reduces the amount of time he or she has for creative enterprises. A young Mozart would be hard pressed to write two operas and a large number of arias, serenades, symphonies, masses, and divertimenti during late childhood today.

Creativity is fostered by adults who are tolerant of unconventional products or responses, who encourage free use of materials, and free flow of conversation, who accept children's own best efforts, and who allow children to proceed on tasks without a lot of specific directions (see Figure 6-17). Messy projects should be permitted and time should not be limited. Creativity is not conducive to maintaining clean, quiet, well-ordered households or to teaching large classrooms of children. Teachers who are firmly committed to developing creativity in their students might find their efforts inhibited by administrators or parents who value conventional academic performance more highly than originality and imagination.

Problems of Learning

Attempts to classify children with learning disabilities have been hampered by the controversies surrounding IQ testing. Minority children (particularly Blacks, Hispanics, and Native Americans) have been overassigned to special-education classes due to test scores, as, to a lesser extent, have been other children from poverty backgrounds and boys in general (Reschly, 1981). An additional problem in classifying learning disabilities centers on labels. Terms such as *dyslexia* (difficulty in reading) and *hyperactivity* are being replaced with more precise labels such as **specific reading disorder** (for dyslexia) and **attentional deficit disorder** (for hyperactivity).

Learning disabilities are now labeled according to the specific disability observed:

- specific reading disorder (basic reading skills and reading comprehension),
- specific arithmetical disorder (mathematics calculation and mathematics reasoning),

- developmental language disorder (oral expression and listening comprehension),
- developmental articulation disorder (oral expression),
- coordination disorder (written expression; other fine or gross motor skills).

Many learning-disabled (LD) children do not fit even into these neater, more well-defined categories. There are many variations of reading problems, for example. Some children have developmental disparities in two or more areas or concurrently have attentional deficit disorders. A learning-disabled child has an imbalance with one (or two) delayed or impaired skill(s) while other abilities are achieved normally. Learning-disabled children can benefit greatly from special-education instruction in the area of their delay or impairment. Specific reading disorders (dyslexias) may affect as many as 15% of elementary school-aged children. They have difficulty learning to read despite conventional instruction, adequate intelligence, and sociocultural opportunity. Since dyslexic children are not all alike, their remedial education should be tailored to their special needs (see Table 6-4).

There are many hypotheses about the causes of learning disabilities. One is that prenatal hormone secretions may have permanent effects on brain structure and function (McEwen, 1983; Marx, 1983). In males, excess prenatal androgens appear to cause the right and left cerebral hemispheres to develop asymmetrically. This may explain why so many more boys than girls show learning disabilities. Other suspect factors include neuroanatomical disorders (Hynd and Hynd, 1984), starting school too early (Ames, 1983), childhood depression (Colbert et al., 1982), genetic inheritance (Moser, 1983), malnutrition during pregnancy (Simopoulos, 1983), prenatal maternal infections (Sever, 1983), prenatal drug use (Gray and Yaffe, 1983), obstetric medications (Broman, 1983), obstetric trauma (Creevy, 1983), low birthweight (Cohen, 1983), socioeconomic factors (Robbins, 1983), and environmental pollutants (Needleman, 1983). In most cases of LD the exact cause cannot be determined with current diagnostic tools. Silver (1984) estimated that approximately 3–7% of the school-age population is affected.

Attentional deficit disorder (ADD) in the past was variously called *hyperactivity, hyperkinesis, minimal brain injury,* and *minimal brain dysfunction.* Although ADD children may have some sort of brain dysfunction, its nature cannot be precisely defined or located. The problem in ADD revolves more around the quality of the child's activities than the amount. Affected children have short attention spans. This inability to focus on a task leads to many irrelevant motor behaviors.

In the "silent" form of ADD (without hyperactivity) the affected child may sit rather quietly through a task, unable to concentrate. In the more common hyperactive form the child may have temper outbursts, rapid mood changes, frequent crying, or explosive and unpredictable behaviors. The child may be demanding, easily frustrated, aggressive, restless and fidgety.

Table 6-4 An Inverted Letters and Numbers List Used to Assess Perceptual Problems Associated with Reading Disorders.

A	И	1	ヤƖ	ANNE	NATHAИ
B	O	ς	15	ᗺOB	O⅃IVIA
C	ꟼ	Ɛ	16	CARO⅃	ꟼAU⅃
ᗡ	Q	4	⟘Ɩ	ᗡAVID	
E	Я	5	18	E⅃IꙅƎ	
Ⅎ	ꙅ	ϱ	ϱƖ	ᖴRAИK	
G	T	⋀	20	GAI⅃	
H	U	8		HARRY	
I	V	9		IRENƎ	
Ⅼ	W	10		JACK	
ꓘ	X	11		KATHY	
L	Y	ςƖ		LARRY	
M	Ƨ	ƐƖ		MARIƎ	

The causes of ADD, like the causes of LD, may lie in genetic inheritance, prenatal factors, postnatal factors, factors related to an early childhood accident, factors related to an early childhood disease, or dietary factors. Hyperactive behaviors can also be caused by some emotional disturbances. The relationship between ADD children and their parents may become emotionally taut due to the ADD problem. The afflicted child is difficult to handle.

Ritalin, a stimulant drug, may be used to treat ADD. It can "quiet" affected children and allow them to attend to tasks and control their motor behaviors. Ritalin works by affecting neurotransmitters (chemicals that transmit signals across the synaptic gap between nerve cell processes). In some communities physicians have overlabeled and overdrugged active, difficult children who are actually free of ADD symptoms. This dangerous practice and its exposure by the mass media with resultant lawsuits has recently made many health professionals wary of any quick diagnoses and drug prescriptions for ADD.

Many other therapies may be tried: hypoglycemic (low-sugar) diets, megavitamin therapy, the Feingold diet (natural foods without artificial colors, flavors, or other additives), use of strong black coffee, and "patterning" exercises of muscles. These therapies have been successful in alleviating ADD in some children and have made it possible for them to attend regular school classes without taking drugs.

The American Association on Mental Deficiency's (AAMD) definition of **mental retardation** has three requirements (Grossman, 1977):

1. significantly subaverage general intellectual functioning,
2. deficits in adaptive behavior, and
3. symptoms manifest in the developmental period.

Significantly subaverage IQ means lower than that obtained by 97 to 98 percent of children the same age. *Mildly retarded* children are considered "educable" to the extent that in special classes they can learn some elementary school subjects. *Moderately retarded* children are considered "trainable." They can be expected, after special education, to learn self-help skills, social skills, and some occupational skill that will be useful in a residential institution or sheltered workshop. *Severely* and *profoundly retarded* children are not able to learn self-care skills, or social or occupational skills, and consequently need to be supervised and cared for throughout their lives.

In many cases of mental retardation, a causative factor cannot be found. In a Swedish study of the causes of mental retardation, Blomquist, Gustavson, and Holmgren (1981) found that the etiology could not be traced in 45% of cases. Prenatal causes were considered relevant in 43%, perinatal in 7%, and postnatal in 5% of the children. There are no cures for mental retardation, only supportive services for the training and care of these special children.

Children with significantly above-average IQ scores are considered intellectually **gifted.** They make up about 2 to 3% of the population. Although giftedness may seem out of place in a discussion of problems of learning, many such children become bored and frustrated in regular school classrooms and fail to be educated to their learning potential. A definition of giftedness at the federal level (Marland, 1972) includes five areas in which the children can be gifted:

1. general intellectual ability,
2. specific academic aptitude,
3. creative or productive thinking,
4. leadership ability,
5. visual and performing arts.

The challenge in educating intellectually gifted children is to find a good fit between child and teacher and between the child's needs and the academic offering (Vail, 1979). Many need help to achieve a balance in their social and emotional as well as intellectual lives (see Box 6-2). While many gifted students are lonely, Ludwig and Cullinan (1984)

BOX
6-2

A Gifted Eleven-Year-Old Boy's Attempt to Explain His "Education."

They laughed at me.
They laughed at me and called me names,
They wouldn't let me join their games.
I couldn't understand.
I spent most playtimes on my own,
Everywhere I was alone,
I couldn't understand.

Teachers told me I was rude,
Bumptious, over-bearing, shrewd,
Some of the things they said were crude.
I couldn't understand.
And so I built myself a wall,
Strong and solid, ten foot tall,
With bricks you couldn't see at all,
So *I* could understand.

And then came Sir,
A jovial, beaming, kindly man,
Saw through my wall and took my hand,
And the bricks came tumbling down,
For *he* could understand.

And now I laugh with them,
Not in any unkind way,
For they have yet to face their day
And the lessons I have learned.
For eagles soar above all birds,
And scavengers need to hunt in herds,
But the lion walks alone,
And now I understand.

SOURCE: "The Wall," from *The World of the Gifted Child*, by P. L. Vail. Copyright © 1980 by Penguin Books. Reprinted by permission.

reported that few have behavioral repercussions. They seem to have the ability to accept the jealousy and resentment of others for what it is and phase it out.

Psychosocial Development

The American family has changed profoundly in the last few years. The majority of mothers of school-age children work outside the home each day. Child-care responsibilities are being shared by neighbors, extended family members, and increasingly by fathers. Persons in the family's social network, the school, and the children's peer group join the parents as major socialization influences. Children from ages six to twelve still identify with and model their behavior after the people they perceive as most nurturant and powerful. Strong family ties relegate peers and school to a position of lesser importance, whereas weak family ties escalate the influence of significant others in the community.

Erikson's Industry versus Inferiority

Erik Erikson's fourth age in his concept of "The Eight Ages of Man" is the nuclear conflict of **industry versus inferiority.** True to his Freudian background, Erikson saw the middle to late childhood period as one characterized by a latent interest in sex. Oral, anal, and genital concerns are supposedly sublimated. As the child becomes master of many of the concerns of early childhood (autonomy, walking, running, talking, toilet training), he or she moves beyond the womb of the family. As Erikson (1963) put it, "The inner stage seems all set for 'entrance into life,' except that life must first be school life, whether school is field or jungle or classroom" (p. 258). The nuclear conflict between developing a sense of industry and acquiring an uncomfortable sense of inferiority remains paramount throughout the elementary school years.

School is an influential force in shaping or negating a sense of industry. In school,

Figure 6-18
Recognition of a group effort gives each individual child a sense of industry and achievement.

children concentrate on the important tools of the adult world: reading, writing, arithmetic, science, and social studies. They must apply themselves to tasks and persist in the work involved until some satisfactory completion point is reached. The ability to bring a productive situation to completion carries with it a sense of pleasure and pride in accomplishment. The more experiences children have winning recognition from others and feeling inner pride, the more anxious they become to finish projects and produce or accomplish things.

Schools foster industry by requiring that tasks be finished. They often teach children to work together toward some stated goal (the division of labor principle). Two or three children may be assigned a joint project, or the whole class may work together on some undertaking. In some places children actually begin working together during their elementary school years to produce articles for sale to the outside community. The recognition that comes to a whole group for their production serves to bolster the sense of industry of each participant (see Figure 6-18).

Although the school has the potential to foster a sense of industry in each pupil, this possibility is not always realized. Tests and report cards can leave some children reproached for mediocrity or inadequacy. When children fail to win recognition for their efforts to accomplish things they are in danger of developing a sense of inferiority. Erikson (1963) wrote that too many experiences of being made to feel inferior in the early years of elementary school may cause a child to revert back to the more isolated, less industry-conscious stage of initiative versus guilt.

The family is an important source of feedback for children to learn that their industry is both recognized and approved. It is important that children be given work to do at home to help foster their growing sense of industry (see Figure 6-19). Although boys and girls may bemoan the addition of chores to their daily activities, such household tasks provide a sense of contributing to the work of the family unit. They also give children a sense of pride in accomplishment.

There are many activities in which elementary school-age children can participate outside of the home and school that serve to enhance their sense of industry. Many organized clubs offer individual recognition in such forms as uniforms, badges, pins, award ribbons, trophies, or even monetary prizes. Erikson (1963) pointed out that it is by no means always in schools with special teachers that children receive systematic instruction. Many adults teach their specialized skills to children simply by dint of gift and inclination. Often the most effective teachers are older siblings, neighbors, and leaders of organized groups.

In discussing inferiority, Erikson (1963) warned of the danger that threatens when

Figure 6-19
Chores help children feel of value and worthwhile to the family unit.

Table 6-5   Erikson's Fourth Nuclear Conflict: Industry Versus Inferiority.

Sense	Eriksonian Descriptions	Fostering Adult Behaviors
Industry	Application of self to given skills and tasks	Give systematic instruction in skills and tasks
	Effort to bring productive situation to completion	Give recognition of things produced
	Attention and perseverance at work with pleasure obtained from effort	Specialized adults and older children outside family also instruct and recognize progress
	Work beside and with others brings sense of need to divide labor	
versus		
Inferiority	Disappointment in own tool use and skills	Family failed to prepare child for life in school and with other adults and unrelated children
	Sense of inadequacy among tool partners	School failed to sustain promises of earlier stages
	Lost hope of association in industrial society	Adult makes child feel that external factors determine worth rather than wish and will to learn
	Sense of being mediocre	

the schoolchild is made to feel that his or her worth is related to skin color, parental background, or fashionable clothes. Parents, teachers, neighbors, or club leaders can be guilty of prejudicial judgments about some children's accomplishments. During the elementary school years children are apt to believe adult evaluations rather than recognize prejudice for what it is. Although some experiences of feeling inadequate are bound to occur during late childhood, a sense of industry can be fostered by sensitive adults who counterbalance criticisms with constructive suggestions, recognition, and praise (see Table 6-5).

Parent–Child Relationships

Children spend less time with their parents during school years than they did in early childhood. The quality of the parent–child relationship becomes very important to the child's socialization. What techniques foster moral and values training, independence, self-esteem, and gender role socialization? A wide array of family behavior can affect psychosocial development.

Moral and Values Training.   The goal of **morality training** is to produce a person whose conscience will direct his or her behaviors toward the good and away from the bad without continual external reminders.

Freud (1953) believed that children learn early moral standards through two kinds of identification with their caregivers: by anaclitic identification (based on a fear of losing love) and by aggressive identification (based on a fear of punishment by the aggressor or authority figures). He believed anaclitic identification is used more by girls in identifying with their mothers, whereas aggressive identification is used more by boys in identifying with their fathers. Freud saw these identifications as a basis for children's knowledge of right and wrong. The fear of losing love and the fear of punishment were the forces that he believed help children avoid unacceptable behaviors.

Social-learning theorists such as Bandura and Walters (1963) emphasized that children model the behavior of adults with whom they most strongly identify. Children's modeling takes the form of striving to incorporate everything about the loved or powerful adults into their own lives, including moral standards and values. Children receive a sense of security and approval when they emulate caregivers' behavior. This modeling of behavior then becomes a need because of the emotional rewards it brings.

Piaget (1965a) distinguished two moral levels in children. The earliest is a morality of constraint that puts wrongdoing in terms of damage done and emphasizes submission to authority. The second moral level is a morality of cooperation that judges wrongdoing by the intent of the doer and establishes rules by mutual agreement.

In the period of morality of constraint, or moral realism, children feel an obligation to comply with rules because they see them as sacred and unalterable. They measure the degree of wrongness of an act by the amount of damage done, without consideration of motivation. Here are two sample stories that Piaget (1965a) used to question children to help him determine their level of morality. Which of the two children is naughtiest?

A. Alfred meets a little friend of his who is very poor. This friend tells him that he has had no dinner that day because there was nothing to eat in his home. Then Alfred goes into a baker's shop, and as he has no money he waits until the baker's back is turned and steals a roll. Then he runs out and gives the roll to his friend.

B. Henriette goes into a shop. She sees a pretty piece of ribbon on a table and thinks to herself that it would look nice on her dress. So while the shop lady's back is turned she steals the ribbon and runs away at once. (p. 123)

A child in Piaget's stage of morality of constraint would judge the first offense as more serious because the roll was bigger and more expensive than the ribbon. In effect, the child would ignore the intent of the transgressor. At this stage children also believe that punishment wipes away the sin. During this stage they see punishment as inherent in the external world, a view that Piaget called *a belief in immanent justice*. (All misdeeds are ultimately punished.) The following question asked by Piaget (1965a) illustrates a belief in an immanent justice:

PIAGET: In a class of very little children the teacher had forbidden them to sharpen their pencils themselves. Once, when the teacher had her back turned, a little boy took the knife and was going to sharpen his pencil. But he cut his finger. If the teacher had allowed him to sharpen his pencil, would he have cut himself just the same?

SIX-YEAR-OLD: He cut himself because it was forbidden to touch the knife.

PIAGET: And if he had not been forbidden, would he also have cut himself?

SIX-YEAR-OLD: No, because the mistress would have allowed it. (p. 252)

If adults fail to punish, nature somehow intercedes. It is common for younger children to believe that accidents, bad dreams, or illnesses are the punishments for their sins of the day.

In late childhood a morality of cooperation, or moral relativism, replaces the morality of constraint. Children begin to see rules as less immutable. They begin to see others' points of view and realize how different motivations underlie different actions. Justice comes to be viewed in a social context and in terms of equity and equality.

Kohlberg (1984) expanded Piaget's ideas of moral development, postulating five stages rather than two. Brief summaries of his stages are presented in Chapter 2, page 47. Kohlberg saw the first two stages, which characterize early childhood, as **pre-morality,** where hedonistic, self-serving urges are paramount. He labeled Stages 3 and 4 as **conventional morality,** where the social context is paramount. School-age children are concerned with maintaining the good relations and approval of others (Stage 3) and grow cognitively aware of the need to show respect for authority and maintain the social order for the sake of having order (Stage 4).

Kohlberg stated that children advance in sequence from one stage to another, rather than by leapfrogging any of them. Some older children may be morally behind due to lack of experience or cognition, whereas younger children may be more advanced. Research by Turiel (1966) supported Kohlberg's theory. Turiel gave his subjects stories like the one below and asked them to choose an ending and explain the reasons for their choices:

> In Europe, a woman was near death from a special kind of cancer. There was one drug that the doctors thought might save her. It was a form of radium that a druggist in the same town had recently discovered. The drug was expensive to make, but the druggist was charging ten times what the drug cost him to make. He paid $200 for the radium and charged $2000 for a small dose of the drug. The sick woman's husband, Heinz, went to everyone he knew to borrow money, but he could only get together about $1000, which is half of what it cost. He told the druggist that his wife was dying and asked him to sell it cheaper or let him pay later. But the druggist said, "No, I discovered the drug and I'm going to make money from it." So Heinz got desperate and broke into the man's store to steal the drug for his wife. Should the husband have done that? (Kohlberg, 1963, pp. 18–19).

Answers such as "You really shouldn't steal the drug" or "The druggist should get some profit from his business" are conventional role-conforming answers, Stages 3 and 4.

In Piaget's and Kohlberg's views, moral development can be influenced by identification and modeling, but it is mainly tied to cognitive development. To reach higher moral levels children need many experiences with choosing right and wrong and opportunities to reason out the whys and wherefores of the choices.

How do parents help provide for optimal moral development? Children need to (1) know right from wrong, (2) be able to control their own urges to do wrong, and (3) consider the rights and needs of others before acting. By middle to late childhood children can be expected to understand most of the things that family and society define as unacceptable, but they cannot always be expected to have control over their urges toward selfish or aggressive acts. Nor can they be expected always to consider the rights and needs of others. Adults can help children learn both self-control and consideration of others.

School-age children learn empathy through inductive reasoning. Parents should tell children how misbehaviors make them feel and ask them how they suppose the wrongful actions make others feel. During late childhood it becomes possible for children to see others' points of view and to consider others' motivations. The more practice children have considering how others feel, what motivates other people's actions, and what other people need, the more apt they are to consider these factors.

Prosocial behaviors are altruistic actions directed at satisfying the wants and needs of others, such as giving and sharing. Infants cannot differentiate between themselves and others and thus cannot be prosocial. In early childhood, preschoolers can learn to take the perspective of another person and sympathize. It is not until late childhood, however, that children can appreciate the perspectives of several other people. They begin to imagine others' emotional states and needs and respond with empathy (Hoffman, 1984).

Prosocial behaviors and empathy are increased in late childhood when parents are affectionate, encourage a positive self-concept, and point out similarities between people (Barnett, 1987). Some research studies suggest that girls become more prosocial than boys (Gilligan, 1982). Some parents encourage daughters to be nurturant and attentive to emotional needs, while they encourage their sons to be assertive and attentive to task mastery. Research has not conclusively demonstrated a sex difference in prosocial behaviors (Eisenberg, 1989): Both girls and boys can learn the value of caring and sharing. Differences in the moral orientations of girls and boys need to be explored further (Gilligan and Attanucci, 1988).

Discipline.   Adults responsible for the care of older children must provide some form of control over misbehavior, although the discipline may take different forms from that used with younger children. Physical punishment leads to hostility toward the punishing parent, as well as a low sense of guilt for the misbehavior. School-age children also model physical punishment and may strike back at the parent or a scapegoat (such as a sibling, friend, or pet). Love-withdrawal discipline leads to resentment of the parent and to a high degree of anxiety about the loss of love. Permissiveness leads to a lack of respect for the parent.

Inductive techniques of discipline are most effective as the child matures cognitively. These are attempts to control the child's actions by explaining reasons for a change of behavior and explaining the consequences of the undesirable deed in terms of its effects on others (see Chapter 5).

Discipline will succeed best if parents avoid any kind of power play with their children (Dreikurs and Stolz, 1964). Dreikurs proposed that children be left to discover the negative consequences of bad behavior for themselves. If they fail to put clothing in the hamper, they will soon find themselves with no clean clothes to wear. If they annoy the cook, their dinner will be delayed. If they leave toys where they do not belong, the toys will disappear. This is actually a form of inductive discipline. The inducement to behave is more felt than heard. (Parents can give reasons for the child's suffered consequences based on the child's own actions whenever they are not immediately apparent). Dreikurs advocated a family democracy where all family members feel loved, wanted, worthwhile, and equally important.

Maccoby and Martin (1983) identified four major patterns of parental behavior: authoritarian, authoritative, indulgent, and neglecting. The **authoritarian parent** assumed complete control over rules and regulations, used physical punishment and stayed somewhat detached and cool toward the children. The **authoritative parent** was in control but allowed feedback from the children about rules and regulations, used inductive techniques of discipline (occasionally backed up by physical punishment), and was receptive and warm toward them. The **indulgent parent** seldom asserted control, made few demands about rules and regulations, and was warm to the children. The **neglecting parent** made few demands on children and was also characteristically detached, cool and unresponsive. (See Chapter 5 for a review of the consequences of such social climates.)

Social responsibility is greatest in children with authoritative parents. Too much authority holds back the socialization of independence and responsibility taking. Lax control sometimes leads to socially disruptive, immature behaviors. Neglecting leads to multiple problems with emotions and behaviors. When Siegal and Cowen (1984) asked school-age children to evaluate the disciplinary climates created by their mothers, they found that authoritative mothering was not only the most effective in terms of positive socialization but was also what children preferred. Induction was rated very favorably as a disciplinary technique. Contrary to what you might expect, children did not advocate permissiveness. Physical punishment was given mild approval.

Both fathers and mothers should be active disciplinarians of children whenever behavior needs correcting. Weintraub (1978) pointed out that the old practice of assigning fathers the roles of breadwinner and ultimate disciplinarian (as in "Wait 'til your father gets home!") may have caused men to feel conflict about their parenting roles. Today's increased reliance on the father's assistance as a warm, nurturing, accepting second parent results in more adequate child socialization. Carlson (1984) found that boys whose fathers share responsibility for child care hold fewer sex-role stereotypes.

Gender Role Socialization.   Chapter 5 presented various theories about how and why children learn to adopt behaviors appropriate to their own sex. Freud believed that boys identify with their fathers and girls identify with their mothers, primarily through repression. Social-learning theorists state that boys identify with their fathers and girls with their mothers because of the rewards and attention such sex-appropriate behaviors bring. Cognitive theorists claim that children model the like-sexed parent because they perceive their resemblance to that parent and want to imitate the person whom they most closely resemble.

When children are old enough to join clubs, stay overnight with friends, and spend at least half of their waking hours outside the home, they develop other **gender-role models** besides their parents. Pitcher and Schulz (1984) presented a strong case for peers becoming major agents of gender-role socialization. The gender-appropriate behaviors children learn at home are tested against a wide sample of men and women, boys and girls. When confusion develops, children are most apt to model the persons who are nurturant and powerful and who dole out rewards. This may mean learning a double or triple standard. For example, a girl may learn that her liberated mom wants her to fight her own battles, that her more traditional schoolteacher believes girls should never fight, and that peers think she should fight verbally but not physically. Or a boy may be told at home that it is appropriate to cry when hurt, by his peers that it is never appropriate to cry, and by a teacher that it is all right to cry when experiencing strong emotion.

Some girls are expected to develop an **expressive orientation** to life. They are supposed to be nurturant, sympathetic, dependent, and emotional. Boys are expected to develop an **instrumental orientation** to life. They are supposed to be task-oriented, brave, independent, and unemotional. Edwards and Whiting (1980) studied three contemporary cultures that socialized expressive and instrumental orientations in their girls and boys: India, Mexico, and Okinawa. Girls were asked to do household tasks, take care of infants, and stay in the company of female adults. In these cultures, a great many statistically significant gender differences were found. In contrast, in three cultures that allowed girls more freedom, the United States, the Philippines, and Kenya, fewer gender differences were found (see Figure 6-20). North American children are not free of gender-typed behaviors, however. The most striking sex difference is the greater rough-and-tumble aggressive behaviors of boys (Maccoby, 1980).

Many books for parents stress the advantages of androgynous child-rearing. An **androgynous** child incorporates positive aspects of both expressive and instrumental

Figure 6-20
Feminine behaviors are not prescribed for school-age children in all countries. Some girls are comfortable doing exactly what boys do from ages 6 through 11. Can you identify the two girls in this photo?

characteristics into his or her personality. Research indicates that androgynous personalities are healthier than those who are highly sex-typed. Both high femininity and high masculinity have been correlated with higher anxiety and lower self-esteem (Bem, 1976).

Beliefs that American girls are more submissive and less assertive than American boys have not been borne out by research studies. Submissiveness is defined as nonhostile, noncoercive behavior that involves taking into consideration the power, authority, or feelings of others while denying one's own feelings. Assertiveness is defined as the direct, nonhostile, noncoercive expression of thoughts, desires, beliefs, or feelings (Deluty, 1979). After observing school-age children over an eight-month period in a wide variety of naturally occurring school-related activities, Deluty (1985) found very few submissive behaviors in either sex and a great many assertive behaviors in both sexes. Both boys and girls were consistently assertive in situations that varied in structure from sitting passively to moving about more actively (such as art and music classes). Girls as well as boys know how to express their thoughts and feelings in a nonhostile manner, make requests for behavior, stand their own ground in arguments, and assert themselves both positively and negatively. They do so frequently, at least until the onset of adolescence (Gilligan, 1982). Deluty's reseach confirmed the finding of many other studies: boys are more aggressive than girls. However, they assert themselves much more frequently than they aggress.

Single Parenting.   A **single-parent family** is composed of one parent and one or more children, for reasons of divorce, desertion, death, unwed mothering, or single-parent adoption. In the United States, about 16% of all children live with a single parent. In Canada, about 9% of families are single-parent (Eiduson, 1990). Single parenting is often only a temporary phenomenon, until marriage or remarriage occurs. About 50% of North American children will spend some portion of their childhood with a single parent. About 7% of one-parent families are male headed (see Box 6-3).

One frequently hears the phrases "Kids are resilient" or "Children bounce back quickly" to assuage fears about the effects of losing a parent. Are they true? Generalizations from one situation to another are of questionable validity, but researchers

---

Single-Parent Fathers.

About 7% of fathers are awarded physical custody of their children in divorce proceedings or become single-parent fathers for reasons of death, desertion, or single-parent adoption. While single-parent fathers are statistically uncommon, there are in fact about 900,000 of them in the United States (Meredith, 1985). Like single mothers, they must combine jobs outside the home with cooking, cleaning, laundry, chauffeuring of children, handling repairs, paying bills, shopping, balancing the budget, functioning as both father and mother, nurturing, disciplining, protecting their children's health and safety, assisting with school-work, and being solely in charge inside the home. The physical and emotional stresses of so doing may exhaust them (just as they do single mothers).

Although caring for younger children might be easier for a father, most children awarded to their father's custody are older (Glick and Norton, 1978). Older children, while they can lend a hand with housework, are harder to discipline, more vocal about their anger, fears, griefs, and displeasures, and more interfering with any attempts on their father's part to develop his own social life.

Single fathers often find housework simple compared to parenting interactions. Fathering of daughters can be especially problematic. Girls without mothers have been rated as less feminine, less independent, and more demanding than those without fathers. In contrast, boys without mothers are more sociable and more mature (Santrock and Warshak, 1979). Santrock and his colleagues (1982) have suggested that father custody may be more beneficial for some boys and mother custody for some girls, although both sexes do better with frequent contact with both parents.

Figure 6-21
Single-parent mothers are often members of minority populations and economically deprived groups.

are finding that a great deal of childhood anguish accompanies the breaking up of the two-parent family, the primary foundation of security. The aftermath is long-lived. In fact, children usually do better during the crisis of the actual loss and have their worst problems with guilt, anger, fear, and depression later. The "bouncing back" seldom occurs until at least a year after the loss of a parent.

When a mother first becomes a single parent, she experiences shock, fears, anxieties, and a loss of self-esteem. Few departing fathers make significant monetary contributions to support their families, so most single-parent mothers must work. Most experience a degree of downward economic mobility. Many must move to more modest housing. More than a fair share of single-parent mothers are from minority, economically deprived groups (Eiduson, 1990) (see Figure 6-21).

The physical and emotional stresses of working, balancing a budget, running the house, functioning as both father and mother, and being solely in charge can exhaust even the best organized and most emotionally stable single parent. Weinraub and Wolf (1983) found that many of them work longer hours, withdraw from their social networks, and become socially isolated. They also become more authoritarian and erratic in the ways they discipline their children (Hetherington, 1979).

Single parenting usually becomes easier with time. Parents can learn how to cope by talking to other single parents in organizations such as Parents Without Partners. Counseling by mental health professionals is also desirable. Single parenting is not as difficult if the parent has help from his or her parents, neighbors, relatives, or friends, and has people with whom to communicate openly and honestly about his or her physical, social, and emotional concerns.

When children first lose one of their parents, they commonly experience anger, fears, guilt, and depression (Hetherington, 1979). They worry about whether their needs will be met, they worry about the absent parent, and they worry whether they are still loved. Kalter and Plunkett (1984) found that about one-third of all children believe their behaviors caused the absent parent to leave. Most fantasize about a parental reunion. If they must move away from old friends, neighbors, and classmates, or if they see less of the remaining parent, they often feel extreme loneliness and depression. Depression in children often takes the form of school setbacks, uncontrolled tempers, destructive acts, and antisocial behaviors. Boys seem to have many more problems adjusting to a father's loss than do girls (Hetherington, Cox, and Cox, 1982). They refuse to comply with many of their mother's requests, adding to her already stressed existence. Father-absent boys have been shown to decline in both achievement motivation and ego strength over time (Fry and Scher, 1984). Wallerstein and Kelly (1976) found that both boys and girls whose fathers are absent had poorer impulse control and lower levels of moral development.

There are several things a single parent can do to help assure good self-esteem and health in a child:

- Assure each child that the break-up was not his or her fault.
- Assure each child that he or she is still loved.
- Communicate with each child about his or her feelings of anger, fear, guilt, and depression.
- Be honest about your own feelings of anxiety, fear, and so on.
- Be honest about the financial situation.
- Don't tear down the reputation of the absent parent.
- Keep quarrels with the absent parent hidden.
- Encourage frequent contact with the absent parent (if he or she is emotionally well adjusted).
- Discourage fantasies and hopes for reconciliation (unless feasible).
- Discuss and reach agreement with the absent parent on rules of child-rearing and discipline and keep them consistently.
- Keep consistent schedules for meals, school, bedtime, and the like.

- Look to others (parents, siblings, friends, competent house-keeper) for support when stressed.
- Seek professional counseling or therapy for self or children if stressed.

Stepparenting.   Within a period of five years, most children who experienced the breakup of their biological parents will have to learn to adjust to a **stepparent** (new spouse of one's biological parent). Jealousy and resentment of the stepparent is common. Blending new families is easier if the stepparent does not try to replace the biological parent but rather becomes a third (or fourth) parent. Relationships develop slowly and should not be rushed. The stepparent and real parent should agree on child-rearing and discipline and be consistent in their use, supporting each other when necessary. Although it is normal for one child to warm up to the stepparent before others, showing favoritism should be studiously avoided. Boys often accept a stepfather sooner than girls (Santrock et al., 1982). Daughter tend to be angry with their mothers for remarrying. They are frequently anxious about any kind of physical contact with the stepfather.

Younger children accept stepparents more easily than do older children (Stapleton and MacCormack, 1981). While initially children may have more behavioral problems in the reconstituted family than in the single-parent family (Nunn, Parish, and Worthing, 1983), over an extended period of time remarriage can mitigate the negative effects of the divorce and single-parent experience. The mother's (or father's) new partner must be supportive, caring, and willing to work at becoming a parent (Rutter, 1979). Designing workable stepparent/stepchild(ren) relationships can seem overwhelmingly difficult at times. Many families cannot meet the challenge. Over 40% of newly blended families end in divorce within five years (Einstein, 1979).

The School's Role in Socialization

A well-liked schoolteacher, especially one who resembles a child in some way (sex, race, religion, ethnicity) may be taken on as a role model by a child. Sometimes a teacher will be aware of the child's modeling; often he or she will not. Consider these examples of teachers' impacts. James Conant (1970), a scientist who helped develop the atom bomb, attributed his early interest in chemistry to a teacher. In his autobiography he wrote "I doubt if any schoolteacher has ever had a greater influence on the intellectual development of a youth than Newton Henry Black had on mine" (p. 160). Helen Keller (1954) paid an even greater tribute to her teacher. She wrote "All the best of me belongs to her—there is not a talent, or an aspiration or a joy in me that has not been awakened by her loving touch" (p. 46).

A classic study by Lewin, Lippitt, and White (1939) helped make educators aware of the ways in which a teacher can influence the social behavior of the members of a group. They compared autocratic (dictatorial), democratic, and laissez-faire (let people do what they choose) teaching styles. They discovered that, although the autocratic teachers ostensibly had good classes, the democratic teachers actually had the better ones. When the autocratic teachers left their groups, fighting broke out immediately. The laissez-faire teachers had fighting occur even in their presence. In the democratic atmosphere policies were established by the group, and the children felt some re-sponsibility for the rules they helped make. They showed little aggression in either the teacher's presence or absence. They also liked the democratic leaders and worked harder for them (see Figure 6-22).

While many persons believe that schools do not make a difference, research suggests differently. In an extensive review of school effects on pupil progress, Rutter (1983) concluded that effective schooling needs to be measured not only by scholastic attainment but also by attitudes toward learning, classroom behavior, social functioning, absenteeism, continuation in education, and ultimate employment. A good teacher, like a good parent, needs to be in control but allow feedback from the children. A good

Figure 6-22
Students are more motivated to achieve for an involved democratic teacher than for either a dictatorial or an indulgent one.

teacher is receptive and warm toward the students and practices inductive techniques of discipline. One good teacher, especially in the first grade, can have remarkably persistent positive effects on students (Pedersen, Faucher, and Eaton, 1978).

Discipline is needed in a classroom whenever one student's behavior prevents other students from learning or the teacher from teaching (Curwin and Mendler, 1980). A teacher should try to induce the misbehaving student to change behaviors without making the student feel stupid or evil. The behavior may be inappropriate, but the student is not bad. Dreikurs and Stolz (1964) believed that children misbehave to get attention when they feel they are not recognized as valued and equal members of a group (see p. 177). Carl Rogers (1969) believed that unconditional positive regard, acceptance, and empathy allow students to solve their own problems (see Chapter 2, p. 49). Ginott (1972), in a classic book about teaching, suggested that students must have firm limits set on behaviors but no limits on the types of activities that foster self-esteem and positive feelings.

Achievement is fostered when teachers hold high expectations for students' success. Deci and his colleagues (1981) showed that democratic teachers contributed most to both students' self-esteem and achievement motivation. All children have high expectancies of success when they first enter school (Dweck and Elliott, 1983). These expectancies may, however, begin to change in a couple of years. Eccles, Midgley, and Adler (1984) wrote that experiences of being assessed as inferior and experiences of being coerced, manipulated, and controlled can lead to drops in achievement motivation.

The Rosenthal effect (see p. 211) can influence children's achievement positively or negatively by eliciting expected classroom performance. Tom, Cooper, and McGraw (1984) found that authoritarian teachers have higher grade expectations for Asians than for whites and for middle-class than for lower-class students. Ball, Newman, and Schewen (1984) also found that teachers lower their performance expectations for children from divorced single-parent families, especially boys.

Is there a carry-over effect on socialization practices from the school to home? Much depends on the child's perceptions of power and importance of school and home. In the best circumstances, both school and home will reinforce each child's accomplishments and joy in learning. When the parents have negative attitudes toward a school, a child may become school phobic (see Box 6-4). When the parents communicate with

BOX
6-4

School Phobia.

A fairly prevalent (and disabling) childhood phobia is **school phobia.** It is a condition where a child actually develops physical symptoms of illness when left at school (headache, vomiting, cramps, diarrhea, hysteria, crying). It is most common when a child first starts school but may also occur after a trauma, such as the loss of a parent by death or divorce. School phobic children are typically more dependent, immature, and anxious than nonphobic children (Trueman, 1984). The root of the child's anxiety is not usually the school or the teacher but a fear of being separated from the parent(s). However, over time the child may also become fearful of teasing or rejection by teacher or peers or of being called on to recite. Symptoms decrease if a parent stays in the classroom. However, this is not a good solution to the problem. The immediate goal is to get the child to remain in school without the parent (usually the mother) on whom he or she has become overly dependent.

To help children overcome school phobia, parents need to be made aware of the ways in which they consciously or unconsciously convey the impression to their child that all will not be well during the separation.

School phobic children may sense that the parent will be lonely without them or that the parent does not believe the school environment is as safe, healthy, and loving as the home environment.

Parents differ in their readiness to accept their own roles in their child's problem. Many need help in adjusting to their child's being in school all day. In some cases, the mother's entry into some out-of-the-home employment will allow her to "untie the apron strings" and more willingly send her child to school. In some cases one or both parents need psychotherapy to work out their underlying conflicts about allowing their child autonomy, and about the safety of the school. This can help to prevent recurrences of the child's perceived need to remain at home.

When a school phobic child does experience physical symptoms in school, he or she should be sent to the nurse's office, not home. As soon as possible, the child should be gently but firmly returned to the classroom. Home teaching should not be prescribed. It creates more psychological invalidism for the school phobic child and encourages continuation of the conscious or unconscious parental domination.

school personnel and both parties share their thoughts, values, and feelings, the child's self-esteem and achievement can be enhanced.

Peer Interactions

Just as a schoolteacher can have an impact on social development, so too can friends. But peers' influence on a child's behavior can be weak or strong depending on several factors, including:

- the age of the child,
- the sex of the child,
- the self-esteem of the child,
- the intelligence of the child,
- the amount of time spent with peers,
- the stoutness of the parent–child affection bond,
- the amount of time spent in positive interactions with the family grouping,
- the family's acceptance of various peer group members,
- the values and activities of the peer group, and
- the child's position in the peer group.

Children use their friends as sounding boards and testing grounds for the values and attitudes they have learned at home. In many cases the **peer group** (group of persons of equal rank or status) can be more democratic than the home. Instead of rules being laid down by authority figures, they are debated, with some or all of the group having a say in what they should be. Home values and attitudes may be upgraded or watered down, depending on the participants in the group.

Children increasingly turn to their peers for assistance. Nelson-LeGall and Gumerman (1984) asked children from whom they would seek help in academic and social contexts and found that their preferences for parental help decrease with age. Peer academic tutoring or collaboration brings with it unique motivational and cognitive benefits for the participating children (Damon, 1984).

During late childhood, friendships become more stable. Friends are usually of the same sex and often of the same race, religion, culture, or socioeconomic standing in the community. Children typically have more than one best friend. This assures them of more dependable companionship if one friend is busy or upset (Davies, 1982). A child without friends needs assistance in finding companionship. Peer rejection in childhood has been correlated with psychological and behavioral problems in adulthood (Parker and Asher, 1987).

Organized activities such as scouting, sports, and religious group projects enhance and strengthen friendships and add a cohesive element to a group. Little League participation for a season, for example, has been shown to enhance the self-esteem of each player involved (Hawkins and Gruber, 1982). When children work together, they learn new respect for each other. Teamwork can create friendships.

Children in groups will often do things they would never do on their own. This can take the form of increased altruism (for example, visiting nursing homes) or increased delinquency (such as destroying property). Many a quiet, well-behaved child has joined fights or used vulgar language along with a supporting peer group. Peers have the potential to influence each other for good or for bad. The direction of friends' influence often depends on the social context for their interactions (religious group, school, neighborhood) (see Figure 6-23).

Being a member of a minority group within a larger community frequently presents special problems for school-age children. If the minority group is large enough so a child can find a cohesive group of same-sex friends, the going is easier. By the elementary school years children have learned many of the prejudices of their parents. Prejudice is an insidious thing. Even members of minority groups may adopt the mainstream culture's prejudice against themselves. Fu and Fogel (1982), for example, found that both black and white children from the South had a white-positive/black-negative bias.

Neighborhood peer groups are important sources of support in late childhood. As more mothers work outside the home, more at-home neighbors are being asked to watch several children after school until parents return. Research on latchkey children (those who are home alone after school) has suggested that they may suffer more fears, loneliness, boredom, and depression (Long and Long, 1983).

Figure 6-23
Peer pressure can reinforce the values and behaviors that are endorsed by adults in some social contexts.

The Effect of Technology

The influences of parents, schools, peers, and neighbors are modified, somewhat, by machines of technology available to children. In addition to the standard television, children now increasingly have videocassette recorders (VCRs). These enable them to tape television programs for later replay or to play movies, games, or music videos on their television sets. Children also have easy access to video games in video arcades or other public places. Many of them are exposed to computers in their schools, and many children now have personal home computers. The effects of television on children are better known than the effects of computers.

The average North American child spends more time watching TV than in any other activity except sleeping (Schramm, 1973). By completion of high school most children will have spent about twice as much time in their lives watching television as learning in school classrooms. Children who feel emotionally insecure or are rejected by peers are likely to be the heaviest viewers (Schramm and Roberts, 1971).

Instructional television is frequently associated with the school classroom. Increasingly, teachers are scheduling televised lessons on topics such as health, music, art, foreign language, science, or history into their lesson plans. The television is an appealing teacher. It can capture and hold children's attention. The quality of education can be enhanced with instructional TV programs (Schramm, 1977). Many video stores and libraries will rent educational programming to families at nominal fees.

Wright and Huston (1983), and Greenfield (1984) argued that television has a rich (although as yet largely untapped) potential for enhancing the cognitive and psychosocial development of children. Information-processing skills and retention of information can be increased and improved by television. Children can also acquire many positive concepts such as the efficacy of moral and prosocial behavior. It is unfortunate that so few programs have been developed to exploit these positive growth possibilities (see Figure 6-24).

Over the past ten years there has been more violence on children's weekend

Figure 6-24
Television influences the social development of children with its own views of reality and pictures of how the "rest of the world" acts and reacts.

programs than on prime-time television. In the past some social scientists felt that watching televised violence would have a cathartic effect and displace or dissipate a child's need to be aggressive in the real world. This theory has not been supported by research. Instead, it has been found that the more violent programming children watch, the more aggressive they become in all aspects of life: conflicts with parents, fighting, and delinquent behaviors. They also view the world with more suspicion and distrust and perceive violence as an effective solution to conflict (Pearl, 1984). Violent television programming has been associated with learning in less positive ways (see Chapter 5, p. 188). The emotions arising from watching violence have been shown to hinder creative cognitive functioning (Kline, Greene, and Noice, 1990).

Commercial time on TV is higher than most people imagine, about 22% of the broadcast day. Commercials rarely last longer than 60 seconds, but they are skillfully designed to stay on their viewers' minds for much longer. Many commercials hire celebrities to endorse foods or toys for children. Ross and her colleagues (1984) found that eight- to fourteen-year-olds prefer products promoted by celebrities and fail to see that the ads are staged, especially when the commercial includes live action. Ads for highly sugared or salted foods with low nutritional value (junk food) are flashed at children frequently, as often as eight times per hour on Saturday mornings. Children in turn beg to be allowed to eat such foods and consider their parents particularly cruel if they deny them the "pleasures" the ad kids have consuming these foods. Feldstein and Feldstein (1982) analyzed televised toy commercials and found that they not only have more males than females per commercial but also are more likely to put females in passive roles. Prime-time adult-oriented commercials do the same (Mackey and Hess, 1982).

Greenfield (1984) described computer technology as another potentially great tool for enhancing children's cognitive and psychosocial development. While children watching television are passive, children playing video games are active. They must plan moves ahead and develop their fine motor skills to play competently. The natures of the video games children play have an effect on their behaviors, however, just as TV programming does. Some video games are terrifyingly violent, with ultimate goals of destruction and annihilation. Ascione and Chambers (1985) reported that children who play violent video games are less likely to help other children (see Figure 6-25).

Some people have worried that computer games are addictive—that children who play a great deal may feel a compulsive need to continue playing. There is little research evidence to support this. Most video games encourage interactions among competitive players. Rather than creating socially isolated children, they often stimulate social involvement. Playing may improve the social acceptance and self-esteem of children who are competent at video games even though they are not good athletes or good scholars. Levin (1985) wrote that mastering a new computer game has much in common

Figure 6-25
Are video arcades sites where friendships bloom, where violence is learned, or both?

with solving a math problem. It absorbs the child's whole attention. The child must modify, augment, delete, or transform behaviors in order to succeed.

Many children now have personal computers in their own homes. They use these home computers not only to play games but also to create new games or other programs. Programming requires that the user provide the machine with a carefully planned series of instructions. This requires patience and a willingness to correct one's mistakes. The computer provides a precise feedback of what it has been told to do. It cannot be intimidated into doing something else. The user must take full responsibility for any "bugs" in the program and find out what he or she has done wrong. Levin (1985) writes that this process teaches children humility and personal responsibility. Many schools have incorporated computer programming courses into their curriculum. There is an optimistic sense that this technology can be beneficial. It will not be a substitute for parents and teachers, but, used wisely, it can enhance the work of adults in rearing children.

Summary

The progression of growth slows in late childhood. Body build is influenced by both nutrition and genetic factors and can influence a child's self-concept. During this age, as in previous ages, good health is maintained through good nutrition, adequate sleep, and satisfying family, school, and peer relationships. Children continue to get many respiratory infections. Tooth decay reaches epidemic proportions. Some children have chronic illnesses or are impeded by psychological problems during late childhood. Accidents, although not as numerous as for younger children, also occur frequently.

The learning process involves metamemory and metacognition. School-aged children can think about strategies for remembering and retrieving the information they need.

Cognitive growth proceeds in what Piaget called the concrete operations stage. With experience children develop abilities to reverse mental operations, see reciprocal relations, conserve, order, classify, conceive of distances in time and space, and understand physical and psychological causation.

Language is fun in late childhood. Children practice accents, secret languages, foreign words, slang, and words with double meanings. Sentences acquire sophistication as understanding of complex syntactical forms develops.

Intelligence is a concept not well understood. Many scholars are attempting to study and define it more precisely. IQ tests give an inexact estimate of children's abilities to learn school subjects. Although both heredity and environment affect intelligence, the relative strength of each influence is unknown. Although creativity is extolled, its development may be inhibited in many structured situations. Problems of learning may take the form of specific disorders, attentional deficits, mental retardation, or giftedness.

Erikson described the nuclear conflict of this age as that of developing a sense of industry versus developing feelings of inferiority. Family members, the school, and peers all have the power to enhance or defeat a child's sense of industry. Children need positive feedback that their efforts are worthwhile.

Moral development is enhanced by identification with and modeling of adults with high ethical standards. It is also tied to cognitive development and disciplinary techniques. Prosocial behaviors are enhanced by affectionate parents who encourage high self-esteem as well as high regard for others. Parents may use authoritarian, authoritative, permissive, or neglectful patterns of discipline. The authoritative pattern is the most effective and is also preferred by children.

Gender-roles may be moving toward androgyny (each human acquiring both male and female traits) with more mothers working outside the home and more fathers participating in child care.

More children are being raised in single-parent families and/or learning to adjust to stepparents as separations, divorces, and remarriages become more common. Separation from a loved parent is traumatic. Behavioral effects are seen for at least a year.

The influence of schoolteachers and the peer group is related to each child's self-concept, parent–child affection bonds, and the amount of time spent with these significant others.

Television and computers can be called electronic socializers. Most children grow up spending more time in front of the TV set than in school. These "family members" can be used wisely and can enhance socialization. They can also teach messages about violence and stereotyped gender behaviors.

Key Concepts

dental caries	mediation	meritocracy	premorality
Heimlich maneuver	metacognition	creativity	conventional morality
hay fever	concrete operational	specific reading disorder	prosocial behaviors
asthma	stage	attentional deficit disor-	gender-role models
diabetes	numbering	der	expressive orientation
epilepsy	reversibility	learning disability	instrumental orientation
enuresis	reciprocity	mental retardation	androgyny
encopresis	conservation	giftedness	single parenting
motor tics	stuttering	industry versus inferior-	stepparenting
metamemory	intelligence quotient	ity	school phobia
encoding	Rosenthal effect	morality training	peer group
	Jensenism		

Questions for Review

1. Outline a day's nutritional program for a school-age child suggesting what you will serve for breakfast, pack in the school lunch, and provide for dinner. Will snacks be provided? Desserts? If so, what will they be?

2. Learning involves an ability to select or discard certain amounts of irrelevant material. How do you think the following affect the learning process: depression, unhappy home atmosphere, poor health, feelings of inferiority? Be specific in your answers. Consider what has been discussed in previous chapters on cognitive development and emotional development.

3. What side would you take on the inheritance of intelligence question? Do you believe that most of intelligence is determined by inheritance and that only a minimal amount of intelligence can be affected by environmental stimulation, or do you believe that intelligence is almost equally affected by inheritance and

environment? Discuss. If possible, use some real-life examples to support your answer.

4. Discuss particular ways in which the family can foster the positive resolution of what Erikson described as the *industry versus inferiority* conflict during middle–late childhood. Also describe the ways the family can negatively influence this resolution.

5. Some individuals argue that male and female children are "born different" and that most sex-role behavior is only minimally influenced by environment. Others argue that "male" and "female" behavior is generally socialized into children and is not innate. To which viewpoint do you subscribe? Discuss.

6. There is often a tug-of-war between the values children are exposed to in the home and those of their peers. How can parents be consistent and adhere to their values without creating greater conflict within the child by putting down the child's friends?

Further Readings

Bolger, N., Caspi, A., Downey, G., and Moorehouse, M. (eds.) (1988). *Persons in context: Developmental processes.* Cambridge, UK: Cambridge University Press.
Chapters by several experts in child development present the issues of raising children within the contemporary human ecology framework. Working mothers, divorce, remarriage, and other social changes have changed family life.

Coles, R. (1986). *The moral life of children.* Boston: Atlantic Monthly Press.
Coles has traveled across America having conversations with children of all races and social statuses. He

reports their views on topics such as social injustice, inequality, school integration, and the threat of war.

Gibbs, J. R., and Huang, L. N. (1989). *Children of color: Psychological interventions with minority youth.* San Francisco: Jossey-Bass.
In this multicultural, pluralistic society, children should be celebrated, whatever their differences. This book helps explain cultural expectations, family structures, language, and discrimination concerns of Native Americans, Asian Americans, Hispanic Americans, and African Americans.

Gilligan, C. (1982). *In a different voice.* Cambridge, MA: Harvard University Press.

Males and females are socialized to different gender roles. In the past, men's behaviors and values have been studied. Gilligan explores the sense of relationship in girls and its effect on empathy, intimacy, and moral choices.

Segilman, M., and Benjamin, R. (eds.) (1989). *Ordinary families, special children*. New York: Guilford Press.
Children with one or more disabilities pose special concerns for parents, school, and friends. This edited book provides several suggestions for ways in which others can respond more effectively to the needs of special children.

Sternberg, R. J. (1988). *The triarchic mind*. New York: Penguin Books.
This book is more than another description of intelligence. It includes exercises to challenge and develop intellectual potential and suggestions on how to apply intelligence to performance tasks.

Physical Development
Puberty
Nutrition
Health Maintenance
Cognitive Development
Piaget's Formal Operations Stage
Sex Differences in Cognition
Psychosocial Development
Erikson's Identity versus Role
  Confusion
Parent–Child Relationships
Alienation
Peer Interactions
School Interactions
Sexual Behaviors

Adolescence 7

Most people cannot recall a particular time when they entered adolescence and left childhood behind. In our society the adolescent period often seems to be a holding pattern between childhood and adulthood (see Figure 7-1). In early adolescence it is easy to slip back into the role of a child to suit a particular purpose. In early adulthood many individuals choose to slip back into adolescent roles.

Adolescence is often defined by both physical and social hallmarks. It is a period of time marked by the biological changes of puberty, and it is a transitional time socially. The adolescent becomes identified as a person increasingly able to make his or her own decisions about school, leisure, employment, and friends. Adolescence ends with an independence from the family of origin, brought about by marriage or a full-time job. For some people adolescence may begin at age eleven or twelve and go on through the middle to late twenties. For others it may start at age fourteen or fifteen and end within a year. Physical, cognitive, and social factors all help determine the length of the adolescent period.

> You cannot teach a person anything. You can only help him to find it for himself.
> —*Galileo*
>
> The main business of the adolescent is through gentle transaction to stop being one.
> —*Arthur Koestler*

Physical Development

The physical changes of adolescence lead to new problems for the growing, developing human. It is not easy to adjust to all the bodily changes that occur. When an adolescent looks in the mirror, he or she is apt to see constant changes in appearance, real or imagined. Increases in height and weight, budding sex organs, body hair, facial blemishes, oversized hands or feet are just some of the changes that may confront the adolescent. The lack of these things, if friends have them, may also worry the teenager.

Puberty

Puberty encompasses the one to two years of rapid growth during which individuals become capable of sexual reproduction. Sexual maturity for a girl is often defined as the time of the first menstrual period, but this is slightly inaccurate. Most girls are not immediately fertile after beginning to menstruate. They may have anovulatory cycles (not productive of mature ova) for one of two years before they can actually bear children.

It is harder to mark a point in time when boys reach sexual maturity or have the

Goldie was born in the Russian Ukraine at the turn of the 20th century into extreme poverty, cold, and hunger. There had been five babies lost between Goldie's older sister Sheyna's birth and her own birth. Her parents wondered if Goldie, too, would die, either of starvation or from Cossack weapons during frequent *pogroms* (organized massacres of Jews).

Goldie survived. She was zealously protected and guided by Sheyna, nine years her senior, who taught her to read and write. Goldie's father escaped to America when she was five, using illegal papers and secret border crossings. While Goldie's mother struggled to keep her family alive, 14-year-old Sheyna joined a Zionist movement. Zionists were regularly abducted and beaten by the police. Sheyna turned a deaf ear to her mother's pleas to disassociate from them. Goldie saw Sheyna as a heroine, a mentor, a shining example of appropriate teenage idealism and defiance.

When Goldie was eight and Sheyna was seventeen, the mother and daughters were able to leave Russia for America by way of more illegal papers, bribes, and boundary runs. They suffered stolen luggage, seasickness, cramped quarters, and starvation, but they arrived alive in the "New World." They went to Milwaukee to join Goldie's father.

Life in the "goldene medina" continued to be difficult. Sheyna was a disobedient sullen adolescent. She missed her boyfriend from the Zionist group in the Ukraine. He had been arrested and jailed for his political activities there. Sheyna soon fell ill with tuberculosis. She had to be sent to a sanitarium in the mountains near Denver.

Goldie wanted to be like her sister. As she later wrote, "Sheyna was the one person whose praise and approval meant most to me."* By the age of eleven, Goldie was involved in her first political cause. She organized a town meeting for the purpose of raising money for school books for children. Milwaukee responded with a considerable outpouring of money and newspaper praise for Goldie.

At age fourteen, Goldie left her parents. She had finished elementary school as valedictorian of her class. She wanted to continue her education in high school, but her parents said no. Her father warned, "It doesn't pay to be too clever. Men don't like smart girls."* Her mother had quietly arranged a marriage for her to a business man in his early thirties, twice her age! Goldie refused to obey. She enrolled in high school and rejected the marriage proposal. The family disputes became bitter. Goldie wrote a furious letter to Sheyna in Denver. Sheyna responded, "Come to me." By this time, Sheyna's boyfriend, Shamai, had escaped from his Russian prison and found his way to Denver to marry Sheyna. They were poor but protective of Goldie's right to do what she wanted to do.

Goldie became politically active in Denver. She joined a Zionist movement with Sheyna and Shamai. She met and fell in love with Morris Meyerson, a Zionist man six years older than she. Suddenly Sheyna ceased to be Goldie's supporter, ordering her to spend less time with Morris. Goldie, at age sixteen, left her sister's home. She moved in with two women with advanced tuberculosis who allowed her to see Morris. Luckily, she did not contract the disease. She continued school, politics, and dating.

When Goldie was seventeen, she returned to Milwaukee to attend a two-year teacher's training college. Her parents let her have her way since she was completely self-supporting. When she was nineteen, she married Morris Meyerson. When she was twenty-three, she and Morris emigrated to Israel. Eventually, Golda Meir became Israel's prime minister.

Would Golda have had such political fervor if it were not for the example set by the adolescent Sheyna? Many teenagers run away from home at age fourteen. Is it an acceptable behavior?

---

*Meir, G. (1975). *My Life by Golda Meir*. New York: G. P. Putnam's Sons.

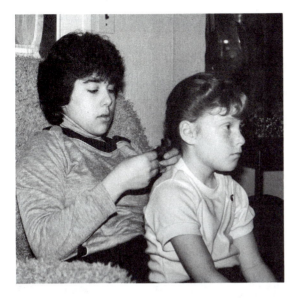

Figure 7-1
An adolescent undergoes rapid changes—from child to adult, from dependent to self-sufficient, from unity to opposition with family members.

ability to produce and ejaculate sperm. One sign sometimes used to mark sexual maturity is the experience of wet dreams. However, wet dreams are environmentally influenced and may occur long after sexual maturity. A more scientific way to deterine male fertility is to examine urine microscopically for evidence of sperm.

In both girls and boys a growth spurt accompanies puberty. If one feels the need to pinpoint sexual maturity, one can keep regular measurements of changes in height, weight, and body proportions during adolescence. The period of most rapid growth is a good indication of the time when sexual maturity is being achieved (see Figure 7-2).

The physical hallmarks of **pubescence** (changes accompanying the arrival of sexual maturity) vary from individual to individual. They are initiated by the periodic secretion of luteinizing hormone releasing hormone (LHRH) by the hypothalamus in the brain (see Figure 7-3). These periodic bursts of LHRH cause the pituitary gland in the brain to release gonadotropic hormones: follicle stimulating hormone (FSH), luteinizing hormone (LH), and interstitial cell stimulating hormone (ICSH). The pituitary also releases a somatotropic hormone: human growth hormone (HGH). *Soma* means body; *tropic*

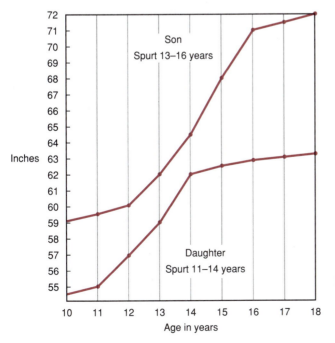

Figure 7-2
The growth spurts in height that accompanied puberty in two siblings.

Figure 7-3
Puberty is triggered when LHRH is released by the hypothalamus. It stimulates the pituitary to send out gonadotropins (FSH, LH, ICSH) which are targeted to the gonads. The female gonads, ovaries, produce estrogen and progesterone. The male gonads, testes, produce testosterone. The adrenal glands produce both estrogens and androgens for both sexes.

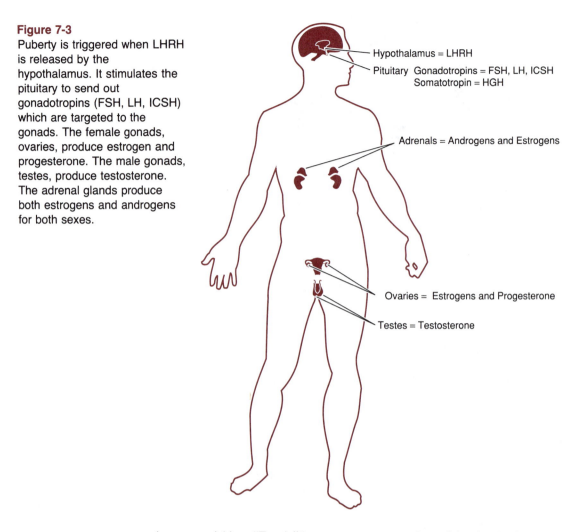

Hypothalamus = LHRH

Pituitary Gonadotropins = FSH, LH, ICSH
Somatotropin = HGH

Adrenals = Androgens and Estrogens

Ovaries = Estrogens and Progesterone

Testes = Testosterone

means turning or nourishing. "Tropic" hormones turn on and nourish other body parts: gonadotropins stimulate the gonads; somatotropins stimulate the body. Many of the secondary sexual characteristics (to be discussed shortly) are turned on by the somatotropic hormone HGH.

Under the influence of gonadotropins (FSH, LH, ICSH), the testes begin the process of spermatogenesis (see Chapter 3, p. 60). A by-product of meiotic cell division (turning primordial sperm into mature sperm) in the testes is the sex hormone testosterone. Testosterone is the most potent of the **androgens** (male sex hormones). The adrenal glands also produce some androgens and some estrogens for both males and females (see Figure 7-3).

Under the influence of the gonadotropins (FSH, LH), the ovaries begin the process of ovulation (see Chapter 3, p. 57, and color plates 9 and 15 in center of textbook). A by-product of meiotic cell divison (turning primordial ova into mature ova) in the ovaries is the sex hormone estradiol. Estradiol is the most potent of the **estrogens** (female sex hormones). The adrenal glands also produce some estrogens and some androgens for females. Once one ovum is ovulated, the remaining corpus luteum produces **progesterone,** a sex hormone that helps prepare the lining of the uterus for implantation of a fertilized ovum.

In both males and females breast budding, characterized by firm nodularity, may be the first indication of increased sex hormone production and the approach of adolescence. Pubic hair grows slowly. Young adolescent males may be very confused about the pain and slight swelling of their breasts at the onset of puberty. It is a normal response to adrenal estrogens. It disappears as testosterone exerts its masculinizing influences.

Increased production of sex hormones and spermatogenesis in boys causes the penis and testes to enlarge. The changes in males and females that contribute to reproductive maturity are called **primary sexual characteristics.** A primary sexual characteristic of females is menstruation.

The onset of menstruation is known as **menarche.** A female begins menstruating when her production of estrogen, in response to gonadotropins, becomes cyclic (see Figure 7-4). An increased production of estrogen occurs approximately once each month as Graafian follicles develop prior to the discharge of an ovum. After ovulation the corpus luteum gradually degenerates unless fertilization of the ovum took place. The corpus luteum's degeneration causes a decreased production of estrogen and progesterone. One or two days after the production of hormones stops, the uterus sheds the lining it had developed for the eventuality of a pregnancy. This discharge of the bloody lining is **menstruation.** The lowered estrogen and progesterone levels also trigger the pituitary to produce more gonadotropins which in turn stimulate the ovaries to ripen more follicles. Rising estrogen levels stimulate growth of the endometrial lining on the inner uterine wall in readiness for a pregnancy. If pregnancy doesn't occur, decreased hormone levels will again trigger the shedding of this lining in another menstrual period. The first several menstrual periods of puberty are often irregular in both amount of flow and timing. The interval between menses may be longer or shorter than is characteristic later in the woman's life (Silver, 1984).

The age at which sexual maturity is reached in American girls varies from nine to seventeen years, with an average age of first menstruation now at twelve years, five months. The range for sexual maturity in American boys is estimated to be from ten to eighteen. Girls, on the average, reach sexual maturity about two years ahead of boys (see Figure 7-5). As noted in Chapter 5, there is a trend toward each generation growing larger than the last. Tanner (1962) reported a similar trend moving the age of puberty down with each successive generation. He reported that in 1840 the average girl's first menstrual period occurred in her seventeenth year. Bullough (1981), after examining ancient Roman, medieval, and nineteenth-century medical documents, questioned Tanner's theory. His data show an onset of menstruation between the ages of twelve and fourteen in the past. Tanner's claim of average menarche at seventeen in the 1840s was based on a small, isolated Norwegian population. Bullough found a slight decline in the twentieth century (about one year), probably due to improved nutrition and health care. Climate apparently has little effect on age of menarche. Nigerian and Eskimo girls begin menstruating at approximately the same ages. Likewise, race appears to have little effect when nutritional and health factors are similar (Silver, 1984).

Menstruation may be accompanied by expectations of physical discomfort, increased emotionality, poor school performance, and the need to interrupt regular activities (Clarke and Ruble, 1978). These negative attitudes and expectations are culture bound and reportedly come from parents, friends, health classes, books, and TV. Such beliefs in menstrual distress can become a self-fulfilling prophecy. Brooks-Gunn and Ruble (1982) found that girls who learned about menstrual distress from male sources rated

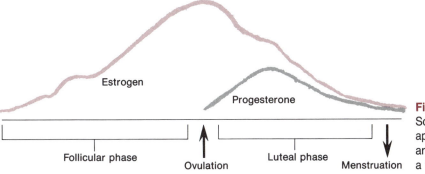

Estrogen

Progesterone

Follicular phase   Ovulation   Luteal phase   Menstruation

Figure 7-4
Schematic presentation of approximate monthly estrogen and progesterone fluctuations in a female after puberty.

menstruation as more debilitating and negative than girls who learned from female sources. Premenarcheal girls (those who have not yet reached menarche) usually expect to experience more distress (pain, water retention, irritability, poor concentration) than postmenarcheal girls. Early maturers and girls who were unprepared for their menarches usually have more negative attitudes about their periods than well-prepared girls and girls who achieved menarche at later ages (Ruble and Brooks-Gunn, 1982). Initially, menarche creates confusion, ambivalence, and inconvenience. Most girls report being scared and upset at their first period (Whisnant and Zegans, 1975; Weideger, 1976) and more self-conscious afterward (Koff, Rierdan, and Jacobson, 1981). However, Greif and Ulman (1982) reported that some postmenarcheal girls later described menarche as a positive event that helped them "fit in" with other girls and reorganize and clarify their sexual identity.

Menstrual cramps are often given as reasons for school absence or refusal to participate in athletics. However, nonprescription medicines containing aspirin or acetaminophen can be used to alleviate cramping if and when it occurs, and few adolescent females need to curtail their regular activities because of menstruation.

Premenstrual syndrome is more common in older women than in adolescents and is discussed in Chapter 9. Mood changes in teenagers related to menstruation can usually be consciously controlled (Muller, 1985).

Secondary sexual characteristics are changes in body shape and size brought on by sex hormones but not necessary for reproduction. Females develop broader hips as they grow older. Hair grows on their arms and legs, in their axillae (armpits), and, in some girls, on the upper lip or near the nipples of the breasts as well. Such facial and chest hair does not grow as coarse and thick as it does on males. Sweat glands become active, causing body odors and acne.

Males also develop acne and increased overall body perspiration at puberty. They develop coarse facial and body hair as well as pubic and axillary hair. Testosterone acts on the receptor cells of their shoulders, causing them to broaden (Tanner, 1974). While females develop more body fat, males develop more muscle tissue. Males average 50% muscle and 15% fat, while females average 40% muscle and 25% fat after puberty.

Before puberty girls and boys are similar in muscle strength. However, during pubescence boys have a greater increase in muscle size and strength and develop more muscle mass and more force per gram of muscle (Tanner, 1974). This is especially true of the upper body. Boys develop proportionately longer limbs, while girls have proportionately larger trunks and wider pelvic girdles (see Figure 7-6). The femurs of females are attached to the pelvis at more oblique angles than those of males (Tanner, 1962). The center of gravity in males is more medially located because of their wider shoulders and narrower hips. Males have still another advantage after puberty: they develop more aerobic power—greater ability to get oxygen to body cells and get rid of waste products. Many of these physical differences between the sexes give the average male an advantage over the average female in our traditional sports, although there are always exceptions. In long-distance swimming, for example, females have an advantage because of their narrower shoulders, lighter muscles, and more fat-cell-insulated and buoyant bodies.

The heart approximately doubles its weight in both sexes during adolescence, growing slightly larger in boys than in girls. Blood pressure also rises appreciably, with males eventually having higher systolic pressure than females.

Both boys and girls experience voice changes. Girls' voices become fuller and richer due to the lengthening of their vocal cords. Boys' voices become lower and louder. The deeper male voice results from enlargement of the larynx (the Adam's apple) and the lengthening of the vocal cords. In the process of acquiring a mature male voice, a boy may occasionally experience embarrassing voice breaks or squeaks in the middle of sentences. Although parents may be proud of this sign that their son is maturing, siblings and friends usually giggle.

When teenagers fail to develop signs of sexual maturity at the time when their friends are changing, their self-concept and self-esteem can be adversely affected. They may feel different, unacceptable, alone. Girls usually are less affected by **late maturation** than boys because a small or flat-chested female is not without sex appeal in our society. A late-maturing girl may also find that her lithe, slender body with narrower hips makes it easier for her to excel in sports. However, late-maturing girls may gravitate toward a younger peer group, or they may be excessively modest among their own age-mates.

Late-maturing boys may feel inferior, less secure, and anxious. Research suggests they are more emotionally expressive (eager, animated, energetic, talkative), resort to more attention-seeking behaviors, and have more body and social acceptance concerns than their normally maturing peers (Clausen, 1975). Occasionally they may withdraw from social activities, possibly due to embarrassment about their small size, smooth faces, and high-pitched voices. Late-maturing boys tend to be more passive in boy–girl relationships. Gillis (1982) discussed the prevalence of **heightism** in our society (similiar to racism and sexism). He felt that late-maturing teenage boys may begin smoking to try to give an older appearance or may turn to drugs to ease anxiety and relieve depression about being smaller. He wrote that the male-taller, female-smaller rule has got to go.

Figure 7-6
Body shapes are sex differentiated after puberty. Boys have broader shoulders, narrower hips, and longer limbs. Girls have breasts, narrower waists, wider hips, and lower centers of gravity.

In rare cases, puberty may begin before age nine in girls or before age ten in boys. This is known as **precocious puberty.** It may be inherited in 5 to 10% of boys but its cause in girls remains a mystery. Occasionally, a benign tumor is found on the hypothalamus, causing early release of LHRH, the hormone that triggers puberty. Children with precocious puberty may feel isolated and socially rejected. Boys often become more aggressive and hyperactive than their peers. Adults often expect the child to act as old as he or she looks, rather than as old as he or she is, which is frustrating for the child. Many physicians try to delay sexual maturation with hormone therapy in precocious children to allow them to begin puberty later, at a more appropriate age (Johnson, 1983).

Nutrition

The nutritional needs of adolescents and the role of good nutrition in maintaining physical and emotional health cannot be overemphasized. Teenagers need to eat more during pubescence to provide their bodies with the nutrients necessary for rapidly accelerating growth. Appetites normally correspond with the need for more food. However, many teenagers get into trouble nutritionally. They eat the wrong kinds of foods, they overeat, or they refuse to eat to keep fashionably slim.

Calcium and iron have been identified as the most common deficiencies in adolescent diets. Protein deficiency also frequently accompanies iron deficiency. The substitution of sodas for milk and snack foods for meals helps to account for these deficits. Refined sugars, salt, and saturated fats are the most common excesses in adolescent diets. They can contribute to many unnecessary health problems (see Figure 7-7).

Iron deficiency results in a reduced amount of blood hemoglobin (the substance that carries oxygen) and anemia (a reduced amount of red blood cells). The anemia may be manifested by lack of energy, quick fatigue on exertion, slow learning, poor concentration, poor muscle tone, shortness of breath, and a pale appearance. Although both sexes may have **iron deficiency anemia,** it is much more common in teenage girls. They lose iron each month in their menstrual flow and may not eat enough of the iron-rich foods (red meats, fortified cereals and breads, green leafy vegetables) to replace it.

Malnourished people can appear of normal weight or even overweight due to their

Figure 7-7

Fast foods and empty calorie snacks are overloading adolescents' diets with saturated fats, sugars, and salt.

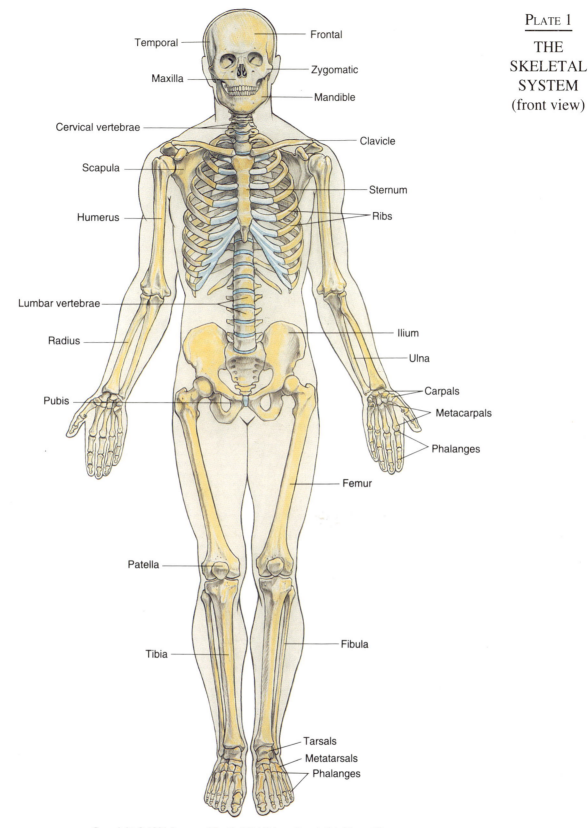

Temporal

Frontal

Maxilla

Zygomatic

Mandible

Cervical vertebrae

Clavicle

Scapula

Sternum

Humerus

Ribs

Lumbar vertebrae

Ilium

Radius

Ulna

Pubis

Carpals

Metacarpals

Phalanges

Femur

Patella

Fibula

Tibia

Tarsals

Metatarsals

Phalanges

PLATE 1

THE
SKELETAL
SYSTEM
(front view)

PLATE 2

THE
SKELETAL
SYSTEM
(side and
back views)

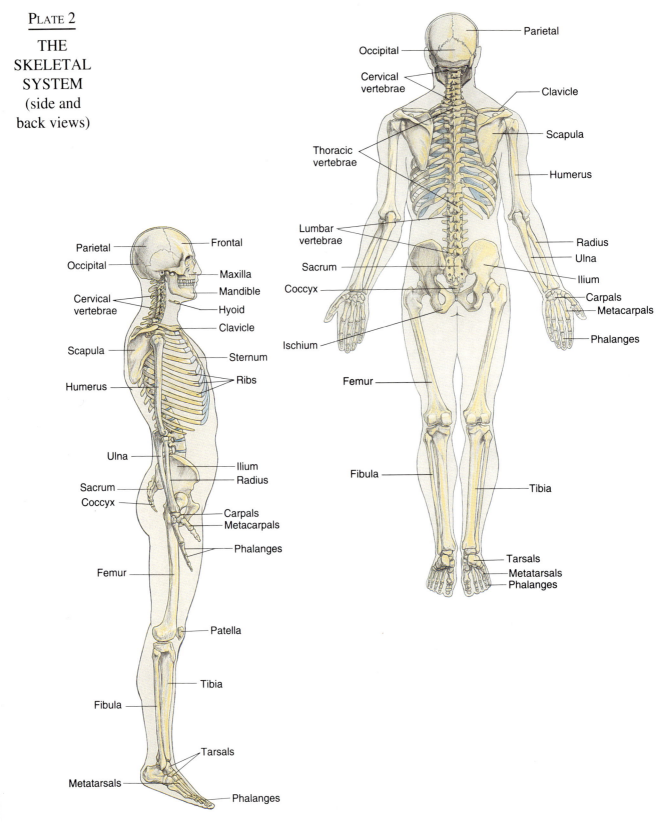

Parietal

Occipital

Cervical
vertebrae

Thoracic
vertebrae

Clavicle

Scapula

Humerus

Lumbar
vertebrae

Sacrum

Coccyx

Ischium

Radius

Ulna

Ilium

Carpals

Metacarpals

Phalanges

Femur

Fibula

Tibia

Tarsals

Metatarsals

Phalanges

Parietal

Occipital

Cervical
vertebrae

Scapula

Humerus

Ulna

Sacrum

Coccyx

Femur

Fibula

Frontal

Maxilla

Mandible

Hyoid

Clavicle

Sternum

Ribs

Ilium

Radius

Carpals

Metacarpals

Phalanges

Patella

Tibia

Metatarsals

Tarsals

Phalanges

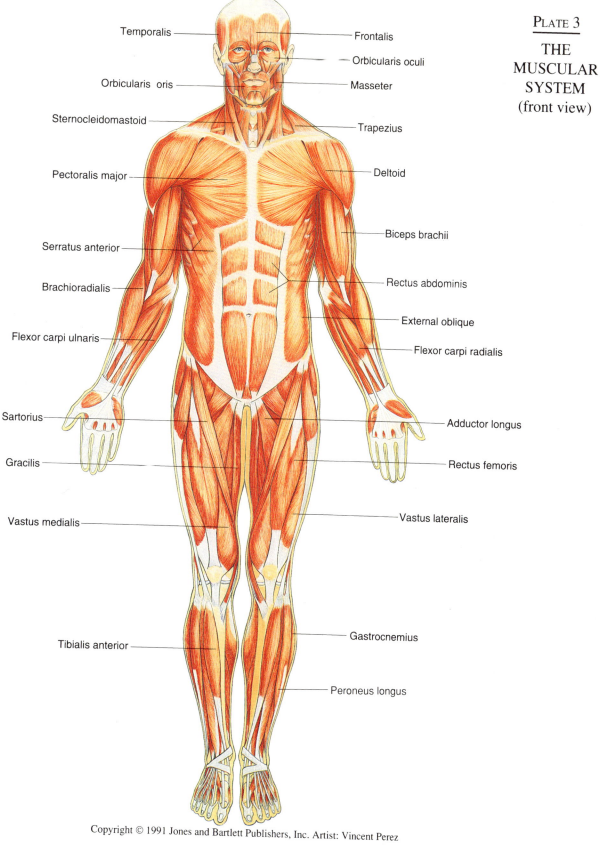

PLATE 3

THE
MUSCULAR
SYSTEM
(front view)

Temporalis

Frontalis

Orbicularis oculi

Orbicularis oris

Masseter

Sternocleidomastoid

Trapezius

Pectoralis major

Deltoid

Biceps brachii

Serratus anterior

Rectus abdominis

Brachioradialis

External oblique

Flexor carpi ulnaris

Flexor carpi radialis

Sartorius

Adductor longus

Gracilis

Rectus femoris

Vastus medialis

Vastus lateralis

Tibialis anterior

Gastrocnemius

Peroneus longus

PLATE 4

THE
MUSCULAR
SYSTEM
(side and
back views)

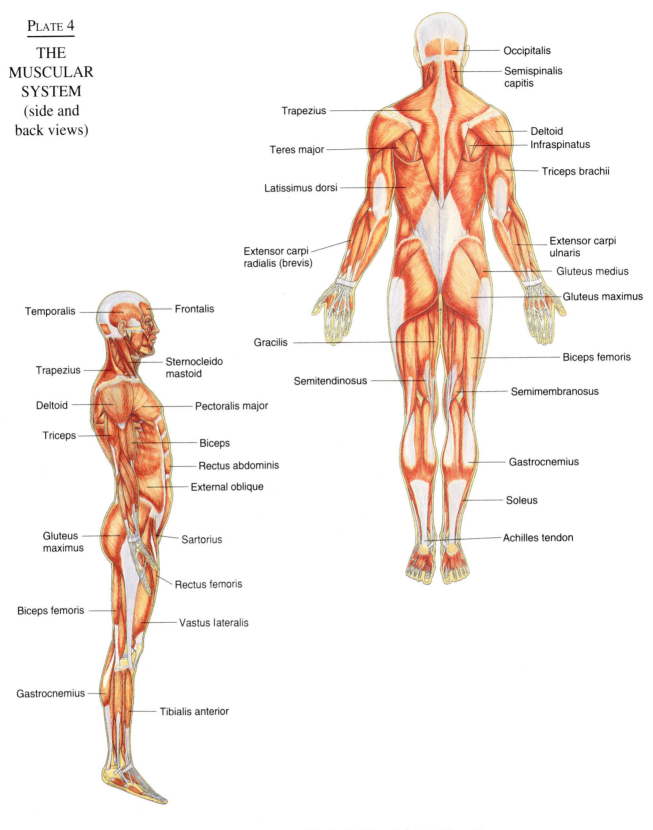

Occipitalis
Semispinalis capitis
Trapezius
Deltoid
Infraspinatus
Teres major
Triceps brachii
Latissimus dorsi
Extensor carpi radialis (brevis)
Extensor carpi ulnaris
Gluteus medius
Gluteus maximus
Gracilis
Biceps femoris
Semitendinosus
Semimembranosus
Gastrocnemius
Soleus
Achilles tendon

Temporalis
Frontalis
Trapezius
Sternocleido mastoid
Deltoid
Pectoralis major
Triceps
Biceps
Rectus abdominis
External oblique
Gluteus maximus
Sartorius
Rectus femoris
Biceps femoris
Vastus lateralis
Gastrocnemius
Tibialis anterior

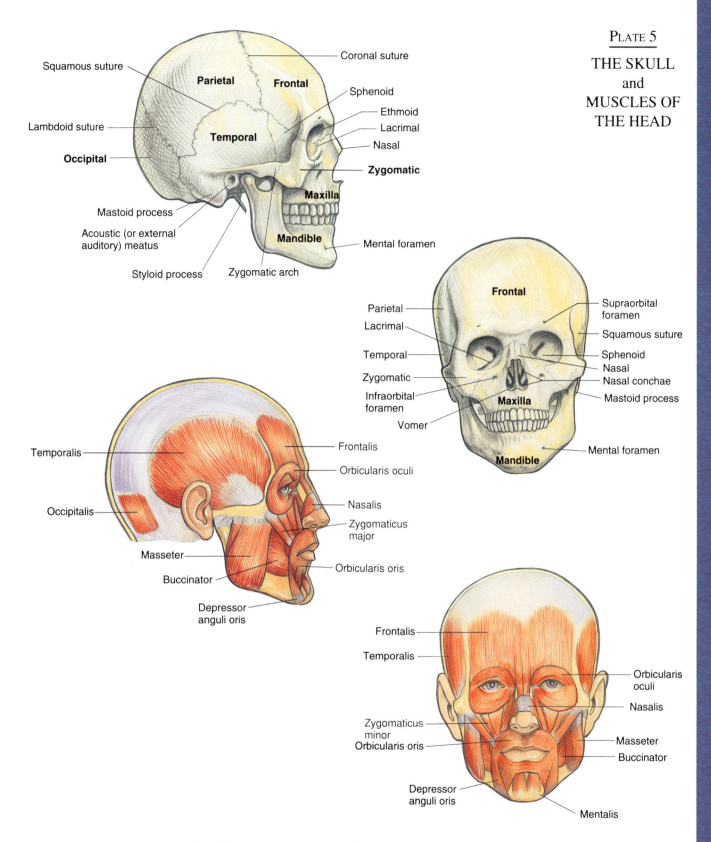

PLATE 5

THE SKULL
and
MUSCLES OF
THE HEAD

Squamous suture

Parietal **Frontal**

Coronal suture

Sphenoid

Ethmoid

Lacrimal

Nasal

Lambdoid suture

Temporal

Occipital

Zygomatic

Maxilla

Mastoid process

Acoustic (or external auditory) meatus

Mandible

Mental foramen

Styloid process

Zygomatic arch

Frontal

Parietal

Supraorbital foramen

Lacrimal

Squamous suture

Temporal

Sphenoid

Nasal

Zygomatic

Nasal conchae

Infraorbital foramen

Mastoid process

Maxilla

Vomer

Mandible

Mental foramen

Temporalis

Frontalis

Orbicularis oculi

Occipitalis

Nasalis

Zygomaticus major

Masseter

Orbicularis oris

Buccinator

Depressor anguli oris

Frontalis

Temporalis

Orbicularis oculi

Nasalis

Zygomaticus minor

Orbicularis oris

Masseter

Buccinator

Depressor anguli oris

Mentalis

PLATE 6

THE
ARTERIAL
SYSTEM
and
THE
VENOUS
SYSTEM

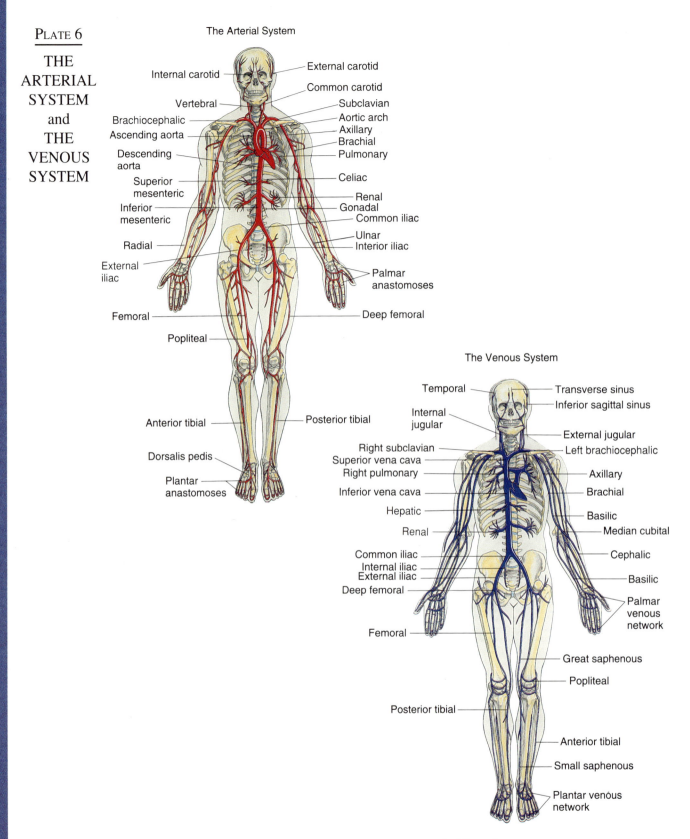

The Arterial System

Internal carotid
External carotid
Common carotid
Vertebral
Subclavian
Brachiocephalic
Aortic arch
Ascending aorta
Axillary
Brachial
Descending aorta
Pulmonary
Superior mesenteric
Celiac
Renal
Inferior mesenteric
Gonadal
Common iliac
Radial
Ulnar
Interior iliac
External iliac
Palmar anastomoses
Femoral
Deep femoral
Popliteal
Anterior tibial
Posterior tibial
Dorsalis pedis
Plantar anastomoses

The Venous System

Temporal
Transverse sinus
Inferior sagittal sinus
Internal jugular
External jugular
Right subclavian
Left brachiocephalic
Superior vena cava
Axillary
Right pulmonary
Brachial
Inferior vena cava
Basilic
Hepatic
Median cubital
Renal
Cephalic
Common iliac
Internal iliac
Basilic
External iliac
Deep femoral
Palmar venous network
Femoral
Great saphenous
Popliteal
Posterior tibial
Anterior tibial
Small saphenous
Plantar venous network

PLATE 7

THE
ARTERIAL-
VENOUS
SYSTEM

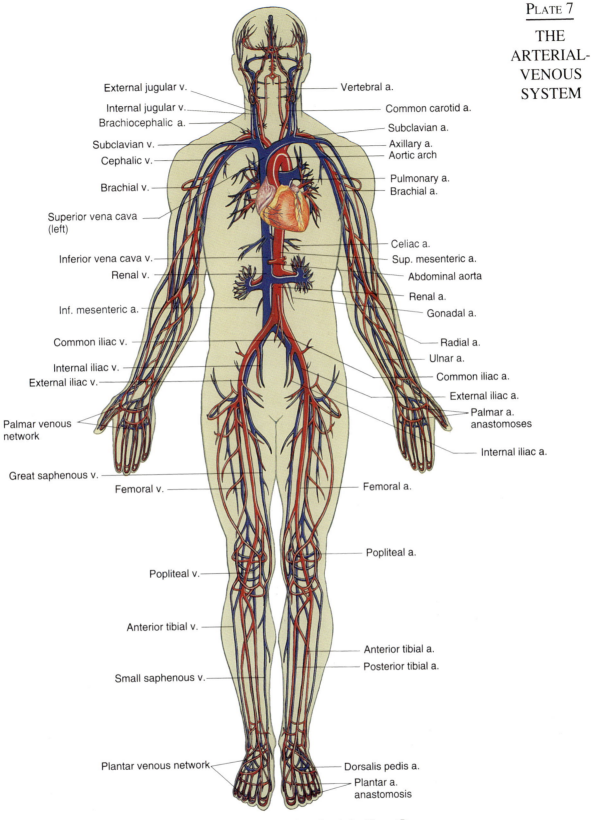

External jugular v.

Internal jugular v.

Brachiocephalic a.

Subclavian v.

Cephalic v.

Brachial v.

Superior vena cava
(left)

Inferior vena cava v.

Renal v.

Inf. mesenteric a.

Common iliac v.

Internal iliac v.

External iliac v.

Palmar venous
network

Great saphenous v.

Femoral v.

Popliteal v.

Anterior tibial v.

Small saphenous v.

Plantar venous network

Vertebral a.

Common carotid a.

Subclavian a.

Axillary a.

Aortic arch

Pulmonary a.

Brachial a.

Celiac a.

Sup. mesenteric a.

Abdominal aorta

Renal a.

Gonadal a.

Radial a.

Ulnar a.

Common iliac a.

External iliac a.

Palmar a.
anastomoses

Internal iliac a.

Femoral a.

Popliteal a.

Anterior tibial a.

Posterior tibial a.

Dorsalis pedis a.

Plantar a.
anastomosis

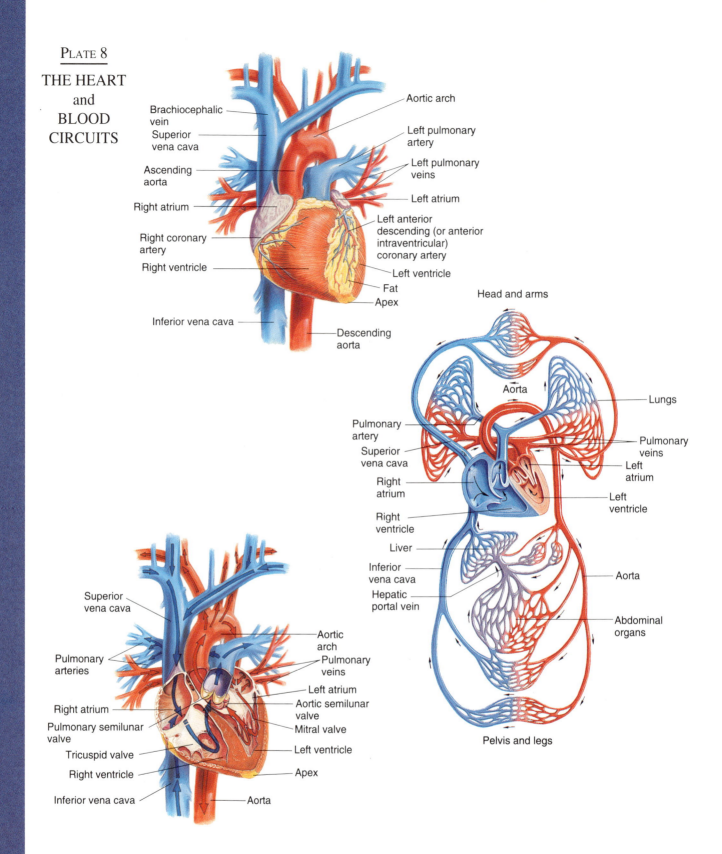

PLATE 8

THE HEART
and
BLOOD
CIRCUITS

Brachiocephalic vein

Superior vena cava

Ascending aorta

Right atrium

Right coronary artery

Right ventricle

Inferior vena cava

Aortic arch

Left pulmonary artery

Left pulmonary veins

Left atrium

Left anterior descending (or anterior intraventricular) coronary artery

Left ventricle

Fat

Apex

Descending aorta

Head and arms

Aorta

Lungs

Pulmonary artery

Superior vena cava

Right atrium

Right ventricle

Liver

Inferior vena cava

Hepatic portal vein

Pulmonary veins

Left atrium

Left ventricle

Aorta

Abdominal organs

Pelvis and legs

Superior vena cava

Pulmonary arteries

Right atrium

Pulmonary semilunar valve

Tricuspid valve

Right ventricle

Inferior vena cava

Aortic arch

Pulmonary veins

Left atrium

Aortic semilunar valve

Mitral valve

Left ventricle

Apex

Aorta

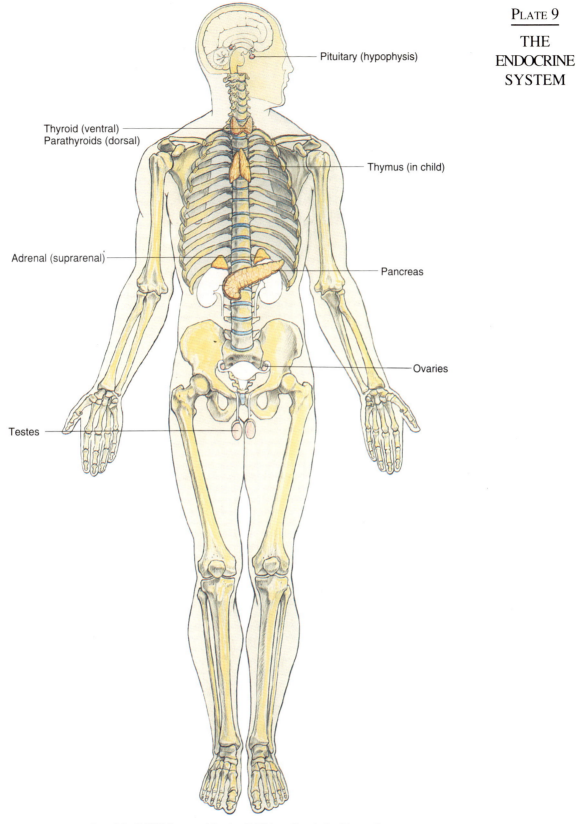

PLATE 9

THE
ENDOCRINE
SYSTEM

Pituitary (hypophysis)

Thyroid (ventral)
Parathyroids (dorsal)

Thymus (in child)

Adrenal (suprarenal)

Pancreas

Ovaries

Testes

PLATE 10

THE
LYMPHATIC
SYSTEM

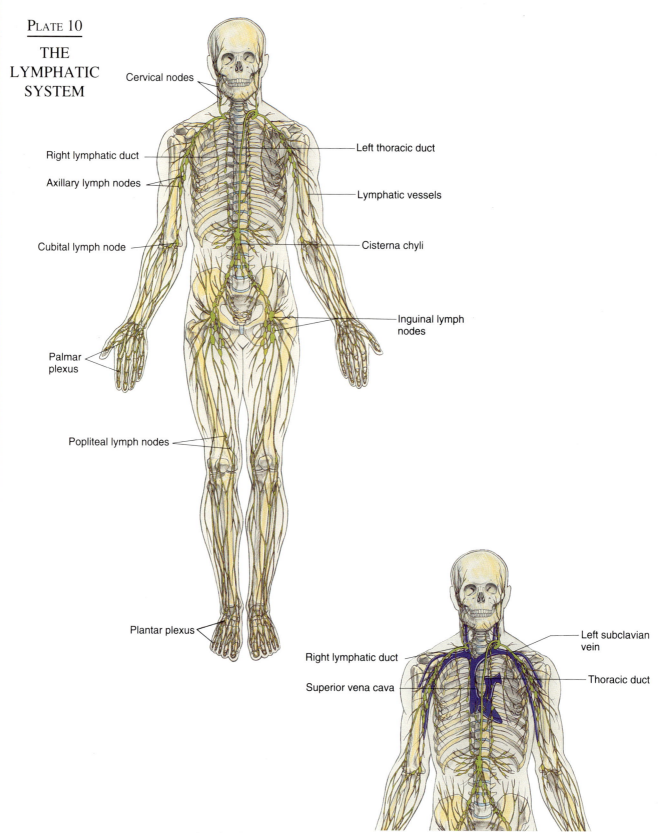

Cervical nodes

Right lymphatic duct

Axillary lymph nodes

Left thoracic duct

Lymphatic vessels

Cubital lymph node

Cisterna chyli

Inguinal lymph nodes

Palmar plexus

Popliteal lymph nodes

Plantar plexus

Right lymphatic duct

Superior vena cava

Left subclavian vein

Thoracic duct

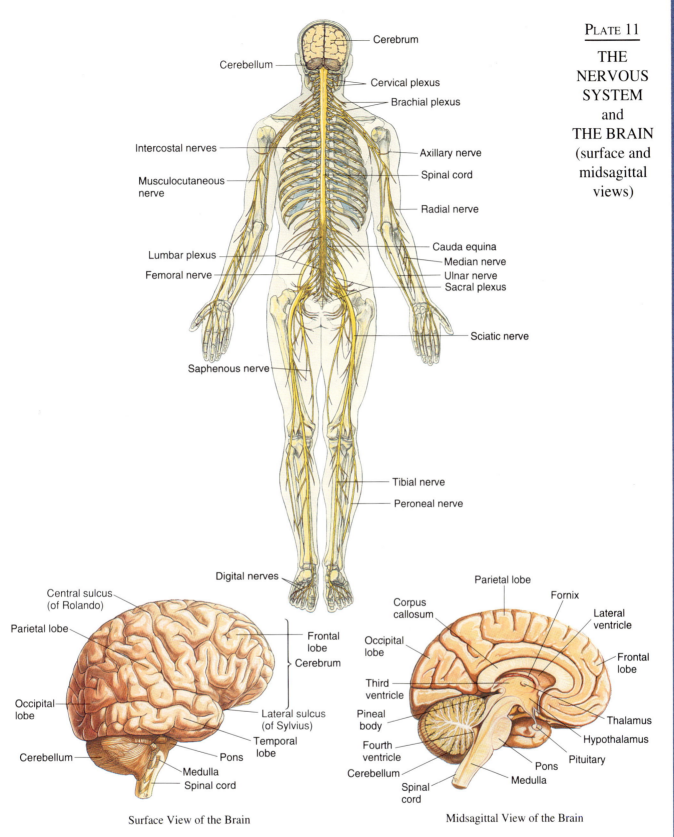

Cerebrum

Cerebellum

Cervical plexus

Brachial plexus

Intercostal nerves

Axillary nerve

Spinal cord

Musculocutaneous nerve

Radial nerve

Lumbar plexus

Cauda equina

Median nerve

Femoral nerve

Ulnar nerve

Sacral plexus

Sciatic nerve

Saphenous nerve

Tibial nerve

Peroneal nerve

Digital nerves

Central sulcus (of Rolando)

Parietal lobe

Occipital lobe

Cerebellum

Medulla

Spinal cord

Frontal lobe

Cerebrum

Lateral sulcus (of Sylvius)

Temporal lobe

Pons

Surface View of the Brain

Parietal lobe

Fornix

Corpus callosum

Lateral ventricle

Occipital lobe

Frontal lobe

Third ventricle

Pineal body

Thalamus

Fourth ventricle

Hypothalamus

Cerebellum

Pituitary

Spinal cord

Pons

Medulla

Midsagittal View of the Brain

PLATE 12

THE
VISCERA

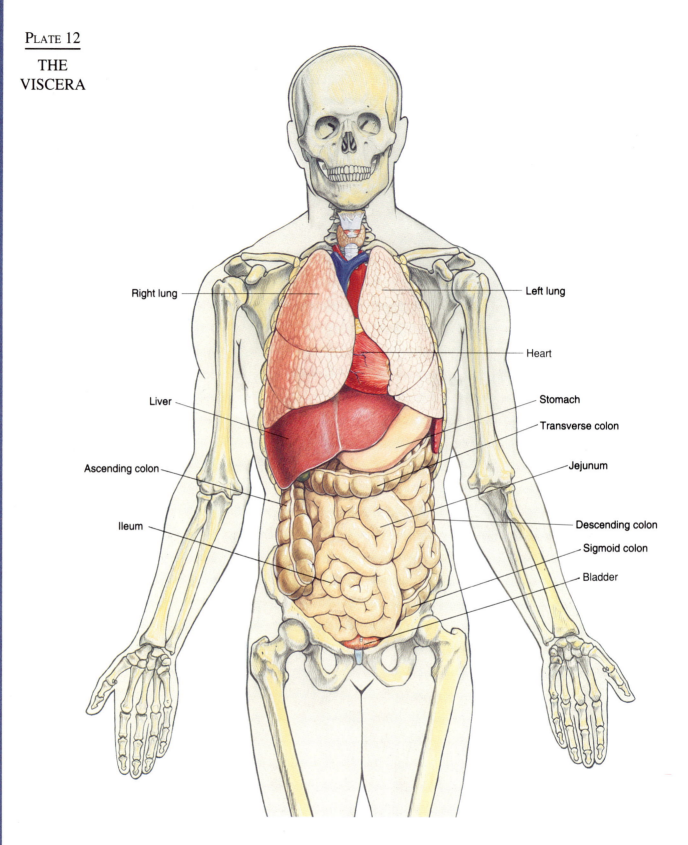

Right lung

Left lung

Heart

Liver

Stomach

Transverse colon

Ascending colon

Jejunum

Ileum

Descending colon

Sigmoid colon

Bladder

PLATE 13

THE
RESPIRATORY
SYSTEM

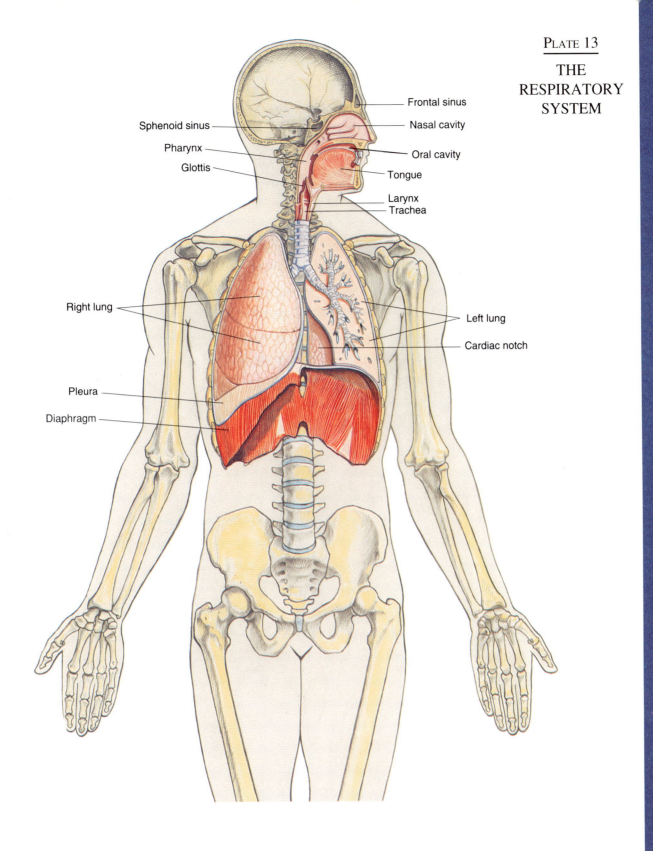

Frontal sinus

Sphenoid sinus

Nasal cavity

Pharynx

Oral cavity

Glottis

Tongue

Larynx
Trachea

Right lung

Left lung

Cardiac notch

Pleura

Diaphragm

PLATE 14

THE
DIGESTIVE
SYSTEM

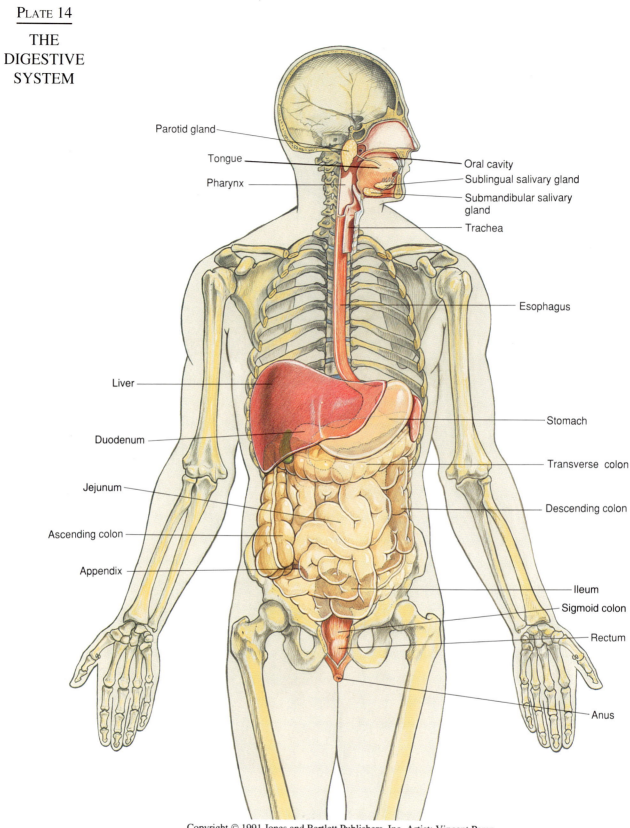

Parotid gland

Tongue

Pharynx

Oral cavity

Sublingual salivary gland

Submandibular salivary gland

Trachea

Esophagus

Liver

Stomach

Duodenum

Transverse colon

Jejunum

Descending colon

Ascending colon

Appendix

Ileum

Sigmoid colon

Rectum

Anus

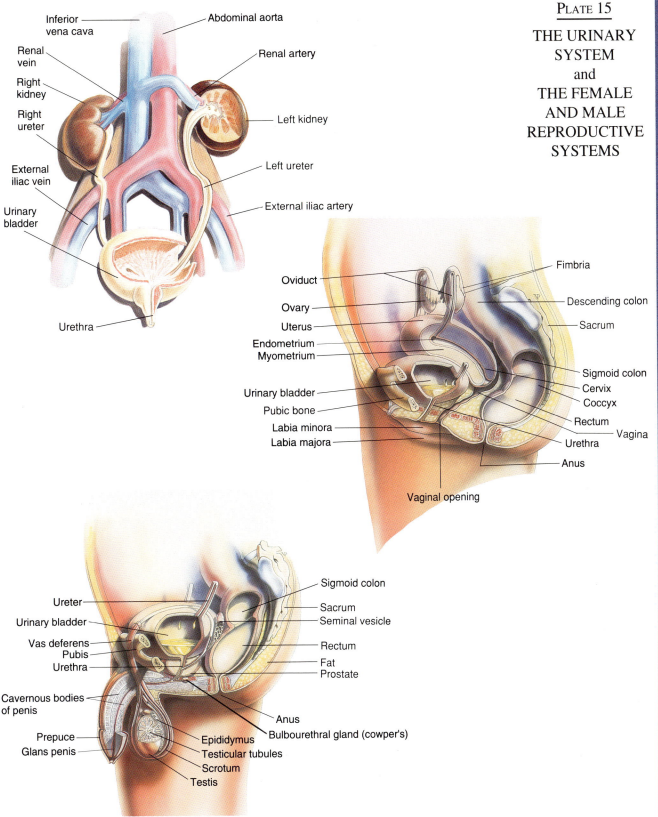

PLATE 15

THE URINARY
SYSTEM
and
THE FEMALE
AND MALE
REPRODUCTIVE
SYSTEMS

Inferior
vena cava

Abdominal aorta

Renal
vein

Renal artery

Right
kidney

Right
ureter

Left kidney

Left ureter

External
iliac vein

External iliac artery

Urinary
bladder

Urethra

Oviduct

Fimbria

Ovary

Descending colon

Uterus

Sacrum

Endometrium
Myometrium

Sigmoid colon

Urinary bladder

Cervix

Pubic bone

Coccyx

Labia minora

Rectum

Labia majora

Vagina

Urethra

Anus

Vaginal opening

Ureter

Sigmoid colon

Urinary bladder

Sacrum

Seminal vesicle

Vas deferens

Rectum

Pubis

Fat

Urethra

Prostate

Cavernous bodies
of penis

Anus

Prepuce

Bulbourethral gland (cowper's)

Glans penis

Epididymus

Testicular tubules

Scrotum

Testis

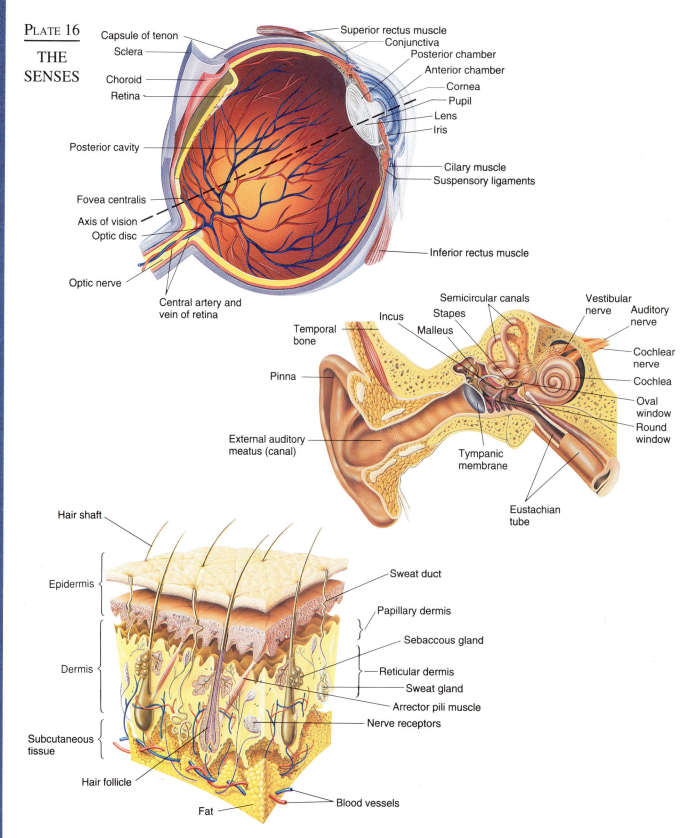

PLATE 16

THE
SENSES

Capsule of tenon
Sclera
Choroid
Retina
Posterior cavity
Fovea centralis
Axis of vision
Optic disc
Optic nerve
Central artery and
vein of retina

Superior rectus muscle
Conjunctiva
Posterior chamber
Anterior chamber
Cornea
Pupil
Lens
Iris
Cilary muscle
Suspensory ligaments
Inferior rectus muscle

Temporal
bone
Pinna
External auditory
meatus (canal)

Incus
Malleus
Stapes
Semicircular canals

Vestibular
nerve
Auditory
nerve
Cochlear
nerve
Cochlea
Oval
window
Round
window

Tympanic
membrane
Eustachian
tube

Hair shaft
Epidermis
Dermis
Subcutaneous
tissue
Hair follicle
Fat

Sweat duct
Papillary dermis
Sebaccous gland
Reticular dermis
Sweat gland
Arrector pili muscle
Nerve receptors
Blood vessels

intake of calories through refined sugars and fats, but they are more susceptible to infections, are mentally sluggish, tend to be irritable, and have the same problems of fatigue that the anemic person has.

Newman and his colleagues (1986) suggested that teenage boys whose diets include a good deal of cholesterol and other saturated fats (as from pork, beef, egg yolks, butter, and cream) may already have fatty streaks of cholesterol and fibrous plaques in their blood vessels, an early sign of atherosclerosis. No fibrous plaques are found in females, who may be protected from early build-ups of plaque due to estrogens.

Nutritionists recommend that daily fat intake should not exceed 30% of total dietary intake (Edlin and Golanty, 1988). Fats are found in protein foods, dairy foods, and in many breads, cereals, and vegetables. Consequently, they do not need to be added to one's diet. Vegetable fats are generally high density (liquid at room temperature) and unsaturated. They are safer. Animal fats are generally low density (solid at room temperature) and saturated. They are the "bad fats" that build up on arteries and threaten health. Cholesterol is also implicated in the build-up of fibrous plaques leading to atherosclerosis. Many foods preferred by teenagers are overloaded with cholesterol and saturated fats (see Table 7-1).

One out of every ten American teenagers suffers from **obesity** (is more than 20% above his or her ideal body weight; McAnarney and Greydanus, 1984). Obese youths usually see themselves as unattractive in appearance and socially less acceptable than their thinner peers. They may spend a great deal of time and money on diets and slimming plans. Lacking immediate improvement, they become discouraged and overeat as a way to assuage their feelings of failure. This vicious circle may repeat itself over and over. Meanwhile the obese youth's self-image remains low. There is evidence from adoption studies that obesity may have a strong hereditary component. Stunkard and his colleagues (1986) reported that 80% of the offspring of two obese parents become obese, as compared with no more than 14% of the offspring of two parents of normal weight, even when raised by adoptive parents.

Rodin (1978) reported that many overweight individuals are highly responsive to the sight and smell of food. Even after dieting they remain extremely responsive to food cues. Any kind of emotional arousal (excitement, distress, amusement) increases the likelihood that hyperresponsive persons will eat. Even nonemotional stimulants like coffee and tea increase the desire to eat. Rand (1979) presented data to show that fear of sexuality, a reason commonly given for the adolescents' layer of protective fat, is rarely a cause of obesity. For most overweight adolescents there is rather a resentment of the cultural stereotype that obesity decreases sexuality. They have sexual desires but less opportunity to find dates.

Overweight adolescents should be encouraged to start good diets and learn how to keep themselves within a normal weight range. Diets should begin with a complete

Table 7-1 Saturated Fat and Cholesterol in Average Servings of Common Foods.

Food	Saturated Fat	Cholesterol
Hamburger	27,120 mg.	90 mg.
Ice cream	13,500 mg.	70 mg.
Hot dog	5,600 mg.	27 mg.
Potato chips	2,100 mg.	15 mg.
Egg	1,800 mg.	270 mg.
French fries	1,700 mg.	10 mg.
Butter	700 mg.	35 mg.
Cheddar cheese	616 mg.	28 mg.
Shrimp	56 mg.	43 mg.

medical examination. Because adolescents frequently rebel against having someone else supervise their eating, they should be given a great deal of nutritional information. If they can understand what they should eat and why, the diet has a greater chance for success. Drugs that suppress the appetite should be used only under the direction of a physican and only for a short time. Self-control must be learned. In order to be effective, any diet plan should include increasing physical activity with a structured and consistent exercise program (see Figure 7-8). Aerobic exercises (swimming, brisk walking, jogging, dancing, bicycling, cross-country skiing) of lower intensity and longer duration are better for obese adolescents than higher intensity, short duration activities (racquet sports, weight lifting). Finally, an adolescent diet should allow the youth to take part in peer-group activities as much as possible, substituting low-calorie nutritious foods for the usual "empty" but high-calorie snacks.

When a person experiences a severe weight loss without the presence of a disease associated with weight loss (such as diseases of the bowel, tumors, or severe infections), **anorexia nervosa** may be suspected. This is often referred to as a diet gone out of control. About 85% of sufferers of anorexia nervosa (called *anorexics*) are teenage girls; the remaining anorexics are males or nonteenagers. Anorexia has existed at least since the middle ages, since young girls have felt the need to use fasting as a way of coping with insecurities (Brumberg, 1989). Anorexics have a morbid fear of fatness and a distorted attitude toward eating, food, or weight that overrides hunger, admonitions, reassurances, and threats. Encouraging an anorexic to eat and/or regain some weight usually generates a hostile response. The American Psychiatric Association (1980) has listed five diagnostic criteria for anorexia nervosa.

1. Intense fear of becoming obese, which does not diminish as weight loss progresses;
2. Disturbance of body image, such as claiming to "feel fat" even when emaciated;
3. Weight loss of at least 25% of original body weight or, if patient is under eighteen years of age, weight loss from original body weight plus projected weight gain expected from growth charts may be combined to make the 25%;
4. Refusal to maintain body weight over a minimal normal weight for age and height;
5. No known physical illness that would account for the weight loss.

There is also frequently amenorrhea (a cessation of menstrual periods), an abnormally slow heartbeat, growth of soft, downy body hair, vomiting (which may be self-induced), social withdrawal, shivering, loss of head hair, constipation, periods of overactivity, and a companion disorder, *bulimia*.

Figure 7-8
The safest way to lose weight is to increase exercise. Aerobic exercises are ideal for obese teenagers.

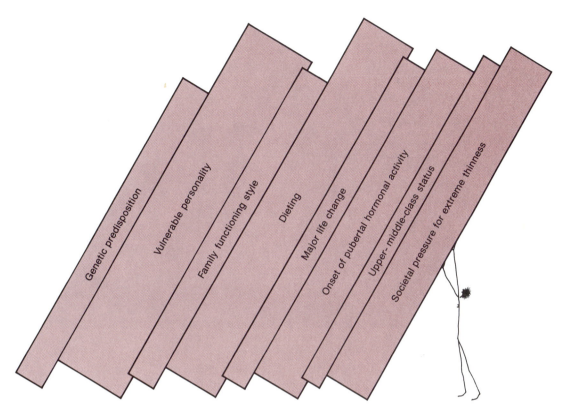

Figure 7-9
Factors contributing to the development of anorexia nervosa.

Typical anorexics are intelligent, ambitious, and anxious to do well. Anorexics may perceive that they are not meeting their family's high standards or that peer-group popularity is not what it should be. Frequently they are perfectionists, work oriented, and preoccupied with rules, schedules, and the like. Many other factors may contribute to the syndrome (see Figure 7-9). It is important that the patient and the patient's family be assured that nobody is to blame for the illness.

A genetic predisposition may exist for eating disorders. Pica, rumination, anorexia nervosa, bulimia, compulsive overeating, and obesity are all more common in some families than others.

Anorexia nervosa frequently begins at puberty. In some patients there is a sense of disgust at sexual maturation (Andersen, 1985). Females become amenorrheic and males show decreased libido and impotence. A disorder of hypothalamic stimulation of sex hormones and appetite may be at work.

With accurate identification and treatment, current starvation mortality rates are about 2% (Andersen, 1985). Treatment includes individual psychotherapy for the anorexic patient, nutritional therapy, and family counseling.

Bulimia is excessive binge eating. In bulimic episodes people may gorge themselves with several times their normal daily caloric intake. After such binges, however, they usually induce vomiting or take several laxatives to assure that the food is not digested.

Bulimia may occur in association with anorexia or may occur apart from it. It may be found in as many as 5% of high school females, 19% of college women, and 5% of college men (Halmi, Falk, and Schwarz, 1981). Binge–purge episodes tend to occur during periods of stress or late in the evening. Food is usually bolted down in private, sometimes in extreme quantities (see Figure 7-10). Bulimics may become distressed

at their inability to control their abnormal eating behaviors. The syndrome may end in suicide or in death from physical complications. Treatment consists of helping the bulimic gain control of eating, dietary therapy, and family therapy.

Health Maintenance

Health maintenance in adolescents requires both education for safe living and an accepting, empathic, nonjudgmental environment that encourages self-esteem and responsible behaviors. The majority of adolescents are blessed with good health, and their maintenance needs are minimal: proper nutrition, adequate sleep, mastery of stress. The infectious diseases of childhood are past and the chronic debilitating diseases of adulthood are still ahead. One of the weakest links in youths' health is their inability to adjust to all the physical changes (rapid growth, sexual maturity) and social changes that occur. Many of the health problems of adolescence are related more to stress than to germs.

Most teenagers have some skin eruptions surrounding puberty. **Acne** is characterized by blackheads, whiteheads (pustules), or cysts of the skin (see Figure 7-11). These most often appear on the face, shoulders, and back. Acne is caused by an increase in the activity and secretions of the sebaceous glands of the skin. Oversecretion is related to increased production of the sex hormones during adolescence and to stress. The thick substance secreted by the glands, called sebum, blocks hair follicles and interacts with other skin substances such as dust, dirt, and bacteria to cause blemishes.

Some teenagers seem to be able to avoid acne simply by normal cleansing of the skin. For others, frequent washing is essential. Some antibiotics are available that help clear up the skin. The drug Accutane, which shrinks the sebaceous glands, is sometimes prescribed for cystic acne. However, it has unpleasant side effects: nosebleeds, dry eyes, dry mouth, chapped lips, and thinning of the hair (Physicians' Desk Reference, 1991). It must not be given to females who might become pregnant while undergoing treatment because it is teratogenic.

Infectious mononucleosis is often referred to as "the kissing disease" because the organisms causing it have a low communicability—they must be spread by direct contact such as kissing or eating or drinking from the same utensils. Mono can occur at any age but is most frequently seen in teenagers (Fulginiti, 1984). A quality of

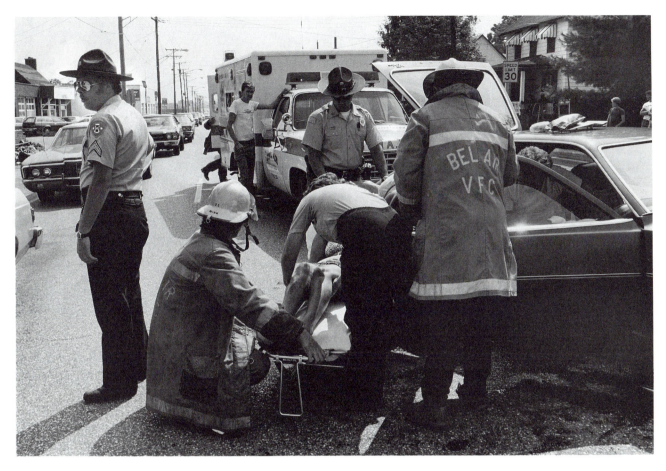

Figure 7-12
Accidents involving motor vehicles are the leading cause of death among American adolescents.

exclusivity may link together the "have-had-mono" sufferers from the "have-nots." The most characteristic symptom of mononucleosis is extreme tiredness. Sufferers also may have fevers or sore throats, develop enlarged spleens, develop faint skin rashes, or have enlarged lymph glands. Many mononucleosis patients develop some temporary abnormal liver functioning. The treatment of infectious mononucleosis varies according to the symptoms that are manifested. It always includes rest. Usually the diet is supplemented with increased protein, vitamins, and iron. The period of convalescence from infectious mononucleosis may be quite prolonged.

Accidents are the leading cause of death among teenagers, and their incidence has been increasing over the last two decades (McAnarney and Greydanus, 1984). Most of these are due to car accidents, many of which are precipitated by driving at excessive speeds under the influence of alcohol or other drugs (see Figure 7-12). Other causes of death that occur with some frequency in the adolescent population are homicide, suicide, drownings, poisonings, and drug overdosing. Many accidents are believed to have an emotional basis. Youths who feel depressed about such things as family strife, school failure, popularity problems, obesity, or poor health may be especially accident prone.

Cognitive Development

New levels of intellectual functioning usually emerge in adolescence. New cognitive abilities, along with the physical changes of puberty, profoundly influence the social development of teenagers. For this reason we will discuss changes in intelligence before describing the social advances of adolescence.

Piaget's Formal Operations Stage

In the period of concrete operations children become proficient at what Piaget (1958) called first-order operations—abilities such as classification, numbering, and one-to-one correspondence. In the **formal operations** stage, youth acquire second-order operations—abilities to see new kinds of logical relationships between classes or between and among several different properties. The reasoning behind first-order operations is called intrapropositional thinking, since it deals within the context of just one property (for example, weight). The more advanced reasoning of second-order operations is called **interpropositional thinking,** since it involves handling relationships among several different properties (density, size, and weight). The term *propositional thinking* simply refers to an ability to take objects that have been ordered into classes or correspondence in one way and then to see relations among the classes in some new, logical ways. Piaget tested youths' level of interpropositional thinking by asking them to discover how rods of different compositions (e.g., iron, aluminum, wood), different thicknesses, and different lengths would bend when weights were attached. When people have the ability to think logically and work systematically, they often enjoy trying to solve such problems.

In formal operations a person becomes proficient at what Piaget (1958) calls **combinatorial analysis** or *combinatorial logic*. This involves seeing all the possible variations of a problem, separating out all the possible variables, and then testing them systematically. Imagine all the possible sums of money one can make from a quarter, a dime, a nickel, and a penny. Formal operators will systematically set about the task of combining the coins in some set order.

no coins	= 0¢	N + D	= 15¢
P alone	= 1¢	N + Q	= 30¢
N alone	= 5¢	D + Q	= 35¢
D alone	= 10¢	P + N + D	= 16¢
Q alone	= 25¢	P + N + Q	= 31¢
P + N	= 6¢	P + D + Q	= 36¢
P + D	= 11¢	N + D + Q	= 40¢
P + Q	= 26¢	P + N + D + Q	= 41¢

People still functioning with concrete operations will combine coins to make various sums but will not do so systematically. They will forget what combinations they may already have used.

Piaget discovered that formal operators become proficient at handling problems of proportional reasoning: If one inch represents 5 miles, how many inches will be needed to represent 52 miles? **Proportional reasoning** refers to the ability to understand ratios, keeping a number or quantity in proportion.

When one sets out on a task with the idea of testing each possible variation to discover the correct solution(s), one is practicing what Piaget (1958) called **hypothetical-deductive reasoning.** Such reasoning involves solutions that are real (what can be seen, or felt, or experienced) and also encompasses abstract "what-if" solutions to the problem—in short, all the possible variations. A set of hypotheses is derived and then tested to deduce the correct answer(s). Piaget described formal operations as the combination of interpropositional thinking, combinational analysis, proportional reasoning, and hypothetical-deductive reasoning (Piaget and Inhelder, 1969). The total process, as he described it, is characterized by painstaking accommodation to detail and careful analyses and observations.

Many of the frustrations parents have with teenagers are created by their new hypothetical reasoning powers. Teenagers may seem to be stupid in their behaviors.

Elkind (1978) describes their actions as evidence of pseudo-stupidity; their thoughts encompass all the possible solutions to a problem. Consider this vignette:

> Carolee was feeling exhausted from the heat. Her air conditioner had been broken all day and it was still close to 100°F. She plugged in a fan and sat down to read. Vinny, her 14-year-old son, unplugged the fan and took it to his room. Carolee angrily told him to bring it back, asking, "Why did you take the fan?" Vinny answered, "I thought your hair was dry." "I didn't wash it." "Oh, were you using it to dry your nails?" "Think, Vinny! I don't have nail polish on." "Oh, are you trying to get rid of the smoke smell?" "Nobody's smoked in this house for days!" "Oh, were you using the fan to muffle the noise of my radio?" Carolee, in exasperation, said "Vinny, try asking if I'm hot!" Vinny laughed as he realized why his mother was using the fan. Still, he had to ask, "May I have the fan now?"

Frequently teenagers egg their parents into debate just for the sake of discussing alternate hypotheses. This may occur even when they approve of a decision.

Using, in Piaget's terms, interpropositional thinking, combinatorial analysis, proportional reasoning, and hypothetical-deductive reasoning, adolescents may construct an ideal society, an ideal religion, an ideal school, or an ideal family. They often compare their ideals with reality and find the adult ways of constructing society lacking. Teenagers, however, seldom make any great efforts to bring about their own best of all possible worlds. As Elkind (1970) put it, "The very same adolescent who professes his concern for the poor spends his money on clothes and records, not on charity."

Piaget (1958) suggested that there are three periods of great egocentrism in the process of development: infancy, early childhood, and early adolescence. He linked **adolescent egocentrism** to cognitive development. In this new form of egocentricity, where all the realms of possibility are viewed, adolescents fail to distinguish between their own conceptualizations and those of the rest of society. They believe everyone should come to terms with their own idealistic schemes. They fail to take into account the fact that others may not like or want what they want.

Youthful egocentrism is also frequently turned into self-criticism. When young people find themselves lacking in some way, they believe the whole world will see the same deficiency. Elkind and Bowen (1979) call this an imaginary audience. Adolescents often believe everybody is watching them, as if they were on stage. This makes adolescents appear very paranoid. They spend hours grooming and preening before a mirror. They believe everyone will admire their faddish clothes, their music, their hair, their bodies, and/or their friends (see Figure 7-13).

Adolescents plunge into self-improvement exercises or write diaries full of resolutions to change. They may also shroud their efforts to better themselves in secrecy. This desire for privacy in adolescence often leads to lying. In the elementary school years children tell lies that are generally tall tales. They may even come to believe their own stories. In early adolescence young people hide behind deceitful screens they

Figure 7-13
Adolescents' egocentrism is a symptom of their ability to conceptualize the thoughts of others. They believe others are as preoccupied with their appearance as they are. This causes them to be both vain and self-conscious at the same time.

erect to confuse others. However, they know the truth full well in their own minds.

A personal fable also develops as a result of early formal operations. The fable is that the unique teenager has a special destiny or is immortal. Adolescents often behave as if they cannot be hurt. They take risks, neglect contraception, experiment with drugs. They seem to believe that nothing bad can happen to them. The personal fable usually fades as adolescents become more proficient at logical, abstract thought.

The abstract reasoning abilities of the formal operations period usher in both new creative skills and renewed creative urges in many teenagers. No longer limited to concrete perceptions of the world, they may express their new visions of possibilities in art forms such as painting, sculpture, music, dance, poetry, short stories, science projects, or inventions. Many creative products of the teenage years show a certain raw-edged sensitivity and originality that is often missing from more mature works. As many creative preschoolers seem to give up original productions when they enter school, many creative teenagers also become inhibited about, or embarrassed by, their creative expressions when they enter the world of adults. Artists who continue to produce as they pass from adolescence to adulthood usually tone down and refine their works so they are more socially acceptable, sometimes at the expense of the freshness of the product.

Piaget saw formal operations as the last phase of cognitive development, the highest level of intellectual functioning. Although his descriptions of earlier intellectual stages have been well accepted and supported by research, the formal operations stage is frequently criticized—for going too far, for not going far enough, and for not adequately describing the new level of thought.

Those who criticize Piaget for going too far cite research studies that show a lack of formal-operational thought in many adults. Written language (symbolic thought) helps children deal with ideas that go beyond concrete here-and-now perceptions of the world. Children who read are helped to think in terms of abstract possibilities as well as in terms of actuality. However, nonreaders, poor readers, and people in cultures that do not ordinarily use written language may not reach formal operations in the Piagetian sense.

Those who feel that a formal stage does not characterize adolescent thought include Keating (1980), who suggested that the new cognitive abilities of adolescents emerge gradually rather than abruptly. He prefers to think of formal-operational reasoning as a general increase in memory span and ability to plan rather than as a new stage. Overton and Newman (1982) suggest that a lack of formal-operational thought in a test situation may reflect a lack of performance ability in the testing situation, or at the task presented, rather than an actual lack of formal-operational structural capacity. Overton and Mechan (1982) found that individuals perform inconsistently across various tasks used to judge a formal operations stage.

Some cognitive psychologists argue that the "formal" structural abilities Piaget described do not go far enough in describing the reasoning abilities of many adults. Commons, Richards, and Kuhn (1982), for example, found that many university undergraduate and graduate students use systematic and metasystematic reasoning, which is more complex and powerful than formal-operational reasoning.

Sex Differences in Cognition

By adolescence most girls show a preference for school subjects involving human relations or verbal skills (literature, composition, foreign languages, history), whereas boys show a preference for subjects with numerical and spatial relationships (math, science). Many people argue that these academic preferences are learned; others contend that they have genetic links.

On the genetic-inheritance side, men are generally physically stronger and predominate in aggressive, protector, provider roles. Women have and care for children. Margaret Mead (1949) found that two cultural universals characterize every human social order. The roles assigned men and women differ, and men have more power. Theoretically, there should be some genetic bases for such invariant findings.

Girls consistently do better at tasks involving word fluency, grammar, spelling, creative writing, and other aspects of language. Boys begin to excel at tasks requiring spatial perception around age seven and accelerate to adult levels by age eleven. Larger sex differences on measures of mental rotation (ability to visualize how a two- or three-dimensional figure will appear when rotated) favoring boys can be detected across the

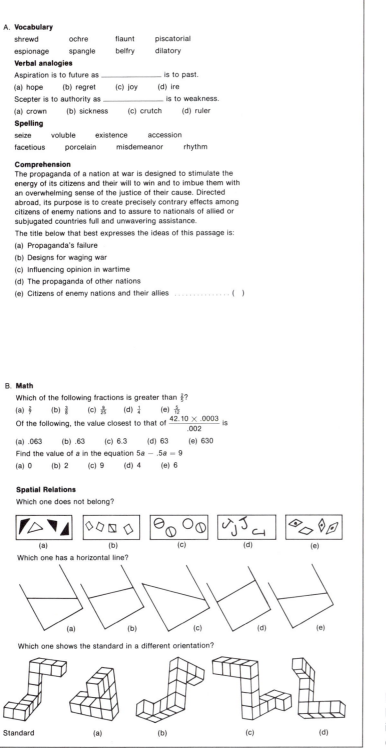

Figure 7-14
Examples of intelligence test items on which (a) females excel and (b) males excel.

life span (Linn and Petersen, 1985). Benbow and Stanley (1983) found that large sex differences in mathematical reasoning ability emerge in adolescence, especially among intellectually gifted students. Boys outnumber girls about 13 to 1 among those students who score 700 or above in the math section of the scholastic aptitude test (see Figure 7-14). Our IQ tests are carefully balanced with tests of math, verbal skills, and spatial abilities to assure that neither boys nor girls will have a scoring advantage over the other. Biologists suggest that these sex differences in mental abilities are best explained by genetically based organizational differences in the brain. In females the dominant cerebral hemisphere of the brain develops earlier than it does in males. The speech center is located in the dominant hemisphere (the left side of the brain for right-handed people). This may account for the earlier use of language by girls. Spatial ability is localized on the nondominant hemisphere. The minor hemisphere appears to become more highly developed in boys after puberty.

On the environmental learning side, most girls are consciously or unconsciously encouraged to like subjects that will make them better wives and mothers. If they voice a desire for a career, they are encouraged to choose one in which they can help others (such as secretary, nurse, teacher). Boys, on the other hand, are encouraged to show off their own individual abilities, to excel as individuals, and to acquire status. Working at self-improvement, it is assumed, is as important for a boy as working to help others is for a girl. Boys are encouraged to pursue occupations where they can be competitive, assertive, and logical (business, law, electronics, mechanics). These are broad generalizations but nevertheless hold true for a great proportion of our society.

Many people contend that the differential treatment of the sexes begins at birth. The pink and blue colors attached to babies cue in adults as to what to expect from and do for the infants. In childhood girls are nearness trained and kept close to home, whereas boys are independence trained and encouraged to behave more like Tom Sawyer. Girls are praised for making good conversation (verbal skills), and boys are attired in reinforced play clothes and expected to wander far afield (spatial skills). Grown-ups tend to worry more about boys who do not go exploring or irreparably stain or tear their clothing than about those who do.

Are the intellectual differences that become more pronounced after puberty due to some females' **fear of success?** Some parents still warn daughters not to be "too smart" or they will never have dates (or get married). In a series of studies, Horner (1972) asked women to finish this story: "After first term finals, Anne finds herself at the top of her medical school class. . . ." About 65% of them wrote endings such as: "Anne is ugly, studies all the time, and will never get married" or "A mistake has been made. Anne is not really at the top of the class" or "Anne feels guilty. She will finally have a nervous breakdown, quit medical school, and marry a successful young doctor." In Horner's studies only about 10% of men wrote similar endings to the story: "After first term finals, John finds himself at the top of his medical school class. . . ." In a replication of Horner's research, Hoffman (1974) found that fear of success was slightly higher in men. Donelson (1977) found different causes for men's fear of success. They may question the value of success, the goals, or the emptiness of achievement. Women's fear of success is more often fear of social rejection. In fact, there are more negative social consequences for intellectual achievement for women.

Hoffman (1972) suggested that women's **affiliation needs** may be higher than their **achievement needs** because they are socialized to value acceptance by others more than being the best at what they do (see Figure 7-15). Erb (1983) found that in early adolescence girls typically show an interest in traditional feminine career areas such as service while boys show an interest in high technology. Elder and Mac-Innis(1983) found that the most achievement-oriented adolescent girls are those whose mothers are well educated, are employed, and have a strong sense of their own personal worth as women. While there are currently almost equal numbers of women and men starting college, women are more apt to drop out before graduation. Men are more

Figure 7-15
The need to achieve versus the need to affiliate is often problematic for females who are torn between a desire to pursue a demanding career and their concerns about wife- and motherhood.

apt either to graduate or to continue to professional schools. Men eventually earn about three-quarters of all doctoral degrees. The question of whether environmental factors or sex differences cause this imbalance is unresolved.

Psychosocial Development

Havighurst (1972) proposed eight developmental tasks to which adolescents must address themselves:

1. accepting one's physique and using the body effectively,
2. achieving new and more mature relations with age-mates of both sexes,
3. achieving a masculine or feminine gender role,
4. achieving emotional independence from parents and other adults,
5. preparing for a career,
6. preparing for marriage and family life,
7. desiring and achieving socially responsible behavior,
8. acquiring a set of values and an ethical system as a guide to behavior—developing an ideology.

Families are often stunned when their obedient children become egocentric, argumentative teenagers. They remember the **generation gap** between themselves and their own parents, but they never thought it would happen with their offspring. All their best efforts to raise understanding, understandable children seem to have been for naught. The physical changes of puberty effect psychosocial changes. Suddenly the more adult-appearing individual feels social pressures to become more independent, make a career choice, make sexual choices, take on more adult responsibilities, and "grow up." In addition, the new level of formal-operational thought can substantially alter the adolescent's outlook on his or her own life.

While not all adolescents experience a generation gap (see Box 7-1) or an identity crisis, most social scientists agree that an identity search and new self-discoveries characterize psychosocial development. The quest for identity affects parent–child relationships, moral development, school and peer interactions, and sexual explorations.

Is Storm and Stress Characteristic of the Adolescent Years?

The American psychologist G. Stanley Hall (1904) wrote two volumes about adolescent development at the turn of the century. His studies led him to conclude that the biological changes of puberty inevitably usher in a period of *Sturm und Drang* (storm and stress). He described adolescents as emotionally unstable, with wide mood swings between elation and depression, extraversion and introversion, energy and lassitude. The American anthropologist Margaret Mead (1928) wrote that storm and stress may characterize adolescents living in Western industrialized nations but not teenagers in cultures such as Samoa who make a smooth, swift transition from child status to adult status after a tribal initiation ceremony. An Australian anthropologist, Derek Freeman (1983), criticized Mead's data and data collection methods and reported that Samoans also experience turmoil during their adolescent years.

What accounts for these different findings? Does the answer lie in cohort differences? Were Samoan teenagers less stressed in the 1920s than in the 1970s? Did Mead and her interpreters look only at the cooperative pleasant Samoans and neglect those who were rebellious, hostile, and alienated? Is turbulence universal between the years of thirteen and nineteen? Jerome Dusek and John Flaherty (1981) conducted a longitudinal study of over 500 adolescents in Syracuse, New York and judged that it is not. Their subjects, who were from a wide range of social class levels and ethnic backgrounds, showed continual and gradual growth characterized by continuity and stability. They concluded, "The person who enters adolescence is basically the same as that who exits it" (p. 39).

Erikson's Identity versus Role Confusion

Erikson, like Freud, recognized the influence of sexual libido on the adolescent's self-concept. Unlike Freud, he did not believe that finding a heterosexual love partner would confer on one a mature self-concept. He proposed the nuclear conflict of **identity versus role confusion** as characteristic of adolescence. The search for a sense of identity, he felt, reaches crisis proportions at this time. Not only does the adolescent need to adjust to a sexually mature body, but he or she also needs to re-resolve all the previous nuclear conflicts (trust versus mistrust, autonomy versus doubt, initiative versus guilt, and industry versus inferiority) in light of the newly sensuous self.

The epigenetic nature of Erikson's theory is especially meaningful during this stage. Erikson proposed that many familial and societal, as well as sexual, forces exert an influence on identity achievement. Also, a sense of identity rests on the resolution of many subconflicts (Erikson, 1968). These include

1. adopting an appropriate gender identity,
2. finding one's own religious ideology,
3. finding one's own political ideology,
4. finding one's own economic ideology,
5. finding one's own social ideology,
6. making an occupational or vocational choice,
7. adopting behaviors consistent with one's self-concept.

Erikson (1980) felt that adolescents need time to experiment with many different roles before they settle into any particular niche. Adolescents use their same- and opposite-sex friends and their family members as sounding boards on which to test their changing identities. Erikson felt that young love is usually more conversational than sexual because young persons need to project their developing self-image confidentially to a second person and then have it reflected back to them (see Figure 7-16). In love relationships teenagers feel more secure that their secrets can be confided without the danger of ridicule, abuse, or broadcasting. But many teenagers prefer to use their family members as sounding boards for the same reasons. Erikson (1963)

Figure 7-16
Early dating gives adolescents a chance to try out a new identity (e.g., egghead, jock, rebel) to see how it feels and to see how a member of the opposite sex will respond.

wrote that the failure of so many teenage marriages may be linked to the fact that one cannot give oneself to another until one knows one's own identity.

Erikson (1968) has been criticized for being sexist in his discussion of the identity strivings of women and men. He wrote that a young woman should keep her identity "open" for the peculiarities of the man to be joined and of the children to be brought up. He did not discuss the converse, that something in the young man's identity must keep itself "open" for the peculiarities of the woman to be joined and the children to be brought up.

Unless adolescents work at affirming and strengthening their identity in adolescence, Erikson feels they will suffer from role confusion. They may imitate others but feel confused about their own sense of self. This role confusion can lead to a progressive sense of identity dissolution. More and more the adolescent will look at others to find out which ones he or she is like, often choosing as most like the self the ones deemed least socially acceptable. When the identity disorder becomes stressful, some outside counseling or therapy is recommended, with parental and sibling participation as well. In some cases the parents project their unfulfilled wishes and desires onto their sons or daughters, asking them to become the person they wanted to, but could not, be. It is especially difficult for adolescents to discover their own uniqueness if parents and peers pressure them to conform and acquiesce to the will of others (see Table 7-2).

Marcia's Identity Statuses. James Marcia (1980) expanded Erikson's beliefs about identity, youth, and crisis. He proposed four different ways in which adolescents resolve (or fail to resolve) their quest for identity and search for commitments: **foreclosure, moratorium, identity diffusion,** and **identity achievement.**

Foreclosed adolescents make a smooth transition from the status of child to that of adult by making a commitment to the adult role laid out for them by others—their parents, their friends, their culture. They do not seem to feel any need to question whether they should comply with the expectations of others; they simply oblige. They appear satisfied with the important life decisions that others have made for them, and they do not experience any crisis of identity (see Table 7-3).

A *moratorium* is a period of time in which one is permitted to delay meeting an obligation—a time out. Marcia believes that adolescents in an identity moratorium postpone the adoption of any set identity. They actively experiment with many different roles and explore a wide range of political, religious, and economic ideologies. They hesitate to make any commitments while searching for all the possibilities of an identity

Table 7-2   Erikson's Fifth Nuclear Conflict: Identity Versus Role Confusion.

Sense	Eriksonian Descriptions	Fostering Behaviors
Identity	Sense of sameness between self-concept and how one appears in the eyes of others.	Others reflect back belief that youth has qualities that match self-image
	Felt continuity between identities prepared in the past, the meaning of one's identity for others, and the promise of career	Opportunity to pursue choice of activities in keeping with aptitudes and endowment
versus Role confusion	Doubt about sexual identity	Lack of interaction with opposite-sex peers
	Inability to find occupational identity	Overidentification with heroes of cliques or crowds
	Personality confusion as evidenced by delinquent, withdrawing, or suicidal behaviors	Lack of attention or feedback as being worthwhile

that might some day be theirs. Eventually they will feel the crisis of needing an identity (see Table 7-3).

Identity-diffused adolescents also lack a commitment to any enduring sense of self. However, they are not actively searching for an identity either. They are more like reeds blowing in the wind. They are easily persuaded to follow others and assume whatever identity is required of them at the moment. They do not seem to experience distress at this status but are content with each new day-to-day self. They seem to be holding their identity open (as Erikson suggested women should do), for the peculiarities of the man (or woman), job, or activity to be joined. Marcia found the identity-diffused status to be more characteristic of the preadolescent, though it also describes some older adolescents (see Table 7-3).

Identity-achieved adolescents have firm commitments and an enduring self-concept. They are beyond the trauma of self-exploration and self-discovery but have experienced a conflict of identity versus role confusion (in the Eriksonian sense) prior to settling on a stable sense of self. They seem to feel comfortable with the choices they have made. They accept the weaknesses as well as the strengths of their personalities and no longer feel pressured to perfect themselves with changes (see Table 7-3).

Archer (1982), in an investigation of the frequency of Marcia's four identity statuses in adolescents, found that the foreclosure and diffusion-identity statuses were most evident. Identity achievement occurred predominantly in the oldest subjects. She found that statuses also varied across content areas. Most adolescents had a foreclosed

Table 7-3   Marcia's Identity Statuses.

Description	Commitment	Crisis
Foreclosure	Yes	No
Moratorium	No	Yes
Identity diffusion	No	No
Identity achievement	Yes	Yes

Figure 7-17
One's self-concept includes internal feelings about the self (self-esteem), self as experienced interacting with others, and self as presented externally to others.

identity in sex-role preference, while in the political area more had a diffused identity. In religious beliefs, adolescents ranged from foreclosed to diffused to identity achieved; few were in a moratorium in their religious identity. Many adolescents were, however, in a moratorium in their vocational identity. Marcia (1980, 1983) wrote that ego identity requires a prolonged period for development. It appears to develop more quickly in some areas than others and at different times in unique individuals.

Savin-Williams and Demo (1984) identified three other areas of ego identity (or self-concept) in which development progresses unevenly: the experienced self, the presented self, and self-feelings (see Figure 7-17). Adolescents are more apt to change the way they experience themselves and their self-images, and the way they present themselves, than they are to change their self-feelings or self-esteem. The evaluation that adolescents make of themselves (self-esteem) is relatively stable from year to year. Higher self-esteem is associated with earlier authoritative parenting practices and use of inductive discipline rather than power assertion or deprivation of love (see Chapter 5). Adolescents who are socialized to be more androgynous (have attributes of both masculinity and femininity in their personalities) usually have higher self-esteem than do other males or females (Lamke, 1982; Rust and McCraw, 1984). Male adolescents with high self-esteem who are more androgynous also engage in fewer aggressive behaviors toward others (LoPresto and Deluty, 1988).

In considering the progression and the impact of an identity search on any given adolescent, one must take into account the self-esteem with which he or she entered adolescence; the identity achieved in the past as it relates to Erikson's psychosocial stages; the level of cognitive functioning; the status of physical maturation; the identities being urged on the adolescent by family members, school, friends, possible employers, the mass media, even the economic and political systems; and the expectations the adolescent may have for his or her future. Any generalization about how a "typical" identity conflict is resolved, or about the effect of the conflict on the adolescent, is, at best, speculative. Some identity searches continue into adulthood.

Parent–Child Relationships

Adolescents typically fluctuate from wanting privileges in keeping with near-adult status (such as learning to drive and use of car, no curfews) to wanting the support and protection afforded them in childhood (no upkeep of clothes, meals prepared). Just as it is difficult for teenagers to achieve a sense of identity during adolescence, so too is it difficult for families to react to adolescents who are esthetes one day and slobs the next or adults one day and children the next. Parents who allow teenagers a great deal of freedom and pay little heed to their coming and going deprive them of some of the direction and support they both need and crave. Likewise, teenagers who have no freedom and too much surveillance feel thwarted in their efforts to be independent.

Independence training is hampered by authoritarian discipline (parents make the rules), by indulgent discipline (teenagers choose their own rules), and by parental indifference or neglect. The authoritative-reciprocal parent–child relationship more successfully allows teenagers to work through their identity crisis and gain a more secure independence—see Goethals and Klos's description (1970) of the ideally adequate parent in Table 7-4.

Any form of discipline is difficult during adolescence. Teenagers often feel that they are too old to be punished. They may rebel against the injustice of power-assertion and love-withdrawal teachniques. They argue about almost every decision made that affects them. Therefore, some adults find it easier to allow teenagers to be responsible for their own behavior. They may hope that their past teaching plus example will be sufficient to keep their teenagers out of trouble. Other adults may become dictatorial and insist that certain behavioral standards be met in exchange for allowance, clothes, privileges, meals, or shelter. Both permissive and authoritarian adults are usually guilty of maintaining a low level of actual involvement with the teenager. They communicate less, show less affection, and offer less companionship. Authoritative adults who can keep "reasoning" communication channels open and provide love, affection, and adequate explanations for their decisions, find that the discipline of teenagers is not impossible and that their behavioral standards are more often obeyed.

How prevalent is storm and stress between adolescents and parents? (Refer back to Box 7-1). Hauser and his colleagues (1984) found that family interactions emphasizing warmth, acceptance, and understanding were peaceful, but found negative correlations between constraining behaviors (devaluing, withholding) and adolescent–parent harmony. Garbarino, Sebes, and Schellenbach (1984) studied two-parent families in which an adolescent had been referred because of problematic adjustment. They found the parents in these families to be more punishing and less supportive of the adolescent, as well as more stressed by changes in their own lives. Adolescents want parental support (Coleman and Coleman, 1984). When they do not get it, they become more self-conscious and more self-focused (Riley, Adams, and Nielsen, 1984). They may also become alienated, delinquent, substance abusers, or pregnant.

Many parents, because of their jobs, second jobs, stresses, commuting, and social or community obligations have little time left to interact with their teenagers. Bronfenbrenner (1972) feared this withering away of family and societal interaction with teenagers contributes to a breakdown in the process of making them human. As he put it:

> By isolating our children from the rest of society, we abandon them to a world devoid of adults and ruled by the destructive impulses and compelling pressures both of the age-segregated peer group and the aggressive and exploitive television screen. . . . (p. 664)

Teenagers spend less time with their parents when the mother works full time. Males also have longer arguments of greater intensity with their mothers if she works outside the home (Montemayor, 1984). On the other hand, maternal employment contributes to greater achievement motivation in daughters (Elder and MacInnis, 1983).

Sibling order influences achievement of independence. The oldest child is generally

Table 7-4 Three Ways Parents Can Facilitate Adolescent Independence.

1. Recognize the adolescent as a separate person in his or her own right, which implies that independent or competent behavior by the adolescent is gratifying rather than threatening.
2. Show genuine care or concern but not overinvolvement; give or offer, but don't impose.
3. Terminate old ways of relating when they no longer are adequate or appropriate, which implies the openness to change that is necessary for any ongoing relationship.

kept dependent longest. Younger children strive to have more privileges to be like the older siblings at earlier ages (see Figure 7-18).

Teenagers from one-parent families are often asked to behave more independently than those from two-parent families (for example, to help support the family with a job, share a greater responsibility for housework and meals). Paradoxically, this may result in greater social and emotional dependence on the custodial parent. How free an adolescent feels from the influence, control, or determination of a parent depends more on his or her self-concept and self-esteem than on quantity or quality of tasks performed. Garbarino, Sebes, and Schellenbach (1984) found that adolescents with stepparents were often at high risk for dysfunction (identity confusion, emotional disturbance).

Moral Development.   Kohlberg (1984) proposed that moral behaviors develop according to the following sequence:

Stage 1: Punishment and obedience orientation.

Stage 2: Acts that are satisfying to self and occasionally satisfying to others defined as right.

Stage 3: Morality of maintaining good relations and approval of others.

Stage 4: Orientation to showing respect for authority and maintaining social order for social order's sake.

Stage 5: Morality of accepting democratically contracted laws.

Kohlberg called Stages 1 and 2 the premoral levels, Stages 3 and 4 conventional morality, and Stage 5 the level of post-conventional morality of **principled moral reasoning.** Refer back to Chapter 6 for a discussion of Stages 1 through 4. In Stage 5 reasoning, there is an emphasis on legalistic contracting of moral principles to guide behavior. If adolescents reach this level, they select for themselves the principles they will follow and show a concern that the rights and needs of others are not violated.

Although many adolescents give answers to the moral dilemmas posed by Kohlberg at the conventional moral reasoning stages, about 10% give answers based on the higher-level, principled reasoning stage (Kohlberg and Gilligan, 1971).

Carol Gilligan (1982) explained the differences between the answers of males and females to moral dilemmas quite differently from Kohlberg. Males are more apt to select behaviors that show a concern for authority, duty, and protecting the rights of unknown others. Females are more apt to select behaviors that show a concern for maintaining relationships with known others. Kohlberg felt that females are less moral, due to their Stage 3 answers. Gilligan felt that females are equally moral, or perhaps more moral, but that they speak in a different voice, based on how they experience themselves and relationships. Boys disconnect from their mothers in early childhood and are rewarded for being autonomous and independent; they are taught to value freedom. Girls usually do not disconnect from their mothers until adolescence, and then they resist the disconnecting. Females tend to perceive themselves as being intimate, empathetic, caring, and mutually dependent; they are taught to value relationships. Therefore, argued Gilligan, their moral reasoning reflects this concern for maintaining good relations and the approval of others.

Gilligan (see Figure 7-19) believed that there are often cognitive conflicts in adolescent girls' conceptions of morality. They know what they really think about issues, but they have been taught not to antagonize others. They bury their real feelings and either give socially acceptable answers or say "I don't know." In an interview at age 12, one preadolescent girl said "I don't know" only 21 times. When she was 14, she was asked the same questions. She said "I don't know" 135 times. She had not suffered brain damage. She had learned to doubt the acceptability of her own opinions and to hide them.

There are interrelationships between reaching the formal operations level of cognitive development (Piaget), being in the nuclear conflict of finding one's identity versus

Figure 7-18
Older siblings may be advocates for younger ones, pleading the case to give them more freedom at an earlier age.

Figure 7-19
Carol Gilligan, who studied the opinions of girls at the edge of adolescence.

feeling role confusion (Erikson), and making moral judgments (Kohlberg, Gilligan). Formal cognitive operating seems to be a necessary condition for reaching higher levels of morality. It certainly is not, however, sufficient in and of itself to lead a person to high-level moral judgments. Such judgments are also based on environmental influences such as modeling, reinforcers, and discipline. A positive resolution of the identity conflict facilitates higher-level moral judgments but is not essential to achieving morality (Cauble, 1976).

Some studies have found that moral reasoning of a cognitive nature such as that required in the moral dilemmas of Kohlberg can be quite different from moral judgments made in actual day-to-day living. Leming (1978), for example, found that adolescents made higher-level moral judgments about moral dilemmas than they did about the actions of others in some practical moral situation. Haan (1978) found that adolescent moral judgments are more frequently based on interpersonal formulations than on formal reasoning. Interpersonal moral solutions are achieved through group discussions that try to come to a consensus of all the participants on action(s) to be taken, rather than on any one individual's beliefs.

Holstein (1976) reported that some adolescents regressed from a higher to a lower level of moral reasoning with age. Kitchener and her colleagues (1984) reported the opposite: moral judgments typically increased over the adolescent years. Colby and her co-workers (1983) found downward moral stage change in only 4% of subjects. Social factors play a role in moral reasoning. More mature moral judgments are possible when one has been taught about, and reinforced for, listening to and considering the obligations and rights of others, seeking the greater good for all humankind, and letting one's conscience be one's guide.

The form of discipline that correlates most highly with moral conduct is use of reasoning to induce changes in behavior (inductive discipline). Providing teenagers with explanations of the pros and cons of each alternative choice of action, exposing them to moral arguments, or even involving them in role-playing exercises to help them see the points of view of others will help them progress to higher levels of moral reasoning.

Alienation

While the majority of adolescents move toward achievement of identity and moral behaviors during their teenage years, some act out against society (delinquency) or try to escape (suicide, substance abuse). These characteristic ways of behaving are not mutually exclusive. Many adolescents move toward people, away from people, and against people, depending on the situation and their moods. When a teenager's major mode of coping with family and social life is to withdraw from it, however, he or she is said to be **alienated.**

Alienated adolescents have been described as more self-conscious, more anxious, and less apt to believe they can control the events in their lives (Moore and Schultz, 1983). They are often academic underachievers. Their tension and anxiety may be evidenced by many phobias, especially social phobias, or by obsessive or compulsive behaviors. They may be neglected by their parents. They may be unpopular or even rejected by their peers (Faust, Forehand, and Baum, 1985). They are consequently more apt to spend time watching TV or listening to music. Loneliness in both boys and girls has also been associated with trying to be stereotypically either very masculine or very feminine. Androgynous teenagers are less often alienated from others (Avery, 1982).

About 25% of teenagers feel both alienated and deeply depressed at some time during adolescence. **Depression** is more common in teenage boys than in girls (Marcoen and Brumagne, 1985). Boys usually feel less connectedness with their mothers and/or fathers. They are also less apt to have an intimate best friend with whom they can discuss their emotional concerns.

The symptoms of depression vary from adolescent to adolescent but usually include some of the behaviors found in Table 7-5. Depression in adolescents has been associated with both overly competitive pressures to succeed and with the decline of the nuclear family (Wetzel, 1989). Approximately 28% of adolescents are living in single parent families; 23% with their mother only, 5% with their father only (Bureau of Labor Statistics, 1989). Aloneness and depression often lead to thoughts about, or attempts at, suicide.

Social scientists are currently describing an epidemic of **suicides.** The rate has quadrupled in the past thirty years without a corresponding rise in the suicide rate in the rest of the population (Lipsitt, 1985a). Adolescent girls attempt suicide more frequently, but adolescent boys are more likely to complete it. Males also have more favorable attitudes about the acceptability of suicide, especially if the victim is another male (Deluty, 1989).

Suicidal teenagers often have family problems. The loss of a parent or sibling through death, divorce, or institutionalization may trigger emotional disturbances within the family and within the teenagers. Teenagers may also react with deep depression and suicidal behaviors to the loss of a significant person outside the family, such as a close friend (Triolo et al., 1984). Some sociologists believe that suicide may be contagious in adolescents (Phillips, 1985). In the late summer of 1985, for example, nine adolescents on the Wind River Indian Reservation in Wyoming followed each other into suicidal deaths. There are numerous other instances of one suicide seeming to trigger others among like-aged persons in the same schools or locale.

The "contagion effect" in suicide doesn't argue against the idea that many problems in suicidal teenagers stem from alienation. On the Wind River Indian Reservation, for example, mental health experts believed that the youths who killed themselves shared problems of alienation, low self-esteem, lack of cultural identity, and a sense of hopelessness about their futures. Grob, Klein, and Eisen (1983) found that among predisposing factors to suicide those related to alienation from the family were most prominent, followed by low self-esteem, difficulty in peer relationships, and economic or ethnic differences.

Most large cities have suicide prevention centers (SPC) and hotlines that troubled adolescents (and adults) can use when they feel they need help. Trained counselors will talk to them for as long as necessary and will help them consider alternatives to suicide. At high risk for suicide are persons who have contemplated their method, those who are depressed, and especially those who have attempted it before. It is a myth that people who talk about or make clumsy attempts at suicide rarely actually kill themselves. Attempts and suicidal talk may be cries for help. If help is not given, the adolescent, feeling hopeless and helpless, may take his or her life. Although SPCs and

Table 7-5 Behaviors that May Signify Depression in an Adolescent Male or Female.

Pessimistic about career	Speaks slowly
Pessimistic about dating	Short attention span
Self-reproach	Increased fidgetiness
Dwells on past errors	Frequent sighing
Hears denunciatory voices	Worries about trivia
Talks about death	Loss of appetite
Can't fall asleep	Always fatigued
Wakes during the night	Loss of libido
Loss of interest in hobbies	Preoccupied with health
Loss of weight	Feelings of unreality
Ignores bathing and/or grooming	Suspicious of others

Figure 7-20
Activities not considered illegal for adults (e.g., school truancy, alcohol use, sexual activity) are considered status offenses. Criminal activities engaged in with the knowledge of adults (e.g., illegal betting, pimping, drug dealing) are considered conduct disorders.

hotlines are helpful in the crises, most youth who have attempted suicide need both individual professional counseling and family counseling to help them overcome alienation and to feel loved and worthwhile within the family unit.

Some alienated teenagers turn their anger against others, rather than against themselves. Juvenile delinquent acts can roughly be classified into three types: status offenses, socialized conduct disorders, and unsocialized conduct disorders.

Status offenses involve conduct that would not be considered illegal if engaged in by an adult: school truancy, ungovernability, running away from home, sexual promiscuity. Depending on the state in which one lives, status offenders are labeled PINS (persons in need of supervision), CINS, JINS, or MINS (children/juveniles/minors in need of supervision). While both males and females commit status offenses, fourteen- to fifteen-year-old females are over-represented in the caseloads of agencies that serve them. Most status offenders are returned to school or home when apprehended in spite of the fact that they usually flee again and again. Individual counseling may be offered if the adolescent shows signs of personal maladjustment. Family counseling is strongly advised to bring to light the family conflicts that the adolescent finds so intolerable. In some cases, when evidence of child neglect or abuse is available, the child is assigned to a foster home while the parents receive counseling. Parents often have little in the way of empathy or positive regard for their runaway adolescents, or vice versa (Spillane-Grieco, 1984). This makes counseling challenging and difficult.

Socialized conduct disorders are illegal activities engaged in with the tacit or expressed approval of others, usually parents. They may be minor infractions of the law (disorderly conduct, smoking marijuana, hunting without a license) or major crimes (drug dealing, car theft). (See Figure 7-20.) The adolescent usually views the behavior as a way to win acceptance and approval from significant others.

Unsocialized conduct disorders are illegal activities committed by adolescents with an undercurrent of hostility and awareness of wrongdoing. Such actions are usually referred to as **delinquent acts.** The extent of juvenile delinquency cannot be understated. The United States has the highest youth crime rate of all the industrialized nations in the world. More crimes are committed by adolescents than by all persons over twenty-five (see Box 7-2). They account for over one-half of the crimes in the United States. Juvenile males are four times more likely to perpetrate criminal activities than are underage females. Juvenile delinquents are frequently out of school and unemployed. Many are alcohol or drug abusers or have serious emotional problems. Many have no parents or have a history of being neglected or abused as children. Loeber (1982) found that most juvenile delinquents show an early onset of antisocial behaviors. They engage in more overt acts (fighting, disobedience) in childhood and escalate to more covert acts (theft, drug use) in adolescence. They not only have signs of maladjustment but also have negative self-images, especially in the areas of body image, moral and ethical self, and family self-concept (Jurich and Andrews, 1984).

A large percentage of **juvenile crimes** are serious: aggravated assault, rape, and murder. The juvenile justice system is frequently lenient with youthful offenders. Rarely are they fingerprinted or photographed before age sixteen or eighteen (depending on the state). Frequently their cases are dismissed rather than tried. When tried, punishments are often merciful: stern lectures, paroles, short stays in juvenile rehabilitation camps or correctional facilities. Many social scientists see rehabilitation as multifaceted: increasing family responsibilities for wayward adolescents, increasing adolescents' feelings of responsibility for their own actions, helping adolescents see the enormity of their offenses and the effects on others. The availability of respected adult role models can be enormously beneficial to these teenagers, as in halfway houses with professionally trained surrogate parents. Nevertheless, because of the deep roots of the problems, rehabilitation is often unsuccessful (Gold and Petronio, 1980). Many juvenile delinquents eventually commit crimes as legal adults and are sentenced, in adult courts, to prison terms.

Substance abuse by minors is usually a sign of alienation and psychological disturbance. A normally curious teenager may want to experiment with mood-altering substances and may want to use them recreationally at parties. However, when an adolescent "needs" some substance on a regular basis and devotes his or her time to seeking and using the substance, alienation is likely.

Jurich and associates (1985) found that substance abusers more often come from

---

BOX

7-2

Juvenile Crime in the United States.

Approximately 8% of all 10- to 17-year-olds in the U.S.A. have been arrested. Each year over 5 million youth are arraigned for criminal activities. The most common juvenile delinquent acts are crimes against property (auto theft, burglary, larceny, arson, vandalism). However, close to one quarter of juvenile offenses are serious and violent actions (murder, aggravated assault, robbery, forcible rape). Other common delinquent acts include status offenses, drug violations, alcohol violations (especially driving under the influence), and parole violations. Property crime arrests peak at age 16 and violent crime arrests peak at age 18. Over 80% of arrested youth are male. Criminals come from all ethnic backgrounds (44% Caucasian, 39% African-American, 15% Hispanic-American, 2% other), but typically grow up in turbulent and/or abusive homes (Wetzel, 1989).

Youth in the United States are frequently the victims of crime. One in every 15 youth experiences a violent crime each year—over 2 million victims. One in every 9 youth experiences a theft each year—over 3½ million victims. Youth are more likely than adults to try to protect themselves during crimes and to get hurt in so doing. About 30% of the youthful victims of crime sustain injuries. Over 5000 youth die in homicides each year (Wetzel, 1989).

Table 7-6 A Comparison of Adolescent Drug Use in the 1970s and the 1980s.

Drug	Percent Who Use 1979	1985
Alcohol	70.3	55.9
Marijuana	30.9	23.7
Cocaine	5.4	5.2

SOURCE: National Institute on Drug Abuse, *Highlights: 1985 National Survey on Drug Abuse*. Washington, D.C.: NIDA.

families with either negligent or authoritarian discipline, hypocritical morality, gaps in communication, or mother–father conflicts. Substance abuse is more common among delinquent and alienated adolescents. It is also frequently associated with father absence (Stern, Northman, and Van Slyck, 1984).

Substance abuse among teenagers declined slightly in the 1980s (see Table 7-6). Fewer teenagers smoked marijuana, used sedatives, hypnotics, barbiturates, or narcotics; fewer sniffed intoxicants or experimented with hallucinogenic drugs. Even cigarette smoking declined. Many adolescents do not want to jeopardize their health with drugs. The exception to the trend toward less substance use or abuse is that more adolescents sought stimulant drugs to get them through the day; caffeine, amphetamines or amphetamine substitutes, and cocaine.

Despite its illegality, alcohol is widely available to adolescents. In 1988, 92% of high school seniors said they had tried alcohol, and 4% said they had used it on a daily basis for at least a month (Wetzel, 1989). Young teenagers are also using alcohol, often

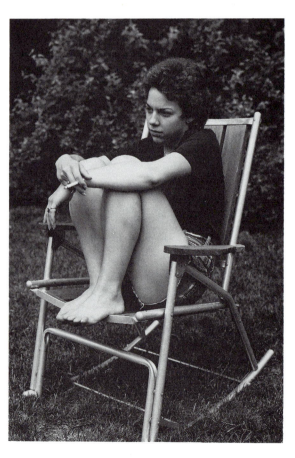

Figure 7-21
At first, many adolescents feel it is cool to smoke. Expense, health complications, and social disapproval may, however, make them reconsider this evaluation.

obtained for them by their own parents. Alcohol use in adolescents is highly correlated with other problems of alienation: depression, suicide and juvenile crime. It is associated with school truancy, diminished school performance, and accident proneness, and with diseases that result from overindulgence, such as acute gastritis, peptic ulcers, pancreatitis, liver cirrhosis, malnutrition, alcohlic stupor, and alcoholism.

The use of other illegal drugs (crack cocaine, amphetamines, marijuana) has adverse legal and medical consequences for many adolescents. About 350,000 teenagers are arrested each year in the U.S.A. for drug-related offenses (FBI Statistics, 1988). About 35,000 U.S. teenagers are rushed to emergency rooms each year for drug-related medical crises (Wetzel, 1989). The adverse effects of these drugs will be discussed in more detail in Chapter 8.

Cigarette smoking tends to begin before adolescence. Close to one half of all middle school students have tried cigarettes. It is often considered "cool," or a way to look grown-up. The cognitive personal fable (nothing bad will happen to me) allows adolescents to ignore the warnings about cigarette smoking and cancer. Many teenagers smoke only for a short while, and then give it up (see Figure 7-21). Smokers in adolescence have been shown to be less stable, less intelligent, less self-confident, and more tense than nonsmokers (Tucker, 1984).

Peer Interactions

Looking back through history, one finds that teenagers have been profoundly influenced through the ages by the convictions of peer groups (for example, Crusaders, Civil Warriors, Hitler's youth, hippies). There are many reasons for believing that teenagers today, and tomorrow, will be affected by the behaviors and beliefs of their peers. When families are less interactive, teenagers increasingly turn to their peers for information, advice, and companionship. **Peer pressures** in adolescence exert a strong force in shaping personalities.

Peer groups can evolve around shared interests such as athletics or the arts; they may grow between persons with common experiences, such as doing well scholastically or becoming popular on the dating circuit. They may reflect neighborhood proximity or be organized around political or religious interests, or they may reflect a fondness for certain modes of behavior like drinking or doing drugs. Any one teenager may belong to two or more peer groups simultaneously. Some groups identify themselves with a certain fashion of dress, grooming, or behavior. More often several groups prefer a certain form of dress that follows the fads and fashions of the day. The kinds and numbers of peer groups any one individual can join and the degree and type of influence the group exerts on the individual (or vice versa) depend on the individual. Personality factors like introversion, extraversion, self-esteem, and motivation, and situational factors like spending money, free time, sex, family rules, and school obligations all determine the strength of peer influence. Every teenager, whether leader or follower, active or passive, accepted or rejected, pays a great deal of attention to the behaviors and opinions of other young people with whom he or she comes in contact. Brown (1982) found that peer pressures for females appeared to be stronger than for males, especially in the areas of dating, sexual activity, and use of drugs and alcohol. "Doing one's own thing" is not typical until early adulthood, when a sense of identity and a degree of independence are established (see Figure 7-22).

Friendships appear to become more stable, more intimate, and more mutually responsive in adolescence (Berndt, 1982). Adolescents spend more time talking to their friends, and describe themselves as more happy doing so, than in any other activity (Csikszentmihalyi, Larson, and Prescott, 1977). Girls and boys appear to differ somewhat in their friendship patterns. Girls' friendships involve higher intimacy (Hunter and Youniss, 1982) and more conversations about themselves and their close relationships (Johnson and Aries, 1983). Boys' friendships, while more intimate than in childhood,

Figure 7-22
The adolescent peer group provides the individual teenager with a sense of security and acceptance and fosters a sense of group loyalty.

appear to be less exclusive than are girls' friendships. Boys' conversations are more apt to center on activity-oriented topics than on personal emotions.

Both girls and boys choose friends who are similar to them in some way: age, sex, race, educational aspirations, attitudes toward school, actual academic achievement, orientation toward contemporary teen culture (music, clothes, leisure-time activities). With increasing age, adolescents become more willing to share with and help their friends rather than compete with them. Adolescents with close and stable friends appear to have higher self-esteem than those with more fleeting, shallow friendships.

Popularity among peers has been investigated along dimensions of both personality characteristics and social status characteristics. Adolescents who are altruistic and able to see others' points of view are more popular than are self-centered teenagers. High self-esteem also contributes to peer popularity. Status correlates of popularity include being an athlete, being in the leading crowd, being a leader in activities, coming from the right family, having high grades, and having a nice car (Thirer and Wright, 1985). Athletic participation is more important for male than for female popularity (see Box 7-3).

Many peer groups consist of teenagers from the same neighborhood, social class, ethnic group, or religion. This kind of exclusive organization can give teenagers a feeling of identity within their own subculture. Although not furthering the American melting pot ideal, such group feeling can provide a sense of security and pride to many teenagers who are confused about their own sense of self. Special interest peer groups may also allow not-so-popular adolescents to belong to some group, especially if membership is determined by religion, social class, parents' group membership (such as Masons-Demolay), or ethnicity. Within segregated peer groups with a heterosexual membership, teenagers can also find opposite-sex friends with whom they share common backgrounds or interests and of whom families may approve.

Segregated peer groups, though good for some teenagers who meet membership requirements, can also have ego-deflating effects on adolescents who are denied mem-

Athletics in the Life of an Adolescent.

Participation in an interschool or community-organized sports program has many advantages for a teenage male. Not only does the training exercise regimen increase physical fitness, but team rules help assure that the boy will eat well and not smoke, drink, use drugs, or even stay out late during the sports season. As a member of the team, the young man learns to compete through cooperation with others, rather than through self-aggrandizement. Such cooperation and team effort builds friendships and enhances self-esteem. To add to the benefits, research by Thirer and Wright (1985) suggests that the foremost criterion for male adolescent popularity with both males and females is having the status of athlete, or "letter-man."

Participation in interschool or community-organized athletic programs should have the same advantages for teenage females, but it does not. Thirer and Wright reported that being an athlete confers a fairly low social status on a girl. Butcher (1985), in a longitudinal study of girls from grades 6 through 10, found that their sports participation decreased or dropped out altogether by high school. In contrast, their secondary participation in sports increased—they vicariously followed sports by viewing live or televised sports events, listening to games on the radio, or reading about athletic contests.

Girls who continued to participate actively, Butcher found, described themselves as assertive and independent. They preferred activity to a sedentary lifestyle and got personal satisfaction from their sports abilities. They also had parents and friends who encouraged their ath-letic participation and had sports equipment available to them. Many adolescent females do not have equipment or encouragement. The physical fitness advantage of sports is the same for female athletes as for males, with an added benefit—girls who engage in regular physical activity have fewer premenstrual and menstrual symptoms.

Are there disadvantages of athletic participation during adolescence as well? Some athletes neglect their schoolwork to have time for sports. However, many others learn to balance studying with playing and earn good grades. A second possible drawback to sports participation is the danger of sports injury. Accidents related to athletic participation rank second after auto accidents as the cause of serious adolescent physical impairment each year.

Psychologists worry about a further effect of some competitive athletic programs. Many coaches encourage a "killer instinct" in their players. Aggression and violence are legitimized on playing fields, whether ice, turf, wood, mat, or ring. Athletes who are highly aggressive toward opponents have been shown to have less mature moral reasoning than less aggressive athletes (Bredemeier and Shields, 1984).

The physical fitness and social status benefits of athletics in the life of an adolescent need to be weighed against the threats of injury and socially sanctioned violence. The latter disadvantage could be minimized with athletic educational programs that discourage intentional infliction of pain and that encourage codes of fair play.

bership. Special interest cliques can be extremely cruel to outsiders. Psychologically mature teenagers can rebound from rejections by enjoying other friendships. Low-maturity teens, however, are much more dependent on peer acceptance for their own sense of self-worth (Josselson, Greenberger, and McConochie, 1977). Rejection, especially if it occurs over and over again, can leave a teenager feeling alienated and bereft of self-confidence. If he or she has also experienced pain and insecurity at home (such as strife with parents, separation or divorce of parents, substance abuse), a rejection by a peer group may precipitate a crisis (depression, suicide attempt).

Some peer groups (gangs) have the additional bad effect of accepting for membership status relatively meek adolescents (good followers) and putting them in positions of having to commit illegal or immoral acts or participate in violence in exchange for permanent membership in the gang. Within such groups many teenagers behave in very uncharacteristic ways. They may eventually begin to see getting into trouble as a desirable way of life because of the social acceptance and status it brings them.

School Interactions

For some teenagers, school is a friendly, stabilizing force in their lives: familiar buildings, rewarding adults, peer support (see Figure 7-23). For some adolescents, school is a source of stress: constant change, threats to safety, threats to self-esteem.

Figure 7-23
Students who excel in areas such as academics or athletics may find school a very rewarding experience.

Young people are required to attend some form of school, usually until they are 16. In the United States, one in every nine students attends private, as opposed to public, school (Nazario, 1988). Depending on locale, public schools may be stimulating and enjoyable, simply boring, or overwhelmingly frightening. They have higher drop-out rates (30% overall, up to 60% in some large cities) than private schools. About one million teenagers drop out of high school each year.

The transition from elementary or middle school to high school is frequently very stressful for an adolescent. It usually means a move from smaller to larger, personal to impersonal, slower-paced to faster-paced, and from the same class with the same teacher to different classes with different teachers. These changes come at the same time as the confusing changes of puberty (raging hormones) and the side effects of new cognitive processes (paranoia, personal fable). Changing schools in the midst of pubertal changes has been associated with both anxiety disorders and depression (Petersen, 1987). Adolescents who are more stressed by school in seventh grade are more apt to drop out of high school (Cairns, Cairns, and Neckerman, 1989). Other factors associated with school dropout are having peers who quit school, getting pregnant, being poor, or being an ethnic minority student in the school.

Learning activities in school may not absorb as much of an adolescent's time and attention as social activities. By their own admission, high school students pay attention in class to the subject of study only 40% of the time (Csikszentmihalyi and Larson, 1984). They also daydream; feel sad, irritable, or bored; whisper; pass notes; or do homework for other classes. Many scholars have suggested that low teacher salaries, overcrowded classrooms, lack of supplies, and teacher burnout make school classes a negative experience. Others have suggested that adolescence is a poor time for requiring memorization of facts and attention to lectures given by teachers. The onset of formal operations is accompanied by a desire to discuss and debate possibilities in subjects as diverse as mathematics and history, art and gym. By encouraging student participation, classes could be made more interesting. However, budget, staff, time, and diploma considerations often make these simple goals unrealistic or impossible.

Discipline in schools is a concern of both teenagers and adults (see Figure 7-24).

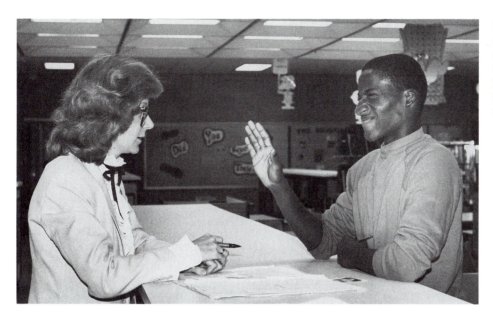

Figure 7-24
Any form of discipline is difficult during adolescence. Teenagers will argue almost every decision that affects them negatively. How should schoolteachers respond?

Some schools are punishment-oriented and have established sanctions to penalize students who violate rules. It is not illegal in many states for teachers to strike students, force them to stand for long periods, force them to eat substances such as soap or cigarettes, tie them to chairs, deprive them of meals, force them to do pushups or run laps, or throw them against objects (Nazario, 1988). On the other hand, some teachers have been assaulted or raped, have had their personal propery destroyed or stolen, or have been subjected to vicious verbal abuse. Public schools cannot expel students under age 16. Students are entitled by law to free and appropriate education in the least restrictive school environment. Suspensions usually cannot exceed two weeks. Schools must ask courts to intervene in extreme cases, but courts are hesitant to sentence unruly juveniles to correctional facilities because of legislation mandating least restrictive educational environments and deinstutionalization. Many schools must change to protect both students and teachers. Inservice training on inductive discipline and behavioral techniques can be instituted. Parents should be involved whenever there is a serious teacher–student dispute. Schools themselves should have human rights review committees to oversee the use and abuse of disciplinary procedures (Singer and Irvin, 1987).

Organized school groups can provide adolescents with safe, acceptable outlets for their energies (see Table 7-7). These groups give adolescents a chance to interact

Table 7-7 Possible School Groups with Which a Teenager May Become Affiliated.

Honor society	Orchestra	Voc-tech club
Student council	Dance band	Folk dancing
School newspaper	School sports teams	Modern dancing
Yearbook staff	Intramural sports teams	Exercise groups
Debate team	Pep squads	Gymnastics
Drama club	Cheerleaders	Ski club
Stamp club	Sororities	Swim club
Coin club	Fraternities	Outdoor clubs
Rifle club	Audio-visual group	International relations
Chorus	Future nurses	Chess club
Ensembles	Future farmers	Academic interest clubs
Band	Home economics group	Ethnic identity groups

with young people who have interests similar to their own. If the organized unit works together for a common goal, its members usually develop a certain amount of cohesiveness and group loyalty. Such special interest groups, organized within a school system, help break down the racial, ethnic, and social class barriers that often characterize outside peer groups. Consequently, school groups can serve two very useful functions: (1) they allow not-so-popular teenagers a chance to experience a sense of belonging and acceptance, and (2) they allow teenagers from different backgrounds to learn more about one another as they work or play together.

Sexual Behaviors

The one aspect of moral training that parents usually postpone until adolescence (or perhaps forever) is the area of responsible sexual behavior. Sex education in schools, popular music with sexual themes, sex on television, sex in the cinema, street language, pornography, and the like are blamed for teenagers' sexual activity. The cultures of most of the Western industrialized nations exude sexuality. The explicit message is that one must have sex appeal. The implicit message is that postpubertal persons are sexually active. Peer pressures may encourage experimentation: "Use it or lose it" is a prevalent myth (see Figure 7-25). Scott-Jones and White (1990) reported that by age fifteen about 28% of Americans have been sexually active. By age eighteen, 70% of males and 52% of females are sexually experienced (Evrard, 1985). The converse is that by age eighteen, 30% of males and 48% of females are still virgins. Not every teenager is sexually active, despite cultural influences. Many feel good about saying "No."

Social scientists often point the finger of blame for sexual activity at the parents, who overuse the defense mechanism of denial. Parents simply do not believe their children are sexually active. Many teenagers do not get information at home about sex. They may be hesitant to ask questions of their embarrassed parents. They may also feel a need to break away from their parents' advice, control, and protection. Erikson (1968) felt that an adolescent's sexual life is a self-seeking, identity-hungry activity in which each partner is really trying to understand himself or herself. McAnarney (1984) wrote that early coitus may be fulfilling a need to be touched, held, and cuddled. Parents become more restrained in physical contact with their children as they grow up and often terminate touching and hugging by adolescence.

Figure 7-25
Coming to terms with sexual urges may be difficult for teenagers.

Efforts to demonstrate that knowledge about birth control contributes to sexual activity have not been supported by research (Schwartz and Ford, 1983). Rather, there is evidence that there is a correlation between a lack of sex education and becoming pregnant (Zelnik and Kim, 1982). Many teenagers believe myths such as the following:

- Plastic wrap makes an effective condom.
- You can't get pregnant the first time.
- You can't get pregnant if you are standing.
- You can't get pregnant if you have your period.
- You can't get pregnant if the male withdraws in time.
- You can't get pregnant if you douche afterward.
- You can't get pregnant if you use foam afterward.
- You can't get pregnant if you take a birth control pill afterward.

Sex education courses fail to teach students that some semen leaks out before ejaculation and applying douches or foam afterward can push sperm through the vagina and cervix into the uterus.

Very few sexually active teenagers take precautions to prevent conception. Guesstimates are that only about one-third of teenagers having coitus use contraceptives on a regular basis. Teenagers who do use contraceptives generally do not begin using them until several months after their first sexual experiences. Teenage couples with good communication patterns are most apt eventually to use effective birth control (Polit-O'Hara and Kahn, 1985). Many teenagers believe pregnancy could not happen to them (personal fable). Only about 40% of American schools provide sex education courses, and 70% of students do not learn about birth control.

Contraceptive devices are not easy to obtain for teenagers. They are often too embarrassed to buy condoms, spermicides, or contraceptive sponges in a drugstore. They believe in the imaginary audience: Everyone is watching; everyone will know. Males often don't use condoms because they believe doing so takes all the pleasure out of intercourse. Many males also believe birth control decisions are the responsibility of the female (Cohen and Rose, 1984).

The effective female contraceptive devices, such as a diaphragm or birth control pills, require medical supervision. Many adolescents are afraid to go to a public clinic, or to a physician, for advice. Many believe that their parents will be notified of the visit and its purpose.

The most popular prescription contraceptive for teenage girls is still the Pill. However, Pill use has declined in recent years (Tyrer and Kornblatt, 1982). Many females are afraid of the Pill because of both myths (it makes your hair fall out) and realities (it may cause nausea; there is a correlation between extended Pill use and thromboembolism formation, visual disorders, gallbladder disease, and hypertension). Intrauterine devices are no longer recommended for teenagers. Teenage girls frequently reject the diaphragm for other reasons. If they have a diaphragm, they are perceived to be announcing that they are sexually active and want sex. Diaphragms require privacy for consistent use. They are also considered messy and inconvenient. Girls with diaphragms may not heed instructions on how to insert them, or the need to use them with a spermicidal jelly or foam, or the need to leave them in place for six or more hours after intercourse. Consequently, they become pregnant. The same problems exist for contraceptive sponges. Some teenagers try to use the rhythm method, but due to insufficient information about a girl's fertile period, and the unpredictability of ovulation in adolescent females (especially those who are stressed), this method is often ineffective as well. Natural family planning (see Chapter 3, p. 59) is often not discussed with adolescents.

Each year over 1 million American teenagers have babies. Over one-quarter of these teenage mothers are under age fifteen (see Figure 7-26) (Gordon and Gilgun, 1987). While some persons believe this is predominantly a phenomenon among non-

Figure 7-26
Children are having children. Many girls conceive at ages 12 or 13. They look more like a sister than a mother to their offspring.

whites, it is not. The rate of **teenage pregnancy** among white American teenagers is more than double the rate among white teenagers in Canada, England, France, Sweden, and the Netherlands. About 70% of teenage mothers are not married. If a pregnant teen marries, she has only a 25% chance of staying married (McAnarney, 1983). Very few teenage mothers relinquish their babies to adoption agencies; about 93% of them choose to raise the child themselves (Zelnik and Kantner, 1978).

Why do so many teenagers become pregnant? A lack of information about contraception is only one reason. Having a baby may be viewed as a sign of maturity, a kind of status symbol. Many girls see motherhood as a way to achieve a feeling of being loved and needed by someone else. Some girls may use pregnancy as an escape from an unhappy home situation. Many teenage mothers have a history of being victims of child abuse or rape. Others may be reacting to the loss of a parent through divorce, death, hospitalization, or institutionalization. Teenage mothers can obtain federal and state aid to support themselves and their babies through programs such as food stamps, Medicaid, and aid to families with dependent children (AFDC). These programs consume over 8½ billion tax dollars for teenagers in the United States each year (Moore and Burt, 1982).

Babies carried by teenage mothers are at high risk for complications of pregnancy and birth. Many pregnant teens starve themselves and exercise rigorously to avoid appearing pregnant. Few seek prenatal care before the second trimester and then few keep their appointments. Their diets are often overloaded with junk foods and deficient in protein, calcium, folic acid, and vitamins. Teenage mothers are often loath to give up late-night dates. They may use alcohol, cigarettes, or other drugs. Teenage mothers have a higher incidence of pregnancy-induced eclampsia and anemia. The mortality rate is 60% greater in teenagers under age fifteen than it is in women over age twenty (Evrard, 1985).

Only about one-half of the teenagers who have babies return to finish high school (McAnarney, 1983). In some areas, high schools have established programs to provide prenatal care and nutritional counseling during pregnancy, and daycare facilities for infants after delivery, in order to allow girls to continue their education. Some programs have reduced the teen mother dropout rate considerably. The exclusion of pregnant students from school is prohibited by law in the United States (Nazario, 1988).

Are teen mothers good mothers? Research suggests that the answer depends on the individual adolescent female. Those who have more knowledge about infants and child development and who have a positive attitude toward motherhood interact with their babies more (LeResche et al., 1983). Younger mothers tend to have less knowledge, to have more negative attitudes, and to be more controlling and less verbal with their babies (Fry, 1985). In general, teenage mothers have been shown to have a low level of verbal interaction with their infants (Landy et al., 1983). At five years of age, children raised by teenage mothers perform less well on tests of vocabulary (Wadsworth et al., 1984). They also tend to be shorter, have smaller head circumferences, and have more behavior difficulties. McAnarney (1983) found that the mother at highest risk of parental dysfunction is a fifteen- to sixteen-year-old, non-black, lower-socioeconomic-status adolescent. She suggested that perhaps both younger and older adolescent mothers have more supports available to them than the 15- to 16-year-olds.

Research has all but ignored teen fathers. Many of them, even if they do not marry the mother, maintain contact with her and show a desire to name the baby and to meet some responsibilities toward the dyad (Barret and Robinson, 1982). However, their support usually drops off, and they tend to disappear, usually after a year (Robinson and Barret, 1985).

Ten to fifteen million new cases of **sexually transmitted diseases** (STDs) (formerly called *venereal diseases*) appear each year in the United States, with a preponderance of the diseases occurring in teenagers and young adults. The most common of the sexually transmitted diseases is not gonorrhea, not syphilis, not even genital herpes, but chlamydia. Many other STDs occur with alarming frequency. Most of the STDs are easily diagnosed and treated. (All but herpes and AIDS can be cured.) However, fears and ignorance keep many teens away from physicians or clinics (see Figure 7-27). They deny the symptoms, try worthless home remedies, or hope that the STD will cure itself. Instead, untreated STDs are spread to unsuspecting others. They create problems such as sterility, cancer, brain damage, arthritis, tubal pregnancies, and miscarriages.

The first symptom of *chlamydia* is usually a purulent discharge from the penis. Pus means infection and should never be ignored. Females are usually without symptoms until they have the disease in their Fallopian tubes (pelvic imflammatory disease). This can cause tubal obstruction, which in turn can lead to an ectopic (tubal) pregnancy, or to infertility. Males have a responsibility to tell all their female sex partners if they discover they have chlamydia. Females must be tested, and treated, to prevent the devastating consequences of chlamydia. If a woman transmits chlamydia to a neonate, it can cause eye and ear infections, which may lead to blindness or deafness. In men, untreated chlamydia can also lead to sterility.

Gonorrhea, also called "the clap," causes painful urination in men and a discharge of thick yellow pus. Women frequently notice no symptoms of disease. Cure can be

Figure 7-27
Many myths surround the topic of sexually transmitted diseases. Teenagers believe the myths and fail to practice safe sex.

achieved with penicillin or a penicillin substitute, but the disease may be contracted again and again. Physicians usually prefer to treat people who even suspect they may have been infected rather than wait for the dubious symptoms, especially in women. Untreated gonorrhea can sometimes lead to infection of the valves of the heart or joints (gonococcal arthritis), skin lesions, gallbladder disease, inflammation of the uterus and oviducts (in women), or sterility (men and women).

Syphilis causes a painless sore called a chancre. It heals fairly quickly and disappears. A man may notice such lesions on his penis, but women cannot detect chancres occurring within their vaginas. Long after the chancre has disappeared, new symptoms develop (secondary syphilis): a rash on the palms or soles, a complete body rash, and hair loss. If syphilis remains untreated, it goes into a latent stage. Untreated syphilis eventually leads to a late tertiary stage characterized by inflammatory diseases of the skin, diseases of the aorta and cardiovascular system, and many forms of neurological disorders including blindness, paralysis, and an organic mental illness called general paresis. Treatment is penicillin or other antibiotic therapy. Physicians must trace sexual contacts and attempt to get them in for treatment when the disease is diagnosed.

AIDS (see Box 7-4) is becoming increasingly common in adolescent populations, especially in those who share needles for drug injections or engage in unprotected sex. Roscoe and Kruger (1990) reported that 90% of adolescents are well-informed about the AIDS virus but only about one-third of them say they have changed their behaviors

BOX 7-4

AIDS.

Acquired immune deficiency syndrome (AIDS) is a sexually transmitted disease that reduces the body's ability to fight infection. AIDS patients invariably die. Many myths have sprung up in the years since AIDS first appeared. Let us look at the simple truths of the disease.

AIDS is caused by a virus. In order to get AIDS, a person must receive the virus directly into the blood. The disease is, consequently, not a highly contagious one. Children who have it usually acquired it in utero or at birth from infected mothers or from blood transfusions. As of March 1985, however, all blood transfusions have been considered safe (free of the AIDS virus), due to testing before use.

Women who have AIDS usually acquired it by sharing needles with an infected person for intravenous injection of heroin, cocaine, or amphetamines. Women also spread it this way or to infants in utero. No one has been able to isolate the virus from vaginal or cervical fluids (Finkbeiner, 1985).

The AIDS virus lives in T-helper cells, which are lymphocytes (white blood cells) that are concentrated most heavily in the blood and also in semen. Any practice that allows infected blood or semen to enter another person's blood (such as during intercourse, sharing intravenous needles) will spread the virus. While saliva and tears may contain a few T-helper cells, there are no known cases of AIDS being spread through saliva or tears. The disease is *not* transmitted by casual contact

with AIDS patients (for example, to family members, to doctors and nurses, to school children in play).

AIDS is a slow-growing virus at first. The incubation period for AIDS can be longer than five years (Food and Drug Administration, 1985). Infection by the virus has three preliminary forms before AIDS, and not all infected persons go on to develop AIDS. In the first form, which may be mistaken for a gastrointestinal flu, symptoms including fever, diarrhea, and weakness occur. After this the patient will develop antibodies. In the second form of infection, the person will be an asymptomatic carrier of the virus (the antibodies will not kill the virus). This second form may be the end of the infectious process. In a small percentage of infected persons, the disease continues to a third form called ARC (AIDS-related complex). The patient again has fever, diarrhea, and weakness, but this time it persists with weight loss and swollen lymph glands. Some people recover from ARC. Others go on to develop AIDS. They keep losing weight, and their immune system fails. They usually die from opportunistic infections (pneumonia, tuberculosis, herpes, toxoplasmosis, Kaposi's sarcoma).

Efforts to cure AIDS are directed at killing the virus before it can progress to the fourth and final form of the disease. This must be accomplished without killing the T-helper cells and destroying the immune system. Prevention of AIDS requires that infected persons do not allow the entrance of their own blood or semen into the blood of noninfected persons.

because of the AIDS threat. They have the personal fable that nothing bad can happen to them. Roscoe and Kruger contend that factual knowledge alone cannot change behaviors of adolescents. They recommend assertiveness training and one-on-one counseling to further prevention efforts.

Genital herpes is a close relative of the cold sore. Like cold sores, genital herpes consists of painful lesions filled with a whitish fluid. They appear around the genitals—on the penis or in the urethra in men, in the vagina or on the labia in women, and occasionally on the thighs and buttocks. Genital herpes is highly contagious when the sores are wet. The sores heal spontaneously in one to three weeks, but the herpes virus remains in the body in a latent stage. It can cause new bouts of painful genital sores periodically, at unpredictable times, such as when the carrier becomes stressed or physically ill. The drug Acyclovir can lessen the severity and duration of bouts of herpes lesions at the time of infection. It cannot, however, cure the disease. Genital herpes has been associated with an increased spontaneous abortion rate and with cancer of the cervix (Barclay, 1984).

Genital warts (condylomata) are another rapidly spreading form of STD. Like other warts, they are benign, virus-induced tumors (Cunningham, Hemsell, and Mickal, 1984). They may be flat, pointed, or cauliflower-like and can grow on the anus, in the perineal area, or in the vagina. They are uncomfortable as well as disfiguring. They can be removed by burning, freezing, chemicals, or surgery.

Vaginal infections caused by the *trichomonas* parasite cause a greenish, frothy, malodorous discharge. In addition, the vulvar area may have burning, itching, and swelling. The parasite, a protozoan, can be eradicated with metronidazole.

Candida albicans, a yeast, causes a thick white vaginal discharge and vulvar itching when it is present. It grows best premenstrually, or in women with a high dietary intake of sugars. In women, it is treated with vaginal suppositories. It sometimes is referred to as *moniliasis.*

All adolescents (or adults) who suspect that they may have a sexually transmitted disease can get information about where to go for confidential tests and treatment by calling the VD National Hot-line's toll free number: (800) 227-8922; (800) 982-5883 in California. They should cease all sexual activity until they have been treated and advise all of their sexual contacts to seek treatment as well.

Summary

The teenage years include vast numbers of interacting changes. Consider, for example, the impact of sexual maturation, formal reasoning abilities, and greater independence. The developing personality is particularly vulnerable to pressures from family members, peers, and school. Turbulence frequently mars the relationships between adults and adolescents in Western industrialized societies.

Puberty, the period of rapid growth preceding sexual maturity, may occur anywhere from ages eight to twenty and may last from a few months to a couple of years. Although both early and late maturers have special problems, late maturation can be especially traumatic because of its impact on self-concept and peer acceptance.

The focal points for health maintenance in adolescence are nutrition, prompt attention to infections, and safety precautions. Accidents are the leading cause of deaths and disabilities. Independence strivings and peer pressures make many teenagers particularly reckless. A plethora of health problems relate to nutrition: obesity, anorexia nervosa, bulimia, anemia, substance abuse, acne, and lowered resistance to infection.

Piaget postulated a stage of formal operations to explain the cognitive changes of adolescence. It is characterized by interpropositional thinking, combinatorial analysis, and hypothetical-deductive reasoning. Persons using formal operations pay close attention to details and thoughtfully analyze new problems and situations. New cognitive abilities during adolescence contribute to a rise in youthful egocentrism, idealism, and argumentativeness.

Adolescent males frequently excel in cognitive tasks requiring spatial abilities. Females often show superior verbal skills. These sex differences in intellectual functioning may be genetically based, environmentally conditioned, or both. They often influence career choices.

The quest for identity, as described by Erikson, is marked by a search for a sense of continuity and sameness between one's own and others' view of the self. Moral development may lead to idealized schemes and a view of others' hypocrisies. Teenagers alienated from their parents may turn to suicidal thoughts, drugs, or delinquent behaviors. Peer and school activities may contribute to an adolescent's positive self-concept. They may also contribute to feelings of alienation or hostility.

Many teens are sexually active. Sexual activity, unless protected, may result in pregnancy. Over one-half of all teenage mothers fail to finish high school. Careless sexual activity may lead to one or more of the sexually transmitted diseases.

Key Concepts

puberty
pubescence
androgens
estrogens
progesterone
primary sexual characteristics
menarche
menstruation
secondary sexual characteristics
late maturation
heightism

precocious puberty
iron deficiency anemia
obesity
anorexia nervosa
bulimia
acne
infectious mononucleosis
formal operations
interpropositional thinking
combinatorial analysis
proportional reasoning

hypothetical-deductive reasoning
adolescent egocentrism
fear of success
affiliation needs
achievement needs
generation gap
identity versus role confusion
foreclosure of identity
moratorium of identity
identity diffusion
identity achievement

principled moral reasoning
alienation
depression
adolescent suicides
status offenses
delinquent acts
juvenile crimes
substance abuse
peer pressures
teenage pregnancy
sexually transmitted diseases (STDs)

Questions for Review

1. Adolescents often feel ugly, ungainly, and not as physically attractive as their peers. Flattery by parents usually doesn't help. How can parents help their teenagers deal with these feelings without sounding superficial?
2. Compare the abilities children have in the concrete operations stage with the abilities adolescents have in the formal operations stage.
3. It might seem that the ability that is developed in adolescence to see all variations of a problem would enable an individual to feel more confident and secure. Is this what happens when adolescents develop this ability? Discuss.
4. Adolescents can be difficult to be around—argumentative at one moment, flattering at another, affectionate at another, and rejecting and angry at another—

often all in the course of one day. Imagine you are an adolescent's parent. What sorts of things would you keep in mind to help *you* in dealing with all these mood changes and the feelings they stir up in you?
5. You are a parent who has spent time discussing sex with your children. You have answered all their questions as openly and honestly as possible. Your daughter, age sixteen, comes to you, telling you she has decided to begin using birth control and wants your help in going to the doctor and choosing a method. She has no steady boyfriend. What would you say to her?
6. There is an increasing trend among pregnant teenagers to keep their babies, even if they decide not to marry. What are the implications of this decision for the girl, her family, the baby, and society?

Further Readings

Berman, A. L. (1990). *Suicide prevention.* New York: Springer.
    The author uses case consultations to present information about how suicides can be prevented through both clinical interventions and community programming efforts.
Brumberg, J. J. (1989). *Fasting girls: A history of anorexia nervosa.* New York: Penguin.
    An overview of eating disorders for contemporary students, exploring how young women have used food

to influence family, medical practice, and themselves for centuries.
Furstenburg, F. F., Brooks-Gunn, J., and Morgan, S. P. (1987). *Adolescent mothers in later life.* Cambridge, UK: Cambridge University Press.
    This volume offers data to guide professionals working with adolescent mothers. What works—limiting more children, finishing high school? The answers come from interviews with 300 young mothers.

Murray-Seegert, C. (1989). *Nasty girls, thugs and humans like us.* Baltimore: Paul Brookes Publishing.
School relations between disabled and nondisabled high school students are discussed. Integration can be mutually empowering for some.

Van Hasselt, V. B., and Hersen, M. (eds.) (1987). *Handbook of adolescent psychology.* New York: Pergamon Press.
Covers a wide range of topics: Theories, history, puberty, cognition, moral development, behavior disorders, teen pregnancy and marriage.

Physical Development
Physical Maturation
Stress Management
Health Maintenance
Substance Abuse

Cognitive Development

Psychosocial Development
Separating from the Family of
   Origin
Searching for Intimacy
Marriage
Parenthood
Preparation for a Career

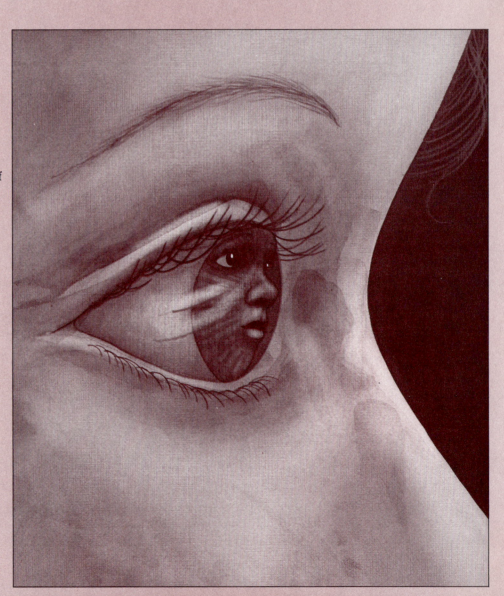

Young Adulthood 8

In our society people in their twenties usually branch out from their families of origin and establish themselves in somewhat independent lifestyles. The activities and patterns of living pursued by various young people may be worlds apart. Consider, for example, the differences between struggling or unemployed ghetto youth and affluent young persons who can move into their families' businesses. Consider the gulf between persons secluded in convents or seminaries and those following rock bands. The examples can go on and on. The lives of young people who get married are vastly different from the lives of those who remain single. Those who pursue advanced education differ from those who never finish high school. Those who earn their own living differ from those whose parents support them. Children and adolescents, because of required school attendance, share similar experiences. People in their twenties often do not. This chapter will describe some of the concerns that face young adults regardless of the path they choose. The choice is profound. As Robert Frost (1949) put it:

> Two roads diverged in a wood, and I—
> I took the one less traveled by,
> And that has made all the difference.

Life is not a matter of holding good cards, but of playing a poor hand well.
—*Robert Louis Stevenson*

Man looks about the Universe in awe at its wonders, and forgets that he himself is the greatest wonder of all.
—*Saint Augustine*

Physical Development

Between ages twenty and thirty the human body reaches its peak condition. The archetypal young adult can expect to have muscles and bones that are strong and resilient, freedom from degenerative disease, normally functioning endocrine glands, an efficient immune system, and a digestive system that functions smoothly. Physical stamina should be sufficient to keep up with all the social, economic, and emotional tasks of this period (see Figure 8-1).

Physical Maturation

Skeletal development is completed as the long bones of the upper legs and arms finish their ossification process (change from cartilage to bone). (See Plate 1 in center of text.) During childhood the head was larger than the trunk and the trunk more developed than the limbs. With the limbs, development proceeded from foot to calf to

The child was really named Orpah, after a woman in the Old Testament, but the midwife misspelled the name *Oprah,* and it stuck.

As a child, Oprah was shuttled frequently between homes. She was raised by her paternal grandparents for six years in a small Mississippi town. There, her grandmother taught her to read and write and even give public speeches by the age of three. Her mother reclaimed her and took her to Milwaukee at age six. At age eight, she went to live with her father in Nashville. Her mother took her back to Milwaukee within the year, where she was eventually raped both by a cousin and by her mother's boyfriend in Milwaukee. By the time she was thirteen, Oprah had a dynamite figure (36–23–36) and an atrocious sense of self-worth. She wore short, tight clothes and too much makeup. She told lies, stole, and ran the streets.

Oprah credits her father with saving her by taking her back to Nashville at age fourteen: "Without his direction, I'd have wound up pregnant and another statistic."*

Oprah started college at Tennessee State University a changed woman. She worked part-time as a radio newscaster and majored in speech and drama. She had a variety of acting roles in college: monologues, dramatic readings, plays. She entered and won beauty contests to help support her education. She was Miss Black Nashville and Miss Black Tennessee, and she competed in the Miss Black America contest in Hollywood.

On the brink of young adulthood, Oprah landed her first television job as a news co-anchor in Nashville. She was a success.

At age twenty-two, Oprah was asked to move to Baltimore to be the TV news co-anchor for a much larger audience. She left the protection of her father's home and began her own independent life.

Oprah did not experience the same success co-anchoring the news in Baltimore. There was bad chemistry between her and her co-anchor. Jealousies and power struggles caused her nine months of co-anchoring to be very unpleasant. She assuaged her frustrations by eating. Even as a teenage beauty queen, Oprah had had difficulties maintaining her figure. In her twenties, her problems were worse.

At age twenty-three, Oprah was asked to move from the newsroom to a local morning talk show slot, competing with the syndicated "Donahue." Oprah had good chemistry with her talk-show co-host, and the program was very successful.

During the six years of co-hosting "People Are Talking" in Baltimore, Oprah had public fame but personal sadness. A supportive boyfriend moved on to a New York City station. She tolerated a new boyfriend who did not recognize her worth. She felt worthless, both with and without this man. She described herself as a doormat. She became a binge eater. She decided to commit suicide. She was twenty-seven years old and felt her wings had been clipped. While thinking of suicide, she had a revelation. She could go it alone. Her lot was not unlike that of a physically abused woman. She needed to get out of destructive affairs. Oprah chose to be positive. Rather than blaming any of the people who had victimized her, she decided to claim victories by overcoming what happened to her. "If you live in the past and allow the past to define who you are, then you never grow."*

Oprah took a job as a talk-show host in Chicago, in part to end her stormy Baltimore relationship. "AM Chicago" with Oprah was so popular that it expanded from a half-hour to an hour after seven months. By the age of thirty, Oprah had indeed overcome. She had a supporting actress role in the movie, *The Color Purple,* and a talk-show that was outdrawing "Donahue." By age thirty-two, "The Oprah Winfrey Show" was syndicated across America. She had proven her worth.

Is it easy for persons who have been victimized to overcome their sense of guilt, shame, and self-blame? Is it easy to forgive the victimizer? Is binge eating related to self-concept and self-esteem? Can adversities motivate success?

*Waldron, R. (1987). *Oprah!* New York: St. Martin's Press.

thigh and from hand to forearm to upper arm. For some adolescents this meant outsized feet or hands, which caused a degree of clumsiness until the near ends caught up with peripheral growth.

As bones ossify, the shaft of the bone develops first. The outlying areas of bones are called *epiphyses*. Between the ossified shaft and the epiphysis there is a nonossified area, the epiphyseal line, from which the bone continues to grow in length. In the twenties these epiphyses fuse with the main shafts of the bones. Once epiphyseal lines are calcified (or closed), the lengthwise growth of bones ceases. Attainment of final adult height coincides with this fusion. A simple radiograph can be used to analyze bone development and determine whether final adult skeletal growth has been achieved. A few millimeters may be added to the width of some bones later by surface deposition. Head length and breadth, facial diameters, and the width of bones in the legs and hands may increase slightly by this process throughout life.

The bones of females tend to be less dense than the bones of males, due to the deposition of less calcium and other minerals. Females can increase bone mass in young adulthood by increasing their calcium intake and adding exercise. Calcium supplementation without exercise or exercise with low calcium intake both have negligible effects on bone mass (Kanders, Lindsay, and Dempster, 1984). Due to a wider pelvic girdle, the femur of the female is attached to her ilium at a much more oblique angle than is a male's. This gives her a lower center of gravity and more support for childbearing, but less agility in running and jumping (see Figure 8-2).

Muscles continue to gain strength throughout the twenties and reach peak strength at about age thirty, depending on exercise and genetic endowment. Men have larger muscles that can produce more force per gram than the muscle tissue of women. They also have a greater aerobic capacity for carrying oxygen in the blood to the muscles and for neutralizing the chemical products of exercising muscle. The stamina needed for endurance tasks peaks in the late twenties and slowly deteriorates after that.

Many young adults, male and female, worry about their physical appearance as it relates to muscles and body build. Men in general are more satisfied with their appearance than women. However, both sexes have a hard time accepting their own appearance if they compare it with body builders or reed thin models. Satisfaction with personal appearance is enhanced by maintaining a normal body weight for size, exercising to keep muscles firm, and accepting one's body with a more realistic view of physical attractiveness. Women normally have more fat and less muscle than men.

The approximate normal percentages of muscle, bone and fat for the two sexes are:

	Male	Female
Muscle	50%	40%
Bone	14%	12%
Fat	15%	25%

Dental maturity is finally achieved in the twenties with the emergence of the last four molars, called wisdom teeth. For some young adults these last teeth are the cause of severe toothaches, as they sometimes become impacted (wedged between the jawbone and the next most forward molars) and need to be removed. The molars, which grind food, are not well utilized by persons who partake of soft, modern diets. The absence of one or more of the wisdom teeth causes no hardship.

The reproductive systems of both men and women are fully mature by the twenties. For men, the maximum capacity for making love several times in a brief interval peaks in the teens. For women, the maximum lovemaking capacity occurs in the early thirties (Labby, 1987). Sex drive remains relatively high, however, in most people for several decades, often into the sixties and seventies. Regardless of libido, the sex hormones

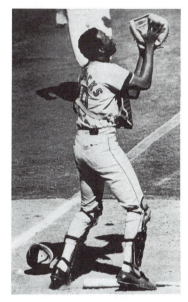

Figure 8-1
The twenties are years characterized by peak physical status: strong muscles, plenty of stamina, resistance to disease, and rapid repair of tissue damage. Retention of these capacities depends on how young adults care for themselves.

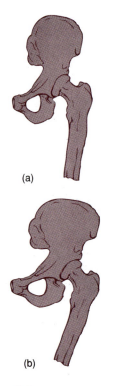

Figure 8-2
Skeletal differences between (a) males and (b) females include a wider pelvic girdle and a less vertical placement of the femur in females.

(testosterone in men, estrogen in women), have their highest rates of production in the twenties.

Evidence suggests that both men and women experience involuntary cyclic alterations in their sex hormone production (Parsons, 1980). They also have involuntary fluctuations of certain adrenal hormones (for example, epinephrine). Hormones vary on a daily basis, called **circadian rhythms,** and on a monthly basis called **lunar cycles.** Changes in production of hormones within each individual occur with clocklike regularity. Low production periods have been associated with apathy, indifference, and a tendency to magnify minor problems out of proportion. High periods correlate with increased energy, a decreased need for sleep, and a feeling of well-being. High testosterone levels in men have been associated with increased feelings of hostility and aggressiveness (Parsons, 1980). High estrogen levels in women have been associated with feelings of increased well-being and mood elevation. This phenomenon has been especially noted during pregnancy, when estrogen levels are much increased, and during the ovulatory phase of the menstrual cycle.

Although some women experience increased anxiety, depression, or a tendency to magnify problems premenstrually, when estrogen levels are low, many do not. Persky (1974) studied twenty-nine healthy young women (average age twenty-two) and found remarkably little change in their moods related to their "periods." Their average values for the psychological variable assessed closely resembled the average values of a control group of male classmates. Some women and men show behavioral effects of high and low hormone levels; some evidence little or no outward signs of these daily and monthly fluctuations.

The effects of the sex hormones on the secretion of oils (sebum) from the sebaceous glands of the skin, which contributed to the acne of adolescence, become less pronounced in the twenties. Acne usually disappears, and young adults' hair is less oily. The body has a remarkable ability to adapt positively to hormone fluctuations.

Stress Management

> José leaves his apartment building to discover it is raining. He uses his briefcase for an umbrella and arrives at the corner just as his bus pulls away. He is soaked by the time another bus gets him to work—late. A note on his desk tells him to call his physician. Another note advises him to see his supervisor. His supervisor tells him he cannot have his requested vacation time (the week of his fiancée's college graduation). Hoping for better news, he calls his physician. His biopsy results revealed skin cancer; he must have the melanoma removed. Fight? Flight? Neither. He must cope.

People differ considerably in their abilities to handle stress. It has been suggested that such simple behaviors as talking or crying can give vent to restrained emotions. Crying especially is credited with helping to restore mental and physical equilibrium during periods of stress, but American men and women are taught not to cry.

Young adults may be experiencing a stress epidemic. College students report a wide variety of stressors (see Table 8-1). Young adults trying to become established in careers report more pressures. Life in the pressure cooker is emerging as the principal threat to the health of young adults. The three best selling categories of drugs for adults are tranquilizers, antihypertensive drugs, and ulcer medications.

People who do not have ways to cope with their stresses, or who are placed in situations where the tension is seemingly too great to handle, increase their probability of a wide range of illnesses. Their immune systems cease to function well (Miller, 1985). **Psychophysiologic disorders** are those that relate to the influence of the mind (emotions, fears, desires, frustrations, anxieties) on the malfunctioning of the body. Psychophysiologic diseases are very real, not imagined. However, successful treatment depends on the removal or alleviation of the sources of stress as well as on pharmaceutical and physical measures. Stress that is restrained and hidden from the

Table 8-1 Some Stressors in the Lives of College Students.

Physical appearance	Moving away from home
Fitness/nutrition	Relationships with parents
Stress management	Shortage of money
Finding time to relax	Changing gender roles
Alcohol and drug use	Intolerance of differences
Study/work habits	Peer pressures for behaviors
Grades/grading policies	Relationships with roommates
Inferior education	Intimacy
Fear of failure	Dating/social life
Fear of success	Sexual identity (homo-, hetero-, bi-)
Career decisions	Fear of commitment to relationship
Choosing job vs. graduate school	Date rape
Planning for an unsure future	Dangers of sexual activity
Few adult role models	Cohabitation
Handling increased responsibilities	Family planning
Changing perception of self	Juggling family and career
Threats to self-esteem	Divorce
Pressures to succeed	Vacation plans
Individuality/independence	Death and dying
Where to live	Suicides

outside world can affect individuals in any number of ways. Skin lesions may erupt, such as neurodermatitis, shingles, psoriasis, or hives. Disorders of the gastrointestinal tract may appear, such as heartburn, chronic diarrhea, constipation, ulcers, bulimia, anorexia nervosa, or diabetes. The respiratory system may show its susceptibility to psychic stimuli, as in hyperventilation, influenza, pneumonia, or aggravation of asthma. The cardiovascular system may be affected by palpitations, fainting spells, hypertension, fibrillation, angina, or large fluctuations in blood pressure. The nervous system may respond with migraine headaches, tics, stuttering, tremors, or multiple sclerosis. Many other diseases have psychophysiologic bases. It is always difficult to separate the physical from the psychological causes of illness. However, we do recognize that stress predisposes persons to disease.

There is a feedback loop between hormones and neurotransmitters that contributes to all of the psychophysiological illnesses. When a person experiences stress, the hypothalamus (the body's thermostat) sends out corticotropic releasing factor (CRF). This stimulates the pituitary to release adrenocorticotropic hormone (ACTH). A tropic hormone is a "turning" hormone; in this case, ACTH turns on the cortical regions of the adrenal glands. ACTH, in a continuation of this loop, stimulates each adrenal cortex to produce stress hormones: cortisol and epinephrine. The stress hormones enter the bloodstream where they have pronounced effects on many physiological functions. They stimulate the sympathetic nervous system to prepare the body for flight (escape) or fight (see Table 8-2). The neurons produce several neurotransmitters that also affect the body: norepinephrine, serotonin, dopamine, and acetylcholine. Neurons also produce endorphins, which are natural painkillers, decreasing one's sensations

Table 8-2 The Physiological Effects of Stress Hormones.

↑ Blood supply to muscles (tension)	↓ Immune system responsivity
↑ Lipids (fats) into blood	↓ Circulation to hands and feet
↑ Sugars into blood	↓ Salivation
↑ Basal metabolic rate	↓ Digestive processes
↑ Heartbeat and blood pressure	↓ Healthy sleep
↑ Pain threshold (numbness)	↓ Sexual libido
↑ Blood supply to brain	↓ Bladder control

of pain during stress. These chemical responses to stress can be either pleasant or unpleasant. Over time, stress chemistry can create one or more psychophysiological disorders.

Selye (1974) differentiated between *eustress* (pleasant and stimulating stress) and *distress*. Our lives would be barren without any stressors. Both eustress and distress can be helpful in small doses and harmful in overloads. Selye described a **general adaptation syndrome** (GAS) that has three stages: (1) alarm, (2) resistance, and (3) exhaustion.

During the alarm phase, the body responds to stress with the hormone neurotransmitter cycle depicted in Figure 8-3. During the resistance phase, the body slows its stress reaction. Outwardly, the signs of stress may disappear, but internally some of the increases and decreases listed on Table 8-2 are still occurring. Gradually, the chemicals needed to respond to stress are depleted, like a pool of water exposed too long to sun and wind. Exhaustion occurs. A psychophysiological disorder, or an accident, is likely.

Our highly industrialized society with its rapid changes (in personal relationships, jobs, residences) requires that we make many decisions and alterations in our lives, leaving us in frequent need of stress hormones. This state is similar to the "culture

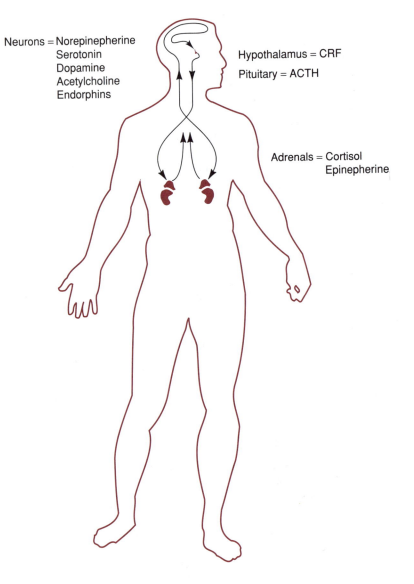

Neurons = Norepinepherine
Serotonin
Dopamine
Acetylcholine
Endorphins

Hypothalamus = CRF

Pituitary = ACTH

Adrenals = Cortisol
Epinepherine

Figure 8-3

The hormone-neurotransmitter feedback loop that regulates our response to stress.

shock" a visitor to a foreign country experiences. Too many changes at once drain our energy resources and exhaust our abilities to cope, adapt, and evolve. Holmes and Rahe (1967), both medical doctors, postulated that too much change in a relatively short period of time lowers one's resistance to stress and increases one's risk of a major health change. They listed the major changes an average adult may experience and asked hundreds of persons to rate them as to the amount of adaptation and readjustment they cause. The averaged mean values assigned to various life events are shown in Table 8-3. Many of these changes are positive. They still require an expenditure of energy, however, for coping with them.

Holmes and Rahe found that persons whose combined life change units (LCU) over a one-year period was 300 or more had about a 90% chance of having a major health change. If one's score was from 150 to 300 points in a year, the chance of a major

Table 8-3   The Social Readjustment Rating Scale.

Life Event	Mean Value
1. Death of spouse	100
2. Divorce	73
3. Marital separation	65
4. Jail term	63
5. Death of close family member	63
6. Personal injury or illness	53
7. Marriage	50
8. Fired at work	47
9. Marital reconciliation	45
10. Retirement	45
11. Change in health of family member	44
12. Pregnancy	40
13. Sex difficulties	39
14. Gain of new family member	39
15. Business readjustment	39
16. Change in financial state	38
17. Death of close friend	37
18. Change to different line of work	36
19. Change in number of arguments with spouse	35
20. Mortgage or loan for major purchase (home, etc.)	31
21. Foreclosure of mortgage or loan	29
22. Change in responsibilities at work	29
23. Son or daughter leaving home	29
24. Trouble with in-laws	29
25. Outstanding personal achievement	28
26. Wife begins or stops work	26
27. Begin or end school	26
28. Change in living conditions	25
29. Revision of personal habits	24
30. Trouble with boss	23
31. Change in work hours or conditions	20
32. Change in residence	20
33. Change in schools	20
34. Change in recreation	19
35. Change in church activities	19
36. Change in social activities	18
37. Mortgage or loan for lesser purchase (car, TV, etc.)	17
38. Change in sleeping habits	16
39. Change in number of family get-togethers	15
40. Change in eating habits	15
41. Vacation	13
42. Christmas	12
43. Minor violations of the law	11

SOURCE: Reprinted with permission from *Journal of Psychosomatic Research*, **11**(2), 213–218, T. H. Holmes and R. H. Rahe, "The Social Readjustment Rating Scale," copyright 1967 Pergamon Press, Ltd.

health change was 50%. A score of 150 or less decreased one's chance of accident or illness to about 30% or less. Holmes and Rahe cautioned that persons who are about to make voluntary changes (such as a job change, a move, marriage) should pace them so they do not all occur at once. One can avoid the danger zone for a stress-related accident or illness by taking the time to readjust and adapt to one or two changes before subjecting oneself to more.

Some persons, after intense stress, develop **posttraumatic stress disorder** (PTSD). This syndrome frequently characterizes soldiers who have returned from battle. However, it also is common in persons who have survived unexpected deaths of family members or close friends, kidnapping, hostage situations, rape, airplane, train, or automobile crashes, floods, fires, tornadoes, or earthquakes. Initially the survivor is disoriented and dazed. When this emotional confusion lifts, the victim goes through a period of denial (resistance). He or she may even seem happy, as if nothing happened. Eventually, however, exhaustion becomes a reality. Several symptoms may develop and persist for extended periods of time: impaired memory, insomnia, nightmares, somnambulism (sleepwalking), guilt, avoidance of close interpersonal relationships, digestive disturbances, accident proneness, frequent illness, work inhibition, aimlessness, displaced anger, increased use of drugs, depression. These aftereffects may not occur until a few months after the trauma. They often persist several months or even over a year. Therapy for PTSD is aimed at helping the victim realize that these reactions are normal, that many others have also had extended posttraumatic stress symptoms. Group therapy with others with similar problems is helpful. Counselors try to help victims reestablish social networks and become involved in meaningful activities (McLeod, 1984). Without psychological help, some emotional distress can continue indefinitely.

Holistic medicine is a developing field that treats the whole person after any illness or injury. Not only are techniques of medicine or surgery applied, but multiple efforts are made to reduce stress responses and increase coping skills. Holistic practitioners make recommendations about diet, exercise, sleep, relaxation, avoidance of drugs, and stress management techniques. Three stress response reducers that have

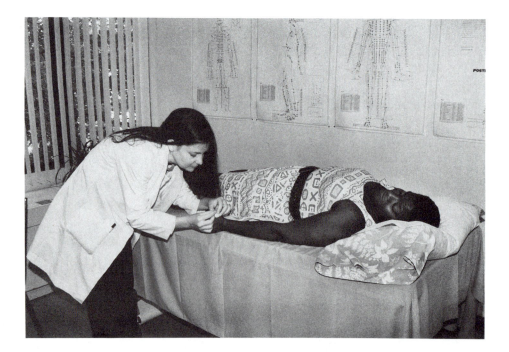

Figure 8-4
Acupuncture can be employed as a health maintenance procedure as well as a pain reliever.

Acupuncture.

Acupuncture is more than just inserting needles to take away pain: It is helpful for many painless conditions, especially those associated with stress.

The ancient Chinese laws of acupuncture teach that illness is a sign that the life energy, called *ch'i,* is not flowing correctly. Illness is classified as either *yin* (wet, cold, slow, quiet, in storage, deep) or *yang* (dry, hot, rapid, in transformation, near the surface). Acupuncture focuses on yin, yang, and five elements: wood, fire, earth, metal, and water. Each element corresponds to organs in the body, activities, emotions, and seasons. Chinese theory interprets all natural phenomena in health and disease.

The placement of acupuncture needles in select locations can rebalance yin, yang, and the five elements and allow ch'i to flow fully and freely in the body (Connelly, 1979). The needles used in acupuncture are as slender as human hairs. They are inserted just below the skin and usually produce only a small ache or tingling sensation. Illnesses often disappear or respond quickly to other medicines or therapies after acupuncture. Acupuncturists often work in conjunction with Western style medical practitioners.

In ancient China, health practitioners were only paid when they maintained health. If a person became sick, the treatment was free (Haas, 1981). The art of acupuncture survived this policy beautifully. It is the oldest, continuously practiced form of health care in human history. In addition to the placement of acupuncture needles, the art keeps yin, yang, and the five elements in balance with diet, exercise, and meditation.

Japanese and Korean acupuncture are different from Chinese acupuncture primarily in technique, not in basic theory.

Acupuncture can be universally applied due to its simplicity (Microcia, 1989). Anger, sadness, guilt, fear, and worry are basic, cross-cultural human feelings. The causes of disease (climate, emotions, diet) apply to all societies. Redirecting ch'i and rebalancing yin, yang, and the five elements can restore health to all peoples.

been demonstrated to be very effective for some young adults are acupuncture (see Figure 8-4 and Box 8-1), biofeedback, and social support groups.

Biofeedback helps a person learn to control bodily responses to stress consciously. The patient is connected to a biofeedback machine with sensors for pulse, respiration, blood pressure, and galvanic skin response. The patient can watch the machine to determine tension levels. By thinking pleasant thoughts, breathing deeply, relaxing (each person uses a slightly different method), the patient can voluntarily reduce the stress response. After only a few sessions, the person can do this without the machine's feedback.

Social support groups reduce stress responses by increasing the stressed person's sense of control. Having a network of compassionate friends can help one reduce tension levels in much the same way as biofeedback.

There are many other techniques that young adults may find effective in reducing the negative effects of stress: massage, aerobic exercise, herbal medicines, meditation, self-hypnosis, muscle relaxation exercises, even hot tubbing.

Health Maintenance

Today's young adults are healthier than those in any previous generation. Advances in health care, immunizations, decreased consumption of fats, scheduled exercise, less smoking, and a variety of other health maintenance measures are contributing to projections of healthier living and a longer life expectancy for youth than for their parents.

Most of the allergies of childhood disappear after the adolescent growth spurt. By the twenties young people have developed natural immunities to many of the infectious agents that troubled them in the past. When immune defense mechanisms are working well, infections that are contracted are not usually life threatening. An exception may be contact with the AIDS virus.

Persons who completed the primary series of immunizations against diphtheria, pertussis, tetanus, and polio (DPT-OPV) in the first year of life and against measles, mumps, and rubella (MMR) in the second year should have a booster immunization against diphtheria and tetanus (DT) every ten years (American College of Physicians, 1985). Physicians now use the mid-decade birthday as the time for each DT booster (ages fifteen, twenty-five, thirty-five, forty-five, and so on). If the person has no record of immunization, no documented history of disease, or no laboratory evidence of immunity to measles, mumps, and rubella he or she should also have the MMR vaccination. This is especially important for young adults living together in close quarters (military barracks, college dormitories, and the like). These diseases are imported frequently by soldiers and students who have traveled abroad or by foreign students and other visitors. There have been many recent outbreaks, especially of measles, on military bases and college campuses. If a woman is pregnant, the MMR vaccination should be postponed until after the delivery of the baby. The live viruses in the vaccine are potentially teratogenic to the fetus.

Young adults living in close proximity to each other and adults at high risk of exposure to influenza (health care professionals, policemen, firemen, school teachers, communications workers, ambulance workers, paramedics) are advised to receive an influenza vaccine on an annual basis. The hepatitis B vaccine is also recommended for doctors, nurses, ambulance workers, and paramedics because of their frequent exposure to blood.

The threats to health that loom largest in the twenties are those related to poor control of emotional stress (accidents, alcohol and drug abuse, stress-related illnesses). Preexisting chronic diseases (diseases of the heart, epilepsy, diabetes) continue to trouble some people in their twenties. Fertility problems may also be discovered in some otherwise healthy young adults. Accidents account for close to half of the total deaths of young adults. A large percentage of these fatalities involve motor vehicles. Many deaths are also due to self-inflicted (suicide) or other-inflicted injuries (homicide). Young adults are the only age group who have shown an increase in death rates during the last two decades, primarily due to accidents, homicides, and suicides.

As with all age groups of the human life cycle, health is maintained most efficiently, and disease forestalled, when each person maintains an appropriate weight for height, eats nutritious meals including foods from the basic four food groups, and avoids excess fats, sugars, and salt. Each human needs restful sleep each day, exercise to the point of perspiration, and time to enjoy life. Everybody needs somebody: A network of supportive friends and relatives, with whom one can speak openly, promotes health. Rather than alleviate stress in helpful ways, some young adults may turn to alcohol or drugs to numb their awareness of their stressful lives.

Substance Abuse

Substance abuse is not a phenomenon seen primarily among young people. It is practiced by all kinds of people in every age bracket. People use drugs for almost every possible effect today. They use them to go to sleep, to wake up, to get hungry, to lose their appetites, to stimulate activity, to relax, to deaden pain, to make sensations more acute—the list can go on and on. Drug abuse is not limited to illegally obtained substances. People abuse laxatives, vitamins, antacids, coffee and tea, cola drinks, aspirin, cigarettes, glue and other volatile (quickly evaporating) materials, and especially alcohol. Any drug is potentially harmful when misused. An estimated 10% of the work force in the United States use alcohol on the job and another 2% struggle with drug addiction (Johnson, 1985).

Young adults may abuse drugs to relieve stress, to keep up with peers, or to rebel against society. Experimenting with different substances is higher in youth who are emotionally withdrawn from their families of origin (Turner, Irwin, and Millstein, 1991). Most young adults have tried some kind of drug at least once (see Table 8-4).

The word *addiction* is being replaced by the term **physical** (or physiological) **dependence** to refer to the physical need for a chemical substance and the experiencing of withdrawal symptoms without it. Withdrawal symptoms differ for each substance on which a person can develop physical dependence but usually resemble a physical illness. Some substances create **psychological dependence** in addition to physical dependence. Withdrawal from a substance on which a person has become psychologically dependent will produce symptoms that resemble a mental disorder (anxiety, hyperactivity, depression). In addition to these two types of dependence, one can develop a **tolerance** to a drug. This means that one needs more and more of the substance to get the effect that one felt initially.

The favorite mood-altering drug in the United States is alcohol (see Figure 8-5). Many people drink more in their twenties than they do during the rest of their lives. This probably reflects a phase of learning about open social drinking (once they reach the legal drinking age) and a phase of wanting to appear mature. Social drinking leads to physical problems in only a small majority of persons in their twenties. It creates social problems for more, but certainly not all, young adults. The amount of **alcohol abuse** in our country far exceeds the amount of abuse of all other drugs. *Abuse* is defined as behavioral and interpersonal difficulties resulting from heavy use of alcohol (or any other chemical substance). About one-half of the fatal automobile accidents each year are directly related to alcohol abuse (Department of Health and Human Services, 1984). In addition, diminished job performance, waning school performance, increased interpersonal aggressiveness, and physical trauma inflicted on self, spouse, children, friends, and others are common sequelae to alcohol abuse.

Although the general effects of alcohol ingestion are the same for all people, the individual effects of a glass of beer, wine, or spirits on each person are unique and change with time. In small quantities, and initially, alcohol has a stimulant effect. In larger quantities, and over time, it acts as a sedative. It is classified as a depressant drug. A large person can ingest more alcohol than a smaller person before becoming intoxicated. Alcohol taken on a full stomach will not reach the bloodstream and cause intoxication as quickly as a drink on an empty stomach. Eating while drinking also slows down the effects of alcohol. Many people believe they will get drunk more quickly on spirits than on beer or wine, or get drunk if they switch from one form of alcohol to another. In fact, it is the blood alcohol content that determines intoxication, not the form of alcohol consumed. A can of beer, a glass of wine, and a shot of spirits all contain about ½ ounce of pure alcohol. It takes about 1½ ounces of pure alcohol (three drinks) to make a smaller person (100 pounds) legally intoxicated. It takes about 3¼ ounces (six and a half drinks) to bring a very large person (240 pounds) to the same degree of intoxication. To impair each person's judgment (and driving ability), however, it

Table 8-4 Estimated Nonmedical Drug Abuse in Young Adults (18–25).

Drug	% Used at Least Once	% Current User
alcohol	93	72
tranquilizers	12	2
sedatives	11	2
heroin	1	—
cocaine	25	8
stimulants	17	4
hallucinogens	12	2
marijuana	60	22

SOURCE: Adapted from Jaffe, S. L. (1978). Inpatient treatment for adolescent drug abusers. *Supplement to Children and Teens Today Newsletter*, December, 1.

Figure 8-5
Social drinking is part of the life style of many young adults.

would take only two drinks and four drinks, respectively. Switching drinks may make a person sick because of the mixture of nonalcoholic ingredients of beverages, not because various forms of alcohol are **synergistic** (enhance each other's effects).

Drunken behavior is no longer considered as socially acceptable as it once was. Rather than being "the life of the party" an intoxicated person is now more often viewed as an annoyance, especially if he or she loses muscular control and coordination, tries to drive, or gets sick.

The difference between a person who abuses alcohol and one who becomes alcoholic is physiological. An alcoholic is defined as a person who organizes his or her behavior around alcohol, continues to drink even though it causes serious personal problems, and suffers withdrawal symptoms whenever he or she sobers up. Withdrawal symptoms include perspiration, cramps, nausea, anxiety, and tremulousness ("the shakes" or "the jitters"). They can also include hallucinations (bad dreams, disordered perceptions), withdrawal seizures ("rum fits"), or delirium tremens ("DTs"). The DTs are characterized by profound confusion, tremors, fever, rapid heartbeat, and profuse perspiration. Each of these withdrawal symptoms can occur alone, but more generally they occur in various combinations. DTs can be fatal if the alcoholic experiences cardiac collapse after an extended period of excitement.

After advanced alcohol abuse a form of irreversible mental illness, called Wernicke-Korsakoff syndrome, occurs. It involves atrophy of cerebral tissue. Although generally believed to be a disease of old men, it can, in fact, be found in young adult alcoholics of both sexes. Occasionally Wernicke-Korsakoff symptoms are the first indication of the amount of drinking that has occurred over time. Some alcoholics, unable to abstain even one day without withdrawal, keep a moderate amount of alcohol in their bloodstream all day, every day, over several years while they continue to function as business executives, college professors, housewives, nurses, physicians, or other workers.

Most people can safely consume alcohol throughout their lives without becoming alcoholic (see Myth 1, Table 8-5). Researchers are actively trying to discover the differences between alcoholics and social drinkers. It is now accepted that alcoholism is a disease not unlike diabetes. It runs in families, suggesting some genetic vulnerability. However, not all offspring of alcoholic parents become alcoholics, so there are probably environmental factors that enhance its appearance. Most of the approximately 10 million alcoholics in the United States first suffered symptoms of the disease (loss of control over drinking, withdrawal sickness) by their middle to late twenties. Some even developed symptoms in adolescence after only minimal drinking. Obviously, their bodies handled alcohol differently than the bodies of nonalcoholics.

A current guess about alcoholism causation is that neurotransmitters become dependent on alcohol in order to function normally in alcoholics. Consequently, when alcoholics become sober, their neurotransmitters misfire, causing withdrawal symptoms (Noble, 1983). Another possibility is that alcoholics may be deficient in certain receptors for neurotransmitters. They may become dependent on alcohol because drinking helps correct the deficiency. Another theory about causation is that the breakdown products of alcohol differ in alcoholics, causing physical dependency (Schuckit, 1984).

Whatever the biological cause of alcoholism, certain reactions and behaviors have been identified that may forewarn that a person is at risk of developing the disease. Nonalcoholics more frequently feel dizzy, drowsy, or nauseated or turn red when their blood alcohol content (BAC) approaches 0.05 to 0.09 percent. They may not want to continue drinking. Future alcoholics more frequently reach legal intoxication without unpleasant symptoms and continue drinking, often gulping drinks, way beyond intoxication. They may experience frequent **blackouts.** These are periods of amnesia (as opposed to passing out) from drinking too much. During a blackout, a person remains conscious and carries out activities of which he or she has no recollection when sober. The high blood alcohol content apparently interferes with the person's ability to store any memories. (This can happen to nonalcoholics who drink too much as well.)

Prealcoholics, more often than nonalcoholics, drink alone, sneak drinks, avoid talking about their drinking, feel guilty about their drinking, and yet continue to drink more and more. Once they have the disease (are alcoholic), drinking is central to their lives. They often neglect job and family, lose interest in sex, neglect their health and nutrition, alibi and rationalize about their behavior, and become ill without alcohol.

Treatment of alcoholism requires permanent cessation of drinking. Detoxification may be protracted with depression, irritability, and anxiety continuing long after the physiological withdrawal symptoms end. Physicians may prescribe short-term therapy

Table 8-5 Common Myths about Alcoholism.

1. Consumption of alcohol over a long period of time causes alcoholism.
2. Family members (wife, husband, parents, children) make a person to turn to drink (become alcoholic).
3. Alcoholics are weak willed (lacking in will power).
4. Alcoholism is a self-inflicted disease.
5. Most alcoholics end up on the street.
6. Beer drinkers do not become alcoholics.
7. Alcohol is a stimulant drug.
8. Alcoholics must want help before they can be treated.
9. Tranquilizers are the best treatment for alcoholism.
10. Recovered alcoholics can safely return to social drinking.

with one of the minor tranquilizers (such as Valium). However, tranquilizers are useful only during the acute withdrawal period. Prolonged use will result in a physical dependence on the tranquilizers as a substitute for alcohol. *Antabuse,* a drug that causes nausea, cramping, and vomiting whenever alcohol is ingested, is frequently prescribed to aid in alcohol abstinence. Motivation to take the daily pill must be good for Antabuse therapy to be effective. Alcoholics Anonymous (AA) is an informal fellowship of recovering alcoholics that teaches a new way of life to combat the strong internal and external pressures to drink. It gives continual support to alcoholics. AA has proved to be the single most effective force in alcoholic rehabilitation.

Very few alcoholics become street people. Estimates of alcoholics who are derelicts range from 3 to 8 percent. Most alcoholics, because of strong pressures from their family, friends, or employers (few are self-motivated) seek treatment of some sort. Some professionals feel it is extremely rare for an alcoholic to resume social drinking without reexperiencing cravings, loss of control, and renewed dependence on alcohol. Consequently, professionals do not use the past tense "recovered alcoholic" but rather the present tense "recovering alcoholic," indicating the lifelong nature of treatment.

The second most commonly abused drugs after alcohol, and the most frequently prescribed substances in the United States, are minor tranquilizers (see Figure 8-6), especially those of the benzodiazepine family (Valium, Librium, Dalmane, Tranxene, Xanax). When taken as directed, usually a small dose three to four times a day for a short period of time, they are relatively safe (*Physician's Desk Reference,* 1991). However, both tolerance and dependence develop rapidly. Many young adults find that they need not only to have their prescriptions renewed but to have their dosages increased in order to cope with life's great bundle of little things. Withdrawal from tranquilizers, once psychological and physical dependence have developed, can result in nearly intolerable anxiety, insomnia, nightmares, tremors, delirium, hallucinations or convulsions. An additional danger of minor tranquilizers is that they are synergistic with alcohol. Mixing of alcohol and one of the benzodiazepines can result in coma and possible death.

Other **depressants** of abuse include antipsychotic drugs, sedatives, and barbiturate substitutes. Young adults more typically abuse depressants over the weekend or on days off to obtain relief from stress and anxieties. The barbiturates or barbiturate substitutes produce a state of intoxication quite similar to that of alcohol. They can also induce stupor, coma, and even death when taken in excess or with large amounts of alcohol.

Depressant overdose is the most common means of suicide among women. Studies indicate that the young American female population is being unnecessarily sedated

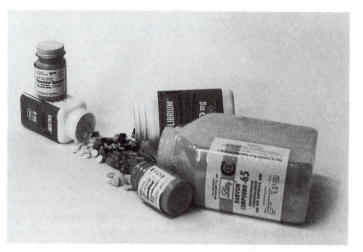

Figure 8-6
Tranquilizers are prescribed more than antibiotics. Prolonged use may result in both physical and psychological dependence. Withdrawal symptoms can be extremely unpleasant. How "mild" are these substances?

(Schiefelbein, 1980). Approximately one-fourth of American women between ages eighteen and twenty-nine have been found to take some prescribed depressant medication in a given calendar year (Scarf, 1979).

The strong tolerance and physical dependence properties of **narcotics** make them especially dangerous drugs. They relieve pain, and, like the barbiturates, they confer tranquillity. When first taken, they produce a euphoria, a buoyancy, and a feeling of well-being. This is followed by apathy, drowsiness, slow respirations, constricted pupils, and blurred vision. Morphine, paregoric, codeine, and Demerol (a synthetic narcotic), when used medically, are injected into a muscle or taken orally. This slows down their entrance into the bloodstream and reduces the initial euphoric rush. Heroin (which has no accepted medical use) can be inhaled (snorted), mixed with other substances and smoked, injected under the skin (popped), or injected directly into blood vessels (mainlined).

The effects of narcotics depend on the method of administration, the dose, and the tolerance of the user. Repeated use leads to the need for larger and larger doses and eventually to physical dependence. Once a person is dependent, he or she must have a continual supply of the drug to avoid withdrawal symptoms. Early signs of withdrawal include dilated pupils, perspiration, watering eyes and nose, restlessness, and insomnia. Later symptoms include nausea, vomiting, diarrhea, violent abdominal cramps, and leg spasms (kicking the habit).

The narcotics drug problem was once predominantly seen in urban ghettos. It is now also found increasingly in middle-class neighborhoods, especially among young adults. The sharing of needles to inject narcotics is one of the major ways in which AIDS and other infectious diseases are spread.

Any drugs taken to make one more alert, including coffee, tea, cocaine, amphetamines, caffeinated soft drinks, and cigarettes, are **stimulants.** Although some are legal, others are strictly illegal or are available by prescription only.

Cocaine (coke) is derived from leaves of the South American coca plant. Some coca leaves are imported legally so that the cocaine can be extracted for medical purposes and the decocainized product used to flavor cola beverages. Cocaine imported illegally is contributing to a vast drug use epidemic and law enforcement problem. Many young adults quickly become psychologically dependent on cocaine for continued feelings of strength, self-confidence, and well-being, even after only short-term experimental use.

Cocaine may be sold on the street as a crystal-like powder, "cut" with other white powders to varying degrees of purity. In its powder form it may be sniffed (snorted), ingested, or injected to produce a "flash" or "rush." Cocaine may also be freebased. To "free the base" is to alter the structure of the cocaine in order to smoke it. Crack, the product of heated cocaine, is nearly 90% pure. It is sold relatively inexpensively in rock form and is smoked through pipes. Smoking crack produces a shorter lived but more intense high than snorting coke. Because large amounts of cocaine reach the brain quickly after smoking crack, fatal overdose can occur. Death comes as a result of seizures, respiratory arrest, and coma, or sometimes by cardiac arrest.

Amphetamines and methamphetamines (speed) decrease fatigue, reduce the appetite, and give an exaggerated sense of well-being. In larger doses they can cause aggressive behavior, delusions of self-importance, hallucinations, or paranoia. In overdoses they cause tremors, convulsions, coma, and sometimes death (Drug Enforcement Administration, 1985).

Amphetamines can be obtained through prescriptions for "diet pills" or on the street. Abuse is common among students, housewives, athletes, truck drivers, and people who need to stay awake for long periods or keep their weight down. Tolerance, physical dependence, and psychological dependence develop rapidly. Amphetamines are sometimes injected directly into the bloodstream, like cocaine or heroin.

Nonamphetamine drugs have been developed to suppress appetite or produce stimulation. Although they are generally less potent than the amphetamines, they have the same effects, create psychological dependence, and can lead to death from overdoses.

Hallucinogens produce subjective perceptions of things that do not exist. Hallucinations may give the impression of things larger or smaller or more vividly colored than life and may simultaneously involve two or more senses. They may even give a person a sense of being outside the self, depersonalized. They may alter a person's sense of time and space and of objects and people in the environment (Schultes, 1980). Some people prefer to use the term *psychedelics* for the hallucinogenic drugs because the perceptual changes may be enticing, pleasure-giving insights into reality rather than hallucinations. In some cases perceptions also mimic psychosis, which has led to the labeling of the drugs as *psychotomimetic*.

Lysergic acid diethylamide (LSD) was once used with some success to produce schizophrenia-like states in studying model psychosis. It is now strictly illegal. Most of the preparations are potentially very dangerous. A poorly understood effect of LSD is its ability to cause *flashbacks*. A person may suddenly fall into another "trip" with hallucinations and disrupted perceptions months after taking the drug.

Phencyclidine (PCP), once used legally in veterinary medicine, can lead to acute antisocial psychotic episodes. It is sometimes called "DOA" (dead on arrival) both because preoccupation with death is common during trips and because lethal trips sometimes result when dangerously potent or contaminated forms are produced in clandestine labs. It has a high potential for creating psychological dependence.

The natural hallucinogens—peyote and mescaline, derived from a cactus, and psilocybin and psilocyn, derived from mushrooms—are sometimes used for religious services, mainly by Indian peoples in western Canada, the United States, and Mexico. The side effects of nausea and vomiting are considered purifying. The feeling of depersonalization can be an aid to meditation and self-understanding, although the altered perceptions caused by these drugs can be dangerous.

Marijuana has properties of depressants, stimulants, narcotics, and hallucinogens. Individual states vary in their laws concerning its use. In some it is now legal to use it and to possess it in small quantities. In others it is criminal to have even traces of it found on one's person or belongings.

Marijuana comes from the hemp plant (*Cannabis sativa*), a weed that grows freely in most parts of the world. Preparations are usually smoked but may also be consumed in drink or food (see Figure 8-7). Users need to increase the dosage needed for a high over time, and they experience withdrawal symptoms when they do not use it. A high from marijuana produces a euphoric release from inhibitions, tensions, and anxieties. In very large doses it may cause vomiting, diarrhea, and loss of muscle coordination. Withdrawal symptoms, after heavy long-term use, include hyperactivity, decreased

Figure 8-7
Marijuana is usually smoked in joints (held with clips) or in water pipes. It can also be consumed in foods.

appetite, weight loss, increased salivation, and increased pressure within the eye (National Academy of Sciences, 1982).

The active ingredient in cannabis leaves is delta-9-tetrahydrocannabinol (THC). THC is synthesized in laboratories or extracted from marijuana grown by the government on special "pot" farms. It is used for treating some glaucoma and reducing the nausea following chemotherapy in cancer patients.

Turner and Waller (1979), after studying many thousands of scientific research reports on cannabis, did not find a single paper that gave it a clean bill of health. Its usual bad effects include lowered fertility, impaired pulmonary function, lowered resistance to infection, a chronic cough, and impairment of intellectual functioning.

Cognitive Development

Brain cell development reaches its peak in the twenties. Actually, the final number of neurons and supportive cells that each individual possesses is determined by the end of the first postnatal year of life, but the cells themselves continue to grow and become more complex during childhood and adolescence. The cell fibers (axon and dendrites) and the myelin sheathing surrounding the fibers increase in size, number, and intricacy. Memory is thought to peak at the time when brain weight peaks. After this the brain cells very slowly begin to degenerate. This gradual shrinking of the brain cells after about age thirty is not a cause for great concern. We hardly begin to use all of the brain cells we have at any point in our lives. The mental processes of many people in their sixties and seventies are still keen enough to control empires or make important contributions to the world of arts and science.

A secular trend has been noticed toward increased height and earlier maturation in successive generations of well-nourished peoples over the past one hundred years (see page 146). There also has been a trend toward increased head circumference and brain weight. Simultaneously, a distinct rise in IQ scores has occurred.

Many people with large heads would like to believe their increased brain size is evidence of superior intelligence. Recent studies, however, have found no correlation between brain size and IQ (Scott, 1983). Acquisition of intelligent behaviors is related to innate intelligence, education, and life experiences. Some small people attain a high level of functioning. In fact, Anatole France, the Nobel laureate French author of such novels as *Thaïs, Penguin Island,* and *The Revolt of the Angels;* and Walt Whitman, one of America's greatest poets, who inspired his readers to a fuller appreciation of the wonders of nature in *Leaves of Grass,* both had unusually small brains. France's brain, which weighed approximately 1000 grams, is one of the smallest on record for an adult human being (Dubos, 1982). The average adult male brain weighs approximately 1570 grams. The brains of both elephants and whales are considerably heavier, averaging 3980 grams and 2488 grams, respectively.

In the twenties young people make considerable use of their "gray cells," as brain cells are called, at whatever level of functioning is available to them. Many American young people go to work (whether outside or inside the home) when they leave high school and must learn new skills, both technical and interpersonal, that relate to their jobs. Many young people continue to pursue formal education in their twenties. They enroll in trade schools, colleges, or graduate schools and may temporarily postpone some of the other kinds of experiential learning.

Psychologists and educators call the need to learn well and do well *achievement need.* It is quite different from innate abilities and cognitive development but enhances the latter. Cognitive ability and achievement need contribute to successful learning far more than either contributes alone. Although caregivers can and do stimulate cognitive development in their children, they have a more potent role to play in stimulating the need to achieve. In a classic study by Rosen and D'Andrade (1959) the characteristics of parents of boys with high achievement need were reported. Fathers were competitive, took pleasure in problem-solving tasks, showed more father–son involvement, gave their sons things to manipulate, and displayed more affection and emotion. Mothers stressed success and achievement and held high aspirations for their sons (see Figure 8-8).

The use of authoritative discipline (reasoning) and giving children a chance to participate in the family's decision-making processes is also associated with high achievement behavior (Klonsky, 1983). Manley (1977) suggested that females are more oriented to achievement when their mothers provide an achieving role model and are moderately nurturing. Males are more achievement oriented when their mothers provide more intense demands for achievement and are highly nurturing.

The achievement needs of women, especially by the time they reach their twenties, are frequently below those of men. They are also below what could be expected of them considering their scores on IQ tests and their past performances in grade school and high school. A popular notion of women's intellect based on their achievement is that they start out ahead of boys, level off, and then retrogress. There is little evidence to support this. Both women and men can reach high levels of cognitive functioning and can maintain their high levels. Evidence, however, does point to a falling off of many women's need to achieve. Horner's (1972) classic study found that college women taking achievement tests could do well, but, when asked to compete with men, they declined.

Horner's data suggesting a fear of success in women were presented in Chapter 7. Her research, and replications of it, have suggested that for some women, the desire to be liked, to be accepted, and to affiliate with others is stronger than the desire to succeed, especially if success brings in its wake jealousy or rejection. In a study of college women at Wellesley, Alper (1974) identified women who were high in feminine traits and who aspired to traditional wife and mother roles and others who were career oriented and more androgynous in their traits. The fear of success that Horner found was present in the traditional women. Such women told stories like the following when shown pictures to describe:

> The lady with the test tube is a movie star who has sunk to doing TV commercials. The other is an admiring nobody [who] pities her. . . . They both fade into oblivion. No one will like them or pay attention to them. . . . The star commits suicide and the other marries a florist and gets fat. (Alper, 1974)

Figure 8-8
The need to achieve is enhanced by independence training, encouragement of intellectual pursuits, and rewards for success.

However, the career-oriented women told "success" stories in response to the same pictures:

> The instructor is showing her student how to do a step in a complicated experimental procedure. The student has been working on the experiment for some time, and is nearly at the end of her work. She is observing carefully what the other woman does, and, when she returns to her own work, will repeat the procedure with care and precision and will be able to finish her project and achieve significant results. The instructor would like the student to become an able scientist, and is pleased with her work.

In addition, they were competitive and high achievers in college, indicating neither a fear of success nor a falling off in their need to achieve.

Different kinds of intellectual behaviors seem to be more appropriate at different times in the life span (Schaie, 1978). Young adults have an achieving, task-related, more competitive style of cognitive behavior. Older adults become more responsible, then more reintegrative (see Chapters 10 and 11). Young adults tend to apply their cognitive skills towards entering the world of work, establishing their own family units, and meeting their own personal goals.

Psychosocial Development

In Chapter 7 we defined adolescence as that period of time between the biological changes of puberty and independence from the family of origin. Using this definition, we find that some teenagers become young adults before reaching age twenty. Likewise, many people in their twenties remain adolescent. (Kenneth Keniston refers to some individuals in their twenties as youth rather than adolescents or young adults. His theory will be described shortly.) Although age is not as good a criterion for life stage as are the pursuits of an individual at a given time, certain pursuits tend to coincide with certain ages (see Figure 8-9).

Figure 8-9
The young adult, unlike the adolescent, has a stable sense of self but is searching for vocational and social roles.

Young adulthood suggests **maturity**. Opinions differ widely as to what constitutes maturity. Freud (1966) wrote that maturity is the ability to discipline oneself in work and in heterosexual relationships. He felt maturity is attained in the postadolescent period for most people. Carl Jung (1923), on the other hand, believed maturity should not be claimed by most people until middle adulthood. First, individuals must go through the trials of many life experiences.

Erik Erikson (1963) wrote that maturity develops gradually as adults work their way through the last three nuclear conflicts of their lives: intimacy versus isolation, generativity versus stagnation, and ego integrity versus despair. Lawrence Kohlberg (1973) described maturity as a cumulative process without a well-defined beginning or end. He saw the highest level of moral development as more mature than the conventional level. He warned that settling too quickly into a static lifestyle can inhibit the development of moral maturity.

Abraham Maslow (1970) also saw maturity as a cumulative process. Individuals progressively meet their physiological needs, safety needs, love and belonging needs, self-esteem needs, and need for self-actualization. Maslow stated that although all people have the innate potential for becoming self-actualized, societal conditions are such that many people only advance as far as trying to meet their love and belonging or self-esteem needs.

This social development section will examine the influence of the **family of origin** (one's parents or surrogate parents and any siblings), and the beginnings of a **family of procreation** (one's spouse and children). The information about twenty- to thirty-year-olds in these sections consists of generalizations, more applicable to describing the masses of young people in this age range than to describing any one particular person.

Separating from the Family of Origin

A great many young people continue to let their primary caregivers provide for part or all of their economic needs during their twenties. It generally takes young adults five or more years to achieve complete independence. It is becoming common practice for postadolescent young people to lay claim to a few years of an **adulthood moratorium** (a period of time in which a person is permitted to delay meeting an obligation). Such a moratorium lengthens the time until the youth declares himself or herself independent from the family of origin: able to satisfy his or her own needs for food, housing, health, safety, and the pursuit of happiness through some productive enterprise. The moratorium may be filled with college, graduate school, exploratory travels, temporary jobs, and, in some cases, military service. The young person in an adulthood moratorium usually still considers "home base" to be the family of origin. However, even without making a declaration of independence, these young adults tend to function with more self-sufficiency than they did in their teenage years.

Moratoriums may postpone the attainment of the developmental tasks of early adulthood, as set forth by Robert Havighurst (1972):

1. Selecting a mate
2. Learning to live with a marriage partner
3. Starting a family
4. Rearing children
5. Managing a home
6. Getting started in an occupation
7. Taking on civic responsibility
8. Finding a congenial social group

Arriving at a legal age (when one no longer has to have parental signatures for loans or licenses, when one can purchase alcoholic beverages, when one can marry and sign contracts) gives most young people a sense of increased independence from their families, even if they choose not to use it.

Once young people have established a stable and satisfying sense of self, they generally prefer to keep and develop more meaningful friendships with a few others. They become interested in who others are and where others are going. They become more tolerant of differences.

Once the "self" is known, young adults can expend more time discovering who the parents are, in all their complex, three-dimensional (past–present–future) personalities. Gradually the hopes and dreams of the parents for themselves become meaningful to the young adult, as well as their hopes and dreams for the youth. In some cases, when the emerging adult rejects both what the parents want for themselves and what they want for him or her, an alienation occurs. For many young people exploring the interests, feelings, values, problems, and welfare of the parents is exciting. They begin to give support and direction as well as take it. This turning of the tables ("You have cared for me, now I will care for you") indicates a real feeling of independence and maturity on the part of the young adult.

Roger Gould (1978), in cross-sectional studies of several hundred men and women between the ages of sixteen and sixty, found that the twenties were characterized by two different kinds of relationships with the family of origin. Young adults in their early twenties, Gould found, typically struggle with leaving their parents' world. However, they feel unprepared to contest the views of their family. They must challenge and resolve several false assumptions from their more childlike consciousness:

1. If I get any more independent, it will be a disaster.
2. I can see the world only through my parents' assumptions.
3. Only my parents can guarantee my safety.
4. My parents must be my only family.
5. I don't own my own body.

Gould found that these battles to change assumptions are replaced with new false assumptions to challenge by the middle to late twenties:

1. Rewards will come automatically if we do what we are supposed to do.
2. There is only one right way to do things.
3. Those in a special relationship with us can do for us what we haven't been able to do for ourselves.
4. Rationality, commitment, and effort will always prevail over all other forces.

The phrase that Gould used to characterize these subjects was "I'm nobody's baby now." (See Figure 8-10.)

Daniel Levinson and associates (1978) labeled the years of separating from one's parents the **early adult transition** and the years of the middle to late twenties as **entering the adult world.** Levinson, like Gould, found questioning the nature of the family of origin and one's place in it a vital part of the novice phase of adulthood. In the early adult transition numerous separations, losses, and transformations are required to terminate old relationships. According to Levinson, entering the adult world involves exploration of self and world, making and testing provisional choices, searching for alternatives, increasing one's commitments, and constructing a more integrated life structure. Finally by age twenty-eight or twenty-nine the **age thirty transition** begins. The young adult feels uneasy, that something is missing or wrong. Levinson found men orienting toward the future to make life more worthwhile: finding a new life direction, making new choices, or strengthening commitments to choices already made. (See Figure 8-11.)

George Vaillant (1977), in his longitudinal study of ninety-four men, found that from twenty to thirty men's major energy expenditures were directed at wooing and winning wives and learning how to get along with them (see Figure 8-10). This happened, Vaillant found, as soon as the men won real autonomy from their parents. Once they found a sense of their own independent identity, they entrusted it to another (a wife). Once they recemented human relationships from the family of origin to a family of

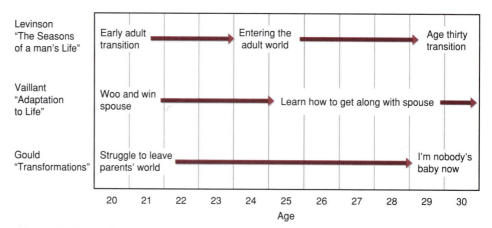

Figure 8-10
Passage through the twenties according to three major researchers.

procreation they devoted themselves to the latter and began to consolidate careers. Vaillant found energy expenditures toward career commitments more characteristic of the decade of the thirties than of the twenties.

Duvall (1977) also saw the establishment of a family of procreation as paramount in the twenties. She described a **family life cycle,** divided into eight stages:

1. Married couples (without children).
2. Childbearing families (oldest child birth to thirty months).
3. Families with preschool children (oldest child thirty months to six years).
4. Families with school children (oldest child six to thirteen years).
5. Families with teenagers (oldest child thirteen to twenty years).
6. Families launching young adults (first child gone, last child leaving).
7. Middle-aged parents ("empty nest" to retirement).
8. Aging family members (retirement to death of both spouses).

Men and women in their twenties, Duvall felt, are primarily concerned with the first three stages of the family life cycle. We will describe the concerns of these stages in the marriage and parenthood sections of this chapter.

Intergenerational family relationships are easier if young adults in their twenties adopt lifestyles similar to, but independent of, their parents. Those who refuse to challenge the childish assumptions, as proposed by Gould (1978), and remain dependent on their families, worry their parents. They seem wary of settling into the existing social order. They may feel chronically incompetent in their dependence while others around them are achieving independence. The greatest conflicts between parents and their twentyish offspring, however, occur when the young adults not only declare their unconditional independence from the family of origin but blatantly reject their parents' views and adopt antagonistic lifestyles.

The majority of American young adults are considered **conventional** in their behavior. They work at becoming a part of the adult culture. Although they may deliberate the need for reform, they spend their time pursuing money or education or enjoying leisure activities. In terms of Marcia's identity statuses (see Chapter 7), conventional young adults are usually either identity foreclosed or identity achieved. They usually have high self-esteem (Prager, 1982). Identity-achieved females are not usually strongly stereotypically feminine sex-typed (Prager, 1983).

Kenneth Keniston (1970) gave the classification **youth stage** to the young people in the Western industrialized world who are between adolescence and adulthood. To come under this rubric a young person must have acquired a stable sense of self.

"Youth," however, are still searching—for a vocation, a social role they can play comfortably, the road to take, a place in the existing society. They feel tension and ambivalence about traditional practices vis-à-vis the developed sense of individuality. Some young people never experience this stage, some pass through it quickly, and others remain in it for prolonged periods.

The youth stage is not limited by race, sex, age, social class, or position in society. As Keniston (1970) pointed out, poor and uneducated men and women, from Abraham Lincoln to Malcolm X, have experienced the youth stage. The classification is applied to those who have outgrown adolescent themes without yet having acquired adult themes. Instead, they have their own themes, which include:

- tension between self and society;
- pervasive ambivalence toward both self and society;
- wary probe of the existing social order;
- alternating estrangement and omnipotentiality;
- refusal of socialization and acculturation;
- youth-specific identities;
- value of change and movement, abhorrence of stasis;
- goals to be moved, to move others, to move through;
- valuation of development;
- fear of death equated with fear of stopping;
- view of adulthood as stasis (equal to death);
- countercultures keep distance from existing social order.

Figure 8-11
Some young adults are activists. Others are minimally involved in social, political, or religious causes.

Different youths experience each of the themes with different intensity. What may be an enormous conflict for one may be relatively unimportant to another. The resolution of the youth stage and the acceptance of adulthood comes when the individual can acknowledge and cope with social reality without feeling that selfhood is static or compromised. It does not mean selling out, simply growing out. Thus the Jerry Rubin of the early 1970s, who in his youth stage presented himself as a Yippie, emerged in the 1980s as a sedate Wall Street analyst, recognizing that the transformation had a great deal of underlying continuity (Rubin, 1981).

Very few young adults are **activists** (see Figure 8-11). They rarely constitute more than 3 to 4 percent of the student population at colleges and universities. Activists are generally intellectually above average. Like youth described by Keniston, they feel a tension between maintaining personal integrity and becoming acceptable in society. Activists are more willing to do something about the estrangements they feel. They plan strikes, lectures, or marches; print and pass out statements; or organize campaigns for change. Activist campaigns are seldom undertaken simply for self-glorification. Keniston (1974) has commented that, given concomitant characteristics of love, compassion, and empathy, they may help make our society a happier place in which to live. However, he has also warned of the truth of the old adage: Compassion without morality is sentimental and effusive, while morality without compassion is cold and inhumane.

Alienated youth try to escape from society through such means as drugs, alcohol, or living in seclusion. They are likely to have had preexisting personal, familial, or social problems before young adulthood descended with its tensions and ambiguities. They most often have had poor relations with their families of origin, and their alienation is both cause and effect of intrafamilial strife.

Searching for Intimacy

To marry or not to marry is an important decision facing people in their twenties. There are a great many pressures, both internal and external, for marriage. Internal pressures include a desire for a true intimacy and mutuality in sex, and a desire to gratify the needs for belonging, love, and self-esteem. External pressures for marriage may include family prodding, watching one's friends get married, peer group prodding, dwindling social life as friends marry, religious convictions, external urgings to marry to improve financial or social status, even the pressure from an employer for marriage in order to enhance career opportunities.

As the twenties pass, many young people feel the exigency to grab hold of life, master it, and establish themselves as self-reliant persons. For some, as Vaillant (1977) found, marriage appears to be the avenue toward accomplishing these goals. For others, staying single seems to be the most desirable course.

Erikson's Intimacy versus Isolation. Erikson described the sixth nuclear conflict of life as that of finding **intimacy versus isolation** (see Table 8-6). Once young adults have acquired a sense of who they are and where they are going (identity), they begin to feel a need to reach out to others. Having severed their former close ties to caregivers, siblings, and schoolmates, they seek new friends with whom to share life's joys and sorrows. The persons with whom one relates do not necessarily have to be prospective marriage partners. A sense of intimacy (defined as closeness) can develop between people who work together, face various kinds of battles or stresses together, share leisure activities, or are roommates. Although intimacy usually develops between marriage partners, Erikson (1963) cautions that some marriages really amount to an *isolation à deux*—two people living in solitude together.

Erikson saw the development of a kind of mature intimacy described by Freud as

Table 8-6   Erikson's Sixth Nuclear Conflict: Intimacy versus Isolation.

Sense	Eriksonian Descriptions	Fostering Behaviors
Intimacy	A fusion of identity with that of others	Others confirm sense that mutuality of efforts is beneficial
	Commitment to concrete affiliations and partnerships	Others prove faithful to co-operative and intimate sharings and interactions
	Strength to abide by commitment to others	Experiences of making sacrifices and compromises to maintain relationships
versus Isolation	Avoidance of contacts that commit to intimacy	Experiences of being victimized, abused, or exploited by others
	Distantiation: readiness to isolate forces and people whose essence encroaches on one's own territory	Shaky sense of identity that causes a repudiation of things foreign to self
	Deep sense of self-absorption	Experiences showing need to compete, not cooperate

being necessarily postponed until after youths have defined themselves in terms of their social, sexual, and career identities. They cannot fully relate to others until they have dealt with the problem of self. Remember from Chapter 7 that Erikson felt young love is usually more conversational than sexual. Young people use their friends as mirrors in which to reflect their developing self-images. Sexual relationships that are self-centered or exploitive or engaged in for erotic pleasure only are immature. Mature love includes self-giving, other-centeredness, or a fusion of one's self with another directed toward mutuality of pleasure. The utopia of intimacy as described by Erikson (1963) should include

1. mutuality of orgasm
2. with a loved partner
3. of the other sex
4. with whom one is able and willing to share a mutual trust
5. and with whom one is able and willing to regulate the cycles of
   a. work
   b. procreation
   c. recreation
6. so as to secure to the offspring, too, all the stages of a satisfactory development.

Even as he defined the utopian, however, Erikson warned that in our complex society factors of tradition, opportunity, health, and temperament interfere with satisfactory mutuality.

Both Eriksonian conflicts of identity and intimacy seem to be more easily resolved by androgynous than by nonandrogynous young adults (Schiedel and Marcia, 1985). Females seem to resolve the conflict of intimacy versus isolation more readily than do males, especially when they are secure in their own ego identities beforehand. Males find it easier to resolve the conflict of intimacy versus isolation after they are secure in their occupational identity (Fitch and Adams, 1983).

Isolation as the alternative to intimacy is fairly common in our culture. Many young people have had little or no experience with making sacrifices or compromises prior to leaving their families of origin. Intimacy cannot develop without a sharing and giving of the self to others. Many young people have also had bad experiences trying to show regard for others. They have been exploited, abused, and victimized. They have learned that competition serves them better than cooperation. They fear openness with others.

Psychotherapy can help people find intimacy in contrast to isolation. Psychoanalysis explores the parent–child relationship to help a person work through reasons for fearing intimacy. Behavior therapies seek to change the environments that stimulate or maintain isolation. Desensitization programs, assertiveness training, modeling, even biofeedback programs (where an individual becomes aware of his or her bodily processes by the use of monitoring instruments) can help people alter the external or internal environments that contribute to their isolation. Perceptual therapies help people assess themselves and improve their self-concepts, allowing them to move toward honest, open interactions with others. Pastoral counseling sessions can also help people understand and appreciate themselves so they can relate more fully to others.

Singlehood.   At least 10% of young adults now resist the pressures for marriage in their twenties for various reasons. This rate has doubled in recent years (Stayton, 1984). Some will eventually marry, but many choose long-term **singlehood** willingly. They no longer fear the labels "spinster" and "bachelor," or criticisms of self-centeredness. Singlehood has advantages: freedom to come and go at any hour, freedom to spend time and money as one chooses, autonomy concerning meals and homework, more career opportunities, more freedom to change, more freedom to move, self-sufficiency, plurality of roles, and psychological autonomy.

Attitudes toward singlehood have changed considerably over the past twenty years. Several hundred Americans were asked the question "Suppose all you knew about a [man/woman] was that [he/she] did not want to get married. What would you guess [he/she] was like?" Two-thirds of contemporary respondents gave either a positive or neutral description of such a person. In the 1950s the majority of respondents gave a decidedly negative description (Veroff, Douvan, and Kulka, 1981).

Some young adults choose singlehood in order to pursue careers that involve frequent traveling or other activities that would be considerably more difficult with a spouse or children. Some may have the responsibilities of caring for older parents or younger siblings. Some may not meet a woman or man they want to marry or one who wants to marry them. Others may form intimate alliances with partners, possibly including cohabitation, but avoid the legal bonds of matrimony.

Schwartz (1976) found six groups that typified single men and women: professionals, socials, individuals, activists, passives, and supportives. Professionally oriented singles spend most of their time at work or in work-related activities (see Figure 8-12). Social life for such persons may revolve around the neighborhood of the job: stores, bars, galleries. Friends are co-workers or people whom they see in the course of going to or from work. Social singles are those to whom one often applies the label "swinging singles." They spend a great deal of time on their social activities. Individuals are those who spend time getting to know themselves or in solitary hobbies. Activists, as described on page 302, devote a great deal of time to social causes that are particularly meaningful to them. The supportive singles spend time doing for others and find meaning to their lives in these endeavors. Passive singles are apt to be the least satisfied being single and may be lonely or depressed. With the exception of the passive singles, Schwartz found her subjects to be satisfied with their chosen lifestyles.

Approximately 80% of singles report some coital involvement between the ages of 25 and 44 (Lauer and Lauer, 1991). The current proportions of sexually active, single men and women are nearly equal (Darling, Kallen, and Van Dusen, 1984). In a study of singles who are virgins compared to single nonvirgins, Jessor and Jessor (1975) found that the nonvirgins are more apt to be independent from their families, more reliant on peers, more unconventional and more tolerant of deviance from social norms by others. Although there is a permissiveness toward premarital sex, many young

Figure 8-12
For some career-centered "professional" singles, work is a major source of pleasure. Work-related activities consume much more than a forty-hour work week.

adults express the belief that sex should be part of a loving relationship without exploitation.

Loving relationships develop slowly. Sternberg (1986, 1988) identified three components of love: passion, intimacy, and commitment (see Figure 8-13). Passion (sexual desire) may develop very rapidly. Intimacy, with a mutuality as described by Erikson, develops more slowly as the partners begin to understand each other's feelings and become friends. The commitment component of love may be the hardest to achieve. It is a rational decision between two people to maintain the relationship and promote each other's well being, with or without marriage. It can hold the love together when the going gets tough.

A love that just involves passion is quite empty. Sternberg (1987) called it infatuation. Some adults marry and even stay in marriages with only infatuation. A love with both passion and intimacy is called romantic. A love with intimacy and commitment but in which passion has ended is called companionate. Both romantic and companionate love are more rewarding than infatuation but not as ideal as a love containing all three components, which Sternberg called **consummate love.** Many couples keep passion alive despite all the stresses that other tasks of adulthood impose on a relationship.

Lee (1973) suggested that there are six different styles of loving: agape, eros, ludus, mania, pragma, and storge (see Table 8-7).

Agape is the kind of love described in the New Testament of the Bible, First Corinthians, Chapter 13: "Looks for a way to be constructive, . . . not possessive, . . . good manners, . . . does not pursue selfish advantage, . . . does not keep

Table 8-7   Styles of Love.

Style	Description
Agape	Unselfish; puts needs of beloved ahead of self; patient and kind
Eros	Passionate; focuses on sex appeal and physical excitement
Ludus	Game playing; "the chase"; may play game with more than one
Mania	Possessive; jealous of beloved being with others; fearful of loss
Pragma	Logical; shopping list of needs; compares beloved against list
Storge	Empathetic; mutual concerns and intimacy; best friends

account of evil, . . . knows no limit to its endurance, no end to its trust, no fading of its hope." Opinions differ as to whether agapic love provides a good foundation for marriage. Consider this vignette:

> Nell met her "ideal husband" on her second day of graduate school and fell instantly in love. She was thrilled when he asked her out. She began to put his needs and desires before her own and spent as much time cleaning his apartment and making his meals as she did on her own studies.
>
> Caleb proposed to Nell but never produced an engagement ring. Twice they filled out the necessary papers for a marriage license, but Caleb found reasons to postpone the wedding until each license expired. On several occasions, one or another of his friends would tell Nell that Caleb was exploiting her while dating other women. She believed this was true but thought that ultimately he would be unable to resist her unselfish agapic style of love.
>
> For two years, Nell tried to be as unconditionally caring, nurturant, compassionate, and loving toward Caleb as was humanly possible. At the end of the second year, Caleb left the university. He called off their engagement.

Could agape become the basis for consummate love if both partners had an agapic style of loving?

Eros is the love commemorated by songwriters: the thrill, the yearning, the flame, the devotion, the fervor, the rapture, the enchantment, the adoration. When struck by Cupid's arrow, the victim becomes "lovesick." Falling in love can create physical symptoms in a person: loss of appetite, insomnia, euphoria. These symptoms subside over time. A person with an eros style of loving may not stay in a relationship once the passion wanes. Can passion remain high forever?

Ludus is the game of love: the chase. To quest for an unattainable goal is exciting. Tally-ho! The ludic style of lover enjoys the pursuit. He or she may engage in every imaginable tactic to break down the resistance of the pursued: hearts, flowers, cards, poems, wining and dining, serenading. When the race is won, however, the ludic lover usually enters a new race. Could a person hold the interest of a ludic style lover by never quite getting caught? Could ludus lead to consummate love?

Manic is possessive: "I want you. I need you. Where have you been? When will I see you? Who are you with? What are you doing? Spend time with me." It is very flattering, at first, to be in a relationship with a manic style of lover. It can be exhausting, however. The manic style of lover appears over time to be too greedy, too grasping, too covetous, too clingy. What would be the result of two manic style lovers entering a relationship with each other?

Pragma is logical. The pragmatic style of lover makes a very rational decision about the object of his or her affection before becoming involved. Involvement only occurs if the list of pros about the beloved far outweighs the list of cons. Marriage brokers are pragmatic. Can arranged marriages result in consummate love?

Storge is intimacy, familiarity, friendship. A storgic style of lover seeks harmony and peace with a partner. The relationship a storgic style of lover seeks is characterized by open, honest communication, sympathy, empathy, cooperation, and interdependency. "I love you like a brother (sister)." Can passion find a place in a relationship between two storgic style lovers?

What style of loving appeals most to you? Can a person combine two or more styles? A person's style of loving can change over time. Reading about these styles of love may cause you to try to alter your loving behaviors.

Cohabitation. (living together and sharing sex without being married) is common. Approximately two million couples live together in the U.S.A. today, representing nearly a fourfold increase since 1970 (Lauer and Lauer, 1991). Clayton and Voss (1977) found that cohabitants are more frequently nonstudents than students. Cohabitation is generally short lived (two years) and ends with marriage or by breaking up. Most cohabitants rate their relationships as rewarding and maturing, with the benefits outweighing the problems (Macklin, 1978). Watson (1983) found that only about 6% of cohabitants have regrets afterward.

Watson studied eighty-four couples during their first year of marriage; fifty-four couples had lived together, and thirty had not. Comparisons revealed that the noncohabitant couples had significantly higher mean adjustment scores in their first year of marriage, due mainly to the responses of the wives. He suggested that this may be due to the noncohabitant woman's delight in establishing her own home and defining her new role, something her previously cohabitated counterpart did a year or two earlier.

Homosexuality.   Cohabitation is becoming increasingly common among homosexual couples (see Figure 8-14). In the past, most homosexuals felt they had to hide their sexual preferences in order to live safely in heterosexual societies. Only a few societies accepted gay men or lesbian women as normal. Today **homosexuality** is considered a normal variation of sexual behavior by the psychiatric community. The American Psychiatric Association removed homosexuality from their list of abnormal behaviors in 1980 (APA, 1980). As the stigma against homosexuality is fading, more couples are "coming out of the closet" and acknowledging their preferred lifestyle.

Nobody knows for sure how many men and women are homosexual or bisexual. Estimates range from 5 to 40% of males and from 2 to 20% of females. Sexologists believe the numbers of homosexuals have not changed very much over the history of human existence: rather, different eras have hidden or acknowledged homosexuality to a greater or a lesser degree. Research evidence is inconclusive as to the origins of homosexuality. It may have a genetic basis (Eckert et al., 1986), a biological basis (Money, Schwartz, and Lewis, 1984), a learned basis (Hoffman, M., 1977), or a blending of biological, learning, and emotional factors (Storms, 1980).

Homosexuals are like heterosexuals. Only the direction of their libidinous urges sets them apart. It is myth that they all are promiscuous or that they all have gender identity disorders. Bell and Weinberg (1978) studied close to 1400 homosexuals. Many lived in couple relationships. They found it rare for one partner to adopt a feminine role and the other to adopt a masculine role. Instead, many couples live in close relationships where sex, monetary, and power roles are shared equitably. Some couples have what is closer to an open marriage. They live together but may have an occasional affair outside of the relationship. Bell and Weinberg found that some homosexuals prefer a single lifestyle. Of the single homosexuals, some are well adjusted, some are troubled

Figure 8-14
Many homosexual couples live in equitable relationships very similar to marriages but with fewer gender-stereotyped roles.

by their libidinous preferences, and some sublimate their urges and live asexual lives. Harry (1983) reported that about one-half of gay men and three-quarters of lesbians live in couple relationships.

Many homosexuals marry before acknowledging their sexual preference. If they have children in their heterosexual marriages, they usually maintain close ties to them after the divorce (Miller, 1979). Homosexual parents can retain custody of their children and/or adopt children. Children raised by homosexuals develop heterosexual libidinous urges at about the same rate as the rest of the population (Hotvedt and Mandel, 1982).

Marriage

Although singlehood or cohabitation may appeal to a portion of young adults, a good marriage and family life is the goal of the majority (see Figure 8-15). Bachman and Johnston (1979) found that 79% of college students and 76% of noncollege youth ranked it as their number one goal, ahead of finding steady work, making a contribution to society or having lots of money. The second-ranked goal of both college and noncollege youth was to have strong friendships. These goals indicate that young adults are extremely interested in resolving the Eriksonian nuclear conflict of intimacy versus isolation.

About 95% of all Americans eventually marry. The median age for a first marriage is now twenty-five for men and twenty-three for women, older than it has been since the turn of the century. This reflects in part the practice of cohabiting before marriage and of postponing marriage until one has finished an education or become established in a career.

The joining of two persons into a legal partnership called marriage is easily accomplished. The molding of the lifestyles of the two people into a workable team involves a great deal of additional effort. Even couples who have lived together prior to marriage agree that the expectations of permanence of the union place new constraints on them. **Marriage** means compromise and sacrifice. It means acceptance of each other's variations in moods, in needs, and in personality. It means trying to achieve consummate love with passion, intimacy and commitment (see p. 305).

Honeymoon. The **honeymoon period** (mutual affection of newlyweds) seldom lasts very long. Major sources of marital disagreements include money, sex, and power. Quarrels can be constructive: they serve to clear the air and relieve tension. Couples should learn how to quarrel, however (see Table 8-8). A willingness to engage in open, honest communication is one of the keys to a workable marriage. Another is to develop

Figure 8-15
Marriage is one way in which young adults meet their needs for belonging and love, esteem, and approval from others.

Table 8-8   The Dos and Don'ts of Quarreling.

Do	Don't
Discuss differences of opinion	Pretend to agree
Take responsibility for your own failures	Make excuses for yourself
Tell mate what you want	Tell mate what to do
Express yourself with "I feel . . ."	Insult mate
Paraphrase what mate has said	Whine
Acknowledge mate's viewpoint	Withdraw from communicating
Listen to mate's feelings	"Mind read" inaccurately
Suggest compromises	Interrupt mid-sentence

SOURCE: Adapted from Gottman, J., and Krokoff, L. (1989). Marital interaction and satisfaction: A Longitudinal view. *Journal of Consulting and Clinical Psychology*, **57**, 47–52.

a relationship where partners are neither completely dependent on each other, nor completely independent from each other, but rather have a certain amount of interdependency.

Kieren, Henton, and Marotz (1975) described and defined **marital morale** as a more accurate indicator of the state of a relationship than happiness or stability. It is a measure of contentment with a marriage based on the number of personal and interpersonal goals that are being achieved. If the expectations of both partners in a marriage are being met, the marriage is likely to persist. If expectations fail, separation usually ensues.

Sternberg (1985) suggested ten factors that form a basic core of love:

1. promoting the welfare of the loved one,
2. experiencing happiness with the loved one,
3. having high regard for the loved one,
4. being able to count on the loved one in times of need,
5. understanding the loved one,
6. sharing oneself and one's things with the loved one,
7. receiving emotional support from the loved one,
8. giving emotional support to the loved one,
9. communicating intimately with the loved one,
10. valuing the loved one in one's own life.

Sternberg found that liking one's partner is a better predictor of satisfaction in a relationship than love. No matter how much a person loves, the union is not apt to work out unless the loved one is liked as well.

Household Organization.   Smooth, efficient running of a household is a major organizational task of persons in their twenties (see Figure 8-16). In spite of the rhetoric on shared roles and equality, most individuals occasionally fall into patterns of boss and bossed.

In the traditional **nuclear family** setting (father–mother–children), the husband is usually perceived as having the managerial role. In fact, the wife expends more energy on household organization, regardless of her employment status (Berardo, Shehan, and Leslie, 1987). When both spouses are employed full time, the wife does about 70% of the housework. When the wife is a full-time homemaker, she does about 83%. Dual income couples still usually consider the home to be the woman's responsibility. Occasionally children are allowed to have input about what is to be done and who is to do it. In nontraditional families (e.g., homosexual couples), the management of the household has more chance of being egalitarian than in families trying to conform to conventional social customs.

Household organization is perceived by some to be simpler today due to modern

Figure 8-16
There are several interdependent tasks, each having a relation to other tasks, that constitute household organization. Some homes run smoothly, some are chaotic.

appliances and convenience foods. Tasks are different from a hundred years ago, but they are not simpler. Society is more complicated. Moves are frequent. Managing a household, even a simple efficiency apartment, means paying bills; organizing time for work, meals, and leisure; socializing and entertaining; struggling with machines; repairing or replacing gadgets that seem engineered to break down; and dealing with meter readers, solicitors, repair people, telephone service, landlords, bill collectors, social service workers, neighbors, garbage collection, and pick-up or delivery of mail, newspapers, laundry, and groceries. People with children must organize and plan time for transportation to school and after-school events as well as cope with children's accidents, illnesses, and disobedience. For some people household organization is untenable. Home means a crowded, chaotic, noisy place where tranquillity reigns only when inhabitants are asleep or absent.

In-Law Relations.   Married adults not only have to adjust to each other's idiosyncrasies, organize a household, and possibly rear children but also have to either design workable **in-law relations** or become estranged from their families of origin. In-law relations require a certain amount of diplomacy, compromise, and sacrifice, even with the best of all possible parents-in-law. The best parents-in-law shoulder many of the necessary sacrifices and compromises themselves for the sake of maintaining ties with their married children (see Figure 8-17).

> Meena eloped with Norman. Early in the marriage, Norman's mother refused to talk to Meena, but after her grandson was born she began visiting Meena frequently. Each time she entered the house she snooped everywhere, looking for something to criticize. She scolded Meena for folding Norman's undershirts wrong and refolded the pile the "right" way. She found a spot on one of Meena's "clean" blouses in the closet. She criticized each meal. Every sneeze or cough from the baby was proof that Meena was a poor mother. At first, Meena cried. She begged Norman to talk to his mother. He refused, pointing out that each remark was superficial and should just be ignored. When Meena fought with her mother-in-law, Norman took his mom's side.

How should Meena and her mother-in-law resolve their problems?

When people marry, they should not expect complete freedom from their families

I never let your father
come home late for meals.

My little girl
never dressed like
that when she lived
under my roof.

Her parents
Why won't they accept our offer
of an interest-free loan to buy that house?

But I don't want my
life exactly like hers.

Dad would have called Mom
if he was going to be late.

Why can't he defend
my ways to his parents?

Why can't she see
that he is happy
with my methods?

She takes her mother's
advice, not mine.

Why can't he understand that
she's not a little girl anymore?
She makes up her own mind.

Why can't she defend
my ways to her parents?

How can he criticize?
I'm making less money
and saving more than he is.

But he *does* prefer
his T-shirts ironed!

He'd do a lot
better if he'd put
his savings in a
money market.

His parents
Why do they spend the
holidays with her parents?

Figure 8-17
Designing workable in-law relationships requires sacrificing, compromising, and a
tolerance of differences.

of origin. What young marrieds can expect is that parents and in-laws will give them
some freedom, tone down or hide some of their concerns, and refrain from too much
advice giving. All relationships with in-laws are potentially problematic. Mothers-in-law
come in for more accusations of interference than fathers-in-law, due partly to the fact
that mothers usually have more to give up in the way of parenting responsibilities.

The wife's mother may feel that she has to help her daughter with cooking, cleaning,
and child care. The daughter may have difficulty gaining a sense of self-esteem as a
mature, capable wife/mother in her own right. She may resent her mother (even while
being thankful for the help), and her husband may resent her, too.

The husband's mother often has difficulty seeing another woman take her place in
her son's life. She may genuinely like her daughter-in-law yet find it hard not to mention

all those things that her son liked when she was mothering him. These suggestions may be taken as veiled criticism or negative advice giving by a sensitive wife rather than as helpful suggestions. Some wives and mothers-in-law actually vie with each other for the attention, affection, and approval of the husband/son.

The wife's father may be problematic in the same way as the husband's mother. Fathers tend to persist in their beliefs that their daughters are naive, unaware, and immature. A father-in-law may be jealous of the husband who has taken his place in his daughter's life and may resent the husband for taking away the daughter's innocence. Daughters may aggravate the problem by comparing their husbands to "Daddy."

The husband's own father may give his son advice about finances, his role in marriage, fathering, or any number of other things to the point where the son has difficulty feeling self-confident about his role as husband/father. The wife may resent her husband's leaning on his father.

Problems usually increase when families give financial aid to their married children. Aid may have certain spoken or unspoken strings attached. It also prolongs the young couples' feelings of dependence on their parents. Although financial aid may contribute to in-law friction, it is also very much needed and appreciated by some married persons. Living with in-laws may be easier than living close to them. When adults exist under the same roof, they work out their misunderstandings sooner and agree upon acceptable roles and responsibilities.

In-law relations can be very rewarding. Some married couples really look forward to weekends and holidays with in-laws. They accept their parents' desire to spoil them, cook, clean, and give gifts and compliments. The older couple welcomes their role as grandparents. The younger couple showers their parents with gifts, compliments, love, and affection in turn. They may both give and accept help with finances, children, illness, and crises. Couples may be able to look on in-laws as role models and learn from them.

Divorce.   Divorces (also annulments and separations) are frequent in our society. The number of new marriages ending in divorce is now approaching 50%. Young people seem to be more ready to divorce than older people. Divorce rates are highest for those marrying young (72% of teen-age marriages) and for those with low incomes, poor education, or uncertain unemployment. Although grounds for divorce are now quite broad in some states (incompatibility, adultery, cruelty, desertion, nonsupport, alcohol or drug addiction, felony conviction, impotence, fraudulent contract, insanity, living separate and apart), the legal costs and the emotional trauma involved make most couples very stressed throughout the divorce process.

Parenthood

Shortly after marriage most couples begin to feel pressure from parents, in-laws, peers, and friends to have children. The desire to conform is frequently given as a reason for procreation. Children can bring a great deal of love, warmth, and laughter into a home. They also bring extra work and added financial responsibilities.

During a woman's pregnancy both fathers and mothers usually begin to anticipate and prepare for the changes that children will bring into their lives (see Chapter 3, p. 89). Husbands may feel a surge in their masculinity as they watch their wife's abdomen expand and feel the unborn child move. They may begin helping and sheltering their wife more. In fact, pregnancy may usher in the first concept in the man that he is the guardian and defender of his wife and family. Women may feel either more or less feminine as they carry children. Some women decry the loss of their figures and the inconveniences of their pregnant stage. Others take great pride in their protruding figures and enjoy the legitimized reduction in their self-help activities.

Life Changes.   Birth is usually a joyous occasion (see Figure 8-18). For a short while parent(s) enjoy receiving congratulations and hearing their very own infant's cry. But, sooner or later, the sound of the baby crying reminds parents of the exhausting work of **parenthood.** LeMasters (1970), after interviews with a wide spectrum of parents, reported that 83% of them experienced a marital crisis after the birth of a baby. In contrast, a reader's poll conducted by *Parents Magazine* (Yarrow, 1982) found that 69% of the write-in respondents felt that having a baby strengthened their marriage. However, most of the women who wrote to the magazine (no husbands responded) also said they were more fatigued, went out less, and were more limited in their activities due to parenthood.

Suddenly the family relationships must change to include the new member. There will be mother–father, mother–child, and father–child. Schisms and jealousies ensue. The problems that existed in maintaining love and marital morale before the child's arrival often become aggravated. Sex is temporarily restricted while the mother heals. Freedom to come and go is inhibited by the need to provide baby care. The extra money from pay checks that once served as a basis for leisure activities is now diverted into baby necessities. In many families the infant's arrival marks a diminution of the mother's wage-earning activities. Exhaustion from night feedings, extra house-work, and tensions related to the baby are common. Feelings of inadequacy are also frequent.

Children seldom, if ever, really improve a marriage by themselves. What may happen is that couples on an upswing work even harder to communicate their problems and needs to each other. Couples on a downswing find their marital adjustment problems magnified. Once children are involved, divorce becomes more complicated. Adults can sever their relationships with each other but usually not with their offspring. Someone must provide for the well-being of a child for eighteen years after birth.

There are reasons to be optimistic about parenthood as an influence on the development of young adults. Children can be immeasurably enriching and rewarding to adults who want them and are ready to love and care for them. (Erik Erikson's seventh nuclear conflict, that of *generativity versus stagnation,* will be discussed in this regard in the next chapter.)

The number of women deciding to postpone parenthood until they are in their late twenties or thirty-something has increased dramatically in the past twenty years (Lauer and Lauer, 1991). This means that they are likely to have fewer children. Women who

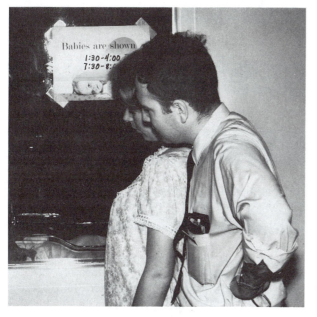

Figure 8-18
Many new parents experience an indescribable surge of wonder as they view the child they have created.

Figure 8-19
Fathers and mothers shoulder the responsibility for helping their offspring grow into trusting, autonomous, initiating, industrious, self-knowledgeable human beings in eighteen years.

are highly educated and pursuing careers are the most apt to delay the birth of a first child. Some couples are deciding that they do not want to have children at all.

Increasing numbers of young adults now approach parenthood with an earnest regard for the seriousness of the task. Courses in child-rearing are popular. Books on child-rearing are in demand in libraries and bookstores. There is also evidence of a growing feeling among men that it is both admirable and desirable to help care for children (see Figure 8-19).

Parke (1982) in a review of the research on fathering, suggested that when men share with their wives the tasks of child care the wife's self-esteem improves, the father's relationship with his children improves, and the children themselves may become both more independent and have higher self-esteem.

Infertility.   About 15% of couples fail to conceive a child after one year of regular coitus without contraception (Marshall, 1984). Reasons for **infertility** are about evenly divided between male and female problems (40% each), with both partners having problems in about 20% of marriages. Not long ago, more than half of all infertility problems were believed to be of psychological origin. Today, many more physical problems have been identified that contribute to the failure to conceive. Fortunately, many more therapeutic techniques have been developed as well. Now infertile couples have a very good chance of achieving a pregnancy after appropriate diagnosis and treatment (Speroff, Glass, and Kase, 1983).

The most frequent physical reason for infertility in women is a blockage of the Fallopian tubes. Blockages often occur as a sequelae to pelvic inflammatory disease (PID), which leaves scar tissue. Chlamydia and gonorrhea (see Chapter 7) are usually the infecting agents in PID. The tubes may also be blocked as a result of endometriosis, tuberculosis, or polyps. They can usually be cleared with microsurgery or laser surgery, restoring fertility to the woman.

Another physical reason for failure to conceive in women is a failure to produce viable ova. Oocytes can be induced to undergo meiosis and produce mature ova with drug and hormone therapy when a woman is ready to conceive. If the reason for female infertility is insufficient cervical mucous, hormone therapy can also be used. If adhesions exist inside the uterus, a dilation and curettage (D&C) and hormone therapy should allow a re-created endometrial cavity to support a pregnancy after three to six months.

Women who exercise vigorously several hours a day (such as distance runners and dancers) may suffer temporary infertility as a result of altered endocrine functioning or of changes in the ratio of body fat to lean tissue that alters their menstrual cycles. Women who fast to diet, who are severely anemic, or who are anorexic may also suffer temporary infertility. These problems are treated by a return to normal eating, nutritional therapy, psychotherapy, or reducing the amount of daily exercise.

A common physical cause of infertility in men is a blocked vas deferens. It may be blocked because of an old inflammatory process from one of the sexually transmitted diseases (chlamydia, gonorrhea). Surgical techniques now allow for the reopening of many blocked tubes. Low sperm counts may also be caused by wearing tight briefs that keep the testicles too close to the body, and too warm, for adequate spermatogenesis. Excess exposure of the scrotum to heat from spas, whirlpools, hot baths, saunas, or sitting in hot environments can also adversely affect sperm production. So, too, can overexposure to radiation. Some drugs, notably marijuana, also decrease fertility. Men with low sperm counts are usually counseled to exercise regularly, lose weight if they are obese, avoid use of alcohol, marijuana, and tobacco, and refrain from daily coitus. Intercourse every other day during the fertile period results in maximal fertility. Prolonged celibacy may depress sperm motility.

Many of the psychological reasons for infertility relate to stress. Fears, guilt, anxieties, hostilities, insomnia, a change in eating habits, an abuse of drugs, and so on will result in a change in endocrine functioning. The body reacts to stress by increasing the production of several "stress" hormones (ACTH, cortisol), which in turn reduce the production of the gonadotropins. Even the stress of wanting a pregnancy can interfere with fertility. (Refer back to Table 8-2 and Figure 8-3, pp. 283–284).

Many couples who fail to conceive after a year or more of intercourse without contraception seek medical advice. The wife is usually the first to seek an evaluation of her status. Physicians prefer to diagnose both partners together, seeing each separately but simultaneously, and reporting and discussing all procedures and findings to both. The uncertainty of the diagnosis creates problems of lowered self-esteem in both men and women. Consequently, a physician must do a great deal of supportive counseling as well as physiological counseling during the evaluation period.

Preparation for a Career

A major element of Erikson's description of the nuclear conflict surrounding identity versus role confusion concerns career choice. During adolescence there may be a host of people to give advice about various careers: guidance counselors, primary caregivers, mentors, peers, siblings, and other relatives. Teenagers can feel tense about making such weighty decisions for their lives. Many steal time by simply saying they are college bound for a liberal arts education that will help them decide, or they declare themselves without choice, saying they must get a job wherever they can.

Advice on career choice often abates somewhat by the twenties. Would-be advisors believe that young people have already made up their minds about a career. Young people often give lip service to the vocational choice they are pursuing or are hoping to pursue. They hesitate to admit their uncertainty. They often seek less advice because they feel they should decide for themselves.

Figure 8-20
The apprenticeship system or a practicum experience helps novice employees see what a job is like from the inside.

Decisions about careers need not be permanent. The young person who starts a career after high school may try out several jobs before deciding on a preferred form of employment. Young persons who choose a career that requires a trade school, college, or graduate school invest more of themselves (time, money) in a future job. They may change jobs later, but at a greater expense. Some will have practicum courses built into their education. These help them decide whether they have made the right choice. If they do not like the work, they may drop out of the particular career program and choose another. When practicum experience is missing, young persons may spend years preparing for a job without any feel for what it will be like (see Figure 8-20).

One may look back wistfully to the days of **apprenticeship learning.** Children once worked alongside their parents and neighbors or at least had more access to places of employment. Children knew a great deal about the world of work. When they decided what job they wanted, they could go to learn the line of trade by working daily with the master craftsman. Contemporary culture offers so many possible kinds of work that deciding on any one direction is now more difficult. Specialization within jobs makes apprenticeship learning complicated. Rapid technological change also makes it less practicable. Finally, education and child labor laws keep children out of much of the work world until they reach the age of sixteen. Most employment today involves on-the-job training no matter how little or how much education the employee has had ahead of time.

Gender Choices. Parental expectations for their offspring are often in stark contrast to the expectations young adults have for themselves. The typical American parents would like to see their sons be successful and respected in their chosen field of work ("My son, the doctor"). Additionally sons should be intelligent, honest, responsible, independent, self-reliant, aggressive, and strong-willed. If they marry, the parents would like the chosen wife to be kind, unselfish, loving, attractive, well-mannered, and a good wife and mother. These same parents would like to see their daughters be kind, unselfish, loving, attractive, well-mannered, and good wives and mothers ("My daughter, Miss America") (Hoffman, 1975). Naturally, they would prefer their daughters to marry men who are successful and respected in their chosen fields. Even professional faculty women interviewed at the University of Michigan, in spite of professing to hold the same goals for offspring of either sex, were found to have higher occupational and academic goals in mind for their sons than for their daughters (Hoffman, L. W., 1977).

In today's changing social structure many more young women have higher academic and occupational goals for themselves than do their parents. Lavine (1982) found that if a daughter is raised perceiving her father to be dominant, she is more apt to select a stereotypically feminine career. However, daughters who perceive their mothers as having egalitarian power or as being dominant tend to select more stereotypically neutral or masculine careers. Parents are not always pleased with these choices. Likewise, many more young men have goals for themselves at odds with their parents' goals. Many of today's young men would prefer to have a wife with some career orientation both to have a second paycheck and to have a more compatible marriage with more shared interests. Many of these same men are more willing and interested than their fathers were in sharing homemaking and child-rearing tasks with their wives. Both young women and young men are expressing more desire than did their predecessors to postpone marriage, postpone parenthood, and have fewer children. This has become feasible because of safe and effective methods of birth control.

For women in our contemporary culture, a commitment to a career has additional concerns. Employers hesitate to hire women of childbearing age for long-term jobs for fear that they will become pregnant and leave. If a woman asks for a maternity leave rather than quitting her job, she is often seen as uncommitted and may be refused

Women versus Men in the Work Place.

Are men being treated as full and equal members of the labor force? Should they be? Or are prejudices against men at work justified? How can a man give his best to an out-of-the-home job while he is also a husband and a father? Can a man ever be fully respected on the job unless we radically alter the basic structures of family life? As it stands now, would you want your staff to be composed entirely of men (unless, of course, the job for which you hired the man was something like child care, nursing, elementary school teaching, cleaning, secretarial work, and the like)?

By and large, men have been socialized to be husbands and fathers first, and workers second. Their attitudes toward a job will always reflect this bias toward home and family. Nonwhite men seem especially inclined to put their wives and children ahead of their jobs. Knowing this, employers do the logical thing. They pay a nonwhite male only about 79% of the white female's average entry hourly wage. If they hire a white male, they pay him 4% more, or about 83% of the white female's average entry hourly wage.*

To the credit of working men, they do not seem to develop as many stress-related illnesses (heart disease, hypertension, peptic ulcers) as women. They also have fewer accidents. Perhaps this is because they are so rarely found in managerial positions. Nevertheless, type A, "cardiac" personality women do make better managers, don't you agree?

Why do men want to be full and equal members of the labor force anyway? Why don't they stay home, raise children, and let the women handle the difficulties of the work place?

*Figures in reverse (substitute female for male).

leave (to test her loyalty) or laid off, usually for some "other" reason (see Box 8-2). Rosen, Jerdee, and Prestwich (1975) found that employers hesitate to give women jobs that require traveling. Women are also seldom considered for jobs that might entail transfers to other cities. A woman is expected to leave her job and follow her husband if and when he is transferred. The reciprocal (that a man will leave his job and follow his wife if and when she is transferred) is not part of the attitude of most employers.

When equally qualified men and women apply for positions, placement officers not only favor the male applicants but also frequently ask more information on the females' personality, marital status, and children. They also ask what the husband and children will do if she is hired. Affirmative action committees have done a great deal to eliminate job discrimination because of sex (also race, age, and country of origin), but old prejudices against women persist. If a job requires aggressive interpersonal behavior and decisive managerial action, men are more apt to be hired.

Although being discriminated against at the time of job seeking is a threat, the more frequent concerns of women contemplating careers are role related. Do I want to be married? Can I combine marriage with a career? Do I want to have children? Can I combine child-rearing with a career? Will daycare centers or babysitters be available so that I can work while I have children? Are daycare centers or babysitters good for children? Are they reasonably priced? Will I be able to take a break from my career to raise children and then return to work?

Social scientists have adopted the term **superwoman syndrome** to describe women who attempt to combine the roles of wife/mother, homemaker, and career woman. They perform all the traditional feminine role functions at home: entertain lavishly, keep an immaculate home, cook gourmet meals, and assume full responsibility for child care. Superwomen most frequently select career areas that are stereotypically feminine. Nearly 70% of all women are employed in traditionally female jobs. More than one-third of all women are employed in ten jobs (Maymi, 1982):

- Secretary
- Bookkeeper
- Sales clerk
- Cashier
- Waitress
- Nurse
- Elementary school teacher
- Private household worker
- Typist
- Nursing aide

In addition to trying to fill the stereotypic female role both at home and at work, superwomen also may conceal their achievements or temporarily reduce their efforts if their accomplishments put them in conflict over their social acceptability. The superwoman syndrome can be hard on a woman's physical and emotional health. Stress management for a working woman may require an overhaul of a woman's entire way of thinking (enough is enough!) and lowering expectations for performance and possessions rather than giving up (Orsborn, 1985) (see Figure 8-21).

Being exclusively a wife and mother is unpaid work and is not given due respect by many people in our culture. In her classic book *The Feminine Mystique,* Betty Friedan (1963) described the loneliness and lack of self-esteem of housewives as "the problem that has no name." Although it is by no means a universal problem, it is not uncommon. The physical and emotional health of women who have no career other than wife and mother may be in more jeopardy today than that of the superwomen. Women have markedly more depression than men, even when matched for such influences as age, marital status, employment, and income (Radloff and Rae, 1979). Homemakers have more depression than working women. They also have more acute illnesses, more chronic conditions, more doctor visits, more disabilities, and more activity limitations (Verbrugge, 1982). Part-time jobs or volunteer work may contribute to improved mental and physical health in homemakers.

Career Mobility.   A worker does not usually perform well in a job until he or she has had a few months to learn the techniques of the work to be done. The settling-in process involves the establishment of interpersonal working relationships with the

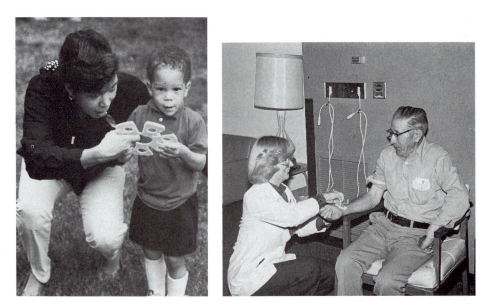

Figure 8-21
Homemakers and career women may envy each other. Each choice has its own advantages and disadvantages.

employer and other employees as well as learning the details of the job. Early career decisions may not be permanent. Most young people need from a few months to a few years to settle into a career. Job changes, job training, and further education prolong the process.

Disillusionment is not uncommon in the months or years spent entering a field of employment. Young persons may choose a job without a realistic understanding of the work entailed. Medicine, for example, is a high-prestige career with an aura of glamour, but doctors and nurses must deal with death and disease, maintain patient rapport, and work under the threat of malpractice suits. Modeling may look glamorous but requires hours of posing for takes and retakes under hot lights with a rigorous regimen of diet and exercise in off-duty hours.

Bachman and Johnston (1979) found that the primary goals of young adults entering jobs were not money, respect, and status but rather (1) interesting work that (2) uses skills and abilities with (3) good chances for advancement and (4) a predictable, secure future, where one can (5) see results of what one does, (6) make friends, and (7) be worthwhile to society.

Many employers try to provide changes and challenges in assignments to keep their employees interested and motivated at their jobs, but this is not always possible. There are many highly technical jobs that must be done one way and one way only by well-trained, practiced hands.

Young persons in search of careers frequently change jobs. These shifts are more easily accomplished when people are young, do not require large salaries, and can travel. However, tight job markets, family pressures, too little or too much education, even fear of discrimination may make young people hesitate to look for better jobs.

Too many job changes can leave young people as dissatisfied with the world of work as can any one routine. Toffler (1970), in his book *Future Shock,* warned of the dangers of too many job changes. There is always a great deal of stress accompanying a change of job. The work is unfamiliar. One must learn quickly and do well to assure job continuance. One's old friends are gone. If the job change involves a move to a new location, there are many extra-career tensions: finding housing, moving the family, starting children in new schools, employment for a spouse. Career commitment consumes a considerable amount of the time and energy of people in their twenties.

Summary

Young adults can be found in many settings: jobs, the military service, institutes of higher education, their families of origin, new families, singles' residences.

Given proper diet, exercise, rest, and freedom from preexisting handicaps or diseases, persons in their twenties should be in peak physical condition. The threat to health that looms largest in young adulthood is stress. Accidents and psychophysiologic illnesses have their origin in persons' inabilities to cope successfully with the stresses of young adult living.

Substance abuse is greater in the twenties than at any other decade of the life span. Many young adults pose serious threats to their mental and physical well-being by abusing alcohol or other drugs.

Cognitive functioning peaks in the twenties. Many young adults have a high need to achieve intellectually. Others subjugate academic achievement to focus on affiliation. Women especially may fear that too many intellectual achievements will stand in the way of their being accepted socially.

The transition from being dependent on one's family of origin to being an economically, socially, and emotionally independent adult is often difficult. Some young adults take a considerable length of time searching for their place in the existing adult social order. Some follow their parents' lead and adhere to conventional customs of the mainstream culture without any conflict. Still others become activists, or become alienated from society.

The nuclear conflict of young adulthood proposed by Erikson is that of finding intimacy versus feeling isolated. Intimacy involves making commitments and fusing one's identity with that of others and is usually seen in the context of marriage, although it can also be achieved outside of marriage.

Many young adults enjoy singlehood or cohabitation. Others choose marriage. Marriages have the greatest potential for lasting when each partner's expectations are being met, when interdependency rather than a dependent or independent relationship exists, and when partners like as well as love each other. Consummate love involves passion, intimacy, and commitment.

Household organization can be complicated, especially with frequent moves, limited space, overextended budgets and all adult members of the household holding part- or full-time jobs.

For both men and women the twenties are the best years for reproducing offspring. Childbearing is often postponed, however, for social, economic, educational, career, or other considerations. Parenthood may bring persons in their twenties both joy, warmth, and laughter, and added work, stress, and financial burdens. Prolonged postpone-

ment of childbearing may result in decreased fertility. As many as 15% of married couples may experience an infertility problem for a variety of reasons.

Entering a suitable field of employment often takes time. Young adults may change jobs frequently before making a commitment to one field. Some persons spend many years in educational centers preparing for a career before they take their first job. Women may choose to be wife/mother/homemaker, to pursue a career, to do one then the other, or to do both simultaneously. Men are increasingly taking more of a role as husband/father/homemaker when the wife also has a career.

Key Concepts

circadian rhythm
lunar cycles
psychophysiologic disorder
general adaptation syndrome
life change units
posttraumatic stress disorder
holistic medicine
physical dependence
psychological dependence

tolerance
alcohol abuse
synergism
blackout
depressants
narcotics
stimulants
hallucinogenic drugs
maturity
family of origin
family of procreation
adulthood moratorium

early adult transition
entering the adult world
age thirty transition
family life cycle
conventionality
youth stage
activists
alienated youth
intimacy versus isolation
singlehood
consummate love
cohabitation

homosexuality
marriage
honeymoon period
marital morale
nuclear family
household organization
in-law relations
parenthood
infertility
apprenticeship learning
superwoman syndrome

Questions for Review

1. Consider the various definitions of maturity presented in Chapter 8. How would you define maturity? Do you agree that young adulthood suggests maturity? Discuss.
2. Why do you think individuals in their twenties, at a peak time of physical and mental ability, have a high incidence of suicide, drug abuse, and stress-related illnesses?
3. Horner found that women fear achievement and success. Some feminists suggest that women learn this fear from the time they are young. Do you agree or disagree? Discuss.
4. Some parents have difficulty accepting their young adults' independence, maturity, and sexuality. Imagine you are a counselor working with a couple who is having difficulty accepting their twenty-year-old's independence. How would you counsel this couple?

5. Describe how the resolution of the sixth nuclear conflict, intimacy versus isolation, is affected by the resolution of earlier nuclear conflicts described by Erikson.
6. Our society has traditionally expected people in their twenties to find a mate, marry, and have children. Much has been written about freedom now to do otherwise. Do you believe individuals are truly any freer to be single, live together, or remain childless? Or do you believe these variations in lifestyle remain stigmatized by the majority of society? Why?
7. Young adulthood is a time of establishing a feeling of self and independence, of choosing a career. Do you think men or women experience more stress and conflict in making these decisions and taking these steps? Or do you think both experience the same amount of stress? Explain your answer.

Further Readings

Bolles, R. N. (1991). *What color is your parachute?* Berkeley, CA: Ten Speed Press.

A how-to-do-it manual for persons trying to find a rewarding career. The author addresses a variety of topics from researching companies to dressing for success.

Bozett, F. W., and Hanson, S. H. (eds.) (1991). *Fatherhood and families in cultural context.* New York: Springer.

The editors have collected a series of articles about the many roles of fathers from many perspectives: health, history, biology, psychology, social welfare, anthropology.

Gerson, K. (1986). *Hard choices: How women decide about work, career and motherhood.* Berkeley: University of California Press.

Using a case study presentation, the author discusses the family vs. career vs. both choices of contemporary women with the pros and cons of such choices.

Miller, T. W. (ed.) (1989). *Stressful life events.* Madison, CT: International University Press.

Renowned stress researchers write about coping mechanisms, coping failures, and assessment and theories of stress and health.

Serpell, R. (1976). *Culture's influence on behavior.* London, UK: Methuen.

To what extent are theories of human development a product of western industrialized norms? The author addresses specific areas in which different cultures affect the personalities of their members.

Sidman, M. (1989). *Coercion and its fallout.* Boston: Authors Coop.

Coercive elements in education, family, law enforcement, diplomacy, even therapy, adversely affect human development. This book suggests practical and moral courses of action to reduce fallout and ways to practice noncoercive control.

The Thirties and Forties   9

Have you ever heard it said, "Never trust a person over thirty"? This generalization about people in their thirties and forties suggests that they have surrendered to the establishment. They have given up youthful idealism and replaced it with a realistic view of what they must do to survive in the world. They behave according to the constraints of their society. They even develop a concern for their reputations.

It is always dangerous to generalize about members of any given group. There are apt to be as many differences between individuals within the group as between members and nonmembers. In fact, not all people in their thirties sell out to the establishment, just as not all individuals in their twenties are idealistic.

The thirties and forties are generally considered to be the most stressful years of adult life. While physical strength, stamina, and coordination decrease, pressures to perform at work, find time for growing children, relate to a tired spouse, and participate in community activities increase. The tumultuous years of early middle adulthood (middlescence) have been compared to adolescence (Kennedy, 1990). By the forties, most adults are tired. They begin to think in terms of time left to live rather than years lived.

> At thirty a man should know himself like the palm of his hand, know the exact number of his defects and qualities, know how far he can go, foretell his failures—be what he is. And above all accept these things.
> —*Albert Camus*

> Life is what happens while you're making other plans.
> —*Tom Smothers*

Physical Development

At some time between thirty and forty-nine, people confront the fact that they have left youth behind them. The physical signs of aging gradually become more obvious. Most people begin to feel some signs of approaching middle age during these decades (for example, muscle or joint stiffness or decreased energy). Some welcome middle age as a sign of maturity, with its concomitant prestige and worldly wisdom. Others spend a good deal of time, effort, and money trying to hide the physical changes that indicate their age (such as gray hair or wrinkles).

Physical Changes

Physically, adults begin to slow down gradually in their thirties and forties. How the body functions is highly dependent on diet, exercise, rest, stress, genetic constitution, and freedom from disease or disabilities.

Muscle size, strength, and reflex speed can be maintained with regular exercise.

The Puerto Rico into which Roberto was born in 1934 was not yet a U.S. Commonwealth, although it was U.S. owned. It had a host of economic and social problems. Puerto Ricans typically labored all day on sugar plantations for subsistence wages. Roberto's father, however, was a plantation foreman. He was able to feed his seven children throughout the great depression and still give Roberto time to play ball.

Roberto was obsessed with baseball. His mother, a talented athlete herself, encouraged him. Before he finished high school, he had been given a contract to play center field for the Santurce, Puerto Rico, baseball team: the same team on which Willie Mays and Orlando Cepeda played. Two Hispanics, Minnie Minoso and Bobby Avila, had already made it to major league baseball in the States, so Roberto had high hopes. By the age of nineteen, he was assigned to a Triple A Dodger farm team, one step away from the majors. By age twenty, he joined the major league Pittsburgh Pirates.

During his twenties, Roberto Clemente became the Pirates' key player. He could hit, field, run, and throw. Each year from twenty-six through age twenty-nine, he had a batting average over .300. Most baseball players slow down at age thirty. Roberto did not. At age thirty, he almost hit .400 (.399) with 211 hits. He was the most consistent batter in baseball, ahead of Willie Mays, Ted Williams, and Hank Aaron.

Roberto continued to bat well in his thirties, maintaining a batting average over .300 for seven years. He did this despite health handicaps. During the break between the baseball seasons of 1964 and 1965, he had a lawn mower accident that resulted in a torn ligament, internal hemorrhage, and surgery on his leg. Then he contracted both malaria and a parathyroid infection. He was underweight and lame, with headaches, fevers, chills, shakes, diarrhea, and vomiting going into his thirty-first year. He still batted .329. The chills, fever, and shakes of malaria recurred periodically the rest of his life.

By age thirty-two, Roberto Clemente won his league's Most Valuable Player award. His batting average dropped to .317, but he had 29 home runs, 71 extra-base hits, batted in 119 runs, scored 105 runs, and had his 2000th career hit. A Los Angeles columnist complained that the award was very late in coming; "That he has never won an MVP, of course, is as big a crime as if Spencer Tracy never won an Oscar."*

At age thirty-seven, Clemente carried his Pirates' teammates to a World Series win over the Baltimore Orioles by hitting .414 and fielding flawlessly. At age thirty-eight, he still hit over .300 (.312) and got his 3000th career hit.

Roberto tried to help correct some of the economic and social problems of his Hispanic people throughout his career. He spent a large portion of his off-season time visiting hospitalized children in Puerto Rico. He set up baseball clinics for juvenile delinquents. He built a "sports city" in San Juan, a facility where young people could choose from a variety of sports until they found one in which they could excel.

On Christmas Eve, 1972, Roberto Clemente asked all Puerto Ricans to give food, clothing, and money to aid Nicaraguans who had just survived a massive earthquake. He spent a week collecting items. Puerto Ricans responded to Roberto out of love. They contributed 26 tons of materials and over $150,000. On New Year's Eve, Roberto loaded the supplies on a propeller-driven airplane. Since he had heard rumors that some earthquake assistance was falling into profiteers' hands, he got on the plane to hand-deliver his items. His wife was worried. The airplane was old and overloaded. She asked him not to go on his mercy mission. He insisted. The supply plane crashed and Roberto Clemente was killed. The Governor of Puerto Rico declared three days of official mourning for the folk hero of their island.

Roberto Clemente was nearing the end of his career as a professional athlete. How would he have restructured his life without baseball? Do you think the risk he took was precipitated by the end of his playing days?

---

*Hano, A. (1973). *Roberto Clemente: Batting King*. New York: G. P. Putnam and Sons.

Without it muscles begin a progressive decline. Size and strength that are lost from disuse, however, can be regained through rigorous exercise. Muscle strength of most men continues to be greater than that of most women throughout the life span. While strength of muscles may be maintained, endurance (the ability to continue to use the same force per mass of muscle tissue over time) decreases. Aging athletes, for example, cannot remain in their game for as long as they could in their twenties. Muscle strains are more common in middlescence when people refuse to acknowledge their decreasing stamina.

Bone elongation ceases in the late teens. By the thirties and forties the bones have already lost some of their mass and density. As the cartilage between the vertebrae start to degenerate from normal wear, the vertebrae become compressed. The spinal column gradually begins to shorten. As adults age, they actually lose some of their height due to this **compression of the spinal column** (see Figure 9-1). By age forty the average adult will stand one-eighth of an inch shorter than he or she did at age twenty (Batten, 1984). With increasing age the cartilage in all joints has a more limited ability to regenerate itself.

In addition to muscular and skeletal changes, there are age-related changes in the endocrine glands, the hormone-producing organs that control stress reactions, reproduction, and metabolism. The adrenal glands (see p. 284 and Plate 9) produce less cortisol and epinephrine in response to stress. The blood levels of stress hormones remain adequate, however, because cortisol is broken down and removed more slowly by the liver (Gregerman and Bierman, 1981). Estrogens, progesterone, and androgens are produced in progressively decreasing amounts by the gonads. In women, the tapering off of estrogen may contribute to problems with **premenstrual syndrome** (see Box 9-1).

Both the **basal metabolic rate** (the body's consumption of oxygen) and secretions

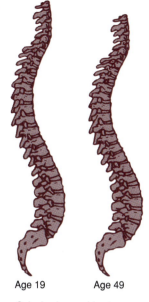

Age 19   Age 49

Spinal column, side view

Figure 9-1
The cartilage between the vertebrae gradually degenerates with age, causing a compression of the spinal column and a consequent loss of height.

BOX 9-1

Moods, Behavior, and Premenstrual Syndrome.

Premenstrual syndrome (PMS) has received a great deal of negative publicity in recent years. Many television shows have portrayed women with PMS as histrionic or hypochondriacal. Some researchers have suggested that women experience symptoms because they look for PMS (Ruble, 1977). Some advertisements for medications for PMS claim to know what causes it and what cures it. Such myths are unfair to the small percentage of women with PMS. It is not a personality disorder, nor a somatoform disorder, nor a fictitious disorder, and its cause (and cure) are still unknown.

Women who experience PMS have both physical and psychological symptoms. Physically, they become edematous (bloated) and have breast pain and engorgement, headaches, joint pain, fatigue, and an increased appetite. Psychologically, they feel anxious, irritable, less able to control their behaviors, and emotionally labile (unstable, rapid mood swings). PMS is more frequent in older women than in teens and young adults (Muller, 1985).

One of the difficulties PMS sufferers face is convincing others that they have a real physiological syndrome. There is currently no test available to diagnose PMS.

So far the only useful drugs are those prescribed for single debilitating symptoms: a diuretic for excess edema, bromocriptine for breast engorgement, an analgesic for joint pain or headache, a sedative for emotional tension. Sometimes these drugs are given together.

The physiological problems of PMS can exacerbate psychological problems, and vice versa. Many PMS sufferers develop low self-esteem and high guilt because of their occasional inabilities to control their physical symptoms, moods, and behavior. Many have thought about suicide. Non-drug therapies have helped some women: diet therapy, massage, acupuncture, exercise, polarity therapy, meditation, and chiropractic. Support groups with other women who share the disorder can also be valuable in alleviating guilt, self-blame, and negative self-imagery.

While prevention may be years away, recognition of the reality of PMS must occur now.

of thyroid hormones decrease with age. The decrease in the basal metabolic rate (BMR) is related to the decrease in the mass of muscle tissue, which is a large oxygen-consuming tissue. The decrease in thyroid hormones (which are involved in the regulation of the BMR) is an adjustment to the progressively slower rate at which it is broken down and removed from the blood (Ingbar and Woeber, 1981). There is a gradual decline of glucose tolerance and an increased prevalence of diabetes mellitus with age (Andres and Tobin, 1977). This is usually due to tissue resistance to insulin, which occurs with age and often weight gain in susceptible individuals.

The respiratory system, heart, and circulatory system have parallel changes occurring with age. The lungs and bronchi become increasingly less elastic, causing a progressive decrease in maximum breathing capacity. Respiratory functioning may decrease as much as 25% between ages thirty and forty-nine (Smith, Bierman, and Robinson, 1978). It takes individuals longer to catch their breaths after exercise in their thirties and forties than when they were younger. Cardiac function may decline by 15 to 20% between ages thirty and forty-nine (Smith, Bierman, and Robinson, 1978). Arteries become less elastic. **Blood pressure** (the force exerted by the heart in pumping blood and the pressure of the blood in the arteries) increases with every decade (see Table 9-1).

High blood pressure, also known as **hypertension,** has many definitions. There is no one set line between normal and abnormal blood pressure. Rather, abnormal is the point at which any individual shows evidence of deleterious effects of his or her own high blood pressure. The values are often used as the upper limits of normal for resting adults. Williams, Jagger, and Braunwald (1980) suggested, however, that a more appropriate definition would take age and sex into account.

Women at any age > 160/95

Men below age 45 > 130/90

Men above age 45 > 140/95

Using these values, from 15 to 20% of the adult population of the United States have abnormal or high blood pressure. The upper value (systolic) refers to the peak pressure and the lower value (diastolic) refers to the bottommost pressure in the arteries during each heart contraction. The diastolic value is considered more important than the systolic value. High diastolic values (over 100) contribute to health risks to many vital organs: heart and arteries, liver, kidneys, eyes, brain. The results of untreated hypertension are worse for men than for women and for blacks than for whites. Young black males are most adversely affected by hypertension (Williams, Jagger, and Braunwald, 1980).

Weight increases are common in middle age due to a decreased energy expenditure without a concomitant decrease in caloric intake. The unneeded calories are stored as fat deposits, commonly in the wall of the abdomen ("spare tire") or the hips and thighs

Table 9-1   Blood Pressure Readings and Their Significance in Adults.

Systolic Pressure (1st, top reading)

Below 140	=	Normal
140-159	=	Borderline systolic hypertension
Above 160	=	Systolic hypertension

Diastolic Pressure (2nd, bottom reading)

Below 85	=	Normal
85-89	=	High normal
90-104	=	Mild hypertension
105-114	=	Moderate hypertension
Above 115	=	Severe hypertension

Figure 9-2
Tanning salons expose skin to light waves that hasten age changes (thinner, drier, more wrinkled skin).

(the "middle-aged spread"). The entire digestive system may slow its process of digesting, absorbing, and eliminating foods. Constipation becomes an increasingly common complaint.

Skin begins to lose its resilience and elasticity. It can no longer stretch as tightly across the muscles and bones. Both women and men usually begin to notice wrinkles. Wrinkle creams may temporarily shrink the skin, but they cannot effect a permanent cessation of these signs of aging. Men usually worry less about wrinkles than women since society considers a lined masculine face to be handsome or to have character. The same lines in women are considered a loss of beauty. Excessive exposure to ultraviolet light accelerates skin changes: dryness, loss of elasticity, susceptibility to cancer. Adults should protect their skin with sun block when outdoors and should not use sunlamps or go to tanning salons (see Figure 9-2).

Hair may grow more slowly, be lost, or occasionally lose its pigmentation (evidenced by gray hair) during the thirties and forties. Genetic predisposition toward baldness or early graying, nutritional factors, disease, drugs, or hormones may cause these changes. Androgens (male sex hormones) often affect hair growth. Masculine balding or a receding hair line after puberty is a well-known and frequent occurrence.

The senses of hearing and vision may begin to show age changes as well. A hearing loss (**presbycusis**) limited first to high pitches may cause persons to stand or sit closer to the source of sound than previously. They may strain to hear or may talk in compensatory louder tones. A visual problem (**presbyopia**) primarily affecting near vision may necessitate reading glasses or bifocals for close work. The lens of the eyes gradually becomes less elastic with age, causing the eyes to lose their ability to bring near-point visual images into clear focus. Presbyopics can usually read far-off signs long before younger passengers in a car but have difficulty reading the numerals on the odometer or the car radio without glasses.

The discussion of the physical changes of the thirties and forties should not cause too much apprehension. Individual differences abound throughout life. Some people may be gray before forty, others not until their sixties or seventies. Some people may grow flaccid and flabby, whereas others remain lithe and limber. Diet, exercise, sleep, control of stress, and avoidance of sunlight, can retard the signs of aging. One may be proud of a physical appearance that shows signs of experience rather than looking young and naive. Most persons in their thirties and forties still consider themselves young, approaching middle age rather than already part of it.

Nutrition

Many adults slow down in their thirties and forties and consequently need fewer calories than they did in their teens and twenties. About 34 million adult Americans, or 25% of the population, are overweight (Van Itallie, 1985). This is defined as being 20% over the desirable weight for one's sex, height, and body build (see Table 9-2). Inadequate calorie intake, or undernutrition, is also becoming more common. In some cases, this is due to poverty. However, in many cases it is due to self-inflicted dieting.

Average adults without special dietary restrictions will be healthier if they choose plenty of dark green leafy vegetables, fresh fruits and vegetables, and whole grain breads, rice, pasta, and cereal products to make up a large proportion of their total daily caloric intake. The recommended daily protein intake for adults is 35 to 40 grams per day (Edlin and Golanty, 1992). Symptoms of "meat intoxication" (headache, lethargy, nausea) may appear if one's protein intake is excessive. A high dietary intake of protein foods containing saturated fats (organ meats, well-marbled steaks or roasts, pork, egg yolks, cream, shellfish) contributes significantly to the risk of

Table 9-2   Desirable Weight According to Height.

Men

Height Feet	Inches	Small Frame	Medium Frame	Large Frame
5	2	128–134	131–141	138–150
5	3	130–136	133–143	140–153
5	4	132–138	135–145	142–156
5	5	134–140	137–148	144–160
5	6	136–142	139–151	146–164
5	7	138–145	142–154	149–168
5	8	140–148	145–157	152–172
5	9	142–151	148–160	155–176
5	10	144–154	151–163	158–180
5	11	146–157	154–166	161–184
6	0	149–160	157–170	164–188
6	1	152–164	160–174	168–192
6	2	155–168	164–178	172–197
6	3	158–172	167–182	176–202
6	4	162–176	171–187	181–207

Women

Height Feet	Inches	Small Frame	Medium Frame	Large Frame
4	10	102–111	109–121	118–131
4	11	103–113	111–123	120–134
5	0	104–115	113–126	122–137
5	1	106–118	115–129	125–140
5	2	108–121	118–132	128–143
5	3	111–124	121–135	131–147
5	4	114–127	124–138	134–151
5	5	117–130	127–141	137–155
5	6	120–133	130–144	140–159
5	7	123–136	133–147	143–163
5	8	126–139	136–150	146–167
5	9	129–142	139–153	149–170
5	10	132–145	142–156	152–173
5	11	135–148	145–159	155–176
6	0	138–151	148–162	158–179

SOURCE: Courtesy Metropolitan Life Insurance Co., 1983.

*Weight in pounds according to frame (in indoor clothing weighing 5 lb for men and 3 lb for women; shoes with 1 in. heels).

Table 9-3 Blood Cholesterol Readings and Their Significance in Adults.

Below 200	= Normal
200–239	= Borderline; have lipoprotein analysis; recheck annually.
Above 240	= High; have lipoprotein analysis; alter diet; recheck frequently.

heart disease. As little as 5 grams per day of fat is sufficient (Walser et al., 1984); most of it should come from unsaturated fats such as soy, sunflower, corn, or safflower oil.

High blood levels of saturated fats and cholesterol contribute to atherosclerosis, coronary heart disease, and cancer. Cholesterol is not a fat but a fat-like substance that can accumulate in tissues and on the walls of arteries. Blood cholesterol levels in adults should be below 200 mg (see Table 9-3). Persons with high blood cholesterol readings usually have a further analysis of their lipoproteins. Low-density lipoproteins (LDLs) are bad fats. They become deposited in body tissues and create many types of health risks, especially heart and artery diseases. High-density lipoproteins (HDLs) are good fats, found in plants and plant oils (e.g., corn, cotton, safflower). The higher the level of HDL, the lower the risk of disease.

About 1 person in 500 has inherited familial hypercholesterolemia (Goldstein and Brown, 1985). Because it is an autosomal dominant disease (see Chapter 3), inheritance of only one gene for the condition (heterozygosity) will produce hypercholesterolemia. It is prevalent in all ethnic groups equally. The disease involves defects in cell receptors for low density lipoproteins (LDL). As a result of reduced cellular intake of LDL, the serum levels of LDL go up (hypercholesterolemia). All persons with hypercholesterolemia have stringent limitations of dietary cholesterol and saturated fat (Goldstein and Brown, 1985).

A high dietary intake of fiber may reduce the risk of atherosclerosis and some forms of cancer. Adults are now being encouraged to consume at least 25 grams of fiber per day, found especially in green leafy vegetables, fruits, berries, bran, whole grain bread and high fiber cereal products.

There is evidence suggesting that the average adult's salt intake (about 4 grams per day) is more than double the safe and adequate intake and may aggravate hypertension. Clearly, persons who have hypertension benefit from a reduction in salt (sodium) intake. Salting food is an acquired habit that can be broken. Many adults have learned to enjoy low-sodium foods in an effort to protect their hearts and their health (Marshall, 1986).

The need for calcium, especially in women, is often not met by daily dietary intake of milk and milk products. Consequently, many adults are advised to supplement their diets with calcium carbonate. Other vitamin supplements are usually not necessary if one is eating a balanced diet. Excessive intake of vitamins A, D, and E can cause physiological problems, and megadoses of vitamin C have been associated with the formation of kidney stones.

While sugar does not cause diabetes, it does contribute to both dental caries and obesity. Many adults consume the bulk of their daily caloric intake from highly sweetened foods (candy, desserts, snack foods, crackers, sodas, alcoholic drinks). Obesity between the ages of twenty and fifty is considerably more dangerous than a similar degree of obesity in later life (Van Itallie, 1985). It puts one in a high-risk group for many illnesses, particularly hypertension, hypercholesterolemia, coronary heart disease, and diabetes (see Figure 9-3). Body weights over 240 pounds in women and over 260 pounds in men constitute extreme health hazards (Kral, 1985). Obesity is considered the single most common preventable factor associated with chronic illness and death in adults under age fifty. Many professionals feel that public health information campaigns should

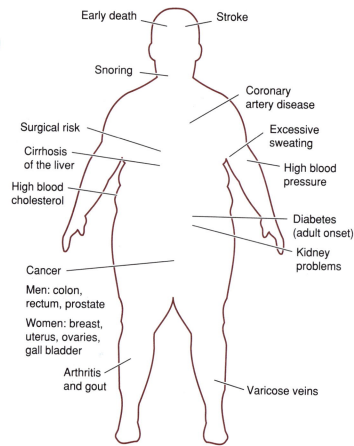

Figure 9-3
Overweight people have a greater likelihood of developing certain health problems than people of normal weight.

be implemented to counteract this increasingly prevalent risk to life. Some have even suggested that legislation be enacted to control the marketing of "junk foods" (those with high calorie and low nutritive values).

Health Maintenance

The decades of the thirties and forties may be a period of excellent health or a time of increased disability due to illness. The state of one's health is strongly related to one's genetic predisposition to diseases, to lifestyle, to the body's immune responses, and to the availability and utilization of medical, surgical, and pharmacological therapeutic aids in the event of disease. As is true of the health of young adults, physical well-being is threatened more by noninfectious agents (alcohol, drugs, smoking, pollution, accidents, obesity, stress, poor diet, and lack of exercise) than by pathogens or degenerative processes.

Accidents as a cause of death drop from about 44% among fifteen- to twenty-four-year-olds to about 16% among twenty-five- to forty-four-year-olds. Alcohol abuse, causing death through liver cirrhosis and gastrointestinal bleeding, climbs steadily. So, too, do heart diseases and mental disorders. Health maintenance in the thirties and forties often requires more than just avoiding or treating infectious diseases. Health spas, diet groups, and exercise programs are some of the ways people invest time and energy toward improving or maintaining their health.

The maximum benefits of exercise are derived from daily exercising, since physical stamina and fitness deteriorate with a lack of training. Many people schedule regular aerobic exercises (jogging, dancing, swimming, cycling) or isometrics (for example, weightlifting) into their daily lives.

Stress. While high-saturated-fat/low-fiber diets are correlated with atherosclerosis and coronary heart disease, diet is not the only risk factor for these medical problems. There is now abundant evidence that when a person is under stress, the body produces more of the adrenal hormones cortisol and epinephrine. They in turn signal the liver to produce more cholesterol. They also signal fat cells to release stored fat and cholesterol into the bloodstream. Often a high blood cholesterol level is associated with daily stress more than with actual daily dietary intake of cholesterol.

People differ considerably in their abilities to handle stress (see Chapter 8). Friedman and Rosenman (1974) described two basic stable personality types: Type A and Type B. Type As have a tendency to compete and challenge others; they have a sense of the urgency of time and strive to accomplish too much or do two things simultaneously; they are aggressive and impatient, disliking repetitious chores, waiting in line, or any inefficiency. Type B personalities are relaxed and easygoing. Rosenman (1978) stated that Type Bs may also be goal directed, but not aggressively so. They tolerate delays without undue tension, and they have learned how to react more calmly to the stresses of daily living (see Figure 9-4). Friedman and Rosenman correlated the onset of stress-related diseases, especially coronary heart disease, with Type A personality.

Type A behavior is now usually called the **coronary-prone behavior** pattern. In the approximate one-half of heart disease patients for whom no causes related to dietary, hereditary, obesity, or smoking factors can be traced, coronary-prone behavior pattern is present. People with this behavior pattern have such a sense of urgency for accomplishing tasks that they ignore warnings of coronary heart disease. They dislike exercises, relaxation techniques, or other procedures that could help them reduce tensions (Mathews and Brunson, 1979). Often they make no real efforts to cope with or control their stresses until after they experience one or more nonfatal heart attacks.

Figure 9-4
Type B personalities are relaxed and able to enjoy the simple pleasures of daily living. They are goal directed, but not aggressively so.

Coronary Heart Disease.   The most prevalent chronic disease condition in men in their thirties and forties is **coronary heart disease** (CHD). It also affects women, though to a lesser extent. It is the single greatest killer of middle-aged adults (Friedman, 1978). Those factors related to CHD that a person can control are diet, cigarette smoking, stress, and exercise. Factors that a person can control with the help of modern medicine are hypertension, hypercholesterolemia, hyperlipidemia (too many lipid fats and oils in the blood), diabetes, and irregular heart rhythms. Factors that a person cannot control are heredity, race, sex, and age. Men and blacks are more susceptible, and the prevalence increases with age, especially in adults with a family history of CHD.

A *myocardial infarction* (MI, heart attack) results from a sudden arrest of blood flow to the muscle of the heart because of a sudden obstruction of the coronary artery supplying it. When it occurs, myocardial (heart muscle) cells become damaged, leading to their death (necrosis). The most common complaint of an MI is uncomfortable pressure, fullness, squeezing, or chest pain lasting two minutes or more. There is some radiation of pain into the upper arms, jaw, and neck. There may also be shortness of breath, sweating, weakness, and fainting (see Figure 9-5). Victims of MIs should be kept warm, quiet, and horizontal and should be taken to a medical facility as quickly as possible.

The inability of the heart to pump effectively can lead to a backup of blood into various organs, a condition known as *congestive heart failure*. The features of congestive heart failure are presence of edema (most commonly in the legs and ankles), shortness of breath, fatigue with exertion, an enlarged heart, a rapid and sometimes irregular pulse, and signs of congestion in various organs due to a backup of blood.

Angina pectoris is a condition characterized by a feeling of heaviness or pressure in the chest that falls short of an MI. Angina pectoris is almost always associated with severe atherosclerosis of the coronary arteries and results from transient relative inadequacy of blood to a portion of the heart. The pain and pressure of the recurrent attacks can be controlled by medication that angina sufferers usually carry with them and use as needed.

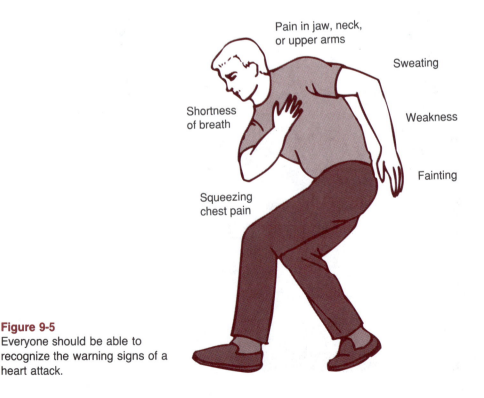

Pain in jaw, neck, or upper arms

Sweating

Shortness of breath

Weakness

Fainting

Squeezing chest pain

Figure 9-5
Everyone should be able to recognize the warning signs of a heart attack.

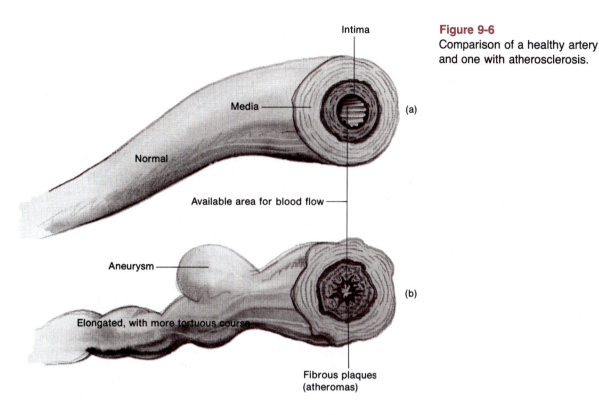

Figure 9-6
Comparison of a healthy artery and one with atherosclerosis.

Irregular heartbeats such as a slow beat or an irregular rhythm should be controlled by the use of drugs or an artificial pacemaker. A pacemaker is a small unit implanted on the chest wall with tiny wires to the heart that will produce the electrical impulses needed to make the heart pump normally.

The most common fatal factor underlying CHD is *atherosclerosis.* It is the most common form of **arteriosclerosis** ("hardening of the arteries"), a thickening and hardening of the walls of the arteries. Atherosclerosis involves mainly the intima (the innermost lining) of the arteries. (Sclerosis refers to any hardening of fibrous tissue.) Arteriosclerosis involves the media (muscle portion) of the arteries as well.

When serum LDL levels are high in any person, the excess cholesterol and other saturated fats are deposited on arterial walls in the form of patchy areas of fatty streaks and fibrous plaques (called atheromas). The coronary arteries and arteries of the brain may begin to contain fatty streaks and fibrous plaques during puberty. Subsequently, there is a progressive rigidity (loss of elasticity) of vessels with plaques. Other changes of arteries include dilation (widening), elongation, tortuosity (winding course instead of a straight course), calcification of the media, and aneurysm formation (ballooning out of vessels) (see Figure 9-6). Although a few fibrous plaques may be asymptomatic and produce no disease, the presence of too many of them may impede blood flow through the arteries and eventually cause coronary heart disease.

Although the exact mechanism of formation of atherosclerosis is unknown, studies suggest that diets high in saturated fats and cholesterol, obesity, physical inactivity, diabetes mellitus, hypertension, cigarette smoking, stress, and Type A behaviors are associated with a premature or accelerated course of the disease. One or more of these factors is generally present when persons in their thirties or forties are diagnosed as having atherosclerosis.

Mental Disorders.   Psychopathology is one of our nation's most important health problems, affecting 20% of the population and costing several billion dollars each year.

Persons in their late thirties and early forties seek the most psychiatric care and also are the age group most frequently admitted to mental hospitals.

There is no single criterion for diagnosing **mental disorders**. Persons showing great personal distress, who disturb others, who become incapable of performing their usual jobs, or who have marked personality changes may be manifesting psychopathology.

Disorders that once were labeled neuroses are now called anxiety disorders, suggesting the role of stress in their onset. There are many varieties of anxiety disorders, including phobias, panic, obsessive-compulsive disorders, posttraumatic shock syndrome, and generalized anxiety. Other conditions once called neuroses are now called somatoform disorders (hypochondriasis, conversion reactions), dissociative disorders (amnesia, multiple personality), psychosexual disorders (transsexuality, paraphilias), personality disorders (antisocial personality, narcissism), or affective disorders (depression). In general, these conditions are less severe than psychoses (in which a person loses touch with reality) and are more easily treated.

The psychotic conditions are characterized by radical and damaging disruptions of consciousness, perception, thinking, and social behavior. The four major psychoses are schizophrenia, bipolar (manic-depressive) disorder, psychotic depression, and organic psychoses (those involving brain trauma or brain degeneration).

Schizophrenia may be of varying severity and have varying symptomatology. Its onset is frequently in early to middle adulthood. Its cause is unknown. Common features include misinterpretation or idiosyncratic distortions of reality, delusions, hallucinations, flat or inappropriate emotions, social withdrawal, ambivalence, and bizarre behavior and appearance. Treatment of schizophrenia may include drug therapy, psychotherapy, and institutionalization. There are many antipsychotic drugs available today that effectively interrupt acute psychotic behaviors.

Bipolar disorder (manic-depressive psychosis) brings periods of excitement (mania) and depression that may each extend for hours or days and have long or short periods of remission in between. In the manic, agitated state a person may show increased energy and accomplish great works. However, mania may also bring in its wake undesirable behaviors such as irrepressible, uninhibited, mischievous speech and actions that hurt others. In the depressed state the individual may be suicidal. Lithium is an alkaline metal element that has been called the "insulin of psychiatry" because it is so

Table 9-4 Prevention of Mental Disorders.

Primary Level of Prevention (Alter conditions that create abnormal behaviors)	Secondary Level of Prevention (Early detection and treatment of abnormal behaviors)	Tertiary Level of Prevention (Reduce long-term consequences of mental disorders)
Prenatal care	Crisis intervention	Sheltered workshops
Quality day care	Support groups	Rehabilitation programs
Affordable medical care	Drug programs	Supervised chemotherapy
Equal justice	Telephone hotlines	Psychotherapy
Clean environment	Psychotherapy	
Nutritious meals	Family therapy	
Exercise/physical fitness	Group therapy	
Responsive parenting	Social services help	
Quality education	Supervised chemotherapy	
Tolerance of differences		
Assertiveness training		
Employment opportunities		
Stress management		
Safety precautions		
Genetic counseling		
Good Samaritanism		

effective in treating and preventing the mood swings of mania and depression. It has few side effects, but the dosages must be carefully monitored to prevent lithium poisoning.

Depression is the "common cold" of psychiatric disorders. Women are afflicted six times more often than men (O'Hara, 1984). Each year several million adults suffer one or more depressive episodes. The usual features of depression are sadness, lack of concentration, indecision, and a waning interest in one's usual pursuits. Psychotherapy, behavioral therapy, and family counseling are used to treat depression. Mood-elevating drugs may be used in conjunction with these forms of therapy to enable the patient to participate.

Prevention of mental illness can be viewed at three levels, as shown in Table 9-4. We can assist each other to achieve better mental health with more supportive and cooperative interpersonal behaviors. Physical health (diet, exercise, stress management, sleep) also improves mental health.

Cognitive Development

Intellectually, the thirties and forties are very good years. Brain cell maturation and brain weight peaked in the late twenties, and a gradual but progressive shrinking is in progress. The weight of the brain decreases due to a loss in the number and size of brain cells and the loss of myelin sheathing. Impulses travel slightly more slowly across neurons and axons, causing a decrease in reaction time. However, mental acumen is still high (see Figure 9-7).

Fluid and Crystallized Abilities

Cattell (1963, 1971) proposed a model of the intellect that makes a distinction between two dimensions of mental abilities: fluid and crystallized intelligence. **Fluid intelligence** refers to capabilities such as associative memory, abstracting, inductive reasoning, dealing with figural relationships and problem solving. These capabilities are not as dependent on learning as they are on neurophysiological functioning and intactness of the central nervous system. **Crystallized intelligence** refers to skills such as verbal comprehension and the handling of word relationships, which are more dependent on learning and experience. Horn and Donaldson (1980) and Horn (1982) presented data suggesting that whereas fluid intelligence may diminish slightly following adolescence, crystallized intelligence may increase with advancing years. The average intelligence may look about the same over the middle years because increases in crystallized abilities balance decreases in fluid abilities (see Figure 9-8).

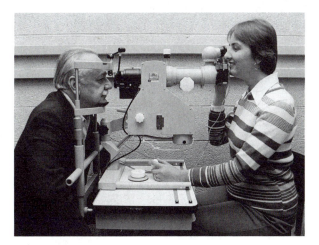

Figure 9-7
Many persons take on tasks requiring greater use of their intellectual functions in their thirties and forties.

Figure 9-8
Different types of measured
intelligences change over time.

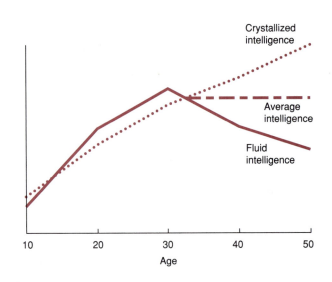

Other Cognitive Stages

It is difficult to detect any actual decline in intellectual performance in healthy adults before age sixty (Schaie and Hertzog, 1983). In fact, the experiences of life are often viewed as tools for improving intellectual performance over time. When work experiences require complex problem solving, adults show more intellectual flexibility in the middle decades (Kohn and Schooler, 1978).

Schaie (1978) proposed that the different experiences of adult life provide different stages of cognition based on situation-specific problems that need to be solved. Childhood is characterized by achieving—applying knowledge to goals. Early and middle adulthood may be characterized by a responsible stage—meeting obligations with cognitive skills—and may also be characterized by an executive style cognition—managing affairs. Finally, later adulthood is characterized as reintegrative—selecting which cognitive skills to apply to chosen tasks to achieve a sense of integrity. Schaie (1978) wrote that traditional tests of intelligence fail to measure the competence type of skills used by adults.

Riegel (1973, 1976) suggested that Piaget's theory stopped short when it proposed formal operations as a final stage of adult cognition. Riegel proposed that **dialectic operations** are a final period of cognitive development. Dialectics involve conflict resolution. In any situation-specific problem, one will encounter a thesis (an affirmation to be proved) and an antithesis (a contrasting affirmation or position). This opposition of ideas requires that the contradictions be resolved toward some synthesis of ideas. Adults are required to use dialectic operations in many aspects of their daily lives. More dialectically skilled adults may be able to achieve more syntheses. They may also achieve more synchronization of their development in relation to other significant people in their lives (spouse, fellow employees, children). Complete synchrony is rare because people and social conditions constantly change. However, a person who uses dialectic operations is able to tolerate more opposition of ideas and resolve more conflicts with successful syntheses.

Horner (1972) suggested that a fear of success may contribute to some decline in women's tested intellectual performance in adulthood. As cited in Chapter 8, Horner found that college women taking achievement tests could do well unless asked to compete with men, at which point they ceased to do their best. Some women's need to achieve drops far below that of men in adulthood. These women prefer the tasks of maintaining good relationships with their husbands, children, and others, and watching over the psychosocial aspects of living. Their affiliative needs may be more socially approved and rewarded. Riegel (1976) suggested that the career development of marriage partners are seldom in synchrony. The wife's progression is traditionally subordinate to her husband's advancements. A woman with a strong career orientation must use dialectic operations to resolve the conflicts of asymmetrical progression.

Women who are more career oriented seldom have a decreased achievement drive, nor do they fear success (Alper, 1974). Older women (in their forties and fifties) with high achievement needs have been shown to express an even greater independence and self-reliance than achievement-motivated women in their twenties (Erdwins, Tyer, and Mellinger, 1982). Erdwins and her colleagues found that achievement needs of traditional homemakers also increase with time, along with their affiliation needs, although they want to achieve in areas characterized by conformity and cooperation rather than those characterized by self-reliance and independence.

Many women and some men return to school in their thirties and forties. Women find they have more time to study once their children enter the elementary grades. They may feel a need for more intellectual stimulation. Perhaps they did not finish high school or attend college earlier because of marriage.

Gender-role changes are occurring. In the 1950s and 1960s, many women felt the most acceptable and socially approved role for them was homemaker. An education was superfluous. Today many women feel that the most acceptable and socially approved role for them is to have a career. An education is a necessity. Women and men return to school to enable themselves to obtain jobs. People in their thirties and forties often achieve higher grade point averages than younger students (Erdwins, Tyer, and Mellinger, 1982).

Creativity

Creativity peaks in the thirties (see Figure 9-9). Lehman (1953), in a classic study of the lives of thousands of creative men and women, reported that the peak years for most creative ventures have been young. The mean peak years for symphony writing have been thirty to thirty-four. Great contributions to chemistry have been made most frequently between ages twenty-six and thirty. Mathematical revelations

Figure 9-9
During their thirties and forties many adults have a high degree of creativity.

have come between the ages thirty and thirty-four, and medical discoveries have been made by men and women most often between the ages of thirty-five and thirty-nine.

Creative people usually continue to produce important works throughout their adult lives, even though they accomplish their more unique and original contributions early. In areas where creative endeavors require a larger amount of accumulated and systematized knowledge (such as medicine), the outstanding productions occur at slightly older ages.

Creativity involves **divergent thinking** (Guilford, 1967). A divergent thinker will be able to see a problem (or any phenomenon) in several new and different ways by moving away from a starting point in several directions. Formal education usually teaches the opposite mode of thinking, convergence. Convergence brings opposing ideas together towards a common finishing point, or a "correct" solution. Creative products are usually completed using both divergent and convergent thinking.

Creative individuals tend to have more visual imagery and curiosity, be able to transfer information from one topic to another, and have a greater ability to see unusual associations between topics (Barron and Harrington, 1981). They may also be more goal-directed, more painstaking in their work, and more daring (Gardner, 1981). Jaquish and Ripple (1981) also found that creative people are high in self-esteem.

A myth exists that highly creative persons are bipolar disordered (see page 334). While some creative geniuses (e.g., Handel) have produced their masterpieces while in a manic phase, most creative people are free of symptoms of clinical mental disorders (Gough, 1979).

Creativity and intelligence, as mentioned in Chapter 6, are not synonymous. Some highly creative individuals may have an average intellect, and some highly intelligent individuals may have an average, or below average, creative quotient.

Psychosocial Development

Havighurst (1972) suggested that the developmental tasks of middle adulthood are to

1. accept and adjust to physiological changes,
2. attain and maintain a satisfactory occupational performance,
3. assist children to become responsible and happy adults,
4. relate to one's spouse as a person,
5. adjust to aging parents,
6. achieve adult social and civic responsibility, and
7. develop adult leisure-time activities

Levinson and his colleagues (1978) characterized the thirties as a time for settling down and establishing a stable niche and the forties as a time for reassessing one's life structure and then restabilizing into middle adulthood. He called the period of reassessment the *midlife transition*. We will discuss its implications later in this chapter.

It must be noted that although people may appear to be much the same in a given age range (or sex, or ethnic, or social group), they are in many ways quite different. Each individual has her or his own preoccupations, goals, tasks, hopes, dreams, problems, and ways of living.

Erikson's Generativity versus Stagnation

Erik Erikson (1963) saw the nuclear conflict of the adult years as that of **generativity versus stagnation** (see Table 9-5). In Erikson's view, generativity involves more than just producing offspring. Mature adults who have achieved a sense of identity and intimacy begin to take a global view of their own lives. They ask "What is life all about?" Generativity involves answers that reflect some benefit to others. The Hindus call it the maintenance of the world (Erikson, 1987): There are things to take care of.

Table 9-5 Erikson's Seventh Nuclear Conflict: Generativity Versus Stagnation.

Sense	Eriksonian Descriptions	Fostering Behaviors
Generativity	Concern for establishing and guiding the next generation	Encouragement and devotion from progeny
	Concern for others including "belief in the species"	Others demonstrate their dependence on and need for the adult's guidance
	Concern for productivity and creativity as well as for progeny	Others reflect back the value of one's productions
versus Stagnation	Self-concern, self-indulgence	Early childhood impressions leading to excessive self-love
	Early physical or psychological invalidism, personal impoverishment	Feedback from others that own resources for generativity are doubtful
	Regression to obsessive need for pseudointimacy as opposed to real intimacy	

Adults can make a contribution to future generations through nurturing, teaching, and serving children or other adults. Producing offspring and guiding them through their nuclear conflicts of developing trust, autonomy, initiative, industry, and identity is an important aspect of generativity. Erikson wrote that one need not have one's own children, however. One can achieve generativity nurturing nieces, nephews, neighbor children, or school children. One can also accomplish a genuine sense of generativity through involvement with the welfare of future generations. Creative skills can be applied to improving the quality of life. Contributions can be made to civic and community causes. One can become a mentor to younger workers on the job. One can also nurture one's own aging parents. Any activity that has a positive influence on another can be viewed as a way to give back to the world as much as or more than one has taken from it.

Stagnation, in Erikson's view, involves a lack of productivity. Instead of leaving one's mark on the world in some contribution (children, work), one behaves parasitically. One takes without repaying. Stagnation is often associated with those persons of low self-esteem who believe any contribution they might make would be worthless anyway. Such persons almost vegetate, simply grinding through the minimal necessities of daily living. However, stagnation may also be applied to active, pompous, selfish individuals who work only to accumulate wealth and possessions for their own self-glorification. Such people exploit others and manage to shut out any thoughts of how they might provide for or give to others in return.

Maslow's Needs Hierarchy

The theories of development that stress the central role of one's self-concept have been given a great deal of attention in recent years. The theories of Abraham Maslow and Carl Rogers, discussed in Chapter 2, stress how a person's perceptions of himself or herself influence his or her choice of activities. Such terms as *perceptual* and *phenomenological* are also used to describe these theories. Each person's perception of his or her life space (past–present–future) and the phenomenological field of experiences that he or she denies, distorts, or incorporates into the self-concept are important factors that shape behavior. This self-concept is the agent that can have either a positive influence on a person in pursuit of a self-actualized life or a negative effect, causing hesitancies and fears.

Maslow defined his concepts as *epi-Freudian* and *epibehaviorist* (*epi* meaning "upon"). He stressed positive growth, normality, and excellence rather than abnormality, depression, and antisocial behaviors. Maslow (1970) postulated a **hierarchy of needs** common to all humans. The highest needs, those for self-actualization, self-understanding, and the understanding of others, can emerge only when lower needs are satisfied. The hierarchy of needs, from lowest to highest, includes the following:

1. *Physical needs*—food, drink, sleep, activity; relief from pain and discomfort.
2. *Safety needs*—freedom from threats to supplies or life; secure, orderly, predictable environment.
3. *Belonging and love needs*—acceptance, affectionate relations with others.
4. *Esteem needs*—competence, confidence, task mastery, recognition, prestige; respect and approval from others.
5. *Self-actualization*—realized potential; feeling that one is what one is capable of being.

According to Maslow, gratification of a need makes a person feel good, but deprivation breeds illness (mental or physical). A deprived person will prefer gratification of the missing need over everything else under conditions of free choice.

The emergence of **self-actualization** rests on prior satisfaction of the other four needs. It is a goal toward which healthy adults continually strive. The characteristics Maslow (1968) attributed to self-actualizing persons include adequate perceptions of reality, comfortable relations with reality, a high degree of acceptance of themselves and others, a feeling of belonging to all humankind, close relationships with a few friends or loved ones, a need for privacy, an unhostile sense of humor, resistance to socialization pressures, autonomy, problem-centeredness, creativeness, spontaneity, a freshness of appreciation, a strong ethical sense, and **peak experiences**. These peaks may occur when one has finished a long-term project or after one has done something special for someone else. While some adults have "peaks" in the Maslowian sense, many more are prevented from approaching self-actualization because of their many unfulfilled needs for belonging and love or for self-esteem in both work and interpersonal relationships.

Career Concerns

Most men and over half of women pursue careers outside their homes in their thirties and forties (see Figure 9-10). Their jobs become part of their identity. Vaillant,

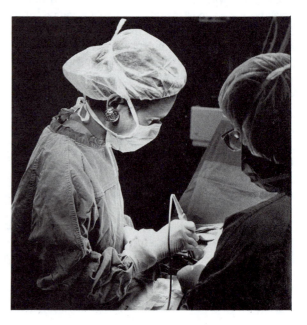

Figure 9-10
Women in their thirties and forties are increasingly pursuing full-time careers. They work outside the home for a variety of personal, social, and economic reasons.

in an interview with one of his subjects, was told: "At twenty to thirty, I think I learned how to get along with my wife. From thirty to forty, I learned how to be a success at my job" (Vaillant and McArthur, 1972). Employees spend half of their waking hours at work and more time preparing for and getting to and from their places of employment. Careers certainly play a central role in social development of adults. Havighurst (1972) felt that attaining and maintaining a satisfactory occupational performance is one of the most important developmental tasks of these years. The work should not only be financially satisfying but also should be interesting to the worker.

People in many fields may devote considerable time in their thirties and forties to pursuing career advancement through night classes, journal reading, studying, experimenting, practicing, working overtime, or attending meetings. Professionals and non-professionals alike may concentrate on gamesmanship skills in hope of speeding up promotions: socializing, being seen at the right places, learning when to compete and when to cooperate, ascertaining when to comply with directives and when to ignore them, studying how to "win friends and influence people," and practicing authority roles. By and large the twenties are considered years for work preparation, job exploration, and settling in. The thirties and forties are considered years for work advancement.

As reported in Chapter 8, young adults preparing to enter the work force want interesting work that uses their skills and abilities and has good advancement possibilities. They are apt to change jobs to accomplish their objectives. By middlescence, employees become more hesitant to leave their companies (Byrne, 1975). They look towards accomplishing their goals within the job they have, perhaps by shifting roles slightly.

Work means different things to different people. Most people can pick and choose a few goals for their jobs. The hierarchy of order for their goals is apt to differ, however, even if people have the same goals. Here are some of many goals of employment:

Use of skills and abilities	Interesting work
Income	Pension benefits
Security	Insurance benefits
Stability	Convenient hours
Social affiliations	Competitive work
Prestige and status	Accomplishment at work
Societal recognition	Responsibility at work
Enjoyable work	Self-direction at work
Serving others	Independence
Self-fulfillment	Creative outlet
Challenging work	Predictable future
Worthwhile to society	Chances for advancement

Terkel (1974), in the book *Working: People Talk about What They Do All Day and How They Feel About What They Do,* pointed out that there are vast differences among humans in the ways they view their jobs. Not all people have the same attitude toward their jobs. Business is almost the only pleasure for some, while pleasure is almost the only business for others. Job satisfaction is a feeling of contentment based on the number of personal and interpersonal goals that are being met by one's position and work. A quick cost accounting of job satisfaction can be done by jotting down goals and rating how well they are being met.

Satisfaction at work is influenced by expectations from others as well as by personal needs. One usually has a certain timetable in one's mind for work progression (for example, "I will probably be advanced to _____ level by the time I am _____ "). One's spouse, parents, or friends may have radically different expectations. Associates may press for salary increments or work promotions when the individual would be quite content to stay put. It may be difficult for a person to feel job satisfaction without some visible signs of upward mobility. Campbell (1981) reported that the role expectations of significant others, and one's salary vis-à-vis one's peers and co-workers, are usually more significant factors in satisfaction than the nature of the role itself. Clausen (1981) suggested that blue-collar workers may be less affected by a lack of upward mobility because they have less personal investment of their identities in their jobs.

Promotions and advancements are usually greatest relatively early in a career. An employee usually settles in at an apprentice level in his or her first years of work, then gradually takes on more responsibilities. By the thirties and forties, some workers will take on a role of **mentor**; they will teach, advise, or sponsor a younger employee. When the younger employee no longer needs (or wants) the mentor, the middle-level employee may sponsor a new worker or may move further up the technical ladder and exert an influence on the functioning of the entire company (Graves, Dalton, and Thompson, 1980).

It is possible for career upward mobility to have a negative as well as (or instead of) a positive effect on social and emotional well-being. One may lose one's friends when promotions put a gap between social status standings. One may also lose one's sense of worth and achievement with a promotion. Peter and Hull (1969) in *The Peter Principle* stated the following premise:

> In a hierarchy, every employee tends to rise to his or her level of incompetence.
>
> In time, every post tends to be occupied by an employee who is incompetent to carry out his or her duties.

Peter and Hull suggested that people who do a job well should stay at the job, not be promoted upward to something they cannot handle. Although many management experts admit the occasional operation of the "Peter principle," they deny its pervasive influence and destructive effect.

Government and big businesses may strip individuals of a sense of personal accomplishment and self-worth. Persons may be at risk of feeling like numbers or simply insignificant cogs in a computerized machine. Good management strives to give employees self-esteem, pleasure, and a sense of achievement at work while also generating a feeling of loyalty to the company. Such things as shares of stock, rewards for completion of units of work, and individual praise in newsletters help bolster employee morale. Negotiation with and consensus of workers when developing directives rather than having them dictated by the power structure also enhance job satisfaction and work morale.

Many women who seek outside jobs can find openings only in tedious, low-paying service or clerical work. As reported in Chapter 8, the gap between men's and women's earnings remains wide. The average male high school dropout often earns more than a female college graduate. Even though the government has been more progressive than the private sector in eliminating pay inequalities, equity has not been achieved. In the federal merit system, women make up 78% of the employees in government service (GS) levels 1–4 and 62% of the workers in GS levels 5–8. In contrast, men make up 96% of the employees in GS levels 14–15 and 97% of the workers in GS levels 16–18 (Friss, 1982). If a woman's salary and advancement are in step with her immediate co-workers of the same ability and seniority, her career satisfaction is usually high. Many companies have a tight-lipped policy about discussion of salaries to prevent dissatisfaction based on knowledge of unequal pay for comparable work. Despite continuing sexual discrimination in the workplace, employed females are generally happier and healthier than their unemployed peers (Coleman and Antonucci, 1983).

Dual-career marriages are rarely equitable, and then only for fleeting periods of time. Regardless of salaries and career work loads, the housework and child care are typically considered the wife's responsibility. Both high-powered career wives and nonprofessional working wives do about 70% of the home tasks (Berardo, Shenan, and Leslie, 1987). Many working wives feel guilty because their jobs, child care, housework, community activities, et cetera, give them very little time for an intimate relationship with their husbands. As reported in Chapter Eight (p. 317), the "Superwoman Syndrome" is exhausting and frustrating. Husbands often feel that they are entitled to a superwoman (Gilbert and Rachlin, 1987), but most couples must make some sacrifices or compromises. Each dual-career couple has to decide whether to hire help, redistribute chores, reduce work loads, separate from the marriage, or create some other way to maintain morale. Many couples do succeed in dual-career marriages (see Figure 9-11). The happiness of dual-career marriages is strongly related to the husband's attitude about his wife's job. If he accepts her employed status, compromises with some adaptations to the demands of her job, helps at home, and gives her emotional support, the arrangement can add to rather than detract from marital happiness (Birnbaum, 1975).

Middle-aged couples tend to communicate more to others about their dual-career grievances than to each other. Zietlow and Sillars (1988) found that they very infrequently confront each other. Instead, they deny or refuse to acknowledge their areas of disagreement. Compared to younger and retired couples, middle-aged couples need to communicate more to resolve their conflicts.

While middle-aged adults are more hesitant to switch jobs than are younger adults, career shifts are common. Persons who change jobs are often high-achievers who feel pressure to progress faster than their current job allows. Sarason (1977) used the status selective *Who's Who* to trace career shifts in high-achievers. Each person had changed careers an average of four times. Some career shifts are mandated by spouse's job transfer, divorce, illness, or by being laid off.

Forced unemployment is one of the greatest threats to a person's sense of self-esteem during the thirties and forties. The nuclear conflict of these decades is that of achieving a sense of generativity. When one's job is terminated, one feels invalidated and impoverished, both psychologically and economically. Coping with this catastrophe requires more than financial assistance. It also requires psychological supports (Voydanoff, 1983). Finding a new job may require months of sending résumés, answering advertisements, and interviewing. It becomes harder and harder to pursue the job search after each rejection. Family and friends should encourage the unemployed person and not criticize his or her periods of seeming self-indulgence. Depression is common. It is hard to continue writing letters and making phone calls when one feels pessimistic and fatigued. Often an outside counselor or support group is necessary to help the unemployed adult cope with a job loss and its concomitant losses of self-worth and self-esteem.

Figure 9-11
Dual-career marriages present challenges to assure that jobs, marriage, and children all get sufficient attention.

Family Concerns

The establishment of a family of procreation (marriage and children) is the conventional behavior that society assumes adults in their thirties and forties will follow. The Puritans punished young people who failed to marry and procreate. Although society is no longer so condemning, it does exert pressures on people to fit the conventional molds. Society rewards adults who marry and procreate with celebrations, gifts, income tax breaks, and ease in obtaining bank loans and credit. People worry about the unmarrieds and persistently try to find eligible mates for them. They pressure married but childless adults to hurry up and have children before they pass their years of fertility or energy for child rearing.

Parent–Child Relationships.   Many of the concerns adults have about children were presented in Chapters 4 through 7 on child and adolescent development. Children can bring a great deal of warmth, love, and laughter into a home (see Figure 9-12). They make adults feel needed. They provide adults with verbal and physical affection. They can be very amusing. Children can help fulfill adults' belonging, love, and self-esteem needs as expressed by Maslow (1970). Children also bring extra work and added financial burdens. The day-to-day provision of food, clothing, shelter, and discipline can be very trying. Some parents find that they appreciate their children most when they are absent from them or when the children are asleep.

Gould (1972) wrote about the many **transformations** that occur in parents through their thirties and forties. Transformations are the changes in one's disposition necessitated by the continual shifts in the structures of one's life. While no pattern fits every unique individual, parents in general have the following transformations of child-life situations and the following personal responses:

Early 30s: Facing challenges of children—Behave like own parents.

Mid 30s: Empathizing with child's hang-ups—Avoid repeating parents' mistakes; Wanting child to adopt good characteristics—Choose parents' pleasing patterns; Acknowledging parenting difficulties—Contemplate divorce.

Late 30s: Controlling growing children—Lose confidence as parent.

Early 40s: Coping with adolescent children—Try to retain power over offspring.

Late 40s: Turning inward to face own needs—Relax parental reins.

Parenthood is one of the most important roles people can take upon themselves in life, yet it is a role for which society offers little formal preparation—people assume it comes naturally. There are books, articles, and columns on child-rearing, although few printed resources can answer the specific questions of individual parents who have unique children, special problems, and extenuating circumstances. Research has indicated that readings and discussions may not have an appreciable effect on parenting behaviors, anyway. Parent-training programs using live models and active role playing would be more effective (Knapp and Deluty, 1989). Parent-training programs are seldom available, however, unless parents and children are already in trouble.

Parents often think the pediatrician, who might be a good resource, is too busy handling life-or-death illnesses to answer questions. Psychologists are thought to be

Figure 9-12
Successes by one member of a family unit can generate a triumphant sense of warmth and pride in all family members.

too expensive. So parents rely on instinct or call their own parents, their friends, or their neighbors for advice. Maybe the advice is good, and maybe it is not, but parents may take it because it's all they have. Then, almost invariably, they hear or read that what they did was wrong. Some parents can maintain their self-esteem and confidence that they are doing their best, given their own particular circumstances. Others find child-rearing fraught with guilt and self-doubt.

As babies grow into toddlers, they test limits. Their pushes for autonomy frequently occur at the worst possible times. Young children interrupt or postpone all kinds of adult behaviors, from sexual intercourse to quarreling. One child seems to double the problems of organizing time. A second child seems to magnify the problems at least three- or four-fold. With one child, the problems and jealousies revolve around mother–father, mother–child, and father–child. With a second child, relationships double to child one–child two, child one–mother, child one–father, child two–mother, child two–father, and mother–father. Each subsequent child further multiplies and complicates the interrelationships (see Figure 9-13).

As children enter school, they begin to make demands on parents for money, excursions with friends, and parental participation in school activities. They want trips to all the places their friends have been; they request fad clothes, junk foods, and all the things that they see so enticingly advertised on television. They also bring home to their parents new worries about grades, adequacy of the school system, disputes with teachers, and behavioral problems that involve parents with neighbors, other parents, school personnel, community workers, or possibly even the law. Discipline—how much and what kind—becomes a primary concern. As with other child-rearing concerns, one can find abundant advice on discipline. Parents may try, at various times, reasoning, behavior modification, love deprivation, power assertion, indulgence, or

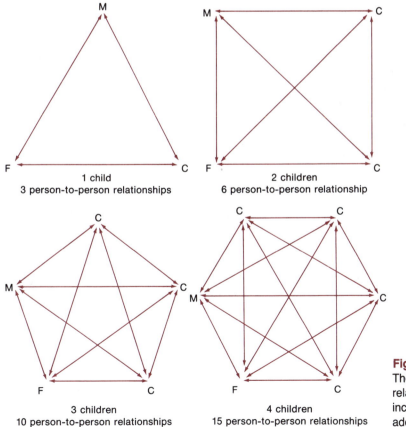

1 child
3 person-to-person relationships

2 children
6 person-to-person relationship

3 children
10 person-to-person relationships

4 children
15 person-to-person relationships

Figure 9-13
The number of different relationships in a family increases dramatically with the addition of each new person.

neglect. The disciplinary techniques that become habitual depend on how the parents were disciplined as children, what they perceive as working best, and what their spouse, relatives, neighbors, and friends reward them for using. In order for the more effective inductive techniques of discipline to predominate, the parents must have positive feedback from significant people in their environment. They must be convinced that reasoning is the best way to help children develop conscience.

Mothering, when it means care of children without help from father, grandparents, or a babysitter, is extremely hard work. Our culture predominantly stresses the mother's responsibility for child care. Consider the job: meals, snacks, nursing, shopping, laundry, dressing, mending, cleaning, entertaining, comforting, assisting, directing, advising, chauffering, cheering, encouraging, motivating, protecting from danger. The entertainments preferred by children are seldom really stimulating or amusing to "Mom." She may miss the hours she once had for work, rest and relaxation, sleep, beauty routines, social activities with companionable adults, and exclusive attention from her husband. The "happy homemaker" image of a wife and mother, so glorified by advertising, imposes an unrealistic ideal. Mothers who remember that the actresses or models in the media are being paid to play a role can accept themselves better than mothers who measure themselves against the yardstick of the glorified Hausfrau. Likewise, mothers whose husbands, families, and friends value their efforts and achievements are usually happier than mothers whose associates criticize and devaluate their daily efforts and exertions.

Tavris (1972) indicated that the more children a woman has, the less satisfied she becomes with her homemaking role. Ragozin and her colleagues (1982) found that the older a woman is when she has her children, the more satisfied she is with mothering and the more time she commits to her role. Bernard (1972) reported that anxiety disorders are very high among housewives. They are nine times as likely to become depressed or attempt suicide as women who are not housewives. The competencies depressed mothers show in caregiving behaviors vary according to life circumstances and the mothers' feelings of self-efficacy in the maternal role (Teti, Gelfand, and Pompa, 1990).

Egalitarianism is gradually emerging as a desirable option for our society. It is a social change emphasizing equality of all peoples, regardless of sex, race, age, religion, or country of origin. As we are moving toward egalitarian and androgynous childrearing (see Chapter 6, page 222), some of the old stereotypes about women's work are disappearing. While housework is still seen as predominantly women's responsibility, childrearing is increasingly being viewed as both parents' responsibility.

Fathering is increasingly being recognized as an important role in the day-to-day socialization of children (see Figure 9-14). Hoffman (1977) found that while fathers rarely assume complete childcare responsibilities if a mother is present in the family, they do take a more active role in caregiving if the mother works outside the home. They can even admit doing so, in some social settings, without damage to their masculine egos.

Although "househusband" is not a label all men welcome, and to be "macho" (masculine, male, vigorous, with connotations of not doing women's work) is still very important to some men, times are changing. Chapter 3 cited the increasing numbers of American parents who attend prepared childbirth classes before their babies are born. These classes strongly recommend the father's participation in the birth event. This is a good start for a father–child relationship. Rooming-in and relaxed hospital visiting arrangements for fathers further allow them to become familiar with their infants. The more a man interacts with his newborn, the more comfortable he feels providing food, clothing, and contact comfort later. Mothers learn in the same way, through observation and experience. If the father participates regularly in caregiving activities, the baby will form a strong attachment bond to him. The infant will smile and coo at him and later show signs of missing him (normal separation anxiety) when he departs.

Single parenting (as discussed in Chapter 6) is difficult but can be done successfully

Figure 9-14
Society has seen several rises and falls in paternal interest in parenting. Contemporary fathers are making themselves increasingly available to their children.

and can be very rewarding. Boys and girls raised without fathers can benefit greatly from having some interactions with a supportive male role model (an uncle, grandfather, teacher, neighbor, "big brother"), especially as they approach adolescence. Boys and girls raised without mothers likewise benefit from close relationships with female role models.

Good parenting (fathering and mothering) becomes particularly important as children approach adolescence. Bronfenbrenner (1977) wrote that the adolescent years are the most critical in terms of a young person's development. Rossi (1980) found that mothers viewed the adolescent years as the most difficult parenting years. Parents must give directions, advice, or assistance on such things as dating and sexuality, drug or alcohol use, independence strivings, and school problems. They may remember things from their own adolescence that they promised they would never inflict on their own children. Yet, due to the changing times, such promises now seem difficult to fulfill.

Generational changes assure that parents and their teenage children do not experience the same social environments or teenage customs. Despite some teens' interest in the old music or clothing styles of their parents, life has changed a great deal. Twenty years ago life was less technological. The mass media were less pervasive. Fewer families had television, and it had predominantly family programming (no music videos). Public transportation was slower and less readily available. Cultural norms, mores and folkways, standards of conduct, etiquette, and moral codes—all were different. Norms today are often ambiguous. Parents can see or hear a full range of language, sex, and aggressive behaviors exhibited by the media, their leaders, and their friends. Are children to do as grownups say, as grownups do, or as other teens do? How many adolescents do drugs? have sex? cut school? stay out all night?

Parents may hope to live vicariously through their teenage children. They have nurtured dreams about their offspring's future for many years. It is not easy for them to realize that their hopes and dreams may not come to fruition. If they must settle for less, or something else, they try to assure themselves that the something else will still reflect well on them.

Many parents see their children as end products of their own parenting and reflections of their own adult worth. The pressures that such attitudes place on both parents and children are sometimes unbearable. Depression is frequently related to overinvolvement and overidentification with children. Parents may become bewildered by their sons' and daughters' behavior: refusing to obey, refusing to study, exhibiting temper tantrums, running away, quitting school, having scuffles with the law, using drugs. They may feel helpless, despondent, and ultimately worthless as parents.

Some parents in our society have a different problem with their teenage children: they see them as standing in the way of their own success. Parents may not want to be bothered with the social, emotional, or financial problems of their offspring when they are struggling so hard to make sense of their own lives. Mothers and fathers may resent their children receiving the complimentary glances that were once thrown their way. They may feel angered and threatened by teenage idealism that criticizes their own lifestyle. They also may intensely dislike having their authority questioned (see Figure 9-15).

Many adults assume **stepparenting** responsibilities when children are adolescents. This is an especially difficult time to establish a relationship with a child (Einstein, 1979). Adolescents are all seeking independence. They do not like an intruder having any power over their lives (Hobart, 1987). While stepparenting of young children is difficult (see Chapter 6, p. 225), stepparenting of teenagers can be even more problematic. Teenage girls particularly resist the entrance of a stepfather into their lives. They are jealous that an intruder has stolen time from their mother–daughter relationship. They also feel a sexual tension with a stepfather, and the confusion of the incest taboo. They may resist any kind of physical contact, even a simple gesture like a handshake (see Figure 9-16). A teenage son may resist a stepfather for reasons of jealousy and resentment but usually not to the same extent as a daughter (Peterson and Zill, 1986). Both male and female adolescents resent stepmothers. The fairy tales about wicked stepmothers set the stage for problems. Stepparents can overcome some of these problems by not rushing the physical relationship (hands off), letting the biological parent mete out discipline, supporting the biological parent (unified front), and maintaining a calm disposition.

All parents find it difficult to assist adolescents. Communicating with teenagers is best achieved by democratic, authoritative parents (see Chapter 6) who have kept an

Figure 9-15
Many compassionate parents find their adolescent children difficult to manage. Grievances seem to be ever-present.

Figure 9-16
Stepparenting of adolescents is fraught with difficulties, especially the fragile relationship between stepfather and stepdaughter.

interchange of thoughts and opinions alive since early childhood. Adolescents (as discussed in Chapter 7) need freedom to exercise their own judgment, within limits. They also need listening persons to turn to as sounding boards. Whatever the difficulties of parenting teenage children and assisting them to assume their own independent lifestyles, it is sometimes comforting to realize that, in time, most children do appreciate the problems their parents had in raising them.

Launching children is the process of moving them out of the family home and into their own independent lives. One often thinks of special events, such as graduation, going to college, or marriage, as the launching points (see Figure 9-17), but it usually takes a few years for parents to completely launch children into independent lives.

Middle adulthood research suggests that the empty nest syndrome, in which parents develop a collection of negative symptoms related to the launching of their last child, is rare. Parents usually look forward to having all the children out of the house (Harkins, 1978; Rubin, 1979). Middle-aged depression, or the empty-nest syndrome, is usually compounded by other problems: divorce, unemployment, failing health, death of a family member. The empty-nest syndrome may be more pronounced if the parents see the child's departure as too early. Bassoff (1988) suggested that the mother–daughter relationship may be more difficult to loosen and let go than other parent–child bonds because of its special closeness.

Figure 9-17
A graduation may signal a launching point for a child to finally become independent of parents.

Spouse Relationships.   Infidelity reaches a peak in the forties. Levinson and associates (1978) found that more than one quarter of the fortyish men they studied were actually involved in affairs, and most of them had fantasies of affairs and wondered about their commitments to their wives. The years when children are adolescents (usually the decade of the forties) are the years in which most married couples are least satisfied with each other. Approximately one quarter of all divorces involve persons over age forty (Jacobson, 1983).

Consider the factors that may contribute to rough going in marriage between a person's thirtieth and fiftieth year: signs of loss of youth, reproductive changes, health, career, and/or personality changes, coping with spouse's uncertainties, maintaining an economic standard of living, managing a home, and guiding children through all the conflicts of childhood and adolescence. Such increased marital stress leads to a decreased self-esteem that in turn leads to more marital stress.

**BOX
9-2**

Men Who Abuse Women.

The doors are closed. Inside the home the male reigns supreme. Home is his sovereignty, his sanctuary. Here his women (wife, daughters, sisters, mother, grandmother) should defer to him and protect, nourish, and cherish him. If they don't, they must be disciplined and taught (again) intrafamilial male versus female roles. This bit of chauvinism is firmly entrenched in the minds of the majority of North American men, women, and children.

Guesstimates are that about one-half of all men resort to some physical form of discipline of at least one adult woman at some time in their lives. About 15% commit some violent act against their wives more frequently. Researchers have studied the differences between men who do not insist on being the supreme rulers behind the family walls of privacy, men who protect their home authority roles verbally rather than physically, and men who resort to abuse of women.

Abusive men exist in every race and in every social and economic walk of life. The wives of prominent doctors, lawyers, politicians, performers, businessmen, and the like are least apt to expose their victimization to public scrutiny. They remain silent because of terror, demoralization, embarrassment, shame or guilt, or confide only in private therapy. The wives of poor or unemployed husbands are somewhat more likely to report their assaults to the police or some other protective social service agency. Many of them, however, also remain silent. The tendency to downplay family violence, or lock trouble in, gives a false impression that few abusive men exist and that violent males are all down and out losers.

Males who perpetrate violence (throwing things, shoving, knocking down, kicking, punching, slapping, choking, and so on) against female family members (wives, grown daughters, sisters, mothers, even grandmothers) usually have several of the following characteristics: few close friends, social isolation, low self-esteem, an inner core of rage about not being given their proper share of something, a lack of trust in others, suspicion of others, anxiety, tension, frustration, insecurity, a belief that violence against women is justified, and a history of having witnessed intrafamilial violence (Queijo, 1984).

Efforts to demonstrate that abused women are masochists who have a secret desire for punishment have not been successful. Abused women do not fit any neat categories. They may be young or old, rich or poor, beautiful or homely, shy or sassy. Some fight back: These women are usually accused of being domineering, hostile, power hungry, and deserving of an occasional battering. Some seek immediate physical protection and take steps to terminate living arrangements with the abuser. Often they are counseled by lawyers, physicians, therapists, family members, religious leaders, or friends to try to work things out. Some women blame themselves, feel ashamed or guilty, and resolve to be still better wives (or daughters, sisters, mothers) to avoid the repetitions of violence. Often they are accused of being "doormats."

After violent acts most men feel guilty about what they have done and become very loving toward the woman they have hurt (Straus and Gelles, 1980). They usually promise never to repeat the behavior. The majority of women want to believe these reassurances. However, without a change in attitudes, social situations, self-esteem, security base, and the like, most men cannot keep such promises. Prevention requires personal counseling, family therapy, societal attitude changes, and enforcement of laws against beating anyone—even someone inside the family.

Husbands often use their wives as scapegoats for their frustrations and lack of satisfactions with personal accomplishments. A husband might, for example, blame his wife for a vocational rut: "She held me back." "She pushed me too much." "She didn't keep pace with me intellectually." "She refused to be cooperative or gracious to my associates." He may somehow feel it is his wife's fault that he is losing his youthful appearance: "She feeds me all the wrong foods." "She interferes with my exercise program." "She causes my gray hairs." Or he might blame his wife for his children's shortcomings: "She was too permissive." "She was too busy with her own concerns to be a good mother." "She did not teach them to value money or property." Or a husband might criticize his wife for spending too much time with the children and not enough time with him. He may suspect her of having an affair or be having one of his own. There are many ways in which husbands blame their wives for their own problems. Some husbands take their frustrations out on their wives physically (see Box 9-2).

Wives, confused about their own life goals and accomplishments, may find their husbands at fault for their shortcomings: "He ignored me for his job." "He held me back and wouldn't let me develop my potential." "He never felt my job was as important as his." "He never gave me enough respect." "He never helped me with the children or the house." They may suspect their husbands of having extramarital affairs or may be having affairs of their own. They may feel that their husbands are totally unsympathetic to their problems of household organization, fatigue, depression, child-rearing, loneliness, or approaching menopause. This is an especially rough period for women who have defined their role predominantly in terms of mothering. As children prepare to leave home, some of these traditional homemakers are left facing a gap in their lives, a feeling of worthlessness.

Women who have continued their careers, combining them with marriage, also have many faults to find with their husbands at this time in their lives: "He always put his needs ahead of mine." "He was jealous or resentful of my successes." "He certainly did not contribute his fair share to household and child-rearing tasks." The research evidence suggests that marriage is a happier state for men than for women in the decades of the thirties and forties (Pearlin, 1975) (see Figure 9-18). Even though men may view their marriage or family responsibilities as a hassle, once they are divorced or widowed they tend to replace the lost wife quite quickly (Reiss, 1980). The adverse consequences on social and emotional health from the loss of a spouse by death or divorce are greater in men than in women (Brown and Fox, 1979).

Divorce.   The U.S. Census Bureau reported that the divorce rate quadrupled between 1960 and 1985 (Lipsitt, 1989). Divorce rates are highest in the first five years of marriage, but there is another peak in divorces in midlife, when spouses are coping with adolescent children and the perennial questions of money, sex, and power. About 15% of divorces occur after fifteen or more years of marriage (Norton and Moorman, 1987).

Divorce in persons approaching middle age is made more painful by the sense of failure after having spent so many years trying to make the marriage work and by fears of loneliness without a partner. Kelly (1982) found that self-doubt, mood swings, and problems adjusting to single living were common sequelae to midlife divorce. Postdivorce adjustment may take several years (Kitson, 1982). Bohannan (1971) wrote that a divorce really involves several facets: the legal divorce, the psychic divorce, the emotional divorce, the economic divorce, the community divorce, the co-parental divorce (if the couple has children). While some people may perceive it as a growth experience, others may be left bereft and quite devastated by a midlife divorce.

If children are involved, the problems of divorce are often compounded. Current projections are that 50% of today's children will experience a separation or divorce of their parents. Children ask for and need to receive reasons for the change in their family. It is important that the reasons given for the divorce do not portray either parent in a bad light. It is also essential to reassure children, even adolescent children,

Figure 9-18
Middle-aged spouses must cope with several marital stressors: economic concerns, career pressures, reproductive changes, threats to self-esteem, feisty adolescents.

that they are not at fault (see Chapter 6). Decisions about custody or financial responsibilities are often problematic. Once custody and visiting privileges have been settled, the absent parent should keep promises to visit as faithfully as possible. The custodial parent should help the children understand if visits are postponed and not use such occasions to try to turn the children against the absent parent.

Dating is problematic for divorced parents with children, especially teenage children. Adolescents may make a parent feel embarrassed or guilty as they compare and pass judgments on the person who is replacing their absent parent (Gardner, 1977). Approximately 75% of women and 80% of men who divorce eventually remarry, nearly one-half of them within three years (Furstenberg, Spanier, and Rothschild, 1982).

Remarriage can also bring jealousies and competition between parent, stepparent, and children. Each new couple resolves in its own way the question of who is to discipline, how, and for what. White and Booth (1985) found that remarriages are usually as satisfactory as first marriages. However, stepchildren do reduce the quality of family life and decrease the quality of parent–child relationships. Remarried couples with children more frequently say they would not remarry if they had to do it over again. They also move their teenage stepchildren out of the home faster than they would natural teenagers. With or without children, remarriage involves the same kinds of issues as first marriages—designing relations with in-laws, organizing the household around belongings, and making decisions about housework, leisure time, and sex.

For those who survive the stresses of marriage during middle adulthood—and many do—marital satisfaction frequently climbs to a new high once the children are gone. Then husbands and wives may redefine their relationship in terms of friends, lovers, or companions rather than as persons trapped together with legal and psychosocial responsibilities toward their offspring.

Relations with Aging Parents.   In their thirties and forties most adults come to sympathize with their own parents and other aging people in a new way. Neugarten (1968) quoted the following statement from an interviewee: "My parents, even though they are much older, can understand what we are going through; just as I now understand what they went through" (p. 95). This change in the way some persons in their thirties and forties view their parents may lead to more confiding in them and more advice seeking from them. The younger adults can appreciate that the older adults understand their problems (see Figure 9-19). Cohler and Grunebaum (1981) suggested that close kinship ties between generations can be an important source of ego strength, identity, and feelings of personal congruence.

At the same time that younger adults acquire a new sympathy for their parents, their parents may turn to them for aid—social, financial, emotional, physical, or the like. This may present new problems for the younger generation. It is difficult to criticize one's own parents, realizing that time is running out for them, yet Gould (1972) found that on occasion the adults he studied were quite vocal in their criticism of their parents. They blamed the older generation for many of their own life problems. Levinson's group (1978) found that having to assist one's aging parents caused a great deal of emotional turmoil. The men he studied had to let go of their dependency on their own parents at this point. They had to redefine their relationships with their parents in terms of changed roles. Consider the following vignette:

Figure 9-19.
Individuals in their thirties and forties often find themselves confiding in and soliciting advice from their parents.

> Urie and Phyllis met in a hospital. Urie's dad was the patient, Phyllis the nurse. They began dating, fell in love, and married. They bought their first home close to Urie's parents, who were both older and in failing health. Although they would have liked to postpone parenthood until they were financially more secure, they had two daughters in the first three years of marriage so that Urie's parents could see and get to know their grandchildren. Urie's dad died on their fourth wedding anniversary. His mother moved in with them soon afterward. She was partially paralyzed after two strokes. They shared the care of their daughters, the mother, the housework, and the cooking for four years, until the mother died.
>
> Urie and Phyllis then moved from the city into a dream cottage in the country so the girls could go to a small school. Life seemed sweet. After six months, bad news came from Phyllis's mother. Her dad had cancer. Her mom did not drive and had no way to take him to and from his hospital treatments. Urie and Phyllis moved again, to be close to *her* parents. Gramps died the year the oldest daughter left home for college. Gram had a series of small strokes shortly afterward and could no longer live alone. Urie and Phyllis wondered whether they'd ever know what it was like to live like other married couples. Would they be selfish if they placed Gram in a nursing home?

Did Urie and Phyllis let go of their dependency on their parents? Was it interdependency? Do you think they would have guilt feelings if they placed a parent in a nursing home? How can a mature adult respond to requests for assistance from parents without giving the exact assistance requested?

Cicirelli (1981) reported that younger generation adults are willing to provide health care assistance to their parents, but older generation adults most frequently request assistance with day-to-day services. A call to assist one's aging parents is a test of maturity that may arrive for some adults very early in life, for others very late in life, and for others not at all. How a person responds to the request for assistance depends not only on the person's maturity and moral values but also on the extent of the request, the previous relationship with the parents, other responsibilities, and other resources for the aging parents.

Community Concerns

People in their thirties and forties define themselves not only in terms of their family successes or failures but also in terms of their position in the community. Common yardsticks against which individuals measure themselves are associates at work, neighbors, brothers, sisters, same-age cousins, former schoolmates, and friends. Although "keeping up with the Joneses" is a common theme of one's community relations, it is not the only concern.

Civic Responsibilities.   Civic responsibilities can be viewed as all the ordinary affairs of social living: obeying laws, paying taxes, working, and maintaining a courteous demeanor toward other people. They also may include more specific roles such as voting, supporting causes, joining civic-minded groups, and running for public office.

Our culture tends to confer positions of leadership to persons of both advanced age and experience. By the time individuals reach their thirties or forties they may receive credit for their accomplishments by election or appointment to status or authority positions such as school board member, church board member, officer of an organization, member of a board of directors of a professional or service organization, or political leader. Many others accrue notable records of accomplishments in community activities of their choice without any desire for external recognition (see Figure 9-20).

Neugarten and Moore (1968) found that persons approaching middle adulthood become more strongly identified with their political party. They are also more apt to run for and get elected to political office. In general, the more responsibility the office carries, the older the person is who gets elected to fill it. At the state levels, Neugarten and Moore found that representatives were younger than senators, who in turn were younger than governors.

Women's roles in the community have changed a great deal in the past thirty years. In the 1950s women generally sought volunteer roles in the community after their children were grown. They worked in church groups, PTAs, charitable organizations,

Figure 9-20
Many adults feel a need to become involved in politics, education, the arts, religion, or volunteer activities.

political parties, hospital auxiliaries, garden clubs, sewing circles, craft classes, and children's groups such as Scouts or 4-H. Many women still do these things. Increasingly, however, they seek careers, elected offices, or paid part-time positions.

The decline of volunteerism among women may be due in part to the societal feeling that only paid work is valuable work. Women, like men, want to feel that their efforts are valuable. Much volunteer work is busy work—address typing, envelope stuffing, or similarly routine, monotonous tasks. When a task is not fulfilling in terms of meeting the needs to feel wanted, needed, goal-oriented, intellectually stimulated, or financially rewarded, a person is not as inclined to persist with the task. Many government and social agencies that once depended heavily on volunteers now have hired employees to do the work to avoid the confusion, tensions, mix-ups, carelessness, and absenteeism that characterized some volunteers.

The volunteer work that survives is the work that allows the performer to meet his or her needs for affiliation and usefulness in well-appreciated, serious jobs. Volunteer jobs are about evenly filled by men and women. A schism exists, however, in work assigned to volunteers. Men tend to get jobs at the policy level, while women work at the operations level, especially in political volunteerism (Towle, 1985). Women volunteers have made an enormous impact, especially in historic preservation and environmental protection, saving many buildings and wildlife areas for posterity.

Friends.   Gould (1972) found that an interest in an active social life climbs in adults between the ages of thirty and fifty (see Figure 9-21). Both men and women show a greater interest in religious activities. They join more clubs and participate in more family gatherings. They also tend to socialize more in career-related functions. This may be due to a desire to hang on to or improve a job or to bid for a promotion, or it may simply be because they want time away from home.

Many of the social, leisuretime pursuits of people in their thirties and forties show a decrease in energy expenditure over their activities of earlier years. They prefer less rigorous sports—golfing, bowling, hunting, fishing. They play more cards or tabletop games. Although some people seek new concerns and hobbies to get them "out of a rut," their interests and attitudes usually reflect their preferred undertakings in the past.

Friends can have a strong impact on each other's emotional adjustment. They do a great deal of data processing for one another. A person tells a friend of joys and sorrows, problems, and worries. A friend may respond in a way that is rewarding and has a favorable influence on a personality or in a way that is upsetting. The same friend may be helpful one day and unresponsive the next. Friends tend to react to each other

Figure 9-21
Male bonding, female bonding, friends, family, social networking: Experts agree that these are important to mental and physical health.

not only on information imparted and received but also with aspects of their own needs, desires, and motivations coming into play. Lynch (1985) wrote that heart-to-heart talking, listening, and otherwise responding to others not only enhances emotional health but also protects one's heart and blood vessels. He argued that the entire cardiovascular system benefits from human dialogue.

Harry Stack Sullivan (1963) based his theory of personality primarily on interpersonal relationships. He felt social approval is as great an influence on one's behavior as shelter, food, and sleep. One's self-concept is formed by the nature of one's relations with others. Rewarding interactions contribute to mental health, whereas upsetting relations lead to a disturbed personality and physical and psychophysiologic disorders. Social living necessitates contacts with many different people. A mature person with a stable self-concept can use communication skills to protect the self from conflict with others. An insecure person with a less well-consolidated self may not be able to escape so readily from the hostility of others.

Sullivan's theory provided the basis for much of the **transactional analyses** of social relationships currently practiced by psychotherapists. These are methods of examining transactions between individuals to determine how they perceive themselves and others. Many adults are insecure and face their friends with the attitude "You're O.K., but I'm not O.K." They continually seek advice and help from their associates. Therapists try to help them develop an "I'm O.K., you're O.K." attitude instead. Two other unhealthy perceptions underlying the behavior of some adults toward their friends are "I'm not O.K., you're not O.K." or "I'm O.K., you're not O.K." Harris (1967) identified the former as a give-up position and the latter as an antisocial position.

Ellis and Harper (1966) stated that rational living necessitates a consideration of interpersonal relationships to determine whether altercations are due to one's own

INGREDIENTS OF FRIENDSHIP

"HOW IMPORTANT TO YOU IS EACH OF THESE QUALITIES IN A FRIEND?"

Numbers represent percentage of respondents who said a quality was "important" or "very important."

Quality	Percentage
Keeps confidences	89%
Loyalty	88%
Warmth, affection	82%
Supportiveness	76%
Frankness	75%
Sense of humor	74%
Willingness to make time for me	62%
Independence	61%
Good conversationalist	59%
Intelligence	57%
Social conscience	49%
Shares leisure (noncultural) interests	48%
Shares cultural interests	30%
Similar educational background	17%
About my age	10%
Physical attractiveness	9%
Similar political views	8%
Professional accomplishment	8%
Abilities and background different from mine	8%
Ability to help me professionally	7%
Similar income	4%
Similar occupation	3%

Figure 9-22
Ingredients of friendship.

behavior or to another person's problems. If a person's own behavior is immature, she or he should try to change. If the source of a conflict is the jealousy, vindictiveness, or greed of another, however, the mature rational adult should accept it as such and maintain his or her own feelings of adequacy and self-esteem.

Parlee (1979) surveyed 40,000 adults to determine what qualities are sought in friends. The characteristics desired most were confidentiality, loyalty, and warmth. Much less important were similarities in education, politics, income, and occupation (see Figure 9-22). Friends play a central role in the psychosocial development of adults. They help determine self-concept, self-esteem, perception of and trust in others, and, to some extent, overall social demeanor in the community.

The Midlife Transition

Most students of the middle adult years agree that a **midlife transition** occurs somewhere between thirty-five and fifty years of age. At some point the adult realizes that she or he is no longer young. This realization sets in motion a process of exploring the past, the present, and the future. One's self-concept in terms of one's current occupation and responsibilities are at the core of this review process. "Am I doing the right thing?" "Is there time to change?" The transition is often called the *midlife crisis,* suggesting the pain, the stress, the crucial decisions, and the alterations that accompany the transition. It is not easy to dispose of dreams that may never come to pass or to face the reality of what is now and what may be left of one's life.

Carl Jung (1923) was one of the earlier social scientists to describe a midlife transition. He believed that it is a crucial period of development. Here decisions for a lifetime must be made to assure a well-adjusted psyche. Jungian theory proposed that maturity does not evolve until the forties, after the trials of a number of life experiences. Before this, adults work at divesting themselves of their childish ways. They face outer reality and come to terms with it. Then, after their forties (transition), they begin to discover their inner selves. They try to unify their former fantasies, hopes, and dreams with the actuality of their lives. Jung described the period of life after the transition period as the **period of individuation**. It is only during these years, in his opinion, that adults finally move toward self-realization (see Figure 9-23).

Bernice Neugarten (1968), after her extensive interviews with middle-aged and aging persons in the 1950s and 1960s, came to a similar conclusion. She described the move inward toward more preoccupation with satisfying personal needs as an increased **interiority of the personality**. This movement generally occurs around the fifth decade. "It is in this period of the life line that introspection seems to increase noticeably and contemplation and reflection and self-evaluation become characteristic forms of mental life" (p. 140).

Figure 9-23
Jungian theory proposed that men and women begin to experience inner growth, a unification of ideas, and self-realization in their forties.

Neugarten found that the transition may begin with a painful awareness of being viewed as old by youth. For example, in her investigations one respondent said, "When I see a pretty girl on the stage or in the movies . . . and when I realize 'My God, she's about the age of my son, it's a real shock. It makes me realize that I'm middle-aged" (p. 94). Another said "Mentally I still feel young, but suddenly one day my son beat me at tennis . . ." (p. 96).

Neugarten found that the midlife transition is clocked more by life contexts—body, career, family—than by chronological age. For example, the family cycle runs its course differently in various social classes. In one study Neugarten and Moore (1968) calculated that the wife of an average unskilled worker finishes school by sixteen, marries by eighteen, and has her last child by twenty-three. An average professional worker's wife finishes school by twenty, marries by twenty-three, and has her last child by thirty. For unskilled workers middle age may arrive in the early to middle thirties. For skilled workers there is usually some realization of whether one will become a supervisor or remain at a lower-level position by the middle to late thirties. A business or professional worker may have a clear picture of whether he or she can reach a desired salary or professional goal (or both) sometime in the forties.

Cultural pressures can also influence the age at which this self-assessment and reposturing occurs. Professional athletes must face a restructuring of their lives relatively early, usually by their mid-thirties. Lerch (1984) wrote that most of them view this transition as a form of social death. For example, Bradley (1977) wrote:

> For the athlete who reaches thirty-five, something in him dies; not a peripheral activity but a fundamental passion. It necessarily dies. The athlete rarely recuperates. He approaches the end of his playing days the way old people approach death. (p. 204)

Athletes do, however, continue to live. After the crisis of retirement they restructure their lives and, unless they've earned enough to avoid subsequent employment, they move on to new projects, often in some way related to their sport.

The stress of the midlife transition leads some individuals to real crises or radical changes in their lives. Some midlife alterations are well known, such as Gauguin's moving to the South Seas to paint, or England's Edward VIII giving up his throne to marry a commoner. Executives may give up positions of power to start their own small corporations, priests and nuns may leave their orders to marry, and the affluent may leave their riches and become involved in work for charitable causes.

Men and women share the problems of a midlife transition, although the bulk of research on the stresses that occur emphasizes the male's transitions (see Figure 9-24). The cross-sectional and retrospective studies of men done by Levinson and his colleagues (1978) led them to describe the stages of **settling down** in the early thirties, **becoming one's own man** (BOOM) in the late thirties, and midlife transition in the forties.

During the settling down stage younger employees often have a mentor. The

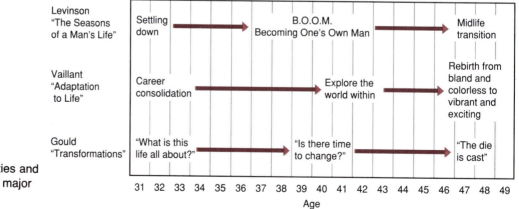

Figure 9-24
Passage through the thirties and forties according to three major researchers.

mentoring relationship usually evolves in the work setting. The mentor supports and facilitates his or her protégé's dream. The relationship lasts two to three years on the average, eight to ten years at the most. It may end with moves or job changes on a cooled-off but still friendly basis, but more often it ends with conflict. The younger employee enters the stage of BOOM. He or she may begin to see a mentor as tyrannical, destructively critical and demanding, or as standing in the way of his or her individuality and independence. The mentor, in turn, may see her or his protégé as inexplicably touchy, unreceptive, rebellious, and ungrateful.

Levinson and colleagues (1978) saw the BOOM stage extending from about thirty-six to forty-one. Employees attempt career advancements, a measure of authority, and less dependence on others. Their desires for affirmation and advancement make them especially vulnerable to social pressures during this time. They want desperately to be understood and appreciated. The culmination of the BOOM stage can be a great success, a failure, or, more frequently, a flawed success—good enough for others but blemished in the eyes of the dreamer. For about 80% of Levinson's subjects this period ended, and the midlife transition began, with a moderate to severe crisis. The adults felt a need to modify their lives, choose new paths, and redirect their futures.

Levinson found adults in this midlife transition anxious and fearful. They became irritated with others whom they perceived as trying to lead them, or push them, or hold them back. Their assessment was personal—something they had to do alone. Many suffered from depression during their transitions. Some tried to bury their troubles in various ways: overeating, alcohol, psychophysiologic disease. Some made radical changes in their lifestyles: leaving a job, leaving the family, having extramarital affairs. In fact, Levinson suggested that most transitional men tend to have fantasies about young, erotic girls and also about older nurturing women. He believed that this may still be related to an attempt to cut free from one's mother. No matter how the assessment process is manifest in a person's life, Levinson stated that it is normal. From his viewpoint, a person cannot go through this stage of life unchanged. Life will have a different meaning, and he or she will emerge on a new personality level.

Not every researcher agrees that a midlife transition involves a personality change. Behavior in midlife is often closely aligned to behavior in the earlier years. Woodruff and Birren (1972) followed a group of adults longitudinally for twenty-five years and found that people who were more neurotic in midlife tended to have been neurotic in college. Those who were well adjusted in college had better mental health in midlife. Costa and McCrae (1980) studied a group of adults longitudinally and found that very little change occurred in basic personalities over the years (see Figure 9-25).

Gould (1978), in his cross-sectional studies of adults, found that the early thirties involve processes of opening up. The major false assumption challenged is that "Life is simple and controllable. There are no significant coexisting contradictory forces within me." Any changes made are tentative and reflect uncertainties. However, by ages thirty-five to forty-five, Gould found, adults see that life is neither simple nor controllable, and this new vision frightens them. They feel an inner demand for action and the pressures of passing time. They see the falsehood of five assumptions left over from the naiveté of younger adulthood:

1. The illusion of safety can last forever.
2. Death can't happen to me or my loved ones.
3. It is impossible to live without a protector (women).
4. There is no life beyond this family.
5. I am an innocent.

Gould found that this reappraisal (an acceptance of death, an acceptance of the "hoax" of life, a recognition of evil within and around) caused periods of passivity, rage, depression, and despair (midlife crisis). However, letting go of childish desires for

Figure 9-25
Are people who join protest marches in their middle years displaying new personality patterns? How many of them also joined marches when they were younger?

absolute safety and innocence brought about a new understanding of the meaning of life—uncontaminated by the need for magical solutions and protective devices. Gould found that his subjects emerged from this midlife transformation with more access to their innermost selves and with an adult sense of freedom. By the late forties a "die is cast" feeling was present and was seen as a relief from the internal tearing apart of the immediately preceding years.

Vaillant (1977), in his longitudinal study of men, found behaviors similar to those described by Levinson and Gould in the decades of the thirties and forties. He found the thirties to be years for career consolidation. In order to achieve success in the workplace, the younger adult is aggressive and assertive. He or she uses the defenses of rationalization and projection to escape inner feelings about career thrusting and maneuvering. By age forty (give or take a few years), workers leave the compulsive busywork of their occupational pursuits and once more become explorers of the world within. Vaillant, however, felt a "crisis" was the exception, not the rule. He saw the growth and change of the forties as a normal progression in the life cycle. Dissatisfactions with careers often reflect desires to be of more service to others. Behaviors that are discontinued are often those that were ill fitting to begin with. By the late forties many of the men Vaillant studied seemed to have experienced a sort of rebirth from bland, colorless characters to vibrant and exciting men. They no longer blamed others for their career ruts and felt in control of their own destinies. They typically were more

---

BOX 9-3

Samples of Feelings Accompanying or Following the Midlife Transition.

1. "There is a difference between wanting to *feel* young and wanting to *be* young. Of course it would be pleasant to maintain the vigour and appearance of youth; but I would not trade those things for the authority or the autonomy I feel—no, nor the ease of interpersonal relationships nor the self-confidence that comes from experience."

2. "I discovered these last few years that I was old enough to admit to myself the things I could do well and to start doing them. I didn't think like this before. . . . It's a great feeling. . . ."

3. "You feel you have lived long enough to have learned a few things that nobody can learn earlier. That's the reward . . . and also, the excitement. I now see things in books, in people, in music that I couldn't see when I was younger. . . . It's a form of ripening that I attribute largely to my present age. . . ."

4. "I know what will work in most situations, and what will not. I am well beyond the trial and error stage of youth. I now have a set of guidelines. . . . And I am practised. . . ."

5. "It is as if there are two mirrors before me, each held at a partial angle. I see part of myself in my mother who is growing old, and part of her in me. In the other mirror,

I see part of myself in my daughter. I have had some dramatic insights, just from looking in those mirrors. . . . It is a set of revelations that I suppose can only come when you are in the middle of three generations."

6. "I sympathize with old people, now, in a way that is new. I watch my parents, for instance, and I wonder if I will age in the same way."

7. "My parents, even though they are much older, can understand what we are going through; just as I now understand what they went through. . . ."

8. "When I think back over the errors I made when I was 28 or 30 or 35, I am amazed at the young men today who think they can take over their companies at 28. They can't possibly have the maturity required. . . . True maturity doesn't come until around 45. . . . And while some of the young men are excellently educated, we middle-aged men are no longer learning from a book. We've learned from past experience. . . ."

9. "I moved at age 45 from a large corporation to a law firm. I got out at the last possible moment, because after 45 it is too difficult to find the job you want. If you haven't made it by then, you had better make it fast, or you are stuck."

SOURCE: From B. L. Neugarten, The awareness of middle age, in B. L. Neugarten (ed.), *Middle Age and Aging* (Chicago: University of Chicago Press, 1968), pp. 93–98. Reprinted by permission.

committed both to their careers and to their personal relationships after their rebirth.

Women may experience midlife transitions that are more closely related to their roles and responsibilities in younger adulthood. Professional career women, like professional career men, usually ascertain by some time in their forties whether or not they will attain their desired goals and status and then alter their directions or alter their self-perceptions accordingly (see Box 9-3). The single woman may have to adjust to the knowledge that her chance of marrying is now low, and that she will probably not have the status of wife and most probably not that of mother. The married professional career woman may experience some doubts as to whether she has done or is doing well in the dual roles of wife and professional or, if she has children, in the triple role of wife/mother/professional. Women who work full-time in skilled, semiskilled, or unskilled jobs will experience the same reevaluations of their lives ("Am I doing the right thing?") but perhaps somewhat earlier since they discover earlier the limits of their advancement and earning power. Women who devoted themselves to the homemaker/mother role in young adulthood generally experience their midlife transitions when their children leave home. The pain, confusion, stress, and changes that women undergo are often explained away as menopausal symptoms. However, women's transitions, like men's transitions, are also rooted in social and emotional aggregates. Transitions in many women occur ahead of their menopause.

Summary

During the decades of the thirties and forties, people struggle for their own place in the social order. At some point they reassess their aspirations and accomplishments, their status, and their life satisfactions. After this midlife survey some make changes. Others work harder at whatever it is they are doing.

Physically, signs of aging appear. Many health problems are related to dietary factors. Others are related to the inability to handle the stresses of everyday living. Chronic illnesses affecting adults in their thirties and forties include coronary heart disease, atherosclerosis, hypertension, and mental disorders.

Intellectually, the thirties and forties are very good years. Crystallized intelligence improves, while fluid reasoning abilities begin to decline. Overall intelligence remains high. Dialectical reasoning is characteristic of the adult years. Intellectual processes are more directed at meeting obligations and managing affairs than at acquiring new information, although many people return to school or continue studying. The output of unique, original materials by creative persons peaks in the decades between thirty and fifty.

Erikson saw the nuclear conflict of the adult years as that of achieving a sense of generativity versus stagnation. Generativity involves nurturing, teaching, and serving children or other adults. One can achieve generativity without having one's own children through creative skills, productivity, and contributions to the quality of life of others and of future generations. Stagnation involves a lack of productivity or concern for others.

Maslow proposed a needs hierarchy common to all humans. Physical needs, safety needs, belonging and love needs, esteem needs, and the need for self-actualization are progressively and cumulatively sought. Although some adults may be struggling with physical and safety needs, most are trying to meet their needs for belonging and love and then for esteem. Self-actualization cannot occur unless the first four needs are being successfully met.

Careers are usually very important to persons in their thirties and forties. While the twenties were years for choosing a vocation, the thirties and forties represent the decades for becoming a success at one's job. Parenthood can bring extra work, financial burdens, and feelings of guilt, anger, and self-doubt. Many parents need the support and reassurances of persons around them that they are competent in child-rearing. Adolescent children are usually the hardest to parent.

Marital relationships are often troublesome. Spouses may be anxious about loss of youthfulness and about their reproductive slowdowns. Spouses' midlife reassessments may take them in different directions, creating problems of readjustment. Often parents have to deal with their children's identity crises as well as their own psychological changes. Research indicates that these are years when married couples are least satisfied with each other. Marriages are not as stable today as in past years. Divorce is made more complicated by the presence of children. A majority of divorced persons do remarry.

Aging parents often turn to their adult children for support—financial, emotional, and physical—as they reach their retirement years. Assisting aging parents can cause emotional turmoil. It is hard to realize that the persons on whom one depended for many years are now dependent instead.

Contributions to civic and community causes often peak in the thirties and forties. Persons may become more strongly identified with their political party, their religion, their social clubs. They may run for, or be appointed to, positions of leadership. The nature of social activities engaged in changes from the more active pursuits of youth to less rigorous sports—golfing, bowling, games—or social or family gatherings.

Friends may reflect upward mobility, status, and job advancement. They also are apt to be people with similar concerns (religion, neighborhood, children). Closest friends are usually those with whom one dares to be more honest. Friends can create situations of conflict and stress or give support and reassurance to each other.

Most persons explore their inner lives sometime during their thirties and forties and restructure their outer lives accordingly. The midlife transition may involve a crisis or may be a realtively smooth transition from the dreams of younger adulthood to the realities of older adulthood.

Key Concepts

compression of the spinal column	coronary heart disease	generativity versus stagnation	stepparenting
premenstrual syndrome (PMS)	arteriosclerosis	hierarchy of needs	launching children
basal metabolic rate	mental disorder	self-actualization	divorce
blood pressure	fluid intelligence	peak experience	remarriage
hypertension	crystallized intelligence	mentor	transactional analysis
presbycusis	dialectic operations	transformations	midlife transition
presbyopia	gender-role changes	egalitarianism	period of individuation
coronary-prone behavior	creativity	generational changes	interiority of personality
	divergent thinking		settling down
			"becoming one's own man"

Questions for Review

1. For a number of years the emphasis in American society has been on the maintenance of youth and the needs of the young. What sorts of implications do you think this has for people in their thirties and forties who are beginning to see signs of their own aging?
2. Describe some of the ways you think diet and stress contribute to the high incidence of coronary heart disease in this country.
3. Erikson stated that stagnation is often associated with persons of low self-esteem. Why do you think this is so? Relate this to the resolution of nuclear conflicts described in earlier chapters.
4. Describe some of the ways husbands and wives can avoid using each other as scapegoats for their failures and insecurities as they go through their lives together, especially during these middle decades of unrest.
5. Imagine you have been married for 15 years, are 40 years old, and are going through a divorce. Would you turn to your friends or family for emotional support? Why?
6. Describe a midlife transition you have witnessed occurring in a friend or a relative. If possible, illustrate your example with conversations you have had with this person about or during this transition.

Further Readings

Forgatch, M. S., and Patterson, G. R. (1989). *Parents and adolescents living together: Family problem solving.* Eugene, OR: Castalia Publishing.
Teaches families with adolescents how to resolve conflicts concerning problems such as sexual behavior, drug and alcohol use, and school achievement.

Gelles, R. J., and Strauss, M. A. (1988). *Intimate violence: The definitive study of the causes and consequences of abuse in the American family.* New York: Simon & Schuster.
Examines the widespread phenomenon of family violence: wife abuse, marital rape, elder abuse, child battering, sibling assault.

Gould, R. L. (1978). *Transformations.* New York: Simon & Schuster.
The whys behind the changes in adult life and sug-

gestions as to how changes can be used to make life fuller and richer.

Grambs, J. D. (1989). *Women over forty.* New York: Springer.
Discusses many of the myths about middle-aged women concerning their physical health, mental health, sexuality, and career concerns.

Levinson, D. J., Darrow, C. N., Klein, E. B., Levinson, M. H., and McKee, B. (1978). *The seasons of a man's life.* New York: Ballantine.
The groundbreaking ten-year study of the experiences and changes in the lives of forty men that stimulated an interest in midlife transitions.

Pogrebin, L. C. (1986) *Among friends.* New York: McGraw-Hill.
Friendships are discussed according to changes with age, differences between the sexes, and activities shared by friends.

Schooler, C., and Schaie, K. W. (eds.) (1987). *Cognitive functioning and social structure over the life course.* Norwood, NJ: Ablex.
Several papers dealing with the changes in intellectual processes over the course of the life span.

The Fifties and Sixties 10

At some point in the decade of their fifties, most people begin to think of themselves as middle-aged. Such hallmarks as launching children and gaining grandchildren serve to remind people where they are chronologically, regardless of how they feel physically and emotionally.

The fifties and sixties are often years of peak status and power (see Figure 10-1). Past accomplishments may be recognized and rewarded with a measure of respect. Financial earnings are probably greater than they have been in the past, while expenses may be lower because of departure of children from the home. Persons in their fifties and sixties are often regarded as reservoirs of wisdom and good judgment. A vast number of them really are in the prime of their lives due to an emphasis on diet, exercise, physical fitness, stress management, and health maintenance.

There is nothing permanent except change.
—*Heraclitus*

Success isn't final; failure isn't fatal; it's courage that counts.
—*Winston Churchill*

Physical Development

The physical changes that normally occur in the fifties were once difficult to ascertain because of the high incidence of debilitating diseases that masked normal development. Now, however, because of improved medical techniques and an increased concern for protection from disease and environmental hazards, a larger number of normal people are surviving, and the changes that are due to aging rather than to illness are becoming more apparent.

Physical Changes

Whereas neurons stop dividing in the prenatal days, other cells (like those of the liver, pancreas, bowel, and skin) continue to divide actively for a much longer time. There are conflicting theories about why some body cells eventually die without replacing themselves and why some lose their ability to function properly over time. There are probably several different causes for cell deterioration and cell malfunctions. Many biologists believe that the aging of cells, including structure and function, may be programmed in the cells' genetic material. Changes seen in the aging of cells include changes in the rate of protein synthesis and breakdown, changes in endocrine organ functions, and changes in cellular responses to many hormones.

Eleanor was a poor little rich girl. Her father was an alcoholic whom she adored. Her mother was a beautiful woman who preferred Eleanor's three little brothers. She nick-named Eleanor "Granny" because she was so homely and such an odd, old-fashioned girl. Eleanor was sent to a convent for a while, even though she wasn't Catholic. Her mother died of diphtheria when she was eight. Soon after, a brother died. Her father died when she was ten. Eleanor was sent to live with her grandmother, who sent her away to a boarding school in England. Eleanor developed many fears: of failure, of displeasing people, of the dark, of death.

When she was twenty-one, Eleanor married an American cousin. Together they had five children. When she discovered he was having an affair with her secretary, she asked for a divorce. He refused, so Eleanor compromised: He gave up the woman; she stayed in the relationship. When Eleanor was thirty-seven, her husband was stricken with polio. She nursed him back to near health, but his legs remained crippled for life.

Eleanor was fifty when her husband, Franklin, was elected President of the United States. He was re-elected an unprecedented three times. Eleanor spent over twelve years as First Lady in the White House. She helped keep her husband's career going. She was the driving force behind many of the programs that shaped the New Deal and helped the U.S. survive the Great Depression. Eleanor also kept her husband's secrets: his new mistress, his paralysis, his failing health. Franklin died of a stroke in Warm Springs, Georgia, in 1945. His mistress, not Eleanor, was at his side.

Eleanor was devastated by Franklin's death. For forty years, she had adjusted to his faults and foibles and had centered her life around meeting his needs. Now what? She described her situation as "a big vacuum which nothing, not even the passage of years, would fill."*

Eleanor still had the same fears of her childhood: She could not remain in a vac-uum, so she set about reorganizing her life. She gave the Roosevelt estate at Hyde Park to the U.S. Government and moved to a smaller home. President Truman accepted her gift and offered her one in return. Would she like to serve as a member of the U.S. delegation to the organizing meeting of the United Nations? Eleanor was sixty-one. She saw the offer as an act of charity. Her first reaction was to decline, but her secretary advised her to give the idea careful thought.

Eleanor decided to accept the United Nations post. Some U.S. Congressmen pro-tested, but her nomination eventually won Senate approval. Mrs. Roosevelt then sur-prised everybody: She was not going to be a figurehead. She took control and wielded power. She read all the secret documents it was her right to see. She argued her own opinions with the men who were supposed to oversee and advise her. She became a tireless worker. She was elected Chairwoman of the U.N. Commission on Human Rights. She then became instrumental in writing the Commission's *Universal Declaration of Human Rights.* She was a social activist at heart, promoting racial and religious equality in an era marked by universal intolerance and bigotry. She walked on eggs. As the only woman on the delegation, she was not very welcome, and as a voice for change, she risked hostile reactions. Eleanor proved her diplomatic skills. She entertained her oppo-nents at small informal sessions where she could cajole and wheedle them. She debated with great skill. She eventually saw her legislation for universal human rights approved.

Eleanor's emptiness after Franklin's death became filled to overflowing with things to accomplish. She had begun writing a newspaper column called "My Day" when she was First Lady. Even after leaving the White House, she continued writing this column five days a week. Her fame as a writer grew. She added a second volume to the autobiogra-phy she had started at the White House. She continued her United Nations work. She found the time to give lectures and travel the world as well.

In the late 1940s, Eleanor was almost the only woman in politics. How did she find the courage to accomplish what she did given her age and the pervasive sexism in soci-ety? Do you think that family traumas and family expectations prevented Eleanor from accomplishing more earlier in her life?

*Roosevelt, E. R. (1961). *The Autobiography of Eleanor Roosevelt.* New York: Harper and Brothers.

Figure 10-1
By middle age, many adults have won recognition, status and power in their chosen fields. The fifties and sixties may be much happier than the trying twenties or the transitional thirties and forties.

The changes of aging are gradual and continue in the same directions described for the thirties and forties, except to a greater and greater extent. Muscles have diminished strength, size, and reflex speed; bones lose mass and density, break more easily, and heal more slowly; skin becomes less elastic, drier, and more wrinkled; nails grow more slowly; hair thins out and grays; vision and hearing become less keen; the senses of taste, touch, and smell become less acute; digestive disturbances occur more frequently; fat accumulation is a threat unless eating habits are curbed; there are changes in the patterns and amounts of production of many hormones (see Table 10-1); voice changes; energy is diminished; and with each passing year it takes slightly longer to catch one's breath after exertions. Baltes and Schaie (1974) reported that a reduction in motor skills may begin to interfere with certain aspects of functioning. Eye–hand coordination, for example, is not as acute as it was in earlier years, and reaction time slows due to a decline in the velocity of nerve impulses.

Considerable retarding of physical decline can be accomplished through regular exercise, stress management, diminished cholesterol and saturated fat intake, adequate

Table 10-1   Changes in Hormones with Age.

Hormone	Change	Function
Antidiuretic hormone	↔	Regulates water reabsorption in the kidney
Growth hormone	↔	Stimulates body growth
Gonadotropins	↑	Influences growth and activity of ovaries and testes
Testosterone	↔ ↓ (?)	Masculinization
Adrenal androgen	↓	Masculinization
Estrogens (female)	↓	Feminization
Estrogens (male)	↔ ↑ (?)	Feminization
Thyrotropin (TSH)	↑	Stimulates growth and function of thyroid gland
Triiodothyronine (T_3)	↔	Involved in regulation of metabolic rate
Thyroxin (T_4)	↔ ↓	Involved in regulation of metabolic rate
Parathyroid hormone	↓	Regulates calcium, phosphate, and bone metabolism
Cortisol	↔	Involved in regulation of body fluids and in carbohydrate, lipid, and protein metabolism
Aldosterone	↓	Regulates body sodium and potassium levels (mainly in kidneys)
Insulin	↔	Regulates carbohydrate, lipid, and protein metabolism
Glucagon	↔	Counters action of insulin (for example, causes elevation of blood sugar)

SOURCE: Modified from R. Gregerman and E. Bierman. Aging and hormones. In R. H. Williams (ed.), *Textbook of Endocrinology*, 6th ed. (Philadelphia: Saunders, 1981). Reprinted by permission.

Figure 10-2
Physical activities, intellectual pursuits, and life satisfaction remain high for mature adults. Don't let the wrinkles or thinning gray hair mislead you.

calcium and protein intake, cessation of cigarette smoking, curbed use of alcohol, and avoidance, whenever possible, of stress and environmental pollutants such as external radiation, exhaust fumes, smoke, and contaminated waters.

Intellectually, people in their fifties and sixties continue to add to their crystallized intelligence: they add words to their vocabulary and organize and process new information they take in from the environment. A person's intellectual functions in middle age are more dependent on motivation, education, experience, intellectual activity, and intellectual stimulation than on age (see Figure 10-2).

Reproductive Changes

The reproductive organs of both men and women begin to atrophy with advancing age. Although records indicate that some men father children into their ninth decade and some women in their sixties bear children, the norm is for humans to cease bearing children in their thirties or forties. The end of the female reproductive cycle is relatively clearly marked by the menopause. The male climacteric is gradual and is less obviously concluded. Neither menopause nor the male climacteric need appreciably affect the sex drive. It may remain powerful throughout the life span.

The term **menopause** comes from two Greek words meaning *month* and *cessation* and refers broadly to all of the physiological changes that occur when a woman experiences a discontinuation of her monthly menstrual function. At the menopause the levels of two pituitary gland gonadotropins—luteinizing hormone (LH) and follicle-stimulating hormone (FSH)—are high, but the ovary, which has been gradually shrinking since the late twenties, responds less to the pituitary hormones and produces less estrogen and progesterone of its own. There are fewer graafian follicles left to ripen and fewer ova left to be released. Menopause is thus a consequence of ovarian "failure."

For at least ten years prior to the cessation of the menses, a woman receives signals that her reproductive organs are changing. In most women, the time between menses gradually shortens. Thus, the menstrual cycle may take 30 days at age thirty, 25 days at age forty, and 23 days by the late forties (Whitbourne, 1985). The mean age for menopause is fifty years, but the age of onset varies widely. It may occur as early as forty-two or as late as sixty (Gregerman and Bierman, 1981). In some women, the time between menses may lengthen. Most women experience more irregular and more anovulatory cycles prior to menopause. They also more frequently develop mild to severe premenstrual distress. When the amount of estrogen/progesterone produced by the few remaining graafian follicles/corpora lutea is so diminished that the endometrium of the uterus is no longer stimulated to prepare it to receive a fertilized ovum, menstruation ceases.

Notman (1980) suggested that a more appropriate term for the menopause would be "the perimenopausal years" since the changes that occur are gradual, not abrupt. An early menopause may occur as the reuslt of an **oophorectomy** (removal of the ovaries), a **hysterectomy** (removal of the uterus), prolonged nursing, poor health, living in an extremely cold climate, or excessive exposure to radiation. The age of onset of menopause also has a link to genetic inheritance.

The decreased levels of estrogen accompanying menopause (or oophorectomy) cause some vasomotor and other physical changes in some, but not all, women. One of the more common vasomotor symptoms of menopause is the **hot flash,** also frequently referred to as the *hot flush.* The body becomes warm and flushed, usually from the breasts up. Perspiration may be followed by chills. The flush may last from a few seconds through several minutes and may recur several times a day. Hot flashes are more common during the months of missed periods and in the evening hours or at night. More rarely, women may experience nausea and vomiting, constipation or diarrhea, gas, frequent or painful urination, low backache, an appetite change, headaches, dizziness, heart palpitations, numbness in the fingers or toes, breast tenderness, depression, anxiety, and insomnia during the perimenopausal period.

While the majority of women experience symptoms of menopause for only a year or two, some may continue to have vasomotor instability (hot flashes or night sweats) for up to eight years following the cessation of their menses. **Estrogen replacement therapy** (ERT) can ameliorate these episodes, although medical opinion differs as to the desirability of giving estrogen (see Table 10-2). Some doctors do not want to interfere with nature. Some give estrogen only for major problems with vasomotor changes. Others give estrogen replacement daily as soon as unpleasant menopausal symptoms begin. Some continue it for several years. Women continue to produce some estrogen from the adrenal glands or by conversion of adrenal androgen in the liver even after menopuase. ERT supplements the naturally produced hormone, bringing it up to a level that provides relief from symptoms related to insufficient hormones.

ERT may be useful in reducing the incidence of osteoporosis (a disease characterized by a porous condition of the bones). There has been much controversy over whether estrogen therapy also increases the risk of gallstone formation, elevated blood pressure, or cancer of the endometrium (the tissue that lines the uterus). The risk depends on the amount and duration of estrogen use (Gregerman and Bierman, 1981). Shapiro and his colleagues (1985) reported that use of ERT not only increases the risk of endometrial cancer during replacement therapy but also increases the risk for up to ten years after estrogen use is discontinued. Wilson, Garrison, and Castelli (1985) reported that long-term ERT also puts women at a 50% elevated risk of death from cardiovascular disease and a twofold risk of death from cerebrovascular disease. Increased rates for myocardial infarctions were also observed, particularly among estrogen users who smoked cigarettes. A study of nurses done by Harvard Medical School did not find that ERT increased the risk of fatal heart disease (Stampfer et al., 1985), but the cutoff age for the nurses studied was fifty-nine. Perhaps further longitudinal studies will reveal increased risk of cardiovascular disease in the estrogen-using nurses as they reach their sixties and beyond.

Currently between two and three million perimenopausal women in the United States rely on ERT to control hot flashes. They have been assured that it will reduce their risk of developing osteoporosis. They are sure to notice that supplemental estrogens also help preserve more youthful skin, hair, and breast tissue. The benefits of ERT have to be weighed against the risks of its use. These risks keep many physicians from prescribing estrogen.

The psychological changes of menopause are often grossly exaggerated. The menopausal woman was once expected to be tearful, unpredictable, forgetful, unattentive, frigid, and haggard, yet the majority of postmenopausal women feel that menopause did not change them in any important way. Only about 50% of women are troubled by hot flashes or night sweats. The remaining 50% are not troubled. Young women are more concerned about it than women experiencing it, perhaps due to fear of the unknown. Many women find an end to their menses a happy relief. Their sex life remains good or even improves after menopause (see Figure 10-3).

Many of the psychological symptoms once associated with menopause (anxiety, depression, and so on) may be related to other concurrent events in a woman's life.

Table 10-2 The Pros and Cons of Estrogen-Replacement Therapy.

Pros	Cons
Reduces hot flashes	Increases risk of some cancers
Reduces osteoporosis	Increases risk of gallstones
Keeps skin softer and moister	Elevates blood pressure
Preserves breast tissue	Increases risk of cardiovascular diseases
Increases vaginal lubrication	Adds to clotting factor abnormalities
Improves sleep	Adds to glucose intolerance
Elevates mood	Causes some breakthrough bleeding

Figure 10-3
A second honeymoon is sensed by many mature adults after the menopause and male climacteric.

Woods (1982) found that women who are satisfied with their lives are less apt to report psychological reactions to menopause than are unhappy women.

Many women experience a renewed interest in sex (and in making their physical appearance more attractive to men) after the menopause. Masters and Johnson (1966) described this unleashed sexual drive as a **second honeymoon phenomenon** and attributed it in part to women's newly found freedom from fears of pregnancy. Social factors such as no children in the home, fewer tiring household tasks, and a desire for more companionship may also contribute to this burst of sexuality. Sexual activity is highest in persons who were sexually active in their earlier lives and who always enjoyed sex. Bachman and Lieblum (1981) found that the direction sexual interest takes is greatly dependent on the woman's premenopausal sexual activity and satisfaction.

The term **climacteric** comes from the Greek term for a critical time. There is a great deal of confusion and debate about whether there really is a male climacteric and, if so, when it occurs. Many men go through a transitional period in their forties. They reexamine their lives, and some may make radical changes in the way they do things. The transition period may erupt in a crisis (such as leaving the wife, leaving the job, turning to drugs or alcohol) for some men. These emotional repercussions were discussed in more detail in Chapter 9. The question of whether these changes are brought about or influenced by the normal male reproductive changes that accompany aging is as moot as the question of whether menopause causes emotional repercussions.

Androgen levels decline slowly with age. As the production of testosterone decreases, men may experience a delayed erection time, a reduced ejaculatory volume, fewer viable sperm, a small decrease in the size of the testes, and a gradual loss of facial, pubic, and underarm hair. These changes occur so slowly that they may go unnoticed or may be detected only in the seventh or eighth decades. A few men may have an abrupt onset of physical symptoms, suddenly becoming impotent. The latter occurrence is felt to be a reaction to aging triggered more by financial, social, familial, or marital problems than by hormones. Such impotence may last for a few weeks, a few years, or forever, depending on emotional health, physical health, and therapy.

For most men, however, the ability to engage in and enjoy sexual activity continues into old age.

Some men do experience a gradual waning of sexual interest with age, uninterrupted by dramatic changes in their levels of sexual libido. This waning of interest varies greatly from man to man and reflects, in part, sexual stimulation received and past history of sexual responsiveness. Masters and Johnson (1966) reported that men in their studies with the most evidence of maintained sexuality in their later years were those who had had more sexual activity in their early years. The men with problems of sexual inadequacy and impotence usually had one or more of the following problems:

1. monotony of a repetitious sexual relationship (usually translated into boredom with his partner),
2. preoccupation with career or economic pursuits,
3. mental or physical fatigue,
4. overindulgence in food or drink,
5. physical and mental infirmities of either the man or his spouse,
6. fear of performance associated with or resulting from any of the former categories.

The cure rate for impotence in men over age fifty is high. Therapy successes indicate that a willingness to return to active sexual practice and an interested partner are more important than any hormonal, medicinal, or other physiological routines in restoring potency.

The physical changes that occur due to decreasing testosterone levels are accompanied by many other normal physical changes of the fifties and sixties (such as decreased muscle strength, wrinkles, graying hair, possible digestive disturbances, or fat accumulation). Potentially traumatic psychological events may occur (seeing a son or daughter become sexually mature, having new financial burdens appear). These events may cause depression, unpredictability, forgetfulness, loss of attention, irritability, headaches, insomnia, fatigue, loss of sex drive, appetite changes, flushes, or, in short, any of the symptoms once associated with female menopause. The male climacteric, when and if it occurs, may have physical and psychological causes compounding the hormonal effects just as the female menopause does.

One hundred years ago, men and women viewed the loss of reproductive abilities as the twilight of their lives. Today menopause and climacteric changes may signal an exciting new phase of the life cycle (Idiculla and Goldberg, 1987). Mature adults may have twenty-five or more years left for exploring, seeking adventures, and enjoying life with sex but without children.

Health Maintenance

The four leading causes of death of persons in their fifties and sixties are coronary heart disease, cancer, vascular disease, and accidents. The fifth leading cause of death is liver **cirrhosis,** usually related to a long-time abuse of alcohol (see Box 10-1). During the last few years the general health of Americans has improved a great deal. The number of deaths from heart disease has declined, but the number of cancer deaths has increased. There has also been a significant rise in the number of deaths from respiratory ailments. In spite of these increases, life expectancy continues to climb slowly. In a study of longevity among nearly 17,000 Harvard alumni, Paffenbarger and his colleagues (1986) found that death rates from all causes were about one-third lower in those who expended 2000 or more kilocalories per week in exercise (walking, climbing stairs, sports) than among less active men, even without consideration of the presence of hypertensive disease, smoking, obesity, or early parental death.) By the age of eighty, the amount of additional life attributable to exercise alone was more than two years.

BOX
10-1

Alcohol and Cirrhosis.

If one is not an alcoholic (does not have a current or past physical dependence on alcohol), one has nothing to fear from regular drinking. Right? What harm can there be in drinking as long as one does not become drunk and disorderly? The fact is that without technically being an alcoholic, a steady drinker can do severe damage to his or her liver.

Cirrhosis of the liver is a disease characterized by cell degeneration, scarring, tissue loss, and deformity of this vital gland. Cirrhosis interferes with the liver's many versatile and vital functions (protein production, sugar storage, bile formation, detoxification). Cirrhosis is often fatal. It is also often the result of chronic alcohol abuse.

The quantity and duration of drinking necessary to cause liver cirrhosis is unknown but usually involves daily imbibing over at least a ten-year period (LaMont, Koff, and Isselbacher, 1980), although alcoholic cirrhosis has been diagnosed in some patients by their early twenties. Some individuals have a low liver tolerance for alcohol and a genetic predisposition for alcohol-induced cirrhotic changes. Annual deaths due to cirrhosis of the liver are highest for black males (about 30 per 100,000), are similar for white males and black females (about 14 per 100,000), and are lowest for white females (about 7 per 100,000) (Jackson, 1982).

Early symptoms of cirrhosis include a firm and enlarged liver, jaundice, intermittent ankle edema, increasing weakness, and fatigability. The treatment is simple: a nutritious diet, added vitamins, and absolutely no further use of any alcoholic beverages for life. Early diagnosis and meticulous attention to diet will prolong life and prevent further liver degeneration. The prognosis is poor, however, for persons who are diagnosed after the appearance of complications of liver disease or who refuse to stop drinking.

In a similar study, Frisch, Wyshak, and their colleagues (1985) surveyed over 5000 women who had graduated from ten American colleges between 1925 and 1981. Those who began athletic training early and remained lean and physically active had two and a half times less cancer of the uterus, ovary, cervix, and vagina, and two times less cancer of the breast, than their less active classmates. Many North Americans take these findings seriously and are now protecting their health with regular sports or exercise programs. They have also learned that such things as a healthful diet (with more lean proteins and green, leafy vegetables and less saturated fat) and a cutback on smoking and drinking can help them avoid costly medical bills (see Table 10-3).

All adults should remember that they need periodic immunizations against preventable disease. The American College and Physicians (1985) recommends that all healthy adults received mid-decade birthday (forty-five, fifty-five, sixty-five) booster doses of tetanus and diphtheria toxoids. In addition, health care personnel should receive an annual immunization against influenza, and persons who have frequent direct contact with blood or infected tissues should be immunized against hepatitis B.

Chapter 9 discussed the causes and ways to avoid coronary heart disease and vascular disorders. It is reemphasized that exercise, dietary discretion, and avoidance of smoking are foremost as preventive measures. The other main causes of death and disability in mature adults are cancer and accidents. We will discuss cancer causation and common forms of cancer in the following pages. Diabetes, visual disorders, and

Table 10-3 Ways to Increase Longevity.

Maintain regular aerobic exercise	Restrict caffeinated beverages
Eat foods from the four food groups	Use stress management techniques
Maintain desirable weight	Avoid cigarettes and smoke
Avoid saturated fats and cholesterol	Get seven to eight hours of sleep per day
Limit sugar and salt	Practice safety precautions
Restrict alcoholic beverages	Develop a social-support network

dental problems, which affect many persons in these decades, will also be presented.

Cancer, from the Latin "crab," is a general term used to describe many diseases that are characterized by an abnormal transformation of a cell and an unlimited proliferation of the same abnormal cell. Because of exponential growth, one abnormal cell advances from 2 to 4 to 16 to 256 to 65,536 abnormal cells, and so on, rather rapidly. The word **malignant** refers to the immortality of the abnormal cells—their ability to continue to grow and invade normal tissue without ceasing; from 65,536 cells to 4,294,967,296 cells to the next exponential leap, and so on. The word **tumor** refers to an abnormal mass of tissue that may form from the proliferation of an abnormal cell. Tumors are not inflammatory. The suffix -*oma* also refers to a tumor (as in *lymphoma*). If the tumor ceases to grow, or grows very slowly and does not invade normal tissue, it is called a **benign** (as opposed to malignant) tumor, and it is not considered cancerous. Some forms of cancer (such as leukemia) do not form tumors (masses). The term **neoplasm,** from the Greek *neo* for "new" and *plasma* for "thing formed," refers to any new growth of cells or tissues, or any cancer. However, it is generally used to refer to a malignant tumor. **Metastasis** means the movement of the abnormal proliferating cells from the part of the body in which they originated to another. Metastasis has occurred, for example, when a brain tumor results from a primary ovarian tumor. **Oncology,** from the Greek *onkos* for mass, is the study of the causes, properties, and treatment of cancers.

A revolution is currently taking place in oncology. For years, the search for the cause of cancer (or different causes for different neoplasms) concentrated on factors external to the human host of the disease. Many **carcinogens** (cancer-producing substances, from the Greek *karkinos* for "cancer" plus *genesis* for "origin") were identified. Tobacco, radiation, some food additives, some industrial products, and some synthetic hormones, for example, are known to trigger cell transformations and then initiate proliferation of the abnormal cells. We all live, breathe, and eat in a world full of carcingens, but carcinogenic agents cause cancer in only some, but not all, people. Today, the search for the cause of cancer has shifted to internal factors. Scientists trained to study such diverse disciplines as ion transport and lipid biochemistry are joining in the search (American Cancer Society, 1990).

Oncogenes, cancer-causing genes, have been discovered in the cells of all humans (Weinberg, 1985). The properties of specific oncogenes and a full understanding of how they mediate abnormal cell change and growth may be years away, however. Oncogenes must be triggered; they normally lie dormant within all cells. How specific carcinogenic agents, or diet, or stress, or lack of exercise interact with or trigger specific oncogenes is not currently well understood.

At present, close to 500,000 Americans die from some form of cancer each year (see Figure 10-4). We will briefly mention the symptoms of and treatments for the most common forms.

The alarming incidence of lung cancer in smoking men and women has been referred to as the **lung cancer epidemic** (Tisi, 1980). Lung cancer is the most prevalent and among the most lethal cancers. Early symptoms of a lung carcinoma—a persistent cough, coughing up blood, difficult breathing—mimic the symptoms of emphysema and chronic bronchitis, which are quite common in smokers. Early diagnosis of lung cancer may be difficult, even with annual or semiannual chest x-rays. Often a malignancy is diagnosed after discovering a metastatic lesion resulting from the spread of the lung cancer to another, usually distant, site. The great distance of metastasis is possible because cancer cells are carried by the blood and lymphatic systems.

Lung cancers are sometimes resected through a lobectomy (removal of one of the lobes of the lung). Inoperable pulmonary cancers may be treated with radiation and chemotherapy. The earlier the tumors are detected and treated, the better, although the overall five-year survival rate for lung cancer is very low, only 13%. Most patients die within two years.

Figure 10-4

American Cancer Society's estimates of cancer death rates per 100,000 Americans.

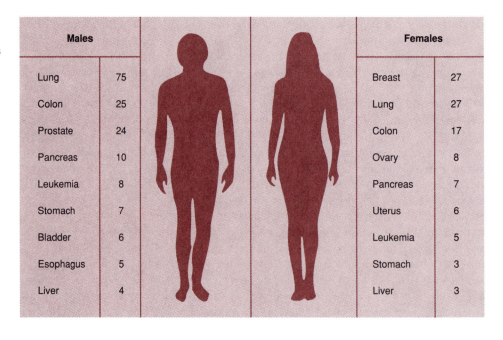

Males				Females	
Lung	75			Breast	27
Colon	25			Lung	27
Prostate	24			Colon	17
Pancreas	10			Ovary	8
Leukemia	8			Pancreas	7
Stomach	7			Uterus	6
Bladder	6			Leukemia	5
Esophagus	5			Stomach	3
Liver	4			Liver	3

The American Cancer Society has produced a list of seven caution signals to alert persons to any possible cancer:

1. **C** hange in bowel or bladder habits,
2. **A** ny sore that does not heal,
3. **U** nusual bleeding or discharge,
4. **T** hickening or lump in breast or elsewhere,
5. **I** ndigestion or difficulty in swallowing,
6. **O** bvious change in a wart or mole,
7. **N** agging hoarseness or cough.

Breast self-examinations and breast screening by mammography have helped to reduce the death rate from breast cancer. When detected early, malignant breast tumors can be completely removed. Undetected breast cancer frequently metastasizes to the nearby lymph nodes, however, lowering the cure rate. Breast cancer is more common in certain groups of women than others (Giuliano, 1984). Seven high-risk factors are

1. Caucasian race,
2. endometrial cancer,
3. family history of breast cancer,
4. fibrocystic breast disease,
5. delayed child-bearing,
6. non child-bearing,
7. early menarche (before age 12).

Cancer of the male prostate may be confined to the prostate or may metastasize (Griffin and Wilson, 1980). Any extension beyond the capsule is associated with a poor prognosis (outcome). This cancer becomes increasingly common from the fifties onward. An early symptom may be some difficulty associated with urination. Surgical removal of the prostate is necessary. With bone or extrapelvic involvement, radiation or chemotherapy may be used in addition. The cure rate is best if the cancer is detected and removed early.

Cancer of the large intestine (colon) accounts for about 20% of cancer deaths in the United States (LaMont and Isselbacher, 1980). Symptoms include changes in bowel habits, constipation, or blood in the stool. If the tumor can be removed before it spreads, the survival rate is high (75 to 80%). Cancer of the colon shows a markedly high intrafamilial occurrence rate. With a known family history, adults should request periodic sigmoidoscopic examinations from middle age onward.

Colon cancer surgery involves establishing an artificial opening (**colostomy**) for the colon through the lower abdominal wall. A person with a colostomy must wear a small bag attached to this opening (stoma) to collect fecal materials that are discharged.

Ostomy societies have sprung up all over the country to enable persons who have had colostomies to share problems, solutions, and self-care techniques with one another. The comradeship of these groups often helps to alleviate the problems of withdrawal and depression that may plague a person. If others can accept that an ostomy is not calamitous or even too unusual, the patient can usually return to his or her normal activities and lifestyle quite successfully.

Leukemias are malignant changes in blood cells originating in any of the blood-forming organs (bone marrow, liver, spleen, lymph nodes, thymus). **Lymphomas** are malignancies arising in the lymph-cell-producing areas (lymph nodes, spleen, liver, and areas in the intestine). Many different forms of leukemias and lymphomas exist. Researchers have recognized several probable contributing factors, including viruses, ionizing radiation, chemical agents, and genetic factors (Clarkson, 1980).

The different subclassifications of leukemia and lymphona require different therapy programs, all aimed at reducing the number and controlling the rate of growth of abnormal cells. Adjunctive therapy may include antibiotics, blood transfusions, and radiation, aimed at controlling complications.

Current beliefs about multifactorial cancer causation have led experts to emphasize healthful living to prevent any neoplastic growths. Since tobacco is implicated in as many as 30% of all cancers, a major thrust of public health campaigns is to persuade people to give up smoking or chewing (see Figure 10-5). Obesity is implicated in cancers of the breast, cervix, ovary, prostate, colon, and gallbladder (Garfinkel, 1985). Persons are advised to maintain weights within the desirable range for their sex, height, and body build. Diets low in saturated fats and high in fiber, whole grains, and green leafy vegetables are recommended. In addition, regular exercise should be a part of each person's daily activities.

Diabetes is one of the most common diseases of metabolism, affecting about 6% of the population (Foster, 1980). Diabetes increases in frequency with every decade of life. The main feature of diabetes is a high blood glucose level (hyperglycemia) often associated with glucose in the urine. The central hormone associated with diabetes is insulin, a product of the pancreas. Insulin promotes entry, storage, and utilization of glucose in tissues. In its absence, glucose cannot enter tissues. The condition is really one of starvation of the body's cells.

Figure 10-5

Persons who smoke or chew tobacco products or inhale second-hand smoke have a higher incidence of many kinds of cancers.

In Chapter 6 insulin dependent diabetes was briefly discussed. It should be pointed out now, for clarification, that in the insulin-dependent form of diabetes there is a total, or almost total, lack of insulin production. In order to survive, the diabetic must have insulin administered.

Tissues become less sensitive to insulin with aging in persons gentically predisposed to the disease (Horton, 1983). The relative lack of insulin seen in noninsulin-dependent diabetes causes hyperglycemia. Diabetics may develop painless breakdown of the skin of their feet, leading to infected ulcers or gangrenous toes. Elevated blood glucose levels also lead to abnormalities in the walls of some blood vessels, resulting in renal (kidney) and retinal (eye) disease.

Often the adult with mild noninsulin-dependent diabetes (mildly elevated blood sugar, no complications) can reduce blood sugar by weight loss, by decreased intake of refined sugars (glucose) in the diet, and by exercise to promote glucose utilization. Drug treatment of noninsulin-dependent diabetes includes agents that promote the release of insulin from the pancreas.

Glaucoma is characterized by increased intraocular pressure due to some impediment of the outflow of the aqueous humor (see Figure 10-6). In 90% of cases the cause is unknown (Victor and Adams, 1980). Glaucoma can and should be easily recognized by physicians and is easily treated with medication.

A **cataract** is a density of the lens of the eye, most often due to degenerative changes in the lens. It also may follow trauma to the eye or lens and is often associated with diabetes. Surgical replacement of the lens is indicated when density produces loss of vision.

Retinal hemorrhage is bleeding within the retina. It is more frequent in persons with kidney disease and diabetes. It can be treated with laser or ophthalmic surgery.

During the first forty years of life, the main cause of tooth loss is dental caries. After the fourth decade, however, gum diseases may become problematic. Bacteria that accumulate in plaques on the surface of the teeth break down the attachments of the teeth to the surrounding bone (Masler, 1975). As a result, middle-aged people may develop **periodontal disease,** sometimes referred to as *pyorrhea*. It is usually manifested by a loosening of the teeth and sometimes with pus from the gingiva (gum) around the teeth (see Figure 10-7). Treatment is largely preventive and is aimed at removing the plaque with frequent, careful brushing and careful flossing. Although proper tooth and mouth cleansing and avoidance of excess sugars can eliminate the need for extractions of teeth in the later years, many Americans fail to pay attention

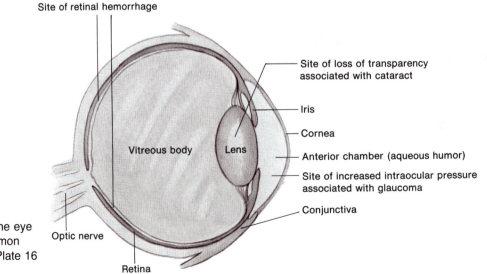

Figure 10-6
Schematic drawing of the eye illustrating sites of common visual disorders. (See Plate 16 in center of text book.)

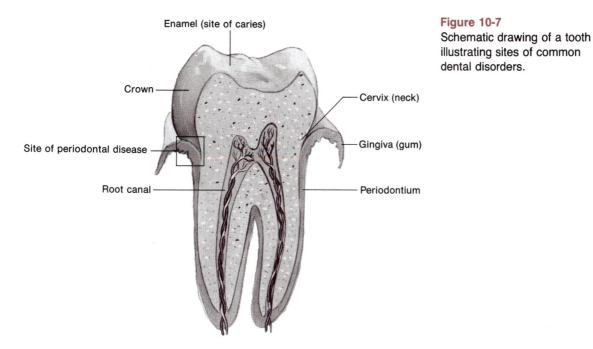

Enamel (site of caries)

Crown

Site of periodontal disease

Root canal

Cervix (neck)

Gingiva (gum)

Periodontium

Figure 10-7
Schematic drawing of a tooth illustrating sites of common dental disorders.

to their teeth until it is too late. Consequently, some people begin wearing partial or complete dental plates by middle age.

Improperly fitted dentures can cause chronic mouth irritations. Denture plates may need periodic adjustments to assure a continued good fit with advancing age because the bony structure of the mouth changes. In spite of preparations that are advertised to hold dentures firmly in place "no matter what one eats," people with false teeth may find it extremely difficult to chew some foods, such as charcoal-broiled steaks and corn on the cob.

Psychosocial Development

People in their fifties and sixties typically have fewer family responsibilities than in earlier decades and more freedom for leisure and social activities. They also tend to view themselves more favorably than they have done in the past. They have more status and power. They begin to reap the rewards of their lifetime of hard work. Just as there is a feeling among youth that people over thirty cannot be trusted, there is a feeling among younger adults that people over fifty have the wisdom of age and experience. Many people are glad to have arrived at fifty and have no desire to relive their thirties and forties. The designation of a distinct period, mature adulthood, begins at around age 50 and continues to retirement at about age 70 (Kennedy, 1990).

Beyond the Empty Nest

Erikson (1963) proposed one nuclear conflict for all the years of middle adulthood, ages 30 through 70, that of generativity versus stagnation (see Chapter 9, p. 339). The work of generating may at first seem to be more easily accomplished while raising children. At second glance, however, the conflict also revolves around careers and community life. Mature adults often feel that they were more stagnant in their thirties and forties. They finally learn how to generate successfully in their fifties and sixties. They act on their desires to create a legacy for themselves. They become mentors to younger adults at work. They become more involved in community activities. If they have grandchildren, they may express their generativity through active involvement with them.

Cytrynbaum and his colleagues (1980) proposed five developmental tasks for mature adults. These are similar, but not identical, to the developmental tasks proposed by Havighurst (1982; see Chapter 9, p. 338):

1. recognition of biological limitations and health risks,
2. restructuring of sexual identity and self-concept,
3. reassessment of primary relationships,
4. reorientation to work, career, creativity, and achievement, and
5. acceptance of death and mortality.

These tasks are usually accomplished after offspring have been launched from the family.

Some adults approach mature adulthood without the experience of an empty nest. They may never have married, never had children. Their experiences are not dramatically different from other fifty- and sixty-year-olds (see Box 10-2). They must still work through developmental tasks such as those proposed by Havighurst and Cytrynbaum.

Today's fifty-year-old married couples can often look forward to spending as much time alone together after launching their children as they spent raising their children. The time when the first child leaves home is a momentous occasion in most families. For some parents the child's going away may be an occasion for grieving. For years the parents may have hovered over and protected the child. To then release the child into the world and to cut off the daily ministrations may bring an acute sense of loss. Sending off the first child is usually the hardest, although families may feel bereaved as each offspring moves out of the family home. Some parents find surrogate children to nurture (their spouses, infirm friends, their aging parents, pets). Some try to hold on to their own children and may meet with varying degrees of success. Parents who

---

BOX 10-2

Middle-Aged Singlehood.

Most studies of psychosocial development through the adult years are studies of married persons. Changes in their lives are assessed in relation to possible family events: marriage, birth of children, parenting of teens, launching of children, grandparenting. Yet about 5% of adults never marry. Another 20% remain single for the remainder of their lives after the death of a spouse or a divorce. What are single childless persons like in their fifties and sixties? Are they swinging singles or lonely and forgotten bachelors and spinsters? How do they maintain a positive self-concept in a marriage-minded society?

With some exceptions, middle-aged single adults behave very much like middle-aged married adults. They invest about the same amount of their time and energy in their jobs. They entertain and are entertained by their friends. They spend time pursuing hobbies and leisure interests. They may be active in political, religious, community, or social groups. They have household responsibilities (meals, cleaning, laundry, bill paying, repairs, shopping). They may be involved in surrogate parenting of nieces and nephews or of their own aging parents.

Unmarried adults at any age are no longer a breed apart. It is less necessary to have a husband or a wife today than at any other time in our history (Blake, 1982). There is legitimate social status for a fully adult, happily unmarried, independent human being. Single women can often achieve and maintain a more clear-cut occupational status without the confounding factor of spouse's status. (Is she a college professor or an insurance salesman's wife?) Many older single women have purposely chosen never to marry. Likewise, many older single men are single by choice, not because they are unattracted by, unattractive to, or rejected by women. More research should be focused on all the psychosocial ramifications of being older and single. Meanwhile, it is a mistake to believe that only the married "live happily ever after" or that all unmarrieds share some stereotypic lifestyle.

refuse to let go are often considered meddlesome and intrusive by their newly independent children. Some parents launch children enthusiastically, however, especially when they have had a stormy relationship with their offspring (Osherson, 1980). They look forward to the adventure of life without children.

Stability of Personality

Carl Jung (1923) described the early years of adulthood as years in which expansion into the outer world is the prevailing manner of operating or working. He felt that middle age brings noticeable personality changes. The maturing adult's manner of dealing with the outer world becomes more contracted. Older individuals begin to integrate outer reality with inner fantasy and move toward more self-realization, which Jung called **individuation** (see Chapter 9, p. 357).

Bernice Neugarten (1968a) held that the reflections of mature adulthood differ from the reminiscences of old age. Middle-aged adults restructure their personalities after their reflecting. They develop new concepts of self, time, and death with a consideration for how they will spend the rest of their lives. Very often they emerge with a feeling of being more fully in charge of their destinies than ever before.

Roger Gould's (1972, 1978) descriptions of the characteristics of personality over the life span supported the conclusions of Jung and Neugarten that persons in their fifties and beyond turn inward. He stated that these patterns of reflection and contemplation result in a mellowing and warming up, with much more self-acceptance and self-approval. They "look within themselves at their own feelings and emotions, although not with the critical 'time pressure' eye of the late thirties or with the infinite omnipotentiality of the early thirties but with a more self-accepting attitude of continued learning from a position of general stability" (Gould, 1972, p. 526).

David Gutmann (1976) found that the increased interiority of personality that occurs during the middle years of life has important repercussions for men's social behaviors. In early adulthood men tend to be bold and active in their dealings with the external environment. They tend to act on their impulses and maintain a position of control over their own lives to the greatest extent possible. After midlife, however, men become less bold. They begin to see the external world as more complex. They conform and accommodate to it more (see Figure 10-8). Gutmann (1977) studied men in a preliterate Mexican farming culture, Navajo Indians, and urban American men and determined that this personality shift occurs with age in all three cultures, regardless of the male sex-role expectations. Although the degree of shift varies from male to male, men generally become less self-assertive and more conforming with age. Gutmann describes this as a shift from **alloplastic** (active) mastery to **autoplastic** (passive) and **omniplastic** (magical) mastery of the outer world.

Feldman, Biringen, and Nash (1981) found that as men become less self-assertive and more conforming, affiliative, and compassionate in middle age, women become more instrumentally competent and more autonomous. This finding has led some people to conclude that middle-aged women become more "masculine." Perhaps with society's gender-role changes this perception of postmenopausal women will disappear. Perhaps society's emphasis on androgynous behaviors will make obsolete the attributions of competence, compassion, nurturance, and other such behaviors as more appropriate for one sex than for the other.

Haan (1981) found that women's personalities change less than men's personalities over the life span. She studied several dimensions of behavior longitudinally. She found more openness, more nurturance, more achievement motivation, and more self-confidence in both middle-aged men and women compared to their behavior as adolescents. Emotional control remained stable over time.

In contrast to the view of change is the view that basic personality characteristics remain stable over the adult life span (see Figure 10-9). As the French put it: *Plus ça change, plus c'est la même chose* (the more it changes, the more it remains the same).

Figure 10-8
Men are often more open and affiliative in their fifties and sixties than they were in their younger years.

Table 10-4   Allport's Four Types of Traits.

Trait pattern	Examples
Cardinal	Martin Luther King, Jr.'s quest for freedom; Albert Schweitzer's reverence for life
Central	Never borrow money; say grace before every meal
Common	Navajos' stoic endurance; Protestant work ethic
Secondary	Drink warm milk before bed; read horoscope every day

Allport (1937) was one of the first theorists to postulate the existence of stable personality traits across the life span. In his view, every individual personality is a unique cluster of traits. Traits, he felt, are autonomous, consistent, self-sustaining forms of readiness for response. He felt that individuals may have all-pervasive, "ruling passion" qualities called **cardinal traits;** characteristics that are consistent and rest on upbringing called **central traits;** and minor ways of behaving known only to a few, called **secondary traits** (see Table 10-4).

No two persons ever have precisely the same traits. Each trait is distinct and individualized within its possessor. Each personality is composed of a cluster of traits, unique to that individual alone.

Allport's theory of personality stressed the concept of a *functional autonomy of motives* as well as traits. Simply stated, a motive that is originally based on one tension or set of tensions (for example, the need to do well in school to earn an allowance from one's parents) can become autonomous (self-governing). One can eventually be motivated to engage in a behavior simply because carrying it through beings a sense of self-satisfaction. Personality, Allport believed, remains relatively stable due to unique traits and the functional autonomy of motives. Allport's theory was once highly controversial, but today more and more psychologists are coming around to this view.

Costa and McCrae (1980a) have argued that personality traits should be viewed as independent variables that function jointly with age and stage to influence some of the outcomes of life, rather than as variables dependent on age or stage. They have presented an eighteen-facet model of personality, with three domains encompassing six dimensions each, as follows:

Neuroticism	**Extraversion**	**Openness**
Anxiety	Attachment	Ideas
Depression	Assertiveness	Feelings
Self-consciousness	Gregariousness	Fantasy
Vulnerability	Excitement-seeking	Esthetics
Impulsiveness	Positive emotions	Actions
Hostility	Activity	Values

A person's score (high to low) in each of the three domains (**neuroticism, extraversion,** and **openness**) is seen as a pervasive part of personality and can be used to predict behaviors. Costa and McCrae (1980b) have demonstrated the endurance over time of these dispositions (see Figure 10-9). They developed their model of **personality stability** after they studied the responses of men from their twenties to their seventies on self-report personality inventories filled out at intervals of from six to ten years apart (Costa and McCrae, 1977, 1978). They found a high degree of stability in how the men responded to the questions over time. Assertiveness in early years, for example, remained assertiveness in midlife and in old age. Block (1981) reported a similar pattern of stability in his longitudinal study of subjects from their early teens through their mid-forties. Vaillant (1977) also followed men from adolescence through

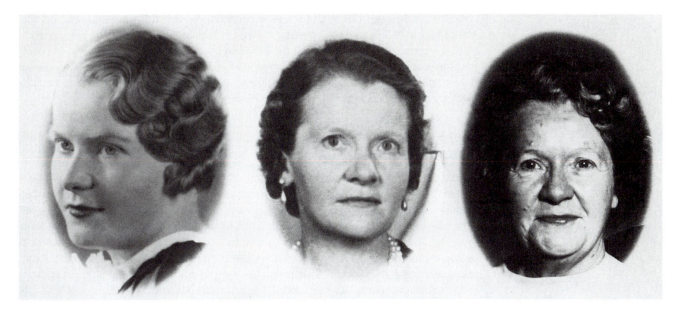

Figure 10-9
Some research suggests that personality remains stable over time. Thus, the sensitive reserved twenty-year-old may remain sensitive and reserved through several decades.

their mid-forties. He suggested that individual adaptability styles remain relatively constant and influence how one copes with each new stress.

In an ongoing Minnesota study of identical twins reared apart and reunited in adulthood, preliminary evidence suggests that some personality characteristics may have a genetic basis (Bouchard et al., 1981). The scores of some sets of twins on personality measures have been closer than might be expected from the same person taking the personality assessment on two different days. Many reunited twins are similar in sociability, energy level, interests, and abilities. This concordance with each other suggests a lifetime stability of personality (see Figure 10-10).

Figure 10-10
Twin research suggests that both twins reared together and twins reared apart are very similar on personality assessment characteristics.

Brim and Kagan (1980) presented a collection of several papers suggesting constancy and several papers suggesting change in human personality. Changes do seem to characterize movement through the life span but with some more stable personality measures influencing the quality and quantity of the change. Scarr (1981) suggested that students of human development should view continuity and change as complementary themes, each making the other more complete and understandable.

Marriage

Campbell (1981) reported an overall greater satisfaction with life in mature adulthood. Part of this satisfaction can be attributed to an upsurge in marital happiness after the nest empties. Whether or not personalities change, husbands and wives usually become more companionable. They use each other as confidants, relating joys and sorrows, interests, worries, satisfactions, annoyances, and dissatisfactions. They are more apt to listen to each other and to rely on each other's advice. Rather than deny problems, as they were more apt to do in the thirties and forties, mature adults begin to communicate about them. This promotes a sense of mutuality and interdependence in the marriage, which increases marital satisfaction (Garrett, 1982).

External situations may also contribute to an improved marriage. Most couples have a more adequate income with fewer expenses when children are gone. Both spouses usually have an increased level of job satisfaction (Skolnick, 1981). Sexual relations frequently improve once children are out of the home and the wife has ceased having PMS. Participation in sexual relationships reinforces feelings of mutuality, sharing, and concern over each other's well-being. It enhances a positive sexual self-image and feelings of sexual competence (Weg, 1983). Wives are usually less tired in their fifties than they were in their forties because of fewer stresses: child-rearing, household responsibilities, other jobs. This reduction in role strain contributes to greater marital satisfaction (Spanier and Lewis, 1980).

Gould's (1972) research on transformations revealed that increased marital happiness and contentment is often associated with a change in attitude toward the spouse. The postparental individual is less likely to view the spouse as a parent or a source of supplies, rather, the sense of inner-directedness finally prevails. Each spouse has the attitude of "I own myself." That awareness helps both husband and wife quit struggling with each other for status and power. They no longer feel guilt or envy toward each other. Change or success in one partner is met with delight by the other. Each looks at the other's transformation as an interesting improvement in the relationship and as a chance for more growth. Marriage can become a route for personal unfolding. Early marriage with its struggles over power, sex, and money is seldom so growth-promoting.

Although marital happiness increases for the majority of postparental couples, others seek divorce soon after the children leave home. In many cases the spouses involved have lost touch with each other long before the empty nest. They have only been biding their time, waiting for the children to depart before separating and divorcing.

In some cases the empty nest proves distressing. The spouses may experience new identity crises: They may have stayed at work more in the preceding years to meet the expense of college educations or weddings. Suddenly they have more time on their hands and no interests to fill the empty hours and days. Hobbies that just occupy time do not relieve boredom and restless feelings. Each partner may be afraid to quit working so hard for fear of demotion, early retirement, or loss of job. These frustrations may be displaced from their real cause and blamed on each other.

Identity crises after the empty nest also may occur in women who have no paid employment. A woman whose predominant role has been mothering is left unemployed when children depart. She may find it difficult to redirect her child-rearing time into new efforts and to find new outlets for her skills. She may begin to make more and more demands on her husband. Although many women find new interests in jobs, school, politics, or religion after the children leave, others wait for their husbands to solve the crises for them and may divorce them if they fail. Marital dissatisfaction in middle age may also be related to heavy drinking, absence of intimate associates, physical disabilities, mental disorders, chronic illnesses, or job dissatisfactions.

Relations with Adult Children

The family both contracts and expands with the launching of children. Although the number of persons living in the family home dwindles, the extended family may grow through marriage to include the new spouses and their offspring (see Figure 10-11). Some parents are pleased with their children's choices of mates. They welcome them into the family with open arms. They may also establish closer ties and frequent contacts with the parents of their children's new spouses.

Some parents have a degree of difficulty in accepting the people their children choose as mates. This is more common when the chosen mate is from a different social class, ethnic group, religion, or region of the country or demonstrates beliefs, values, or lifestyles that are distasteful to the parents. As reported in Chapter 8, there are often special problems that arise between in-laws. A mother may resent her son's preference for his new bride's attention. A father may be especially bitter toward the groom who has taken away his "little girl." All interactions may be problematic. A mother and father may resent the fact that their daughter now seeks her husband's advice, or they may want their son to take social and economic favors and advice from them, not from his wife or his wife's family.

Designing good in-law relations takes a great deal of tact and skill. Parents must remember that their children need to be independent to be mature human beings. It is difficult, however, not to be intrusive or overgenerous with advice or financial or social assistance after years of practice. On the other hand, parents who sever all ties with their offspring at the launching phase may be contributing to their own future conflicts and stresses with their sons- and daughters-in-law and alienation from their possible grandchildren. Some interactions and interdependencies are conducive to the establishment of good relationships that remain workable over time.

Parents are more apt to intrude in their offsprings' lives if children marry while still quite young rather than waiting until they have finished their education and begun a career. Mothers are more apt to intrude in their offsprings' lives than are fathers,

Figure 10-11
Parenting relations with adult children require many adjustments. The adult–adult–children family can still be a supportive and dynamic unit.

probably due to their greater investment in the nurturing role. Family interference is much more pronounced if the young couple borrows money or accepts financial aid from the mature couple. Money almost always has some strings attached.

It is not always the parents who intrude into or sever ties with their offsprings' mates. Many problematic relations with adult children relate to the fact that the departed child and spouse cut off ties with the parents. Many mothers and fathers would dearly love to give housekeeping or childcare aid, gifts, and the like to their children but find their offers of assistance rejected. This causes some parents to suffer great pangs of confusion and disappointment. Invariably they question their own performance as parents. Many initial problems of parent-in-law and children-in-law discord are worked out in time with honest communcation and a bit of pride swallowing on both sides. However, some problems may persist for years.

Grandparenthood

In spite of an American vision of grandparents as old, heavy-set, rosy-cheeked, wrinkled, benevolent persons enjoying rocking chairs and home-baked foods, most grandparents are quite different from this stereotype. Today's grandparents are more apt to be actively working, involved, middle-aged persons (see Figure 10-12). Troll (1983) reported that the average age for a first-time grandmother is about forty-nine to fifty-one, and the average for first becoming a grandfather is only a couple of years older, fifty-one to fifty-three. Great-grandparents, or great-great-grandparents (and there are many of them alive today) are much more apt to approach the popular notion of how a grand-parent should appear.

Approaching grandparenthood may improve relationships with adult children. Many middle-aged parents see a grandchild as a wonderful gift—a way of assuring their own immortality (Kivnick, 1982). Grandmothers, in particular, are often anxious to have some input into both the care of the new grandchild and the nurturing of the daughter (or daughter-in-law) who has produced progeny. Daughters, in turn, may not want as much independence from the mother (or mother-in-law) when they realize the weighty responsibility of sheltering, protecting, feeding, changing, and loving a baby. Contact

Figure 10-12
Today's grandparents are usually youthful, vital members of the community who must juggle their schedules in order to spend time with their grandchildren.

between new mothers and their own mothers generally increases after the birth of a grandchild (Fischer, 1981). Many young mothers depend on their own mothers to share infant care—especially teen mothers, single-parent mothers, and mothers who return to full-time employment shortly after their infant's birth.

Grandmothers and grandfathers can play a potent role in the social, emotional, and cognitive development of their grandchildren when they live together (Hetherington, 1989). Increasing numbers of divorced mothers live with their parents for a while until they can become financially independent. Grandparents serve as buffers when life is difficult. "Grandparents in America are like volunteer firefighters: They are required to be on the scene when needed" (Cherlin and Furstenberg, 1986, p. 183).

Fathers and sons frequently grow closer because of grandchildren. A son may turn to his father for financial advice (life insurance, budgeting) or personal social advice (fathering, dealing with the changed marital relationship) (Tinsley and Parke, 1983).

Grandparenthood speeds on the realization of aging for many people. It may contribute to the process of personality restructuring that leads to a more conforming, accommodating alloplastic mastery of the external world. Grandparents are expected to conform to, supplement, and support the decisions and rules about their grandchildren handed to them by their children. The former pattern of active mastery and control is usurped by the younger generation.

In a study of American grandparents, Neugarten and Weinstein (1968) found that about 60% of the persons they interviewed felt comfortable in the role of grandparenthood. About 30% of them were uncomfortable, however. Some had difficulty viewing themselves as grandparents. Some had conflicts with the parents about the rearing of the grandchildren. Some found that their grandparenting responsibilities were void of positive rewards and full of disappointments. Some grandparents had all three problems.

Neugarten and Weinstein identified five major classifications into which grandparents fall in terms of style of interacting with grandchildren:

1. formal,
2. fun seeking,
3. parent surrogate,
4. reservoir of family wisdom, or
5. distant.

Formal grandparents do no child-rearing beyond occasional babysitting. They maintain a clearly demarcated line between parents' responsibilities and grandparents' roles. When grandchildren enter the formal grandparents' home, they know that there are rules that must be obeyed.

> Glenn loved his Nana and Pop, but he wished they would visit him at his house instead of vice versa. Every time he entered their house, he had to take off his shoes so he wouldn't muddy the white carpet. Then he had to wash his hands. He could only sit on the chair with the plastic cover, never on the velvet sofa. If he was hungry, he had to ask for food. Then he had to listen to a lecture about how he should eat vegetables instead of sweets. They only let him watch educational television. Glenn was always glad when the visits ended.

Fun-seeking grandparents see their role primarily as playmates. Authority lines are irrelevant. The principal goal is that all parties involved should enjoy the interaction. Fun-seeking grandparents are typified by the signs that many post on a wall somewhere:

If mother says no, ask Grandmother.

If all else fails, ask Grandfather.

Parent-surrogate grandparents take on all the caregiving responsibilities for the grandchildren and are more parents than grandparents. It is more common to have parent-surrogate grandparents when the mother is young and unmarried. She may return to school and allow her parents to take care of both her and her baby. Grandparents can become parent surrogates for a number of other reasons. They may offer to raise a grandchild, for example, if one or both parents, or another sibling, is seriously ill or accidentally disabled.

The **reservoir of family wisdom** is a grandparent who is really an authority figure for parents as well as grandchildren. Such a grandparent uses interaction time to pass on special skills or resources. Alex Haley's classic book *Roots* (1976) illustrated how reservoir-of-wisdom grandparents serve to pass on family history. Generation after generation of the descendants of Kunta Kinte learned about his kidnapping from an African village, his importation to America in shackles in the hold of a ship, and his early life as a plantation slave from a reservoir-of-wisdom grandparent. Two hundred years later, Alex Haley was able to document a great deal of his family's history and write it in his book.

The **distant figure** stays remote from grandchildren except possibly to observe rituals such as birthdays or religious holidays. Distant-figure grandparents often are geographically distant from their grandchildren. They may live so far away that a visit must involve airplane travel or days in a train, bus, or automobile.

The fun seekers, surrogates, and distant figures are now the most common styles of grandparents in their fifties and sixties. Older grandparents and great-grandparents are more apt to be formal or reservoirs-of-family wisdom grandparents.

Grandmothers tend to have warmer relationships with their grandchildren than do grandfathers (Troll, 1980). On topics where the generations perceive some similarity of attitudes, there is an exchange of views. However, on topics where grandparents and grandchildren perceive some disagreement, discussions are avoided. General religious or political attitudes are more apt to be discussed than specific practices. Grandmothers' influences cover such topics as lifestyle, values, interpersonal relationships, work, and education. Grandfathers more often limit their areas of advice to work and education (Troll and Bengtson, 1979).

Relations with Aging Parents

Bernice Neugarten and Roger Gould both report that during the fifties people tend to mellow and develop warmer, more sympathetic feelings toward their own parents. One of Neugarten's (1968b) interviewees said:

> I was shopping with my mother. She had left something behind on the counter and the clerk called out to tell me that the "old lady" had forgotten her package. I was amazed. Of course, the clerk was a young man and she must have seemed old to him. But the interesting thing is that I myself don't think of her as old. . . . She doesn't seem old to me. . . .(p. 95)

Gould (1972) reported that middle-aged adults less frequently see their parents as the source of their problems. They begin to call them "Mom" and "Dad" with more warmth and affection.

Although feelings mellow, responsibilities for aging parents often grow. The older generation may gradually require more assistance in managing their own lives and households. Housekeeping chores, shopping trips, transportation, financial arrangements, holiday preparations, and the like may be more and more troublesome for aging parents. They are more likely to turn to their children than to strangers for help and are more likely to request assistance from their daughters than from their sons (see Figure 10-13). Not all older parents turn to their middle-aged children for help, however. Many prefer to remain independent as much as possible.

Some aging parents, particularly lonely widows or widowers, move in with their daughters or sons. The tensions of trying to share a household are usually not as great as they are among younger adults with live-in parents. The middle-aged adult tends to be more sympathetic toward the older adult. Many over-fifty persons also tend to be

Figure 10-13
Mature women are often sandwiched between two generations who need assistance: their aging parent and their adult children.

more conforming and accommodating toward one another. If the nest is empty, the frictions commonly associated with differences of opinion about child-rearing do not exist. The older parent can often be a help with light housework and may even be able to contribute some financial assistance for equipping and maintaining the household. In addition, aging parents can be a source of companionship to the postparental middle-aged adults with whom they live.

Career Concerns

Middle-aged persons are expected to be stable. They seldom make the radical shifts or impulsive moves that may have characterized their younger years. They are expected to remain in their present jobs until retirement. By this time the threat of being fired or laid off is usually low due to seniority status. Society tends to worry about mature adults who threaten their own security. Consider the following vignette:

> Marvin and Coretta had their last child when they were ages forty-two and forty, respectively. Consequently, their nest did not empty until they were in their sixties.
>
> When all the children became financially independent, Marvin went back to school. Many of his relatives and friends rebuked him. They told him that he was too old to start a new career.
>
> For three years, Marvin and Coretta struggled while he studied. When he completed his studies, he sent out résumés and interviewed for jobs. Nobody wanted to hire a sixty-five-year-old man who had just finished school and had no experience in his new field.
>
> After a new job that lasted only one year, Marvin again looked for work. He could not find another position. He eventually resumed his old work.
>
> Both Marvin and Coretta were glad they had made their little adventure, even if it hadn't worked out well. Had they been foolish, or was there wisdom in their mid-sixties undertaking?

Men and women who have worked throughout their adult lives generally reach the zenith of their careers in their fifties and sixties. Not only are their salaries as high as they will probably go, but their prestige and power are at their peak. Persons at all other stages of life—children, adolescents, young adults, older adults—look to middle-aged experts for advice and direction and expect middle-aged adults to help them solve their problems and make appreciable changes in the society.

For many people the years of work between approximately ages fifty and seventy are the most comfortable, satisfying years of their careers. They are doing what they know how to do best with fewer threats of moves or job changes. Many middle-aged adults become mentors to younger co-workers (see Chapter 9). Mentoring is one way in which an adult can achieve a sense of generativity. By offering guidance and support to new employees, the mature adult gives back what some mentor gave him or her earlier. Mature workers are generally more content with their jobs, perhaps because they have better jobs (Wright and Hamilton, 1978), or perhaps because they have learned to appreciate such things as the benefit package, the hours, and the familiar surroundings (Kalleberg and Loscocco, 1983). Younger employees are more apt to eye promotions and power-brokering opportunities. Mentors have learned "If you can't get what you want, want what you get." They can help younger workers learn tolerance and patience.

Some people are now opting to retire early, at fifty, or sixty, or whenever they have enough money to live at a level they deem comfortable. Work for them may be so boring or onerous that they give it up gladly to do what they prefer to do for the

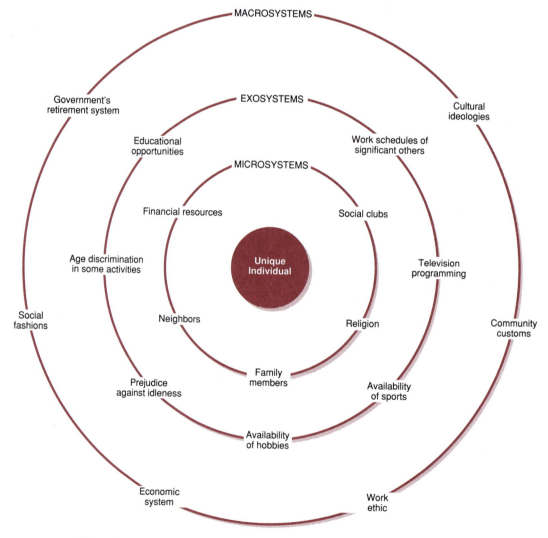

Figure 10-14

An overview of some of the macrosystem, exosystem, and microsystem influences that may impact on early retirement.

Figure 10-15
Many women embark on second careers after they have launched their children. They are freer to explore the limits of their creative talents in their fifties and sixties than when they were in their thirties.

rest of their lives. Early retirement may bring unexpected stresses in psychosocial realms. Despite sufficient finances and the approval of one's spouse, the early retiree may discover that forces from the macrosystem and exosystem exert a disapproving influence (see Figure 10-14). Our mainstream society expects male adults to work until they qualify for social security benefits at age 65. Increasingly, women are also expected to work until they are eligible for retirement benefits. **Idiosyncratic transitions** (life changes out of step with common practice) may not be socially approved (Neugarten and Neugarten, 1987). Events that are out-of-sync leave other people uncertain as to how to react and behave. Do you give a retirement party and a gold watch to a man who voluntarily quits his job at age 55? How do you adjust to his new freedoms? Many people are distressed by the ripple effects brought about by one other person's untimely role transition.

For women who have been predominantly homemakers until the launching of children, a first retirement occurs in their forties. Many women then choose to embark on a second career (see Figure 10-15). For this group, jobs are approached with expectations of upward mobility during their fifties. They do not view themselves as winding down their lives but rather as renewing themselves—starting all over again. Some go back to school before embarking on a job. Career boredom is less apt to occur in women who begin their out-of-the-home jobs later in life.

Some men may be jealous of their wives' new careers. A history professor told Neugarten (1968b): "I'm afraid I'm a bit envious of my wife. She went to work a few years ago, when our children no longer needed her attention, and a whole new world has opened to her. But myself? I just look forward to writing another volume, and then another volume. . . ." (p. 97).

Leisure and Activities

Neugarten (1974) noted an interesting facet of our changing American society: "A hundred years ago, the higher one's education and income, the more leisure one had. Now . . . the best educated and the most skilled professionals . . . put in sixty- and eighty-hour weeks. As you go down the occupational scale, people are working fewer hours. . . . It is the blue-collar worker who has gained leisure over the past 100 years" (p. 36).

The postparental phase often brings in its wake increased pocket money and greater opportunities to get up and go out for many adults. Although some couples may strike out anew and attempt to go places and do things foreign to their previous lifestyles, it is more common for leisure pursuits to follow habits of the past: watching television, eating out, socializing with friends, attending cultural or sports events, or participating in activities centered around religion, politics or extended families.

Friendships remain important sources of support for mature adults. The adage, "Old friends are the best friends," is often a good characterization of fifties and sixties friendships. Younger adults are more apt to strike up new friendships with co-workers, new neighbors, or parents of their children's friends. Mature adults have both fewer opportunities to meet new people and less desire to court new friends. They prefer to spend time with a few trusted companions (Weiss and Lowenthal, 1975). Friendships in the middle adult years are less age-segregated than they were in earlier years. Social groups are forty-, fifty- and sixty-something rather than thirty-something. Close friends are usually very similar in lifestyles and attitudes (e.g., religion, politics).

Many people in their fifties and sixties have a limited amount of actual time for pursuing enjoyable leisure activities. The professional workers may be tied up with eighty-hour work weeks. They may spend considerable amounts of their free time getting to and from work or doing work-related reading, entertaining, or preparations. Blue-collar workers, who supposedly have the most leisure time, often take on a second job to supplement the income from the first job. Most people have work to do at home (such as do-it-yourself projects, home repairs, meals, housework) that also cuts into their planning of leisure and social activities (see Figure 10-16).

Kelly (1972) proposed that people's use of their nonworking time can be classified according to whether they choose an activity for the free time or have it determined for them and whether the free-time activity is independent of their career or dependent on it. A great deal of a person's nonworking time is actually used in career-related activities. Kelly labeled the work-related activities that are freely chosen by individuals **coordinated leisure.** Examples include reading in one's professional field or improving one's technical skills at home. Work-related activities that are determined by others are called **preparation and recuperation** by Kelly. Examples may include entertaining clients or preparing teaching aids at home. Free time that is not used in career-related activities is classified by Kelly as either **complementary leisure** or **unconditional leisure.** Complementary leisure is determined directly or indirectly by others. It includes those activities that a person pursues because he or she is expected to do

Figure 10-16
Leisure time in middle adulthood is often spent in activities that are neither freely chosen nor fun.

	Determined by others	**Chosen for self**
Dependent on job	Transportation to and from work Talking to co-workers about job Socializing with boss or co-workers Entertaining clients after hours Taking work home by request	Dressing for work Improving job skills Reading in work-related areas Attending work-related seminars Voluntarily taking work home
Independent of job	Religious participation Community responsiblities Household chores Social invitations Childrearing responsibilities	Television Movies Theatre Concerts Hobbies

Figure 10-17
Leisure time may be determined by others or freely chosen, dependent on a job or independent of it. Unconditional leisure time is rare for many mature adults.

so (religious activities, voluntary services, household chores, community activities). Unconditional leisure includes the things freely chosen because one enjoys doing them (see Figure 10-17). Many people have little free time left over in their lives for unconditional leisure. When one does have this ideal leisure, he or she often chooses to do enjoyable work (hobbies, handicrafts).

Kimmel, Price, and Walker (1978) suggested that as much as a decade or two before retirement adults should develop a few interests that may deepen into satisfying leisure pursuits during retirement. Kimmel called this projecting **preretirement planning,** or anticipatory socialization. This pursuit of new enjoyable leisure activities should include making a new circle of friends to help replace those one will be leaving at the job. Kimmel and his colleagues felt preretirement planning should also include considering the source of income after retirement, maintaining health after retirement, and planning, in general, to accept the changed role that an eventual retirement will bring. The actual event of retirement with its economic and psychosocial implications will be discussed further in Chapter 11.

Summary

The fifties and early sixties can be years of peak status and power: in the family, in the community, in the world of work. Health may continue to be excellent or begin to decline. Physical strength and stamina are diminished, and signs of aging are evident, yet vast numbers of persons in this age span still feel in the prime of their lives.

The end of the female reproductive cycle is marked by menopause. Menopausal symptoms vary from woman to woman and range from negligible to psychologically and physically difficult. The end of the male reproductive cycle is gradual and less obviously concluded.

Health maintenance requires attention to diet, exercise, safety precautions, rest and relaxation, and prompt treatment of disease symptoms. Common health problems of this age are heart disease, cancer, diabetes, cirrhosis, visual disorders, and dental problems.

Family responsibilities are less problematic—children are launched and the empty nest may be very comfortable. Transitions include marital relationships, relating to adult children, and helping aging parents.

Introspection, a looking into one's own mind, feelings, and reactions, is a common tendency in the fifties. Individuals often restructure their concepts of self and time and plan for the rest of their lives. Most tend to be more self-accepting and less self-assertive than in previous decades. Whether or not basic personality changes occur (such as decreased assertiveness) is currently an area of active research with data arguing both for and against the stability of personality.

Marriages tend to become more stable and satisfying after the launching of offspring. Spouses may look to each other more for advice, approval, and companionship.

Specific circumstances and points of view may make the experiences of maintaining son- and daughter-in-law relationships problematic, gratifying, or both for persons in their fifties and sixties. Likewise, grandparenting and caring for one's own aging parents can be hard work, rewarding, or a little of each.

Women and men who have been pursuing careers for many years often find that in their fifties and early sixties they are regarded as experts by their co-workers. Many become mentors (loyal advisors and friends) to younger adults who are just starting careers.

Leisure time is divided between work- and home-related activities and is rarely unconditional. Friends remain important determinants of satisfaction with life.

Key Concepts

menopause	benign	retinal hemorrhage	fun-seeking grandparents
oophorectomy	neoplasm	periodontal disease	parent-surrogate grand-
hysterectomy	oncology	alloplastic mastery	parents
hot flash	metastasis	autoplastic mastery	reservoir-of-wisdom
estrogen replacement	carcinogen	omniplastic mastery	grandparents
therapy	oncogenes	cardinal traits	distant-figure grandpar-
second honeymoon phe-	lung cancer epidemic	central traits	ents
nomenon	colostomy	common traits	idiosyncratic transitions
climacteric	leukemia	secondary traits	coordinated leisure
cirrhosis	lymphomas	neuroticism	preparation and recuper-
cancer	diabetes	extraversion	ation
malignant	glaucoma	openness	complementary leisure
tumor	cataract	personality stability	unconditional leisure
		formal grandparents	preretirement planning

Questions for Review

1. Recent articles indicate a revitalized interest in physical activity and exercise. What do you think are some of the causes of this renewed interest?
2. Menopause is often more feared by younger women than by women experiencing it. Why do you think society has perpetrated so many myths about the horrors of menopause?
3. Individuals who have cancer often speak of rejection, avoidance by others, and inability to discuss their feelings with others. Why do you think these reactions prevail? What sorts of information would help others react more openly to the cancer patient?
4. "Happily ever after" occurred right after marriage in fairy tales. Why is it more apt to occur after the empty-nest in real life?
5. Do you believe personality changes or remains stable after midlife? If possible, use some real life examples to support your answer.
6. How do you think family and friends affect a person's use of leisure time? Should mature adults claim more unconditional leisure time for themselves?

Further Readings

Aronoff, J., Rabin, A. I., and Zucker, R. A. (eds.) 1989). *The emergence of personality.* New York: Springer.
The editors have collected the views of several eminent personality theorists to explore the basis of personality in our nature and in our nurture.

Eichorn, D. H., Clausen, J. A., Haan, N., Honzik, M. P., and Mussen, P. H. (eds.) (1981). *Present and past in middle life.* New York: Academic Press.

Presents findings of a major longitudinal study of human development from adolescence through middle adulthood.

Garner, J. D., and Mercer, S. O. (eds.) (1989). *Women as they age.* New York: Haworth Press.
Written by women about women for women. Highlights the challenge that older women present to

professionals as well as their triumphs, accomplish-ments, and contributions.

Rossi, A. S (ed.) (1985). *Gender and the life course.* New York: Aldine.

Theories of aging are not adequate without a speci-fication of gender. This volume addresses the differ-ential concerns of men and women over the life span.

Schumaker, S. A., Schron, E., and Ockene, J. K. (eds.) (1990). *Handbook of health behavior change.* New York: Springer.

Encompasses behaviors for disease prevention (such as lifestyle interventions) and disease management. Discusses issues for specific populations.

Weg, R. B. (ed.) (1983). *Sexuality in the later years: Roles and behavior.* New York: Academic Press.

Includes discussions of both physical and psychological aspects of human sexual functioning beyond repro-duction.

The Later Years 11

Consider the leadership of septuagenarian political leaders such as Ronald Reagan, Josip Tito, David Ben-Gurion, Golda Meir, Charles DeGaulle, Leonid Brezhnev, Winston Churchill, Mohandas Gandhi, or Mao Tse-tung. Consider old age in octogenarian entertainers such as Bob Hope, Claudette Colbert, Cary Grant, Sir John Gielgud, Sir Lawrence Olivier, or Henny Youngman. George Burns has starred in television specials in his nineties. Classical guitarist Andres Segovia and classical cellist Pablo Casals performed solos in their nineties. Georgia O'Keeffe and Pablo Picasso painted masterpieces in their nineties. Grandma Moses painted her landscapes until age 101 (she did not start painting until age 74). Many individuals maintain their vim, zest, vitality, and a real *joie de vivre* (keen enjoyment of the pleasures of life) well into and beyond their seventies.

Old age is a difficult topic for many to discuss. Our youth-loving culture generally fears growing old. Sometimes this fear translates into a fear of older persons. Society creates euphemisms for them: senior citizens, retirees, golden-agers, the sunshine crowd. Some older individuals are healthy, some are ill, some are crippled. Some are rich, some poor. Some are venerable and revered, some feisty, some mellow, some ageless. In every imaginable category they account for 30 million persons in the United States, about 12% of the population. Some people refer to the increased numbers of old people in the population as "the graying of America." By the year 2030, it is projected that one quarter of the population will be over age sixty-five. Half of all the people on earth who ever lived past the age of sixty-five are alive today.

Life expectancy, the average number of years that a person may be expected to live, has climbed dramatically in the past two millennia. Life expectancy in the Roman Empire averaged in the early twenties. Today it averages in the mid-seventies (see Figure 11-1). Women, on the average, live seven years longer than men. Attempts to explain this phenomenon focus on both biology and environment. Biologically, having two X chromosomes, more of the hormone estrogen, and greater immune responsivity may extend women's lives (Holden, 1987). On the environmental side, men's lives are more frequently shortened by violence as measured in homicides, suicides, and accidents. Their occupational stresses may contribute more to stress-related illnesses such as hypertension, coronary heart disease, pulmonary disease, and alcohol-induced liver cirrhosis. The differences in male–female longevity are still poorly understood. They are probably determined by a multitude of factors.

At 70, I could follow the dictates of my own heart; for what I desired no longer overstepped the boundaries of right.

—*Confucius*

When I examined myself, and my methods of thought, I came to the conclusion that the gift of fantasy has meant more to me than my talent for absorbing positive knowledge.

—*Albert Einstein*

Agnes' father was a famous playwright. Her grandfather was a famous economist. Her mother was a famous crusader for her father's tax-reform ideas and also for music, dance, and the arts. Her uncle achieved the most fame: Cecil B. de Mille revolutionized the Hollywood film industry.

Agnes met prominent stage and screen figures at family parties, prompting an early resolve to become an actress. Later, after seeing a ballet, she resolved to become a ballerina. Her parents discouraged this, and she went off to college to study writing. Agnes graduated cum laude, then went to London to do what she wanted to do: dance.

Agnes' young adult years as a dancer were not very successful. Her first secure job came not as a dancer, but as a choreographer. Her choreography got rave reviews in England. Returning to the United States, Agnes de Mille worked on her uncle's film, *Cleopatra.* She also choreographed a film version of *Romeo and Juliet.* She then found her own fame on Broadway. Agnes choreographed such blockbusters as *Rodeo, Oklahoma!, Carousel, Brigadoon, Gentlemen Prefer Blondes,* and *Paint Your Wagon.* She also achieved a measure of fame as a dancer.

Throughout her adult years, Agnes worked to create an American dance style, different from European dances. She won a Tony Award for choreographing *Kwamina,* using African dance motifs. In her sixties, she persuaded Congress to establish the National Endowment for the Arts. She also founded the Heritage Dance Theatre, to train young dancers in traditional American dance forms.

Agnes began her seventieth year bursting with energy. She planned a gala fund raiser for her beloved Heritage Dance Theatre. It would be a lecture–concert called *Conversations About the Dance.* There would be a lecture by her and performances by Heritage's finest students, doing everything from ballet to square dancing. Several thousand supporters backed her. On the night of the performance, Agnes suffered a stroke. The concert had to be canceled. As an aftermath of the stroke, Agnes was paralyzed on the right side and confined to a wheelchair.

In the next years, Agnes earned the nickname "Agnes, the Indomitable de Mille." She had surgery, physical therapy, and speech therapy. She struggled against the odds to learn to stand and walk, crediting her career as a dancer for her perseverance: "I learned patience that the ordinary nondancer never experiences."* She taught herself to write with her left hand and wrote a memoir of her childhood, *Where the Wings Grow.* It received excellent reviews.

A year after her stroke, Agnes went to Washington, D.C., to see her friend, Martha Graham, receive a Presidential Medal of Freedom. After the ceremony, she suffered a heart attack. Again, she refused to stay down. In less than three weeks, she left the hospital.

At age seventy-two, Agnes persuaded Robert Joffrey, head of the Joffrey Ballet, to help her revive *Conversations About the Dance. Conversations* was performed two years after her stroke and thirteen months after her heart attack. The City Center Opera House of New York was packed with supporters. Agnes not only choreographed the dances, she narrated the performance and gave her own lecture. Usually confined to a wheelchair, she stood, without support, for the ovation. The experience gave her "the sense of living and the rejoining of the active human race."*

Throughout her seventies and into her eighties, Agnes continued to help choreograph revivals of her works. She worked behind the scenes to support and increase funding for the arts. She also wrote the story of her later life illnesses and her recoveries in the book *Reprieve.* It is an outstanding example of courage from which others can draw inspiration.

What gives some old people the indomitable will to survive? Did the achievements of Agnes' famous family inspire her achievements into old age? Did her stage presence help give her strength to stand alone after *Conversations?*

*de Mille, A. (1981). *Reprieve.* New York: Doubleday.

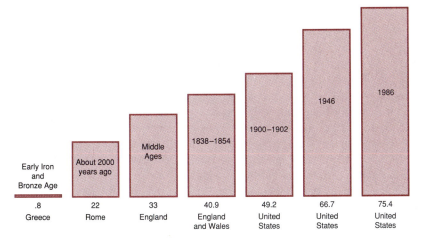

Figure 11-1
Average length of life from ancient to modern times. (Source: L. Hayflick, The aging of humans and their cultured cells, *Resident and Staff Physician,* 1984, 30(8), 37. Reprinted with permission.)

Physical Development

The physical appearance of individuals over seventy varies as much as does the appearance of individuals of earlier decades. Call forth mental images of two or more persons you know who are beyond seventy. Consider various aspects of these persons: hair color, skin tone, posture, mobility, voice, eating behavior. These persons may have few if any similarities. The physical changes that accompany aging appear at different times and in different ways in all individuals. Persons who have escaped chronic or debilitating diseases into their later years and who exercise regularly and watch their diets carefully stand a much better chance of retaining a vigorous appearance than persons who have experienced debilitating illness, chronic disease, obesity, or muscular atrophy.

Chronological age cannot be used as a predictor of physical decline. In some cultures (Hunza, Pakistan; Georgia, Russia; Vilcabamba, Ecuador) and even in some American families **longevity** (long life) is the rule, not the exception.

Benign Senescence

The term **senescence** refers to the process of growing old, with the accompanying decrease in functional abilities. The term **benign** often precedes senescence to prevent confusing the term with senility. *Benign* means manifesting kindness and gentleness, or favorable, from the old French *bene* for "well," plus the root of *genus* for "kind." Medically, benign is used to suggest mild character, as opposed to a malignant character. **Senility** refers to a degenerative condition of the brain with problems of confusion and disorientation. It does not occur in all old persons, as sensecence does.

Gerontology is the study of the normal aging process. It has grown rapidly since the mid-twentieth century. At the turn of the century, only 4% of the population lived past 65. Today, there are ten times more elderly, most living reasonably healthy, active lives. This demographic change is due, in part, to improved nutrition and health care. Gerontologists are actively searching for other explanations for increased longevity today.

There are a myriad of explanations about how benign senescence proceeds, and why it occurs. Some biologists feel that human cells have a genetically preprogrammed, fixed life span. Even if we could eliminate accidental, homicidal, and disease-related causes of death, humans might still die from normal physiological decrements in the vicinity of one hundred years of age (Hayflick, 1984).

Some biologists believe that the endocrine system, and one or more of the hormones

Figure 11-2
Regular exercise is one of the best ways to maintain cardiovascular fitness in old age.

it secretes, directs the gradual decline of a variety of human physiological functions. Research by Denckla (1975) suggested that aging occurs partially because the pituitary gland controlled by the hypothalamus of the brain stimulates the production of smaller quantities of thyroid hormones by the thyroid gland. Denckla's research suggested the possibility that the pituitary gland secretes another hormone, called DECO (decreased consumption of oxygen), that may have a blocking effect on cells, preventing them from using the thyroid hormones normally circulating in the blood.

Zatz and Goldstein (1985) suggested that hormones secreted by the thymus gland, which controls the immune system, might wane with age. The thymus gland is known to shrink to about one-tenth of its original size by old age. A slowdown in the functional abilities of the immune system to produce antibodies increases one's vulnerability to disease, and, in turn, diseases speed decrements in organ, tissue, and cellular functioning.

Some scientists believe we are aged by an increased production of, or altered sensitivity to, prostaglandins, especially of the E series (Licastro and Walford, 1986). Prostaglandins are potent biologically active compounds, derived from fatty acids, that can function as "local" hormones and change cell functioning.

Many researchers are looking at dietary elements that may speed up, or prolong, the aging process. Walford suggested that marked food restriction with some vitamin supplementation might increase the human life span (Batten, 1984). Others have suggested that only certain foods or condiments (saturated fats, refined sugars, salt) be restricted while others (green leafy vegetables, whole grains) be increased. Most agree that tobacco use and alcohol abuse shorten life expectancy. Regular exercise, on the other hand, seems to slow down the rate at which tissues become debilitated, especially those of the cardiovascular, respiratory, muscular, and psychomotor systems (Whitbourne, 1985) (see Figure 11-2).

It seems likely that many interactions between the brain, the endocrine system, the immune system, genes, environmental stresses, exercise, and diet affect the aging process. Look at some of the specific functional changes that are a part of benign senescence:

1. Heart reduces its stroke volume;
2. Lungs ventilate less efficiently;
3. Muscles receive less aerobic support;
4. Basal metabolic rate decreases;
5. Bones lose density and mass and break more easily;
6. Spinal cord compresses, causing loss of height;
7. Cartilage degenerates, causing smaller range of movement;
8. Collagen and elastin degenerate, causing skin wrinkles.

Older persons usually do most tasks slowly. James McCracken (1976) offered this remembrance of how his elderly father got out of a chair. "He'd sit in his chair just thinking about getting up. He'd run his hands up the arms of the chair a little way, brace, and push. And he'd stand up. Well, he was up. He'd stand for a moment, put his hands on the back of his hips. He'd still be bent over a little bit. But then he'd straighten up and be off about his business."

There is a relative increase in the body's fat content in the elderly. Although some old persons have problems with obesity, appetites are usually less keen. Less than half of the taste buds are still active, making all foods less interesting. The sense of smell is also diminished, which reduces the perception of taste of foods. A reduced amount of saliva and digestive juices of the stomach makes indigestion more common (Stare, 1977). Reduced absorption from the intestines, lowered esophageal and intestinal peristalsis, and decreased secretions of the intestinal mucosa add to constipation problems, as do diets low in bulk and fiber. A loss of teeth may make chewing of many foods difficult. Diets are often unbalanced for reasons of economics (lean protein foods and fresh fruits and vegetables may be expensive) and preparation procedures (cooking may be difficult due to arthritis and visual problems).

Sweat glands become less active in old age. Most older persons find it increasingly difficult to adapt to changing temperatures. They are especially sensitive to cold temperatures and may require higher room temperatures, or more clothing, than would be comfortable for a younger person. Some older persons occasionally develop **hypothermia,** a subnormal body temperature. This can be life-threatening. It is more common in persons with preexisting chronic conditions such as diabetes, cardiovascular disorders, coronary heart disease, cirrhosis, or alcoholism.

Vision deteriorates steadily beyond the sixties, and problems of cataracts, glaucoma, retinal disease, and presbyopia (change in accommodation power in the eyes) continue (see Figure 11-3). The iris constricts or dilates more slowly, affecting the rapidity with which older persons can accommodate to variations between dark and light. Vision may be adequate when the darkness or light is constant, but sudden changes to more or less light may cause temporary blindness. Night driving is more hazardous for older persons for this reason. Color perception and depth perception also become less accurate.

The muscles supporting the eardrum lose fibers, contributing to hearing losses. Hearing losses are so common among old people that persons should habitually raise their voices to all older persons. Higher tones are more difficult to hear than low ones. Many old people, either unaware of their hearing losses or hesitant to admit such a loss, may pretend to understand messages that they actually did not hear completely. Or they may try to piece together what they did hear and fill in the blanks. As a result, they may receive the wrong message and/or appear paranoid (suspicious). Noise pollution (background noises) may further distort or mask messages for hard-of-hearing persons.

A loss of vestibular function in the inner ears may give old people difficulty with balance. They may sway slightly when standing or experience dizziness when rising, when viewing heights, or when trying to climb hills. They may lose their balance and fall quite frequently.

Hair may turn white in old age due to loss of pigmentation at the roots. Pigment deposits in skin cells may produce "age spots" on the hands, face, and other body surfaces. The skin gradually loses its elasticity and may develop folds or jowls. If an old person loses weight, skin is apt to hang loosely for a long time in areas once filled by deposits of fat. Skin surfaces that are allowed to dry out may take on a withered look. Decubitus ulcers (bedsores, pressure sores) may develop in places where circulation is impaired by prolonged sitting or lying.

All of the above descriptions may make growing old seem painful or cruel. Remember that the types and degrees of change occur gradually over a long period of time and vary greatly from individual to individual. A great many older people enjoy their lives. They would argue, quite persuasively, that being sixteen or twenty-six or thirty-six is more difficult.

Figure 11-3
Most elderly persons must wear
corrective lenses to improve
their vision.

Health Maintenance

Over 75% of the elderly have at least one chronic health problem. Many of the problems that are chronic in the elderly had their origins in childhood or earlier adulthood. Most of these long-term or recurrent conditions have been discussed in preceding chapters. The most common chronic health problems of the elderly are coronary heart disease, hypertension, cancer, degenerative diseases of bones and joints, and disabilities from accidents. Whereas the number of deaths from heart disease declined in the past decade (due both to improved medical care and to greater individual concern for disease-prevention measures), the incidence of cancer, arthritis, respiratory diseases, cirrhosis, and diabetes climbed.

Many of the respiratory diseases of the elderly can be made less severe by prompt medical attention to symptoms (cough, congestion, sore throat). The immune response is much slower than it was in previous decades, and the common cold can become complicated by bronchitis or pneumonia before it runs its course. Elderly persons are especially susceptible to infections of the lower respiratory tract. Influenza, which is the fifth leading cause of death in persons over sixty-five, and pneumococcal pneumonia can be prevented by immunization. Physicians are now advised to immunize all persons age sixty-five or older with pneumococcal vaccine once (no boosters are necessary) and with influenza vaccine each year (American College of Physicians, 1985). In addition, they should receive booster doses of tetanus and diphtheria toxoids during mid-decade years (sixty-five, seventy-five, eighty-five).

Two important concerns for health maintenance in the elderly are the rising costs of health care and the decreasing numbers of physicians willing to provide such care. Young doctors today tend to continue their education in one of the specialized branches of medicine or surgery after completion of their internships. Few choose either family practice or **geriatrics** (the branch of medicine that treats old people). Geriatrics is both a difficult subspecialty and an unprofitable one. Many elderly persons are inaccurately diagnosed as having senile dementia rather than given the expensive and time-consuming tests required to evaluate their presenting symptoms. Many elderly people do not take the medicines prescribed for daily use because they cannot afford them. Many old people also neglect dental care or vision and hearing problems, because dentures, glasses, or hearing aids are too expensive.

The remainder of this section will examine problems not previously discussed: osteoporosis, osteoarthritis, the special accident hazards of the elderly, cerebrovascular accidents (strokes), and Alzheimer's disease.

Osteoporosis is characterized by a progressive reduction in the mass of bone and greater inner bone porosity (see Figure 11-4). It occurs in both men and women, although, since women have less bone mass than men in youth, their loss is more pronounced in old age and is more apt to lead to fractures, especially of the wrist, hip, or vertebrae. The shorter, thinner, and smaller the bone structure of the person, the more apt she or he is to develop osteoporosis.

Caucasians and Asians are born with less bone mass than are people of African descent, so their incidence of osteoporosis is higher. Most African-Americans have a greater blood concentration of the hormone calcitonin, which provides a relatively greater protection to their skeletons from bone loss (Avioli, 1986). Osteoporosis seems to be especially common in whites originating from northern Europe. In Britain, for example, 40% of women over age seventy have suffered vertebral fractures and another 10% have had fractures of the wrist (Gregerman and Bierman, 1981). In the United States, 25% of women over age seventy have had at least one vertebral fracture, and an estimated 200,000 break their femurs (thighbones) annually.

The demineralization that leads to osteoporosis begins early, between the ages of twenty-five and thirty. Current emphasis is on preventing osteoporosis. Little can be done to treat it once the bone has become porous and fragile. To prevent bone loss in younger adults and retard further demineralization in osteoporotic patients, calcium

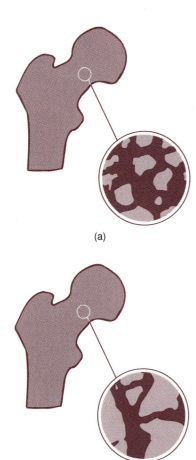

Figure 11-4
Schematic view of the inside of the femur (thigh bone) in a younger adult (a) and an older adult (b). Inner bone loss in the elderly contributes to frequent bone fractures.

(a)

(b)

supplementation is recommended. Women in their twenties, thirties, and forties should consume 1 gram of calcium every day. This is the amount found in one quart of milk. Women in their fifties, sixties, seventies, and eighties should consume at least 1.5 grams of calcium daily (Avioli, 1986). Since few women care to drink 1½ quarts of milk each day, they are advised to supplement their diets with other calcium-rich foods (hard cheese, salmon, sardines, nuts, broccoli) or to take calcium tablets. They must also be sure to take at least 400 units of vitamin D each day to help the body absorb the calcium (milk is already fortified with vitamin D).

Other factors that may play a role in bone loss are a lack of exercise, alcohol abuse, drinking carbonated beverages, heredity, cigarette smoking, and low estrogen levels. Calcium supplementation without exercise, or exercise with low calcium intake both have less effect on bone mass than calcium plus exercise (Kanders, Lindsay, and Dempster, 1984). Cigarette smoking lowers blood estrogen levels and increses bone demineralization (Jensen, Christiansen, and Rodbro, 1985). Although estrogen is greatly diminished in all postmenopausal women, the use of ERT to prevent osteoporosis is a debated issue (see Chapter 10). Many osteoporotic persons wear special corsets or back braces to help support their curving spines and prevent compound fractures. Simple, painless photon absorptiometry procedures can measure bone mass and mineral density and provide valuable information about bone loss at any time of life (see Figure 11-5).

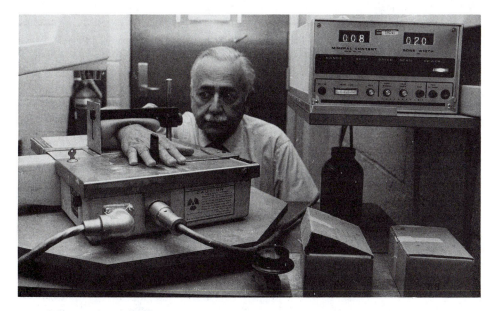

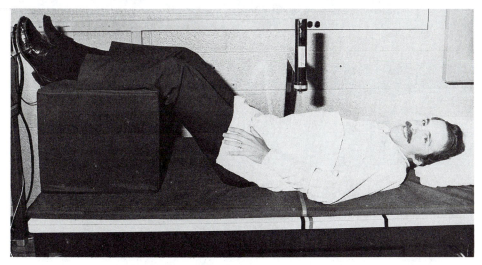

Figure 11-5
Photon absorptiometry procedures: (a) A single beam scans the forearm; (b) Dual beams scan the lower spine. Both machines measure bone mass and density.

There are over one hundred kinds of arthritis, and one in five adults are disabled by these conditions (Pardini, 1984). After age seventy, 85% of persons have some **osteoarthritis** (Mannik and Gilliland, 1980). This condition is characterized by degeneration and loss of the cartilage at the ends of the bones and by sharp "spur" formations (see Figure 11-6). Pain is confined to the joints, especially on motion and weight bearing. It affects the hips and knees, vertebrae, ankles, and fingers. Obesity, or the bearing of too much weight on weakened joints, is thought to contribute to osteoarthritis, as do the normal jolts of everyday living. Treatment is usually aimed at relieving pain and preventing further joint trauma; aspirin or nonsteroidal anti-inflammatory drugs may be prescribed (Salzman, 1983). Diet regimens for weight loss may also be prescribed, and regular range-of-motion exercises for the affected joints may be recommended. Surgical replacement of a painful, crippled joint with a prosthesis is occasionally used for persons with a great deal of pain and joint destruction.

Accidents are the fourth leading cause of death in the elderly. Motor vehicles account for about half of all accidental deaths. Several million of the drivers on our roads are elderly. Most of them drive cautiously. They fear revocation of their licenses if they are arrested. Driving for them signifies freedom, independence, and a relatively safe form of transportation. Most elderly people prefer back roads to super highways and often avoid night driving. Many are also duly cautious not to drive when tired or under the influence of alcohol. Nevertheless, the traffic accident rate per miles driven is approximately the same for old people as it is for teenagers. Whereas teenagers generally err in the direction of high speed, elderly drivers have more mishaps while failing to yield, signaling incorrectly, changing lanes, making turns, missing stop signs and stop lights, or parking.

Home accidents cause more disabilities than motor vehicles, especially in the elderly. Falls, fires, burns, poisonings, firearms, choking, suffocation, and heat stroke cause many impairments. Waxed floors, loose carpets, slippery bathtubs, high beds, misplaced furniture, and stairs cause many old people to trip and fall. Living quarters of the elderly should have elevators or well-lighted, well-railed, wide, nonslippery steps

Figure 11-6
The bones, cartilage, and synovial membranes of a normal hand (a) and an arthritic hand (b). Note the degenerative changes that contribute to osteoarthritis.

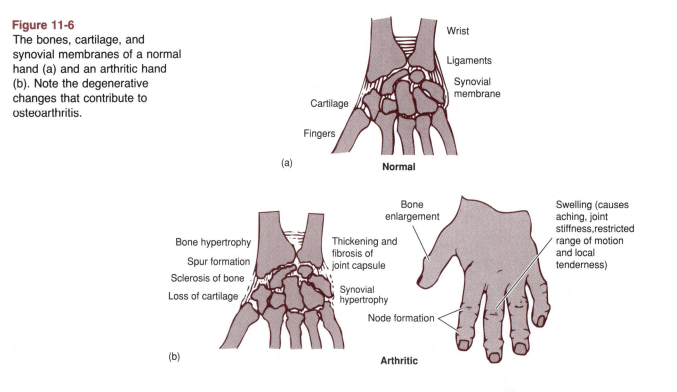

or should be on one level to help avoid some of these disasters. Many elderly accident victims must use walking aids to help them get around (see Figure 11-7).

A frequent cause of poisoning in older persons is **accidental drug overdosing.** Over 95% of the elderly population take some prescription daily medications. In addition, most older people buy over-the-counter drugs and practice self-medication for respiratory or gastrointestinal disorders or to help them sleep. Sleeping pills are more often a cause of insomnia than a cure for it (see Box 11-1). While taking both prescription and nonprescription medicines, many elderly people also drink alcoholic beverages that increase central nervous system depression. The effects of combining alcohol with tranquilizers, sleeping pills, and some allergy medications are often multiplied rather than just combined. This result is known as drug synergism (see Chapter 8). Drug synergism may result in stupor, or even coma or death.

Many pharmacists now keep computer records of the prescription drugs their customers use. They can call a physician if he or she prescribes a drug that will have a synergistic or toxic reaction with a drug prescribed by another physician. This is especially important when persons go to many different specialists (cardiologist, oncologist, ophthalmologist, gynecologist, endocrinologist) and fail to remember or fail to tell each doctor what the others have prescribed. However, a pharmacist can supply

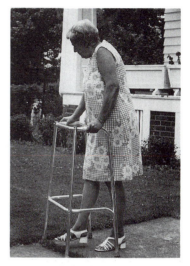

Figure 11-7
Physical disabilities are common in the elderly. Many old persons continue to get around by using walkers or canes.

BOX 11-1

Sleep Disturbances in Old Age.

Compared to younger adults, persons over age seventy need more time to fall asleep, spend much less time in deep sleep, have a reduced amount of rapid-eye-movement sleep (that in which dreams take place), and awaken more readily; they may spend up to 20% of the night in periods of wakefulness (Whitbourne, 1985). They also frequently have sleep disorders, especially sleep apnea and nocturnal myoclonus (Dement, Miles, and Bliwise, 1982).

Apnea means without breath or respiration. There are two kinds of apnea that occur during sleep. In *obstructive apnea,* the muscles that control the airway relax to the point that the airway is blocked. This usually occurs in persons born with narrow airways that become further narrowed by obesity or in those who sleep on their backs through the night. In *central sleep apnea,* which for unknown reasons becomes increasingly common in old age, the brain simply misses occasional signals to the lungs and diaphragm to breathe during sleep. Persons suffering from either form will not be aware of the apnea; even though they may stop breathing for from a few seconds to up to two minutes, on up to a few hundred occasions each night, they realize only that they have had a restless sleep, have experienced periods of wakefulness, or are fatigued throughout the day.

Any prescription for sleeping pills will aggravate both of these sleep disorders. Sleeping pills may even cause death in central sleep apnea by sedating the central nervous system to the point where it forgets for longer than a few minutes to send out signals for breathing. Both types of sleep apnea can be treated with a nasal mask for sleep, which provides positive air pressure. Obstructive sleep apnea may also be treated surgically by widening the narrow airway (Mendelson, 1984).

Nocturnal myoclonus is characterized by leg spasms, jerks, and kicking, up to a hundred times a night. As with sleep apnea, the victim is unaware of his or her behavior. The cause is unknown. The myoclonus (muscle contractions and relaxations) may awaken the sleeper, who does not know the reason for so much wakefulness. Victims of nocturnal myoclonus may complain of some tingling in their legs, or of leg pressure, while awake. Sleeping pills cannot cure nocturnal myoclonus. If given over an extended period of time, they leave the patient physically and psychologically dependent on them for sleep. They can also cause patients to be disoriented during the day, to have impaired memories, and in some cases, to have slurred speech. Regular bedtime and wake-up schedules to stabilize body rhythms, daily exercise, weight loss, and a change of sleeping position may help reduce nocturnal myoclonus. Sometimes warm milk before bed promotes a more peaceful sleep. In some cases, physicians may prescribe a mild anticonvulsive drug for nocturnal myoclonus.

Any persons, young or old, who have difficulty sleeping should be evaluated at a sleep disorder clinic for the possible physiologic causes of their insomnia. These specialized centers now exist in most of the major cities in the United States and Canada.

this invaluable service only if the person has all prescriptions filled at the same pharmacy. Persons should ask their pharmacist about the drugs they are taking. They should tell him or her about the over-the-counter preparations they use as well. While the pharmacist can be a safety officer for preventing accidental drug overdosing or drug synergism in the elderly, he or she must be given accurate and complete information and must be asked for advice. Drugstore clerks cannot substitute for pharmacists. And the pharmacist must know about all other medicines the person is taking, even those purchased from other pharmacies or grocery stores.

The term *stroke* is often used to describe a **cerebrovascular accident** (CVA), a sudden, crippling, sometimes fatal occurrence. Although young people, and even children, occasionally suffer strokes, they most typically affect older people. When a stroke occurs, the blood flow through one or more blood vessels of the brain is disrupted. If the disruption is severe and prolonged enough to deprive adjacent brain tissue of blood and oxygen, the involved tissue will cease to function and subsequently die. The death of the tissue that results from the arrest of circulation in the artery supplying the part is called an *infarct.*

The warning signals of a CVA include dizziness, unsteadiness, sudden falls, temporary dimness or loss of vision, particularly in one eye, temporary loss of speech or trouble in speaking or understanding speech, or sudden weakness or numbness of the face, arm, and leg on one side of the body (American Heart Association, 1985). Many major CVAs are preceded by **transient ischemic attacks** (TIAs) or "little strokes." Many little strokes are referred to as **multiple infarcts.** They may be a cause of dementia (see page 405).

There are several factors that may cause the disruption of blood flow in the brain. The majority of strokes, especially in the elderly, are caused by thrombosis, embolism, hemorrhage, or a ruptured aneurysm. Cerebral thrombotic strokes occur because a **thrombus** (a blood clot) forms in one of the blood vessels of the brain. Thrombotic strokes are slow to develop, over a few hours. They may be referred to as thrombosis-in-evolution or stroke-in-evolution. TIAs may precede the actual stroke (confusion, weakness, numbness, difficulty with speech, trouble understanding speech, dizziness, or diminished vision).

An **embolus** is a clot that forms in the blood vessels in one part of the body and travels to another. An embolus may be a plaque from atherosclerotic deposits in the arteries or some other foreign material such as air, fat, or tumor cells (Mohr, Fisher, and Adams, 1980). Embolic strokes are usually abrupt in onset, like a bolt out of the blue. They are often associated with a recent heart attack, a diseased or recently surgically replaced heart valve, or the abnormal heart rhythm called atrial fibrillation.

A **hemorrhage** is a flow of blood, often profuse. Hemorrhagic strokes may result when a cerebral blood vessel ruptures and bleeds into an area of the brain. Such ruptures are frequently the consequence of an **aneurysm** (an outpouching of an artery) produced in the cerebral blood vessels in severe and prolonged hypertension.

Treatment of strokes may be aimed at the primary cause, at preventing complications and recurrences, and at restoring as much function as possible. Anticoagulant drugs may be given to prevent a thrombus from enlarging and to prevent new thrombi from forming. Antihypertensive drugs may be given to control high blood pressure, which is a leading cause of hemorrhagic strokes and aneurysm formation.

Aspirin has been shown to be an effective drug for preventing the formation of emobli and thrombi (Fields, 1983). It can be used both in persons who have had TIAs and in those who have had CVAs. Only a small amount (about half of a 325 mg aspirin tablet per day) is needed to achieve an antithrombotic effect. Larger doses may cause gastrointestinal irritation.

Restoration of function after a stroke depends on the extent of the CVA and the parts of the body affected. The kinds of therapy given the patient may include physical rehabilitation therapy, speech therapy, and psychotherapy. It is important that family members be involved so that they will know what to expect, both physically and mentally, when the stroke victim returns home. The current goal is to make survivors as independent and productive as possible and to prevent additional CVAs in the future.

The term *senility* is from the Latin root *senilis,* meaning old. It is used most often to describe old persons with organic brain syndromes (damage to, or degeneration of, brain tissue). It is not, however, a true diagnosis of any specific disease condition. Unfortunately, senility is often used as a label or diagnosis for older persons who have acute, reversible problems. Medical personnel are sometimes guilty of gross neglect for diagnosing old people as being "senile" without searching for reversible disease conditions and providing them with proper and adequate medical care (see Table 11-1).

Dementia refers to a general mental deterioration usually characterized by confusion, memory loss, disorientation, and disordered thinking. If dementia occurs in older people, it is called **senile dementia.** Today researchers believe that as much as 80% of senile dementia may be due to Alzheimer's disease, another 10% to multiple infarcts,

Table 11-1   Reversible, Treatable Conditions That May Be Mistaken for Senile Dementia.

1. Nutritional disorders
    Malnutrition
    Pernicious anemia (B_{12} deficiency)
    Iron deficiency anemia
    Pellagra (niacin deficiency)
    Beriberi (thiamine deficiency)
2. Endocrine disorders
    Myxedema (hypothyroidism)
    Graves' disease (hyperthyroidism)
    Addison's disease (insufficient adrenal hormone)
    Cushing's syndrome (excessive adrenal hormone)
3. Toxicities
    Bromide intoxication
    Lead encephalopathy
    Mercury poisoning
    Manganese poisoning
    Carbon monoxide poisoning
    Overmedication
    Adverse side effects of medicine
4. Depression
5. Sensory deprivation ("cabin fever")
6. Alcohol or drug abuse
7. Head injury; concussion, contusion
8. Brain tumor
9. Other untreated or poorly controlled diseases
    Diabetes
    Chronic obstructive pulmonary disease
    Epilepsy
    Hypertension
    Atherosclerosis
    Congestive heart failure
    Angina pectoris
    Abnormal heart rhythms
    Nephrosis
10. Cerebrovascular accident
11. Transcient ischemic attacks
12. Normal-pressure hydrocephalus (obstruction to cerebrospinal fluid)
13. Subdural hematoma
14. Brain infection
15. High fever
16. Hypothermia
17. Migraine headaches
18. Anxiety disorders
19. Situational reaction (bereavement, move to new residence)

and another 10% to loss of neural tissue for other reasons (many still unknown).

Alzheimer's disease can affect adults of any age but is more common in old age. It probably affects between 5 and 10% of persons over age sixty-five. There is currently no way to diagnose absolutely the disease prior to death. On autopsy, however, the diagnosis can be confirmed by a loss of neurons in the basal forebrain and the presence of neurofibrillary tangles (Whitehouse et al., 1982).

Persons with Alzheimer's show a progressive loss of intellectual abilities and increasingly abnormal behaviors over time. They may have swings from relatively good hours to bad hours, or from good days with near normal functioning to bad days marked by memory loss and antisocial behaviors. They become increasingly neglectful of their personal hygiene. They may show marked personality changes—for example, becoming obsessed with some unusual interest or activity or becoming exceedingly aggressive or impulsive. They may have auditory or visual hallucinations. Their memory loss is often limited to recent events. It is not uncommon for a patient to have near perfect recall of some childhood event yet be unable to remember what was just seen on television. Communications often become jumbled. Emotions become labile (unstable, liable to change quickly).

BOX
11-2

The Home Caregiver of the Demented or Disabled Elderly.

Increasingly, attention is being focused on the impact on the spouse or other family members of caring for victims of stroke, Alzheimer's disease, or any of the other dementing or debilitating diseases of the elderly.

When the diagnosis of an incurable, irreversible disease with a steady downhill course is first given, most people react with disbelief and denial. However, when the patient is sent home, the caregiver gradually becomes aware that the diagnosis is real. The disease begins to permeate the caregiver's entire quality of life, for the worse. Despite love for the affected patient, resentment and hostility are typical. The caregiver often feels a lack of support from others, confusion about the disease and what to expect, a lack of information from the physician, a trapped feeling, isolation, depression, and a loss of self-identity (Barnes et al., 1981). Feelings of resentment are almost invariably followed by feelings of guilt. One of the most difficult aspects of caring for a beloved but severely disabled person is the constant view of the disintegrated condition of one who was once so healthy. The emotions of love, pity, resentment, and guilt become inextricably intertwined.

If a patient is mentally but not physically disabled (as in Alzheimer's disease), the caregiver may be both physically abused by the belligerent, irascible victim of disease and physically exhausted trying to prevent the confused, disoriented person from wandering outside the home. When the disabled patient is less mobile, the caregiver may be physically exhausted from the work of transferring him or her from bed to wheelchair, from changing wet clothing or sheets, from feedings, and from all other aspects of daily care. If the caregiver has a preexisting chronic illness (such as coronary heart dis-

ease, osteoporosis, arthritis, diabetes, hypertension), this care is especially difficult. It is not unusual for a caregiver to die before the disabled person for whom he or she has been providing care.

The financial price of caring for a disabled person, even at home, is steep. One must hire or impose on another person to watch the patient while buying medicines, groceries, and supplies or leaving the home for any reason. Alternately, one can have others do the shopping, banking, and other out-of-the-home duties. The caregiver can no longer be employed at any job other than caregiving, and the expenses must be covered by pension or social security checks. Medicaid will provide funding for home health care only for persons who qualify as indigent (very low income and few salable assets). Often long-term care of the disabled leaves little income for the unaffected spouse when the patient dies.

Some support groups now exist in which caregivers of the disabled give each other mutual emotional encouragement and practical problem-solving advice. Some telephone support lines have been established for the same purpose. However, most caregivers need the respite of an occasional outside meeting in addition to a telephone support network. In a book entitled *The 36 Hour Day,* Mace and Rabins (1984) have outlined many ways to manage more successfully the care of an elderly disabled family member. Each home caregiver needs all the support and encouragement he or she can get to manage each "36 hour" day. Changes in social and funding policies for long-term care of the disabled at home are needed to lighten caregivers' burdens in the future.

In the later stages of Alzheimer's, patients may become incontinent (lose the ability to prevent discharge of urine or feces) and incoherent and often fail to recognize even their closest friends and relatives. Even memory for the distant past fails. They may exist in a vegetative state, requiring total custodial care.

The cause of Alzheimer's disease remains elusive. There is probably a genetic predisposition to the degenerative process, although it can also strike persons with no known family involvement. Since Down syndrome individuals who live into adulthood often develop Alzheimer's disease, the defect might involve the twenty-first chromosome pair (Sinex and Myers, 1982).

The care of an Alzheimer's patient can be grueling physically, mentally, and financially on family members (see Box 11-2). Many Alzheimer's victims end their lives in nursing homes because their care becomes more than family members can handle.

Multiple infarct dementia is caused by multiple small areas of infarction after TIAs. The blood supply is blocked by clots in the blood vessels with resultant tissue death, but the damage is slow and cumulative and, therefore, not recognized as a cerebrovascular accident. The cause may not be discovered until autopsy. Persons with multiple infarct dementia have symptoms very similar to those just described for Alzheimer's patients. Caring for them is very grueling. Family members often place them in nursing homes for long-term care.

Cognitive Changes

Just as not all people become senile, not all people experience cognitive disabilities in old age. Some crystallized abilities (such as vocabulary) decline little or not at all in a majority of older people, while other abilities (such as inductive reasoning) gradually decline in a large segment of the aging population (Horn and Donaldson, 1980). Baltes and Schaie (1976) pointed out that there is a great deal of plasticity as well as vast individual differences related to adult cognitive behaviors. Current knowledge is not sufficient to make broad generalizations about cognitive abilities or about all the factors related to the stability or decline of intellectual functioning in the aged.

The idea that intellectual abilities do fall off with age has been suggested and demonstrated in numerous cross-sectional research studies. For example, using the Wechsler Adult Intelligence Scale (WAIS) to appraise the IQs of larger numbers of aging persons, Wechsler (1958), Eisdorfer (1963), and Botwinick (1970) all reported that the oldest people scored less well than the younger subjects. However, the latter two research reports expressed concern about interpreting the results as conclusive of an age-related IQ decline. In cross-sectional research the subjects cannot be matched for their initial level of intelligence, since they are tested only once. Even if chance allowed for an equal distribution of persons of initially high, average, and low IQ to be tested in each age group, other factors make the results inconclusive. Even high IQ older persons may not have had any formal schooling beyond adolescence. The availability of high school and college educations to anyone other than the privileged classes is a relatively new phenomenon. In addition, the 1930s Depression and the 1940s World War interfered with the education of many of today's old people. The WAIS questions are geared to various academic subjects. They are not particularly relevant to the concerns or types of knowledge of old people. Many elderly become bored or tired or lack the motivation to do well on the examinations. Younger adults are apt to be both better educated and more "test-wise" than their elders. (Test wisdom refers to one's knowledge of how to choose right answers on an examination. Some students may know less of the material covered in a course than others but score better on tests because of this "test wisdom.") There are also sex, culture, and language-bound factors that influence how well or how poorly one performs on standardized intelligence tests (see Chapter 6). These factors may also influence the IQ test scores of older immigrant or first-generation adults.

Some cross-sectional researchers have used nonverbal and less culture-bound tests of intelligence with old people. For example, Heron and Chown (1967) used the Raven Progressive Matrices Test, and Schaie (1958) used Thurstone's Primary Mental Abilities Test. These studies also reported results indicating that older subjects perform below the level of younger adults (see Figure 11-8).

Longitudinal studies are felt to be more accurate indicators of intellectual changes, since they test and retest the same persons over a period of years. Schaie and Strother's (1968) seven-year longitudinal study and Eisdorfer and Wilkie's (1973) ten-year study are representative of this kind of research. They found some IQ decline with age, but results were highly individualistic. Although some persons showed a decline, others demonstrated quite stable ability levels over time. The elderly may send new information into a long-term memory store more slowly than youth (Kline & Szafran, 1975), but they can still store new memories. Most old persons also take longer to retrieve information from their memory, but they can still recall it given sufficient time.

Intellectual loss in old age may reflect many interrelated physiological decrements due to disease. For example, blood vessels that are narrowed by atherosclerosis can cause diminished blood supply to the brain as well as cause coronary heart disease with its associated sequelae. Malignancies may metastasize to the brain as well as to other body parts or may interfere with circulation. Cardiovascular disease, hypertension, emphysema, acute infections, poor nutrition, lack of exercise, injuries, or surgery may all temporarily or permanently diminish, to some degree, the blood supply of oxygen to the brain. Hearing or visual losses may interfere with comprehension of incoming information. Old people process information from their senses more slowly than young people (Schaie and Parr, 1981). Horn (1982) suggested that these types of biological processes cause a slow but gradual decline in fluid intelligence throughout the adult years (see Chapter 9). Crystallized intelligence, which is more culture bound (dependent on learning and experience) may show less decline or may even increase in some persons. Although biological processes may set limits on the intellectual functioning of some elderly persons, learning, problem solving, reasoning, and judgment are still possible. The worldwide reliance on the wisdom of many persons who are well into their seventies or even eighties attests to many people's beliefs that this is so.

Physical fitness, especially cardiovascular fitness, helps maintain intellectual functioning with age (see Figure 11-9). Intellectual exercises (e.g., crossword puzzles, continuing education, writing) may also help maintain cognitive functioning. Do you think "use it or lose it" can apply to mental abilities?

Wilkie and Eisdorfer (1974), Riegel and Riegel (1972), and others have suggested that there is probably a **terminal decline** in intelligence. A signifcant drop in IQ test scores often precedes death. Researchers have repeatedly observed that old persons who score poorly have died before the next year's retest period.

Figure 11-8
The intelligence of old people may be determined with nonverbal, culture-fair tests of mental abilities.

Figure 11-9
Exercise, diet, and a healthy lifestyle can retard age changes in mental abilities as well as age changes in physical functions.

Psychosocial Development

Robert Havighurst (1972) saw the following as development tasks to be accomplished in old age:

1. adjusting to decreasing physical strength and health,
2. adjusting to retirement and reduced income,
3. adjusting to the death of a spouse,
4. establishing an explicit affiliation with one's age group,
5. adjusting and adapting social roles in a flexible way, and
6. establishing satisfactory physical living arrangements.

Each unique old person accomplishes these tasks in his or her own way. The individual differences between the aged in our society are vast. Try answering these questions about old people:

Does decreasing metabolism in old age lead to heart problems?

Will vigorous physical activity in old age cause a heart attack?

Is memory loss a normal consequence of aging?

Will retirement cause "shock" with negative sequelae?

Does crabbiness increase with age?

Are married old people sexually impotent?

Does the death of a spouse in old age lead to depression?

Do most old people end up in nursing homes to die?

Each of these questions should be answered *no.* If you believe some of the answers should be *yes,* you lack sufficient information about old age. Misinformation about age is common. Even the elderly agree with some of the negative stereotypes about old age.

Butler (1969) described a sentiment in our society similar to racism and sexism, but aimed at old persons, that he termed **ageism.** It is a process of systematic stereotyping of old people in which they are seen as old-fashioned in morality, rigid in thought and manner, sexless, and senile. Ageism allows younger adults to see the elderly as something very different from themselves and consequently permits them to stop identifying with old people. Ageism takes a cruel turn where sexuality is concerned. Old people often become the butt of sexual jokes; they are portrayed as exhibitionists, dirty old men, lusty old women, or as never-say-quit impotents who will try every quack nostrum or gadget offered them to improve libido. In fact, young adults buy more of the sexual gadgets and potions. The average age of a "dirty old man" is about twenty-seven, not seventy.

Retirement

The move from an agrarian society to a predominantly industrialized society brought in its wake the phenomenon of **retirement.** Not too long ago people worked until they became physically incapacitated or until they died. They worked less as they got older or did more advising and less manual labor, but they still felt a part of the job. When Congress established the Social Security Act in 1935, it arbitrarily set sixty-five as the age when men could first collect government retirement benefits (sixty-two for women). Many industries in turn set sixty-five as a a mandatory retirement age for men and sixty-two for women. In the late 1970s Congress banned rules setting sixty-five as mandatory retirement age for most employees at the request of senior citizens' groups. Many companies have readjusted their policies and now require retirement at age seventy. Some corporations with their own pension plans ask employees to retire earlier or allow them to work beyond age seventy. Each state has the right to set its own rules concerning mandatory retirement. Many workers in occupations where the lives of others can be affected by their efficiency (fire fighters, police, pilots) are forced to retire as early as age fifty-five. Census bureau figures show that about 86% of Americans retire or are already retired when they first become eligible for social security benefits, and about 12% continue to work past age seventy (see Figure 11-10).

There is a prevalent belief in our society that the transition from working to retirement brings in its wake a shock syndrome, a collection of symptoms such as a decline into illness, depression, loneliness, anxiety, self-doubt, feelings of uselessness, or financial worries. Consider the following vignette:

Figure 11-10
Some old people never retire, especially if they are self-employed. For them, work is a source of profit, pleasure and identity, and they choose not to give it up.

Bertram began working as a bookkeeper for a small roofing company during World War II. He was a forty-year-old immigrant with only a grade school education. He quickly learned the ins and outs of the roofing business. Bertram eventually became indispensable to the business as it expanded into other areas. When Bert turned 70, nothing was said about retirement. Bert was healthy. The boss realized that it would take two or more employees to replace him.

When Bert was 75 his boss had a serious heart attack. The boss retired and sold the business. The new owners wanted their own bookkeepers. Bert was without a job, and he had had little time to prepare himself.

Seventeen days after his last day on the job, Bertram was admitted to the hospital for emergency surgery of a strangulated hernia. His doctor suggested that the reason for the sudden change in his health was the shock of retirement.

Although it is true that the transition requires substantial changes in one's lifestyle, it is not true that shock and decline are necessary results. For some people retirement is a welcomed relief from the toils of daily labor. For others it means a change from a disliked job to a more enjoyable, self-directed form of employment. For still others it does generate feelings of uselessness and impending death. There are a great many differences in how retirees view their changed status, just as there are a wide variety of ways in which people handle every other developmental milestone throughout life.

Research suggests that the majority of retirees are happy in retirement. Less than 20% of retirees reported that it was worse than they expected and less than 10% reported being unhappy (Brody, 1985). Feelings of job deprivation and lack of a role are often related to the kind of work performed prior to retirement. Upper-status workers (executives and professionals) object more to forced retirement and often fear the consequences of being unemployed. The higher the level of occupation, the longer people want to pursue it. Their self-concept is dependent on being a success at work, and they find it difficult to relinquish such an identity (Neugarten, 1987). Once professionals are retired, however, they organize and plan for their leisure hours in such a way as to minimize some of their feelings of job deprivation. Unskilled workers may have less to lose with retirement. They had low autonomy, low pay, and often little or no satisfaction in their jobs. Interestingly enough, however, they are often less able to adapt to loss of work roles.

Many factors help retirees make better retirement adjustments. Persons who retire early tend to adjust better than employees who continue at their jobs beyond the expected age of retirement. Persons who voluntarily retire fare better than persons who are compelled to retire. Preretirement planning and a prior involvement with hobbies and leisure activities makes the transition easier, as does experience in allocating time.

Recall from Chapter 10 (p. 391) that the leisure time of an employed person is used in many job-dependent ways:

- dressing for work,
- transportation to and from work,
- talking to co-workers about the job after hours,
- talking to or entertaining clients after hours,
- socializing with one's employer or co-workers,
- taking work home,
- improving job skills,
- reading in work-related areas, and
- attending work-related seminars, meetings, etc.

Persons who can easily fill their leisure hours with activities independent of their former jobs make a more satisfactory retirement adjustment than do people who find themselves with time on their hands and nothing to do.

Cox and Bhak (1979) found that the single most critical determinant of retirement adjustment may be the attitudes of the retiree's significant others. When one's family members, close personal "confidants," and friends in social clubs or religious organizations view the retirement as a positive move, the retiree's adjustment is significantly better than it is when others feel that the end of employment is a mistake or a disaster.

What do you think a retiree would miss most about the former job: money, the work itself, the people at work, feeling useful, miscellaneous reasons, or nothing? If current retirees are like those of the past, they will miss money the most. Shanas and colleagues (1968) surveyed 700 retirees and found they missed the things listed above in the presented order.

Retirement is a financial blow for many persons. On the average, social security benefits and other pension plans total less than 50% of preretirement income. It is often easier for persons with low preretirement wages to learn to live on their social security checks than it is for persons who were once more affluent.

Many of today's retirees fought in World War II or worked in war-related industries at home. They participated in the booming postwar economy and contributed a portion of each paycheck to social security. Many believed that this government-sponsored program would enable them to retire at sixty-five and live their retirement years in a sunny southern climate. For many retirees, this bright dream has not materialized. Inflation has made the cost of retirement much steeper than anticipated. The average social security payment provides for income just slightly above the poverty level. The majority of today's retirees do not have corporate pension plans to supplement their social security payments. In general, corporate pension funds go to the people who need them the least. Few of today's retirees established their own individual retirement accounts (IRAs), even though social security was never designed to be one's only source of retirement income. Retirement may hit widows especially hard. Close to two-thirds of them have no income other than a social security check. About 70% of today's elderly poor are women.

Many retired persons who are struggling to pay their bills would rather have part-time, flexible-hours jobs with diminished physical demands than more government handouts. Both public and private sectors should make available more part-time, flexible-time jobs for older workers. Returned elderly employees are usually good employees. They have fewer accidents and less absenteeism than their younger colleagues.

Many retired persons become active as volunteers in hospitals, churches, and other community facilities. One of the more popular volunteer projects for old people today is the **Foster Grandparents Program,** in which old people become involved in teaching, supporting, and helping children with special needs (see Figure 11-11).

There is a special affinity between children and old people that serves to round out the life cycle. Each helps the other in very important ways. Eisdorfer (1975) recalls having lunch with a group of Foster Grandparents working at a home for profoundly retarded children. He found them a lively, aggressive, involved group of human beings. A child psychiatrist then told him that when the elderly first arrived for in-service training sessions, they were a pitiful, depressed group of old people. They even refused to talk. After giving love and affection to the children, however, they changed as much as, if not more than, the children. Although some volunteer projects provide a tremendous feeling of self-worth to the elderly, others are fraught with difficulties. Volunteer work does not necessarily enhance well-being. The work must be meaningful and must be rewarded with honest praise and genuine appreciation if the worker is to feel good about it.

Retirement can have either a beneficial or an adverse effect on marriages. After years of one or both partners hurrying to dress, eat breakfast, and depart for a job, the change to both persons staying home can be stupefying. Many adjustments are needed. Conversation may be difficult. Partners may get in each other's way. Disputes often arise about how to do even the most trivial of household tasks. One woman in a study by Maas and Kuypers (1974) summarized her feelings this way: "I think it's harder on a wife when her husband retires. I mean, he was around underfoot all the time—and it meant three meals a day—you know—to get and prepare and clean up

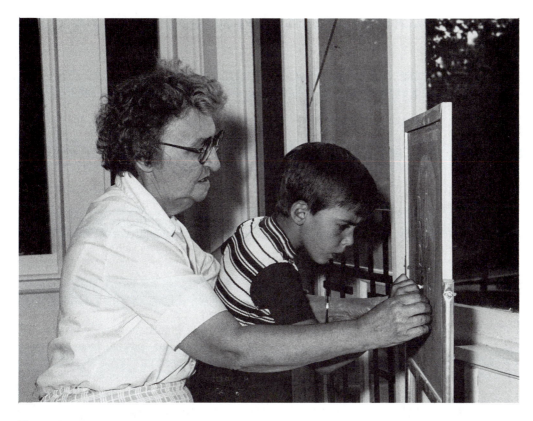

Figure 11-11
Many retirees work as foster grandparents. They are patient, persevering, and compassionate. They can often elicit more motivation to achieve than can a teacher working simultaneously with several children.

after and so on" (p. 140). Peterson and Payne (1975) found that marital satisfaction prior to retirement is the best predictor of the effects of more leisuretime on a marriage. Couples who were accustomed to sharing pleasurable leisure hours together before retirement had less trouble adjusting than couples who had a history of marital conflict.

Erikson's Ego Integrity versus Despair

Erik Erikson (1963) saw the nuclear conflict of the later adult years as that of achieving **ego integrity versus despair** (see Table 11-2). In Erikson's view, ego integrity involves an acceptance of the fact that one's life and work and leisure have been one's own responsibility. Attaining a sense of ego integrity necessitates a great deal of self-acceptance as well as acceptance of other family and community members.

Although aspects of this last stage of Erikson's "eight ages of man" theory are suggestive of the midlife transition described in Chapter 9, this final Eriksonian stage goes far beyond the self-assessment of a midlife transition. An individual in the process of achieving ego integrity looks back over his or her own life experiences. Mistakes, faults, failures, and disappointments are not denied or overlooked. Accomplishments, assets, successes, and satisfactions are appreciated. The individual comes to feel content with the outcome of his or her life. Family and community members are accepted in a new way. The individual no longer wishes that others had been different but accepts responsibility for the course of many life experiences based on the way he or she acted and reacted to the deeds of others.

The opposite of ego integrity is despair. If an individual cannot accept what his or her life has been by the later adult years, a feeling of hopelessness develops. Despair,

Table 11-2   Erikson's Eighth Nuclear Conflict: Ego Integrity Versus Despair.

Sense	Eriksonian Descriptions	Fostering Behaviors
Ego integrity	Ego's accrued assurance of its proclivity for order and meaning	Associates recognition of ego's lifestyle as meaningful
	Love of the human ego	Demonstrations of human integrity and human dignity by others
versus	Acceptance of one's life cycle as something that had to be and that permitted no substitutions	Recognition of style of integrity of culture and civilization
Despair	Fear of death	Lack of ego integration
	Nonacceptance of one's life cycle	Feedback from others that own resources have not been sufficient during life cycle

in Erikson's view, involves low self-esteem, feelings of incompetence, speculation on what one would like to change about one's past, a lack of acceptance of one's age and status and lifestyle, and a fear of death. Failures are emphasized more than accomplishments and successes. Despairing persons would like to start life again but realize that it is too late and consequently become discouraged, frustrated, and resentful rather than accepting.

Just as different people work at the eight nuclear conflicts of life at varying rates and lengths of time, different persons resolve their conflicts in contrasting ways. It is possible for a person to go through a period of despair before achieving a sense of ego integrity or to have some despair along with a sense of integrity. As Erikson (1987) said: "How could anybody have integrity and not also despair about certain things in his own life, about the human condition? Even if your own life was absolutely beautiful and wonderful, the fact that so many people were exploited or ignored must make you feel some despair" (pp. 134–135).

The prayer used by Alcoholics Anonymous sums up the feeling that old persons achieve along with ego integrity:

> God grant me the serenity to accept things I cannot change, courage to change the things I can, and wisdom to know the difference.

When a person can look back on life with the satisfaction of ego integrity, death becomes much more acceptable. The whole process of achieving ego integrity may take many years.

Personality in Old Age

Costa, McCrae, Block, and others (see Chapter 10) argued that personality remains relatively stable over the adult life span. Maas and Kuypers (1974) reported that some personality changes occurred over a forty-year time span in the 142 persons they studied longitudinally. The Maas and Kuypers data argued against the stereotype of all old people being crabby, depressed, and in poor health. Every old person is individual, even down to his or her physical manifestations of age.

Cumming and Henry (1961) theorized that **disengagement** is a natural part of aging. They believed that old people and society mutually separate from each other. Kuhlen (1964), after looking at the data on disengagement, felt that the separation is due more to the attitudes of society—old people withdraw because they feel unloved and unwanted, and they often resent being neglected. Havighurst, Neugarten, and Tobin (1968) found that in older people feelings of satisfaction with life are correlated more with participation than with disengagement. Robert Butler (1975a) stated in his

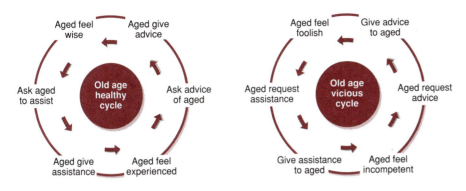

Aged feel wise — Aged give advice — Ask advice of aged — Aged feel experienced — Aged give assistance — Ask aged to assist — **Old age healthy cycle**

Aged feel foolish — Give advice to aged — Aged request advice — Aged feel incompetent — Give assistance to aged — Aged request assistance — **Old age vicious cycle**

Figure 11-12
How old people feel and what old people do are related to how younger people relate to them.

Pulitzer Prize-winning book, *Why Survive? Being Old in America,* that disengagement of all old people from society is a myth. It is merely one of many patterns of reaction to old age that may be affected by society's reactions to the aged (see Figure 11-12).

In some North American families, the old reside with the young and are an integral, honored part of the household, whether they help with the work load, add to it, or do a little of both. More often in our culture the old live apart from the young. Families differ in the ways they regard their elders: as beloved grandparents or great-grandparents; as dons or dowagers to be courted with favors in hopes of an inheritance; as burdens; as persons already three-quarters dead. Just as younger adults vary in the ways they regard their elders (sentimentally, solicitously, disdainfully, neglectfully), old persons vary in the ways in which they treat the younger generations (lovingly, angrily, disparagingly). Research has not shown that any particular racial, religious, or cultural group categorically experiences a better old age or increases the likelihood that a personality change will emerge by old age. Factors such as health, wealth, longevity, past experiences, surviving kin, and intrafamilial communication patterns make the personalities and lifestyles of old persons highly diverse (see Figure 11-13).

Charlotte Bühler (1968) reported that most of the older European people she studied in the 1920s and 1930s could be classified into one of four personality types: (1) those who were satisfied with their past lives and were content to relax; (2) those who would not sit back but felt they must strive to the end; (3) those who were dissatisfied with their past lives and sat back with an unhappy air of resignation; and (4) those who were dissatisfied with their lives and continued to experience regrets, frustrations, and feelings of guilt until the end (see Table 11-3).

Neugarten, Havighurst, and Tobin (1968) described eight personality types that fit into four similar personality patterns of older Americans: (1) **integrated personalities,** (2) **armored-defended personalities,** (3) **passive-dependent personalities,** and (4) **unintegrated personalities** (see Table 11-3). Although integrated persons all faced up to their emotions and experienced rich inner lives, their outward

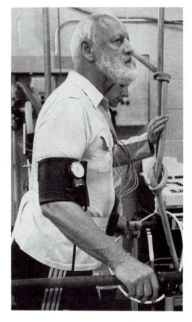

Figure 11-13
The energy, stamina, and ambition of some old people make it impossible to categorize old people by any personality traits, abilities, activities, or life styles.

Table 11-3 Comparison of Personality Orientations of Aging.

Bühler (1968)	Neugarten, Havighurst, and Tobin (1968)
1. Satisfied and content to relax	(Integrated) 1. Reorganizers 2. Focused 3. Disengaged
2. Striving to the end	(Armored-defended) 4. Hanging-on 5. Constricted
3. Dissatisfied, unhappy, resigned	(Passive-dependent) 6. Apathetic 7. Succorance-seekers
4. Dissatisfied, frustrated, guilt-ridden	8. Unintegrated

Table 11-4 Personality Patterns of the Elderly.

Label	Description
Fearful-ordering mothers	Low activity, depressed, poor self esteem, afraid, withdrawn, reassurance-seeking.
Anxious-asserting mothers	Anxious, tense, assertive, need to share, histrionic, self-dramatizing, moody, hostile.
Autonomous mothers	Good self esteem, aloof, critical, cheerful, independent, productive, self-defensive.
Person-oriented mothers	Warm, close, good interpersonal relations, sympathetic, well liked.
Person-oriented fathers	Warm, sympathetic, giving, reassurance-seeking, popular.
Active-competent fathers	Good self esteem, nonconforming, direct, power conscious, verbally fluent.
Conservative-ordering fathers	Overcontrolled, conservative, self-satisfied, repressive, conventional.

behaviors varied from those who reorganized their activities, substituting new ones for old ones, to those who focused on one or two activities, to those who disengaged and chose a rocking-chair approach to old age. Armored-defended personalities held their impulses and emotions in tight harness. They were either achievement driven and wanted to work until the end or were limited in their social interactions and energy expenditures so they could concentrate on taking care of themselves without outside assistance. Passive-dependent personalities were less satisfied with life. Although some remained apathetic, others gleaned a measure of contentment from leaning on and receiving succor from other persons. Unintegrated personalities were characterized by dissatisfactions, disorganization, and low activity levels.

Maas and Kuypers (1974) described seven personality patterns of the elderly. Four of the patterns picture women and three depict men (see Table 11-4). Person-oriented mothers were giving, sympathetic, warm, and well liked. Fearful-ordering mothers were withdrawn, reassurance-seeking, anxious individuals who found little personal meaning to their worlds. Autonomous mothers were involved more with formal organizations than with their families. They kept others at a distance and were independent, productive, and self-defensive. Anxious-assertive mothers were histrionic and self-dramatizing and were apt to be moody and hostile as well as talkative. Person-oriented men were warm, sympathetic, and giving. They sought more reassurance and were less poised than the person-oriented women but were still popular. Active-component men were power-conscious, aloof, verbally fluent, charming persons who were also rebellious and nonconforming to social expectations. Conservative-ordering men were similar to the fearful-ordering women; however, they were not as anxious and afraid. They were self-satisfied but also overcontrolled, repressive, and conventional.

While some personality changes may seem pronounced after retirement, there is probably a great deal of stability in the underlying behavior patterns of each person. These patterns influence the quality and quantity of each person's changes. Attempts to place old people into personality groupings such as those just described may successfully characterize the majority of the elderly, but there will always be unique old people. You may be able to think of at least one old person you know who does not fit comfortably into any of the descriptions just presented.

Marriage

A myth about personality in the aged attacked by Butler (1975b) but still prevalent in our society is a belief that emotions become dulled as people age. The **myth of serenity** portrays the elderly as peaceful, carefree, relaxed persons, beyond the storms

Figure 11-14
Marital satisfaction in old age tends to be higher than at any other time in the couple's lives.

and stresses of their earlier years. In fact, emotional reactions of the elderly remain powerful enough to trigger divorces, marriages, outbursts of rage, ecstatic happiness, laughter, tears, depressions, or any of the other manifestations of tumultuous emotions that affect younger adults.

Marriages tend to be happier and more companionable in older persons. The satisfaction of both marital partners tends to be greater in old age than at any other time in the marriage, including the newlywed period, although husbands are, on the average, more satisfied with marriage in old age than are wives (Rollins and Feldman, 1970). Approximately 75% of men are satisfied with marriage after the honeymoon while 90% of men are happily married in old age. Approximately 60% of women are happy in marriage after the honeymoon, while 65% of women report marital satisfaction in old age.

The second honeymoon phenomenon reported by Masters and Johnson (1966; see also Chapter 10) occurs for some people after the last child is launched. For other couples, it occurs (or a third honeymoon occurs) after retirement (Guilford, 1984). Spouses take trips, enjoy leisure time together, visit children, begin spending their retirement savings, and, in general, find a great deal of mutual satisfaction (see Figure 11-14). Satisfaction may drop somewhat later in retirement as income dwindles and/or disabling illnesses make it more difficult to enjoy recreational leisure time together.

Wives, over time, may become more assertive with or more dominant over their husbands, especially if the husband's health is failing (Troll, Miller, and Atchley, 1979). Some aging husbands and wives perceive that they have lost their power to accomplish change by giving vent to their emotions. Consequently, they may practice silence or make noncommittal comments. This reaction, however, does not indicate that they are immune to emotional reactions. Analytic remarks that attempt to clarify what the spouse is thinking, feeling, or saying, become more common in aged marriages (Zietlow and Sillars, 1988). This type of communication is healthy and can enhance marital satisfaction.

Many people believe sexual desire is dulled with age. Butler and Lewis (1982) found five components of a **myth of a sexless old age:**

1. Old people do not desire sex.
2. Old people cannot physically perform intercourse.

3. Sex is hazardous to the health of old people.
4. Old people are not sexually desirable.
5. The thought of old people having sex is perverse.

As reported in Chapter 10, however, sexual interests and performance need not cease after menopause or after a male experiences slowed erection time and diminished ejaculatory volume. When partners are interested and willing to help each other find ways to stimulate libido, sexual activity can often be maintained throughout the life span. The majority of old married people continue having sexual relations, including intercourse. Erikson (1987) proposed that sexuality in old age is a potential to be enjoyed, not an obligation. He believed many old people have a generalized sensuality. Sex is no longer for reproduction. It becomes playful, recreational, potentially child-like. It includes real intimacies and mutuality with a great deal more caressing and tender lovingness.

Not all old age marriages are happy. Some elderly persons become increasingly hostile toward each other. They separate or file for divorce. Extramarital affairs are not unknown among the elderly. Nor are late-life marriages or remarriages. About 60% of late-life remarriages are of older men to younger women. Occasionally, an older woman will marry a younger man, although many persons in this culture still frown on this breach of custom. Many older women prefer not to remarry after the death of a spouse. They are tired from their nursing/caregiving duties to their late husbands and want respite. Many cannot imagine replacing a loved and lost companion with anyone new, believing it would show disrespect. Despite some widows' hesitations, however, many older women do remarry. Butler (1975b) found that a poignant sense of tenderness—a feeling that each encounter is precious because it may be the last—often exists and characterizes the relationships between persons who have met and married late in life.

Widows and Widowers

There are many more widows than widowers in the world, due to the longer life expectancy of women. Since the custom for women to marry men older than themselves is so prevalent, many women outlive their husbands by a decade or more.

The last chapter of this book will focus on death and bereavement and examine the ways in which people handle their emotions at the time of death. The death of a beloved person, especially one with whom another has had an amiable, daily relationship over a number of years, leaves the survivor feeling lost and threatened and as if some part of the self had died. A numbness and disbelief follow immediately after death. The more difficult period of bereavement occurs a month or more after the loss (see Chapter 12).

A person's reactions to losing a spouse vary according to how companionable the marriage was, how much warning the person had of the approaching death, how independent the person is, how supportive family and friends are, and how many financial burdens are left to the widow or widower. In general, women have a less difficult time adjusting to the death of a spouse than men. A widow is more apt to have observed the reactions of other women to their husbands' deaths. She is more apt than her husband to put herself in the widow's place and imagine what life will be like without a spouse. This is referred to as rehearsal for widowhood. Men seldom do such rehearsing because it is expected that a man will predecease his wife. The transition to widowerhood is made difficult by this cultural expectation and by the fact that the widower seldom has a strong support network (Lopota, 1973). A woman usually knows other widows to whom she can talk confidentially, pouring out her grief, fears, loneliness, or bitterness. Women are more apt to have harmonious ties to many persons, both within and outside the family, from whom they can seek sympathy, nurturance, and support (see Figure 11-15).

Figure 11-15
Women tend to have more interactions with other women for purposes of consoling, sharing, and lending one's aid and assistance.

Having adequate financial resources makes adjustment to widowhood much easier. Greater difficulties arise for those who are saddled with debts from their marriage or from the funeral or who must cope with diminished income because of the spouse's death.

The widower is more apt to suffer acute loneliness after the death of his wife. Often she was his only true confidante. A man may feel that he has to be courageous and unemotional in his bereavement. He may refuse to discuss death with others, hiding his intense emotions rather than defusing them through conversation. Widowers are also apt to be less independent in terms of living alone than are widows. Only about 8% of older widowers live alone compared to about 32% of older widows. Although they may have been fiercely independent in their work-a-day worlds, many men know little about cooking, laundry, and the like.

The mortality rate for older widowed men is about 60% higher than it is for married men of the same age (Helsing and Szklo, 1981). It is not unusual for a man to die of cardiovascular disease, coronary heart disease, a cerebrovascular accident, cancer, or some other disorder within a year of his wife's death. Suicide rates are higher in widowed persons than in the married; they are especially high in older widowed men. The incidence of alcohol abuse is also high in widowers over age seventy. In addition, elderly widowers have a high rate of depression, anxiety disorders, and lowered self-esteem.

Many cities have organized self-help groups for widows and widowers to encourage them to help each other through the bereavement and readjustment process after the loss of a spouse. Although widowers may be more in need of such support groups, they are less apt to attend meetings or establish social networks with other grieving men or women. They are more apt to try to hide their emotions or to seek out a single woman for support and remarry.

Extended Family Relationships

The fact that about three-quarters of the 30 million old people in the nation today live apart from their families is not entirely a matter of ageism or the young rejecting the old. Sussman (1976) found that a majority (60%) of younger adults indicated they would be willing to let their elderly parents move in with them. Many old people prefer to live alone, maintaining their privacy and their sense of competence and self-determination for as long as possible. They do not want to impose on their children or become burdens to them. It is difficult for parents to move in and become dependent on children, a reversal from the years and years of having their children dependent on them.

A preference for self-help as long as possible generally does not mean that old

Figure 11-16
Left to right, a grandmother, great-great-grandmother, great-grandmother, great-great-great-grandmother, and mother welcome a sixth living generation to their family.

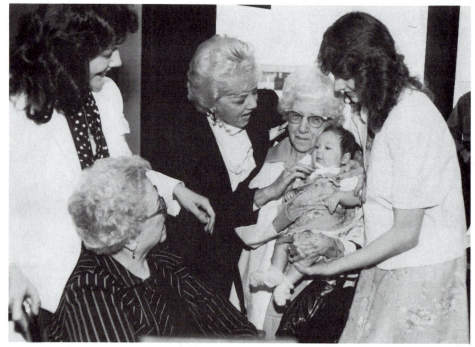

people prefer to be disengaged from their families and friends. Parents still appreciate phone calls, letters, and visits from children, grandchildren, and great-grandchildren if the reasons for the communications are friendly, not demanding or hostile.

A majority of elderly people live within a half hour's drive of at least one member of their family. Families differ greatly in the amount and quality of time spent with their old people. In general, contact with children and grandchildren is frequent and may increase as the second generation move into their teens, become young adults, and have children of their own. Close to half of the grandparents over age seventy are also great-grandparents. It is not uncommon for the elderly to enjoy great-great-grandchildren as the years pass. There have been at least eleven cases of great-great-great-grandparents reported in the past twenty years (see Figure 11-16).

Due to some physical disabilities, elderly persons frequently prefer to have family members come to visit them rather than making trips to see family. Here are three typical comments about children and grandchildren (Maas and Kuypers, 1974): (1) "The children always want me to come more than I can, . . ." (2) "I kind of wish they did live closer. . . . When you get older, you miss them," and (3) "It's a pleasure for a little while [to be with grandchildren]. I wouldn't say that I could be with them all day long" (pp. 137, 143, 146). Cicirelli (1981) pointed out that the extended family, particularly adult children, help elderly parents with physical chores (home repairs, housework, shopping). Increasingly, elderly persons help each other, revoking the need for visits from children for these reasons.

Much has been written recently about the abuse of elderly persons perpetrated by younger extended family members. The extent of **elder abuse** is unknown but is guessed to affect about 4% of the aged population. It is more apt to happen when an older person lives with a younger abusive adult. Very few cases come to the attention of appropriate authorities. This may be because the older, frailer person is intimidated by the younger, stronger family member or because the elderly person still loves the son, daughter, or other family member too much to report him or her. In some cases, the elderly person may actually be taking care of the younger abusive adult more than vice versa. The characteristics of a person who abuses an elderly family member are often similar to the characteristics of a child abuser (see page 176) or a spouse abuser (see page 350):

- history of abuse,
- powerless feeling,
- low self-esteem,
- few close friends,
- un- or under-employed,
- marital problems,
- health problems,
- belief in aggression.

Laws now exist for child and spouse abuse protection. New laws are needed to assure that neighbors, friends, medical personnel, or even other family members will report elder abuse. In addition, shelters or other alternative living facilities are needed to protect older persons while younger abusers are prosecuted.

Social Relationships

Humans are social beings. Retirement often means the loss of contact with friends at work. With each passing year older people are also apt to experience through death the loss of other relatives, friends, and acquaintances. The diminution of social contacts can mean low morale, low self-esteem, and depression for many persons. Gerontologists believe that old people who remain socially active have a higher level of satisfaction with their lives. One must remember that factors such as family relationships, health, and finances influence how much activity a given old person can have. Some elderly persons resent the fact that their health, their spouse's health, or their lack of finances prevent them from getting about and socializing more. Other elderly persons accept their limitations and their diminished social contacts and are still satisfied.

The recreational activities available to retired persons who want them and are able to enjoy them vary from community to community and from state to state. Because of the great numbers of retirees who move to warmer regions of the country, areas such as southern California, southern Arizona, and Florida have a considerable selection of recreations planned, produced, and maintained for older adults. Northern and midwestern cities and larger towns are also becoming increasingly aware of the large numbers of retired persons who compose their population and are planning, building, and supporting centers for senior citizens.

Grandparenting is identified as one of the most satisfying social relations in old age (Kennedy, 1990). As reported earlier, grandparents and grandchildren frequently have a special affinity for each other. Old people continue to eat out, attend their clubs or religious services, go shopping, dance, participate in sports, or pursue whatever interests they had in their younger years (see Figure 11-17).

At-home activities pursued by many old persons include socializing with friends, gardening or raising plants, reading, watching television, caring for a spouse or younger family member (grandchild or great-grandchild), household tasks, repairs, cooking, laundering, hobby or handicraft projects, reading, and card or game playing. Television programming is not, in general, aimed at older viewers. Many elderly persons prefer news programs to entertainments such as game shows, detective stories, or situation comedies (Kubey, 1980). Often reruns of older shows bring more enjoyment to them than do the newer programs.

Maas and Kuypers (1974) identified ten different lifestyles into which the elderly were clustered (see Table 11-5). The lifestyles into which women were clustered were (1) husband-centered wives, (2) uncentered mothers, (3) visiting mothers, (4) work-centered mothers, (5) disabled-disengaging mothers, and (6) group-centered mothers. Husband-centered women are more interested in their spouses than in their children, grandchildren, and siblings. Uncentered women are most apt to live alone, be in poor health, and have meager financial resources. Visiting women have frequent social interactions in churches, clubs, and their own or others' homes. Work-centered women

Figure 11-17
The choice of activities of old people usually reflects the activities they enjoyed when they were younger.

are more apt to be widows or divorcees, to live alone, to be in good health, and to enjoy full- or part-time jobs. Disabled-disengaging mothers are frequently in poor health but live with others from whom they withdraw. The group-centered mothers differ from the visiting mothers in that they prefer formal social functions. They are usually from well-to-do families and have high education levels.

Lifestyles of the men were seen to develop independently from those of women. A husband-centered wife is not, for example, necessarily married to a family-centered man. The four groupings into which elderly men were placed were (1) family-centered fathers, (2) hobbyists, (3) remotely sociable fathers, and (4) unwell-disengaged fathers. Family-centered men have children living nearby whom they visit often. The hobbyists live farther from their children. The core of their lives is their leisuretime interests and activities. Remotely sociable fathers are more involved in formal activities (politics, social organizations) than in interpersonal relationships. Unwell-disengaged fathers are most apt to be in poor health and have few friends.

The lifestyles of the men Maas and Kuypers studied showed more continuity over the forty-year span into old age than did the living modes of women. This may be due to the fact that women are more affected by loss of children, loss or gain of outside employment, and changing marital and family situations than men. They make more adaptations in their lifestyles to cope with these altered circumstances.

The value of this research is to show the diversity of lifestyles and social relationships of the elderly. Even these ten categories provide broad generalizations in order to fit unique individuals. Remember, old people are as different from each other as are infants, teenagers, or young adults.

Table 11-5   Lifestyles of the Later Years.

Women	Men
Husband-centered wives	Family-centered fathers
Uncentered mothers	Hobbyists
Visiting mothers	Remotely sociable fathers
Work-centered mothers	Unwell-disengaged fathers
Disabled-disengaging mothers	
Group-centered mothers	

SOURCE: Adapted from Henry S. Maas and Joseph A Kuypers, *From Thirty to Seventy* (San Francisco: Jossey-Bass, 1974).

Living Facilities

As has been mentioned, about three-quarters of the elderly live apart from their families. The large majority of them still live in homes of their own. Many live in rented facilities. Only about 5% live in hospitals or homes for the aged.

For many persons who still enjoy relatively good health, few physical disabilities, and adequate income, living at home may bring great happiness (see Figure 11-18). While many retired persons remain in the homes in which they have lived during early adult years, others opt to sell and buy something smaller, or something in a sunnier climate. They must compete for available housing with younger families.

Condominiums, cooperative homes, or small homes in specially designed retirement communities are popular places for people to move in their later years. Carp (1975) studied many old persons who moved to a community for the elderly. He reported that after one year 99% of them rated the project as a very good place to live. More importantly, after eight years 90% of them still rated the place as very good, with another 9% rating it as okay. They were able to adjust to the modern setting and make new friends in the Senior Center. He suggested that morale is generally good in planned societies where the inhabitants are of a comparable age range and activities are designed to be of interest and within the ability levels of the participants.

Increasingly, retired persons are choosing to live in mobile homes located in well-managed parks designed for the elderly. They select them for the low demands on their energy, the low maintenance costs, and the independence associated with owning one's own home rather than renting from someone else. Most older mobile home dwellers show a high level of satisfaction with their living arrangements (Mackin, 1985).

Another alternative that allows older persons to own their own home, to maintain privacy and independence, and to cut maintenance chores and upkeep costs, is an ECHO house (Hare and Haske, 1984). This is a small living unit placed in the yard of another single-family home. An older person can rent out his or her larger home and live in the ECHO. Or the elderly can choose to live in an ECHO close to, but separate from, extended family members. Some middle-aged adults build accessory apartments within their homes for their aging parents. This allows older persons to maintain some privacy and independence but may make them feel more like renters, or boarders, than homeowners.

Figure 11-18
Many old people continue to live in the homes they purchased to accommodate their children when they were young.

Figure 11-19
Many old people live in substandard homes. They are unable to pay for repairs, unable to sell, and unable to move elsewhere.

Poverty is prevalent in the aged population, especially among women. Moen (1983) reported that nearly a quarter of the elderly women she surveyed were living in poverty. Many exist in substandard, self-owned dwellings. It is difficult for them to keep up their homes. Without an adequate income, household repairs and upkeep costs can be staggering. Plumbing, electrical wiring, furnaces, pipes, and drains require attention. Termites or rodents create problems; heavy winds or rains do damage, and there are continual bills for utilities, heating, and taxes. Many women live in dwellings without flush toilets, or hot water showers or baths, with minimal heat in winter, and with general conditions of deterioration. Many of the severely impoverished elderly homeowners are trapped in their poverty. They cannot find buyers for their homes or afford to move elsewhere (see Figure 11-19).

Many of the elderly poor live in rural areas, in the mountains, or on small farms scattered across the prairies. Many old people live without any means of transportation (public or private), far from the nearest towns or sources of supplies and medical care. Some do not even have telephones. Often, mail delivery is the closest link to society.

Some elderly people rent dwellings for their later years. Satisfaction or dissatisfaction is very much dependent on what one can afford to rent and the services provided by the landlord or landlady. Although all repairs and services should be the responsibility of the owner of the rental property, rentals are often neglected. Tenants may be afraid of being evicted if they complain. Most retirees have a fixed income. Regular rent increases are a hardship to them. Some rental properties available to the elderly are in poor condition (walk-up flats, dingy rooms in hotels or boarding houses, poorly heated trailers), and they reflect the meager amount spent to maintain them.

The government has tried to alleviate some of the problems of inadequate housing for the aged by making public housing units available to them. Tenants generally are not required to pay more than 25% of their income to rent such federally supported dwellings. However, annual income eligibility requirements generally are fixed at levels that exclude both the elderly who are too poor or slightly too rich. There is a shortage of federally subsidized senior rental housing (and also of units subsidized by state or local governments). Even when the elderly meet income eligibility requirements, they may be placed on a waiting list. It may then be well over a year before a unit is available. In the meantime, they must try to find some other temporary alternative living facility. When an older person knows that a subsidized rental unit may become available on short notice, he or she tries to find a place to live with a short-term lease. Owners of rentals usually prefer long-term leases. This can prove very frustrating for seniors with limited fixed incomes.

About 30% of old persons live alone. For those who have neighbors, friends, and family around or some outside employment, the arrangement may be satisfactory. Some older persons, in fact, jealously guard their freedom to live alone. They prefer to come and go as they please.

There are many programs to help solitary old persons feel less alone. **Meals-on-Wheels** can provide one or two meals delivered to the old person in the home each day. Often the visitor bringing the food is as welcome and as beneficial as the food itself. Pets-on-Wheels can bring companionship, love, and laughter on a regular basis. Often an old person feels more inclined to give love to an animal than to a strange human visitor. The old person can choose whether to have a dog, a cat, a bird, or some other animal visitor.

Home care is a program that matches the needs of an old person with the services available in the community (DeNike, 1987). The social service agency sponsoring home care will decide if light housekeeping assistance, shopping assistance, meals-on-wheels, medical visits, companionship, or other services are needed. Such services can keep many old people out of nursing homes (see Figure 11-20).

Adult day care programs also postpone or prevent nursing home placements. With **adult day care,** the old person is taken out of his or her own home each day to a community facility for recreational activities and/or rehabilitative services. Adult day

Figure 11-20
Social service programs for the elderly in their homes can be an alternative to nursing home placements.

care has been one of the fastest growing old-age programs in the last decade. The impact of day care is often profound. Wolf-Klein and her colleagues (1988) reported the following comment from a woman with Parkinson's disease:

> I couldn't even blow my nose when I came here. Now I can write again. I can crochet again. I couldn't do it for two years. [The center] does you more good than any hospital. You move around and you do things . . . It's a whole new life opening up for me here (p. 529).

Home health care, unlike simple home care, provides nursing assistance each day to disabled or infirm old people in their own home. It is provided after recommendation by a physician, usually only if the patient can cope without more extensive medical supervision (e.g., hospital or nursing home).

When health problems become too disabling, the best solution, especially for poverty-stricken old people with no significant family, is to move into a nursing home. Three times more females than males choose this option, reflecting both the greater number of widows than widowers in the aged population and the widows' relative greater poverty.

Nursing homes are generally regarded as a last resort as a living facility for the aged. They are not, however, the place where most old people go to die. Less than 20% of the aged population ever live in a nursing home. At any given moment in time, only about 5% of the aged population reside in such facilities (see Table 11-6).

Nursing homes have pros and cons. The pros generally concern problems of family, economics, and health. About 50% of all older persons in nursing homes have a distant cousin, niece, or nephew somewhere but no relation who could reasonably be expected to take care of them. The poverty that affects the elderly also makes nursing homes desirable. Widows, in particular, often cannot financially cope with self-care. Finally, the majority of nursing home residents have several chronic health problems. These leave them in need of around-the-clock medical supervision beyond that which can be provided by family members or nurses in private homes. Thus, for many persons nursing homes or extended-care hospital settings are the best living facilities available for the later years.

Table 11-6   The Elderly in Nursing Homes.

Age	Percent in Nursing Home
65–74	1.25
75–84	5.77
85 +	21.94

SOURCE: D. S. Kolb and A. E. Balsano (1988). Balancing efficiency and effectiveness in day-care programs for the elderly. *J. Ambul. Care Manage.*, **11**, 53–62.

Nursing homes may be foul-smelling, barracks-like facilities. Problems in poor facilities include giving patients the wrong medicines, giving them overdoses of medicines, failing to report allergic responses or side effects to medicines, spoiled food, poorly balanced meals, insufficient food, food served too hot or too cold, mildew in ice machines, mildew in showers, roaches, mice or rats in rooms, and deteriorated floors, walls, or ceilings. Some nursing homes have refused to allow married couples to share the same bedroom or to have privacy together (Corbett, 1981). The poorest facilities are gradually being closed down after unannounced visits from state or local inspection teams.

Good nursing homes are very home-like. They offer privacy, dignity, an array of dietary plans, excellent medical supervision, laundry facilities, recreation, occupational therapy, physical therapy and personal, group, or pastoral counseling services.

Nursing homes are big business in North America. They receive over $30 billion annually for the care of the aged and infirm. Most homes have over one hundred beds. Many are chain-operated—run by the same owner as several other nursing homes in the region. Chains large enough to be listed on the Stock Exchange control many of the old-age homes. With such far-reaching interests, it is sometimes difficult for the administrators of the large homes to be concerned about the problems of individual patients. In the best homes the staff members show concern for each person, using respectful titles ("Mr. Hine") rather than nicknames ("Pops," "Gramps") or diagnoses ("the coronary in room 402"). However, personnel in some homes are poorly trained, disrespectful, or even cruel to the patients. In the best homes the residents are helped to get out of bed, dress, and participate in exercises and social activities. In some homes, however, the highlight of the day is television. Some patients are never dressed and taken out of bed.

Just as nursing homes differ and patients differ, so too do families who place an older and infirm relative in a nursing home. Some love the old person very much but simply cannot provide adequate care at home any longer. Others do, unfortunately, abandon the elderly relative for whom they have little compassion or tolerance. For some middle-aged children, placing a parent in a nursing home can have positive effects. Smith and Bengtson (1979) found that in about 15% of families they studied, the middle-age child found a new sense of love and affection to replace an old sense of duty and obligation to the aged parent after nursing home placement. Rather than having to cope with the strenuous physical task of caregiving, the child visited the parent to share and communicate (see Figure 11-21). In another approximate 30% of families, Smith and Bengtson found that nursing home placement of the aged and infirm parent strengthened the already existing bond of love and affection, and in about 25% of families, it kept the bond at a continued level of closeness. In the remaining 30% of families, nursing home placement continued the pattern of separateness, gave parent and child feelings of anger and guilt, respectively, or was seen as a virtual "dumping" of parent by child, where the child abdicated all his or her responsibilities to the nursing home.

If a man or woman has no living family or few friends left, he or she may find friends among the residents of the home. If a person cannot afford nursing home care, Medicaid will pay the costs. Medicaid rules vary from state to state. In some states a person must be rid of all financial assets (home, stocks and bonds, savings for a funeral) before he or she is eligible. In others they may hold on to a few possessions and valuables and still receive Medicaid. Medicaid, Medicare, veteran's benefits, and social security checks go right to the nursing home once a person resides there. However, the law provides that each resident of a nursing home should receive an allowance for his or her own personal use. While medical attention varies from home to home, nursing homes are theoretically better equipped to handle medical emergencies than most private residences could be. At present, our society is struggling to answer the question of how much and for how long Medicare or Medicaid should be provided to sustain the lives of terminally ill patients in both hospitals and nursing homes. This question has both moral and legal implications and will not be easily resolved.

Figure 11-21
High quality nursing homes can improve the relations between the patient and extended family members.

There are questions to ask and observations to make in assessing a potential nursing home for a friend or relative. Are most patients up and dressed? Do patients receive regular baths? Are their teeth well cared for? Do doctors make regular visits? Is there enough staff? Is the place clean and well maintained? Often, local social service agencies or offices for the aging can provide information about nearby facilities and answers to these questions above and beyond what one sees on a visit through a facility. Some facilities are not certified to care for patients covered by Medicaid. If it is likely that private resources will be exhausted and Medicaid payments will be needed eventually, it is important to select a facility that is certified.

Every nursing home must guarantee its residents and their families certain rights. Among these are 30 days' advance notice before a transfer or discharge, the right to receive up-to-date information on diagnosis, treatment, and prognosis, the right to refuse treatment, a written explanation of services provided, the right to privacy in medical examination and treatment, the right to privacy with visitors, the right to receive and send unopened mail and untapped telephone calls, and the right to present grievances about the facility to a state agency that protects the rights of nursing home residents.

Summary

The later years may be spent in active pursuit of goals or at a leisurely pace, by healthy individuals or by those debilitated by disease. The ecological settings of persons over seventy are as varied as those of other humans at any time in the life span.

Benign senescence, the process of growing old, is marked by body changes in structure and function. The changes are gradual and often begin quite early in adulthood.

Health in old age can be maintained best when the old person attends to diet, exercise, rest, stress management, safe living, and prompt treatment of symptoms of illness. The most common chronic health problems in old age include degenerative diseases of bones and joints and coronary heart disease. While cerebrovascular accidents (strokes), transient ischemic attacks (TIAs), Alzheimer's disease, or unknown factors may cause senile dementia in some old people, "senility" is not synonymous with old age. Strokes and TIAs are not always associated with senile dementia. Alzheimer's disease is.

Research has not sufficiently demonstrated that cognitive disabilities occur in all older persons. Many persons demonstrate stable cognitive abilities until very late in life.

Mandatory retirement at age seventy can be a blow to the finances, social life, and self-esteem of men and women after years of steady, paid employment outside the home. Conversely, it may be welcomed. Some workers opt to retire even before age seventy. Many retired persons become active as volunteers in hospitals, churches, and community projects. Many also pursue leisure activities planned for older adults in their communities.

Erik Erikson saw the conflicts associated with old age as leading either to a state of ego integrity or one of despair. When elderly adults can acknowledge that their work and leisure are their own responsibility and accept the accomplishments, failures, satisfactions, and disappointments of their lives, they move toward ego integrity. Despair results if they overemphasize their failures, blame others for them, and refuse to accept their life patterns.

Personality remains relatively stable in the later years. Most old people continue to behave in patterns similar to those they established early in life. Retirement adjustment, marital adjustment, bereavement reactions, living facilities, and many other phenomena are handled differently by each unique old person. Personalities may range from integrated to armored-defended, to passive-dependent, to unintegrated, with many variations of personalities in each category.

Marriages in old age, like marriages in younger adult years, range from very happy to very unhappy. Divorces and remarriages are not foreign to the aged population.

Life expectancy for women exceeds that of men by about seven years, making many more widows than widowers in our country. Many more widowers than widows remarry. Becoming single after years of marriage alters one's lifestyle in many ways, most of which require difficult readjustments.

About three-quarters of the nation's older people live apart from their children, but a majority live close enough to visit or be visited by one or more children or grandchildren at frequent intervals. Most older persons maintain their own homes or apartments for as long as possible. Only a small minority live in hospitals or homes for the aged.

Lifestyles may range from spouse-centered to family-centered, visiting-centered, work-centered, group-centered, uncentered, hobby-centered, remotely sociable, disabled, unwell, and disengaged.

Key Concepts

life expectancy
longevity
senescence
benign senescence
senility
gerontology
hypothermia
geriatrics
osteoporosis
osteoarthritis

accidental drug overdosing
cerebrovascular accident
transient ischemic attacks
multiple infarcts
thrombus
embolus
hemorrhage
aneurysm
senile dementia
Alzheimer's disease

terminal decline
ageism
retirement
Foster Grandparents
   Program
ego integrity versus despair
disengagement
integrated personalities
armored-defended personalities

passive-dependent personalities
unintegrated personalities
myth of serenity
myth of a sexless old age
elder abuse
meals-on-wheels
adult day care
nursing homes

Questions for Review

1. Describe the various physical changes that occur during benign senescence.
2. Your neighbor's father has been diagnosed as probably having Alzheimer's disease. She asks you what to expect. What will your answer be?
3. Mandatory retirement has recently come under attack. Do you believe people should be forced to retire at a specific age?
4. Describe some examples of ageism that exist in the mass media—newspapers, magazines, and television.
5. Why do you think it is true that widowers tend to remarry at a much greater rate than widows?
6. Would you feel guilty about putting one of your parents in a nursing home? Explain your answer.

Further Readings

Bengtson, V. L., and Schaie, K. W. (eds.) (1989). *The course of later life: Research and reflection.* New York: Springer.

Contributions from renowned gerontologists cover topics such as neurobiology and social processes. Analysis is integrated with data to provide models for behavioral aging.

Ferraro, K. F. (ed.) (1990). *Gerontology: Perspective and issues.* New York: Springer.

An introduction to the major themes of the study of the aging process and all of the contemporary controversial issues.

Kaplan, L. (1987). *Retiring right: Planning for your successful retirement.* New York: Avery.

A discussion of the areas in which people need to make changes in order to adapt to and enjoy retirement.

Kingson, E. R., Hirshorn, B. A., and Cornman, J. M. (1986). *Ties that bind: The interdependence of generations.* Cabin John, MD: Seven Locks Press.

A persuasive argument for generational interdependency. Presents the challenge of embracing an aging society with family caregiving, social security, research, and public policies.

Tobin, S. S. (1991). *Personhood in advanced old age.* New York: Springer.

Case studies illustrate how the elderly cope with stress; includes advice on how to incorporate knowledge about aged mental processes into practice working with the elderly and their families.

World Health Organization (1989). *Health of the elderly,* Technical Report No. 779. Geneva.

A review of recent advances in knowledge about the biology of aging and special health needs of the elderly.

Death and Bereavement 12

Thanatology, the study of death, is growing as a field of scientific inquiry. Mortality and immortality have always been concerns of theologians and philosophers. Meanwhile, most humans remain afraid of death. According to Shakespeare, Julius Caesar reasoned thus with his wife:

> Cowards die many times before their deaths;
> The valiant never taste of death but once.
> Of all the wonders that I yet have heard,
> It seems to me most strange that men should fear;
> Seeing that death, a necessary end,
> Will come when it will come.

Freud (1966) felt that fear of death is related to a destructive or death instinct (Thanatos), which has parity with a self-preservation instinct (Eros). Humans hate to die, they see no reason for it, and it becomes their agony (Burton, 1974).

Today social scientists probing death and dying are attempting to break down the taboos against discussing the end of life. By discussing death they hope to help us all learn to live more comfortably with a knowledge of our finite state.

Let no man fear to die; we love to sleep all
And death is but the sounder sleep.

—*Francis Beaumont*

I have lost friends, some by death . . . others by sheer inability to cross the street.

—*Virginia Woolf*

Perspectives on Death

The emotions a loved one's death evokes are disquieting: fear, anger, anxiety, jealousy, recriminations, weeping, and anguish. And yet, Kübler-Ross (1969) tells us that a proximity to death can be an enriching, growth-promoting experience. If a dying person can honestly express a host of negative and confusing feelings, he or she can move to a final stage of peaceful acceptance of death. If a mourner can express a host of chaotic, anguished feelings, he or she can move to a stage of rebuilding a rewarding life. And if doctors, nurses, social workers, and religious and other counselors can learn to accept their own fears and concerns about death, they can be enormously helpful to dying patients. They can help terminally ill persons grow and find harmony. In addition, they can be inspired rather than depressed by such experiences.

In this chapter death will be examined first from the point of view of the dying individual: child, young adult, and older adult. Then the ways in which death affects bereaved persons will be discussed. Finally, death will be viewed as a catalyst to enjoying life more fully. The text will end by exploring some perspectives on living.

Johnny Gunther was an only child. He was born in Paris to wealthy parents. He lived in Austria for six years, where he frolicked in the Alps and started school. He spent a year in England and moved to the U.S. at age eight. His parents divorced but Johnny continued to see them both. He was sent to boarding schools and summer camps. He went to New York City for school holidays with his father and spent some of his summer with his mother in Connecticut. He enjoyed sailing and swimming, music and math, chess and chemistry. A school official told his parents he was the brightest child the school had ever had.

A brain tumor was discovered when Johnny was fifteen. He had had a stiff neck, and his boarding school roommate feared he might have polio. Johnny had surgery soon after the diagnosis. The best brain surgeons spent six hours removing half of the tumor. The rest had spread like a spider web deep into the crevasses of his brain, where it couldn't be removed. In fifteen months, Johnny had two brain operations, chemotherapy, radiation therapy, and diet therapy. These procedures allowed him to live with normal thinking abilities and a degree of dignity. He died when he was seventeen.

Johnny's story, as told in *Death Be Not Proud,* is not a story of death, but a story of courage: how patient, father, and mother dealt with dying.

When Johnny heard the truth of his fatal tumor, he first asked the doctor to help protect his parents from the news. He then set about experiencing all the wonderful miraculous things to see, hear, taste, smell, and enjoy doing until death. He especially loved physics. Twelve days after his first surgery, he wrote a letter to Albert Einstein. He asked Einstein's opinion about an idea he had about gravitation. Einstein answered "I hope to see you when you have recovered so that we may have a conversation."* Johnny had tutors teach him his senior year subjects. He did homework between therapies. He took and passed all his examinations. He also applied to, and was accepted by, Harvard. A fortnight before his death, he slowly, very slowly, trod up the aisle of his prep school to receive his diploma. "The applause began and then rose, and the applause became a storm . . . when Johnny finally reached the pulpit."* With a sublime strength of will, he triumphed.

Johnny's father knew within five minutes of hearing about the brain tumor that his only son would die. He visited him often and let him read drafts of his writings (he was a war correspondent and an author). He put together the memoir of his son that became *Death Be Not Proud.* The heartbreak he suffered is evident in the lovingly written pages.

Johnny's mother continued the experiment she had been conducting since his birth. She wanted to make him "an aware person, without fear, and with love."* She read him the Bible, Buddha, Confucius, Mahomet, Spinoza, Einstein, Plato, and St. Exupéry. She prayed continually and felt God's presence but felt that God, in all His omnipotence, was helpless too.

After Johnny died, his mother wrote, "One feels that it is not right to live when one's child has died."* She wished she had loved Johnny more, although she didn't know how she could have. She wished she hadn't divorced his father, hadn't sent him to boarding school. She wanted to cry out to parents who showed vexation toward children, "They are alive, think of the wonder of that!"* She struggled with her philosophy of life and death, things physical and things spiritual.

In the fifteen months that Johnny was dying, he lived each day with *élan.* Why? Johnny's parents pretended with him that he would recover. Was this wise? The Gunthers did not fight death. Should one look death in the face and not be afraid?

*Gunther, J. (1949). *Death Be Not Proud.* New York: Harper & Row.

Approaches of Children to Death

Children are minimally aware of death when very young. In fact, the finality of death may not be fully realized until children approach the end of their elementary school years. Each child's understanding is very much dependent on his or her own experiences with death, teachings about death, and cognitive maturity.

Preschool children view death as changed circumstances. They believe that powerful adults should be able to make things that have disappeared reappear. They do not recognize death as a final process. Rather, they seem to believe that the deceased will someday return or come to life again at the will of a parent, or perhaps, God. For many preschool children death is experienced first through the loss of a pet. The fact that pets are often rather quickly replaced with new pets may help perpetuate a young child's belief that death is temporary or causes only a slight change in ongoing situations. Children also have ample opportunities to witness reincarnations of heroes, heroines, villains, cartoon characters, and the like on television programs. It is difficult for preoperational children to separate fantasy from reality (see Figure 12-1).

School-age children develop a greater understanding of death with each passing year, with each new experience of learning about death of another animal or person, and with each new lesson about death taught to them by caregivers, teachers, religious leaders, or friends. Lansdown and Benjamin (1985) found that approximately 60% of the children they studied had a fairly well developed notion of the reality and finality of death by age five, and all of them understood it by age nine. Between the ages of five and nine, many children still believe that death does not have to be permanent. They believe that a dead person may come back to life for a while to finish some tasks or see loved ones. A school-age child whose grandfather and mother had both died within a few months of each other wrote a letter to God asking to have his mother returned. He explained, "You have my Grandpa and all the angels to make you laugh. I need my mother."

Very often school-age children engage in the **personification of death**. They see it as some invisible force that carries people off. The personification of death is often individualistic and ranges from night, to invisible animal, to monster, to some deceased person, to skeleton, to angel of death, to God. Another school-age child exemplified the personification of death as God. "You know, God is going to come down from Heaven and take me back with Him" (Morrissey, 1965). Death is generally believed to occur at night, in the dark, when nobody can see. Many nightmares and night terrors of children may stem from their anxieties about the link between death and night. Many bedtime prayers reinforce this link: for example, "If I die before I wake, I pray Thee Lord my soul to take." Adults often refer to death as eternal rest or eternal sleep. In fact, more deaths occur while people are pursuing waking activities than while they sleep, most often in the hours between six in the evening and midnight (Lamberg, 1984). It is important for adults to avoid equating death with sleep while talking with children, lest they become anxious about taking naps or falling asleep at night.

Some children equate death with risk taking or with traveling far from home and caregivers. The media coverage of distant wars, coups, police actions, assassinations, or violence in general and reports of other distant disasters with many fatalities, such as volcanic eruptions, earthquakes, tornadoes, hurricanes, and airplane crashes, make many children fearful of the safety of leaving home. After the 1986 tragedy of the space shuttle *Challenger,* many children felt that Christa McAuliffe would not have died if she had only stayed home (Lipsitt, 1986).

With increasing cognitive maturity, adolescents begin to work on personal philosophies of both life and death. They often take an intense interest in the concepts of death and afterlife offered by their own and other people's religions. The age at which a child is allowed to attend a funeral varies from family to family, and from situation to situation, but most adolescents are considered old enough to attend a funeral if they

Figure 12-1
Cartoon characters are regularly killed and reincarnated. This gives children an unrealistic view of death.

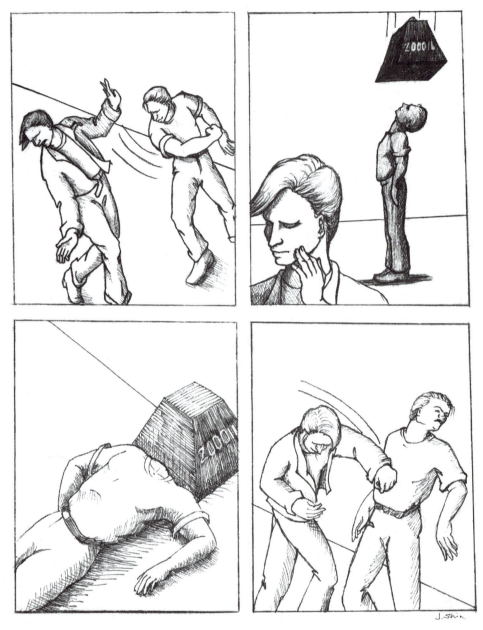

so desire. They may be profoundly affected by the experience. Elkind (1981) described a **personal fable** that develops in most adolescents. This is a belief in one's own immortality and invulnerability. Adolescents may view a casket, or the deceased's body, and decide that death happens only to others. Freud (1966), as well as Elkind, noted adolescents' increased risk taking as evidence of the great distance they feel from death. Freud believed that id impulses of the Thanatos (death force) type are discharged against others (aggression) or against the self (risk taking) in increased intensity during the adolescent years. While some adolescents may believe in their own immortality, others may develop a serious intention to experience death, as evidenced by the high attempted and completed suicide rates among teenagers (see Figure 12-2).

When preschool children are hospitalized with terminal illnesses, their reactions of fright are more related to fear of separation and pain than to any awareness or fear of death. Preschoolers are still very much dependent on their caregivers for physical help with their activities and for emotional support and nurturance. When caregivers are replaced by doctors or nurses, as often occurs in hospital settings, the preschooler

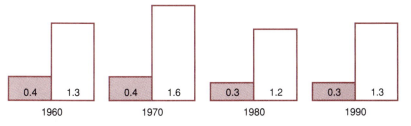

Figure 12-2
U.S. deaths per 1000, comparing deaths between the ages of five and fourteen (shaded) to deaths between the ages of fifteen and twenty-four. (Source: National Center for Health Statistics.)

may become anxious. Not only are caregivers absent, but all of the other familiar sights and sounds (home, siblings, pets, friends) that add to a feeling of security are lost. The terminal illness itself is seldom a threat beyond the fact that the child may experience pain and discomfort from it.

School-age children who are hospitalized with terminal illnesses often have more anxiety about medical procedures (such as intravenous feedings, blood transfusions, x-rays, bone marrow aspirations, blood tests, or injections) than about approaching death.

If a school-age child still views death as a temporary phenomenon, he or she will have hopes of everything eventually returning to normal, despite death. In some children, especially younger ones, parents and medical personnel may have tried to shield the patient from knowledge of the seriousness of the illness. Even when a prognosis has not been given, the child often perceives the seriousness of the situation. The grief of the parents becomes obvious to the child. Eventually the child may ask "Am I going to die?"

Opinions differ as to how best to answer children's questions about their own deaths. Marlow (1973) stated her belief that honesty is best. For example, an answer may be worded carefully: "Yes, but we are not certain when this will be." Many professionals feel that a physician or nurse should not answer without the parents' permission, since they may prefer to do it themselves or with the help of a religious counselor. If parents or professionals hedge on such questions, the child may become extremely anxious. The fear of death is worse when one cannot discuss it. It is especially traumatic for a child to be left alone when family members are feeling that death is too terrible to mention. Many children want the reassurance that someone will be with them when they die, and that death will not be too painful.

Binger, Mikkelsen, and Waechter (1970) believed that in some cases children may realize that they are dying and try to shield their parents from the fact. This lack of open, honest communication can prevent acceptance of death and the growth that accompanies acceptance in both the dying child and the parents. The dying child is still alive. He or she needs comforting, loving, and help to overcome some of the overwhelming terrors being experienced. If parents and professionals listen, children will usually give an indication of how much they know or suspect and what particular concerns they wish to discuss. Morrissey (1965) found that once a child is aware of impending death, one of three patterns of reaction may occur:

1. anxiety expressed symbolically and physiologically,
2. anger with acting-out behaviors, or
3. depression with withdrawal.

The reactions may be sequential or may even occur almost simultaneously. There is a danger that the dying child who misbehaves and makes demands on the parents may be overindulged. Such overindulgence can be more upsetting than helpful. Children feel more secure when they know their limits. When limits are stripped away, the child may make preposterous requests to test the parents. Parents will invariably come to resent this. The dying child usually senses this resentment and may accuse them of not being loving any longer. If demands are then met to prove love, a vicious cycle is begun (see Figure 12-3). The child will make more and more requests. The parents will become more and more frustrated and resentful. The child will sense the hostility,

Figure 12-3
Parents and their terminally ill child may experience either a helpful communication cycle or a vicious one.

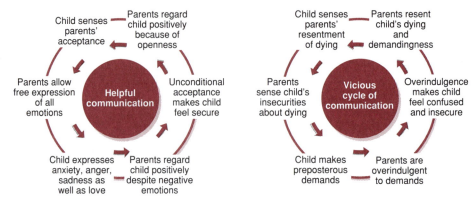

and, ultimately, the child may die feeling unloved or rejected. The parents may feel relieved of their demanding child as well as grieved. The guilt feelings for feeling relieved can be enormous (Marlow, 1973).

Approaches of Adults to Death

Keller, Sherry, and Piotrowski (1984) studied adults' evaluation of death in general, beliefs in the hereafter, and death anxiety related to the self in six age groups from young adulthood through old age. Many middle-age and late middle-age persons show less anxiety about death than younger and older adults. Becker (1973) suggested that such persons may deny the threat of death by sublimating themselves in activities related to family, career, and achievements. Younger and older adults show more anxiety about death in general, but older adults show less anxiety about their own death. Older adults evidence more beliefs in a hereafter than younger adults, and women have more beliefs in an afterlife than do men at all ages.

Adults with fatal illnesses usually know or guess their prognosis quite soon after physicians and family members learn the facts of the disease. The physician is responsible for imparting the information to the patient, although this is often fraught with difficulties. Many adults resist having the prognosis spoken aloud. They may not be ready to deal with this information about their own death. In addition, many physicians, nurses, aides, orderlies, clerks, and volunteers avoid talking to dying patients, especially about death. If they do so, they soften the blow with euphemisms such as hyperplastic tissue, lesion, or neoplastic proliferation (for cancer) or cerebral ischemia (for strokes). Most doctors admit that they learned not to inform patients through experience, not in school. Kastenbaum and Aisenberg (1972) questioned 200 nurses and attendants about how they responded to patients' talk about death. Five patterns emerged:

1. Reassurance: "You're doing so well now. You don't have to feel this way."
2. Denial: "You don't really mean that . . . you're not going to die. Oh, you're going to live to be a hundred."
3. Changing the subject: "Let's think of something more cheerful. You shouldn't say things like that; there are better things to talk about."
4. Fatalism: "We are all going to die sometime, and it's a good thing we don't know when. When God wants you, He will take you."
5. Discussion: "What makes you feel that way today? Is it something that happened, something somebody said?"

Discussion is most helpful to the patient, but changing the subject and avoiding any discussion of death is most common. Such neglect, denial, fatalism, or "turning off" the patient makes it especially difficult for an adult to approach the fact that he or she has but a short time left to live.

Elisabeth Kübler-Ross (1969) identified five stages through which persons pass when they realize death is imminent. (Teenagers and cognitively mature children may also progress through the same stages in trying to accept their deaths.) The **Kübler-Ross stages of dying** are

1. denial,
2. anger,
3. bargaining,
4. depression,
5. acceptance.

Some persons may move back and forth across these stages or experience two of them simultaneously. On occasion they occur out of the sequence presented. Some persons may never reach the acceptance stage. It is important to remember that Kübler-Ross's research was conducted with patients who knew that they were dying.

Kübler-Ross, a Swiss physician and psychiatrist who immigrated to the United States in 1958, spent many years working with dying patients at the University of Chicago. She voluntarily spent many hours with each person, rather than providing the more typical brief physician-to-patient visit. She listened and gave each dying person her own unconditional love and acceptance. The same stages may not be descriptive of persons who have not been told, or have not learned or even guessed, the terminal nature of their illness. These stages may also not be descriptive of patients who, because of extreme pain, are kept in a heavily drugged state of impaired consciousness.

In the first stage, that of **denial**, the patient may vigorously oppose the notion that the end is near. As Thomas Bell (1961) wrote:

> This can't be happening to me. Not to me. Me with a malignant tumor? Me with only a few months to live? Nonsense. . . . Such things happen, should happen, only to other people. . . . People who are strangers . . . born solely to fill such quotas.

The patient may hop from doctor to doctor, or from clinic to health spa to faith healer to miracle worker seeking a different diagnosis or a cure for the illness. He or she may become isolated, insulated from friends or acquaintances who know the truth. A reaction of shock, in which the person seems dazed, temporarily helpless, and confused, may ensue. Eventually, when the patient can no longer say, "This can't be happening to me," he or she will move to the second stage, that of anger. The question becomes, "Why me?"

At the **anger** stage the patient may strike out especially hard at loved ones. The terminal illness may be blamed on the spouse, parents, siblings, children, best friend, doctor, employer, or God. Frequently, a vehement jealousy arises against people in good health. It is not unusual at this time for the patient to behave in agonized ways: cursing, accusing, condemning, screaming, being aggressive, being destructive, demonstrating hate and bitterness. The venting of such strong emotions may help a patient pass through this stage more readily than trying to choke back the mental and physical anguish being experienced.

The next stage, that of **bargaining**, usually begins when the anger is somewhat dissipated. The patient may agree to alter his or her behavior, become devoted to a religion, give away goods, buy some special treatments, or purchase wares for doctors or persons responsible for his or her health; in short, he or she may attempt to strike almost any kind of bargain in exchange for a longer life. Bargaining with God through prayers or exchanges with a religious representative are common. Variations of the Faust legend, in which people try to sell their souls to the devil to prolong their lives, have also been written, based on the tumultuous experiences of this stage (see Figure 12-4).

Eventually, when the patient gives up hope that bargaining will effect a cure, he or she usually becomes **depressed**. The patient may refuse visitors, show little interest in external events, be silent even with loved family members and friends, and simply cry softly or stare into space. It is as if the patient is preparing for the time when he

Figure 12-4
According to legend, a 15th century German named Faust made a pact with the devil: his soul in exchange for years of magical powers and pleasures on earth. He repented his bargain as he was finally carried off to hell.

or she will no longer be able to see or hear others. This mourning need not be the final stage before death.

Kübler-Ross identified a fifth stage that many persons reach: **acceptance**. The patient leaves depression behind and goes about saying and doing all the unfinished business of his or her life. Rather than acting defeated or bitter, the patient seems to accept impending death with a peaceful, quiet sense of expectation. Often the acceptance is expressed by a desire to have just one or two close friends near, to hold hands, to listen to reading or quiet music, or simply to share silence. The patient seems to have reached the ego integrity described by Erikson (1963): "acceptance of one's one and only life cycle as something that had to be and . . . permitted of no substitutions." The fear of death is removed. Consider the acceptance of death in the following vignette:

> Margaret's diagnosis was an acute leukemia, a rare type for which there is no effective therapy. Her physician wanted to transfer her to a major research facility in a distant city for experimental chemotherapy. The drugs could possibly extend her life for a few additional months. Margaret said no. She preferred to stay close to her husband, home, and friends.
>
> An adult daughter arrived from out of town to spend time with Margaret in the hospital. Margaret did not want to be in the hospital. After a week, she persuaded her physician to discontinue the blood transfusions and let her go home to be cared for by her daughter.
>
> Although she was very weak, Margaret had her daughter help her prepare to die. They made phone calls and wrote good-bye letters to her friends. They went through closets and drawers and she asked that her daughter give certain things away to special people or organizations. When relatives and friends visited her, she spoke reassuringly. She was not afraid to die. She viewed death only as a transition.
>
> She often lay with her head in her daughter's lap while her daughter read to her. They held hands as much as possible. She liked physical contact.
>
> Margaret died in her daughter's arms two weeks after her discharge from the hospital.
>
> Margaret probably could have lived a little longer if she had agreed to a transfer to a cancer center for chemotherapy, or even if she had remained in her local hospital for blood transfusions. Should her family have allowed her to make the choices she made?

Kübler-Ross (1975) not only described the stages through which dying persons pass but also identified what others can do to be of most help to terminally ill patients. She taught many physicians, nurses, social workers, religious counselors, and others at seminars around the world to overcome their own anxieties about death. In doing so, they became better able to communicate with dying persons. In *Death: The Final Stage of Growth* (1975) she presented five rules from a seminar:

1. . . . I must try to be myself. If the dying patient repulses me, for whatever reason, I must face up to that repulsion. I also must let the other person be himself. . . .
2. . . . when we talk to each other about ourselves, we will find something in common.
3. . . . let the patient "tell him" (the counselor) how he feels . . . "let the patient be." This simple rule does not imply granting all of the patient's demands and jumping whenever the patient wants the counselor to jump. . . . The belief that "I know what's best for the patient" is not true. The patient knows best.
4. I must continually ask myself "What kind of a promise am I making to this patient and to myself?" . . . [Is it to] save this person's life or to make him happy in an unendurable situation(?) . . . stop trying to attempt both. If I can learn to understand my own feelings of frustration, rage, and disappointment, then I believe I have the capacity to handle these feelings in a constructive manner.
5. My fifth and last rule . . . is expressed in the Alcoholics Anonymous prayer: "God grant me the serenity to accept the things I cannot change, the courage to change the things I can, and the wisdom to know the difference."(p. xviii)

The persons who are most helpful to a dying person are those who allow communication to proceed honestly and those who have come to terms with their own frustrations and anxieties about death. Family members, however, may find it extremely difficult to talk about death or to understand and control their own emotions. They may go through stages similar to those of the patient—denial, anger, bargaining, and depression—before they can accept the prognosis. Their own grief sometimes leaves them as much in need of support as the patient approaching death. Occasionally, the patient may try to help family members or may simply prefer not to see them.

In order to meet the needs of dying patients, medical practitioners, social service personnel, family, and friends should be aware of their major requirements: (1) the need to control pain, (2) the need to retain dignity or feelings of self-worth, and (3) the need for love and affection (Schulz, 1978). Dignity can be enhanced by allowing the dying adult as much control over decisions affecting his or her death as over the rest of the life span. Love and affection can be shown by listening, imparting desired information, perceiving the patient's approach to death (allowing for self-respect and dignity), and reassuring him or her that others will be there to provide love until the end. It can also be shown through the tender touch: holding hands, stroking, touching.

The Elderly and Death

Old people are generally less afraid of their own death than are young adults who have not yet had a chance to pursue careers or raise families. However, the approaches of individual old people to death vary tremendously. Whereas some welcome death, others try to postpone it in every way possible. Some will discuss it; to others it is a taboo topic. The variety of views old people have about death were expressed in interviews conducted by Maas and Kuypers (1974):

"Life and death go together—that's the natural way. . . . I don't like to—just—think about death. . . . We're ready to die before we're ready to know how to live." (p. 137)
"Talk about death? No, we never have thought to talk about it. We're always too busy doing something." (p. 140).
"I think death would be wonderful. . . . There's a time for everybody and when it comes, it comes. . . . Death to me is a way out of this troubled world that we're in. And I think sometimes that death is going to be peaceful." (p. 141)

Old persons have all had experience witnessing the deaths of others around them. This practice in mourning and coming to terms with grief and anxieties concerning the death of others gives them some degree of preparation for facing their own finiteness. Butler

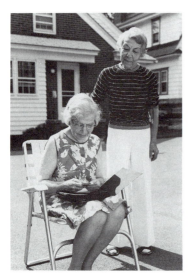

Figure 12-5
Elderly family members often get together to reminisce about their earlier years. This can give them a sense of peace about both their lives and the eventuality of their deaths.

(1975) pointed out that many older persons show a perseveration in reminiscing about their lives. Did they make sense? Were they worthwhile? By so doing, they seek to find some way to assure themselves that their lives were meaningful and thus prepare themselves to face death more peacefully (see Figure 12-5).

When an elderly person is terminally ill, he or she is still apt to go through the stages described by Kübler-Ross: denial, anger, bargaining, depression, and finally acceptance. Physicians or family members may try to shelter the elderly from knowledge that his or her illness will be fatal, although dying persons usually know their status, whether or not the prognosis is put in words. They may have financial or personal matters that they want to put in order. Older persons should be allowed to take care of such matters when they desire. The terminal decline in intelligence that precedes death (see Chapter 11) may render some individuals incapable of accomplishing logical, ordered thinking when death is near.

Fanslow (1984) wrote about the calming effect of touch on elderly dying patients. She has taught nurses and family members to hold hands, to place one's hand near the patient's heart, or to stroke the patient rhythmically to decrease predeath anxiety and provide the sense of peace needed for finishing business with surviving relatives and friends. Touching is therapeutic for family and friends as well. It helps them adjust to the reality of the imminent death and to cope with the difficulties of holding on and letting go.

Some persons sign what is called a **living will** earlier in their lives or when a terminal illness is diagnosed. This legal document, which must be witnessed and notarized, states that the individual does not desire to be kept alive by artificial means but rather would like to be allowed to die with dignity (see Figure 12-6). A standardized "living will" is available from euthanasia societies throughout the United States. The concept of **euthanasia** (literally meaning good death) has become a controversial one, generally associated with mercy killing. Various religious and philosophical groups differ in their opinions of where one draws a line between not making heroic efforts to sustain life and actually allowing or even hastening death by withholding life-supporting equipment or medicines (see Box 12-1).

The **hospice** movement, which is growing in popularity throughout Europe and North America, is not as controversial as the euthanasia movement. A hospice attempts to provide the most supportive climate possible, both physically and psychologically, for dying patients. Although a hospice is usually a specialized physical facility, hospice services may also be provided in one's own home (Munley, 1983). Since the amendment of the Social Security Act in 1982, Medicare funds have been allowed to pay for hospice services for up to three years. Specially trained doctors, social workers, nurses, chaplains, physical therapists, and volunteers associated with the hospice system carefully regulate activities and pain-relieving substances (morphine, cocaine, gin) in such a way as to alleviate fears, pain, and discomfort without creating an agitated, depressed, or comatose state. They also attend carefully to the patient's emotional, social, and spiritual status. The environment is kept as loving and caring and peaceful as possible. Each dying person is respected as a unique individual with his or her own needs and desires. Each patient has autonomy regarding decisions about his or her own care. Constant attention is given by staff, volunteers, relatives, or friends: listening, holding hands, touching (see Figure 12-7).

By including family members in the hospice services, the hospice staff can also simultaneously help them work through their relationship to the dying person, help them work through the difficulties of holding on and letting go, and give some anticipatory guidance for what will occur after the death.

Anticipatory guidance involves preparing survivors for their probable actions and reactions at the time of death and bereavement. Families can do some **anticipatory grief** work as well: recognizing and coping with their feelings of denial, anger, and depression. Counselors can make them aware of their needs for supportive relationships

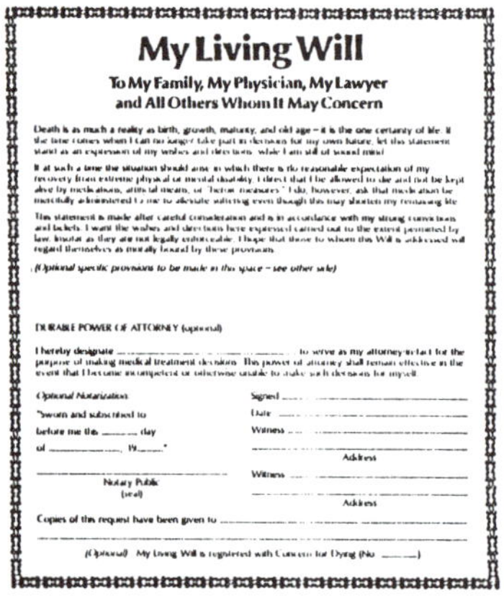

My Living Will

To My Family, My Physician, My Lawyer and All Others Whom It May Concern

Death is as much a reality as birth, growth, maturity, and old age – it is the one certainty of life. If the time comes when I can no longer take part in decisions for my own future, let this statement stand as an expression of my wishes and directions, while I am still of sound mind.

If at such a time the situation should arise in which there is no reasonable expectation of my recovery from extreme physical or mental disability, I direct that I be allowed to die and not be kept alive by medications, artificial means, or "heroic measures." I do, however, ask that medication be mercifully administered to me to alleviate suffering even though this may shorten my remaining life.

This statement is made after careful consideration and is in accordance with my strong convictions and beliefs. I want the wishes and directions here expressed carried out to the extent permitted by law. Insofar as they are not legally enforceable, I hope that those to whom this Will is addressed will regard themselves as morally bound by these provisions.

(Optional specific provisions to be made in this space – see other side)

DURABLE POWER OF ATTORNEY (optional)

I hereby designate ______________ to serve as my attorney-in-fact for the purpose of making medical treatment decisions. This power of attorney shall remain effective in the event that I become incompetent or otherwise unable to make such decisions for myself.

Optional Notarization:

"Sworn and subscribed to before me this ______ day of ______________, 19____."

____
Notary Public
(seal)

Signed ______________
Date ______________
Witness ______________
____
Address
Witness ______________
____
Address

Copies of this request have been given to ______________

(Optional) My Living Will is registered with Concern for Dying (No. ______)

Figure 12-6
The living will sets guidelines for terminal medical interventions.

Should Life Be Sustained in a Permanent Vegetative State?

Varying versions of the Hippocratic Oath have been taken for over 2000 years by physicians entering the practice of medicine. A current version, approved by the American Medical Association, includes the phrase "That you will exercise your art solely for the cure of your patients." Physicians are also advised by the American Medical Association's Council on Ethical and Judicial Affairs that they may discontinue all life supports (respirators, dialysis, even food and water) for patients who are in irreversible comas from which there is no hope of cure. This directive does not mandate the discontinuance of life supports; it simply allows that such action is not unethical in cases where it is the wish of the family and perhaps also the previously stated wish of the patient (as in a living will signed prior to the comatose state). Each physician must examine his or her own conscience to decide for how long to attempt to cure a patient, or alternatively, whether to allow the comatose incurable patient to die with dignity minus a roomful of life-sustaining apparatuses.

The problem goes beyond a moral–ethical dilemma. Should life be maintained at costs in excess of $250 per day ($8000 a month, $100,000 a year) in patients who are in a permanent vegetative state? Few families can afford such long-term care. The fees, instead, are usually paid by private insurance companies or government Medicare/Medicaid. Some patients can survive for many years in irreversible comas. The price of insurance for each insuree goes up in proportion to these costs of comprehensive medical care.

In some cases, families must go to court to obtain an injunction requiring that physicians, hospital staff, or nursing home staff cease to care for persons in permanent vegetative states. The life-or-death decision is then in the hands of neither the medical community nor the close family members but rather an impartial judge or jury.

Who should determine how and for how long to treat a person in an irreversible coma? The question will not be an easy one to decide, and the answers may be years in coming.

and good communication within their support networks after the death. Although hospice staff are trained to help relatives and friends as well as dying patients cope with death, their anticipatory guidance procedures can and should be used by all medical, paramedical, and social services personnel.

Most people would prefer to die in their own homes (Kalish and Reynolds, 1976). Unfortunately, few families allow this to happen. Many people are afraid of continued close proximity to a dying person. Family members may not want to feel in any way responsible for the death finally occurring. In addition, many persons feel that the spirit of the dead person will continue to dwell in the room or in the home where death took place. They prefer that death occur in a distant place (hospital, nursing home, hospice).

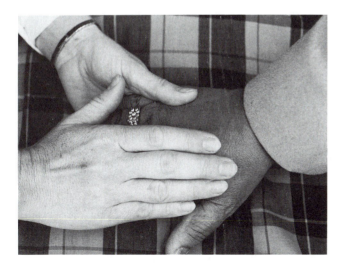

Figure 12-7
The tender touch has a calming effect on both patient and family members. Often hand-holding or rhythmic stroking is more beneficial than verbal communication.

Bereavement and Grief

Thus far this chapter has focused on the reactions of persons to their own approaching deaths. The reactions of others to the death of a loved one are also painful. It does not matter that death may relieve the suffering of the loved person or, depending on religious convictions, that the departed is believed to have made a transition into a better afterlife. Surviving individuals will still miss a loved person who dies and will need to work through an assortment of disturbing emotions concerning the meaning of that death to their lives.

Each year an estimated 8 million Americans experience the death of an immediate family member. Each type of death (death of a child, death of a spouse, death of a parent, suicide) carries with it a special kind of acute pain. Most researchers concerned with stress agree that it is the most potent kind of stress in life. It can produce major changes in the functioning of the immune, respiratory, cardiovascular, endocrine, and autonomic nervous systems, with resulting changes in physical and mental health. The Committee for the Study of Health Consequences of the Stress of Bereavement (1984) provided the following definitions for reactions to a death of a loved person:

> **Grief**: The feeling (affect) and certain associated behaviors such as crying.
>
> **Grieving process**: The changing affective state over time.
>
> **Bereavement**: The fact of loss through death.
>
> **Bereavement reactions**: Any psychological, physiological, or behavioral response to bereavement.
>
> **Bereavement process**: The emergence of bereavement reactions over time.
>
> **Mourning**: The social expressions of grief, including funeral rituals and associated behaviors. (pp. 9-10)

Mourning rituals are vastly different across cultures, ethnic groups, social classes, and even rural and urban areas. What many people do not realize is that bereavement reactions and grief vary greatly as well, not only across social settings but also from individual to individual. The grieving process may involve rapid mood swings and uncontrollable emotions (from sadness, to anger, to fear, to love, to happiness) (see Figure 12-8). These feelings are unexpected and intense. They may leave the bereaved confused or ashamed. They may also leave other bereaved family members angry at what they perceive to be inappropriate affective reactions.

Researchers have found that the grieving process may begin before death (in cases of terminal illnesses) and may continue over a year beyond death. Books, magazines, articles, and radio and television shows are just beginning to educate the public about the different reactions to bereavement. Physicians, nurses, psychiatrists, psychologists, social workers, chaplains, and the like are becoming better prepared to support bereaved families as more and more information about reactions becomes known. In the remainder of this chapter we present an overview of some of the current knowledge about the grieving and bereavement processes.

Lindemann (1944), in a classic paper, described seven physical signs that characterize **acute grief**:

1. bodily distress,
2. a feeling of tightness in the throat,
3. choking,
4. a need for sighing,
5. an empty feeling in the abdomen,
6. loss of muscular power,
7. mental pain.

Figure 12-8
Grieving persons may feel an intense need to hug and show affection to others. This is not an inappropriate bereavement reaction.

The duration of these symptoms may vary depending on the relationship between the deceased and the survivors. They are common during the first week after death when the funeral or memorial service is being held (see Box 12-2).

Intermediate grief reactions soon replace acute grief. They differ depending on age, sex, ethnicity, relationship to the dead person, prior experiences with grief, support networks, and preexisting mental or physical health. Let us look at different grief reactions depending on the age of the deceased.

Reactions to a Child's Death

There is no one way all parents react when one of their offspring dies. Some parents go into a state of shock. They may be confused and unable to act or react. Some parents may refuse to believe that the death has occurred. They behave as if the child will return soon. Some parents have brief psychotic reactions. Some become agitated and acutely anxious about trivia and unnumerable smaller events. Some parents are overcome with unreasonable fears. Others may become deeply depressed. Some parents show their grief in emotional outpourings. Others give no visible signs of their feelings although the grieving process is very much a part of their inner lives. The sorrow parents feel manifests itself in different ways for different people.

The death of a child generally leaves everyone feeling that a great injustice has been done. The child had no chance to live out his or her life. A sense of bitterness compounds the grief. The work of mourning, called **grief work**, is to come to terms with the fact of death and to work out some of the bitterness, sense of loss, hurt, disappointment, and frustrations that accompany it. Parents who can express their feelings and allow others to comfort them are able to emerge more rapidly from their bereavement process (see Figure 12-9).

The initial acute grief reaction to a death of a child usually gives way to a period of crying and extended sorrow. Parents should be encouraged to weep openly. After a few days to weeks the rate of crying will decrease and an intermediate grief phase will commence (Glick, Weiss, and Parkes, 1974). In this phase the parents will review the child's life. It is common for parents to search for their dead child in places where

Funerals.

Much attention has been directed toward the high price of burial in recent years. The average traditional funeral costs about $3500, but it is not unusual for families to pay two to three times this amount for a funeral to honor their dead. Why so much? Consider the services: a casket, a cemetery plot, opening the grave, a vault to line the grave, embalming of the body, use of the funeral home, flowers, transportation of the body to the cemetery, additional limousines for the family, the graveside service, closing of the grave, a grave marker, and fees for services for funeral director, staff, and clergy.

Many persons are opting to bequeath their bodies to science. In such cases, the funeral is usually replaced by a memorial service. Such a service allows mourning rites and early grief work, as well as a memorialization of the life and contributions of the deceased.

The number of persons who opt for cremation has doubled in recent years, to close to 10% of bodies. Many funeral directors handle cremations as well as body burials. In fact, they may sell the family a casket for transportation to the crematorium, provide use of the funeral home, sell a cemetery plot and marker for the cremated remains, and direct the graveside service as well. Most states do not require a casket for a body destined for a crematorium. If the family elects to bypass a funeral home and deal directly with the crematorium, fees may be considerably lowered. Most persons elect to hold a memorial service for the dead even if they do not have a funeral to bury the ashes. Laws governing the disposal of ashes vary from state to state. Many crematoriums will provide a variety of urns or vaults for cremated remains in a wide range of prices. Cremation can be as expensive as a funeral.

Many states require neither embalming nor vaults to line the grave for body burials. A simple pine box in a simply lined grave will meet most legal requirements. It is often difficult, however, to find a place to purchase an inexpensive casket or to find a cemetery willing to bury the dead in an inexpensively lined grave.

Funeral expenses are occasionally covered by union pension funds, fraternal orders, insurance policies, bank trusts, or church organizations. In some cases, families can also qualify for financial assistance from social security or the Veterans Administration.

Many persons opt to arrange their own prepaid funerals. Some mortuaries are owned by giant corporations that also own cemeteries, monument works, flower stores, and other related services. For one fee, all services will be provided at the time of death. The law requires that all the money prepaid on such contracts be placed in escrow. Preneed contracts can be cancelled and all money refunded on written demand at any time prior to death. Preneed contracts allow people to elect a lower-priced (or even higher-priced) service than they believe their families might select in the emotionally taut, vulnerable days following death. Unless a will specifies funeral, cremation, or donation-to-science plans, the next of kin will be asked to make all decisions about burial soon after death occurs.

he or she spent a lot of time (bedroom, playroom, parks). It is also common for them to experience a sense of personal guilt for their child's death. Johnson-Soderberg (1983) found that guilt is more common in parents who had only a short time (under two weeks) to prepare for their child's death and is more common in mothers than in fathers. Guilt often complicates the intermediate grief phase and may contribute to the high divorce rate of parents who have lost a child by death. Johnson-Soderberg found that parents often believe that they committed an actual wrongdoing, either by commission (action) or omission (inaction) to oneself or to another, that caused harm and somehow related to the child's death. In many cases, the guilt is based on some deviation from a social norm (getting pregnant before marriage, mother working outside the home). Many parents experience obsessive, repetitive "movie scenes" about the death of their child during the intermediate grief phase. If such torturing movies are kept secret, the parent may feel that he or she is going crazy. Sharing them with others, and learning that other bereaved parents have also experienced such recurrent scenes, both alleviates guilt and provides relief from the movie.

Eventually the survivors will understand the futility of self-reproach or searches and will work at accepting the fact of death. This is the **recovery phase of bereavement**. They may make an appointment with the dead child's doctor and repeat the

Figure 12-9
Supportive friends who permit or elicit emotional release are important to the bereavement process.

same questions they asked earlier. They may seek support from other bereaved parents, social workers, religious counselors, community counseling centers, psychologists, psychiatrists, relatives, or friends. They come to terms with their guilt, disappointment, and loss and accept the finality of the death. They decide to live again and resume social activities. They feel more self-assured. They turn their attention back to their living children (if they have others), to each other, and to other relatives and friends.

A danger inherent in parents' recovery from the death of a child is that they will overprotect or smother surviving persons. Parents need to be helped and encouraged to allow each other, other children, and all other surviving family members to live out their own unique lives, in their own way, without feeling pressured to take on the roles of the lost child. Some parents may try to have another child as soon as possible. They realize that they cannot replace the dead child, but they hope that a new baby will fill their void and further ameliorate their feelings of loss.

Parents who refuse to discuss or deal with their child's death and who refuse sympathy, compassion, and support from others may delay recovery interminably. Grief that is hidden may burst forth later. Delayed emotional responses to death are abnormal and are termed **morbid grief reactions**. Parkes (1972) reported morbid-grief patients developed serious psychophysiologic illnesses and suffered from alcoholism, deep depressions, severe anxiety disorders, or psychosis.

Siblings and close playmates of a dead child also experience a number of painful emotions associated with death. They often feel guilty, believing that some action or angry thought of theirs caused their brother, sister, or playmate to die. They may develop an overwhelming fear of death in general: "If it could happen to my friend, it can happen to me." In addition, due to their limited understanding of death, they may be angry at the dead child for leaving them. Children need to be given a chance to express all of their emotions openly and freely after experiencing the death of a sibling or friend (see Figure 12-10). They will cue adults on what they most want to know: Will it happen to me? Was I responsible? Will I ever see him (or her) again? Bereaved children should be encouraged to cry. They should be given extra emotional support and a sense of security in their environments. A sudden change in rules, discipline, schedules, or living arrangements can be especially upsetting to them when they are trying to cope with their anxieties and fears about death.

Some children who cannot cope with their guilt, fears, or anger at the death of another child turn their emotions inward and become depressed and withdrawn or

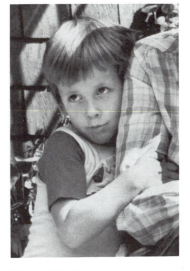

Figure 12-10
Bereaved children often feel guilty, as if something they did caused their friend's/sibling's death. They need to be helped to express all of their feelings (guilt, fear, anger, sadness) to a compassionate adult.

develop physical symptoms (Sargent, 1979). They may need professional help if these behaviors persist over several months.

Reactions to a Younger Adult's Death

In general, the death of a young adult is met with feelings of injustice in much the same way as is the death of a child. It is especially hard to understand or accept the death if the adult had many persons dependent on him or her (children, employees), or if he or she were doing some important work.

The death of young adults not only brings grief to loved ones but also causes a sense of discomfort in most associates. An untimely death makes us all remember how unpredictable our own futures are, how finite we all are. However, the process of grieving, although painful, can be a growth-promoting experience. If people can come to terms with their pain and loss and their concerns and fears of death, they may gain a sense of competence from mastering what seemed insurmountable grief. With this new self-confidence they may begin to live each day in a more meaningful way.

The ways in which adults express their grief over the loss of an adult friend or relative vary from tight control of emotions to hysterical outpourings of anguish. Initially, persons are disbelieving. When the realization of death finally sets in, protests (silent or otherwise) are common. Confusion follows. Survivors may feel hopeless, without direction, desperate. They may move slowly, think slowly, and detach themselves from others and from the course of everyday living.

Shortly after the death of a significant adult the bereaved may find it difficult to be aware of the things that are happening around them. They may not react to events in their customary fashion. Personalities may change (for example, short tempers replacing patience, or reserve replacing gregariousness). During the acute periods of grieving, persons may be unusually sensitive to criticism.

One of the more difficult aspects of the intermediate period of grieving is coping with the feeling of regret at things left undone or unsaid to the departed. Guilt feelings are a common ingredient in grief work and must be resolved. So, too, are feelings of anger. Most people can accept their feelings of guilt or regret more readily than they can their hostility toward the deceased. They feel they have no right to be angry at someone who paid the ultimate price, death, yet anger is a common affective response to a loved person's departure. Survivors may feel betrayed, stranded, rejected, as if, by dying, the deceased has pulled the rug from under their own feet.

Fear is yet another emotion common to grieving. On occasion real reasons for fear exist (economic instability, deprivation of primary social–emotional support). On other occasions the dread is nameless and often more frightening because its cause cannot be ascertained.

Another difficult aspect of grieving may be coping with the attitudes of certain friends and neighbors. Some persons do not recognize the necessity of grief work. They feel it would be better if the bereaved would forget, quit talking about the dead, and stop crying. The grieving process may be viewed as a form of self-indulgence. On the other hand, having supportive medical, social, or religious counselors or family and friends helps a grieving person to work through his or her emotions, to reach the stage of accepting the death. Gorer (1965) suggested three things that must be done:

1. The bereaved must separate himself or herself from the deceased by breaking the bond that holds them together.
2. He or she must readjust to an environment from which the deceased is missing.
3. He or she must form new relationships.

Separations are part of "grief work". Bereaved persons must break their emotional ties to the past and rid themselves of the hopes and dreams they shared with the dead person. Grief work can take months to accomplish (see Figure 12-11).

Reactions during the grieving process may include a host of behavioral, physiolog-

Figure 12-11
Grief work includes removing the deceased person's clothing and personal effects from the home. Although difficult, this acknowledges the finality of death.

ical, and psychological responses. There is evidence that many accidents are linked to bereavement. In general, grief tends to exacerbate preexisting accident proneness. Thus, poor drivers may make even more errors in judgment on the road, or persons with poor motor coordination may have more falls. In a similar vein, grief may aggravate preexisting physical illnesses. Thus, the person with asthma or emphysema may have greater respiratory distress, the person with coronary heart disease may have more angina attacks, or the person with chronic ulcers may have flareups or bleeding of their lesions. Healthy individuals may also find themselves more susceptible to infections during the grieving process. An increase in use of alcohol, tobacco, tranquilizers, or sleeping pills by persons who previously used them is common. Finally, a small percentage of bereaved individuals may develop symptoms of real clinical depression four months or more after their loss. Clinical depression puts a person at high risk for suicidal behaviors and should be treated professionally.

When a child loses a parent, grief and bereavement are especially agonizing. When a child loses a father, the attachment and dependency on the mother become intensified. Often the expression of anger is repressed and turned inward, against the self. Sometimes the anger comes out as defiance against the mother, creating, in turn, guilt at defying the mother on whom one is so dependent (Grossberg and Crandall, 1978). When a child loses a mother, the attachment and dependency on the father become intensified. Because the mother is usually the primary caregiver, the loss may have more negative sequelae. Children often hesitate to accept a new mother or mother-figure: Nobody can compare with the idealized image of their dead mother. They may be very jealous of people who still have their mothers. They more frequently turn their feelings of rage, frustration, and jealousy toward the father who is trying to be a mother-substitute. Then, in turn, they feel guilty for aggressing against their only remaining parent. This may cause them to turn their anger inward, against themselves.

Behaviors that have been identified as possible childhood consequences of the death of a parent include changes in personality, changes in sex-role identity and sexual behaviors, moral changes, antisocial behaviors, emotional disturbances, and cognitive and achievement-related changes (Berlinsky and Biller, 1982). Some long-term consequences of the death of a parent on a child that have been reported include mental illness (especially depression), an increased risk of suicide, impaired sexual identity, impaired capacity for intimacy, and lack of autonomy (Committee for the Study of Health Consequences of the Stress of Bereavement, 1984).

Each child's reaction to the loss of a parent will be individual and will depend on the child's age, sex, personality, developmental concept of death, and previous experience with death; on the sex of the lost parent; on the reason for the parent's death; and on the support provided by surviving caregivers.

Some children react with loud protesting and increased aggressiveness. Others withdraw and become detached. Recurrent attacks of anxiety are common whenever a reminder of the dead parent appears. Guilt is often a part of a child's grief. The child may believe that he or she was in some way responsible for the parent's disappearance. Children must be told the truth about the parent's death. They must also be encouraged to cry, to ask questions, and to do grief work to come to terms with all their feelings of anger, hurt, loneliness, guilt, fear, and anxiety. Grief work, though painful, can prevent more serious consequences.

Children's grief work is a threefold task: to cope with the immediate impact of the loss of a parent, to mourn, and to resume and continue their emotional development in harmony with their level of maturity (Furman, 1974). Some alternate caregivers should become available to meet the kinds of bodily and psychological needs previously met by the deceased parent. In addition, the surviving caregiver should create a milieu in which the child can mourn. This can be especially difficult with a very young child who may not know how to communicate and who cannot differentiate or tolerate emotions such as anger or sadness. Some thanatologists feel that children cannot mourn until about age three (Furman, 1973). Others place it much later, even until adulthood

Figure 12-12
After the death of a parent, children usually show changes in emotional responses and personality patterns.

is reached (Wolfenstein, 1969; Miller, 1971). Many children have difficulties going forward with their emotional development. They often regress in emotional behaviors instead, becoming more fearful, insecure, withdrawn and detached, aggressive and hostile and less able to control their shifting moods (see Figure 12-12).

Like adults, children often become more susceptible to illness and become more accident prone while going through the grieving process. It is not unusual for them to have appetite and sleep disturbances and complain of pain, especially abdominal cramps. School-age children often have difficulty remembering or concentrating, and their academic performance may decline. With adequate support and encouragement, children can eventually recover from the loss of a parent, usually within a year, without long-term negative consequences. How much support, for how long, and whether professional assistance will be required depend on each child's unique circumstances.

Reactions to an Older Adult's Death

Mourning for an aged person who dies is generally less painful than mourning the death of a child or younger adult. One senses that the death is more a part of a natural process. The aged person can be viewed as having lived a long and full life. Death in the elderly is also generally anticipated, consciously or unconsciously, for a period of time before it occurs and some anticipatory grief work may be done. Family and friends have a chance to prepare for what life will be like when the older person dies.

Grief is most severe in elderly persons who were dependent on the departed (for example, the widow or widower). Clayton and her colleagues (1972) and Bornstein, Clayton, and others (1973) studied depression in older widows and widowers. They found that almost half of the older surviving spouses were depressed at some point during the first bereavement year and nearly 15% were depressed for the entire year. Many of the older persons who were not clinically depressed had individual depressive symptoms of varying durations.

Lynch (1977) described the medical consequences of unresolved (morbid) grief, as the **broken heart syndrome**, which can lead to death. Lynch pointed out that years ago "grief" was openly recognized as a cause of death. Today our sophisticated, medical-wise society does not tolerate such an ill-defined diagnosis. Death may occur due to coronary heart disease, a stroke, an accident, cancer, some other illness, or even suicide, but the physical or mental illness was exacerbated by the bereavement (see

Figure 12-13
Do you know of two older
married persons who died within
a year of each other? The
phenomenon may reflect the
broken heart syndrome.

Figure 12-13). Lynch's research suggested that the increased incidence of older married persons dying within one or two years of each other may reflect the difficulty surviving spouses have in working through the intense emotional stresses of grieving.

The sequence of feelings in accepting the death of an elderly person is the same as the sequence following the death of a younger person: acute grief with disbelief, possibly anger and confusion, and finally the painful process of intermediate grief and disassociating oneself from the departed. Survivors must find a meaning and purpose to their own lives that no longer center around or include the dead person in order to recover and return to normal functioning.

Bereavement Interventions

Most friends are not sure how to help a recently bereaved person. What can one say or do? Thanatologists recommend that the process of mourning should not be cut short. It is a healing process. Good friends should be there for the bereaved and should listen to whatever feelings are expressed in an accepting, nonjudgmental way. It is not helpful to say, "I know how you feel." One can never know the most intimate thoughts of another. "How do you feel?" is a more helpful query, but one must phrase this question gently, with a desire to learn and be supportive, not with a desire to instruct.

It is wrong to try to tell a bereaved person how he or she should feel. Rebukes or advice will complicate bereavement, not ease the pain. In most cases, the less said, the better. "I'm sorry," and an embrace or tender touch shows caring. One may also inquire whether the bereaved needs any assistance (such as with meals, shopping, transportation). In time, the bereaved may express his or her desire to have help resolving feelings of guilt, anger, and despair. It is helpful then to put the bereaved in contact with trained counselors or support groups. Hospices, physicians, specially trained nurses, community support groups, clergy, social workers, psychologists, and psychiatrists may be able to provide assistance, insight, and understanding with the grieving process.

The hospice movement includes services to family members as well as to terminally ill patients. Although Medicare will not reimburse hospice personnel for the counseling they provide to family members of a dying patient, the hospice cannot qualify for Medicare collection unless it includes such counseling services. While participating in a hospice program, anticipatory guidance is provided and some anticipatory grief work can be done. During the early bereavement period, family members can continue to talk to and receive support from hospice workers. This support can be invaluable to each person involved and can help prevent many of the complications of bereavement as well as morbid grief reactions.

Support groups consisting of other bereaved persons, usually headed by a specially trained nurse, social worker, psychologist, psychiatrist, or member of the clergy, can enhance each individual's personal coping strategies. It can be beneficial to learn that other people are experiencing frightening emotions, rapid mood swings, forgetfulness, or physical and psychological symptoms. Attentive listening and empathy for others are often as helpful as sharing one's own turmoil. The person-to-person exchange can reveal coping techniques and solutions to problems and enhance the bereaved person's sense of personal worth. Many support groups are focused on specific circumstances (suicide, homicide, the death of a child, SIDS death, widow-to-widow support). Others serve the needs of any bereaved person (see Figure 12-14).

Some individuals seek medical care for their behavioral, physiological, and psychological reactions to bereavement. Many physicians order extensive tests to diagnose specific disorders responsible for whatever symptoms are reported. While this is often necessary (bereavement exacerbates physical illnesses), physicians should also assist the individuals to accomplish their grief work. They can provide counseling themselves or they can help the bereaved find either a support group or an individual counselor such as a qualified nurse, social worker, religious counselor, psychologist, or psychiatrist. Physicians should exercise caution in prescribing medications for bereaved individuals. There is some evidence that antidepressant drugs, sometimes used to suppress intense, distressing, or disabling grief reactions, may have later adverse consequences. Many physicians prescribe minor tranquilizers (Valium, Librium) to help grieving persons. There have been virtually no controlled trials on the efficacy of these drugs with the bereaved (Committee for the Study of Health Consequences of the Stress of Bereavement, 1984). Sedatives or hypnotics prescribed for insomnia may, over time, become the cause of insomnia. The grieving and bereavement processes should not be completely suppressed but should be worked through for healing and growth to occur.

Figure 12-14
There are many free or inexpensive services available in most communities to help with dying and bereavement.

Circle of support. For people who have lost a loved one. Sponsored by Hospice

Compassionate Friends Inc. For parents who have experienced the death of a child. Meets first Wednesday each month, 8 p.m.

Bereavement Seminar
Dates: Nov. 3 – Dec. 8
Time: 10–11:30 am
Fee: $12
A program for those who have experienced the death of a loved one.

Seminar on Death and Dying
For three Sundays in March, following the Lenten Luncheons, there will be a session of our seminar. We plan to meet after lunch in the Parlor. Therefore, each session should be from about 1:45 to 3:00 p.m. All members and friends are invited. The schedule is as follows:
March 6 - The Traditional Funeral
March 13 - The Medical Donor Program
March 20 - Psychological Issues

Homicide survivors. The Family Bereavement Center provides counseling and legal services for survivors of homicide. Sponsored by State's Attorney's Office.

Holiday grief. On managing the holidays, for those who have experienced the death of a loved one. Dec. 16, 1 p.m. to 3 p.m. Arundel Hospice.

Bereavement program. Individual counseling to help families cope with death or terminal illness of a loved one.

Suicide bereavement. For people who have experienced the loss of a loved one by suicide. Meets third Tuesday each month, 8 p.m. to 10 p.m. Spangler Hall adjacent to St. Paul's Church.

Partners in Survivorship. For people who lost a loved one. Meets first Sunday of each month, 7 p.m. to 9 p.m., Mount Washington United Methodist Church.

AIDS services. Referrals, counseling, legal services, emergency assistance and prevention education availble to people who are HIV-positive. Sponsored by HERO.

Perspectives on Living

An understanding and acceptance of the totality of the human life span, including death, can make us all feel more akin to each other, whatever one's age or life stage. Experiencing death can be a catalyst to living more fully. Many people have had what is known as a near-death experience (Perry, 1988). They "die" and feel themselves rising out of their bodies to view themselves from above. They frequently experience a life review, seeing their own actions and the effects of their deeds on people in their lives. People may find this near-death experience so overwhelming that they do not want to return to life, but they are resuscitated by medical personnel. They are usually profoundly moved by their close brush with death: The experience dramatically and positively alters their values, their personality, and their outlook on life (Kurtz, 1988).

The concept of death, the idea that our future is limited, is one of the major keys to continued personal growth and giving. As Kübler-Ross (1975) put it, "When you fully understand that each day you awaken could be the last you have, you take the time, that day, to grow, to become more of who you really are, to reach out to other human beings."

One of the secrets of happy living is to spend a portion of each day reaching out to others. This must be done lovingly and unselfishly, not because one wants something in return but simply because it is in us to care for others. When concern and affection are given another, the reward is not only the appreciation of the one served but, more important, a feeling of self-esteem and personal growth. By repeated giving, one is able to learn to like and understand other human beings more fully (see Figure 12-15).

Most people have good intentions. Most people would like to live lives that benefit others, but, when one lives as if life will go on forever, it is too easy to postpone until tomorrow all those things that ought to be done today. Eventually one looks back and sees one's life as being self-absorbed, selfish, and not very beneficial to others. This is embarrassing and unpleasant. Such negative feedback from the internal valuing system prevents one from becoming all one is capable of being.

Take a moment to consider who you really are. How and where do you fit into the fellowship of humankind? Consider the wise command spoken by Socrates: "Know thyself."

Figure 12-15
Giving to one another as part of human kindness can make each of us happier and healthier.

Figure 12-16
Think globally. Act locally. Our planet needs the help and support of every human being.

Humans have existed on earth for about 100,000 years. Most of this time they have been hunters and gatherers. Farming in a primitive form only started about 10,000 years ago. The industrial revolution occurred only 200 years ago. Now every single generation sees fantastic changes in the way society lives. Society must take risks to survive. The future is uncharted, unpredictable. There are difficult problems in trying to adapt and cope with the ever-changing world around us. Life exists with conditions of stress and fear. Alvin Toffler (1970) called this "future shock." Shock can prevent us from behaving rationally with respect to future planning. How does one plan for a world that may in a short time include such things as cloning, a depletion of the ozone layer, robots capable of holding jobs, a prevention of aging, toxic nuclear wastes, the spread of anarchism over large parts of the world, and destruction of the rain forests (see Figure 12-16)? Try to view living in the world today and tomorrow from a more positive perspective. There are several special kinds of environments that should be reasonably available to all people to help shape a more peaceful, humane world.

The first is an environment of health. All members of society should be able to afford medical attention to prevent and treat disease processes. A vital part of this environment of health is physically fit parents of our future generations. Our world should make it possible for expectant parents, especially mothers, to confer optimum health benefits to offspring. The mother should not have to conceive at too young an age or in a malnourished, drug-addicted, or chronically diseased state, all of which could adversely affect the baby-to-be.

A second environment that all people should reasonably expect to enjoy is a quality home life. One cannot become all one is capable of being without love and a sense of belonging at home. People also need family environments that are free from racial discrimination and abject poverty.

A third specialized kind of environment that should be available to all humans is that of quality education. One of our priorities must be to provide educational opportunities flexible enough to allow all people to learn to read and reason about the various areas of human knowledge.

A fourth environment needed is that of constructive outlets for aggression, which Lorenz (1966) and others have postulated to be an instinctual behavior in the human species. It is not in the best interests of humankind for persons to turn their aggression and hostilities against each other. Persons of all races, ethnicities, and religions are now economically, socially, and politically interdependent. (see Figure 12-17). Humans should work together to solve the food, fuel, pollution, and population problems of the future. Society needs to provide opportunities for persons to direct their aggressive urges at righting environmental obstacles to a quality life.

Figure 12-17
Our "melting-pot" world has created an interdependence among peoples of every age, race, religion, education, and lifestyle.

A fifth environment necessary is that of employment. Jobs should be structured to allow for more cooperative efforts among employees rather than competition for employment in a tight job market. The dual hardships of unemployment plus inflation can quickly destroy the quality of everyone's life. Feelings of impotence among the unemployed may contribute to destructive aggressive outbursts such as child abuse, spouse abuse, elder abuse, and crimes against society.

A sixth environment that should be available to all persons is equal treatment under the law. We must not have a double standard of justice, one divided between the rich and powerful and the poor and powerless. Every human being needs dignity as part of the fellowship of humankind.

Where do you see yourself in the scheme of the total environment? What will you give to the population of the world in order to assure a better quality of life and a peaceful, humane future for all people?

Summary

The study of death (thanatology) is a growing research area. Scholars have identified different ways in which children, younger adults, and older adults approach death. Included in thanatology is a study of bereavement and grief. Reactions differ according to age and available coping mechanisms.

Children generally view death as a transient phenomenon. Older children and adolescents may appreciate the permanence of death but believe they, themselves, are invulnerable. When faced with their own approaching death, children are more often concerned about the reactions of persons around them than they are with their own terminal condition.

Kübler-Ross identified five stages through which adolescents and adults pass when faced with their own imminent death: denial, anger, bargaining, depression, and acceptance. Some persons may move back and forth between stages or experience two of them simultaneously, and not every dying person reaches the acceptance stage. Acceptance of death is fostered by significant others who allow communications to proceed honestly.

Older adults typically show more anxiety about death in general than do middle-aged adults but are less afraid of their own deaths. Dying persons often sign living wills, asking that their lives not be sustained by artificial means when there is no reasonable expectation of recovery. Hospices provide both physical and psychological care for dying persons and their families. They use medications to help alleviate the suffering of the patient and help survivors prepare for their actions and reactions surrounding death and bereavement.

The grieving process involves changing affective states over time. Acute grief, common in the first week after death, may be manifested by tightness in the throat, choking, loss of muscle power, mental pain, and somatic distress. Intermediate grief involves crying and extended sorrow. Other emotions typical of intermediate grief include guilt, fear, and anger. Grief work involves coming to terms with the fact of death and coping with one's loss, guilt, hurt, disappointment, frustration, and changing emotions over time. Unresolved grief may result in morbid grief reactions, which can lead to serious psychophysiological disorders.

Bereavement reactions, the behavioral responses to a loss through death, vary according to the age of the dead person, the unique characteristics of bereaved individuals, and ethnic or cultural mourning rituals.

The death of a child or young adult generally leaves survivors feeling that a great injustice has been done. Such a loss may precipitate loud protesting. Mourning for an older adult is usually less painful since the aged person can be viewed as having lived a long and full life.

Experiencing death can be a catalyst to living each day more fully. Successful living involves reaching out to other persons. Humans could live together more peacefully with environments of health, quality home life, education, constructive outlets for aggression, employment, and equal treatment under the law available to everyone around the world.

Overview of Human Development

This text has discussed development throughout the life span, considering physical, cognitive, and psychosocial components. Development should be viewed as occurring throughout life and even into a terminal illness.

Development through infancy and childhood proceeds from sensory and motor responses to verbal communication, thinking, conceptualizing, and learning from others. In adolescence the individual begins to test out sexual maturity. Values and identity are questioned.

Early adulthood usually establishes the individual as an independent person. Employment, further education, the beginning of one's own family are all aspects of setting up a distinct life, with both its own characteristics and the characteristics and customs of previous generations.

During middle adulthood persons have new situations to face, new transitions with which to cope. Children grow up and leave home. Signs of aging become apparent. Relationships change, roles shift. New abilities may be found and opportunities sought.

Finally, during late adulthood, people assess what they've accomplished. Some are pleased. Some feel they could have done more or lived differently. In the best of instances, individuals accept who they are and are comfortable with themselves.

People should discuss and consider the end of the life span—death. The processes of grieving and bereavement are the focus of much new research. Social supports through these processes are important to prevent negative physical or psychosocial consequences. This healthy opening up of discussions about death and bereavement has enabled individuals to consider their own mortality, their own finiteness. Rather than being gruesome, such awareness can be liberating. An awareness of one's mortality can help a person to look at each day as one filled with opportunity and potential for accomplishment. Rather than living one's life in the future, this awareness can help people to focus on what can be achieved here and now.

The human developmental process is always changing. It is exciting and scary, joyful and disappointing. As each person's development progresses, he or she brings unique characteristics and contributions to surrounding settings. The environment that is established and continues for future generations hinges upon what each person contributes and values. Step by step, the process continues.

Key Concepts

thanatology	anger stage	hospice	grief work
personification of death	bargaining stage	anticipatory guidance	recovery phase of bereavement
personal fable	depression stage	anticipatory grief	
Kübler-Ross stages of dying	acceptance stage	mourning rituals	morbid grief reactions
	living will	acute grief	broken heart syndrome
denial stage	euthanasia	intermediate grief	

Questions for Review

1. Some researchers say that proximity to death can be a growth-producing experience. Do you agree or disagree with this? Explain your answer.
2. Describe some ways in which parents, other relatives, friends, and medical personnel can help alleviate the fears of a seven-year-old who is terminally ill and is hospitalized.
3. Kübler-Ross defined five stages that terminally ill persons experience in facing their own deaths. Describe the characteristics of each of these stages.
4. Are you in favor of "living wills," or do you believe it is best left up to a person's loved ones to determine whether to maintain life-sustaining equipment? Explain your answer.
5. Describe the special kinds of environments that should be reasonably available to all people for a more peaceful, humane, and healthy life span.

Further Readings

Dietrich, D. R., and Shabad, P.D. (eds.) (1989). *The problem of loss and mourning: Psychoanalytic perspectives.* Madison, CT: International University Press.
Presents papers dealing with trauma, defenses, ego, psychopathology, object relations and clinical consequences of loss and mourning.
Klass, D. (1988). *Parental grief.* New York: Springer. Examines the emotions parents experience on a child's death; discusses the role of support groups in helping parents redefine their sense of self and their other relationships.
Kübler-Ross, E. (1975). *Death: The final stage of growth.* Englewood Cliffs, NJ: Prentice-Hall.
A spectrum of views on the subject of death and dying

stressing the growth-promoting aspects of facing it openly.

Kübler-Ross, E. (1987). *Working it through.* New York: Macmillan.

Dying can be hard, but Kübler-Ross has written this short book to help make it easier. People can cope with the stages of dying when they are prepared and supported.

Rando, T. A. (1984). *Grief, dying, and death.* Champaign, IL: Research Press.

Focuses on why bereavement is necessary and how to work with grieving persons. Also presents information on how to help the terminally ill patient through the dying process.

Worden, J. W. (1991). *Grief counseling and grief therapy,* 2nd ed. New York: Springer.

Describes how health practitioners can help clients cope with grief reactions; includes AIDS, grief and the elderly, and grief counseling in groups.

Glossary

A

Acceptance stage: Kübler-Ross's fifth stage of dying, characterized by a consent and willingness to die.

Accidental drug overdosing: Frequent cause of poisoning in older persons, who forget whether they have taken their medication or self-medicate and take combinations of drugs.

Accommodation: Piagetian term refering to changes in existing schemas to include new experiences.

Achievement needs: Needs to learn well and perform well.

Acne: A common skin disease characterized by chronic inflammation of the sebaceous glands, usually causing pimples on the face, back, and chest.

Activists: Persons with a cause who seek to bring about change with energy and decisiveness.

Acute grief: Lindemann's description of several disturbing emotions that accompany loss, misfortune, or death of a loved one.

Adolescent egocentrism: Belief held by the adolescent that other people are preoccupied with his or her appearance and behavior.

Adolescent suicides: The act of teenagers killing themselves intentionally; a serious, and growing, health concern in North America.

Adult day care: Social and rehabilitative activities provided for old or infirm persons during the day at a community facility.

Adulthood moratorium: A period of time during which a person is permitted to delay meeting the obligations of adulthood.

Affiliation needs: Needs to unite or associate oneself with other persons.

Age thirty transition: Levinson's stage description for men roughly between ages 28 and 32.

Ageism: A widely prevalent social attitude that overvalues youth and discriminates against the elderly.

Alcohol abuse: Misuse of any alcoholic substance; habitual use.

Alienated youth: Youth who feel estranged from society and try to escape through such means as drugs, alcohol, or adherence to socially unacceptable lifestyles and actions.

Alienation: A feeling of estrangement from and hostility toward others.

Alleles: Pair of genes affecting a trait. When alleles are identical, an individual is homozygous for a trait; when alleles are dissimilar, the individual is heterozygous.

Alloplastic mastery: Gutmann's description for active world mastery.

Alzheimer's disease: A dementia involving rapid intellectual deterioration, speech impairment, loss of body control, and death, usually within five to ten years of onset.

Androgens: Male sex hormones, produced primarily by the testes.

Androgyny: A sex-role identity that incorporates some positive aspects of both traditional male and traditional female behaviors.

Androsperm: Y-carrying sperm.

Aneurysm: A vessel dilation in which a weak part of the vessel wall balloons out.

Anger stage: Kübler-Ross's second stage of dying, characterized by anguish and rage.

Animism: Piagetian term for the attribution of life to inanimate objects.

Anorexia nervosa: Chronic failure to eat for fear of gaining weight; characterized by an extreme loss of appetite that results in severe malnutrition, semistarvation, and sometimes death.

Anoxia: A severe deficiency in the supply of oxygen to the tissues, especially the brain.

Anticipatory grief: Recognizing and coping with feelings of denial, anger, and depression that precede a person's death.

Anticipatory guidance: Preparation of survivors for their probable actions and reactions at the time of death of a loved person; usually done by trained counselors or clergy.

Antigens: Any foreign materials (such as microorganisms, viruses, toxins, or proteins) that stimulate the immune system to produce antibodies when they come in contact with appropriate body tissues.

Apgar scale: Medical technique to measure adjustment of neonate at birth; measures appearance, pulse, grimace, activity, and respiration.

Applied research: Research based on the desire to know for the sake of being able to do something better or more efficiently.

Apprenticeship learning: Education by legally agreeing to work a specified length of time for a master craftsman to learn the craft or trade.

Archetypes: Jungian term for prototypes of great figures in human literature, religion, mythology, and art believed to emerge from the collective unconscious in dreams and fantasies.

Armored-defended peronalities: Neugarten's description for persons who hold their impulses and emotions in tight harness and restrain their creativity.

Arteriosclerosis: Commonly called "hardening of the arteries." Includes a variety of conditions that cause the artery walls to thicken and lose elasticity.

Artificialism: Piagetian term for the belief that the universe is made by humans, for humans.

Assimilation: Piagetian term referring to the process of making new information part of one's existing schemas.

Asthma: A chronic disorder characterized by wheezing, coughing, difficulty in breathing, and a suffocating feeling.

Astigmatism: Unequal curvature of one or more of the refractive surfaces of the eye that interferes with visual focus.

Attachment: An active, affectionate, reciprocal relationship specifically between two individuals; their interaction reinforces and strengthens the bond.

Attentional deficit disorder: A childhood disorder characterized by an inability to focus attention.

Authoritarian parents: Parents who are directive and who firmly control their children, yet are somewhat emotionally distant and cold.

Authoritative parents: Parents who combine high controls with warmth, receptivity, and encouragement.

Autonomy versus shame and doubt: According to Eriksonian theory, the second nuclear conflict of personality development. The child develops either a sense of autonomy (independence, self-assertion) or the feelings of doubt and shame.

Autoplastic mastery: Gutmann's description for passive world mastery.

Autosomes: The chromosomes of a cell, excluding those that determine sex.

B

Bargaining stage: Kübler-Ross's third stage of dying, characterized by an attempt to trade or barter something in exchange for a longer life.

Basal metabolic rate (BMR): Measurement of the consumption of oxygen by a body at rest.

Basic research: Research conducted for the satisfaction of knowing or understanding.

"Becoming one's own man": Levinson's stage description for men in their late thirties.

Behaviorism: School of psychology based on the study of observable behavior and the patterns of stimulus and response that govern it.

Behavior modification: An intervention approach using procedures based on principles of learning.

Benign: Nonmalignant character of a neoplasm, or the mild character of an illness.

Benign senescence: Normal decreases in functional abilities that accompany aging.

Birth order effects: Any behaviors believed to be brought about by birth position in the family relative to siblings.

Blackout: A momentary lapse of consciousness. In alcoholism a period of temporary amnesia when the alcoholic functions but of which he or she has no memory when sober.

Blastocyst: The cluster of cells resulting from cell division of a zygote in the first week after conception.

Blood pressure: The force or pressure exerted by the heart in pumping blood; the pressure of blood in the arteries.

Bonding: An attachment between neonate and parent that occurs in the first few hours after birth under conditions of close physical contact.

Braxton-Hicks contractions: Irregular painless contractions of the uterus during the last trimester of pregnancy before the onset of labor. Also called *false labor.*

Brazelton scale: Scale used to assess the neurological integrity and behaviors of neonates.

Broken heart syndrome: Lynch's term for the severe, unresolved, morbid grief that can result in the death of the bereaved.

Bulimia: Excessive overeating or uncontrolled binge eating followed by purging.

C

Caesarean section: Surgical delivery of a baby through an incision made through the abdomen and uterus of the mother.

Cancer: Growth of abnormal cells that spread and behave differently from the cells of the body part in which they develop.

Carcinogen: Any substance that produces cancer.

Cardinal traits: Allport's term for all-pervasive, "ruling passion" qualities.

Case study: An observational study in which one person is studied intensively.

Cataract: A loss of transparency of the crystalline lens of the eye or of its capsule.

Catch-up growth: A period of rapid growth, following a period of illness or malnutrition, that continues until the child has attained the height of his or her previous normal growth curve.

Central traits: Allport's term for consistent characteristics that rest on upbringing.

Centration: Tendency to focus on one aspect of a situation and to neglect the importance of other aspects; characteristic of preoperational thought in Piaget's theory.

Centromere: The spindle arrangement with the chromatids at the equator of chromosomes as produced in the metaphase of mitosis and meiosis.

Cephalocaudal development: Development that proceeds in a head-to-toe direction; upper parts of the body develop before lower parts do.

Cerebrovascular accident: An impeded blood supply to some part of the brain; also called *stroke.*

Child abuse: The intentional, nonaccidental physical or sexual abuse of a child by a parent or other adult entrusted with the child.

Child neglect: Failure to attend to important aspects of child care such as provision of physiological needs, safety, a sense of love and belonging, and discipline.

Chromosomes: The long strands of hereditary material containing the genes and composed exclusively of nucleic acids; found in the nucleus of the cell.

Circadian rhythm: Around-the-clock, twenty-four-hour cycle of some bodily functions.

Cirrhosis: A disease of the liver characterized by degeneration, fatty infiltration, atrophy, and inflammation.

Classical conditioning: A basic learning process in which a previously neutral stimulus (conditioned stimulus) is paired with one that elicits a known response (unconditioned stimulus) until the neutral stimulus comes to elicit a similar response (conditioned response).

Climacteric: Term used to suggest a critical time or transitional period in men's lives influenced by male reproductive changes.

Clinical investigations: In-depth studies of the course of an individual's life experiences and personal history.

Cognition: Knowing the world through the use of one's perceptual and conceptual abilities.

Cohabitation: Living together and maintaining a sexual relationship without being legally married.

Cohort: A person born about the same time and into the same social environment as another person.

Colic: Unexplained, explosive, inconsolable crying in infants from two weeks to three months of age.

Collective unconscious: According to Jung, the unconscious life of all human beings, which is composed of many common elements and not just sexual strivings as Freud contended.

Colostomy: The surgical operation of forming an artificial anal opening in the colon.

Colostrum: The fluid secreted by the breasts for several days after childbirth preceding the secretion of milk.

Combinatorial analysis: A Piagetian term referring to the ability to see all the possible variations of a problem and to test each one systematically.

Common traits: Allport's term for behaviors typical of all members of a culture.

Complementary leisure: Leisure that is determined directly or indirectly by others.

Compression of the spinal column: The process by which the spinal column is made more compact by pressure of gravity with age, resulting in a slight loss of height.

Concrete operational stage: Third stage of Piagetian cognitive development, during which children develop logical, but not abstract, thinking.

Confidence intervals: Mathematical expressions that define a range into which a certain proportion of the values of a variable or feature of a population will fall.

Conservation: Piagetian term for the awareness that two substances of equal amount remain equal in the face of perceptual alteration, so long as nothing has been added to or taken away from either substance.

Consummate love: An ideal loving style with passion, intimacy, and commitment.

Contact comfort: Cuddling and other forms of warm physical caressing that bring consolation, relaxation, or ease.

Control group: Those subjects in an experiment who are not exposed to whatever conditions are being studied.

Conventionality: The quality of behaving or acting according to the prevailing norms for conventional behavior.

Conventional morality: According to Kohlberg, the second level of moral development; characterized by observation of standards of others because one wants to please other people.

Coordinated leisure: Work-related activities that are freely chosen by individuals.

Coronary heart disease (CHD): An inclusive term for diseases of the heart and blood vessels, including heart attacks, angina, irregular heartbeat, and congestive heart failure.

Coronary-prone behavior: Highly competitive, tense, hyperalert, achievement-oriented, aggressive, hostile, and impatient habitual modes of action.

Corpus luteum: Body formed in the ovary by a ruptured Graafian follicle that has discharged its ovum.

Correlational research: Studies of the relationship (positive or negative) of variables to each other rather than of cause and effect.

Correlation coefficient: A statistical index for measuring correspondence in changes occurring in two variables.

Creativity: The ability to think flexibly, divergently, imaginatively, inventively, or productively.

Crossing over: A process during meiosis in which individual genes on a chromosome cross over to the opposite chromosome.

Cross-sectional study: A research method using different subjects studied at the same time.

Croup: An inflammation of the respiratory passages, with labored breathing, hoarse coughing, and laryngeal spasm.

Crystallized intelligence: A broad area of intelligence that includes verbal reasoning, comprehension, and spatial perception; may increase during the life span.

D

Deductive reasoning: Thinking about experiences from generalities to particulars, or from the universal to the individual.

Defense mechanisms: In psychodynamic theory, self-protective, usually unconscious psychological devices that help block the ego's awareness of anxiety-provoking memory and instinct.

Delinquent acts: Illegal or offensive activities committed by minors who are aware of wrong-doing.

Denial stage: Kübler-Ross's first stage of dying. A refusal to believe or accept impending death as it is and instead perceiving it as one wishes it would be.

Dental caries: Decay of teeth.

Dependent variable: In an experiment, the behavior that is measured and is expected to change with manipulation of an independent variable.

Depressants: Drugs that act on the central nervous system to reduce pain, tension, and anxiety, to relax and disinhibit, and to slow down intellectual and motor reactivity.

Depression: An emotional state characterized by intense and unrealistic sadness.

Depression stage: Kübler-Ross's fourth stage of dying, characterized by intense sadness.

Descriptive psychology: The study of human and animal behavior that describes patterns of behavior.

Descriptive statistics: Numerical data assembled, classified, and tabulated to describe and summarize the characteristics of the data.

Developmental psychology: The study of humans focusing on developmental changes from conception through death.

Diabetes: A chronic disorder of carbohydrate metabolism due to insulin deficiency or a disturbance of normal tissue responsiveness to insulin.

Dialectic Operations: A stage of adult intelligence characterized by conflict resolution: thesis, antithesis, and synthesis.

Dilation: Enlargement of an opening, blood vessel, canal, or cavity.

Discipline: Training that develops self-control, character, orderliness, and efficiency.

Disengagement: The false belief that all old people withdraw and detach themselves from obligations, occupations, and relationships.

Disequilibrium: Piagetian term referring to the lack of balance between assimilation and accommodation. Most learning takes place in states of disequilibrium.

Distant-figure grandparents: Those who stay remote from their grandchildren except for birthday, religious, or other special observances.

Divergent thinking: Moving from a starting point in many directions to see something in new or different ways.

Divorce: Legal dissolution of a marriage.

Dreikurs's stages: Stages—from being annoying, to rebelliousness, to revenge, to noninteraction—that Dreikurs believed a child goes through unless he or she feels accepted as a valued and equally loved family member.

E

Early adult transition: Levinson's stage description for men from the years of separating from parents until the early to middle twenties.

Ecology: The study of the relations between people and sociocultural patterns in their environment.

Eclecticism: Method or system of thought in which one chooses various sources and selects materials from many doctrines.

Eczema: A stress-related skin disorder that encompasses conditions ranging from an itching rash to a cluster of open wounds.

Effacement: A thinning out; becoming less conspicuous.

Egalitarianism: A belief in the equality of people, regardless of sex, age, race, education, physique, or other characteristics.

Ego: In psychodynamic theory, the rational self-concept, which mediates between the instinctual demands of the id and the externally oriented pressures of the superego.

Egocentrism: Inability to consider another's point of view.

Ego integrity versus despair: According to Eriksonian theory, the eighth and last nuclear conflict of personality development, characterizing old age.

Eidetic memory: The ability to remember minute details of a situation.

Elder abuse: The intentional, nonaccidental physical or sexual abuse of an aged person by adult children or other adults entrusted with elder care.

Embolus: A blood clot that forms in the blood vessels in one part of the body and travels to another.

Embryonic period: The second prenatal period, which lasts from the beginning of the second week to the end of the seventh week after conception. All the major structures and organs of the individual are formed during this time.

Encoding: Categorizing incoming information.

Encopresis: Lack of bowel control.

Endometrium: The mucous membrane lining the uterus.

Entering the adult world: Levinson's stage description for persons in their middle to late twenties.

Enuresis: Lack of bladder control.

Environment: All the external conditions and influences affecting the life and development of an organism.

Epilepsy: A brain disorder in which abnormalities in the electrical activity of the brain produce loss of consciousness and convulsions.

Episiotomy: Surgical incision of the vulva for obstetrical purposes to prevent uneven laceration during delivery.

Equilibrium: Piagetian term referring to a relative state of balance between assimilation and accommodation. This state seldom lasts long.

Eros: According to Freud, the constructive life instinct of the id, which deals with survival, self-propagation, and creativity.

Estrogen replacement therapy (ERT): Estrogen given to bring the level of hormone up to that once produced naturally, to provide relief from symptoms associated with insufficient estrogen.

Estrogens: Female sex hormones, produced primarily in the ovaries.

Euthanasia: Literally, "good death"; the practice of withholding life-sustaining procedures so that death will occur naturally.

Exosystem: A setting that does not involve a person as an active participant but in which events occur that affect the person.

Experiment: A study in which the investigator manipulates one or more variables to determine the effect on another variable.

Experimental psychology: The study of human and animal behavior that stresses knowledge based on countable or measurable actions and reactions.

Expressive orientation: Stereotypic "feminine" behaviors aimed at serving others' physical, social, and emotional needs through nurturance and emotional expressions.

Extinction: Dying out of a response as the result of withdrawal of positive reinforcement.

Extraversion: An attitude in which a person directs his or her interest to outside phenomena rather than to feelings within.

Extravert: A personality whose thoughts, feelings, and interests are directed toward other persons, social affairs, and external phenomena.

F

Failure-to-thrive syndrome: Decline of growth, with height and weight below the norm, in infancy.

Family life cycle: Duvall's description of the eight family stages from marriage to the death of both spouses.

Family of origin: One's biological (or surrogate) parents and any siblings.

Family of procreation: One's spouse and children.

Fear of success: Horner's term for the avoidance of too much success found in some men and women.

Fetal period: Final stage of prenatal development (eight weeks to birth).

Field study: Observational study in which only specified activities and events are catalogued.

Fixation: The inability to progress normally from one stage of psychosexual development to the next due to overgratification or excessive deprivation during that stage.

Fluid intelligence: A type of intelligence involving the ability to solve novel problems.

Forceps: Tongs used for grasping and rotating the fetal head without compressing it during delivery.

Foreclosure of identity: Marcia's term for adolescents' early acceptance of the identity laid out for them by others without any search for self-definition.

Formal grandparents: Those who maintain a clear line between parents' responsibilities and grandparents' roles and who do little or no child-rearing.

Formal operations: According to Piaget, the stage of cognition characterized by the ability to think abstractly.

Foster Grandparents Program: Program that allows older persons to become involved in teaching, supporting, and helping children with special needs.

Free association: A technique in which therapy patients verbalize whatever thoughts come to mind without editing, structuring, or censoring.

Fun-seeking grandparents: Those who serve as playmates to their grandchildren.

G

Gender-role changes: Alterations in the behaviors seen as appropriate for males or females.

Gender-role models: Any persons who demonstrate gender-appropriate behaviors and are imitated.

General adaptation syndrome: Selye's description of the three stages one goes through when faced with intolerable stress: alarm, resistance, and exhaustion.

General to specific development: Development from the main, overall use of body parts to use of limited, distinct body parts.

Generation gap: A distance or difference in ideas between parents and offspring or between people spaced a generation (about thirty years) apart.

Generational changes: Societal changes that assure that parents and offspring will not experience the same norms at the same ages.

Generativity versus stagnation: According to Eriksonian theory, the seventh nuclear conflict of personality development concerned with guiding the next generation.

Genes: The basic units of heredity located on the chromosomes.

Genetic epistemology: The study of the origin, nature, method, and limits of knowledge.

Genotype: Actual genetic composition of an individual.

Geriatrics: Branch of medicine concerned with the elderly.

Germinal period: The first prenatal period, which lasts from fertilization through implantation. The zygote (one cell) changes to a blastocyst (over 100 cells).

Gerontology: Study of the processes of aging and the elderly.

Giftedness: Characterized by one or more of the following attributes: above-average intellectual ability; specific academic aptitude; creative or productive thinking; leadership ability; skill in visual or performing arts.

Glaucoma: Disease of the eye characterized by increased intraocular pressure leading to gradual impairment of sight.

Graafian follicle: One of the small round sacs in the ovaries, each of which contains an ovum.

Grief work: The work of mourning in which one comes to terms with the fact of death and deals with the bitterness, hurt, disappointment, and sense of loss.

Growth trajectory: The curved path that a normal child follows in terms of growth in height and weight.

Gynosperm: X-carrying sperm.

H

Hallucinogenic drugs: Drugs that induce hallucinations; some are also called *psychedelics*.

Hay fever: Seasonal nasal obstruction, itching, sneezing, mucous discharge, and eye irritations as a result of exposure to specific wind-borne pollens.

Heightism: Prejudice directed against shorter people.

Heimlich maneuver: A method of dislodging objects blocking the airway by applying sudden pressure just under the rib cage.

Hemorrhage: A flow of blood from any blood vessel caused by injury or rupture of the vessel.

Heredity: The transmission of physical and psychical characteristics of parents to their offspring by means of genes passed to the offspring through the ovum and sperm at the moment of conception.

Hierarchy of needs: Maslow's concept of a series of needs that must be satisfied one by one in the process of development before the adult can begin pursuing self-actualization.

Holistic medicine: Treatment of the whole person; removal or alleviation of any sources of stress as well as pharmaceutical and physical treatment of symptoms of illness.

Holophrases: One-word sentences that occur early in language acquisition.

Homosexuality: Sexual libido excited by members of one's own sex.

Homozygous: Having allelic genes carrying the same message for the manifestation of a trait.

Honeymoon period: Period of mutual affection of newlyweds.

Hospice: A residence for the terminally ill that allows them to live out their days as independently and as painlessly as possible.

Hot flash: A vasomotor symptom of menopause that causes a flush from the breasts up and an overheated feeling.

Household organization: The task of arranging and maintaining a home.

Humanistic psychology: The view that humans have free will and both the right and capacity for self-determination based on purpose and values (in contrast to Freud's emphasis on unconscious forces).

Hyperopia: Farsightedness.

Hypertension (high blood pressure): An unstable or persistent elevation of blood pressure above the normal range.

Hypothermia: Subnormal body temperature.

Hypothetical-deductive reasoning: Piagetian term referring to the ability to test each possible variation of a problem in order to discover the correct solution.

Hysterectomy: Surgical removal of the uterus or part of the uterus.

I

Id: According to Freud, the mass of biological drives with which the individual is born.

Identification: Process by which an individual acquires the characteristics of a model.

Identity achievement: Acquisition of a firm sense of one's stable and enduring self.

Identity diffusion: Marcia's term for adolescents' failure to seek an identity and lack of commitment to any enduring sense of self.

Identity versus role confusion: According to Eriksonian theory, the fifth nuclear conflict of personality development, in which an adolescent must determine his or her own sense of self (identity).

Idiosyncratic transitions: Life changes out of step with common practice.

Implantation: The embedding of the prenatal organism in the uterine wall.

Independent variable: The variable that is controlled by the experimenter to determine its effect on the dependent variable.

Indifferent parents: Parents who show little interest in controlling their children's behaviors or in responding to them.

Individual differences: Denotes the belief that each human being is born with and has a unique physical and psychological makeup, unlike that of any other human being.

Inductive discipline: A technique employed by parents who try to control their children's behavior by carefully explaining how they want their children to behave and by use of reason.

Inductive reasoning: Reasoning from particular facts to a general conclusion or from the individual to the universal.

Indulgent parents: Parents who combine little or no control with high levels of responsiveness, receptivity, and encouragement.

Industry versus inferiority: According to Eriksonian theory, the fourth nuclear conflict of personality development, which occurs during middle childhood. Children must learn the skills of their culture or face feelings of inferiority.

Infant daycare: A situation in which several infants are cared for all day by a few adults in a setting specifically designed for infant care.

Infectious mononucleosis: A disease causing fever and enlargement of the lymph nodes.

Inferential statistics: The assembling, classifying, and tabulating of numerical data in such a way that the characteristics of the population from which the data were drawn can be inferred.

Inferiority: Term used to describe the feelings of inadequacy that characterize some people.

Infertility: The state of being unable to produce offspring.

Initiative versus guilt: According to Eriksonian theory, the third nuclear conflict of personality development, which characterizes children from three to six years.

In-law relations: The reciprocal dealings of persons related by marriage, not blood.

Inner speech: Term denoting the language of the mind, the private speech we use only for our own thinking and reasoning.

Instrumental orientation: Stereotypic "masculine" behaviors characterized by task-orientation, self-serving actions, independence, and tight rein on emotional expression.

Integrated personalities: Neugarten's description for persons who face up to their emotions and experience rich inner lives.

Intelligence quotient (IQ): Mathematical score computed by dividing an individual's mental age by chronological age and multiplying by 100: IQ = MA/CA X 100.

Interiority of personality: Neugarten's description of the move inward toward more preoccupation with satisfying personal needs that occurs in middle age.

Intermediate grief: A period of crying and extended sorrow after the acute grief accompanying loss, in which one often reviews one's life and engages in self-reproach for things done or left undone.

Interpropositional thinking: According to Piaget, the ability to handle relationships among several different properties at the same time.

Interview: A method for learning about people through purposeful communication.

Intimacy versus isolation: According to Eriksonian theory, the sixth nuclear conflict of personality development, which occurs during young adulthood.

Introvert: One whose orientation is toward the self rather than toward association with others.

Iron deficiency anemia: A reduction in the amount of hemoglobin in the blood due to a dietary deficiency of iron.

J

Jensenism: Belief that genetic factors play the major role in the average black/white intelligence difference.

Juvenile crimes: Crimes committed by persons under the legal age of adulthood.

K

Kübler-Ross stages of dying: Denial, anger, bargaining, depression, and acceptance.

L

Lactation: Secretion of milk by the mammary glands; breastfeeding.

Lamaze delivery: Approach to childbirth in which expectant parents attend classes prior to labor and delivery.

Language acquisition device (LAD): Inborn mental structure that enables children to build a system of language rules.

Lanugo: Fuzzy prenatal and neonatal body hair.

Late maturation: Puberty that occurs significantly later than the average.

Launching children: The process of moving offspring out of the family home and into independent lives.

Learning disability: Extreme difficulty in learning with no detectable physiological abnormality.

LeBoyer delivery: Delivery in a warm, darkened, soothing environment reducing as much trauma to the neonate as possible.

Leukemia: Cancer of the blood-forming tissues characterized by an abnormal increase in the number of leukocytes.

Libido: In psychodynamic theory, the energy of the life instinct, which Freud saw as the driving force of personality.

Life change units: The average mean values assigned to various life events by Holmes and Rahe.

Life expectancy: The average number of years that a person of a given age may expect to live.

Limbic system: The part of the brainstem forming a border around the lower forebrain that is involved in emotional reactivity.

Living will: A legal document stating that a person does not wish to be kept alive by artificial means, signed while a person is healthy.

Longevity: Long life.

Longitudinal study: A research method that involves examining the same subjects over a long period.

Long-term memory: Type of memory that involves long-term storage of material; appears to last forever.

Love-withdrawal discipline: Method of discipline that predominantly uses a loss of affection and approval as a consequence of misbehaving.

Lunar cycles: Events that recur over a period of about one month.

Lung cancer epidemic: The alarming, rapid increase in lung cancer in recent years.

Lymphomas: Cancerous growths arising in the lymph-cell-producing areas.

M

Macrosystem: The belief systems or ideologies underlying a given culture or subculture.

Malignant: Having the property of uncontrollable growth and dissemination.

Marital morale: A measure of contentment with a marriage based on the number of personal and interpersonal goals that are being achieved.

Marriage: Relation between a man and woman who have become husband and wife.

Maturity: The quality of being fully developed, complete, full-grown, or perfect.

Meals-on-Wheels: A social service program that brings meals to the homes of disabled or elderly clients.

Mediation: Using skills already developed to help acquire new skills or greater dexterity at old skills.

Menarche: The time of the first menstrual period.

Menopause: The period in a woman's life when menstruation ceases.

Menstruation: The periodic discharge of the bloody endometrial lining from the uterus.

Mental disorder: An unhealthy or abnormal condition of some mental function(s).

Mental retardation: A condition of mental deficiency, defined as being two standard deviations below the norm in IQ with deficits in adaptive behavior, manifest in the developmental period.

Mentor: An older adult who acts as a counselor or guide.

Meritocracy: Term used by Herrnstein to describe an educational system that would provide teaching in keeping with inherited abilities to learn.

Mesosystem: The interrelations among two or more microsystems in which a person actively participates.

Metacognition: The knowledge of how and when to apply memory strategies in order to retain information or master new skills.

Metamemory: Conscious or intuitive knowledge about memory.

Metastasis: The shifting of a cancer from one part of the body to another.

Microsystem: The interpersonal relations, activities, and roles experienced by a person in a given setting with particular physical and material characteristics.

Midlife transition: Turmoil precipitated by the review and reevaluation of one's past, typically occurring in the early to middle forties.

Modeling: In behavioral theory, the learning of a new behavior by imitating another person performing that behavior.

Molding: The temporary misshaping or elongation of a newborn's head caused by pressure on the soft bones during the birth process.

Morality training: Education that directs behaviors toward the good and away from the bad.

Moratorium of identity: Marcia's term for adolescents' postponement of the adoption of a stable sense of self, characterized by experimentation with different roles.

Morbid grief reactions: Delayed emotional responses to loss, misfortune, or death of a loved one that may be expressed in a serious psychosomatic disorder, drug abuse, depression, or serious anxiety disorder.

Mores: Fixed customs imbued with an ethical significance, often having the force of law.

Morula: The mass of cells resulting from early mitotic cell division of the zygote.

Motor milestones: The major developmental tasks of a period (such as infancy) that depend on muscular movements.

Motor norms: Standards for achievement of activities related to muscle use set for various ages of childhood.

Motor tics: Involuntary, repetitive, nonpurposeful movements of a part of the body.

Mourning rituals: The social expressions of grief, including funeral rituals and associated behaviors.

Multiple infarcts: Multiple small strokes.

Myelin: A white fatty covering on many neural fibers that serves to channel impulses along fibers and to reduce the random spread of impulses across neurons.

Myopia: Nearsightedness.

Myth of serenity: False belief that all old people are peaceful, relaxed, and carefree.

Myth of a sexless old age: False belief that all old people have lost their sexual desires.

N

Narcotics: Drugs that induce relaxation and provide relief from anxiety and physical pain.

Neonate: Newborn infant up to two to four weeks.

Neoplasm: Growth of abnormal cells or tissues; cancer.

Neuroticism: State of being partially disorganized due to anxieties.

Neurotransmitters: A group of chemicals that facilitate the transmission of electrical impulses between nerve endings in the brain.

Nuclear conflict: Eriksonian term applied to major conflicts characterizing each of his eight stages.

Nuclear family: The family that consists of only parents and children.

Numbering: Designating the place of objects in a series, taking into account classes and orders within classes.

Nursing homes: Residences providing needed care for the infirm, disabled, and chronically ill.

O

Obesity: The quality or state of being more than 20% above one's ideal body weight for size, age, and sex.

Objectivity: State or quality of observing phenomena without bias, in a detached, impersonal way.

Observation: An act of noting and recording facts and events as they occur in the real world; also the data so noted and recorded.

Omniplastic mastery: Gutmann's description for magical world mastery.

Oncogenes: Cancer-causing genes present in the cells of humans.

Oncology: The study of the causes, properties, and treatment of cancer.

Ontogeny: Origin and development of an individual organism and its functions from conception to death.

Oophorectomy: Incision into and removal of an ovary or ovarian tumor.

Openness: State of being frank and forthright with an absence of secrecy, prejudice, or bigotry.

Operant conditioning: Basic learning process in which behaviors are repeated or reduced as functions of environmental consequences (reinforcements and punishments).

Ossification: The change from cartilage to bone.

Osteoarthritis: Degeneration and loss of cartilage at the ends of bones that cause joint pain.

Osteoporosis: A disease of bone characterized by increased porosity and softness from absorption of the calcareous material.

Otitis media: Inflammation of the middle ear.

Ovulation: Expulsion of an ovum from the ovary, which occurs once about every twenty-eight to thirty-two days from puberty to menopause.

P

Parenthood: Taking responsibility for protecting and raising one's offspring or adopted children.

Parent-surrogate grandparents: Those who take on all the caregiving responsibilities for the grandchildren.

Participant observation: A method of research in which the researcher attempts to become immersed in the way of life to be studied to the point of temporarily becoming part of the social context.

Passive-dependent personalities: Neugarten's description for persons who are dissatisfied with their lives and apathetic and who lean on others for succor and support.

Peak experience: Maslow's term for a momentary state of ecstasy and a sense of unity with the whole world.

Peer group: The group of persons who constitute one's associates, usually of the same age and social status.

Peer pressures: Compelling influences to behave in certain ways brought to bear by one's age cohorts.

Period of individuation: Jung's description of the period of life after a discovery of one's inner self in the forties.

Periodontal disease: Loosening of the teeth and occasionally infection of the gum that is characteristic of the older mouth when neglected.

Personal fable: A belief in one's own immortality and invulnerability.

Personality stability: Costa and McCrae's term for the endurance over time of many personality dispositions.

Personification of death: Embodiment of death as a human figure.

Phenomenological approach: Attempts to see the subject's world from the vantage point of the subject's own internal frame of reference.

Phenotype: Observable characteristics of a person: may vary from genotype (genetic characteristics).

Phonetic drift: The tendency of an infant learning language to produce predominantly the phonemes that he or she hears spoken.

Phylogeny: Evolution of traits and features common to a species or race.

Physical dependence: A physical need for some chemical substance; withdrawal from its use produces symptoms of illness.

Pica: Hunger for nonfood substances.

Pincer grasp: Hold between thumb and forefinger.

Placenta: Organ that conveys food and oxygen to the prenatal organism and carries away its body wastes.

Placental barrier: Barrier to substances created by the fact that only molecules small enough to diffuse through the villi of the placenta reach the fetus.

Posttraumatic stress disorder: An anxiety reaction to a disaster or severe stress characterized by numbness, recurrent dreams, and excessive reactivity.

Power-assertive discipline: Disciplinary techniques used by parents who rely on punishment, fear, and material rewards.

Precipitous delivery: Sudden delivery of a fetus after less than three hours of labor.

Precocious puberty: Puberty beginning before age nine in girls or before age ten in boys.

Premenstrual syndrome (PMS): Group of physical and behavioral changes that affect some women in the week before a menstrual period, including tension, bloating, fatigue, irritability, and moodiness.

Premorality: According to Kohlberg, the first level of moral development, characterized by hedonistic, self-serving urges.

Preoperational thought: Thought that characterizes children from about two to seven, in Piaget's second stage of cognitive development.

Preparation and recuperation: Kelly's term for work-related activities that are determined by others.

Preretirement planning: The development of special interests or leisure pursuits a decade or two before retirement in anticipation of more time to enjoy them after retirement.

Presbycusis: Physiological changes in auditory perception, especially of high-tone frequencies, in advancing age.

Presbyopia: Physiological changes in accommodation power in the eyes in advancing age.

Primary sexual characteristics: Changes in breasts, ovaries, uterus, and vagina, or in the penis and testes, that occur at puberty and lead to reproductive maturity.

Principled moral reasoning: Kohlberg's descriptive term for the last stage of his sequence of moral development; also called postconventional morality.

Probability: Chance stronger than possibility but falling short of certainty.

Progesterone: A principal female sex hormone, secreted by the corpus luteum.

Prolonged labor: Dilation and effacement of the cervix of the uterus that progresses very slowly, lasting over 24 hours.

Proportional reasoning: Piagetian term referring to the ability to understand ratios, keeping a number or quantity in proportion.

Prosocial behaviors: Altruistic behaviors; giving, caring, sharing.

Proximal-distal development: Development that proceeds in a near-to-far direction; parts of the body near the center develop before the extremities do.

Psychodynamic: Referring to the assumption that human behavior is a function of events occurring inside the mind and is explainable only in terms of those mental events.

Psychological dependence: The emotional need for continued use of a drug or for support from another person.

Psychophysiologic disorder: Physical disorders involving actual tissue damage that result from continual emotional activation of the autonomic nervous system.

Puberty: The period of life during which an individual's reproductive organs become functional.

Pubescence: Time of life span characterized by rapid physiological growth, maturation of reproductive functioning, and appearance of primary and secondary sex characteristics.

R

Random sample: A method of selecting research subjects that allows all members of the population under study an equal chance of being selected.

Rational-emotive theory: Albert Ellis's theory that self-defeating thoughts and feelings underlie disordered behavior.

Reaction formation: A defense mechanism in which the individual distorts a drive to its opposite; for example, acting kindly toward a person whom one dislikes.

Realism: Piagetian term for the confusion of psychological events with objective reality.

Reciprocity: Corresponding, complementary, inverse relationships.

Recovery phase of bereavement: A period during which survivors work at accepting the fact of death.

Reflexes: Those actions performed involuntarily by infants in response to some external excitation.

Reliability: The degree to which the same observations or procedures will produce the same or similar results each time they are repeated.

Remarriage: Marrying a new spouse after death or divorce.

Replication: Reproduction of the original; important in experimental research to give more confidence that the research results did not occur by chance.

Reservoir-of-wisdom grandparents: Those who serve as authority figures for parents and grandchildren, passing on special skills, resources, and family history.

Respiratory distress syndrome: Breathing disorder of the newborn caused by under-expansion of the lungs and reduced lung volume; also called *hyaline membrane disease.*

Retinal hemorrhage: Bleeding within the retina of the eye.

Retirement: A withdrawal from an activity such as business, service, or public life, especially because of advanced age or poor health.

Retrospective study: A research method of investigating subjects' development, examining their histories by means of interviews and records.

Reversibility: Piagetian term for the awareness that an operation can be reversed to bring back the original situation.

Rh factor: An agglutinizing factor present in the blood of most humans; when it is introduced into blood lacking the factor, antibodies form in the blood.

Rosenthal effect: Treatment of a person according to some preconceived notion of how he or she will behave intellectually, which has the effect of eliciting the expected academic performance.

S

Schema: Piagetian term for a basic cognitive unit.

School phobia: Fear of going to school or separating from parents, accompanied by somatic symptoms of illness.

Scientific method: Practice of acquiring knowledge by systematically stating problem, forming hypotheses, experimenting, observing, and drawing conclusions.

Second honeymoon phenomenon: Renewed interest in one's spouse and in sexual activities after the menopause.

Secondary sexual chacteristics: Physical characteristics that appear in humans around the age of puberty and that are sex differentiated but not necessary for sexual reproduction.

Secondary traits: Allport's term for minor personality characteristics or ways of behaving known only by a few close associates.

Secular growth trend: A trend toward increased height in each new generation of children seen in well-nourished children over the past 100 years.

Self-actualization: According to Abraham Maslow, the need to develop one's true nature and fulfill one's potentialities.

Senescence: Period of the life span accompanied by decrement in bodily functioning; begins at different ages for different people.

Senile dementia: A pathological degenerative disorder resulting from severe organic deterioration of the brain in old age in some persons.

Senility: Senile dementia; an organic brain syndrome characterized by problems of confusion and disorientation in some old persons.

Sensorimotor intelligence: Cognitive development characterizing the infant (birth to two years) in which children actively engage in contact with their environment and thus gain information about their world.

Sensory memory: The second-long retention of a visual or auditory sensation.

Settling down: Levinson's stage description for men in their early thirties.

Sex chromosomes: The one pair of chromosomes that determines the sex of the organism (XX is female; XY is male).

Sex typing: Process by which children acquire attitudes and behaviors deemed by their culture to be appropriate for members of their sex.

Sexually transmitted diseases (STDs): Diseases transmitted through sexual intercourse or other direct genital, oral, or anal sexual contact.

Short-term memory: Memory retained for brief periods of time—about 30 seconds.

Sibling rivalry: Competition between brothers and sisters.

SIDS (sudden infant death syndrome): A major cause of death for American infants between one week and six months of age. The cause is unknown. Also called *crib death.*

Singlehood: The state of being alone, not united with another.

Single parenting: Taking on the responsibilities for protecting and raising one's offspring or adopted children alone.

Social-learning theory: School of thought based on the belief that new behaviors are acquired through observational learning and imitation and are maintained through either direct or vicarious reinforcements.

Social network: A system of socially interrelated persons who serve to support each other.

Soft spots: The spaces (fontanelles) between the bones of the neonate's skull that have not yet changed from cartilage to bone.

Specific reading disorder: Difficulty with basic reading skills or reading comprehension.

Spermatogenesis: The formation of mature sperm.

Standard deviation: A statistical technique for expressing the extent of variation of a group of scores from the mean.

Standardized tests: Tests administered to a large group of people in order to determine statistical norms or standards for the population.

Statistical significance: Characteristic of a variable if it is unusual and if its chance of occurring is less than a value arbitrarily set by a researcher, usually less than 1% or 5% of the time.

Status offenses: Conduct considered illegal if engaged in by a juvenile but not if engaged in by an adult.

Stepparenting: Taking on the responsibilities for protecting and raising the children of one's spouse.

Stimulants: A class of drugs whose major effect is to provide energy, alertness, and feelings of confidence.

Stimulus–response learning: Learning that takes place when a reaction is repeatedly paired with a stimulus to obtain some reward or avoid some undesirable consequence.

Strabismus: Crossed eyes; walleyes.

Stranger anxiety: Phenomenon that often occurs during the second half of the first year, when infants express fear of strange people and places and protest separation from parents.

Strep infection: An infection, usually in the throat, resulting from the presence of streptococci bacteria.

Stuttering: The interruption of speech fluency through blocked, prolonged, or repeated words, syllables, or sounds.

Subconscious: Partial unconsciousness. The state in which mental processes take place without the conscious perception of the individual.

Subjectivity: State or quality of imposing personal prejudices, thoughts, and feelings into one's work.

Substance abuse: Chemical abuse characterized by a minimum of one month's physiological or psychological dependence and difficulty in social functioning.

Superego: In Freudian theory, that part of the mind in which the individual has incorporated the moral standards of the society.

Superiority: Adlerian term used to describe the exaggerated feeling of high value and worth that characterizes some people.

Superwoman syndrome: Situation in which a woman who holds a job also assumes major responsibility for child care and performs all the traditional role functions at home.

Synapse: The junction of two neurons; the locale where an electrical impulse is transmitted from one neuron to another.

Syncretism: Belief that co-occurring events belong together.

Synergism: The interaction of drugs in which the total effect is much greater than the sum of their individual effects.

T

Teenage pregnancy: Conception and gestation by an adolescent female.

Telegraphic speech: Early speech that uses salient words (nouns and verbs) and omits auxiliary parts of speech.

Temperament: Unique style of behavior, arousal, and expression of emotions.

Teratogenic drugs: Any drugs that cause malformations of the embryo/fetus within the uterus.

Terminal decline: A significant decline in intellectual abilities that often precedes death.

Thanatology: The study of death.

Thanatos: In Freudian theory, the death instinct of the id.

Thrombus: A blood clot that forms inside a blood vessel or cavity of the heart.

Toilet training: Teaching a child to defecate and urinate in the proper place.

Tolerance: The physiological condition in which the usual dosage of a drug no longer provides the desired effect.

Transactional analysis: An interpersonal therapy in which one becomes aware of one's unconscious games and controls one's own fate.

Transformations: Changes in nature, disposition, or the like that accompany age.

Transient ischemic attacks: Mild forms of obstruction to the flow of blood in the vessels of the brain, causing dizziness, unsteadiness, slurred speech, and numbness; also called *little strokes*.

Transductive reasoning: Piaget's term for associative reasoning instead of induction or deduction.

Trust versus mistrust: Erikson's first nuclear conflict of personality development in which an infant develops a sense of whether the world and its inhabitants are safe and can be trusted.

Tumor: An abnormal mass of tissue that forms from the proliferation of an abnormal cell.

U

Unconditional leisure: Leisure that is freely chosen by an individual.

Unconscious: In Freudian theory, the largest level of consciousness, containing all memories not readily available to the perceptual conscious because they have been either forgotten or repressed.

Unintegrated personalities: Neugarten's description for persons who are dissatisfied and disorganized and have a low activity level.

Uterus: Pear-shaped muscular organ in which the fertilized egg develops until birth; also known as the *womb*.

V

Validity: Truthfulness and trustworthiness of a research finding. *Internal validity* refers to the research procedures, and *external validity* refers to the generalizability of the data to the larger population.

Vernix caseosa: Waxy covering of the fetus in utero; also found on the neonate.

Villi: Capillaries of the placenta that link the developing unbilical veins and arteries of an embryo with the uterine wall.

Y

Youth stage: Keniston's classification for young people between adolescence and adulthood with a stable sense of self but still searching for a vocation and a social role they can play comfortably.

Z

Zygote: A new individual formed by the union of ovum and sperm at fertilization.

References

CHAPTER 1

American Psychological Association (1981). Ethical principles of psychologists. *American Psychologist,* **36,** 633–638.

Applebaum, M. I., and McCall, R. B. (1983). Design and analysis in developmental psychology. In W. Kessen (ed.), *History, theory and methods.* Vol. 1 of P. H. Mussen (ed.) *Handbook of child psychology,* 4th ed. New York: Wiley.

Aries, P. (1962). *Centuries of childhood.* New York: Vintage/Random House.

Block, J., Block, J. H., and Keyes, S. (1988). Longitudinally foretelling drug usage in adolescence: Early childhood personality and environmental precursors. *Child Development,* **59**(2), 336–355.

Bouchard, T. J., and McGue, M. (1981). Familial studies of intelligence: A review. *Science,* **212,** 1055–1059.

Bronfenbrenner, U. (1979). *The ecology of human development.* Cambridge, MA: Harvard University Press.

Courage, M. L. (1989). Children's inquiry strategies in referential communication and in the game of twenty questions. *Child Development,* **60**(4), 877–886.

Darwin, C. (1859). *On the origin of species by means of natural selection.* London: John Murray.

Darwin, C. (1877). A biographical sketch of an infant. *Mind,* 7, 285–294.

Descartes, R. (1972). *Treatise of man* (T. S. Hall, trans.). Cambridge, MA: Harvard University Press.

Elder, G. H., Jr., Van Nguyen, T., and Caspi, A. (1985). Linking family hardship to children's lives. *Child Development,* **56**(2), 361–375.

Galton, F. (1892). *Hereditary genius.* London: Macmillan Ltd.

Green, B. F. (1981). A primer of testing. *American Psychologist,* **36**(10), 1001–1011.

Greer, T. H. (1982). *A brief history of the Western world.* New York: Harcourt Brace Jovanovich.

Hall, G. S. (1904). *Adolescence* (2 vols.) New York: Appleton.

Hall, G. S. (1922). *Senescence: The last half of life.* New York: Appleton.

Jasnow, M., Crown, C. L., Feldstein, S., Taylor, L., Beebe, B., and Jaffe, J. (1988). Coordinated interpersonal timing of Down-syndrome and nondelayed infants with their mothers. *Biological Bulletin,* **175,** 355–360.

King, L. (1982). *Larry King by Larry King.* New York: Simon & Schuster.

Lester, B. M., and Dreher, M. (1989). Effects of marijuana use during pregnancy on newborn cry. *Child Development,* **60**(4), 765–771.

Mead, M. (1928). *Coming of age in Samoa.* New York: Morrow.

Mead, M. (1953). *Growing up in New Guinea.* New York: New American Library.

Pinon, M. F., Huston, A. C., and Wright, J. C. (1989). Family ecology and child characteristics that predict young children's educational television viewing. *Child Development,* **60**(4), 846–856.

Society for Research in Child Development (1990). Committee on ethics research with children. *SRCD Newsletter* (Winter), 3–4.

Stanovich, K. E., Nathan, R. G., and Zolman, J. E. (1988). The developmental lag hypothesis in reading: Longitudinal and matched reading-level comparisons. *Child Development,* **59**(1), 71–86.

Stevenson, D. L., and Baker, D. P. (1987). The family–school relation and the child's school performance. *Child Development,* **58**(5), 1348–1357.

Stocker, C., Dunn, J., and Plomin, R. (1989). Sibling relationships: Links with child temperament, maternal behavior and family structure. *Child Development,* **60**(3), 715–727.

Tieger, T. (1980). On the biological basis of sex differences in aggression. *Child Development,* **51,** 943–963.

CHAPTER 2

Adler, A. (1971). *The practice and theory of individual psychology.* New York: Humanities Press. (Originally published, 1929).

Bandura, A. (1969). *Principles of behavior modification.* New York: Holt, Rinehart & Winston.

Bandura, A. (1977). *Social learning theory.* Englewood Cliffs, NJ: Prentice-Hall.

Bandura, A., and Rosenthal, T. (1966). Vicarious classical conditioning as a function of arousal level. *Journal of Personality and Social Psychology,* **3,** 54–62.

Bandura, A., and Walters, R. (1963). *Social learning and personality development.* New York: Holt, Rinehart & Winston.

Bruner, J. (1966). *Toward a theory of instruction.* Cambridge, MA: Harvard University Press.

Cohen, D. (1983). *Piaget: Critique and assessment.* New York: St. Martin's Press.

Colby, A., Kohlberg, L., Gibbs, Jr., and Lieberman, M. (1983). A longitudinal study of moral judgment. *Monographs of the Society for Research in Child Development,* **48** (1–2, Serial No. 200).

Ellis, A. (1974). Rational–emotive theory. In A. Burton (ed.), *Operational theories of personality.* New York: Brunner/Mazel.

Ellis, A., and Harper, R. (1961). *A guide to rational living.* Englewood Cliffs, NJ: Prentice-Hall.

Erikson, E. H. (1963). *Childhood and society,* 2nd ed. New York: Norton.

Erikson, E. H. (1968). *Identity, youth and crisis.* New York: Norton.

Flavell, J. H. (1982). On cognitive development. *Child Development,* **53,** 1–10.

Freud, S. (1966). *Introductory lectures on psychoanalysis* (J. Strachey, ed. and trans.). New York: Norton. (Originally published, 1920).

Horney, K. (1937). *The neurotic personality of our time.* New York: Norton.

Jones, M. C. (1924). A laboratory study of fear: The case of Peter. *Journal of Genetic Psychology,* **31,** 308–315.

Jung, C. (1931). *Psychology of the unconscious.* New York: Dodd, Mead.

Jung, C. (1968). *Analytical psychology.* New York: Pantheon. (Originally published, 1916).

Keller, H. (1902). *The story of my life.* New York: Doubleday.

Kohlberg, L. (1984). *The psychology of moral development.* San Francisco: Harper and Row.

Luria, A. R. (1976). *Cognitive development: Its cultural and social foundations.* Cambridge, MA: Harvard University Press.

Luria, A. R. (1982). *Language and cognition.* New York: Wiley.

Maslow, A. (1954). *Motivation and personality.* New York: Harper Brothers.

Maslow, A. (1965). Lessons from the peak experience. In R. Farson (ed.), *Science and human affairs.* Palo Alto, CA: Science and Behavior Books.

Maslow, A. (1968). Some educational implications of the humanistic psychologies. *Harvard Educational Review,* **38,** 685–696.

Miller, N., and Dollard, J. (1941). *Social learning and imitation.* New Haven, CT: Yale University Press.

Piaget, J. (1962). *Play, dreams and imitation in childhood* (C. Gattegno and F. Hodgson, trans.). New York: Norton.

Rogers, C. (1951). *Client-centered therapy.* Boston: Houghton Mifflin.

Rogers, C. (1961). *On becoming a person.* Boston: Houghton Mifflin.

Sears, R. (1957). Identification as a form of behavior development. In D. B. Harris (ed.) *The concept of development* (pp. 149–161). Minneapolis: University of Minnesota Press.

Sears, R., Rau, L., and Alpert, R. (1965). *Identification and child-rearing.* Stanford, CA: Stanford University Press.

Skinner, B. F. (1948). *Walden two.* New York: Macmillan.

Skinner, B. F. (1971). *Beyond freedom and dignity.* New York: Knopf.

Vygotsky, L. (1962). *Thought and language* (E. Hanfmann and G. Vakar, trans.). Cambridge, MA: MIT Press. (Originally published, 1934).

Watson, J. B. (1928). *Psychological care of infant and child.* New York: Norton.

Watson, J. B. (1930). *Behaviorism.* New York: Norton.

Watson, J. B. and Raynor, R. (1920). Conditioned emotional reactions. *Journal of Experimental Psychology,* **3,** 1–4.

CHAPTER 3

American Academy of Pediatrics Committee on Drugs (1978). Effect of medication during labor and delivery on infant outcome. *Pediatrics,* **62,** 402–403.

Ayala, F. A., and Kiger, J. A., Jr. (1984). *Modern genetics,* 2nd ed. Menlo Park, CA: Benjamin Cummings.

Bancroft, J., Axworthy, D., and Ratcliffe, S. G. (1982). The personality and psychosexual development of boys with 47 XXY chromosome constitution. *Journal of Child Psychology and Psychiatry,* **23,** 169–180.

Benson, R. C. (1987). Psychological aspects of obstetrics and gynecology. In M. L. Pernoll and R. C. Benson (eds.), *Current obstetric and gynecologic diagnosis and treatment,* 6th ed. Los Altos, CA: Appleton & Lange.

Bhatia, R., Sokol, R. J., and Pernoll, M. L. (1987). Detection of high-risk pregnancy. In M. L. Pernoll and R. C. Benson (eds.), *Current obstetric and gynecologic diagnosis and treatment,* 6th ed. Los Altos, CA: Appleton & Lange.

Bodde, T. (1984). *Facts about pregnancy and smoking* (NICHD Fact Sheet 461–309:52). Washington, D.C.: U.S. Government Printing Office.

Brent, R. L. (1986). Radiation teratogenesis. In J. L. Sever and R. L. Brent (eds.), *Teratogen update: Environmentally induced birth defect risks.* New York: Alan R. Liss.

Brody, J. E. (1981). As Caesarean birth rate grows, so does a debate. *The New York Times,* Sunday, September 20, p. E22.

Broman, S. H. (1983). Obstetric medications. In C. C. Brown (ed.), *Childhood learning disabilities and prenatal risk: Pediatric round table series; 9.* Skillman, NJ: Johnson & Johnson Baby Products Company.

Campbell, S. B., and Werry, J. S. (1986). Attention deficit disorder (hyperactivity). In H. C. Quay and J. S. Werry (eds.), *Psychological disorders of childhood,* 3rd ed. New York: Wiley.

Chasnoff, I. J., Griffith, D. R., MacGregor, S., Dirkes, K., and Burns, K. A. (1989). Temporal patterns of cocaine use in pregnancy. *Journal of the American Medical Association,* **2651**(12), 1741–1744.

Darby, B. L., Streissguth, A. P., and Smith, D. W. (1981). A preliminary follow-up of eight children diagnosed with fetal alcohol syndrome in infancy. *Neurobehavioral Toxicology and Teratology,* **3,** 157–159.

Dick-Read, G. (1972). *Childbirth without fear: The original approach to natural childbirth.* New York: Harper and Row.

Drillien, C. M., Thomson, A. J. M., and Bargoyne, K. (1980). Low birthweight children at early school-age: A longitudinal study. *Developmental Medicine and Child Neurology,* **22,** 26–47.

Durfee, R. B. (1987). Obstetric complications of pregnancy. In M. L. Pernoll and R. C. Benson (eds.), *Current obstetric and gynecologic diagnosis and treatment,* 6th ed. Los Altos, CA: Appleton & Lange.

Dwyer, J. (1984). Impact of maternal nutrition on infant death. *Resident and Staff Physician,* **30**(8), 19–30.

Edwards, R. G. (1981). Test-tube babies. *Nature,* **293,** 253.

Ericsson, R. J., and Glass, R. H. (1982). *Getting pregnant in the 1980s: New advances in infertility treatment and sex preselection.* Berkeley: University of California Press.

Furey, E. M. (1982). The effects of alcohol on the fetus. *Exceptional Children,* **49,** 30–34.

Ganong, W. F. (1983). *Review of medical physiology,* 11th ed. Los Altos, CA: Lange.

Ganong, W. F. (1987). Physiology of reproduction. In M. L. Pernoll and R. C. Benson (eds.), *Current obstetric and gynecologic diagnosis and treatment,* 6th ed. Los Altos, CA: Appleton & Lange.

Garn, S. M., Johnston, M., Ridella, S. A., and Petzold, A. S. (1981). Effect of maternal cigarette smoking on Apgar scores. *American Journal of Diseases of Children,* **135,** 503–506.

Githins, J. H., and Hathaway, W. E. (1984). Hematologic disorders. In C. H. Kempe, H. K. Silver, and D. O'Brien (eds.), *Current pediatric diagnosis and treatment,* 8th ed. Los Altos, CA: Lange.

Golden, N. L., Sokol, R. J., and Rubin, I. (1980). Angel dust: Possible effects on the fetus. *Pediatrics,* **65**(1), 18–20.

Hale, R. W. (1984). Diagnosis of pregnancy and associated conditions. In R. C. Benson (ed.), *Current obstetric and gynecologic diagnosis and treatment,* 5th ed. Los Altos, CA: Lange.

Hartland, E. S. (1909). *Primitive paternity.* Washington, D.C.: American Medical Society.

Hemsell, D. L., Cunningham, F. G., Mickal, A., and Wendel, G. D. (1987). Pelvic infections and sexually transmitted diseases. In M. L. Pernoll and R. C. Benson (eds.), *Current obstetric and gynecologic diagnosis and treatment,* 6th ed. Los Altos, CA: Appleton & Lange.

Hollenbeck, A. R., Gewirtz, J. L., Sebris, S. L., and Scanlon, J. W. (1984). Labor and delivery medication influences parent–infant interaction in the first postpartum month. *Infant Behavior and Development,* **7,** 201–109.

Holzman, I. R. (1982). Fetal alcohol syndrome (FAS)—A review. *Journal of Children in Contemporary Society,* **15,** 13–19.

Householder, J., Hatcher, R., Burns, W. J., and Chasnoff, I. (1982). Infants born to narcotic-addicted mothers. *Psychological Bulletin,* **92,** 453–468.

Jacklin, C. N., and Maccoby, E. M. (1982). Length of labor and sex of offspring. *Journal of Pediatric Psychology,* **7,** 355–360.

Johnston, C. (1981). Cigarette smoking and the outcome of human pregnancies: A status report on the consequences. *Clinical Toxicology,* **18,** 189–209.

Katchadourian, H. (1989). *Fundamentals of human sexuality,* 5th ed. New York: Holt, Rinehart & Winston.

Kennell, J. H. (1982). The physiologic effects of a supportive companion (doula) during labor. In M. H. Klaus and M. O. Robertson (eds.), *Birth, interaction and attachment: Pediatric round table series; 6.* Skillman, NJ: Johnson & Johnson Baby Products Company.

Lamaze, F. (1958). *Painless childbirth: Psychoprophylactic method.* London: Burke.

Mabie, B. C., and Sibai, B. M. (1987). Hypertensive states of pregnancy. In M. L. Pernoll and R. C. Benson (eds.), *Current obstetric and gynecologic diagnosis and treatment,* 6th ed. Los Altos, CA: Appleton & Lange.

Meyer, M. B. (1978). How does maternal smoking affect birth weight and maternal weight gain? Evidence from the Ontario Perinatal Mortality Study. *American Journal of Obstetrics and Gynecology,* **8,** 888–893.

Miller, G. (1989). Addicted infants and their mothers. *Zero to Three,* **9**(5), 20–23.

Moore, K. L. (1988). *The developing human: Clinically oriented embryology,* 4th ed. Philadelphia, PA: W. B. Saunders.

Mulvihill, J. L. (1986). Fetal alcohol syndrome. In J. L. Sever and R. L. Brent (eds.), *Teratogen update: Environmentally induced birth defect risks.* New York: Alan R. Liss.

Naeye, R. L. (1981). Nutritional/nonnutritional interactions that affect the outcome of pregnancy. *American Journal of Clinical Nutrition,* **34,** 727–731.

Needham, J. (1959). *A history of embryology,* 2nd ed. Cambridge: Cambridge University Press.

Osofsky, H. J. (1983). Coping with pregnancy and parenthood. In V. J.

Sasserath (ed.), *Minimizing high-risk parenting.* Skillman, NJ: Johnson & Johnson Baby Products Company.

Physicians Desk Reference (1988), 42nd ed. Oradell, NJ: Medical Economics Co.

Ratcliffe, S. G., and Field, M. A. S. (1982). Emotional disorder in XYY children: Four case reports. *Journal of Child Psychology and Psychiatry,* **23,** 401–406.

Robinson, A., Goodman, S. I., and O'Brien, D. (1984). Genetic and chromosomal disorders, including inborn errors of metabolism. In C. H. Kempe, H. K. Silver, and D. O'Brien (eds.), *Current pediatric diagnosis and treatment,* 8th ed. Los Altos, CA: Lange.

Robison, J. T. (1988). Pregnancy and childbirth in an age of technology. Paper presented at the meeting of the American Psychological Association, Atlanta, GA.

Rovet, J., and Netley, C. (1983). The triple X chromosome syndrome in childhood: Recent empirical findings. *Child Development,* **54,** 831–845.

Saco-Pollitt, C. (1981). Birth in the Peruvian Andes: Physical and behavioral and consequences of the neonate. *Child Development,* **52,** 839–846.

Sadler, T. W. (1985). *Langman's medical embryology,* 5th ed. Baltimore: Williams & Wilkins.

Sever, J. L. (February, 1983). Perinatal infections and damage to the central nervous system. Paper presented at the Symposium on Prenatal and Perinatal Factors Relevant to Learning Disabilities. ACLD 20th International Conference, Washington, D.C.

Sexton, M., and Hebel, J. R. (1984). A clinical trial of change in maternal smoking and its effect on birth weight. *Journal of the American Medical Association,* **251**(7), 911–915.

Shiono, P. H., Klebanoff, M. A., and Rhoads, G. G. (1986). Smoking and drinking during pregnancy: Their effects on preterm birth. *Journal of the American Medical Association,* **255**(1), 82–84.

Simopoulos, A. P. (1983). Nutrition. In C. C. Brown (ed.), *Childhood learning disabilities and prenatal risk: Pediatric round table series; 9.* Skillman, NJ: Johnson & Johnson Baby Products Company.

Snowman, M. (1986). *Foods and fitness.* Syracuse: New Readers Press.

Stein, Z., Susser, M., Saenger, G., and Moralla, F. (1975). *Famine and human development: The Dutch hunger winter of 1944/45.* New York: Oxford University Press.

Stenchever, M. A., and Jones, H. W., Jr. (1987). Genetic disorders and sex chromosome abnormalities. In M. L. Pernoll and R. C. Benson (eds.), *Current obstetric and gynecologic diagnosis and treatment,* 6th ed. Los Altos, CA: Appleton & Lange.

Streissguth, A. P. (1983). Smoking and drinking. In C. C. Brown (ed.), *Childhood learning disabilities and prenatal risk: Pediatric round table series; 9.* Skillman, NJ: Johnson & Johnson Baby Products Company.

Streissguth, A. P., Barr, H. M., and Martin, D. C. (1983). Maternal alcohol use and neonatal habituation assessed with the Brazelton Scale. *Child Development,* **54,** 1109–1118.

Streissguth, A. P., Martin, D. C., Barr, H. M., Sandman, B. M., Kirchner, G. L., and Darby, B. L. (1984). Intrauterine alcohol and nicotine exposure: Attention and reaction time in 4-year-old children. *Developmental Psychology,* **20,** 533–541.

Sutton, H. E. (1980). *An introduction to human genetics,* 3rd ed. Philadelphia: Saunders.

Tatum, H. J. (1987). Contraception and family planning. In M. L. Pernoll and R. C. Benson (eds.), *Current obstetric and gynecologic diagnosis and treatment,* 6th ed. Los Altos, CA: Appleton & Lange.

Taylor, C. M., and Pernoll, M. L. (1987). Normal pregnancy and prenatal care. In M. L. Pernoll and R. C. Benson (eds.), *Current obstetric and gynecologic diagnosis and treatment,* 6th ed. Los Altos, CA: Appleton & Lange.

Thorneycroft, I. H. (1987). In vitro fertilization and related techniques. In M. L. Pernoll and R. C. Benson (eds.), *Current obstetric and gynecologic diagnosis and treatment,* 6th edition. Los Altos, CA: Appleton & Lange.

Tjossem, T., De La Cruz, F. F., and Muller, J. Z. (1984). *Facts about Down syndrome* (NICHD Fact Sheet 421-948:15). Washington, D.C.: U.S. Government Printing Office.

Trattner, E. R. (1942). *The story of the world's great thinkers.* New York: J. B. Lippincott.

Turkington, C. (1987). Special talents. *Psychology Today,* **21**(9), 42–46.

Warkany, J. (1986). Anti-tuberculous drugs. In J. L. Sever and R. L. Brent (eds.), *Teratogen update: Environmentally induced birth defect risks.* New York: Alan R. Liss.

Weaver, R. F., and Hendrick, P. W. (1989). *Genetics.* Dubuque, IA: William C. Brown.

Whitehead, M. B. (1989). *A mother's story.* New York: St. Martin's Press.

Zuckerman, B., Frank, D., Hingson, R., Amaro, H., Levenson, S., Kayne, H., Parker, S., Vinci, R., Aboagye, K., Fried, L., Cabral, H., Timperi, R., and Bauchner, H. (1989). Effects of maternal marijuana and cocaine use on fetal growth. *New England Journal of Medicine,* **320,** 762–768.

CHAPTER 4

Agran, P. F. (1981). Motor vehicle occupant injuries in noncrash events. *Pediatrics,* **67,** 838–840.

Agras, W. S. (1990). Influence of early feeding style on adiposity at 6 years of age. *Journal of Pediatrics,* **116,** 805–809.

Ainsworth, M. D. S. (1982). Early caregiving and later patterns of attachment. In M. H. Klaus and M. O. Robertson (eds.), *Birth, interaction and attachment: Pediatric round table series; 6.* Skillman, NJ: Johnson & Johnson Baby Products Co.

Ainsworth, M. D. S., Blehar, M. C., Waters, E., and Wall, S. (1978). *Patterns of attachment.* Hillsdale, NJ: Lawrence Erlbaum.

Als, H., Lester, B. M., and Brazelton, T. B. (1982). Towards a research instrument for the assessment of preterm infants' behavior. In H. E. Fitzgerald, B. M. Lester, and M. W. Yogman (eds.), *Theory and research in behavioral pediatrics,* vol. 1. New York: Plenum.

Apgar, V. (1953). Proposal for a new method of evaluation of the newborn infant. *Anesthesia and Analgesia,* **32,** 260.

Aslin, R. N., Pisoni, D. B., and Jusczyk, P. W. (1983). Auditory development and speech perception in infancy. In M. M. Haith and J. J. Campos (eds.), *Infancy and developmental psychobiology,* Vol. 2 of P. H. Mussen (ed.), *Handbook of child psychology,* 4th ed. New York: Wiley.

Baillargeon, R. (1987). Object permanence in 3½- and 4½-month-old infants. *Developmental Psychology,* **23,** 655–664.

Baillargeon, R., and Graber, M. (1988). Evidence of location memory in 8-month-old infants in a nonsearch AB task. *Developmental Psychology,* **24,** 502–511.

Baillargeon, R., DeVos, J., and Graber, M. (1989). Location memory in 8-month-old infants in a nonsearch AB task: Further evidence. *Cognitive Development,* **4,** 345–367.

Baillargeon, R., Graber, M., DeVos, J., and Black, J. (1990). Why do young infants fail to search for hidden objects? *Cognition,* **36,** 255–284.

Banks, M. S., and Salapatek, P. (1983). Infant visual perception. In M. M. Haith and J. J. Campos (eds.), *Infancy and developmental psychobiology,* Vol. 2 of P. H. Mussen (ed.), *Handbook of child psychology,* 4th ed. New York: Wiley.

Barbero, G. (1982). Failure-to-thrive. In M. H. Klaus, T. Leger, and M. A. Trause (eds.), *Maternal attachment and mothering disorders: Pediatric round table series; 1.* Skillman, NJ: Johnson & Johnson Baby Products Co.

Barnard, K. E., and Bee, H. L. (1983). The impact of temporally patterned stimulation on the development of preterm infants. *Child Development,* **54,** 1156–1167.

Beedle, G. L. (1984). Teeth. In C. H. Kempe, H. K. Silver, and D. O'Brien (eds.), *Current pediatric diagnosis and treatment,* 8th ed. Los Altos, CA: Lange.

Bell, S. M., and Ainsworth, M. D. S. (1972). Infant crying and maternal responsiveness. *Child Development,* **43,** 1171–1190.

Berberian, K. E., and Snyder, S. S. (1982). The relationship of temperament and stranger reaction for younger and older infants. *Merrill-Palmer Quarterly,* **28,** 79–94.

Bowlby, J. (1951). *Maternal care and mental health.* Geneva: World Health Organization.

Brackbill, W. Y. (1979). Obstetrical medication and infant behavior. In J. D. Osofsky (ed.), *Handbook of infant development.* New York: Wiley.

Brazelton, T. B. (1973). *Neonatal Behavioral Assessment Scale.* Philadelphia: Lippincott.

Brodish, M. S. (1982). Relationship of early bonding to initial infant feeding patterns in bottle-fed newborns. *Journal of Obstetric, Gynecologic and Neonatal Nursing,* **11,** 248–252.

Bruner, J. S. (1973). Organization of early skilled action. *Child Development, 44,* 1–11.

Burns, K. A., Deddish, R. B., Burns, W. J., and Hatcher, R. P. (1983). Use of oscillating waterbeds and rhythmic sounds for premature infant stimulation. *Developmental Psychology, 19,* 746–751.

Call, J. D. (1984). Child abuse and neglect in infancy: Sources of hostility within the parent-infant dyad and disorders of attachment in infancy. *Child Abuse and Neglect: The International Journal, 8,* 185–202.

Campos, J., Langer, A., and Krowitz, A. (1970). Cardiac responses on the visual cliff in prelocomotor human infants. *Science, 170,* 196–197.

Campos, J. J., Barrett, K. C., Lamb, M. E., Goldsmith, H. H., and Stenberg, C. (1983). Socioemotional development. In M. M. Haith and J. J. Campos (eds.), *Infancy and developmental psychobiology,* Vol. 2 of P. H. Mussen (ed.), *Handbook of child psychology,* 4th ed. New York: Wiley.

Carey, W. B. (1981). The importance of temperament-environment interaction for child health and development. In M. E. Lewis and L. A. Rosenblum (eds.), *The uncommon child.* New York: Plenum Press.

Carey, W. B., and McDevitt, S. C. (1978). Revision of the infant temperament questionnaire. *Pediatrics, 61,* 735–739.

Cernoch, J. M., and Porter, R. H. (1985). Recognition of maternal axillary odors by infants. *Child Development, 56,* 1593–1598.

Chess, S., and Thomas, A. (1982). Infant bonding: Mystique and reality. *American Journal of Orthopsychiatry, 52,* 213–222.

Chomsky, N. (1968). *Language and mind.* New York: Harcourt, Brace & World.

Clarke-Stewart, K. A., and Fein, G. G. (1983). Early childhood programs. In M. M. Haith and J. J. Campos (eds.), *Infancy and developmental psychobiology,* Vol. 2 of P. H. Mussen (ed.), *Handbook of child psychology,* 4th ed. New York: Wiley.

Crook, C. K. (1978). Taste perception in the newborn infant. *Infant Behavior and Development, 1,* 52–68.

Crnic, K. A., Greenberg, M. T., Ragozin, A. S., Robinson, N. M., and Basham, R. B. (1983). Effects of stress and social support on mothers and premature and full-term infants. *Child Development, 54,* 209–217.

Dennis, W., and Najarian, P. (1957). Infant development under environmental handicap. *Psychological Monographs, 71,* (Whole No. 436).

DeStefano, C. T., and Mueller, E. (1982). Environmental determinants of peer social activity in 18-month-old males. *Infant Behavior and Development, 5,* 175–183.

Drotar, D., and Malone, C. (1982). Family-oriented intervention with the failure-to-thrive infant. In M. H. Klaus and M. O. Robertson (eds.), *Birth, interaction and attachment: Pediatric round table series; 6.* Skillman, NJ: Johnson & Johnson Baby Products Co.

Duffy, F. H., Burchfield, J. L., and Lombroso, C. T. (1979). Brain electrical activity mapping (BEAM): A method for extending the clinical utility of EEG and evoked potentials data. *Annals of Neurology, 5,* 309–321.

Durrett, M. E., Otaki, M., and Richards, P. (1984). Attachment and the mother's perception of support from the father. *International Journal of Behavioral Development, 7,* 167–176.

Egeland, B., and Farber, E. A. (1984). Infant-mother attachment: Factors related to its development and changes over time. *Child Development, 55,* 753–771.

Entwisle, D. R., and Doering, S. G. (1980). *The first birth.* Baltimore: Johns Hopkins University Press.

Erikson, E. (1963). *Childhood and society,* 2nd ed. New York: Norton.

Fairweather, H. (1976). Sex differences in cognition. *Cognition, 4,* 31–280.

Feldstein, S., DiGregorio, I., Crown, C., Jasnow, M., Beebe, B., and Jaffe, J. (1990a). Infant temperament and coordinated interpersonal timing. *Infant Behavior and Development, 13,* 369. (Abstract.)

Feldstein, S., Jasnow, M. D., DiGregorio, I., Crown, C. L., Beebe, B., and Jaffe, J. (1990b). *The possible heritability of dialogic time patterns.* Poster presented at the Eastern Psychological Association, Philadelphia.

Fernald, A. (1985). 4-month-old infants prefer to listen to motherese. *Infant Behavior and Development, 8,* 181–195.

Fernald, A. (1989). Intonation and communicative intent in mothers' speech to infants: Is the melody the message? *Child Development, 60,* 1497–1510.

Fomon, S. J. (1974). *Infant nutrition,* 2nd ed. Philadelphia: Saunders.

Frankenburg, W. K., and Dodds, J. B. (1967). *Denver developmental screening test manual.* Denver: University of Colorado Medical Center.

Fulginiti, V. A. (1984). Immunization. In C. H. Kempe, H. K. Silver, and D. O'Brien (eds.), *Current pediatric diagnosis and treatment,* 8th ed. Los Altos, CA: Lange.

Gagan, R. J., Cupoli, J. M., and Wakins, A. H. (1984). The families of children who fail to thrive: Preliminary investigations of parental deprivation among organic and nonorganic cases. *Child Abuse and Neglect, The International Journal, 8,* 93–103.

Galler, J. R., Ramsey, F., and Solimano, G. (1984). The influence of early malnutrition on subsequent behavioral development: III. Learning disabilities as a sequel to malnutrition. *Pediatric Research, 18,* 309–313.

Gibson, E. J. (1969). *Principles of perceptual learning and development.* New York: Appleton-Century-Crofts.

Gibson, J. J. (1966). *The senses considered as perceptual systems.* Boston: Houghton Mifflin.

Gill, W. L. (1987). Essentials of normal newborn assessment and care. In M. L. Pernall and R. C. Benson (eds.), *Current obstetric and gynecologic diagnosis and treatment.* Norwalk, CT: Appleton & Lange.

Githens, J. H., and Hathaway, W. (1984). Hematologic disorders. In C. H. Kempe, H. K. Silver, and D. O'Brien (eds.), *Current pediatric diagnosis and treatment,* 8th ed. Los Altos, CA: Lange.

Goldberg, S. (1983). Parent-infant bonding: Another look. *Child Development, 54,* 1355–1382.

Goldsmith, H. H., and Gottesman, I. I. (1981). Origins of variation in behavioral style: A longitudinal study of temperament in young twins. *Child Development, 52,* 91–103.

Grantham-McGregor, S. M., Powell, C., Stewart, M., and Schofield, W. N. (1982). Longitudinal study of growth and development of young Jamaican children recovering from severe protein-energy malnutrition. *Developmental Medicine and Child Neurology, 24,* 321–331.

Greenough, W. T., and Juraska, J. M. (1979). Experience-induced changes in brain fine structure: Their behavioral implications. In M. E. Hahn, C. Jensen, and B. C. Dudek (eds.), *Development and evolution of brain size: Behavioral implications.* New York: Academic Press.

Guilleminaut, C., Ariagno, R. L., Forno, L. S., Nagle, L., Baldwin, R., and Owen, M. (1979). Obstructive sleep apnea and near miss for SIDS: Report on an infant with sudden death. *Pediatrics, 63,* 837–843.

Harding, C. M. (1985). Whooping cough vaccination: The case presented by the British national press. *Child: Care, Health & Development, 11,* 21–30.

Harlow, H. F., and Harlow, M. (1965). The affectional systems. In A. Schrier, H. Harlow, and F. Stollnitz (eds.), *Behavior of nonhuman primates,* vol. II. New York: Academic Press.

Harvey, D., Prince, J., Burton, J., Parkinson, C., and Campbell, S. (1982). Ability of children who were small for gestational age babies. *Pediatrics, 69,* 296–300.

Hazen, N. L., and Durrett, M. E. (1982). Relationship of security of attachment to exploration and cognitive mapping abilities in 2-year-olds. *Developmental Psychology, 18,* 751–759.

Holmes, D. L., Reich, J. N., and Pasternak, J. F. (1984). *The development of infants born at risk.* Hillsdale, NJ: Lawrence Erlbaum.

Holt, K. (1977). *Developmental pediatrics.* Reading, MA: Butterworths.

Honig, A. S. (1983). Evaluation of infant/toddler intervention programs. *Studies in Educational Evaluation, 8,* 305–316.

Honig, A. S., and Lally, J. R. (1972). *Infant caregiving: A design for training.* New York: Media Projects.

Honig, A. S., and Oski, F. A. (1984). Solemnity: A clinical risk index for iron deficient infants. *Early Child Development and Care, 16,* 69–84.

Howes, C. (1983). Caregiver behavior in center and family day care. *Journal of Applied Developmental Psychology, 4,* 99–107.

Hsu, C., Soong, W., Stigler, J. W., Hong, C., and Liang, C. (1981). The temperamental characteristics of Chinese babies. *Child Development, 52,* 1337–1340.

Hunt, J. M. (1964). How children develop intellectually. *Children, 11*(3), 83–91.

Huntington, L., Hans, S. L., and Zeskind, P. S. (1990). The relations among cry characteristics, demographic variables, and developmental test scores in infants prenatally exposed to methadone. *Infant Behavior and Development, 13,* 533–538.

Jenkins, S., and Pederson, D. R. (1985). *Maternal responses to premature birth*. Poster paper presented at the meeting of the Society for Research in Child Development, Toronto.

Kagan, J. (1978). The baby's elastic mind. *Human Nature, 1*(1), 66–73.

Kagan, J. (1979). Structure and process in the human infant: The ontogeny of mental representation. In M. H. Bornstein and W. Kessen (eds.), *Psychological development from infancy: Image to intention.* Hillsdale, NJ: Lawrence Erlbaum.

Kagan, J., Kearsley, R. B., and Zelazo, R. P. (1978). *Infancy: Its place in human development.* Cambridge, MA: Harvard University Press.

Keller, W. D., Hildebrandt, K. A., and Richards, M. E. (1985). Effects of extended father-infant contact during the newborn period. *Infant Behavior and Development, 8,* 337–350.

Kennell, J. H., Voos, D. K., and Klaus, M. H. (1979). Parent-infant bonding. In J. Osofsky (ed.), *Handbook of infant development.* New York: Wiley.

Kent, R. D. (1980). Articulatory and acoustic perspectives on speech development. In A. P. Reilly (ed.), *The communication game: Pediatric round table series; 4.* Skillman, NJ: Johnson & Johnson Baby Products Co.

Klaus, M. M., Jerauld, R., Kreger, N., McAlpine, W., Steffa, M., and Kennell, J. (1972). Maternal attachment: Importance of the first postpartum days. *New England Journal of Medicine, 286,* 460–463.

Klaus, M. H., and Kennell, J. H. (1982). *Parent-infant bonding.* St. Louis: Mosby.

Klein, R. P. (1985). Caregiving arrangements by employed women with children under 1 year of age. *Developmental Psychology, 21,* 403–406.

Koop, C. B. (1983). Risk factors in development. In M. M. Haith and J. J. Campos (eds.), *Infancy and developmental psychobiology,* Vol. 2 of P. H. Mussen (ed.), *Handbook of child psychology,* 4th ed. New York: Wiley.

Koops, B. L., and Battaglia, F. C. (1984). The newborn infant. In C. H. Kempe, H. K. Silver, and D. O'Brien (eds.), *Current pediatric diagnosis and treatment,* 8th ed. Los Altos, CA: Lange.

Korner, A. F., Zeanah, C. H., Linden, J., Berkowitz, R. I., Kraemer, H. C., and Agras, W. S. (1985). The relation between neonatal and later activity and temperament. *Child Development, 56,* 38–42.

Kotelchuck, M. (1976). The infant's relationship to the father: Experimental evidence. In M. E. Lamb (ed.), *The role of the father in human development.* New York: Wiley.

Lally, J. R., and Honig, A. S. (1977). The family development research program. In C. Day and R. Parker (eds.), *The preschool in action.* Boston: Allyn & Bacon.

Lamb, M. E., and Bornstein, M. H. (1987). *Development in infancy,* 2nd ed. New York: Random House.

Leifer, A., Leiderman, P. H., Barnett, C. R., and Williams, J. A. (1972). Effects of mother-infant separation on maternal attachment behavior. *Child Development, 43,* 1203–1218.

Lenard, L. (1983). The dynamic brain. *Science Digest,* 65–67, 118–119.

Lipsitt, L. P. (October, 1979). Critical conditions in infancy: A psychological perspective. *American Psychologist, 34*(10), 973–980.

Lounsbury, M. L., and Bates, J. E. (1982). The cries of infants of differing levels of perceived temperamental difficultness: Acoustic properties and effects on listeners. *Child Development, 53,* 677–686.

Maccoby, E. E., and Jacklin C. N. (1974). *The psychology of sex differences.* Stanford, CA: Stanford University Press.

Main, M. (1983). Exploration, play, and cognitive functioning related to infant-mother attachment. *Infant Behavior and Development, 6,* 167–174.

McIntosh, K., and Lauer, B. A. (1984). Infections: Bacterial and spirochetal. In C. H. Kempe, H. K. Silver, and D. O'Brien (Eds.), *Current pediatric diagnosis and treatment,* 8th ed. Los Altos, CA: Lange.

Mizukami, K., Kobayashi, N., Ishii, T., and Iwata, H. (1990). First selective attachment begins in early infancy: A study using teletethermography. *Infant Behavior and Development, 13,* 257–271.

Nazario, T. A. (1988). *In defense of children.* New York: Scribner.

O'Brien, D., and Hambridge, K. M. (1984). Normal childhood nutrition and its disorders. In C. H. Kempe, H. K. Silver, and D. O'Brien (eds.), *Current pediatric diagnosis and treatment,* 8th ed. Los Altos, CA: Lange.

Oller, D. K. (1980). Patterns of infant vocalization. In A. P. Reilly (ed.), *The communication game: Pediatric round table series; 4.* Skillman, NJ: Johnson & Johnson Baby Products Co.

Pape, K. E., and Fitzhardinge, P. M. (1981). Perinatal damage to the developing brain. In A. Milunsky, E. A. Friedman, and L. Gluck (Eds.), *Advances in perinatal medicine,* vol. 1. New York: Plenum.

Parke, R. D. (1982). The father's role in family development. In M. H. Klaus and M. O. Robertson (eds.), *Birth, interaction and attachment: Pediatric round table series; 6.* Skillman, NJ: Johnson & Johnson Baby Products Co.

Pedersen, F. A. (1981). Father influences viewed in a family context. In M. E. Lamb (ed.), *The role of the father in child development,* 2nd ed. New York: Wiley.

Pedersen, F. A., Rubenstein, J. L., and Yarrow, L. J. (1980). Infant development in father-absent families. *Journal of Genetic Psychology, 135,* 51–61.

Piaget, J. (1952). *The origins of intelligence in children* (M. Cook, trans.). New York: International Universities Press.

Pollitt, E., Consolazio, B., and Goodkin, F. (1981). Changes in nutritive sucking during a feed in two-day- and thirty-day-old infants. *Early Human Development, 5,* 201–210.

Power, T. G., and Parke, R. D. (1982). Play as a context for early learning: Lab and home analysis. In L. M. Laosa and I. E. Sigel (eds.), *The family as a learning environment.* New York: Plenum Press.

Ridenour, M. V. (1982). Infant walkers: Developmental tool or inherent danger. *Perceptual and Motor Skills, 55,* 1201–1202.

Rodholm, M., and Larsson, K. (1982). The behavior of human male adults at their first contact with a newborn. *Infant Behavior and Development, 5,* 121–130.

Roffwarg, H. P., Muzio, J. N., and Dement, W. C. (1966). Ontogenetic development of the human sleep-dream cycle. *Science, 152,* 604–619.

Ross, G. S. (1984). Home intervention for premature infants of low-income families. *American Journal of Orthopsychiatry, 54,* 265–270.

Rubin, R. (1963). Maternal touch. *Nursing Outlook, 11,* 828–831.

Russell, M. J. (1976). Human olfactory communication. *Nature, 260,* 520–522.

Scafidi, F. A., Field, T. M., Schanberg, S. M., Bauer, C. R., Tucci, K., Roberts, J., Morrow, C., and Kuhn, C. M. (1990). Massage stimulates growth in preterm infants: A replication. *Infant Behavior and Development, 13,* 167–188.

Scarr, S. (1985). *Mother care, other care.* New York: Basic Books.

Silver, H. K. (1984). Growth and development. In C. H. Kempe, H. K. Silver, and D. O'Brien (eds.), *Current pediatric diagnosis and treatment,* 8th ed. Los Altos, CA: Lange.

Sinclair, D. (1978). *Human growth after birth,* 3rd ed. London: Oxford University Press.

Spitz, R. (1946). Anaclitic depression. *Psychoanalytic Study of the Child, 2,* 313–342.

Sroufe, L. A. (1979). The coherence of individual development: Early care attachment and subsequent developmental issues. *American Psychologist, 34*(10), 834–841.

Sroufe, L. A., Fox, N. E., and Pancake, V. R. (1983). Attachment and dependency in developmental perspective. *Child Development, 54,* 1615–1627.

Steiner, J. E. (1979). Human facial expressions in response to taste and smell stimulation. In H. Reese and L. Lipsitt (eds.), *Advances in child development and behavior,* vol. 13. New York: Academic Press.

Steinschneider, A. (1972). Prolonged apnea and the sudden infant death syndrome. *Pediatrics, 50,* 646–654.

Stunkard, A. J., Sorensen, T. I. A., Hanis, C., Teasdale, T. W., Chakraborty, R., Schull, W. J., & Schulsinger, F. (1986). An adoption study of human obesity. *The New England Journal of Medicine, 314*(4), 193–198.

Teti, D. M., and Ablard, K. E. (1989). Security of attachment and infant-sibling relationships: A laboratory study. *Child Development, 60,* 1519–1528.

Thomas, A., and Chess, S. (1977). *Temperament and development.* New York: Brunner/Mazel.

Torgersen, A. M., and Kringlen, E. (1978). Genetic aspects of temperamental differences in infants: A study of same-sexed twins. *Journal of the American Academy of Child Psychiatry, 17,* 433–444.

Trelease, J. (1982). *The read-aloud handbook.* New York: Penguin.

Ungerer, J. A., and Sigman, M. (1983). Developmental lags in preterm infants from one to three years of age. *Child Development, 54,* 1217–1228.

Wegman, M. E., (1987). Annual summary of vital statistics—1986. *Pediatrics, 80,* 817–827.

Weissbluth, M. (1982). Chinese-American infant temperament and sleep duration: An ethnic comparison. *Developmental and Behavioral Pediatrics,* **3**(2), 99–102.

Weissbluth, M. (1985). *Crybabies. Coping with colic: What to do when your baby won't stop crying!* New York: Berkley.

Weissbluth, M., and Green, O. C. (1984). Plasma progesterone concentrations and infant temperament. *Developmental and Behavioral Pediatrics,* **5**(5), 251–253.

White, B. L. (1975). *The first three years of life.* Englewood Cliffs, NJ: Prentice-Hall.

Winick, M. (1976). *Malnutrition and brain development.* Oxford: Oxford University Press.

Wolfe, R. R., and Wiggins, J. W., Jr. (1984). Cardiovascular diseases. In C. H. Kempe, H. K. Silver, and D. O'Brien (Eds.), *Current pediatric diagnosis and treatment,* 8th ed. Los Altos, CA: Lange.

Zeskind, P. S. (1980). Adult responses to cries of low and high risk infants. *Infant Behavior and Development,* **3**, 167–177.

Zeskind, P. S. (1983). Production and spectral analysis of neonatal crying and its relation to other biobehavioral systems in the infant at risk. In T. Field and A. Sostek (eds.), *Infants born at risk: Physiological, perceptual and cognitive processes.* New York: Grune & Stratton.

Zeskind, P. S., and Iacino, R. (1984). Effects of maternal visitation to preterm infants in the neonatal intensive care unit. *Child Development,* **55**, 1887–1893.

Zeskind, P. S., and Lester, B. M. (1978). Acoustic features and auditory perceptions of the cries of newborns with prenatal and perinatal complications. *Child Development,* **49**(3), 580–589.

CHAPTER 5

Albert, M. L., and Obler, L. K. (1978). *The bilingual brain.* New York: Academic Press.

Ames, L. B., and Chase, J. A. (1974). *Don't push your preschooler.* New York: Harper & Row.

Anderson, D. R. (1989). Television and children: Not necessarily bad news. *The Brown University Child Behavior and Development Letter,* **5**(9), 4.

Ashton, E. (1983). Measures of play behavior: The influence of sex-role stereotyped children's books. *Sex Roles,* **9**, 43–47.

Atkinson, R. C., and Shiffrin, R. M. (1968). Human memory: A proposed system and its control processes. In K. Spence (ed.), *The psychology of learning and motivation,* Vol. 2. New York: Academic Press.

Bandura, A. (1977). *Social learning theory.* Englewood Cliffs, NJ: Prentice-Hall.

Bandura, A., Ross, D., and Ross, S. (1963). Imitation of film-mediated aggressive models. *Journal of Abnormal and Social Psychology,* **66**, 3–11.

Baskett, L. M. (1985). Sibling status effects: Adult expectations. *Developmental Psychology,* **21**, 441–445.

Bearison, D. J., and Cassel, T. Z. (1975). Cognitive decentration and social codes: Communication effectiveness in young children from differing family contexts. *Developmental Psychology,* **11**, 29–36.

Bergomi, M., Borella, P. Fantuzzi, G., Vivoli, G., Sturloni, N., Cavazzuti, G., Tampieri, A., and Tartoni, P. L. (1989). Relationship between lead exposure indicators and neuropsychological performance in children. *Developmental Medicine and Child Neurology,* **31**, 181–190.

Block, J. H. (1979). Another look at sex differentiation in the socialization behavior of mothers and fathers. In J. Sherman and F. L. Denmark (eds.), *Psychology of women: Future directions of research.* New York: Psychological Dimensions.

Block, J. H. (1983). Differential premises arising from differential socialization of the sexes: Some conjectures. *Child Development,* **54**(6), 1335–1354.

Breland, H. M. (1974). Birth order, family configuration, and verbal achievement. *Child Development,* **45**, 1011–1019.

Bronfenbrenner, U., Alvarez, W. F., and Henderson, C. R., Jr. (1984). Working and watching: Maternal employment status and parents' perceptions of their 3-year-old children. *Child Development,* **55**, 1362–1378.

Buffery, A. W. H., and Grey, J. A. (1972). Sex differences in the development of spatial and linguistic skills. In C. Ounsted and D. C. Taylor (eds.), *Gender differences: Their ontogeny and significance.* London: Churchill.

Chance, P. (1979). *Learning through play: Pediatric round table; 3.* Skillman, NJ: Johnson & Johnson Baby Products Co.

Chomsky, N. (1957). *Syntactic structures.* The Hague: Mouton.

Clarke-Stewart, A. (1982). *Day care.* Cambridge, MA: Harvard Univ. Press.

Cook, A. S., Fritz, J., McCornack, B. L., and Visperas, C. (1985). Early gender differences in the functional usage of language. *Sex Roles,* **12**, 909–915.

Dasen, P. R., and Heron, A. (1981). Cross-cultural tests of Piaget's theory. In H. C. Triandis and A. Heron (eds.), *1981 Handbook of cross-cultural psychology,* Vol. 4. Boston: Allyn & Bacon.

Diaz, R. M. (1985). Thought and two languages: The impact of bilingualism on cognitive development. *Review of Research in Education,* **10**, 23–54.

Dolgin, K. G., and Behrend, D. A. (1984). Children's knowledge about animates and inanimates. *Child Development,* **55**, 1646–1650.

Dreikurs, R., and Soltz, V. (1964). *Children: The challenge.* New York: Hawthorn.

Dunn, J. (1983). Sibling relationships in early childhood. *Child Development,* **54**(4), 787–811.

Dunn, J., and Shatz, M. (1989). Becoming a conversationalist despite (or because of) having an older sibling. *Child Development,* **60**(2), 399–410.

Easterbrooks, M. A., and Goldberg, W. A. (1985). Effects of early maternal employment on toddlers, mothers, and fathers. *Developmental Psychology,* **21**(5), 774–783.

Egeland, B., and Sroufe, L. A. (1981). Attachment and early maltreatment. *Child Development,* **52**, 44–52.

Elkind, D. (1981). *The hurried child.* Reading, MA: Addison-Wesley.

Elkind, D. (1987). *Miseducation: Preschoolers at risk.* New York: Knopf.

Ellis, P. O. (1984). Eye. In C. H. Kempe, H. K. Silver, and D. O'Brien (eds.), *Current pediatric diagnosis and treatment,* 8th ed. Los Altos, CA: Lange.

Erikson, E. H. (1963). *Childhood and society,* 2nd ed. New York: Norton.

Faller, K. C. (1984). Is the child victim of sexual abuse telling the truth? *Child Abuse and Neglect, The International Journal,* **8**, 473–481.

Field, T., and Reite, M. (1984). Children's responses to separation from mother during the birth of another child. *Child Development,* **55**, 1308–1316.

Finkelhor, D. (1984). The prevention of child sexual abuse: An overview of needs and problems. *SIECUS Report,* **13**(1), 1–5.

Frankenburg, W. F. (1981). Early screening for developmental delays and potential school problems. In C. C. Brown (ed.), *Infants at risk: Pediatric round table; 5.* Skillman, NJ: Johnson & Johnson Baby Products Co.

Freud, S. (1965). *New introductory lectures on psychoanalysis.* New York: Norton. (Originally published, 1933.)

Freud, S., and Breuer, J. (1955). *Studies on hysteria.* London: Hogarth. (Originally published, 1895.)

Furman, W., and Buhrmester, D. (1985). Children's perceptions of the qualities of sibling relationships. *Child Development,* **56**, 448–461.

Ganong, W. F. (1980). *Review of medical physiology,* 8th ed. Los Altos, CA: Lange.

Garcia, E. E. (1980). Bilingualism in early childhood. *Young Children,* **35**, 52–66.

Gerbner, G. (1972). Violence in television drama: Trends and symbolic functions. In G. A. Comstock and E. A. Rubenstein (eds.), *Television and social behavior, vol. I: Media content and control.* Washington, DC: US Government Printing Office.

Glass, D. C., Neulinger, J., and Brim, O. G., Jr. (1974). Birth order, verbal intelligence, and educational aspiration. *Child Development,* **45**, 807–811.

Goodwin, J., Cormier, L., and Owen, J. (1983). Grandfather–granddaughter incest: A trigenerational view. *Child Abuse and Neglect, The International Journal,* **7**, 163–170.

Haber, R. N. (1969). Eidetic images. *Scientific American,* **220**, 36–44.

Hakuta, K. (1987). Degree of bilingualism and cognitive ability in mainland Puerto Rican children. *Child Development,* **58**(5), 1372–1388.

Havighurst, R. (1972). *Developmental tasks and education,* 3rd ed. New York: McKay.

Hay, D. F. (1985). Learning to form relationships in infancy: Parallel attainments with parents and peers. *Developmental Review,* **5**, 122–161.

Hoffman, M. L. (1975). Altruistic behavior and the parent–child relationship. *Journal of Personality and Social Psychology,* **31,** 937–943.

Holobow, N. E., Genesee, F., Lambert, W. E., Gastright, J., and Met, M. (1987). Effectiveness of partial French immersion for children with different social class and ethnic backgrounds. *Applied Psycholinguistics,* **8,** 137–152.

Honig, A. S., Lally, J. R., and Mathieson, D. H. (1982). Personal–social adjustment of school children after 5 years in a family enrichment program. *Child Care Quarterly,* **11,** 138–146.

Hunt, J. M. (1964). How children develop intellectually. *Children,* **11,** 83–91.

Huston, A. C. (1983). Sex typing. In E. M. Hetherington (ed.), *Socialization, personality and social development.* Vol. 4 of P. H. Mussen (ed.), *Handbook of Child Psychology,* 4th ed. New York: Wiley.

Huston, A. C., Wright, J. C., Rice, M. L., Kerkman, D., and St. Peters, M. (1990). Development of television viewing patterns in early childhood: A longitudinal investigation. *Developmental Psychology,* **26,** 409–420.

Kalliopuska, M. (1984). Empathy and birth order. *Psychological Reports,* **55,** 115–18.

Kempe, C. H., Silverman, F. N., Steele, B. F., Droegemueller, W., and Silver, H. K. (1985). The battered-child syndrome. *Child Abuse and Neglect, The International Journal,* **9,** 143–154.

Kendall, J. R., LaJeunesse, G., Chmilar, P., Shapson, L. R., and Shapson, S. M. (1987). English reading skills of French immersion students in kindergarten and grades 1 and 2. *Reading Research Quarterly,* **22,** 135–159.

Kidwell, J. S. (1982). The neglected birth order: Middleborns. *Journal of Marriage and the Family,* **44,** 225.

Kohlberg, L. A. (1966). A cognitive-developmental analysis of children's sex role concepts and attitudes. In E. E. Maccoby (ed.), *The development of sex differences.* Stanford, CA: Stanford University Press.

Kohlberg, L. (1984). *The psychology of moral development.* San Francisco: Harper & Row.

Kunkel, D. L., and Watkins, B. A. (1985). Children and television. *Washington Report,* **1**(4), 1–8.

Lally, J. R. (1984). Three views of child neglect: Expanding visions of preventive intervention. *Child Abuse and Neglect, The International Journal,* **8,** 243–254.

Lennenberg, E. (1967). *Biological foundations of language.* New York: Wiley.

Liebert, R. M., Sprafkin, J. N., and Davidson, E. S. (1982). *The early window: Effects of television on children and youth.* New York: Pergamon Press.

Lipsitt, L. P. (1990). Statistics reflect increase in child abuse. *The Brown University Child Behavior and Development Letter,* **6**(8), 1.

Luria, A. R. (1968). *The mind of a mnemonist.* (L. Solotaroff, trans.) New York: Basic Books.

Lynch, A. (1982). Maternal stress following the birth of a second child. In M. H. Klaus and M. O. Robertson (eds.), *Birth, interaction and attachment: Pediatric round table; 6.* Skillman, NJ: Johnson & Johnson Baby Products Co.

Maccoby, E. E., and Martin, J. A. (1983). Socialization in the context of the family: Parent-child interaction. In E. M. Hetherington (ed.), *Socialization, personality, and social development.* Vol. 4 of P. H. Mussen (ed.), *Handbook of child psychology,* 4th ed. New York: Wiley.

Martin, C. L., and Halverson, C. F., Jr. (1981). A schematic processing model of sex typing and stereotyping in children. *Child Development,* **52,** 1119–1134.

McLoyd, V. C., and Ratner, H. H. (1983). The effects of sex and toy characteristics on exploration in preschool children. *Journal of Genetic Psychology,* **142,** 213–224.

Minnett, A. M., Vandell, D. L., and Santrock, J. W. (1983). The effects of sibling status on sibling interaction: Influence of birth order, age spacing, sex of child, and sex of sibling. *Child Development,* **54,** 1064–1072.

Mischel, W. (1966). A social-learning view of sex differences in behavior. In E. E. Maccoby (ed.), *The development of sex differences.* Stanford, CA: Stanford University Press.

Mueller, E. L. (1989). Toddlers' peer relations: Shared meaning and semantics. In W. Damon (ed.), *Child development today and tomorrow.* San Francisco: Jossey-Bass.

Murray, J. P. (1989). Using TV sensibly. *The Brown University Child Behavior and Development Letter,* **5**(9), 5.

O'Keefe, E. S. C., and Hyde, J. S. (1983). The development of occu-

pational sex-role stereotypes: The effects of gender stability and age. *Sex Roles,* **9,** 481–492.

Pederson, F. A., Cain, R. L., Zaslow, M. J., and Anderson, B. J. (1982). Variation in infant experience associated with alternative family roles. In L. Laosa and I. Sigel (eds.), *Families as learning environments for children.* New York: Plenum.

Petersen, A. C. (1979). Hormones and cognitive functioning in normal development. In M. A. Wittig and A. C. Petersen (eds.), *Sex related differences in cognitive functioning.* New York: Academic Press.

Piaget, J. (1933). Children's philosophies. In C. Murchinson (ed.), *A handbook of child psychology.* Worcester, MA: Clark University Press.

Piaget, J. (1962). *Play, dreams and imitation in childhood* (C. Gattegno and F. Hodgson, trans.). New York: Norton.

Piaget, J., and Inhelder, B. (1956). *The child's conception of space* (F. Langdon and J. Lunzer, trans.). London: Routledge & Kegan Paul.

Pinon, M. F., Huston, A. C., and Wright, J. C. (1989). Family ecology and child characteristics that predict young children's educational television viewing. *Child Development,* **60,** 846–856.

Roche, A. F. (1979). Secular trends in human growth, maturation and development. *Monographs of the Society for Research in Child Development,* Serial No. 179.

Rosenfield, I. (1988). *The invention of memory: A new view of the brain.* New York: Basic Books.

Rumack, B. H. (1984). Poisoning. In C. H. Kempe, H. K. Silver, and D. O'Brien (eds.), *Current pediatric diagnosis and treatment,* 8th ed. Los Altos, CA: Lange.

Rutter, M. (1987). *Developmental Psychiatry.* Washington, DC: American Psychiatric Assoc.

Schilling, L. S. (1985). Imaginary companions: Considerations for the health profession. *Early Child Development and Care,* **22,** 211–223.

Schmitt, B. D. (1984). Ambulatory pediatrics. In C. H. Kempe, H. K. Silver, and D. O'Brien (eds), *Current pediatric diagnosis and treatment,* 8th ed. Los Altos, CA: Lange.

Schmitt, B. D., and Berman, S. (1984). Ear, nose and throat. In C. H. Kempe, H. K. Silver, and D. O'Brien (eds.), *Current pediatric diagnosis and treatment,* 8th ed. Los Altos, CA: Lange.

Sears, R. R., Rau, L., and Alpert, R. (1965). *Identification and child rearing.* Stanford, CA: Stanford University Press.

Silbert, M. H., and Pines, A. M. (1981). Sexual child abuse as an antecedent to prostitution. *Child Abuse and Neglect, The International Journal,* **5,** 407–411.

Silver, H. K. (1984). Growth and development. In C. H. Kempe, H. K. Silver, and D. O'Brien (Eds.), *Current pediatric diagnosis and treatment,* 8th ed. Los Altos, CA: Lange.

Silverman, A., and Roy, C. C. (1984). Liver and pancreas. In C. H. Kempe, H. K. Silver, and D. O'Brien (eds.), *Current pediatric diagnosis and treatment,* 8th ed. Los Altos, CA: Lange.

Shugar, G. W., and Bokus, B. (1986). Children's discourse and children's activity in the peer situation. In E. C. Mueller and C. R. Cooper (eds.), *Process and outcome in peer relationships.* Orlando, FL: Academic Press.

Snow, M. E., Jacklin, C. N., and Maccoby, E. E. (1981). Birth order differences in peer sociability at 33 months. *Child Development,* **52,** 589–595.

Springer, S. P., and Deutsch, G. (1981). *Left brain, right brain.* San Francisco: W. H. Freeman.

Starr, R. H. Jr., (1978). The controlled study of the ecology of child abuse and drug abuse. *Child Abuse and Neglect,* **2,** 19–28.

Starr, R. H., Jr. (1988). Physical abuse of children. In V. B. Van Hasselt, A. S. Bellack, R. L. Morrisson, and M. Hersen (eds.), *Handbook of family violence.* New York: Plenum.

Steele, B. F. (1975). *Working with abusive parents from a psychiatric point of view.* U. S. Department of Health, Education, and Welfare Publication OHD75-70. Washington, D.C.: U.S. Government Printing Office.

Stocker, C., Dunn, J., and Plomin, R. (1989). Sibling relationships: Links with child temperament, maternal behavior, and family structure. *Child Development,* **60,** 715–727.

Suransky, V. P. (1982). *The erosion of childhood.* Chicago: University of Chicago Press.

Sutton-Smith, B., and Rosenberg, B. G. (1970). *The sibling.* New York: Holt, Rinehart & Winston.

Teti, D. M., and Ablard, K. E. (1989). Security of attachment and infant–

sibling relationships: A laboratory study. *Child Development,* **60,** 1519–1528.

Teti, D. M., Bond, L. A., and Gibbs, E. D. (1986). Sibling-created experiences: Relationships to birth-spacing and infant cognitive development. *Infant Behavior and Development,* **9,** 27–42.

Thomas, J. H. (1983). The influence of sex, birth order, and sex of sibling on parent–adolescent interaction. *Child Study Journal,* **13,** 107–114.

Tubergen, D. G. (1984). Neoplastic disease. In C. H. Kempe, H. K. Silver, and D. O'Brien (eds.), *Current pediatric diagnosis and treatment,* 8th ed. Los Altos, CA: Lange.

Tulving, E. (1974). Cue-dependent forgetting. *American Scientist,* **62,** 74–82.

Vihman, M. M. (1985). Language differentiation by the bilingual infant. *Journal of Child Language,* **12,** 297–324.

Vygotsky, L. (1962). *Thought and language* (E. Hanfmann and G. Vakar, trans.) Cambridge, MA: Harvard University Press. (Originally published 1934.)

Weinraub, M., Clemens, L. P., Sockloff, A., Ethridge, T., Gracely, E., and Myers, B. (1984). The development of sex role stereotypes in the third year: Relationships to gender labeling, gender identity, sex-typed toy preference, and family characteristics. *Child Development,* **55,** 1493–1503.

Weitzman, N., Birns, B., and Friend, R. (1985). Traditional and non-traditional mothers' communication with their daughters and sons. *Child Development,* **56**(4), 894–898.

White, B. (1971). *Experience and psychological development.* Englewood Cliffs, NJ: Prentice-Hall.

Will, B. E., Rosensweig, M. R., Bennett, E. L., Herbert, M., and Morimoto, H. (1977). Relatively brief environmental enrichment aids recovery of learning capacity and alters brain measures after post-tweaning brain lesions in rats. *Journal of Comparative and Physiological Psychology,* **91,** 33–50.

Wolfe, D. A. (1985). Child-abusive parents: An empirical review and analysis. *Psychological Bulletin,* **97,** 462–482.

Wolock, I., and Horowitz, B. (1984). Child maltreatment as a social problem: The neglect of neglect. *American Journal of Orthopsychiatry,* **54,** 530–543.

Zajonc, R. B. (1976). Family configuration and intelligence. *Science,* **160,** 227–236.

CHAPTER 6

Ames, L. B. (1983). Learning disability: Truth or trap? *Journal of Learning Disabilities,* **16,** 19–20.

Ascione, F. R., and Chambers, J. H. (1985). Videogames and prosocial behavior: The effects of prosocial and aggressive video games on children's donating and helping. Paper presented at the meeting of the Society for Research in Child Development, Toronto, April.

Ball, D. W., Newman, J. M., and Scheuren, W. J. (1984). Teachers' generalized expectations of children of divorce. *Psychological Reports,* **54,** 347–353.

Bandura, A., and Walters, R. (1963). *Social learning and personality development.* New York: Holt, Rinehart & Winston.

Barnett, M. A. (1987). Empathy and related responses in children. In N. Eisenberg and J. Strayer (eds.), *Empathy and its development.* Cambridge, UK: Cambridge University Press.

Bem, S. L. (1976). Probing the promise of androgyny. In A. Kaplan and J. Bean (eds.), *Beyond sex-role stereotypes: Readings toward a psychology of androgyny.* Boston: Little, Brown.

Blomquist, H. K., Jr., Gustavson, K. H., and Holmgren, G. (1981). Mild mental retardation in children in a northern Swedish county. *Journal of Mental Deficiency Research,* **25,** 169–186.

Broman, S. H. (1983). Obstetric medications. In C. C. Brown (ed.), *Childhood learning disabilities and prenatal risk: Pediatric round table; 9.* Skillman, NJ: Johnson & Johnson Baby Products Co.

Bryant, B. K. (1985). The neighborhood walk: Sources of support in middle childhood. *Monographs of the Society for Research in Child Development,* **50**(3, Serial No. 210).

Carey, S. (1978). The child as word learner. In M. Halle, J. Bresnan, and G. A. Miller (eds.), *Linguistic theory and psychological reality.* Cambridge, MA: MIT Press.

Carlson, B. E. (1984). The father's contribution to child care: Effects on children's perceptions of parental roles. *American Journal of Orthopsychiatry,* **54,** 123–136.

Carroll, J. B., and Horn, J. L. (1981). On the scientific basis of ability testing. *American Psychologist,* **36**(10), 1012–1020.

Cattell, R. B. (1971). *Abilities: Their structure, growth, and action.* Boston: Houghton Mifflin.

Chomsky, N. (1972). *Language and mind.* New York: Harcourt Brace Jovanovich.

Cohen, S. L. (1983). Low birthweight. In C. C. Brown (ed.), *Childhood learning disabilities and prenatal risk: Pediatric round table; 9.* Skillman, NJ: Johnson & Johnson Baby Products Co.

Colbert, P., Newman, B., Ney, P., and Young, Jr. (1982). Learning disabilities as a symptom of depression in children. *Journal of Learning Disabilities,* **15,** 333–336.

Conant, J. (1970). *My several lives.* New York: Harper & Row.

Creevy, D. C. (1983). Obstetrical trauma. In C. B. Brown (ed.), *Childhood learning disabilities and prenatal risk: Pediatric round table; 9.* Skillman, NJ: Johnson & Johnson Baby Products Co.

Curwin, R. L., and Mendler, A. (1980). *The discipline book: A complete guide to school and classroom management.* Reston, VA: Reston Publishing.

Damon, W. (1984). Peer education: The untapped potential. *Journal of Applied Developmental Psychology,* **5,** 331–343.

Davies, B. (1982). *Life in the classroom and playground.* Boston: Routledge & Kegan Paul.

Deci, E. L., Schwaratz, A. J.., Sheinman, L., and Ryan, R. M. (1981). An instrument to assess adults' orientations toward control versus autonomy with children: Reflections on intrinsic motivation and perceived competence. *Journal of Educational Psychology,* **73,** 642–650.

Deluty, R. H. (1979). Children's action tendency scale: A self-report measure of aggressiveness, assertiveness, and submissiveness in children. *Journal of Consulting and Clinical Psychology,* **47,** 1061–1071.

Deluty, R. H. (1985). Consistency of assertive, aggressive, and submissive behavior for children. *Journal of Personality and Social Psychology,* **49**(4), 1054–1065.

Dreikurs, R., and Stolz, V. (1964). *Children: The challenge.* New York: Hawthorn Books.

Dweck, C. S., and Elliott, E. S. (1983). Achievement motivation. In E. M. Hetherington (ed.), *Socialization, personality and social development.* Vol. 4 of P. H. Mussen (ed.), *Handbook of child psychology,* 4th ed. New York: Wiley.

Eccles, J., Midgley, C., and Adler, T. F. (1984). Grade related changes in the school environment: Effects on achievement motivation. In M. Maehr (ed.), *Advances in motivation and achievement: The development of achievement motivation; 3.* Greenwich, CT: JAI Press.

Edwards, C. P., and Whiting, B. B. (1980). Differential socialization of girls and boys in light of cross-cultural research. In C. M. Super and S. Harkness (eds.), *New directions for child development: Anthropological perspectives on child development.* San Francisco: Jossey-Bass.

Eiduson, B. T. (1990). One-parent families. In R. M. Thomas (ed.), *The Encyclopedia of human development and education theory, research and studies.* New York: Pergamon Press.

Einstein, E. (1979). Stepfamily lives. *Human Behavior,* April, 63–68.

Eisenberg, N. (1989). Empathy and sympathy. In W. Damon (ed.), *Child development today and tomorrow.* San Francisco: Jossey-Bass.

Erikson, E. H. (1963). *Childhood and society,* 2nd ed. New York: Norton.

Feldman, D. H. (1989). Creativity: Proof that development occurs. In W. Damon (ed.), *Child development today and tomorrow.* San Francisco: Jossey-Bass.

Feldstein, J. H., and Feldstein, S. (1982). Sex differences on televised toy commercials. *Sex Roles,* **8,** 581–587.

Flavell, J. H. (1970). Developmental studies of mediated memory. In H. Reese and L. Lipsitt (eds.), *Advances in child development and behavior; 5.* New York: Academic Press.

Freud, S. (1953). *A general introduction to psychoanalysis* (J. Rivere, trans.). New York: Permabooks. (Originally published, 1935).

Fry, P. S., and Scher, A. (1984). The effects of father absence on children's achievement motivation, ego-strength, and locus-of-control orientation: A five-year longitudinal assessment. *British Journal of Developmental Psychology,* **2,** 167–178.

Fu, V. R., and Fogel, S. (1982). Pro-white/anti-black bias among southern preschool children. *Psychological Reports,* **51,** 1003–1006.

Gardner, H. (1983). *Frames of mind: The theory of multiple intelligences.* New York: Basic Books.

Gelman, S. A., and Markman, E. M. (1987). Young children's inductions from natural kinds: The role of categories and appearances. *Child Development,* **58,** 1532–1541.

Gemelli, R. J. (1982). Classification of child stuttering: Part II. Persistent late onset male stuttering, and treatment issues for persistent stutterers—psychotherapy or speech therapy, or both? *Child Psychiatry and Human Development,* **13,** 3–34.

Gilligan, C. (1982). *In a different voice: Psychological theory and women's development.* Cambridge, MA: Harvard University Press.

Gilligan, C., and Attanucci, J. (1988). Much ado about . . . knowing? noting? nothing? A reply to Vasudev concerning sex differences and moral development. *Merrill-Palmer Quarterly,* **34,** 451–456.

Ginott, H. G. (1972). *Teacher and child: A book for parents and teachers.* New York: Macmillan.

Glick, P. G., and Norton, A. J. (1978). Marrying, divorcing and living together in the U.S. today. *Population Bulletin,* **32,** 3–38.

Gray, D. B., and Yaffe, S. L. (1983). Prenatal drugs. In C. C. Brown (ed.), *Childhood learning disabilities and prenatal risk: Pediatric round table; 9.* Skillman, NJ: Johnson & Johnson Baby Products Co.

Greenfield, P. M. (1984). *Mind and media: The effects of television, video games, and computers.* Cambridge, MA: Harvard University Press.

Grossman, H. (1977) (Ed.). *Manual on terminology and classification in mental retardation.* Washington, D.C.: American Association on Mental Deficiency.

Gruber, H. (1981). *Darwin on man: A psychological study of scientific creativity,* 2nd ed. Chicago: University of Chicago Press.

Guilford, JP. (1967). *The nature of human intelligence.* New York: McGraw-Hill.

Hagen. J. W., Anderson, B. J., and Barclay, C. R. (1986). Issues in research on the young chronically ill child. *Topics in Early Childhood Special Education,* **5**(4), 49–57.

Haggerty, R. J. (1984). Forward: chronic disease in children. *Pediatric Clinics of North America,* **31,** 1–2.

Hawkins, D. B., and Gruber, J. J. (1982). Little League baseball and players' self-esteem. *Perceptual and Motor Skills,* **55,** 1335–1340.

Hearnshaw, L. S. (1979). *Cyril Burt, psychologist.* Ithaca, NY: Cornell University Press.

Herrnstein, R. (1971). IQ. *Atlantic Monthly,* September, 43–64.

Hetherington, E. M. (1979). Divorce: A child's perspective. *American Psychologist,* **34**(10), 851–858.

Hetherington, E. M., Cox, M., and Cox, R. (1978). The aftermath of divorce. In J. Stevens and M. Matthews (eds.), *Mother/child, father/child relationships.* Washington, D.C.: National Association for the Education of Young Children.

Hetherington, E. M., Cox, M., and Cox, R. (1982). Effects of divorce on parents and children. In M. Lamb (ed.), *Nontraditional families.* Hillsdale, NJ: Erlbaum.

Hoffman, M. L. (1984). Interaction of affect and cognition on empathy. In C. E. Izard, J. Kagan, and R. B. Zajonc (eds.), *Emotions, cognition and behavior.* Cambridge, UK: Cambridge University Press.

Hynd, G. W., and Hynd, C. R. (1984). Dyslexia: Neuroanatomical/neurolinguistic perspectives. *Reading Research Quarterly,* **19,** 482–498.

Jensen, A. (1969). How much can we boost IQ and scholastic achievement? *Harvard Educational Review,* **39,** 1–123.

Jensen, A. (1980). *Bias in mental testing.* New York: Free Press.

Kalter, N., and Plunkett, J. W. (1984). Children's perceptions of the causes and consequences of divorce. *Journal of the American Academy of Child Psychiatry,* **23,** 326–334.

Keller, H. (1954). *The story of my life.* New York: Doubleday.

Kline, L. M., Greene, T. R., and Noice, H. (1990). The influence of violent video material on cognitive task performance. *Psychology in the Schools,* **27,** 228–232.

Kohlberg, L. (1963). The development of children's orientations toward a moral order. I: Sequence in the development of human thought. *Vita Humana,* **6,** 11–33.

Kohlberg, L. (1984). *The psychology of moral development.* San Francisco: Harper & Row.

Levin, G. (1985). Computers and kids: The good news. *Psychology Today,* **19**(8), 50–51.

Lewin, K., Lippitt, R., and White, R. (1939). Patterns of aggression in experimentally created social climates. *Journal of Social Psychology,* **10,** 271–299.

Long, T., and Long, L. (1983). *The handbook for latchkey children and their parents.* New York: Arbor House.

Ludwig, G., and Cullinan, D. (1984). Behavior problems of gifted and nongifted elementary school girls and boys. *Gifted Child Quarterly,* **28,** 37–39.

Maccoby, E. E. (1980). *Social development: Psychological growth and the parent-child relationship.* New York: Harcourt Brace Jovanovich.

Maccoby, E. E., and Martin, J. A. (1983). Socialization in the context of family: Parent–child interaction. In E. M. Hetherington (ed.), *Socialization, personality, and social development.* Vol. 4 of P. H. Mussen (ed.), *Handbook of child psychology,* 4th ed. New York: Wiley.

Mackey, W. D., and Hess, D. J. (1982). Attention structure and stereotype of gender on television: An empirical analysis. *Genetic Psychology Monographs; 106,* 199–215.

Marland, S. P. (1972). *Education of the gifted and talented.* Report to the Congress of the United States by the U.S. Commissioner of Education. Washington, D.C.: U.S. Government Printing Office.

Marx, J. L. (1983). The two sides of the brain. *Science,* **220**(4595), 488–490.

McEwen, B. S. (1983). Hormones and the brain. In C. C. Brown (ed.), *Childhood learning disabilities and prenatal risk: Pediatric round table; 9.* Skillman, NJ: Johnson & Johnson Baby Products Co.

McGhee, P. (1979). *Humor: Its origin and development.* San Francisco: Freeman.

Meijer, A. A. (1981). A controlled study on asthmatic children and their families: Synopsis of findings. *Israel Journal of Psychiatry and Related Sciences,* **18,** 197–208.

Menyuk, P. (1977). *Language and maturation.* Cambridge, MA: MIT Press.

Meredith, D. (1985). Dad and the kids. *Psychology Today,* **19**(6), 62–67.

Moser, H. W. (1983). Genetics. In C. C. Brown (ed.), *Childhood learning disabilities and prenatal risk: Pediatric round table; 9.* Skillman, NJ: Johnson & Johnson Baby Products Co.

Needleman, H. L. (1983). Environmental pollutants. In C. C. Brown (ed.), *Childhood learning disabilities and prenatal risk: Pediatric round table; 9.* Skillman, NJ: Johnson & Johnson Baby Products Co.

Nelson-LeGall, S. A., and Gumerman, R. A. (1984). Children's perceptions of helpers and helper motivation. *Journal of Applied Developmental Psychology,* **5,** 1–12.

Nunn, G. D., Parish, T. S., and Worthing, R. J. (1983). Perceptions of personal and familial adjustment by children from intact, single-parent, and reconstituted families. *Psychology in the Schools,* **20,** 166–174.

O'Brien, D., and Hambidge, K. M. (1984). Normal childhood nutrition and its disorders. In C. H. Kempe, H. K. Silver, and D. O'Brien (eds.), *Current pediatric diagnosis and treatment,* 8th ed. Los Altos, CA: Lange.

Olmedo, E. L. (1981). Testing linguistic minorities. *American Psychologist,* **36**(10), 1078–1085.

O'Shea, J. S. (ed.) (1988). *Under three.* New York: Van Nostrand Reinhold.

Parker, J. G., and Asher, S. R. (1987). Peer relations and later personal adjustment: Are low-accepted children "at risk"? *Psychological Bulletin,* **102**(3), 357–389.

Pearl, D. (1984). Violence and aggression. *Society,* **21**(6), 17–22.

Pearlman, D. S. (1984). Allergic disorders. In C. H. Kempe, H. K. Silver, and D. O'Brien (eds.), *Current pediatric diagnosis and treatment,* 8th ed. Los Altos, CA: Lange.

Pedersen, E., Faucher, T. A., and Eaton, W. W. (1978). A new perspective on the effects of first grade teachers on children's subsequent adult status. *Harvard Educational Review,* **48,** 1–1.3.

Piaget, J. (1965a). *The moral judgment of the child* (M. Gabain, trans.). New York: Free Press. (Originally published, 1932.)

Piaget, J. (1965b). *The child's conception of number.* New York: Norton. (Originally published, 1941.)

Pitcher, E. G., and Schultz, L. H. (1984). *Boys and girls at play: The development of sex roles.* New York: Praeger.

Pollitt, E., Leibel, R. L., and Greenfield, D. (1981). Brief fasting, stress, and cognition in children. *American Journal of Clinical Nutrition,* **34,** 1526–1533.

Reschly, D. J. (1981). Psychological testing in educational classification and placement. *American Psychologist,* **36**(10), 1094–1102.

Robbins, F. C. (1983). Forum. In C. C. Brown (ed.), *Childhood learning disabilities and prenatal risk: Pediatric round table; 9.* Skillman, NJ: Johnson & Johnson Baby Products Co.

Rogers, C. R. (1969). *Freedom to learn: A view of what education might become.* Columbus, OH: Merrill.

Rosenthal, R., and Jacobson, L. (1968). *Pygmalion in the classroom: Teacher expectation and pupils' intellectual development.* New York: Holt, Rinehart & Winston.

Ross, R. P., Campbell, T., Wright, J. C., Huston, A. C., Rice, M. L., and Turk, P. (1984). When celebrities talk, children listen: An experimental analysis of children's responses to TV ads with celebrity endorsement. *Journal of Applied Developmental Psychology,* **5,** 185–202.

Rutter, M. (1975). *Helping troubled children.* New York: Plenum.

Rutter, M. (1979). Protective factors in children's response to stress and disadvantage. In M. W. Kent and J. E. Rolf (eds.), *Primary prevention of psychopathology, vol. 3: Social competence in children.* Hanover, NH: University Press of New England.

Rutter, M. (1983). School effects on pupil progress: Research findings and policy implications. *Child Development,* **54,** 1–29.

Samuda, R. J. (1975). *Psychological testing of American minorities: Issues and consequences.* New York: Dodd, Mead.

Santrock, J. W., and Warshak, R. A. (1979). Father custody and social development in boys and girls. *Journal of Social Issues,* **35**(4), 112–125.

Santrock, J. W., Warshak, R. A., Lindbergh, C., and Meadows, L. (1982). Children's and parents' observed social behavior in stepfather families. *Child Development,* **53,** 472–480.

Scarr, S. (1978). From evolution to Larry P., or what shall we do about IQ tests? *Intelligence,* **2,** 325–342.

Schiff, M., Duyme, M., Dumaret, A., and Tomiewicz, S. (1982). How much could we boost scholastic achievement and IQ scores? A direct answer from a French adoption study. *Cognition,* **12,** 165–196.

Schmitt, B. D. (1984). Ambulatory pediatrics. In C. H. Kempe, H. K. Silver, and D. O'Brien (eds.), *Current pediatric diagnosis and treatment,* 8th ed. Los Altos, CA: Lange.

Schramm, W. L. (1973). *Men, messages and media: A look at human communication.* New York: Harper & Row.

Schramm, W. L. (1977). *Big media, little media: Tools and technologies for instruction.* Beverly Hills, CA: Sage.

Schramm, W. L., and Roberts, D. F. (1971). Children's learning from the mass media. In W. L. Schramm and D. F. Roberts (eds.), *The process and effects of mass communication.* Urbana, IL: University of Illinois Press.

Sever, J. L. (1983). Maternal infections. In C. C. Brown (ed.), *Childhood learning disabilities and prenatal risk: Pediatric round table; 9.* Skillman, NJ: Johnson & Johnson Baby Products Co.

Shapiro, A. K., and Shapiro, E. S. (1980). *Tics, Tourette syndrome and other movement disorders.* Bayside, NY: The Tourette Syndrome Association.

Sheldon, W. H. (1940). *The varieties of human physique.* New York: Harper & Row.

Shockley, W. (1972). Dysgenics, genecity, raceology: A challenge to the intellectual responsibility of educators. *Phi Beta Kappan,* **53,** 297–307.

Siegal, M., and Cowen, J. (1984). Appraisals of intervention: The mothers' versus the culprits' behavior as determinants of children's evaluations of disciplinary techniques. *Child Development,* **55,** 1760–1766.

Silver, H. K. (1984). Growth and Development. In C. H. Kempe, H. K. Silver, and D. O'Brien (eds.), *Current pediatric diagnosis and treatment,* 8th ed. Los Altos, CA: Lange.

Silver, H. K., Gotlin, R. W., and Klingensmith, G. J. (1984). Endocrine disorders. In C. H. Kempe, H. K. Silver, and D. O'Brien (eds.), *Current pediatric diagnosis and treatment,* 8th ed. Los Altos, CA: Lange.

Simopoulos, A. P. (1983). Nutrition. In C. C. Brown (ed.), *Childhood learning disabilities and prenatal risk: Pediatric round table; 9.* Skillman, NJ: Johnson & Johnson Baby Products Co.

Spearman, C. (1927). *The abilities of man.* London: Macmillan.

Stapleton, C., and MacCormack, N. (1981). When parents divorce, DHHS Publication No. (ADM)81-1120. Washington, D.C.: U.S. Government Printing Office.

Sternberg, R. J. (1988). *The triarchic mind: A new theory of human intelligence.* New York: Penguin Books.

Tanner, J. M. (1978). *Fetus into man: Physical growth from conception to maturity.* Cambridge, MA: Harvard University Press.

Thurstone, L. L. (1938). *Primary mental abilities.* Chicago: University of Chicago Press.

Tom, D. Y. H., Cooper, H., and McGraw, M. (1984). Influences of student background and teacher authoritarianism on teacher expectations. *Journal of Educational Psychology,* **76,** 259–265.

Trueman, D. (1984). What are the characteristics of school phobic children? *Psychological Reports,* **54,** 191–202.

Turiel, E. (1966). An experimental test of the sequentiality of the developmental stages in the child's moral judgments. *Journal of Personality and Social Psychology,* **3,** 611–618.

Vail, P. L. (1979). *The world of the gifted child.* New York: Walker.

Wallerstein, J. S., and Kelly, J. B. (1976). The effects of parental divorce: Experiences of the child in later latency. *American Journal of Orthopsychiatry,* **46,** 256–269.

Wechsler, D. (1949). *The Wechsler Intelligence Scale for Children.* New York: Psychological Corp.

Weinraub, M. (1978). Fatherhood: The myth of the second-class parent. In J. Stevens and M. Mathews (eds.), *Mother/child, father/child relationships.* Washington, D.C.: National Association for the Education of Young Children.

Weinraub, M., and Wolf, B. M. (1983). Effects of stress and social supports on mother–child interactions in single- and two-parent families. *Child Development,* **54,** 1297–1311.

Wilson, J. Q., and Herrnstein, R. (1985). *Crime and human nature.* New York: Simon & Schuster.

Wolf, T. H. (1973). *Alfred Binet.* Chicago: University of Chicago Press.

Wright, J. C., and Huston, A. C. (1983). A matter of form: Potentials of television for young viewers. *American Psychologist,* **38,** 835–843.

CHAPTER 7

American Psychiatric Association (1980). *Diagnostic and statistical manual of mental disorders (DSM-III),* 3rd ed. Washington, D.C.: American Psychiatric Association.

Andersen, A. E. (1983). Anorexia nervosa and bulimia: A spectrum of eating disorders. *Journal of Adolescent Health Care,* **4,** 15–21.

Andersen, A. E. (1985). *Practical comprehensive treatment of anorexia nervosa and bulimia.* Baltimore: Johns Hopkins University Press.

Archer, S. L. (1982). The lower boundaries of identity development. *Child Development,* **53,** 1551–1556.

Avery, A. W. (1982). Escaping loneliness in adolescence: The case for androgyny. *Journal of Youth and Adolescence,* **11,** 451–459.

Barclay, D. L. (1984). Disorders of the vulva and vagina. In R. C. Benson (ed.), *Current obstetric and gynecologic diagnosis and treatment,* 5th ed. Los Altos, CA: Lange.

Barret, R. L. and Robinson, B. E. (1982). A descriptive study of teenage expectant fathers. *Family Relations,* **31,** 349–352.

Benbow, C. P., and Stanley, J. C. (1983). Sex differences in mathematical reasoning ability: More facts. *Science,* **222,** 1029–1031.

Berndt, T. J. (1982). The features and effects of friendship in early adolescence. *Child Development,* **53,** 1447–1460.

Bredemeier, B. J., and Shields, D. L. (1984). Divergence in moral reasoning about sport and life. *Sociology of Sport Journal,* **1,** 348–357.

Bronfenbrenner, U. (1972). The roots of alienation. In U. Bronfenbrenner (ed.), *Influences on human development.* Hinsdale, IL: Dryden Press.

Brooks-Gunn, J., and Ruble, D. N. (1982). The development of menstrual-related beliefs and behaviors during early adolescence. *Child Development,* **53,** 1567–1577.

Brown, B. B. (1982). The extent and effects of peer pressure among high school students: A retrospective analysis. *Journal of Youth and Adolescence,* **11,** 121–133.

Brumberg, J. J. (1989). *Fasting girls: A history of anorexia nervosa.* New York: Penguin.

Bullough, V. L. (1981). Age at menarche: A misunderstanding. *Science,* **213**(7), 365–366.

Bureau of Labor Statistics (1989). *Employment and earnings,* **36**(1). Washington: U.S. Government Printing Office.

Butcher, J. (1985). Longitudinal analysis of girls' participation in physical activity. *Sociology of Sport Journal,* **2,** 130–143.

Cairns, R. B., Cairns, B. D., and Neckerman, H. J. (1989). Early school dropout: Configurations and determinants. *Child Development,* **60,** 1437–1452.

Cauble, M. A. (1976). Formal operations, ego identity, and principled morality: Are they related? *Developmental Psychology,* **12**(4), 363–364.

Clarke, A. E., and Ruble, D. N. (1978). Young adolescents' beliefs concerning menstruation. *Child Development, 49,* 231–234.

Clausen, J. A. (1975). The social meaning of differential physical and sexual maturation. In S. E. Dragastin and G. H. Elder, Jr. (eds.), *Adolescence in the life cycle: Psychological change and social context.* New York: Wiley.

Cohen, D. D., and Rose, R. D. (1984) Male adolescent birth control behavior: The importance of developmental factors and sex differences. *Journal of Youth and Adolescence,* **13,** 239–252.

Colby, A., Kohlberg, L., Gibbs, J., and Lieberman, M. (1983). A longitudinal study of moral judgment. *Monographs of the Society for Research in Child Development,* **48**(1-2, Serial No. 200).

Coleman, J., and Coleman, E. (1984). Adolescent attitudes to authority. *Journal of Adolescence, 7,* 131–141.

Commons, M. L., Richards, F. A., and Kuhn, D. (1982). Systematic and metasystematic reasoning: A case for levels of reasoning beyond Piaget's stage of formal operations. *Child Development, 53,* 1058–1069.

Csikszentmihalyi, M., and Larson, R. (1984). *Being adolescent: Conflict and growth in the teenage years.* New York: Basic Books.

Csikszentmihalyi, M., Larson, R., and Prescott, S. (1977). The ecology of adolescent activity and experience. *Journal of Youth and Adolescence, 6,* 281–294.

Cunningham, F. G., Hemsell, D. L., and Mickal, A. (1984) Pelvic infections. In R. C. Benson (ed.), *Current obstetric and gynecologic diagnosis and treatment.* 5th ed. Los Altos, CA: Lange.

Deluty, R. H. (1989). Factors affecting the acceptability of suicide. *Omega, 19,* 315–326.

Donelson, E. (1977). Development of sex-typed behavior and self-concept. In E. Donelson and J. Gullahorn (eds.), *Women: A psychological perspective.* New York: Wiley.

Dusek, J. B., and Flaherty, J. F. (1981). The development of the self-concept during the adolescent years. *Monographs of the Society for Research in Child Development, 46*(4, Serial No. 191).

Edlin, G., and Golanty, E. (1992). *Health and wellness: A holistic approach,* 4th ed. Boston: Jones & Bartlett.

Elder, G. H., Jr., and MacInnis, D. J. (1983). Achievement imagery in women's lives from adolescence to adulthood. *Journal of Personality and Social Psychology,* **45,** 394–404.

Elkind, D. (1970). *Children and adolescents: Interpretive essays on Jean Piaget.* New York: Oxford University Press.

Elkind, D. (1978). Understanding the young adolescent. *Adolescence,* **13,** 127–134.

Elkind, D. (1985). Egocentrism redux. *Developmental Review,* **5,** 218–226.

Elkind, D., and Bowen, R. (1979). Imaginary audience behavior in children and adolescents. *Developmental Psychology,* **15,** 38–44.

Erb, T. O. (1983). Career preferences of early adolescents: Age and sex differences. *Journal of Early Adolescence, 3,* 349–359.

Erikson, E. (1963). *Childhood and society,* 2nd ed. New York: Norton.

Erikson, E. (1968). *Identity, youth, and crisis.* New York: Norton.

Erikson, E. (1980). *Identity and the life cycle.* New York: Norton.

Evrard, J. R. (1985). Teen sexuality at root of rise in pregnancies. *Brown University Human Development Letter,* **1,** 8–9.

Faust, J., Forehand, R., and Baum, C. G. (1985). An examination of the association between social relationships and depression in early adolescence. *Journal of Applied Developmental Psychology,* **6,** 291–297.

Federal Bureau of Investigation (1988). *Crime in the United States: 1987.* Washington: U.S. Government Printing Office.

Finkbeiner, A. (1985). AIDS: Just the facts. *Johns Hopkins Magazine,* **37**(6), 23–28.

Food and Drug Administration (1985). Progrss on AIDS. *FDA Drug Bulletin, 15*(3), 27–32.

Freeman, D. (1983). *Margaret Mead and Samoa: The making and un-making of an anthropological myth.* Cambridge, MA: Harvard University Press.

Fry, P. S. (1985). Relations between teenagers' age, knowledge, expectations and maternal behavior. *British Journal of Developmental Psychology, 3,* 47–55.

Fulginiti, V. A. (1984). Infections: Viral and rickettsial. In C. H. Kempe, H. K. Silver, and D. O'Brien (eds.), *Current pediatric diagnosis and treatment,* 8th ed. Los Altos, CA: Lange.

Garbarino, J., Sebes, J., and Schellenbach, C. (1984). Families at risk for destructive parent–child relations in adolescence. *Child Development,* **55,** 174–183.

Gilligan, C. (1982). *In a different voice: Psychological theory and women's development.* Cambridge, MA: Harvard University Press.

Gillis, J. S. (1982). *Too tall, too small.* Champaign, IL: Institute for Personality and Ability Testing.

Goethals, G. W., and Klos, D. S. (1970). *Experiencing youth: First person accounts.* Boston: Little, Brown.

Gold, M., and Petronio, R. (1980). Delinquent behavior in adolescence. In J. Adelson (ed.), *Handbook of adolescent psychology.* New York: Wiley.

Gordon, S., and Gilgun, J. F. (1987). Adolescent sexuality. In V. B. Van Hasselt and M. Herson (eds.), *Handbook of adolescent psychology.* New York: Pergamon.

Greif, E. B. and Ulman, K. J. (1982). The psychological impact of menarche on early adolescent females: A review of the literature. *Child Development, 53,* 1413–1430.

Grob, M. C., Klein, A. A., and Eisen, S. V. (1984). The role of the high school professional in identifying and managing adolescent suicidal behavior. *Journal of Youth and Adolescence,* **12,** 163–173.

Haan, N. (1978). Two moralities in action contexts: Relationships to thought, ego, regulation, and development. *Journal of Personality and Social Psychology,* **36,** 286–305.

Haan, N., Aerts, E., and Cooper, B. (1985). *On moral grounds: The search for practical morality.* New York: New York University Press.

Hall, G. S. (1904). *Adolescence* (2 vols.). New York: Appleton.

Halmi, K. A., Falk, J. R., and Schwartz, E. (1981). Binge-eating and vomiting: A survey of college population. *Psychological Medicine,* **11,** 697–706.

Hauser, S. T., Powers, S. I., Noam, G. G., Jacobson, A. M., Weiss, B., and Follansbee, D. J. (1984). Familial contexts of adolescent ego development. *Child Development,* **55,** 195–213.

Havighurst, R. J. (1972). *Developmental tasks and education,* 3rd ed. New York: McKay.

Hoffman, L. W. (1972) Early childhood experiences and women's achievement motives. *Journal of Social Issues,* **28,** 129–155.

Hoffman, L. W. (1974). Fear of success in males and females: 1965 and 1971. *Journal of Consulting and Clinical Psychology,* **18,** 806–811.

Holstein, C. B. (1976). Irreversible, stepwise sequence in the development of moral judgment: A longitudinal study of males and females. *Child Development,* **47,** 51–61.

Horner, M. (1972). Toward an understanding of achievement-related conflicts in women. *Journal of Social Issues,* **28,** 157–175.

Hunter, F. T. and Youniss, J. (1982). Changes in functions of three relations during adolescence. *Developmental Psychology,* **18,** 806–811.

Inhelder, B., & Piaget, J. (1958). *The growth of logical thinking from childhood to adolescence.* (A. Parsons and S. Milgram, trans.) New York: Basic Books.

Johnson, F. L., and Aries, E. J. (1983). Conversational patterns among same-sex pairs of late-adolescent close friends. *Journal of Genetic Psychology,* **142,** 225–238.

Johnson, S. (1983). *Facts about precocious puberty.* (NICHD Fact Sheet 0-418-065). Washington, D.C.: U.S. Government Printing Office.

Josselson, R., Greenberger, E., and McConochie, D. (1977). Phenomenological aspects of psychosocial maturity in adolescence. *Journal of Youth and Adolescence, 6,* 25–55; 145–167.

Jurich, A. P., and Andrews, D. (1984). Self-concepts of rural early adolescent juvenile delinquents. *Journal of Early Adolescence, 4,* 41–46.

Jurich, A. P., Polson, C. J., Jurich, J. A., and Bates, R. A. (1985). Family factors in the lives of drug users and abusers. *Adolescence,* **20,** 143–159.

Keating, D. P. (1980). Thinking processes in adolescence. In J. Adelson (ed.), *Handbook of adolescent psychology.* New York: Wiley.

Kitchener, K. S., King, P. M., Davison, M. L., Parker, C. A., and Wood, P. K. (1984). A longitudinal study of moral and ego development in young adults. *Journal of Youth and Adolescence,* **13,** 197–211.

Koff, E. Rierdan, J., and Jacobson, S. (1981). The personal and interpersonal significance of menarche. *Journal of the American Academy of Child Psychiatry,* **20,** 148–158.

Kohlberg, L. (1984). *The psychology of moral development.* San Francisco: Harper & Row.

Kohlberg, L., and Gilligan, C. (1971). The adolescent as a philosopher: The discovery of the self in a postconventional world. *Daedalus,* **100,** 1051–1086.

Lamke, L. K. (1982). Adjustment and sex-role orientation in adolescence. *Journal of Youth and Adolescence,* **11,** 249–259.

Landy, S., Clark, C., Schubert, J., and Jillings, C. (1983). Mother–infant interactions of teenage mothers as measured at six months in a natural setting. *Journal of Psychology,* **115,** 245–258.

Leming, J. S. (1978). Intrapersonal variations in stage of moral reasoning among adolescents as a function of situational context. *Journal of Youth and Adolescence,* **7,** 405–416.

LeResche, L., Strobino, D., Parks, P., Fischer, P., and Smeriglio, V. (1983). The relationship of observed maternal behavior to questionnaire measures of parenting knowledge, attitudes, and emotional state in adolescent mothers. *Journal of Youth and Adolescence,* **12,** 19–31.

Linn, M. C., and Petersen, A. C. (1985). Emergence and characterization of sex differences in spatial ability: A meta-analysis. *Child Development,* **56,** 1479–1498.

Lipsitt, L. P. (1985a). Birth stress and adolescent suicide. *The Brown University Human Development Letter, Whole Special Report.*

Lipsitt, L. P. (1985b). Who commits juvenile crime? *The Brown University Human Development Letter,* **1,** 9.

Loeber, R. (1982). The stability of antisocial and delinquent child behavior: A review. *Child Development,* **53,** 1431–1446.

LoPresto, C. T., and Deluty, R. H. (1988). Consistency of aggressive, assertive, and submissive behavior in male adolescents. *Journal of Social Psychology,* **128,** 619–623.

Marcia, J. E. (1980). Identity in adolescence. In J. Adelson (ed.), *Handbook of adolescent psychology.* New York: Wiley.

Marcia, J. E. (1983). Some directions for the investigation of ego development in early adolescence. *Journal of Early Adolescence,* **3,** 215–223.

Marcoen, A., and Brumagne, M. (1985). Loneliness among children and young adolescents. *Developmental Psychology,* **21,** 1025–1031.

McAnarney, E. R. (1983). The vulnerable dyad—adolescent mothers and their infants. In V. J. Sasserath (ed.), *Minimizing high risk parenting.* Skillman, NJ: Johnson & Johnson Baby Products Co.

McAnarney, E. R. (1984). Touching and adolescent sexuality. In C. C. Brown (ed.), *The many facets of touch.* Skillman, NJ: Johnson & Johnson Baby Products.

McAnarney, E. R., and Greydanus, D. E. (1984). Adolescence. In C. H. Kempe, H. K. Silver, and D O'Brien (eds.), *Current pediatric diagnosis and treatment,* 8th ed. Los Altos, CA: Lange.

Mead, M. (1928). *Coming of age in Samoa.* New York: Morrow.

Mead, M. (1949). *Sex and temperament in three primitive societies.* New York: Dell. (Originally published, 1935).

Montemayor, R. (1984). Maternal employment and adolescents' relations with parents, siblings, and peers. *Journal of Youth and Adolescence,* **13,** 543–557.

Moore, D., and Schultz, N. R., Jr. (1983). Loneliness at adolescence: Correlates, attributions, and coping. *Journal of Youth and Adolescence,* **12,** 95–100.

Moore, K. A., and Burt, M. R. (1982). *Private crisis, public cost: Policy perspectives on teenage childbearing.* Washington: The Urban Institute Press.

Muller, J. Z. (1985). *Dysmenorrhea and premenstrual syndrome.* (NICHD Fact Sheet 461. 338-814/25320). Washington, D.C.: U.S. Government Printing Office.

National Institute on Drug Abuse (1985). *National Survey on Drug Abuse.* Washington, D.C.: NIDA.

Nazario, T. A. (1988). *In defense of children.* New York: Scribners.

Newman, W. P., III, Freedman, D. S., Voors, A. W., Gard, P. D., Srinivasan, S. R., Cresanta, J. L., Williams, G. D., Webber, L. S., and Berenson, G. S. (1986). Relation of serum lipoprotein levels and systolic blood pressure to early atherosclerosis. *The New England Journal of Medicine,* **314**(3) 138–144.

Overton, W. F., and Mechan, A. M. (1982). Individual differences in formal operational thought: Sex role and learned helplessness. *Child Development,* **53,** 1536–1543.

Overton, W. F., and Newman, J. (1982). Cognitive development: A competence activation/utilization approach. In T. Field,

A. Houston, H. Quay, L. Troll, and G. Finley (eds.), *Review of human development.* New York: Wiley.

Petersen, A. C. (1987). Those gangly years. *Psychology Today,* **21,** 28–34.

Phillips, D. P. (1985). The Werther effect: Suicide and other forms of violence are contagious. *The Sciences,* **25**(4), 32–39.

Physician's Desk Reference (1991). Oradell, NJ: Medical Economics Co.

Piaget, J. (1958). *The growth of logical thinking from childhood to adolescence.* (A. Parsons and S. Seagrin, trans.) New York: Basic Books.

Piaget, J., and Inhelder, B. (1969). *The psychology of the child.* (H. Weaver, trans.) New York: Basic Books.

Polit-O'Hara, D., and Kahn J. R. (1985). Communication and contraceptive practices in adolescent couples. *Adolescence,* **20,** 33–43.

Rand, C. S. (1979). Obesity and human sexuality. *Medical Aspects of Human Sexuality,* **13**(1), 141–151.

Riley, T., Adams, G. R., and Nielsen, E. (1984). Adolescent egocentrism: The association among imaginary audience behavior, cognitive development, and parental support and rejection. *Journal of Youth and Adolescence,* **13,** 401–417.

Robinson, B. E., and Barret, R. L. (1985). Teenage fathers. *Psychology Today,* **19,** 66–70.

Rodin, J. (1978). The puzzle of obesity. *Human Nature,* **1**(2), 38–47.

Roscoe, B., and Kruger, T. L. (1990). AIDS: Late adolescents' knowledge and its influence on behavior. *Adolescence,* **25,** 39–47.

Ruble, D. N., and Brooks-Gunn, J. (1982). The experience of menarche. *Child Development,* **53,** 1557–1566.

Rust, J. O., and McCraw, A. (1984). Influence of masculinity–femininity on adolescent self-esteem and peer acceptance. *Adolescence,* **19,** 359–366.

Savin-Williams, R. C., and Demo, D. H. (1984). Developmental change and stability in adolescent self-concept. *Developmental Psychology,* **20,** 1100–1110.

Schwartz, M., and Ford, J. H. (1982). Family planning clinics: Cure or cause of teenage pregnancy? In U. S. House of Representatives, *Teen parents, and their children: Issues and programs.* Hearings before the Select Committee on Children, Youth, and Families, July. Washington: U.S. Government Printing Office.

Scott-Jones, D., and White, A. B. (1990). Correlates of sexual activity in early adolescence. *Journal of Early Adolescence,* **10,** 221–238.

Silver, H. K. (1984). Growth and development. In C. H. Kempe, H. K. Silver, and D. O'Brien (eds.), *Current pediatric diagnosis and treatment.* Los Altos, CA: Lange.

Singer, G. S., and Irvin, L. K. (1987). Human rights review of intrusive behavioral treatments for students with severe handicaps. *Exceptional Children,* **54,** 46–52.

Spillane-Grieco, E. (1984). Characteristics of a helpful relationship: A study of empathic understanding and positive regard between runaways and their parents. *Adolescence,* **19,** 63–75.

Stern, M., Northman, J. E., and Van Slyck, M. R. (1984). Father absence and adolescent "problem behaviors": Alcohol consumption, drug use and sexual activity. *Adolescence,* **19,** 301–312.

Stunkard, A. J., Foch, T. T., and Hrubec, Z. (1986). An adoption study of human obesity. *New England Journal of Medicine,* **314**(4), 193–198.

Tanner, J. M. (1962). *Growth at adolescence,* 2nd ed. Oxford: Blackwell Scientific Publications.

Tanner, J. M. (1974). Sequence, tempo, and individual variation in the growth and development of boys and girls aged twelve to sixteen. In A. E. Winder (ed.), *Adolescence: Contemporary studies,* 2nd ed. New York: Van Nostrand.

Thirer, J., and Wright, S. D. (1985). Sports and social status for adolescent males and females. *Sociology of Sport Journal,* **2,** 164–171.

Triolo, S. J., McKenry, P. C., Tishler, C. L., and Blyth, D. A. (1984). Social and psychological discriminants of adolescent suicide: Age and sex differences. *Journal of Early Adolescence,* **4,** 239–251.

Tucker, L. A. (1984). Psychological differences between adolescent smoking intenders and nonintenders. *Journal of Psychology,* **118,** 37–43.

Tyrer, L. B., and Kornblatt, J. E. (1982). Teens' contraceptive needs. *Planned Parenthood Review,* **2,** 11–13.

Wadsworth, J., Taylor, B., Osborn, A., and Butler, N. (1984). Teenage mothering: Child development at five years. *Journal of Child Psychology and Psychiatry,* **25,** 305–313.

Weideger, P. (1976). *Menstruation and menopause: The physiology and psychology; the myth and the reality.* New York: Knopf.

Wetzel, J. R. (1989). *American youth: A statistical snapshot.* Washington: The Wm. T. Grant Commission on Work, Family, Citizenship.

Whisnant, L., and Zegans, L. A. (1975). A study of attitudes toward menarche in white middle-cass American adolescent girls. *American Journal of Psychiatry, 132,* 809–814.

Zelnik, M., and Kantner, J. F. (1978). First pregnancies in women aged 15–19: 1976 and 1971. *Family Planning Perspectives, 10,* 11–20.

Zelnik, M., and Kim, Y. J. (1982). Sex education and its association with teenage sexual activity, pregnancy, and contraceptive use. *Family Planning Perspectives, 14,* 3.

CHAPTER 8

Alper, T. G. (1974). Achievement motivation in college women: A now-you-see-it-now-you-don't phenomenon. *American Psychologist, 29*(3), 194–203.

American College of Physicians (1985). *Guide for adult immunizations.* Philadelphia.

American Psychiatric Association (1980). *Diagnostic and statistical manual of mental disorders.* Washington, D.C.

Bachman, J. G., and Johnston, L. D. (1979). The freshmen, 1979. *Psychology Today, 13*(4), 78–87.

Bell, A., and Weinberg, M. (1978). *Homosexualities: A study of diversity among men and women.* New York: Simon & Schuster.

Berardo, D. H., Shehan, C. L., and Leslie, G. R. (1987). A residue of tradition: Jobs, careers, and spouses' time in housework. *Journal of Marriage and the Family, 49,* 381–390.

Clayton, R., and Voss, H. (1977). Shacking up: Cohabitation in the 1970s. *Journal of Marriage and the Family, 39*(3), 273–283.

Connelly, D. M. (1979). *Traditional acupuncture: The law of the five elements.* Columbia, MD: Center for Traditional Acupuncture.

Darling, C. A., Kallen, D. J., and Van Dusen, J. E. (1984). Sex in transition, 1900–1980. *Journal of Youth and Adolescence, 13,* 385–399.

Department of Health and Human Services (1984). *Alcohol and health: Report to the U.S. Congress.* Rockville, MD.

Drug Enforcement Administration (1985). *Drugs of abuse.* Washington, D.C.: U.S. Government Printing Office.

Dubos, R. (1982). Being human. *The Sciences, 22*(1), 16–18.

Duvall, E. M. (1977). *Marriage and family development,* 5th ed. Philadephia: Lippincott.

Eckert, E. D., Bouchard, T. J., Bohlen, J., and Heston, L. L. (1986). Homosexuality in monozygotic twins reared apart. *British Journal of Psychiatry, 148,* 421–425.

Erikson, E. (1963). *Childhood and society,* 2nd ed. New York: Norton.

Fitch, S. A., and Adams, G. R. (1983). Ego identity and intimacy status: Replication and extension. *Developmental Psychology, 19,* 839–945.

Freud, S. (1966). *Introductory lectures of psychoanalysis* (J. Strachey, ed. and trans.). New York: Norton. (Originally published, 1917.)

Friedan, B. (1963) *The feminine mystique.* New York: Norton.

Frost, R. (1949). *Complete poems of Robert Frost.* New York: Holt, Rinehart and Winston.

Gottman, J. M., and Krokoff, L. J. (1989). Marital interaction and satisfaction: A longitudinal view. *Journal of Consulting and Clinical Psychology, 57,* 47–52.

Gould, R. (1978). *Transformations.* New York: Simon & Schuster.

Haas, E. M. (1981). *Staying healthy with the seasons.* Berkeley, CA: Celestial Arts.

Harry, J. (1983). Gay male and lesbian relationships. In E. D. Macklin and R. H. Rubin (eds.), *Contemporary families and alternative lifestyles: Handbook on research and theory.* Beverly Hills, CA: Sage Publications.

Havighurst, R. J. (1972). *Developmental tasks and education,* 3rd ed. New York: McKay.

Hoffman, L. W. (1975). The value of children to parents and the decrease in family size. *Proceedings of the American Philosophical Society, 119,* 430–438.

Hoffman, L. W. (1977). Changes in family roles, socialization, and sex differences. *American Psychologist, 32*(8), 644–657.

Hoffman, M. (1977). Homosexuality. In F. A. Beach (ed.), *Human sexuality in four perspectives.* Baltimore: Johns Hopkins University Press.

Holmes, T. H., and Rahe, R. H. (1967). The social readjustment rating scale. *Journal of Psychosomatic Research, 11*(2), 213–218.

Horner, M. (1972). Toward an understanding of achievement-related conflicts in women. *Journal of Social Issues, 28*(2), 157–176.

Hotvedt, M., and Mandel, J. (1982). Children of lesbian mothers. In J. Weinrich and B. Paul (eds.), *Homosexuality: Social, psychological, and biological issues.* Beverly Hills, CA: Sage Publications.

Jaffe, S. L. (1987). Inpatient treatment for adolescent drug abusers. Supplement to *Children and Teens Today Newsletter,* December, 1.

Jessor, S. L., and Jessor, R. (1975). Transition from virginity to non-virginity among youth: A social-psychological study over time. *Developmental Psychology, 11*(4), 473–484.

Johnson, A. T. (1985). Municipal employee assistance programs: Managing troubled employees. *Public Administration Review, 45,* 383–390.

Jung, C. G. (1923). *Psychological types or the psychology of individuation.* New York: Harcourt Brace.

Kanders, B., Lindsay, R., and Dempster, D. W (1984). Determinants of bone mass in young healthy women. *Osteoporosis, 3,* 337–340.

Keniston, K. (1970). Youth: A "new" stage of life. *American Scholar,* Autumn, 39*(4), 631–654.

Keniston, K. (1974). Moral development, youthful activism, and modern society. In H. Kraemer (ed.), *Youth and culture: A human development approach.* Monterey, CA: Brooks/Cole.

Kieren, D., Henton, J., and Marotz, R. (1975). *Hers and his: A problem-solving approach to marriage.* Hinsdale, IL: Dryden.

Kinsey, A. C., Pomeroy, W. B., and Martin, C. E. (1948). *Sexual behavior in the human male.* Philadelphia: Saunders.

Kinsey, A. C., Pomeroy, W. B., Martin, C. E., and Gebhard, P. H. (1953). *Sexual behavior in the human female.* Philadelphia: Saunders.

Klonsky, B. G. (1983). The socialization and development of leadership ability. *Journal of Psychology Monographs, 108,* 97–135.

Kohlberg, L. (1973). Continuities in childhood and moral development revisited. In B. P. Baltes and K. W. Schaie (eds.), *Life-span developmental psychology: Personality and socialization.* New York: Academic Press.

Labby, D. H. (1987). Marriage, marital counseling, and sex therapy. In M. L. Pernoll and R. C. Benson (eds.), *Current obstetric and gynecologic diagnosis and treatment,* 6th ed. Los Altos, CA: Appleton & Lange.

Lauer, R. H., and Lauer, J. C. (1991). *The quest for intimacy.* Dubuque, IA: Wm. C. Brown.

Lavine, L. O. (1982). Parental power as a potential influence on girls' career choice. *Child Development, 53,* 658–663.

Lee, J. A. (1973). *The colors of love: An exploration of the ways of loving.* Don Mills, Ontario: New Press.

LeMasters, E. E. (1970). *Parents in modern America.* Homewood, IL: Dorsey.

Levinson, D. J., Darrow, C. N., Klein, E. B., Levinson, M. H., and McKee, B. (1978). *The seasons of a man's life.* New York: Knopf.

Macklin, E. (1978). Review of research on nonmarital cohabitation in the U.S. In B. I. Murstein (ed.), *Exploring intimate lifestyles.* New York: Springer.

Manley, R. O. (1977). Parental warmth and hostility as related to sex differences in children's achievement orientation. *Psychology of Women Quarterly, 1,* 229–245.

Marshall, J. R. (1984). Infertility. In R. C. Benson (ed.), *Current obstetric and gynecologic diagnosis and treatment,* 5th ed. Los Altos, CA: Lange.

Maslow, A. (1970). *Motivation and personality,* 2nd ed. New York: Harper & Row.

Maymi, C. R. (1982). Women in the labor force. In P. W. Berman and E. R. Ramey (eds.), *Women: A developmental perspective.* Bethesda, MD: NICHD/NIH (Publication No. 82-2298).

McLeod, B. (1984). In the wake of disaster. *Psychology Today, 18,* 54–57.

Microcia, G. (1989). *The foundations of Chinese medicine.* London: Churchill Livingstone.

Miller, B. (1979). Unpromised paternity: The lifestyles of gay fathers. In M. Levine (ed.), *Gay men.* New York: Harper & Row.

Miller, N. (1985). Effects of emotional stress on the immune system. *Pavlovian Journal of Biological Sciences, 20,* 47–52.

Money, J., Schwartz, M., and Lewis, V. G. (1984). Adult erotosexual status and fetal hormonal masculinization and demasculinization. *Psychoneuroendocrinology, 9,* 405–414.

National Academy of Sciences, Institute of Medicine (1982). *Marijuana and health.* Washington, D.C.: National Academy Press.

Noble, E. P. (1983). Social drinking and cognitive function: A review. *Substance and Alcohol Actions/Misuse,* **4**(2–3), 205–216.

Orsborn, C. (1985). Enough is enough. *Superwomen Anonymous,* **1,** 2–4.

Parke, R. D. (1982). The father–infant relationship: A family perspective. In P. W. Berman and E. R. Ramey (eds.), *Women: A developmental perspective.* Bethesda, MD: NICHD/NIH (Publication No. 82-2298).

Parsons, J. E. (1980). Psychosexual neutrality: Is anatomy destiny? In J. E. Parsons (ed.), *The psychobiology of sex differences and sex roles.* New York: McGraw Hill.

Persky, H. (1974). Reproductive hormones, moods, and menstrual cycle. In R. C. Friedman, R. M. Richart, and R. L. Vande Wiele (eds.), *Sex differences in behavior.* New York: Wiley.

Physician's Desk Reference (1991). Oradell, NJ: Medical Economics Co.

Prager, K. J. (1982). Identity development and self-esteem in young women. *Journal of Genetic Psychology,* **141,** 177–182.

Prager, K. J. (1983). Identity status, sex-role orientation, and self-esteem in late adolescent females. *Journal of Genetic Psychology,* **143,** 159–167.

Radloff, L. S., and Rae, D. S. (1979). Susceptibility and precipitating factors in depression: Sex differences and similarities. *Journal of Abnormal Psychology,* **88,** 174–181.

Rosen, B., and D'Andrade, R. (1959). The psychosocial origins of achievement motivation. *Sociometry,* **22,** 185–195, 215–217.

Rosen, B., Jerdee, T. H., and Prestwich, T. L. (1975). Dual-career marital adjustment: Potential effects of discriminating managerial attitudes. *Journal of Marriage and the Family,* **37,** 565–572.

Rubin, Z. (1981). Does personality really change after 20? *Psychology Today,* **15**(5), 18–27.

Scarf, M. (1979). The more sorrowful sex. *Psychology Today,* **12**(11), 44–52, 89–90.

Schaie, K. W. (1978). Toward a stage theory of adult cognitive development. *Journal of Aging and Human Development,* **8,** 129–138.

Schiedel, D. G., and Marcia, J. E. (1985). Ego identity, intimacy, sex role orientation, and gender. *Developmental Psychology,* **21,** 149–160.

Schiefelbein, S. (1980). The female patient—Heeded? Hustled? Healed? *Saturday Review,* March 29, 12–16.

Schuckit, M. A. (1984). Relationship between the course of primary alcoholism in men and family history. *Journal of Studies on Alcohol,* **45**(4), 334–338.

Schultes, R. E. (1980). *The botany and chemistry of hallucinogens,* 2nd ed. Springfield, IL: Charles C. Thomas.

Schwartz, M. A. (1976). Career strategies of the never married. Paper presented at the 71st Annual Meeting of the American Sociological Association, New York, September 3.

Scott, D. H. (1983). Brain size and "intelligence." *British Journal of Developmental Psychology,* **1,** 279–287.

Selye, H. (1974). *Stress without distress.* Philadelphia: Lippincott.

Speroff, L., Glass, R. H., and Kase, N. G. (1983). *Clinical gynecologic endocrinology and infertility,* 3rd ed. Baltimore: Williams & Wilkins.

Stayton, W. R. (1984). Lifestyle spectrum 1984. *SIECUS Report,* **12,** 1–4.

Sternberg, R. J. (1985). The measure of love. *Science Digest,* **60,** 78–79.

Sternberg, R. J. (1986). A triangular theory of love. *Psychological Review,* **93,** 119–135.

Sternberg, R. J. (1987). Liking vs. loving: A comparative evaluation of theories. *Psychological Bulletin,* **102,** 331–345.

Sternberg, R. J. (1988). Triangulating love. In R. J. Sternberg and M. Barnes (eds.), *The psychology of love.* New Haven, CT: Yale University Press.

Storms, M. D. (1980). Theories of sexual orientation. *Journal of Personality and Social Psychology,* **38,** 783–792.

Toffler, A. (1970). *Future shock.* New York: Random House.

Turner, C., and Waller, C. (1979). *Marijuana: An annotated bibliography.* New York: Macmillan.

Turner, R. A., Irwin, C. E., Jr., and Millstein, S. G. (1991). Family structure, family processes, and experimenting with substances during adolescence. *Journal of Research on Adolescence,* **1,** 93–106.

Vaillant, G. E. (1977). *Adaptation to life.* Boston: Little Brown.

Verbrugge, L. M. (1982). Women's social roles and health. In P. W. Berman and E. R. Ramey (eds.), *Women: A developmental perspective.* Bethesda, MD: NICHD/NIH (Publication No. 82-2298).

Veroff, J., Douvan, E., and Kulka, R. A. (1981). *The inner American: A self-portrait from 1957 to 1976.* New York: Basic Books.

Watson, R. E. L. (1983). Premarital cohabitation vs. traditional courtship: Their effects on subsequent marital adjustment. *Family Relations,* **32**(1), 139–147.

Yarrow, L. (1982). What a baby does to your marriage. *Parents,* **57,** 47–51.

CHAPTER 9

Alper, T. G. (1974). Achievement motivation in college women: A now-you-see-it-now-you-don't phenomenon. *American Psychologist,* **29**(3), 194–203.

American Heart Association (1985). *Heart facts: 1985.* Dallas: American Heart Association's Office of Communications.

Andres, R., and Tobin, J. D. (1977). Endocrine systems. In C. E. Finch and L. Hayflinch (eds.), *Handbook of the biology of aging.* New York: Van Nostrand Reinhold.

Bardwick, J. M. (1971). *The psychology of women.* New York: Harper & Row.

Barron, F., and Harrington, D. M. (1981). Creativity, intelligence, and personality. *Annual Review of Psychology,* **32,** 439–476.

Bassoff, E. (1988). *Mothers and daughters: Loving and letting go.* New York: New American Library.

Batten, M. (1984). Life spans. *Science Digest,* February, 46–51, 98.

Berardo, D. H., Shehan, C. L., and Leslie, G. R. (1987). A residue of tradition: Jobs, careers, and spouses' time in housework. *Journal of Marriage and the Family,* **49,** 381–390.

Bernard, J. (1972). *The future of marriage.* New York: World.

Birnbaum, J. (1975). Life patterns and self-esteem in gifted, family-oriented, and career-committed women. In T. S. Mednick, S. Tangri, and L. W. Hoffman (eds.), *Women and achievement.* Washington, D.C.: Hemisphere.

Bohannan, P., (1971). *Divorce and after.* New York: Anchor Books.

Bradley, W. (1977). *Life on the run.* New York: Bantam Books.

Breen, J. L. (1981). Premenstrual tension. *Medical Aspects of Human Sexuality,* **15**(6), 52.

Bronfenbrenner, U. (1977). Nobody home: The erosion of the American family. *Psychology Today,* **10**(12), 41–47.

Brown, P., and Fox, H. (1979). Sex differences in divorce. In E. S. Gomberg and V. Franks (eds.), *Gender and disordered behavior: Sex differences in psychopathology.* New York: Brunner/Mazel.

Byrne, J. D. (1975). Mobility rate of employed persons into new occupations. *Monthly Labor Review,* **2,** 53–59.

Campbell, A. (1981). *The sense of well-being in America.* New York: McGraw-Hill.

Cattell, R. B. (1963). Theory of fluid and crystallized intelligence: A critical experiment. *Journal of Educational Psychology,* **36,** 1–22.

Cattell, R. B. (1971). *Abilities: Their structure, growth and action.* Boston: Houghton Mifflin.

Cicirelli, V. G. (1981). *Helping elderly parents: The role of adult children.* Boston: Auburn House.

Clausen, J. A. (1981). Men's occupational careers in the middle years. In D. E. Eichorn, J. Clansen, N. Haan, M. Honzik, and P. Mussen (eds.), *Present and past in middle life.* New York: Academic Press.

Cohler, B. J., and Grunebaum. H. U. (1981). *Mothers, grandmothers, and daughers: Personality and child care in three-generation families.* New York: Wiley.

Coleman, L. M., and Antonucci, T. C. (1983). Impact of work on women at midlife. *Developmental Psychology,* **19,** 290–294.

Costa, P. T., Jr., and McCrae, R. R. (1980). Still stable after all these years: Personality as a key to some issues in adulthood and old age. In P. B. Baltes and O. G. Brim, Jr. (eds.), *Life span development and behavior,* vol. 3. New York: Academic Press.

Edlin, G., and Golanty, E. (1988). *Health and wellness: A holistic approach.* Boston: Jones and Bartlett.

Einstein, E. (1979). Stepfamily lives. *Human Behavior,* **4,** 63–68.

Ellis, A., and Harper, R. (1966). *A guide to rational living.* Hollywood, CA: Wilshire.

Erdwins, C. J., Tyer, Z. E., and Mellinger, J. C. (1982). Achievement and affiliation needs of young adult and middle-aged women. *Journal of Genetic Psychology,* **141,** 219–224.

Erikson, E. (1963). *Childhood and society,* 2nd ed. New York: Norton.

Erikson, E. (1980). *Identity and the life cycle.* New York: Norton.

Erikson, E. (1987). The father of the identity crisis. In E. Hall (ed.), *Growing and changing: What the experts say.* New York: Random House.

Friedman, M. (1978). Type A behavior: Its possible relationship to pathogenic processes responsible for coronary heart disease. In T. M. Dembroski (ed.), *Coronary-prone behavior.* New York: Springer-Verlag.

Friedman, M., and Rosenman, R. H. (1974). *Type A behavior and your heart.* New York: Knopf.

Friss, L. (1982). Equal pay for comparable work: Stimulus for future civil service reform. *Review of Public Personnel Administration,* **2,** 39.

Furstenberg, F. F., Spanier, G., and Rothschild, N. (1982). Patterns of parenting in the transition from divorce to remarriage. In P. W. Berman and E. R. Ramey (eds.), *Women: A developmental perspective.* Bethesda, MD: NICHD/NIH (Publication No. 82-2298).

Gardner, H. (1981). Breakaway minds. *Psychology Today,* **15**(7), 64–71.

Gardner, R. (1977). *The parents' book about divorce.* New York: Doubleday.

Gilbert, L. A., and Rachlin, V. (1987). Mental health and psychological functioning of dual-career families. *The Counseling Psychologist,* **15,** 7–49.

Goldstein, J. L., and Brown, M. S. (1985) Familial hypercholesterolemia: A genetic receptor disease. *Hospital Practice,* **20**(11), 35–46.

Gough, H. G. (1979). A creative personality scale for the adjective check list. *Journal of Personality and Social Psychology,* **37,** 1398–1405.

Gould, R. L. (1972). The phases of adult life: A study in developmental psychology. *American Journal of Psychiatry,* **129**(5), 33–43.

Gould, R. L. (1978). *Transformations.* New York: Simon & Schuster.

Graves, J. P., Dalton, G. W., and Thompson, P. H. (1980). Career stages in organizations. In C. B. Derr (ed.), *Work, family and career.* New York: Praeger.

Gregerman, R. I., and Bierman, E. L. (1981). Aging and hormones. In R. H. Williams (ed.), *Textbook of endocrinology,* 6th ed. Philadelphia: Saunders.

Guilford, J. P. (1967). *The nature of human intelligence.* New York: McGraw-Hill.

Harkins, E. B. (1978). Effects of empty-nest transition on self-report of psychological and physical well being. *Journal of Marriage and the Family,* **40,** 549–558.

Harris, T. (1967). *I'm O.K.—You're O.K.* New York: Harper & Row.

Havighurst, R. J. (1972). *Developmental tasks and education,* 3rd ed. New York: McKay.

Havighurst, R. J. (1982). The world of work. In B. Wolman (ed.), *Handbook of developmental psychology.* Englewood Cliffs, NJ: Prentice-Hall.

Hobart, C. (1987). Parent–child relations in remarried families. *Journal of Family Issues,* **8,** 259–277.

Hoffman, L. W. (1977). Changes in family roles, socialization, and sex differences. *American Psychologist,* **32,** 644–657.

Horn, J. L. (1982). The aging of human abilities. In B. Wolman (ed.), *Handbook of developmental psychology.* Englewood Cliffs, NJ: Prentice-Hall.

Horn. J. L., and Donaldson, G. (1980). Cognitive development II: Adulthood development of human abilities. In O. G. Brim, Jr., and J. Kagan (eds.), *Constancy and change in human development: A volume of review essays.* Cambridge, MA: Harvard University Press.

Horner, M. (1972). Toward an understanding of achievement-related conflicts in women. *Journal of Social Issues,* **28**(2), 157–176.

Ingbar, S. H., and Woeber, K. A. (1981). The thyroid gland. In R. H. Williams (ed.), *Textbook of endocrinology,* 6th ed. Philadelphia: Saunders.

Jacobson, G. F. (1983). *The multiple crises of marital separation and divorce.* New York: Grune & Stratton.

Jaquish, G. A., and Ripple, R. E. (1981). Cognitive creative abilities and self-esteem across the adult life-span. *Human Development,* **24,** 110–119.

Jung, C. G. (1923). *Psychological types, or the psychology of individuation.* New York: Harcourt Brace.

Kelly, J. B. (1982). Divorce: The adult perspective. In B. Wolman (ed.), *Handbook of developmental psychology.* Englewood Cliffs, NJ: Prentice-Hall.

Kennedy, C. E. (1990). Adulthood. In R. M. Thomas (ed.), *The encyclopedia of human development and education.* New York: Pergamon.

Kitson, G. C. (1982). Attachment to the spouse in divorce: A scale and its application. *Journal of Marriage and the Family,* **44,** 379–393.

Knapp, P. A., and Deluty, R. H. (1989). Relative effectiveness of two behavioral parent training programs. *Journal of Clinical Child Psychology,* **18,** 314–322.

Kohn, M., and Schooler, C. (1978). The reciprocal effects of the substantive complexity of work and intellectual flexibility: A longitudinal assessment. *American Journal of Sociology,* **84,** 24–52.

Kral, J. G. (1985). Morbid obesity and related health risks. *Annals of Internal Medicine,* **103**(6), 1043–1047.

Lehman, H. (1953). *Age and achievement* (Vol. 33, Memoirs Series). Princeton, NJ: Princeton University Press.

Lerch, S. (1984). Athletic retirement as social death: An overview. In N. Theberge and P. Donnelly (eds.), *Sport and the sociological imagination.* Ft. Worth: T.C.U. Press.

Levinson, D. J., Darrow, C. M., Klein, E. B., Levinson, M. H., and McKee, B. (1978). *The seasons of a man's life.* New York: Knopf.

Lipsitt, L. P. (1989). American family in transition. *Brown University Child Behavior and Development Letter,* **5,** 6.

Lynch, J. J. (1985). *The body's response to human dialogue.* New York: Basic Books.

Marshall, E. (1986). Diet advice, with a grain of salt and a large helping of pepper. *Science,* **231,** 537–539.

Maslow, A. (1968). Some educational implications of the humanistic psychologies. *Harvard Educational Review,* **38,** 685–696.

Maslow, A. (1970). *Motivation and personality,* 2nd ed. New York: Harper & Row.

Mathews, K. A., and Brunson, B. I. (1979). Allocation of attention and the type A coronary-prone behavior pattern. *Journal of Personality and Social Psychology,* **37,** 2081–2090.

Muller, J. Z. (1985). *Dysmenorrhea and premenstrual syndrome.* Washington, D.C.: U.S. Government Printing Office.

Neugarten, B. (1968). The awareness of middle age. In B. Neugarten (ed.), *Middle age and aging.* Chicago: University of Chicago Press.

Neugarten, B., and Moore, J. (1968). The changing age-status system. In B. Neugarten (ed.), *Middle age and aging.* Chicago: University of Chicago Press.

Norton, A., and Moorman, J. (1987). Current trends in marriage and divorce among American women. *Journal of Marriage and the Family,* **49,** 3–14.

O'Hara, J. (1984). The depression mystery. *World Press Review,* June, 29–30.

Parlee, M. B. (1979). The friendship bond. *Psychology Today,* **13**(4), 43–54, 113.

Pearlin, L. I. (1975). Sex role and depression. In N. Datan and L. H. Ginsberg (eds.), *Lifespan developmental psychology: Normative life events.* New York: Academic Press.

Peter, L., and Hull, R. (1969). *The Peter principle.* New York: Morrow.

Peterson, J. L., and Zill, N. (1986). Marital disruption, parent–child relationships, and behavior problems in children. *Journal of Marriage and the Family,* **48,** 295–307.

Queijo, J. (1984). The paradox of intimacy. *Bostonia Magazine,* 21–25.

Ragozin, A. S., Basham, R. B., Crnic, K. A., Greenberg, M. T., and Robinson, N. M. (1982). Effects of maternal age on parenting role. *Developmental Psychology,* **18,** 627–634.

Reiss, I. L. (1980). *Family systems in America,* 3rd ed. New York: Holt, Rinehart & Winston.

Riegel, K. F. (1973). Dialectic operations: The final period of cognitive development. *Human Development,* **16,** 346–370.

Riegel, K. F. (1976). The dialectics of human development. *American Psychologist,* **31,** 689–700.

Rosenman, R.H. (1978). The interview method of assessment of the coronary-prone behavior pattern. In T. M. Dembroski (ed.), *Coronary-prone behavior.* New York: Springer-Verlag.

Rossi, A. S. (1980). Aging and parenthood in the middle years. In P. B. Baltes and O. G. Brim (eds.), *Life-span development and behavior,* vol. 3. New York: Academic Press.

Rubin, L. B. (1979). *Women of a certain age.* New York: Harper & Row.

Ruble, D. (1977). Premenstrual symptoms: A reinterpretation. *Science,* **7,** 291–292.

Sarason, S. B. (1977). *Work, aging and social change.* New York: Free Press.

Schaie, K. W. (1978). Toward a stage theory of adult cognitive development. *Journal of Aging and Human Development,* **8,** 129–138.

Schaie, K. W., and Hertzog, C. (1983). Fourteen-year cohort-sequential analyses of adult intellectual development. *Developmental Psychology,* **19,** 531–543.

Smith, D. W., Bierman, E. L., and Robinson, N. M. (1978). *The biologic ages of man,* 2nd ed. Philadelphia: Saunders.

Straus, M., and Gelles, R. J. (1980). *Behind closed doors: Violence in the American family.* New York: Doubleday.

Sullivan, H. S. (1963). *The interpersonal theory of psychiatry.* New York: Norton.

Tavris, C. (1972). Woman and man. *Psychology Today,* **5**(10), 34–42.

Terkel, S. (1974). *Working: People talk about what they do all day and how they feel about what they do.* New York: Pantheon.

Teti, D. M., Gelfand, D. M., and Pompa, J. (1990). Depressed mothers' behavioral competence with their infants: Demographic and psychosocial correlates. *Development and Psychopathology,* **2,** 259–270.

Towle, L. H. (1985). The dilemma of the female volunteer. *Cornell Human Ecology Forum,* **15**(2), 24–25.

Vaillant, G. E. (1977). *Adaptation of life.* Boston: Little, Brown.

Vaillant, G. E., and McArthur, C. C. (1972). Natural history of male psychologic health: I. The adult life cycle from 18–50. *Seminars in Psychiatry,* **4,** 415–427.

Van Itallie, T. B. (1985). Health implications of overweight and obesity in the United States. *Annals of Internal Medicine,* **103**(6), 983–988.

Voydanoff, P. (1983). Unemployment: Family strategies for adaptation. In C. R. Figley and H. I. McCubbin (eds.), *Stress and the family: Vol. II. Coping with catastrophe.* New York: Brunner/Mazel.

Walser, M., Imbembo, A. L., Margolis, S., and Elfert, G. A. (1984). *Nutritional management: The Johns Hopkins handbook.* Philadelphia: Saunders.

White, L. K., and Booth, A. (1985). The quality and stability of remarriages: The role of stepchildren. *American Sociological Review,* **50,** 689–698.

Williams, G. H., Jagger, P. I., and Braunwald, E. (1980). Hypersensitive vascular disease. In K. J. Isselbacher, M. M. Wintrobe, G. W. Thorn, R. D. Adams, E. Brunwald, and R. G. Petersdorf (eds.), *Harrison's principles of internal medicine,* 9th ed. New York: McGraw-Hill.

Woodruff, D., and Birren, J. (1972). Age changes and cohort differences in personality. *Developmental Psychology,* **6**(2), 252–259.

Zietlow, P. H., and Sillars, A. L. (1988). Life stage differences in communication during marital conflicts. *Journal of Social and Personal Relationships,* **5,** 223–245.

CHAPTER 10

Allport, G. (1937). *Personality: A psychological interpretation.* New York: Holt, Rinehart & Winston.

American Cancer Society (1990). *Cancer manual.* Boston: American Cancer Society Massachusetts Division.

American College of Physicians (1985). *Guide for adult immunizations.* Philadelphia.

Bachman, G. A., and Leiblum, S. R. (1981). Sexual expression in menopausal women. *Medical Aspects of Human Sexuality,* **15**(10), 96B–96H.

Baltes, P. B., and Schaie, K. W. (1974). Aging and IQ: The myth of the twilight years. *Psychology Today,* **7**(10), 35–38, 40.

Blake, J. (1982). Demographic revolution and family evolution: Some implications for American women. In P. W. Berman and E. R. Ramey (eds.), *Women: A developmental perspective.* Bethesda, MD: NICHD/NIH (Publication No. 82-2298).

Block, J. (1981). Some enduring and consequential structures of personality. In A. I. Rabin (ed.), *Further explorations in personality.* New York: Wiley.

Bouchard, T. J., Heston, L., Eckert, E., Keyes, M., and Resnick, S. (1981). *The Minnesota study of twins reared apart: Project description and sample results in the developmental domain.* In L. Gedda, P. Parisi, and W. E. Nance (eds.), *Twin Research 3: Intelligence, personality and development.* New York: Alan R. Liss.

Brim, O. G., Jr., and Kagan, J. (eds.) (1980). *Constancy and change in human development: A volume of review essays.* Cambridge, MA: Harvard University Press.

Campbell, A. (1981). *The sense of well-being in America.* New York: McGraw-Hill.

Cherlin, A., and Furstenberg, F. F., Jr. (1986). *The new American grandparent: A place in the family, a life apart.* New York: Basic.

Clarkson, B. (1980). The acute leukemias. In K. J. Isselbacher, M. M. Wintrobe, G. W. Thorn, R. D. Adams, E. Braunwald, and R. G. Petersdorf (eds.), *Harrison's principles of internal medicine,* 9th ed. New York: McGraw-Hill.

Costa, P. T., Jr., and McCrae, R. R. (1978). Age differences in personality structure revisited: Studies in validity, stability, and change. *Aging and Human Development,* **8,** 261–275.

Costa, P. T., Jr., and McCrae, R. R. (1978). Objective personality assessment. In M. Storandt, I. C. Siegler, and M. F. Elias (eds.), *The clinical psychology of aging.* New York: Plenum.

Costa, P. T., Jr., and McCrae, R. R. (1980a). Still stable after all these years: Personality as a key to some issues in adulthood and old age. In P. B. Baltes and O. G. Brim, Jr. (eds.), *Life-span development and behavior,* vol. 3. New York: Academic.

Costa, P. T. Jr., and McCrae, R. R. (1980b). The influence of extroversion and neuroticism on subjective well-being: Happy and unhappy people. *Journal of Personality and Social Psychology,* **38**(4), 668–678.

Cytrynbaum, S., Blum, L., Patrick, R., Stein, J., Wadner, D., and Wilk, C. (1980). Midlife development: A personality and social systems perspective. In L. W. Poon (ed.), *Aging in the 1980s.* Washington: American Psychological Association.

Duvall, E. (1977). *Marriage and family development,* 5th ed. Philadelphia: Lippincott.

Erikson, E. (1963). *Childhood and society,* 2nd ed. New York: Norton.

Feldman, S. S., Biringen, Z. C., and Nash, S. C. (1981). Fluctuations of sex-related self-attributions as a function of stage of the family life cycle. *Developmental Psychology,* **17,** 24–35.

Fischer, L. R. (1981). Transitions in the mother–daughter relationship. *Journal of Marriage and the Family,* **43,** 613–622.

Foster, D. W. (1980). Diabetes mellitus. In K. J. Isselbacher, M. M. Wintrobe, G. W. Thorn, R. D. Adams, E. Braunwald, and R. G. Petersdorf (eds.), *Harrison's principles of internal medicine,* 9th ed. New York: McGraw-Hill.

Frisch, R. E., Wyshak, G., Albright, N. L., Albright, T. E., Schiff, I., Jones, K. P., Witschi, J., Shiang, E., Koff, E., and Marguglio, M. (1985). Lower prevalence of breast cancer and cancer of the reproductive system among former college athletes compared to nonathletes. *British Journal of Cancer,* **52**(6), 885–891.

Garfinkel, L. (1985). Overweight and cancer. *Annals of Internal Medicine,* **103,** 1034–1036.

Garrett, W. R. (1982). *Seasons of marriage and family life.* New York: Holt, Rinehart & Winston.

Giuliano, A. E. (1984). Diseases of the breast. In R. C. Benson (ed.), *Current obstetric and gynecologic diagnosis and treatment,* 5th ed. Los Altos, CA: Lange.

Gould, R. L. (1972). The phases of adult life: A study in developmental psychology. *American Journal of Psychiatry,* **129**(5), 33–43.

Gould, R. L. (1978). *Transformations.* New York: Simon & Schuster.

Gregerman, R., and Bierman, E. (1981). Aging and hormones. In R. H. Williams (ed.), *Textbook of endocrinology,* 6th ed. Philadelphia: Saunders.

Griffin, J. E., and Wilson, J. D. (1980). Diseases of the testes. In K. J. Isselbacher, M. M. Wintrobe, G. W. Thorn, R. D. Adams, E. Braunwald, and R. G. Petersdorf (eds.), *Harrison's principles of internal medicine,* 9th ed. New York: McGraw-Hill.

Gutmann, D. (1976). Individual adaptation in the middle years: Developmental issues in the masculine mid-life crisis. *Journal of Geriatric Psychiatry,* **9,** 41–59.

Gutmann, D. (1977). The crosscultural perspective: Notes toward a comparative psychology of aging. In J. E. Birren and K. W. Schaie (eds.), *Handbook of the psychology of aging.* New York: Van Nostrand Reinhold.

Haan, N. (1981). Common dimensions of personality development: Early adolescence to middle life. In D. Eichorn, J. Clausen, N. Haan, M. Honzik, and P. Mussen (eds.), *Present and past in middle life.* New York: Academic Press.

Haley, A. (1976). *Roots.* New York: Doubleday.

Harkins, E. B. (1978). Effects of empty-nest transition on self-report of psychological and physical well-being. *Journal of Marriage and the Family,* **40,** 549–558.

Havighurst, R. J. (1982). The world of work. In B. Wolman (ed.), *Handbook of developmental psychology.* Englewood Cliffs, NJ: Prentice-Hall.

Hetherington, E. M. (1989). Coping with family transitions: Winners, losers and survivors. *Child Development, 60,* 1–14.

Hill, E. C. (1984). Disorders of the uterine cervix. In R. C. Benson (ed.), *Current obstetric and gynecologic diagnosis and treatment,* 5th ed. Los Altos, CA: Lange.

Horton, E. S. (1983). Role of environmental factors in the development of noninsulin-dependent diabetes mellitus. *The American Journal of Medicine,* **75**(5B), 32–40.

Idiculla, A. A., and Goldberg, G. (1987). Physical fitness for the mature woman. In D. M. Barbo (ed.), *Medical clinics of North America: The postmenopausal woman,* vol. 71/No. 1. Philadelphia: W. B. Saunders.

Jackson, J. J. (1982). Death rate trends of black females, United States, 1964–1978. In P. W. Berman and E. R. Ramey (eds.), *Women: A developmental perspective.* Bethesda, MD: NICHD/NIH (Publication No. 82-2298).

Jung, C. G. (1923). *Psychological types or the psychology of individuation.* New York: Harcourt Brace.

Kalleberg, A. L., and Loscocco, K. A. (1983). Aging, values, and rewards: Explaining age differences in job satisfaction. *American Sociological Review,* **48,** 78–90.

Kelly, J. (1972). Work and leisure: A simplified paradigm. *Journal of Leisure Research,* 4(1), 50–62.

Kennedy, C. E. (1990). Adulthood. In R. M. Thomas (ed.), *The encyclopedia of human development and education.* New York: Pergamon Press.

Kimmel, D. C., Price, K. F., and Walker, J. W. (1978). Retirement choice and retirement satisfaction. *Journal of Gerontology,* **33**(4), 575–585.

Kivnick, H. O. (1982). *The meaning of grandparenthood.* Ann Arbor: University of Michigan Press.

LaMont, J. T., and Isselbacher, K. J. (1980). Diseases of the colon and rectum. In K. J. Isselbacher, M. M. Wintrobe, G. W. Thorn, R. D. Adams, E. Braunwald, and R. G. Petersdorf (eds.), *Harrison's principles of internal medicine,* 9th ed. New York: McGraw-Hill.

LaMont, J. T., Koff, R. S., and Isselbacher, K. J. (1980). Cirrhosis. In K. J. Isselbacher, M. M. Wintrobe, G. W. Thorn, R. D. Adams, E. Braunwald, and R. G. Petersdorf (eds.), *Harrison's principles of internal medicine,* 9th ed. New York: McGraw-Hill.

Macara, I. G. (1985). Oncogenes, ions, and phospholipids. *American Journal of Physiology,* 248, **C3**–C11.

Massler, M. (1975). Dental considerations in the later years. In E. Brown and E. Ellis (eds.), *Quality of life: The later years.* Acton, MA: Publishing Sciences Group.

Masters, W. H., and Johnson, V. E. (1966). *Human sexual response.* Boston: Little, Brown.

Neugarten, B. (1968a). Adult personality: Toward a psychology of the life cycle. In B. Neugarten (ed.), *Middle age and aging.* Chicago: University of Chicago Press.

Neugarten, B. (1968b). The awareness of middle age. In B. Neugarten (ed.), *Middle age and aging.* Chicago: University of Chicago Press.

Neugarten, B. (1974). The roles we play. In E. Brown and E. Ellis (eds.), *Quality of life: The middle years.* Acton, MA: Publishing Sciences Group.

Neugarten, B. L., and Neugarten, D. A. (1987). The changing meanings of age. *Psychology Today,* **21,** 29–32.

Neugarten, B., and Weinstein, K. (1968). The changing American grandparent. In B. Neugarten (ed.), *Middle age and aging.* Chicago: University of Chicago Press.

Notman, M. T. (1980). Adult life cycles: Changing roles and changing hormones. In J. E. Parsons (ed.), *The psychobiology of sex differences and sex roles.* Washington: Hemisphere.

Osherson, S. D. (1980). *Holding on or letting go: Men and career change at midlife.* New York: The Free Press.

Paffenbarger, R. S., Jr., Hyde, R. T., Wing, A. L., and Hsieh, C. C. (1986). Physical activity, all-cause mortality, and longevity of college alumni. *The New England Journal of Medicine,* **314**(10), 605–613.

Scarr, S. (1981). Steps in the stream. *The Sciences,* **21**(3), 24–26.

Shapiro, S., Kelly, J.P., Rosenberg, L., Kaufman, D. W., Helmrich, S. P., Rosenshein, N. B., Lewis, J. L., Knapp, R. C., Stolley, P. D., and Schottenfeld, D. (1985). Risk of localized and widespread endometrial cancer in relation to recent and discontinued use of conjugated estrogens. *The New England Journal of Medicine,* **313**(16), 969–972.

Skolnick, A. (1981). Married lives: Longitudinal perspectives on marriage. In D. E. Eichorn, J. A. Clausen, N. Haan, M. P. Honzik, and P. H. Mussen (eds.), *Past and present in middle life.* New York: Academic Press.

Spanier, G. B., and Lewis, R. A. (1980). Marital quality: A review of the seventies. *Journal of Marriage and the Family,* **42,** 825–839.

Stampfer, M. J., Willett, W. C., Colditz, G. A., Rosner, B., Speizer, F. E., and Hennekens, C. H. (1985). A prospective study of postmenopausal estrogen therapy and coronary heart disease. *The New England Journal of Medicine,* **313**(7), 1044–1049.

Tinsley, B. R., and Parke, R. D. (1983). Grandparents as support and socialization agents. In M. Lewis (ed.), *Beyond the dyad.* New York: Plenum.

Tisi, G. M. (1980). Neoplasms of the lung. In K. J. Isselbacher, M. M. Wintrobe, G. W. Thorn, R. O. Adams, E. Braunwald, and R. G. Petersdorf (eds.), *Harrison's principles of internal medicine,* 9th ed. New York: McGraw-Hill.

Troll, L. E. (1980). Grandparenting. In L. W. Poon (ed.), *Aging in the 1980s.* Washington, D.C.: American Psychological Association.

Troll, L. E. (1983). Grandparents: The family watchdog. In T. Brubaker (ed.), *Family relationships in later life.* Beverly Hills, CA: Sage.

Troll, L. E., and Bengtson, V. (1979). Generations in the family. In W. Burr, R. Hill, F. I. Nye, and I. Reiss (eds.), *Contemporary theories about the family.* New York: Free Press.

Vaillant, G. (1977). *Adaptation to life.* Boston: Little, Brown.

Victor, M., and Adams, R. D. (1980). Common disturbances of vision, ocular movement, and hearing. In K. J. Isselbacher, M. M. Wintrobe, G. W. Thorn, R. D. Adams, E. Braunwald, and R. G. Petersdorf (eds.), *Harrison's principles of internal medicine,* 9th ed. New York: McGraw-Hill.

Weg, R. B. (1983). The physiological perspective. In R. B. Weg (ed.), *Sexuality in later years.* New York: Academic Press.

Weinberg, R. A. (1985). The action of oncogenes in the cytoplasm and nucleus. *Science,* **230,** 770–776.

Weiss, L., and Lowenthal, M. (1975). Life-course perspectives on friendship. In M. Lowenthal, M. Thurner, and D. Chiriboga (eds.), *Four stages of life.* San Francisco: Jossey-Bass.

Whitbourne, S. K. (1985). *The aging body: Physiological changes and psychological consequences.* New York: Springer-Verlag.

Wilson, P. W. F., Garrison, R. J., and Castelli, W. P. (1985). Postmenopausal estrogen use, cigarette smoking, and cardiovascular morbidity in women over 50. *The New England Journal of Medicine,* **313**(17), 1038–1043.

Woods, N. F. (1982). Menopausal distress: A model for epidemiologic investigation. In A. M. Voda, M. Dinnerstein, and S. R. O'Donnell (eds.), *Changing perspectives on menopause.* Austin: University of Texas Press.

Wright, J. D., and Hamilton, R. F. (1978). Work satisfaction and age: Some evidence of the 'job change' hypothesis. *Social Forces,* **56,** 1140–1158.

CHAPTER 11

American College of Physicians (1985). *Guide for adult immunizations.* Philadelphia: American College of Physicians.

American Heart Association (1985). *Heart facts.* Dallas.

Avioli, L. V. (1986). Osteoporosis: A guide to detection. *Modern Medicine,* February, 28–42.

Baltes, P. B., and Schaie, K. W. (1976). On the plasticity of intelligence in adulthood and old age: Where Horn and Donaldson fail. *American Psychologist,* **31**(10), 720–725.

Barnes, R. F., Raskind, M. A., Scott, M., and Murphy, C. (1981). Problems of families caring for Alzheimer patients: Use of a support group. *Journal of the American Geriatric Society,* **29**(2), 80–85.

Batten, M. (1984). Life spans. *Science Digest,* February, 46–51, 98.

Botwinick, J. (1970). Geropsychology. *Annual Review of Psychology,* **21,** 239–272.

Brody, R. (1985). New research dispels myths about unhappy retirements. *San Diego Union,* December 20.

Bühler, C. (1968). The developmental structure of goal setting in group and individual studies. In C. Bühler and F. Massarik (eds.), *The course of human life.* New York: Springer.

Butler, R. (1969). Ageism: Another form of bigotry. *Gerontologist,* **9,** 243–245.

Butler, R. (1975a). *Why survive? Being old in America.* New York: Harper & Row.

Butler, R. (1975b). Sex after sixty-five. In L. Brown and E. Ellis (eds.), *Quality of life: The later years*. Acton, MA: Publishing Sciences Group.

Butler, R., and Lewis, M. I. (1982) *Aging and mental health*. St. Louis: Mosby.

Carp. F. (1975). Housing and living arrangements. In L. Brown and E. Ellis (eds.), *Quality of life: The later years*. Acton, MA: Publishing Sciences Group.

Cicirelli, V. G. (1981). *Helping elderly parents: The role of adult chiildren*. Boston: Auburn House.

Corbett, L. (1981). The last sexual taboo: Sex in old age. *Medical Aspects of Human Sexuality*, **15**(4), 117–131.

Cox, H., and Bhak, A. (1979). Symbolic interaction and retirement adjustment: An empirical assessment. *International Journal of Aging and Human Development*, **9**(3), 279–286.

Cumming, E., and Henry, W. (1961). *Growing old: The process of disengagement*. New York: Basic Books.

Dement, W. C., Miles, L. E., and Bliwise, D. L. (1982). Physiological markers of aging: Human sleep pattern changes. In M. E. Reff and E. L. Schneider (eds.), *Biological markers of aging*. Bethesda, MD: NIH (Publication No. 82-2221).

Denckla, W. D. (1975). Pituitary inhibitor of thyroxine. *Federation proceedings: Federation of American societies for experimental biology*, **34**(1), 96.

DeNike, L. G. (1987). Eldercall update. *Keynotes*, **3**, 22–24.

Eisdorfer, C. (1963). The WAIS performance of the aged: A retest evaluation. *Journal of Gerontology*, **18**, 169–172.

Eisdorfer, C. (1975). Making life worth living. In L. Brown and E. Ellis (eds.), *Quality of life: The later years*. Acton, MA: Publishing Sciences Group.

Eisdorfer, C., and Wilkie, F. (1973). Intellectual changes. In L. Jarvik, C. Eisdorfer, and J. Blum (eds.), *Intellectual functioning in adults*. New York: Springer.

Erikson, E. (1963). *Childhood and society*, 2nd ed. New York: Norton.

Erikson, E. (1987). The father of the identity crisis. In E. Hall, (ed.), *Growing and changing: What the experts say*. New York: Random House.

Fields, W. S. (1983). Aspirin for prevention of stroke: A review. *American Journal of Medicine*, **74**(6A), 61–65.

Gregerman, R. I., and Bierman, E. L. (1981). Aging and hormones. In R. H. Williams (ed.), *Textbook of endocrinology*, 6th ed. Philadelphia: Saunders.

Guilford, R. (1984). Contrasts in marital satisfaction throughout old age: An exchange theory analysis. *Journal of Gerontology*, **39**, 325–333.

Hare, P. H., and Haske, M. (1984). Innovative living arrangements: A source of long-term care. *Aging Magazine*, January, 3–8.

Havighurst, R. (1972). *Developmental tasks and education*, 3rd ed. New York: McKay.

Havighurst, R., Neugarten, B., and Tobin, S. (1968). Disengagement and patterns of aging. In B. Neugarten (ed.), *Middle age and aging*. Chicago: University of Chicago Press.

Hayflick, L. (1984). The aging of humans and their cultured cells. *Resident and Staff Physician*, **30**(8), 36–44.

Helsing, K. J., and Szklo, M. (1981). Mortality after bereavement. *American Journal of Epidemiology*, **114**, 41–52.

Heron, A., and Chown, S. (1967). *Age and function*. Boston: Little, Brown.

Holden, C. (1987). Why do women live longer than men? *Science*, **238**, 158–160.

Horn, J. L. (1982). The aging of human abilities. In B. Wolman (ed.), *Handbook of developmental psychology*. Englewood Cliffs, NJ: Prentice-Hall.

Horn, J. L., and Donaldson, G. (1980). Cognitive development II: Adulthood development of human abilities. In O. G. Brim, Jr., and J. Kagan (eds.), *Constancy and change in human development: A volume of review essays*. Cambridge, MA: Harvard University Press.

Jensen, J., Christiansen, C., and Rodbro, P. (1985). Cigarette smoking, serum estrogens, and bone loss during hormone-replacement therapy after menopause. *The New England Journal of Medicine*, **313**(16), 973–975.

Kanders, B., Lindsay, R., and Dempster, D. W. (1984). Determinants of bone mass in young healthy women. In C. Christiansen (ed.), *Osteoporosis*. Copenhagen: Aalborg Stiftsbogtrykkeri.

Kennedy, C. E. (1990). Old age. In R. M. Thomas (ed.), *The encyclopedia of human development and education theory, research, and studies*. New York: Pergamon Press.

Kline, D. W., and Szafran, J. (1975). Age differences in backward monoptic masking. *Journal of Gerontology*, **30**, 307–311.

Kolb, D. S., and Balsano, A. E. (1988). Balancing efficiency and effectiveness in day care programs for the elderly. *Journal of Ambulatory Care Management*, **11**, 53–62.

Kubey, R. W. (1980). Television and aging: Past, present and future. *The Gerontologist*, **20**, 16–35.

Kuhlen, R. (1964). Developmental changes in motivation during the adult years. In J. Birren (ed.), *Relations of development and aging*. Springfield, IL: Thomas.

Licastro, F., and Walford, R. L. (1986). Effects exerted by prostaglandins and indomethacin on the immune response during aging. *Gerontology*, **32**, 1–9.

Lopota, H. Z. (1973). *Widowhood in America*. Cambridge, MA: Schankman.

Mass, H., and Kuypers, J. (1974). *From thirty to seventy*. San Francisco: Jossey-Bass.

Mace, N., and Rabins, P. (1984). *The 36 hour day: Family guide to caring for persons with Alzheimer's disease, related dementing illness and memory loss in later life*. Baltimore: Johns Hopkins University Press.

Mackin, J. (1985). Mobile homes popular with elderly. *Human Ecology Forum*, **15**(2), 21–22.

Mannik, M., and Gilliland, B. C. (1980). Degenerative joint disease. In K. J. Isselbacher, M. M. Wintrobe, G. W. Thorn, R. D. Adams, E. Braunwald, and R. G. Petersdorf (eds.), *Harrison's principles of internal medicine*, 9th ed. New York: McGraw-Hill.

Masters, W. H., and Johnson, V. E. (1966). *Human sexual response*. Boston: Little, Brown.

McCracken, J. (1976). The company tells me I'm old. *Saturday Review*, August 7.

Mendelson, W. B. (1984). Sleep after forty. *American Family Physician*, **29**(1), 135–139.

Moen, P. (1983). Is employment the solution to the poverty of female headed households? Paper presented at the meeting of the National Council on Family Relations, Minneapolis, October.

Mohr, J. P., Fisher, C. M., and Adams, R. D. (1980). Cerebrovascular diseases. In K. J. Isselbacher, M. M. Wintrobe, G. W. Thorn, R. D. Adams, E. Braunwald, and R. G. Petersdorf (eds.), *Harrison's principles of internal medicine*, 9th ed. New York: McGraw-Hill.

Neugarten, B. (1987). Acting one's age: New rules for old. In E. Hall (ed.), *Growing and changing: What the experts say*. New York: Random House.

Neugarten, B., Havighurst, R., and Tobin, S. (1968). Personality and patterns of aging. In B. Neugarten (ed.), *Middle age and aging*. Chicago: University of Chicago Press.

Pardini, A. (1984). Exercise, vitality, and aging. *Aging*, April–May, 19–29.

Peterson, J. A., and Payne, B. (1975). *Love in the later years*. New York: Associated Press.

Riegel, K. F., and Riegel, R. M. (1972). Development, drop, and death. *Developmental Psychology*, **6**, 306–319.

Rollins, B. C, and Feldman, H. (1970). Marital satisfaction over the family life cycle. *Journal of Marriage and the Family*, **32**, 20–37.

Salzman, R. T. (1983). Management of rheumatoid arthritis and osteoarthritis. *American Journal of Medicine*, **75**(48), 91.

Schaie, K. W. (1958). Rigidity-flexibility and intelligence: A cross-sectional study of the adult life span from twenty to seventy years. *Psychological Monographs*, **72** (Whole No. 462).

Schaie, K. W., and Strother, C. R. (1968). The effects of time and cohort differences on the interpretation of age changes in cognitive behavior. *Multivariate Behavior Research*, **3**, 259–294.

Schaie, K. W, and Parr, J. (1981). Intelligence. In A. W. Chickering (ed.), *The modern American college*. San Francisco: Jossey-Bass.

Shanas, E., Townsend, P., Wedderburn, D., Friis, H., Milhoj, P., and Stehouwer, J. (1968). *Older people in three industrial societies*. New York: Atherton.

Sinex, F. M., and Myers, R. H. (1982). Alzheimer's disease, Down's syndrome, and aging: The genetic approach. In F. M. Sinex and C. R. Merril (eds.), *Alzheimer's disease, Down syndrome and aging*. New York: New York Academy of Sciences.

Smith, K. F., and Bengtson, V. L. (1979). Positive consequences of institutionalization: Solidarity between elderly parents and their middle-aged children. *The Gerontologist, 19*(5), 438–447.

Stare, F. (1977). Three score and ten plus more. *Journal of the American Geriatric Society, 25,* 529–533.

Sussman, M. B. (1976). Family life of old people. In R. H. Binstock and E. Shanas (eds.), *Handbook of aging and the social sciences.* New York: Van Nostrand Reinhold.

Troll, L. E., Miller, S. J., and Atchley, R. C. (1979). *Families in later life.* Belmont, CA: Wadsworth.

Wechsler, D. (1958). *The measurement and appraisal of adult intelligence.* 4th ed. Baltimore: Williams & Wilkins.

Whitbourne, S. K. (1985). *The aging body: Physiological changes and psychological consequences.* New York: Springer-Verlag.

Whitehouse, P. J., Price, D. L., Struble, R. G., Clark, A. W., Coyle, J. T., and DeLong, M. R. (1982). Alzheimer's disease and senile dementia: Loss of neurons in the basal forebrain. *Science, 215,* 1237–1239.

Wilkie, F, and Eisdorfer, C. (1974). Terminal changes in intelligence. In E. Palmore (ed.), *Normal aging II: Reports from the Duke longitudinal studies, 1970–1973.* Durham, NC: Duke University Press.

Wolf-Klein, G. P., Marr, V. K., and Foley, C. J. (1988). Adult day care—A recent past and a growing future. *New York State Journal of Medicine,* October, 528–530.

Zatz, M. M., and Goldstein, A. L. (1985). Thymosins, lymphokines, and the immunology of aging. *Gerontology, 31,* 263–277.

Zietlow, P. H., and Sillars, A. L. (1988). Life-stage differences in communication during marital conflicts. *Journal of Social and Personal Relationships, 5,* 223–245.

CHAPTER 12

Becker, E. (1973). *The denial of death.* New York: Free Press.

Bell, T. (1961). *In the midst of life.* New York: Atheneum.

Berlinsky, E. B., and Biller, H. B. (1982). *Parental death and psychological development.* Lexington, MA: D. C. Heath.

Binger, C., Mikkelsen, C., and Waechter, E. (1970). Terminal illness: Implications for patient, family, and staff. In H. Thorpe (ed.), *The hospitalized child, his family, and his community.* San Francisco: American Association for Child Care in Hospitals.

Bornstein, P. E., Clayton, P. J., Halikas, J. A., Maurice, W. L., and Robins, E. (1973). The depression of widowhood after 13 months. *British Journal of Psychiatry, 122,* 561–566.

Burton, A. (1974). *Operational theories of personality.* New York: Brunner/Mazel.

Butler R. (1975). *Why survive? Being old in America.* New York: Harper & Row.

Clayton, P. J., Halikas, J. A., and Maurice, W. L. (1972). The depression of widowhood. *British Journal of Psychiatry, 120,* 71–78.

Committee for the Study of Health Consequences of the Stress of Bereavement (1984). *Bereavement: Reactions, consequences and care.* Washington, D.C.: National Academy Press.

Elkind, D. (1981). *The hurried child.* Reading, MA: Addison-Wesley.

Erikson, E. (1963). *Childhood and society,* 2nd ed. New York: Norton.

Fanslow, C. A. (1984). Touch and the elderly. In C. C. Brown (ed.), *The many facets of touch.* Skilman, NJ: The Johnson & Johnson Baby Products Co.

Freud, S. (1966). *Introductory lectures on psychoanalysis* (J. Strachey, ed. and trans.). New York: Norton. (Originally published, 1920).

Furman, E. (1974). *A child's parent dies: Studies in childhood bereavement.* New Haven, CT: Yale University Press.

Furman, R. A. (1973). A child's capacity for mourning. In E. J. Anthony and C. Koupernik (eds.), *The child in his family: The impact of disease and death. Yearbook of the International Association for Child Psychiatry and Allied Professions,* Vol. 2. New York: Wiley.

Glick, I. O., Weiss, R. S., and Parkes, C. M. (1974). *The first year of bereavement.* New York: Wiley.

Gorer, G. (1965). *Death, grief and mourning.* Garden City, NY: Doubleday.

Grossberg, S. H., and Crandall, L. (1978). Father loss and father absence in preschool children. *Clinical Social Work Journal, 6,* 123–134.

Johnson-Soderberg, S. (1983). Parents who have lost a child by death. In V. J. Sasseroth (ed.), *Minimizing high-risk parenting.* Skilman, NJ: The Johnson & Johnson Baby Products Co.

Kalish, R. A., and Reynolds, D. K. (1976). *An overview of death and ethnicity.* Farmingdale, NY: Baywood.

Kastenbaum, R., and Aisenberg, R. (1972). *The psychology of death.* New York: Springer.

Keller, J. W., Sherry, D., and Piotrowski, C. (1984). Perspectives on death: A developmental study. *Journal of Psychology, 116,* 137–142.

Kurtz, P. (1988). Scientific evidence: Near-death experiences. *Psychology Today, 22,* 15.

Kübler-Ross, E. (1969). *On death and dying.* New York: Macmillan.

Kübler-Ross, E. (1975). *Death: The final stage of growth.* Englewood Cliffs, NJ: Prentice-Hall.

Lamberg, L. (1984). *The American Medical Association's straight-talk, no-nonsense guide to better sleep.* New York: Random House.

Lansdown, R., and Benjamin, G. (1985). The development of the concept of death in children aged 5–9 years. *Child: Care, health and development, 11,* 13–20.

Lindemann, E. (1944). Symptomatology and management of acute grief. *American Journal of Psychiatry, 101,* 141–148.

Lipsitt, L. P. (1986). The Challenger tragedy. *The Brown University Human Development Letter, 2*(2),2.

Lorenz, K. (1966). *On aggression* (M. Wilson, trans.). New York: Harcourt, Brace & World.

Lynch, J. J. (1977). *The broken heart: The medical consequences of loneliness.* New York: Basic Books.

Maas, H. S., and Kuypers, J. A. (1974). *From thirty to seventy.* San Francisco: Jossey-Bass.

Marlow, D. (1973). *Pediatric nursing,* 4th ed. Philadelphia: Saunders.

Miller, J. B. M. (1971). Reactions to the death of a parent: A review of the psychoanalytic literature. *Journal of the American Psychoanalytic Association, 19*(4), 697–719.

Morrissey, J. (1965). Death anxiety in children with a fatal illness. In H. Parad (ed.), *Crisis intervention.* New York: Family Service Association.

Munley, A. (1983). *The hospice alternative: A new context for death and dying.* New York: Basic Books.

Parkes, C. M. (1972). *Bereavement: Studies of grief in adult life.* New York: International University Press.

Perry, P. (1988). Brushes with death. *Psychology Today, 22,* 14–17.

Sargent, M. (1979). *Caring about kids: Talking to children about death.* (DHEW Publication No. ADM 79-838). Washington, D.C.: U.S. Government Printing Office.

Schulz, R. (1978). *The psychology of death, dying and bereavement.* Reading, MA: Addison-Wesley.

Toffler, A. (1970). *Future shock.* New York: Random House.

Wolfenstein, M. (1969). Loss, rage and repetition. *Psychoanalytic Study of the Child, 24,* 432–462.

Author Index

Subject Index

Photo credits continued from page iv.